POLITICAL IDEOLOGIES AND THE DEMOCRATIC IDEAL

TENTH EDITION

TERENCE BALL

Arizona State University

RICHARD DAGGER

University of Richmond

DANIEL I. O'NEILL

University of Florida

Routledge
Taylor & Francis Group

NEW YORK AND LONDON

Tenth edition published 2017
by Routledge
711 Third Avenue, New York, NY 10017

and by Routledge
2 Park Square, Milton Park, Abingdon, Oxon, OX14 4RN

Routledge is an imprint of the Taylor & Francis Group, an informa business

First edition published by Harpercollins, 1991
Second edition published by Pearson Education, Inc., 1995
Third edition published by Pearson Education, Inc., 1999
Fourth edition published by Pearson Education, Inc., 2001
Fifth edition published by Pearson Education, Inc., 2003
Sixth edition published by Pearson Education, Inc., 2005
Seventh edition published by Pearson Education, Inc., 2009
Eighth edition published by Pearson Education, Inc., 2011
Ninth edition published by Pearson Education, Inc., 2014; and Routledge, 2016

Library of Congress Cataloging in Publication Data
Names: Ball, Terence, author. | Dagger, Richard, author. | O'Neill, Daniel I., 1967- author.
Title: Political ideologies and the democratic ideal / Terence Ball, Arizona State University, Richard Dagger, University of Richmond, Daniel I. O'Neil, University of Florida.
Description: Tenth edition. | New York : Routledge, 2017.
Identifiers: LCCN 2016006819| ISBN 9781138650008 (hardback) | ISBN 9781138650015 (pbk.) | ISBN 9781315625553 (ebook)
Subjects: LCSH: Political science--History. | Democracy--History. | Right and left (Political science)--History. | Ideology--History.
Classification: LCC JA81 .B25 2017 | DDC 320.509--dc23
LC record available at https://lccn.loc.gov/2016006819

ISBN: 978-1-138-65000-8 (hbk)
ISBN: 978-1-138-65001-5 (pbk)
ISBN: 978-1-315-62555-3 (ebk)

Typeset in Galliard
by Saxon Graphics Ltd, Derby

Visit the eResource: www.routledge.com/cw/Ball

To

Andrew, Alexandra and Eliana Nicole Lopez Ball

Emily and Elizabeth Dagger

and

Cassidy and Jackson O'Neill

PRAISE FOR THE TENTH EDITION

For philosophical depth and breadth of coverage, *Political Ideologies and the Democratic Ideal* is simply without peer. It is the best political-ideologies textbook on the market, and its use of the concept of freedom to unify the analyses of ideologies as diverse as socialism, liberalism, conservatism, fascism, and political Islam is both innovative and insightful. The tenth edition does an even better job than earlier editions of connecting these ideologies to practical politics, as in its new discussions of *Citizens United*, the Black Lives Matter movement, and Putin's expansionist foreign policy.

Robert S. Taylor, *University of California-Davis, USA*

Ball, Dagger, and O'Neill cover a staggering range of material in this carefully conceived and cogently written text. That they do so while balancing serious attention to the historical contexts out of which ideologies emerge, with a keen sense of their relevance to contemporary problems and debates, makes this an impressive achievement.

Michael Goodhart, *University of Pittsburgh, USA*

It is a real pleasure to see a new edition of this classic in the field of political theory and political ideologies. This edition retains the original perceptive framework of analysis, but it now also includes crucial and insightful updates on topics like Black Lives Matter and the Islamic State (ISIS). It should remain an excellent vehicle for instruction.

Stephen K. White, *University of Virginia, USA*

I have used *Political Ideologies and the Democratic Ideal* through multiple editions as required reading for an Intro to Political Science course. I particularly appreciate its exploration of a comprehensive array of both historical and contemporary ideologies and its writing at a level to make those understandable to an undergraduate audience. The latest edition combines new scholarship about long-standing ideologies and coverage of new developments regarding freedom of speech, Islamist ideologies, environmentalism, and so on.

Ralph G. Carter, *Texas Christian University, USA*

Ball, Dagger, and O'Neill's *Political Ideologies and the Democratic Ideal* is what students of politics have been waiting for—a thoughtful, critical, accessible, and engaging analysis of political ideologies. An outstanding update to previous editions, this text will serve students and professors of politics well.

Michael Cairo, *Transylvania University, USA*

BRIEF CONTENTS

CONTENTS

Part Three   Political Ideologies Today and Tomorrow 257

Chapter 8   Liberation Ideologies and the Politics of Identity 257

Chapter 9   Green Politics: Ecology as Ideology 307

Chapter 10   Radical Islamism 332

PREFACE

An ancient Chinese curse says, "May you live in interesting times." That is, may you live in times of social, political, and economic upheaval, of mass misery, and maybe even of death. Some times are more trying and dangerous than others. We should count ourselves fortunate for not living during a world war, or civil war, or some other variety of violent internecine conflict. But we *are* living in an era of national and international economic crises, of global warming and environmental degradation, of domestic and international terror, of military coups and civil wars, of genocide in the Sudan and elsewhere, of hot wars fought with weapons and culture wars fought with competing ideas. And because our world keeps changing and hurling new challenges at human beings, people's ideas—and especially those systems of ideas called "ideologies"—change accordingly in hopes of helping people cope with those crises.

In this, the tenth edition of *Political Ideologies and the Democratic Ideal*, we have tried to track and take account of changes in our world and in how people interpret those changes with the aid of one or another ideology. This is no easy task, and we sometimes fear that any account, including our own, must fall short of the mark. Nevertheless, we have here done our best to offer a reasonably up-to-date and systematic account of the ideologies that have shaped and continue to reshape the world in which we live. As before, we have described in some detail the deeper historical background out of which these ideologies emerged and developed.

NEW TO THIS EDITION

In this tenth edition we have once again made numerous changes, large and small. Among the larger changes are the following:

- Discussion questions at the end of each chapter.
- Additional graphs and photos.
- In Chapter 1 we ask—and attempt to answer—the question, "Why *political* ideologies? That is, what exactly is the connection between practical politics and the seemingly abstract systems of ideas called "ideologies"?
- In Chapter 2 we have added an expanded account of the long and still-continuing struggle for the right to vote, and the U.S. Supreme Court's *Citizens United* decision and recent voter ID laws and their implications for

American democracy. Does "dark money" corrupt democratic politics? And: are there some issues—same-sex marriage, for example—that democratic majorities should *not* decide?

- In Chapter 3 we offer a more extended discussion of Adam Smith's contributions to the liberal tradition, and a new discussion of John Stuart Mill's harm principle—more specifically, is it always possible to distinguish between "offense" and "harm"?—and T. H. Green's welfare-liberal conception of freedom. And, in light of recent terrorist attacks, is there a necessary trade-off between liberty and security?

- Chapter 4 includes an account of how and why the "law of unintended consequences" makes traditional or classical conservatives wary of even the most well-intended innovations. More on the divide between religious-right conservatives and libertarian-leaning "conservatarians." We have also added a new section on "fusionist" conservatism that attempts to ally different kinds of conservatives.

- In Chapter 6 we discuss Putin's post-Soviet expansion of Russia's territory and influence, as well as the apparent rebirth of "Mao Zedong thought" in China and the oddly idiosyncratic ideology of *Juche* in North Korea. And: has "socialism" lost its negative connotation in twenty-first-century America in the wake of "democratic socialist" Bernie Sanders's presidential campaign?

- In Chapter 7 we provide a greatly expanded discussion of the role of "myth" and the intellectual and aesthetic origins of fascism. We also discuss Nazism's antipathy to modern art and its "Aryan" alternative, and attempts to resist Hitler's Nazi regime. And we trace the increasing prominence of neofascist and neo-Nazi parties in the wake of the refugee crisis in Europe and elsewhere.

- In Chapter 8 we offer a more in-depth account of the origins of black liberation and the current and continuing obstacles it faces, and a discussion of the new Black Lives Matter movement. We also discuss new directions in feminist theory, the impact of the Supreme Court's decision on same-sex marriage, and other current issues. And we offer an account of how "ag-gag" laws attempt to limit the access and influence of animal liberationists. Included also is an in-depth discussion of different faith traditions' views of animals and their treatment by human beings.

- Chapter 9 includes an account of Pope Francis's 2015 encyclical on the environment and humans' duty to protect it. We also ask whether protecting the environment requires a radically new ethic.

- In this new edition we have once again expanded the discussion of radical Islamism in Chapter 10, especially with regard to the varieties of Islamism (from legal-constitutional to violent jihadist), the rise of the Islamic State (ISIS), and the effects of recent terrorist attacks on national and international politics.

- Finally, we have supplied a short summary and review in Chapter 11.

- We have made these and many other changes to make the text as clear, accurate, readable, and up-to-date as we can.

FEATURES

As in previous editions, we have tried in this new one to improve upon *Political Ideologies and the Democratic Ideal* without sacrificing the qualities that have made the book attractive to many students and teachers. Our principal aims continue to be the two that have guided us since we set out, in the late 1980s, to write the first edition. We try, first, to supply an informed and accessible overview of the major ideologies that shaped the political landscape of the twentieth century and now begin to give shape to that of the twenty-first. Our second aim is to show how these ideologies originated and how and why they have changed over time. In addition to examining the major modern "isms"—liberalism, conservatism, socialism, and fascism—we try to provide the reader with a sense of the history, structure, supporting arguments, and internal complexities of these and other, recently emerging ideologies.

The basic structure of the text remains the same as in previous editions. We begin by constructing a fourfold framework—a working definition of "ideology" and of the four functions that all ideologies perform—within which to compare, contrast, and analyze the various ideologies. We also show how each ideology interprets "democracy" and "freedom" in its own way. Democracy is not, in our view, simply one ideology among others; it is an *ideal* that different ideologies interpret in different ways. Each ideology also has its own particular conception of human nature and its own program for promoting freedom. We use a simple three-part model to illustrate this, comparing and contrasting each ideology's view of freedom in terms of agent, obstacle, and goal. In every chapter devoted to a particular ideology, we explain its basic conception of freedom in terms of the triadic model, discuss the origin and development of the ideology, examine its interpretation of the democratic ideal, and conclude by showing how it performs the four functions of political ideologies. We do this not only with liberalism, conservatism, socialism, and fascism but also with newly emergent ideologies. These include "liberation ideologies"—black liberation, women's liberation, gay liberation, native peoples' liberation, liberation theology, and animal liberation—as well as the emerging environmental or "Green" ideology and the ideology of radical Islamism.

This text is twinned with an accompanying anthology, *Ideals and Ideologies: A Reader,* also published in a newly revised tenth edition by Routledge. Although each book can stand alone, they are arranged to supplement and complement each other. Other instructional materials are available from the publisher.

SUPPLEMENT

Instructor's Manual/Test Bank This resource includes learning objectives, lecture outlines, multiple-choice questions, true/false questions, and essay questions for each chapter.

ACKNOWLEDGMENTS

We first undertook this collaborative effort in the belief that two heads are better than one. We found in writing the first and subsequent editions that a project of this sort requires more, or better, heads than the authors could muster between themselves, and revising the book for the subsequent editions has only strengthened that conclusion. To those who shared their time, energy, and wisdom with us in preparing this new edition, especially our families and the staff at Routledge, we offer our deepest thanks. We would also like to thank Professor Avital Simhony of Arizona State University for reading and commenting on our treatment of T. H. Green and welfare liberalism in Chapter 3, Professor Tracy Munsil of Arizona Christian University for her advice regarding religious-right and "fusionist" conservatism in Chapter 4, Dr. Jeffery Zavadil for his assistance on far-right and neo-Nazi parties in Europe in Chapter 7, and Rabbi Lawrence Raphael of Congregation Sherith Israel in San Francisco for his help on Jewish teachings about the treatment of animals in Chapter 8. We are once again indebted to Dr. Zhipei Chi of Renmin University Beijing for his advice regarding Chinese communism in Chapter 6, Professor Mary Dietz of Northwestern University for extensive and astute advice on Chapter 8 (particularly feminism and LGBT), and Professor Michaelle Browers of Wake Forest University, for assistance with radical Islamism. And for his helpful advice about the affinities between hunters and environmentalists, we again thank Steven Kingsbury.

We would also like to express our heartfelt gratitude to those scholars and fellow teachers whose thoughtful reviews of the previous edition of this book helped us to prepare this new one: Dilshod Achilov, East Tennessee State University; Robert Brem, College of Alameda and California State University, East Bay; Ralph Carter, Texas Christian University; Nicholas Damask, Scottsdale Community College; Gretchen Knudson Gee, Northern Arizona University; and Patrizia Longo, St. Mary's College of California. We are in their debt.

We are no less indebted to our students and our far-flung student readers in the United States and abroad, whose questions and requests for clarification of this or that point have led us time and again to improve our prose and clarify our meaning. This book is almost as much theirs as ours.

Terence Ball
Richard Dagger
Daniel I. O'Neill

TO THE READER

We want to call three features of this book to your attention. First, many of the primary works quoted or cited in the text are also reprinted, in whole or in part, in a companion volume edited by the authors, *Ideals and Ideologies: A Reader*, Tenth Edition. When we cite one of these primary works in this text, we include in the note at the end of the chapter a reference to the corresponding selection in *Ideals and Ideologies*.

Second, the study of political ideologies is in many ways the study of words. For this reason we frequently call attention to the use political thinkers and leaders make of such terms as "democracy" and "freedom." In doing so, we have found it convenient to adopt the philosophers' convention of using quotation marks to mean the word—as in "democracy" and "freedom."

Third, a number of key words and phrases in the text are set in boldface type. Definitions of these words and phrases appear in the Glossary at the back of the book, just before the Index.

We also invite you to send us any comments you have on this book or suggestions for improving it. You may email Terence Ball at tball@asu.edu, Richard Dagger at rdagger@richmond.edu, and Daniel O'Neill at doneill@ufl.edu.

Terence Ball
Richard Dagger
Daniel I. O'Neill

ABOUT THE AUTHORS

TERENCE BALL received his Ph.D. from the University of California at Berkeley and is Emeritus Professor of Political Science and Philosophy at Arizona State University. He taught previously at the University of Minnesota and has held visiting professorships at Oxford University, Cambridge University, and the University of California, San Diego. His books include *Transforming Political Discourse* (Blackwell, 1988), *Reappraising Political Theory* (Oxford University Press, 1995), and a mystery novel, *Rousseau's Ghost* (SUNY Press, 1998). He has also edited *The Federalist* (Cambridge University Press, 2003), *James Madison* (Ashgate, 2008), *Abraham Lincoln: Political Writings and Speeches* (Cambridge University Press, 2013), and coedited *The Cambridge History of Twentieth-Century Political Thought* (Cambridge University Press, 2003).

RICHARD DAGGER earned his Ph.D. from the University of Minnesota and has taught at Arizona State University and Rhodes College, and the University of Richmond, where he is currently the E. Claiborne Robins Distinguished Chair in the Liberal Arts. He is the author of many publications in political and legal philosophy, including *Civic Virtues: Rights, Citizenship, and Republican Liberalism* (Oxford University Press, 1997) and the forthcoming *Playing Fair: Political Obligation and the Problem of Punishment* (Oxford University Press).

DANIEL I. O'NEILL holds a Ph.D. from the University of California at Los Angeles and is now Associate Professor of Political Science at the University of Florida. He is the author of *The Burke-Wollstonecraft Debate: Savagery, Civilization, and Democracy* (Penn State University Press, 2007), coeditor of *Illusion of Consent: Engaging with Carole Pateman* (Penn State University Press, 2008), and author, most recently, of *Edmund Burke and the Conservative Logic of Empire* (University of California Press, 2016).

CHAPTER 1

IDEOLOGY AND IDEOLOGIES

It is what men think, that determines how they act.

John Stuart Mill, *Representative Government*

On a warm June evening in 2015, a prayer service was beginning at "Mother Emanuel"—the Emanuel AME church in Charleston, South Carolina—when a 21-year-old white man entered and asked the black worshippers if he could join them. They welcomed him warmly. After nearly an hour of praying with them (or perhaps pretending to), the young man took out a newly purchased pistol and began to shoot the congregants without regard to age or sex and with regard only to the color of their skin. While shouting racist epithets and slogans, he killed nine people, including the pastor, and wounded another before fleeing into the night. Arrested the next day, he told police that he had hoped to start a "race war." The investigation that followed showed the shooter to have been a racist, a white supremacist, and a neo-Nazi sympathizer. Photos posted on his Facebook page showed him holding weapons, flanked by a Confederate flag; in another photo he is burning an American flag. He had also written a 2,500-word "manifesto" denigrating African-Americans and defending white supremacy. The FBI deemed the crime an act of "domestic terrorism." And, far from starting his hoped-for race war, the shooter's murderous attack backfired. The conservative Republican governor and a majority of the Republican-led state legislature agreed to remove the Confederate flag from the state capitol grounds, where it had flown for decades. In the scale of things, this is a somewhat positive outcome of a negative act. Yet his was hardly the only instance of home-grown terrorism.

The annual Boston Marathon is a joyous occasion, attracting the best runners from across the country and around the world. But the 2013 Marathon, which had begun so happily on a sunny New England morning, ended abruptly and violently at 2:49 in the afternoon as two homemade bombs exploded near the finish line, killing three onlookers and grievously injuring 264 others. The bombers, two brothers who were self-radicalized Islamists, saw themselves as defenders of their faith, engaged in a **jihad**, or "holy war," against its Western, and especially its American, enemies. Violent and deadly as they were, however, the Boston Marathon bombings pale in comparison to an earlier terrorist attack.

On the morning of September 11, 2001, nineteen terrorists hijacked four American airliners bound for California from the East Coast and turned them toward targets in New York City and Washington, D.C. The hijackers crashed two of the airplanes into the twin towers of the World Trade Center in New York and a third into the Pentagon in Washington. Passengers in the fourth plane, which crashed in a field in Pennsylvania, thwarted the hijackers' attempt to fly it into another Washington target. In the end, nineteen al-Qaeda terrorists had taken the lives of nearly 3,000 innocent people. Fifteen of the terrorists came from Saudi Arabia; all nineteen professed to be devout Muslims fighting a "holy war" against Western, and particularly American, "infidels." Condemned in the West as an appalling act of terrorism, this concerted attack was openly applauded in certain Middle Eastern countries where al-Qaeda's now-deceased leader, Osama bin Laden, is widely regarded as a hero and its nineteen perpetrators as martyrs.

These terrorist attacks were not the first launched by radical Islamists, nor have they been the last. Since 9/11, Islamist bombings have taken more than 200 lives in Bali, more than 60 in Istanbul, more than 190 in Madrid, and more than 50 in London, to list several prominent examples. And in Syria and Iraq, ISIS (or Islamic State) uses social media to broadcast the beheadings and burnings-alive of its captives. How anyone could applaud or condone such deeds seems strange or even incomprehensible to most people in the West, just as the deeds themselves seem purely and simply evil. Evil they doubtless were. But the terrorists' motivation and their admirers' reasoning, however twisted, is quite comprehensible, as we shall see in the discussion of radical Islamism in Chapter 10 of this book.

Nor should we think that all terrorists come from the Middle East or act in the name of Allah or Islam. For evidence to the contrary, we need only look back to 9:02 on the morning of April 19, 1995, when a powerful fertilizer bomb exploded in front of the Murrah Federal Building in Oklahoma City. One hundred sixty-eight people, including nineteen children, died in that act of terror by American neo-Nazis. More than 500 people were seriously injured. The building was so badly damaged that it had to be demolished. The death and destruction attested not only to the power of the bomb. It also attested to the power of ideas—of neo-Nazi ideas about "racial purity," "white power," Jews, and other "inferior" races and ethnic groups. At least one of the bombers had learned about these ideas from a novel, *The Turner Diaries* (discussed at length in Chapter 7). The ideas in this novel, and in contemporary neo-Nazi ideology generally, have a long history that predates even Hitler (to whom *The Turner Diaries* refers as "The Great One"). This history and these ideas continue to inspire various "skinheads" and militia groups in the United States and elsewhere.

These are dramatic, and horrific, examples of the power of ideas—and specifically of those systems of ideas called *ideologies*. As these examples of neo-Nazi and radical Islamic terrorism attest, ideologies are sets of ideas that shape people's thinking and actions with regard to race, nationality, the role and function of government, the relations between men and women, human responsibility for the natural environment, and many other matters. So powerful are these ideologies that Sir Isaiah Berlin (1909–1997), a distinguished philosopher and historian, concluded that there are two factors that, above all others, have shaped human history in [the twentieth] century. One is the development of the natural sciences and technology... The other, without doubt, consists in the great ideological storms that have altered the lives of virtually all mankind: the Russian Revolution and its aftermath—totalitarian tyrannies of both right and left and the explosions of nationalism, racism, and, in places, of religious bigotry, which, interestingly enough, not one among the most perceptive social thinkers of the nineteenth century had ever predicted.

When our descendants, in two or three centuries' time (if mankind survives until then), come to look at our age, it is these two phenomena that will, I think, be held to be the outstanding characteristics of our century—the most demanding of explanation and analysis. But it is as well to realise that these great movements began with ideas in people's heads: ideas about what relations between men have been, are, might be, and should be; and to realise how they came to be transformed in the name of a vision of some supreme goal in the minds of the leaders, above all of the prophets with armies at their backs.[1]

Acting upon various visions, these armed prophets—Lenin, Stalin, Hitler, Mussolini, Mao, and many others—left the landscape of the twentieth century littered with many millions of corpses of those they regarded as inferior or dispensable, or both. As the Russian revolutionary leader Leon Trotsky said with some understatement, "Anyone desiring a quiet life has done badly to be born in the twentieth century."[2]

Nor do recent events, such as 9/11 and subsequent terrorist attacks, suggest that political ideologies will fade away and leave people to lead quiet lives in the twenty-first century. We may still hope that it will prove less murderous, but so far it appears that the twenty-first century will be even more complicated politically than the twentieth was. For most of the twentieth century, the clash of three political ideologies—liberalism, communism, and fascism—dominated world politics. In World War II, the communist regime of the Soviet Union joined forces with the liberal democracies of the West to defeat the fascist alliance of Germany, Italy, and Japan. Following their triumph over fascist regimes, the communist and liberal allies soon became implacable enemies in a Cold War that lasted more than forty years. But the Cold War ended with the collapse of communism and the disintegration of the Soviet Union, and the terrifying but straightforward clash of ideologies seemed to be over. What President Ronald Reagan had called the "evil empire" of communism had all but vanished. Liberal democracy had won, and peace and prosperity seemed about to spread around the globe.

Or so it appeared for a short time in the early 1990s. In retrospect, however, the world of the Cold War has been replaced by a world no less terrifying and certainly more mystifying: a world of hot wars, fought by militant nationalists and racists bent on "ethnic cleansing"; a world of culture wars, waged by white racists and black Afrocentrists, by religious fundamentalists and secular humanists, by gay liberationists and "traditional values" groups, by feminists and antifeminists, and many others besides; and a world of suicide bombers and terrorists driven by a lethal combination of anger, humiliation, rage, and religious fervor. How are we, as students—and, more important, as citizens—to make sense of this new world with its bewildering clash of views and values? How are we to assess the merits of, and judge between, these very different points of view?

One way to gain the insight we need is to look closely at what the proponents of these opposing views have to say for themselves. Another is to put their words and deeds into context. Political ideologies and movements do not simply appear out of nowhere, for no apparent reason. To the contrary, they arise out of particular backgrounds and circumstances, and they typically grow out of some sense of grievance or injustice—some conviction that things are not as they could and should be. To understand the complicated political ideas and movements of the present, then, we must understand the contexts in which they have taken shape, and that requires understanding something of the past, of history. To grasp the thinking of neo-Nazi skinheads, for example, we must study the thinking of their heroes and ideological ancestors, the earlier Nazis from whom the neo- (or "new-") Nazis take their bearings. And the same is true for any other ideology or political movement.

Every ideology and every political movement has its origins in the ideas of some earlier thinker or thinkers. As the British economist John Maynard Keynes observed in the mid-1930s, when the fascist Benito Mussolini, the Nazi Adolf Hitler, and the communist Joseph Stalin all held power,

> The ideas of economists and political philosophers, both when they are right and when they are wrong, are more powerful than is commonly understood. Indeed the world is ruled by little else. Practical men, who believe themselves to be quite exempt from any intellectual influences, are usually the slaves of some defunct economist. Madmen in authority, who hear voices in the air, are distilling their frenzy from some academic scribbler of a few years back.[3]

In this book we shall be looking not only at those "madmen in authority" but also at the "academic scribblers" whose ideas they borrowed and used—often with bloody and deadly results.

All ideologies and all political movements, then, have their roots in the past. To ignore or forget the past, as the philosopher George Santayana remarked, is to risk repeating its mistakes. If we are fortunate enough to avoid those mistakes, ignorance of the past will still keep us from understanding ourselves and the world in which we live. Our minds, our thoughts, our beliefs and attitudes—all have been forged in the fires and shaped on the anvil of earlier ideological conflicts. If we wish to act effectively and live peacefully, we need to know something about the political ideologies that have had such a profound influence on our own and other people's political attitudes and actions.

Our aim in this book is to lay a foundation for this understanding. In this introductory chapter our particular aim is to clarify the concept of ideology. In subsequent chapters we will go on to examine the various ideologies that have played an important part in shaping and sometimes radically reshaping the political landscape on which we live. We will discuss liberalism, conservatism, socialism, fascism, and other ideologies in turn, and in each case we will relate the birth and the growth of the ideology to its historical context. Arising as they do in particular historical circumstances—and typically in response to real or perceived crises—ideologies take shape and change in response to changes in those circumstances. These changes sometimes lead to perplexing results—for instance, today's conservatives sometimes seem to have more in common with early liberals than today's liberals do. Such perplexing results would not occur, of course, if political ideologies were fixed or frozen in place, but they are not. They respond to the changes in the world around them, including changes brought about by people acting to promote their political ideologies.

That is to say that ideologies do not react passively, like weather vanes, to every shift in the political winds. On the contrary, ideologies try to shape and direct social change. The men and women who follow and promote political ideologies—and almost all of us do this in one way or another—try to make sense of the world, to understand society and politics and economics, in order either to change it for the better or to resist changes that they think will make it worse. But to act upon the world in this way, they must react to the changes that are always taking place, including the changes brought about by rival ideologies.

Political ideologies, then, are dynamic. They do not stand still, because they cannot do what they want to do—shape the world—if they fail to adjust to changing conditions. This dynamic character of ideologies can be frustrating for anyone who wishes to understand *exactly* what a liberal or a conservative is, for it makes it impossible to define liberalism or conservatism or any other ideology with mathematical precision. But once we recognize that political ideologies are rooted in, change with, and themselves help to change historical circumstances, we are on the way to grasping what any particular ideology is about.

WHY *POLITICAL* IDEOLOGY?

To answer this question we first need to ask and answer another even more elementary question: Why politics? The answer, quite simply, is that people cannot live solitary, self-sufficient lives; they need the presence of other people if they are to survive and flourish. But within any group of mutually interdependent people, differences will inevitably arise. Politics is the art of resolving these differences without resorting to force or coercion. At its best, politics is about discussion, debate, talking and listening, and compromise—the "political arts," as they are sometimes called. But why political *ideologies?* The answer is that within or between societies, some differences—those based on ideas, ideals, and principles— are harder to resolve than more practical problems. An example might help here.

Imagine a town whose citizens agree that a new school is needed. The question arises as to where that school should be built. Some want it located on the west side of town, others on the east. A meeting is called to discuss and resolve the matter. Chances are that the townspeople will compromise and decide to locate the new school in the center of the town, if that option is open. This is a simple solution to a practical problem. But suppose that the question arises, should the school be a taxpayer-supported public school or a tuition-supported private school? Matters now cease to be purely practical, and ideological differences come quickly into play. Some citizens favor the former option, others the latter. Those in the first group contend that education is a shared public good that should be freely available to all alike, regardless of wealth, income, or social standing. Those in the second contend, on the contrary, that the only "real" goods are private ones, paid for by individuals according to what they wish and what they can afford for their children; other people's children are not their concern. Here we have a very real and deep difference of outlook traceable to different *ideas*—to *ideological* differences—not only about education but about individual versus shared responsibility, about public versus private, and so on through a long list. Such differences tend to be more intractable and perhaps even insoluble—in which case the citizens are likely to split the difference, compromise, and create a system in which public schools are available to those who want them, and private schools are available for those who do not.

Of course, matters are likely to be much more complicated than our simple example suggests. Consider, for example, differences arising over the school's curriculum. What should students be taught about the origins and development of different species, including our own? Should Darwin's theory of natural selection (often mistakenly called the theory of evolution) be taught alongside, or instead of, the theory of Intelligent Design? Should there be sex education and, if so, of what should the curriculum consist and at what age should it be taught? Should prayers and other forms of religious practice be permitted in the classroom, in school assemblies, and at athletic contests? Needless to say, these are not hypothetical questions but ones debated in school districts all across the nation. And they are, in the end, not merely pedagogical questions but *political* questions that require some knowledge of ideologies and ideological differences if they are to be understood at all.

We now need to inquire into these enigmatic entities called "ideologies." What are they? And how do they work?

A WORKING DEFINITION OF "IDEOLOGY"

There is at first sight something strange about the word "ideology." Other terms ending in "-ology" refer to fields of scientific study. So, for example, "biology"—the prefix coming from the Greek *bios*, or "life"—is the scientific study of life. "Psychology" is the study of psyche, or mind. "Sociology" is the study of society. It seems only logical, then, that "ideology" would be the scientific study of ideas. And that is just what ideology originally meant when the term *idéologie* was coined in eighteenth-century France.[4]

Over the last two centuries, however, the meaning of the term has shifted considerably. Rather than denoting the scientific study of ideas, "ideology" has come to refer to a set of ideas that tries to link thought with action. That is, ideologies attempt to shape how people *think*—and therefore how they *act*.

As we shall use the term, then, *an ideology is a fairly coherent and comprehensive set of ideas that explains and evaluates social conditions, helps people understand their place in society, and provides a program for social and political action.* An ideology, more precisely, performs four functions for people who hold it: the (1) *explanatory*, (2) *evaluative*, (3) *orientative*, and (4) *programmatic* functions. Let us look more closely at these four functions.

Explanation. An ideology offers an explanation of why social, political, and economic conditions are as they are, particularly in times of crisis. At such times people will search, sometimes frantically, for some explanation of what is happening.

Why are there wars? Why do depressions occur? What causes unemployment? Why are some people rich and others poor? Why are relations between different races so often strained, difficult, or hostile? To these and many other questions, different ideologies supply different answers. But in one way or another, every ideology tries to answer these questions and to make sense of the complicated world in which we live. A Marxist might explain wars as an outgrowth of capitalists' competition for foreign markets, for instance, while a fascist is apt to explain them as tests of one nation's "will" against another's. A libertarian will probably explain inflation as the result of government interference in the marketplace, while a black liberationist will trace the roots of most social problems to white racism. Their explanations are quite different, as these examples indicate, but all ideologies offer a way of looking at complex events and conditions that tries to make sense of them. Moreover, **ideologues**—people who try to persuade others to accept their ideology—typically want to reach as many people as possible, and this desire leads them to offer simple, and sometimes simplistic, explanations of puzzling events and circumstances.

Evaluation. The second function of ideologies is to supply standards for evaluating social conditions. There is a difference, after all, between explaining why certain things are happening and deciding whether those things are good or bad. Are all wars evils to be avoided, or are some morally justifiable? Are depressions a normal part of the business cycle or a symptom of a sick economic system? Is full employment a reasonable ideal or a naive pipe dream? Are vast disparities of wealth between rich and poor desirable or undesirable? Are racial tensions inevitable or avoidable? Again, an ideology supplies its followers with the criteria required for answering these and other questions. If you are a libertarian, for example, you are likely to evaluate a proposed policy by asking if it increases or decreases the role of government in the lives of individuals. If it increases government's role, it is undesirable. If you are a feminist, you will probably ask whether this proposed policy will work for or against the interests of women, and then either approve or disapprove of it on that basis. Or if you are a communist, you are apt to ask how this proposal affects the working class and whether it raises or lowers the prospects of their victory in the class struggle. This means that those who follow one ideology may evaluate favorably something that the followers of a different ideology greatly dislike—communists look upon class struggle as a good thing, for instance, while fascists regard it as an evil. Whatever the position may be, however, it is clear that all ideologies provide standards or cues that help people assess, judge, and appraise social policies and conditions so that they can decide whether those policies and conditions are good, bad, or indifferent.

Orientation. An ideology supplies its adherent with an orientation and a sense of identity—of who he or she is, the group (race, nation, sex, and so on) to which he or she belongs, and how he or she is related to the rest of the world. Just as hikers and travelers use maps, compasses, and landmarks to find their way in unfamiliar territory, so people need something to find their social identity and location. Like a compass, ideologies help people orient themselves—to gain a sense of where they are, who they are, and how they fit into a complicated world. If you are a communist, for example, you most likely think of yourself as a member of the working class who belongs to a party dedicated to freeing workers from capitalist exploitation and oppression, and you are therefore implacably opposed to the ruling capitalist class. Or if you are a Nazi, you probably think of yourself as a white person and member of a party dedicated to preserving racial purity and enslaving or even eliminating "inferior" races. Or if you are a feminist, you are apt to think of yourself as first and foremost a woman (or a man sympathetic to women's problems) who belongs to a movement aiming to end sexual oppression and exploitation. Other ideologies enable their adherents to orient themselves, to see their situation or position in society, in still other ways, but all perform the function of orientation.

Political Program. An ideology, finally, tells its followers what to do and how to do it. It performs a programmatic or prescriptive function by setting out a general program of social and political action. Just as doctors prescribe medicine for their patients and fitness trainers provide a program of exercise for their clients, so political ideologies prescribe remedies for sick societies and treatments designed to keep the healthy ones in good health. If an ideology provides a diagnosis of social conditions that leads you to believe that conditions are bad and growing worse, it will not be likely to win your support unless it can also supply a prescription or program for action that seems likely to improve matters. This is exactly what ideologies try to do. If you are a communist, for example, you believe it important to raise working-class consciousness or awareness in order to prepare for the overthrow of capitalism, the seizure of state power, and the eventual creation of a cooperative, communist society. If you are a Nazi, however, you think it important for the "superior" white race to isolate, separate, subordinate—and perhaps exterminate—Jews, blacks, and other "inferior" peoples. If you are a libertarian, your political program will include proposals for reducing or eliminating government interference in people's lives and liberties. But if you are a traditional conservative, you may want the state or government to intervene in order to promote morality or traditional values. Different ideologies recommend very different programs of action, as these examples demonstrate, but all recommend a program of some sort.

Political ideologies perform these four functions because they are trying to link thought—ideas and beliefs—to action. Every ideology provides a vision of the social and political world not only as it is, but as it *should* be, in hopes of inspiring people to act either to change or to preserve their way of life. If it does not do this—if it does not perform all four functions—it is not a political ideology. In this way our functional definition helps to sharpen our picture of what an ideology is by showing us what it is—and is not.

One thing an ideology is *not* is a scientific theory. To be sure, the distinction between an ideology and a scientific theory is sometimes difficult to draw. One reason for this is that the proponents of political ideologies often claim that their views are truly scientific. Another reason is that scientists, particularly social scientists, sometimes fail to see how their own ideological biases shape their theories. And political ideologies frequently borrow from scientific theories to help explain why the world is as it is. For example, some anarchists and some liberals have used Darwin's theory of evolution for their own purposes, as have Nazis and some communists.

Difficult as it may sometimes be to separate the two, this does not mean that there is no difference between a theory, such as Darwin's, and an ideology that draws on—and often distorts—that theory. Scientific theories are **empirical** in nature, which means that they are concerned with *describing* and explaining some feature or features of the world, not with *prescribing* what people *ought* to do. To the extent that these theories carry implications for how people *can* live, of course, they also carry implications for the **normative** problem of how people *should* live. This is especially true of theories of society, where empirical and normative concerns are remarkably difficult—some say impossible—to separate. But to say that scientific theories have implications for action is not to accept that they are ideologies. The scientist is not directly concerned *as a scientist* with these implications, but the ideologue certainly is.

We can also use our functional definition to distinguish political ideologies from some of the other "isms," such as terrorism, that are occasionally mistaken for ideologies. Because the names of the most prominent ideologies end with the suffix "ism," some people conclude that all "isms" must be political ideologies. This is clearly a mistake. Whatever else they are, alcoholism, magnetism, and hypnotism are not political ideologies. Nor is terrorism. Terrorism may offer a program for social and political action, thus performing the programmatic function, but it does not itself explain and evaluate conditions or provide people with an orientation. Terrorism is a strategy that some ideologues use to try to advance their causes, but it is not itself an ideology. Nor are **nationalism** and **anarchism**, as we shall see shortly.

This functional definition, finally, helps distinguish democracy from political ideologies. Unlike socialism, conservatism, and the other ideologies, democracy offers no explanation of why things are the way they are, and it is only in a very vague and loose sense that we can say that democracy serves the evaluative, orientative, or programmatic functions. Almost all political ideologies claim to be democratic, furthermore, which is something they could hardly do if democracy were an ideology itself. One can easily claim to be a conservative democrat, a liberal democrat, or a social(ist) democrat, for instance—much more easily than one can claim to be a socialist conservative, say, or a liberal fascist. This suggests that democracy, or rule by the people, is an *ideal* rather than an ideology—a topic to be pursued further in the next chapter.

In all of these cases, the functional definition helps to clarify what an ideology is by eliminating possibilities that do not perform all four functions. There are other cases, however, where our functional definition is not so helpful. The task of distinguishing a political theory or philosophy from an ideology is one of them. In this case the functional definition offers little help, for political theories can also perform the same four functions. The chief difference is that they do so at a higher, more abstract, more principled, and perhaps more dispassionate level. The great works of political philosophy, such as Plato's *Republic* and Rousseau's *Social Contract*, certainly attempt to explain and evaluate social conditions, just as they try to provide the reader with a sense of his or her place in the world. They even prescribe programs for action of a very general sort. But these works and the other masterpieces of political philosophy tend to be highly abstract and complex—and not, therefore, the kind of writing that stirs great numbers of people into action. Political ideologies draw on the works of the great political philosophers, much as they draw on scientific theories to promote their causes. But because their concern to link thought to action is so immediate, political ideologies tend to simplify, and even to oversimplify, the ideas of political philosophers in order to make them accessible—and inspiring—to masses of ordinary people. The difference between a political philosophy and a political ideology, then, is largely a difference of degree. Although they can do the same things, political ideologies do them in much simpler, less abstract ways because their focus is more tightly fixed on the importance of action.[5] This, in the end, marks an important difference between political theories, on the one hand, and political ideologies, on the other.

Similar problems arise with regard to religion. Most religions, perhaps all, perform the explanatory, evaluative, orientative, and programmatic functions for their followers. Does this mean they are ideologies? It does if we define an ideology to be simply a "belief system," as some scholars propose.[6] Many scholars and quite a few ideologues have noted, moreover, the ways in which political ideologies take on the characteristics of a religion for their followers; one account of communism by disillusioned ex-communists, for instance, is called *The God That Failed*.[7] There is no denying that religious concerns have played, and continue to play, a major role in ideological conflicts—as we shall see in subsequent chapters. Still, there is an important difference between religions and political ideologies. Religions are often concerned with the supernatural and divine—with God (or gods) and the afterlife (or afterlives)—while ideologies are much more interested in the here and now, with this life on this earth. Rather than prepare people for a better life in the next world, in other words, political ideologies aim to help them live as well as possible in this one.

This difference, again, is a matter of degree. Most religions take an active interest in how people live on earth, but this is neither their only nor necessarily their main concern. But for a political ideology, it is. Even so, drawing sharp and clear distinctions between political ideologies, on the one hand, and scientific theories, political philosophies, and religions, on the other, is not the most important point for someone who wants to understand ideologies. The most important point is to see how the different ideologies perform the four functions and how they make use of various theories, philosophies, and religious beliefs in order to do so.

HUMAN NATURE AND FREEDOM

For a political ideology to perform these four functions—the explanatory, evaluative, orientative, and programmatic—it must draw on some deeper conception of human potential, of what human beings are capable of achieving. This means that implicit in every ideology are two further features: (1) a set of basic beliefs about *human nature* and (2) a conception of *freedom*.

Human Nature

Some conception of human nature—some notion of basic human drives, motivations, limitations, and possibilities—is present, at least implicitly, in every ideology. Some ideologies assume that it is the "nature" of human beings to compete with one another in hopes of acquiring the greatest possible share of scarce resources; others hold that people are "naturally" inclined to cooperate with one another and to share what they have with others. So, for example, a classical liberal or a contemporary libertarian is likely to believe that human beings are "naturally" competitive and acquisitive. A communist, by contrast, will hold that competitiveness and acquisitiveness are "unnatural" and nasty vices nurtured by a deformed and deforming capitalist system—a system that warps people whose "true" nature is to be cooperative and generous. Still other ideologies take it for granted that human beings have a natural or innate racial consciousness that compels them to associate with their own kind and to avoid associating or even sympathizing with members of other races. Thus, Nazis maintain that it is "natural" for races to struggle for dominance and "unnatural" to seek interracial peace and harmony. They also deny that there is a single, universal human nature shared by all human beings; each race, they say, has its own unique "nature."

These competing conceptions of human nature are important to the understanding of political ideologies because they play a large part in determining how each ideology performs the four functions that every ideology must perform. They are especially important because each ideology's notion of human nature sets limits on what it considers to be politically possible. When a communist says that you ought to work to bring about a classless society, for instance, this implies that he or she believes that a classless society is something human beings are capable of achieving, and something, therefore, that human nature does not rule out. When a conservative urges you to cherish and defend traditional social arrangements, on the other hand, this implies that he or she believes that human beings are weak and fallible creatures whose schemes for reform are more likely to damage society than to improve it. Other ideologies take other views of human nature, but in every case the program a political ideology prescribes is directly related to its core conception of human nature—to its notion of what human beings are truly like and what they can achieve.

Freedom

Strange as it may seem, every ideology claims to defend and extend "freedom" (or "liberty," its synonym). Freedom figures in the performance of both the evaluative and programmatic functions, with all ideologies condemning societies that do not promote freedom and promising to take steps to promote it themselves. But different ideologies define freedom in different ways. A classical conservative's understanding of freedom differs from a classical liberal's or contemporary libertarian's understanding, for instance; both, in turn, disagree with a communist's view of freedom; and all three diverge radically from a Nazi's notion of freedom. This is because freedom is an **essentially contested concept**.[8] What counts as being free is a matter of controversy, in other words, because there is no one indisputably correct definition of "freedom."

Because every ideology claims to promote freedom, that concept provides a convenient basis for comparing and contrasting different ideologies. In later chapters, therefore, we will explicate each ideology's conception of freedom by fitting it within the triadic, or three-cornered, model proposed by Gerald MacCallum. According to MacCallum,[9] every conception of freedom includes three features: (A) an agent, (B) a barrier or obstacle blocking the agent, and (C) a goal at which the agent aims. And every statement about freedom can take the following form: "A is (or is not) free from B to achieve, be, or become C."

To say that someone is free, in other words, is to say that he or she is *free from* something and therefore *free to do* something. The *agent* is the person or group that is or should be free. But an agent is not simply free; to be free, an agent must be *free to* pursue a *goal*, whether it is speaking one's mind, practicing one's religion, or merely going for a stroll in the park. No one can be free to pursue a goal, however, unless he or she is also free from particular *obstacles*, barriers, or restraints. These may take a wide variety of forms—walls, chains, prejudices, and poverty, to name a few—but the point is that no one can be free when there are obstacles that prevent him or her from doing what he or she wants to do. So "freedom" refers to a relationship involving an agent who is both free from some obstacle and free to achieve some goal.

We can visualize this relationship in a diagram (see Figure 1.1).

Consider how these three aspects of freedom are present even in so ordinary a question as, Are you free tonight? The agent in this case is "you," the person being asked the question. There are no obvious obstacles or goals specified in the question, but that is because the point of the question is to learn whether some obstacle keeps the agent from pursuing a particular goal. That is, when we ask someone whether he or she is free tonight, we are trying to determine whether anything—such as the need to study for a test, to go to work, or to keep a promise to someone else—prevents that person from doing something. If not, then the agent in this instance is free.

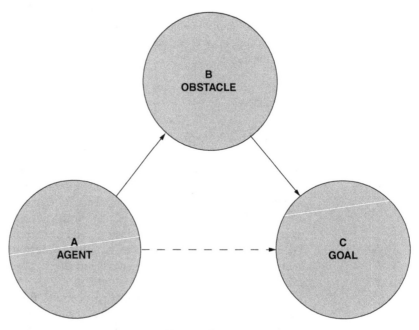

FIGURE 1.1   The triadic model of freedom.

But what of *political* freedom? According to MacCallum, people have different views of what counts as freedom in politics because they identify A, B, and C in different ways. Let us examine each of these, beginning with the agent, proceeding to a consideration of the agent's goals, and returning to examine the barriers or obstacles facing the agent in pursuing those goals.

The Agent. The agent can be an individual, a class, a group, a nation, a sex, a race, or even a species. As we shall see in Chapter 3, liberals typically talk of freedom as the freedom of the individual. Marx and the Marxists, by contrast, focus their attention on the freedom of a particular class—the working class (Chapter 5). Mussolini and the Italian Fascists identified the agent as a nation-state, and German fascists (Nazis) identified it as a race (Chapter 7). For feminists, the gender identity of the agent is all-important (Chapter 8). And other ideologies identify the agent in different ways.

The Goal. Agents have goals. Different kinds of agents have different kinds of goals. A Nazi's goal is the "purity" and supremacy of the white race. A communist's goal is the achievement of a classless communist society. A liberal's goal is for everyone to live in his or her own way, without undue interference from others. A feminist's goal is to live in a society that recognizes and rewards the capacities and worth of women. And so on for all other ideologies.

Obstacles. In pursuing their goals, agents often encounter obstacles in their path. These obstacles can take a variety of forms—material or physical conditions (poverty or physical disabilities, for instance); crime; or social, political, and economic ideas, ideologies, institutions, practices, traditions, and beliefs. Women confront sexism and sexual discrimination. Communists confront the apathy and **"false consciousness"** of the workers and the economic and political power of the capitalist class. Nazis confront Jews, blacks, and other so-called "inferior races." Ideologies also frequently view other ideologies as obstacles or barriers to be removed. Fascists, for instance, see the liberal emphasis on the individual and the socialist emphasis on equality as obstacles in the way of a united, disciplined, and free society. Whatever form the obstacles take, they must be overcome or removed. The more obstacles these agents can remove, the freer they will be. To the degree that they are unable to overcome the barriers, they are not free but "unfree." When the individuals—or class or race or gender—a political ideology takes to be its agent are not free to realize their goals, then the ideology will call for action to remove the obstacles to their freedom. Throughout the history of political ideologies, that action has often taken the form of revolution.

IDEOLOGY AND REVOLUTION

In its original political use, the word **"revolution"** referred to a return to an earlier condition. Like the revolution of the earth around the sun, or a wheel turning full circle, a political revolution was a revolving back to a starting point. But after the American and French revolutions of the eighteenth century, "revolution" took on a more radical meaning. The American Revolution began as an attempt to *restore* the colonists' rights as Englishmen, but it ended with the creation of a new country with a new system of government. Then, while that new system was still taking shape, the French Revolution began with the intention not of returning to the old ways but of introducing a radically new social and political order. As we shall see in Chapter 3, this revolution went further than the men who launched it intended, and it ended in a way that none of them wanted. But it did bring about sweeping changes in the social, economic, and political life of France. Indeed, the French Revolution sent shock waves through all of Europe and much of the rest of the world, waves so strong that their effects are still felt today. One sign of this is the way political positions are now commonly described as **left**, **right**, or **center**. These terms come from the seating arrangements in the National Assembly of the revolutionary period. Those who favored more or less radical change congregated on the left side or "wing" of the chamber, and those who resisted change gathered on the right. That is why, even today, we talk of the right wing, the left wing, and the moderate centrists in politics.

Modern revolutionaries do not simply want to replace one set of rulers or leaders with another or to make minor changes or reforms in the political structure. Their aim is to overthrow the old order, which they believe to be fundamentally rotten or corrupt. Changes or reforms are not enough, in their view, if the government and society are diseased at the roots. When this is the case, they say, the only solution is to uproot the whole social order and replace it with something better. This is literally a radical approach, for the word "radical" comes from the Latin *radix*, meaning "root."

Of course, people will not undertake anything so radical as a revolution unless they believe that it is indeed possible to bring about a fundamental change for the better in society. This is why conservatives tend to be suspicious of revolutions; their low estimate of human nature generally leads them to believe that sweeping improvements in society are practically impossible. Conservatism differs from the other ideologies in this respect, however. Almost all of the others hold that human reason and action can bring about great advances in society, politics, and the quality of life. Each ideology has its own idea of what counts as an advance or improvement, to be sure, but all except traditional or classical conservatism have been generally optimistic about the possibility of dramatic progress and significant improvement in the quality of human life.

In this respect, political ideologies are products of the modern world. In earlier times, most people had every reason to believe that their lives would be much the same as their parents' and grandparents' lives. Most people made their living from the soil or the sea, and changes in their ways of life were so slow in coming that they usually had little reason to believe that their children's or grandchildren's lives would be significantly different from their own. In the modern world, however, the pace of change has become so rapid that we now have "futurists" (or futurologists), who make careers of anticipating the changes to come; others, meanwhile, fear that they will not be able to adjust or keep up with change as their jobs and perhaps even their attitudes become obsolete. For better or worse, we live in an age of innovation. And ours, for better or worse, is also an age of ideology.

Ideologies and innovation are connected in an important way. The scientific, technical, and even artistic advances that mark the beginnings of the modern world in Europe instilled in many people a faith in progress, a belief that life on earth could become far more rewarding for many more people than it had ever been before. Before people could enjoy the fruits of progress, however, society itself would have to be reordered. The old ways of life retarded progress, especially when they prevented creative and vigorous individuals from using their energies and initiative to improve life for themselves and others. So the institutions that upheld the old ways of life—notably the Roman Catholic Church and the economic order of feudalism—came under attack from those who sought to free individuals to make the most of themselves in a new world of opportunity, progress, and reason. This attack took a number of forms, including the philosophical movement known as the **Enlightenment**, which saw the world as something to be comprehended by human reason and perfected by human action.

The attack on the old ways of life also took the form, even before the Enlightenment, of liberalism, the first of the political ideologies. How liberalism arose as a protest against religious conformity and feudalism in the name of tolerance and opportunity is a story told in Chapter 3. For now, the important point is that first liberalism and later all of the other political ideologies except conservatism grew out of a conviction that human life and society can and should be dramatically changed. It is this conviction that inspires people to lead or join movements to reshape and even revolutionize their societies. It is this conviction, in short, that gives rise to political ideologies.

NATIONALISM AND ANARCHISM

Two important political forces remain to be discussed in this introductory chapter. These forces, **nationalism** and **anarchism**, are sometimes considered ideologies in their own right. We disagree. Nationalism and anarchism take so many forms and are so entwined with so many different ideologies that we think it better not to treat them as distinct ideologies. Few nationalists are simply nationalists, for instance. They are, instead, liberal or conservative or communist or fascist nationalists. Anarchists are also divided, with most of them following either liberalism or socialism to their extreme conclusions. For these reasons, it seems better to weave the discussions of nationalism and anarchism into the discussions of those ideologies most closely connected with them. But first we need to have some idea of what nationalism and anarchism are.

Nationalism

One of the most powerful forces in modern politics, nationalism grows out of the sense that the people of the world fall more or less naturally into distinct groups, or nations. A person's nationality, in this view, is not something he or she chooses but something acquired at birth. Indeed, "nation" and "nationality" come from the Latin word *natus*, meaning "birth." A nation, then, is a group of people who in some sense share a common birth. In this way, a person's nationality may be separate from his or her citizenship. A member of the Cherokee nation, for example, may also be a citizen of the United States. From the perspective of the ardent nationalist, however, nationality and citizenship *should not* be separate. The people who share a common birth—who belong to the same nation—should also share citizenship in the same political unit, or state. This is the source of the idea of the **nation-state**, a sovereign, self-governing political unit that binds together and expresses the feelings and needs of a single nation.

Although nationalistic sentiments have been present through much of history, they became especially powerful following the Napoleonic Wars of the early 1800s. As Napoleon's French armies conquered most of Europe, they stirred the resentment, and sometimes the envy, of many of the conquered peoples. This was particularly true in Germany and Italy, neither of which was then a unified country. Germany was a scattered collection of separate political units, ranging in size and strength from the Kingdom of Prussia and the Austrian Empire to tiny duchies or baronies ruled by the local nobility. Even so, the people of these scattered communities spoke a common language and shared a common literature, as well as many customs and traditions. Italy's condition was similar. The victories of Napoleon's armies—the victories of the French *nation*—created a backlash of sorts, then, by inspiring many people in Germany, Italy, and elsewhere to recognize their respective nationalities and to struggle for unified nation-states of their own.

In the nineteenth and twentieth centuries this nationalistic struggle spread to virtually every part of the globe. Nationalistic sentiments and antagonisms helped to provoke World Wars I and II, for example, as well as the anticolonial "wars of national liberation" in Asia and Africa. For all their emotional power and political force, however, the ideas of nation and nationalism are plagued by difficulties. One is the difficulty of determining just what a nation is. What is it that marks a group of people as members of the same nationality? There is no clear answer to this question, although nationalists often appeal to such characteristics as shared race, ethnicity, culture, language, religion, customs, or history. These traits, however, are themselves notoriously difficult to define.

Even if we can determine what nationality is, another difficulty remains for nationalism. Many states—Canada, Switzerland, and the United States among them—include people of apparently different nationalities. Should each group have its own state? Should Switzerland be taken apart, for instance, with France, Germany, and Italy absorbing the French-speaking, German-speaking, and Italian-speaking parts, respectively? Should this happen even though the Swiss seem to be prospering under their present arrangement? Or should we say that together they form a new nation, the Swiss? If so, when and how did these people, with their different languages and cultures, become a single nation?

Despite these difficulties, there is no doubt that many people not only feel the pull of national sentiment but identify and orient themselves primarily in terms of nationality. These sentiments have been especially evident in the events following the collapse of communism in Eastern Europe. When the communist regimes that held together the Soviet Union and Yugoslavia fell, both countries split apart into states divided largely along lines of nationality. In those areas where no national group was powerful enough to establish an independent state, as in the Bosnian section of the former Yugoslavia, bitter warfare between former neighbors was the result. The tug of nationalism even pulled apart Czechoslovakia, which in the 1990s peacefully divided itself into a Czech and a Slovakian state. For all the difficulties of defining what a nation is, then, nationalism remains a real and powerful force in politics.

Anarchism

Contrary to popular misconception, anarchy does not mean chaos or confusion, nor do anarchists favor chaos and confusion. The word comes from the Greek *an archos*, meaning "no rule" or "no government." An anarchist, then, is someone who advocates abolishing the state and replacing its coercive force with voluntary cooperation among freely consenting individuals. As the anarchist sees it, government by its very nature is immoral and evil. All governments force people to do things they do not want to do—pay taxes, fight in wars, follow orders, and so on—so all governments engage in immoral, coercive actions. One could agree with this assessment, of course, yet maintain that government or the state is simply a necessary evil that people should continue to obey. But the anarchist believes that the state is not necessary but is simply evil. Given the chance, anarchists insist, people can live together peacefully and prosperously with no coercive authority over them.

All anarchists agree, then, that the state is an evil to be abolished in favor of a system of voluntary cooperation. But there the agreement ends. Some anarchists are radical individualists who advocate a competitive, capitalist—but stateless—society. Others are communalists who detest capitalism and believe that anarchism requires the common ownership and control of property. Some anarchists advocate the violent overthrow of the state; others are pacifists who believe that only a peaceful path can lead to a cooperative society. In other words, anarchism takes so many different forms—right, left, communist, capitalist-libertarian, feminist, ecological, violent, non-violent, etc.—that it is difficult to the point of impossibility to characterize and analyze it as a single ideology. The disagreements and differences among anarchists, in short, overwhelm the single point on which they agree. As one student of anarchism has said, "anarchism is not really *an* ideology but rather the point of intersection of several ideologies."[10] That is why instead of having a single chapter dealing with all the varieties of anarchism, we give each its due in different chapters. Thus anarchism receives extensive treatment, though not in a chapter of its own.

Like nationalism, anarchism has played a major part in the development of modern political ideologies. In the late nineteenth and early twentieth centuries, in particular, it was a potent political force in many parts of the world. Since then its influence has waned. Small bands of anarchists continue to argue that the state is immoral and that anarchy is possible, but few now take direct action against the state.

CONCLUSION

We began by noting how important ideologies are in the conflicts that characterize modern political life. We then defined "ideology" as a more or less coherent and comprehensive set of ideas that performs four functions for those who accept it: (1) it *explains* why social conditions are the way they are; (2) it *evaluates* those conditions; (3) it *orients* people so they can see how they fit into society; and (4) it *prescribes a program* for social and political action. In every ideology, moreover, there are core assumptions about *human nature* and *freedom*—assumptions that have led most ideologies, at one time or another, to call for revolution.

In later chapters we will examine the history and structure of different ideologies. Before doing that, however, we need to look more closely at *democracy*. As we explain in the following chapter, democracy is not itself an ideology but an *ideal* that different ideologies either reject outright or, more often, pursue in different ways.

Discussion Questions

1   What is the triadic model of freedom? What are its parts, and how can they be used to analyze political ideologies?
2   What is a political ideology? In what ways is an ideology similar to, and in what ways different from, a scientific theory or a religion?
3   How do different ideologies arise in the first place?
4   Why are conceptions of or ideas about human nature and freedom so important to political ideologies?
5   Ball, Dagger, and O'Neill maintain that nationalism and anarchism are not political ideologies in their own right. Do you agree with them? Explain why you agree or disagree.

NOTES

1   Isaiah Berlin, *The Crooked Timber of Humanity: Chapters in the History of Ideas* (New York: Vintage Books, 1992), p. 1.
2   As quoted in Isaiah Berlin, *Liberty* (Oxford: Oxford University Press, 2002), p. 55.
3   John Maynard Keynes, *The General Theory of Employment, Interest, and Money* (New York: Harcourt, Brace & World, 1936), p. 383.
4   For accounts of the origin and history of "ideology," see Terrell Carver, "Ideology: The Career of a Concept," in Terence Ball, Richard Dagger, and Daniel I. O'Neill, eds., *Ideals and Ideologies: A Reader*, 10th ed. (New York and London: Routledge, 2017), selection 1.1; Mark Goldie, "Ideology," in Terence Ball, James Farr, and Russell L. Hanson, eds., *Political Innovation and Conceptual Change* (Cambridge: Cambridge University Press, 1989), pp. 266–291; and George Lichtheim, *The Concept of Ideology, and Other Essays* (New York: Random House, 1967).
5   For further discussion of the relationship between political philosophies and political ideologies, see Michael Freeden, *Ideologies and Political Theory: A Conceptual Approach* (Oxford: Clarendon Press, 1996), pp. 27–46.
6   Philip Converse, "The Nature of Belief Systems in Mass Publics," in David Apter, ed., *Ideology and Discontent* (New York: Free Press, 1964).
7   Arthur Koestler et al., *The God That Failed*, R. H. S. Crossman, ed. (Freeport, NY: Books for Libraries Press, 1972; originally published 1949).
8   For a detailed explanation of this term, see W. B. Gallie, "Essentially Contested Concepts," *Proceedings of the Aristotelian Society* 56 (1955–1956): 167–198.
9   Gerald MacCallum, Jr., "Negative and Positive Freedom," *Philosophical Review* 76 (1967): 312–334. This now-classic essay is reprinted in David Miller, ed., *The Liberty Reader* (Boulder and London: Paradigm, 2006), pp. 100–122.
10   David Miller, *Anarchism* (London: Dent, 1984), p. 3.

FOR FURTHER READING

Arendt, Hannah. *On Revolution*. New York: Viking, 1963.

Berlin, Isaiah. *Liberty. Ed. Henry Hardy*. Oxford: Oxford University Press, 2002.

——. "Nationalism: Past Neglect and Present Power," in Berlin, *Against the Current: Essays in the History of Ideas*. Harmondsworth, U.K.: Penguin, 1982.

Bookchin, Murray. *Post-Scarcity Anarchism*. London: Wildwood House, 1974.

Carter, April. *The Political Theory of Anarchism*. London: Routledge & Kegan Paul, 1971.

Dunn, John. "Revolution," in Terence Ball, James Farr, and Russell L. Hanson, eds., *Political Innovation and Conceptual Change*. Cambridge: Cambridge University Press, 1989. pp. 333–355.

Freeden, Michael. *Ideology: A Very Short Introduction*. Oxford: Oxford University Press, 2003.

—— ed., *Oxford Handbook of Political Ideologies*. Oxford: Oxford University Press, 2013.

Journal of Political Ideologies. Oxford: Carfax Publishing, 1996–.

Kohn, Hans. *Nationalism: Its Meaning and History*. Princeton, NJ: D. Van Nostrand, 1955.

Lichtheim, George. *The Concept of Ideology, and Other Essays*. New York: Random House, 1967.

McLellan, David. *Ideology*. Minneapolis: University of Minnesota Press, 1986.

Miller, David. *Anarchism*. London: Dent, 1984.

Pfaff, William. *The Wrath of Nations: Civilization and the Furies of Nationalism*. New York: Simon & Schuster, 1993.

Wolff, Robert Paul. *In Defense of Anarchism*. New York: Harper & Row, 1970.

Woodcock, George. *Anarchism*. Harmondsworth, U.K.: Penguin, 1963.

Yack, Bernard. *The Longing for Total Revolution*. Princeton, NJ: Princeton University Press, 1986.

From the Ball, Dagger, and O'Neill Reader *Ideals and Ideologies*, Tenth Edition

Part I: The Concept of Ideology

1.1 Terrell Carver—Ideology: The Career of a Concept

CHAPTER 2

THE DEMOCRATIC IDEAL

No one pretends that democracy is perfect or all-wise. Indeed, it has been said that democracy is the worst form of Government except all those other forms that have been tried from time to time.

Winston Churchill

For most of recorded human history, "democracy" was reviled as rule by the mob or by the unwashed and ignorant. By contrast, one of the most striking features of contemporary politics is the almost universal popularity of democracy. There are few people nowadays, whether major political leaders or ordinary citizens, who do not praise (or at least pay lip service to) democracy and claim to be democrats. Except for fascists, Nazis, and radical Islamists, in fact, almost everyone seems to agree that democracy is desirable. But this agreement comes in the midst of vigorous, sometimes violent, ideological conflict. How can this be? How can men and women of almost all ideological persuasions—liberal and socialist, communist and conservative—share this belief in the value of democracy?

One possible explanation is to say that many people use the word "democracy" in a hypocritical or deceptive way. Democracy is so popular that everyone will try to link his or her ideology, whatever it may be, to democracy. The formal title of East Germany before the collapse of its communist regime in 1989–1990 was the German Democratic Republic, for instance. Yet the government of this "democracy" strictly limited freedom of speech and effectively outlawed competition for political office. With this and other examples in mind, some critics have complained that the word "democracy" has been misused so often as to rob it of any clear meaning.

A second explanation is that followers of different ideologies simply have different ideas about how to achieve democracy. Almost all agree that democracy is a good thing, but they disagree on how best to bring it about. Most people in the United States regard a dictatorship as an obviously undemocratic regime, but Mao Zedong, the leader of the Chinese Communist Party for more than forty years, maintained that his government was a "people's democratic dictatorship." Mao apparently saw no contradiction in this term because he believed that China needed a period of dictatorship to prepare the way for democracy. Perhaps, then, there is a genuine and widespread agreement that democracy is the true *end* or *goal* of ideological activity, with disagreement arising only over the proper *means* for achieving that end.

Although there may be merit in both of these positions, we think that a third explanation provides a deeper insight into the problem. This is that different people quite simply mean different things by democracy. They may all say that they want to achieve or promote democracy, but they disagree about *how* to do this because they disagree about *what* democracy truly is. With respect to political ideologies, we may say that democracy is an *ideal* that most ideologies espouse; but because people have very different understandings of what democracy is, they pursue it in very different ways. They may even come into conflict with one another in their attempts to achieve or promote democracy as they understand it.

Democracy, then, like freedom, is an **essentially contested concept**. The democratic ideal is itself deeply involved in the ideological conflict of the modern world. To understand this conflict, we need to know more about democracy and the democratic ideal. In particular, we need to know what "democracy" originally meant and why it is only in the last two centuries or so that democracy has been widely regarded as a desirable form of government.

THE ORIGINS OF DEMOCRACY

"Democracy" the word and democracy the form of political life both began in ancient Greece. The word comes from a combination of the Greek noun *demos*, meaning "people" or "common people," and the verb *kratein*, "to rule." For the Greeks, *demokratia* meant specifically "rule or government by the common people"—that is, those who were uneducated, unsophisticated, and poor. Because these people made up the majority of the citizenry, democracy was identified, as it often is today, with majority rule. But it is important to note that this majority consisted mainly of a single class, the *demos*. Many Greeks thus understood democracy to be a form of class rule—government by and for the benefit of the lower or working class. As such, it stood in contrast to aristocracy, rule by the *aristoi*—the "best"—those supposedly most qualified to govern.

The center of activity in ancient Greece, which was not united under a single government, was the self-governing *polis*, or city-state. Athens, the largest *polis*, provides the best example of a democratic city-state. Throughout most of the second half of the fifth century BCE, the period renowned as the Golden Age of Athens, Athenians called their *polis* a democracy. Not everyone willingly accepted this state of affairs, but those who did seemed to embrace democracy enthusiastically. This attitude is evident in the words attributed to Pericles, the most famous leader of the Athenian democracy, in his Funeral Oration:

> Our form of government does not enter into rivalry with the institutions of others. We do not copy our neighbors but are an example to them. It is true that we are called a democracy, for the administration is in the hands of the many and not of the few. But while the law secures equal justice to all alike in their private disputes, the claim of excellence is also recognized; and when a citizen is in any way distinguished, he is preferred for the public service, not as a matter of privilege but as the reward of merit. Neither is poverty a bar, but a man may benefit his country [*polis*] whatever be the obscurity of his condition.[1]

Pericles's words hint at the tension between aristocrats and democrats in ancient Athens. The aristocrats generally believed that only the well-established citizens, those with substantial property and ties to the noble families, were wise enough to govern. Pericles and the democrats, however, believed that most citizens were capable of governing if only they could afford to take the time away from their farms and work. To this end, the Athenian democracy paid citizens an average day's wages to enable them, poor as well as rich, to go to the assembly and decide policy by the direct vote of the citizens. Citizens also were paid to serve on juries, sometimes for as much as a year at a time. As further testimony to their faith in the *demos*, the Athenians filled a number of their political offices not by election but by randomly selecting citizens through a lottery.

Pericles's Funeral Oration also suggests another distinction of great significance to the Athenians, that between the public-spirited citizen (*polites*) and the self-interested individual who preferred a private life (*idiotes*). In Athens, Pericles said,

> an Athenian citizen does not neglect the state [*polis*] because he takes care of his own household; and even those of us who are engaged in business have a very fair idea of politics. We alone regard a man who takes no interest in public affairs, not as harmless, but as a useless character; and if few of us are originators, we are all sound judges of a policy.[2]

Even more significant to Athenian democracy was another aspect of citizenship, as Athenians understood it. To be a citizen, one had to be an adult, free, male Athenian. Women, resident foreigners, and slaves (who together made up a majority of the population) were all excluded. In fact, only about one out of ten inhabitants of Athens was a citizen. From the vantage point of the twenty-first century, then, it appears that Athenian democracy was hardly democratic at all.

This judgment becomes even more striking when we consider that Athenian democracy provided little if any protection for minority rights. Although citizens were equal in the eyes of the law, this did not mean that any citizen was free to express his opinions regardless of how unpopular those opinions might be. The Athenian assembly sometimes banished citizens temporarily from Athens, without trial and even without legal charges being brought against them, simply because the majority of the assembly thought these citizens posed a danger to the *polis*. This was the practice of *ostracism*, so called because of the shell or piece of pottery (*ostrakon*) on which Athenian citizens wrote the names of those they wished to banish.

Sometimes the punishment for voicing unpopular views was even harsher. We know this especially from the case of Socrates (469–399 BCE), the philosopher who saw himself as a gadfly whose mission it was to sting the sluggish citizens of Athens out of complacency by raising questions about their most basic beliefs. "I never cease to rouse each and every one of you," he said, "to persuade and reproach you all day long and everywhere I find myself in your company."[3] In 399 BCE, when the democratic faction was in control, some citizens stung back, falsely accusing Socrates of religious impiety and corrupting the morals of the youth of Athens. Socrates was tried, convicted, and condemned to death by poison. Thus Athens, the first democracy, created the first martyr to the cause of free thought and free speech.

In the fifth and fourth centuries BCE, however, those who favored democracy found themselves facing a different criticism. This was the complaint that democracy is a dangerously unstable form of government. Foremost among those who made this complaint was Socrates's student and friend, Plato (427–347 BCE).

Plato believed that democracy is dangerous because it puts political power into the hands of ignorant and envious people. Because they are ignorant, he argued, the people will not know how to use political power for the common good. Because they are envious they will be concerned only with their own good, which they will seek to advance by plundering those who are better off. Because they are both ignorant and envious they will be easily swayed by demagogues—literally, leaders of the *demos*—who will flatter them, appeal to their envy, and turn citizen against citizen. From democracy, in short, comes civil war and anarchy, the destruction of the city-state. When democracy has left the *polis* in this wretched condition, according to Plato's analysis, the people will cry out for law and order. They will then rally around anyone strong enough to bring an end to anarchy. But such a person will be a despot, Plato said, a tyrant who cares nothing about the *polis* or the people because he cares only for power. So from democracy, rule by the people, it is but a series of short steps to tyranny.[4]

This argument against democracy found favor with a number of political thinkers, including Plato's student Aristotle (384–322 BCE). Aristotle maintained that democracy is one of six basic kinds of political regimes or constitutions. Governing power, he said in his *Politics*, may be in the hands of one person, a few people, or many; and this power may be exercised either for the good of the whole community—in which case it is good or true—or solely for the good of the rulers—in which case it is bad or perverted. By combining these features, Aristotle arrived at the six-cell scheme illustrated in Figure 2.1.

Two features of Aristotle's classification of regimes are especially noteworthy. The first, of course, is that he followed Plato in considering democracy to be bad or undesirable. For Aristotle, democracy is a corrupt form of rule because the *demos* tends to be shortsighted and selfish. The common people will recklessly pursue their own interests by taking property, wealth, and power from the few with little or no regard for the peace and stability of the *polis* as a whole. But this serves their interests only in the short run, and in the end they will bring chaos, and ultimately tyranny, to the whole *polis*.

In Book V of the *Politics* Aristotle analyzes the close connection between democracy and tyranny by showing how the former can and often does turn into the latter. First, a demagogue persuades the common people that their democracy is in grave danger from some real or imagined enemy, whether foreign or domestic. Next, he endears himself to the people by presenting himself as their friend and their savior from this foe. He then starts a war against this real or imagined enemy, based on bogus reasons which the gullible people accept (fear having made them even more gullible), and leaving them "always in need of a leader." This war serves to distract the people, preventing them from paying attention to what the demagogue-turned-tyrant is doing domestically, including undermining the constitution, making his cronies and hangers-on wealthy at public expense, and expanding his powers into areas that were previously constitutionally off-limits. The tyrant maintains and increases his power by distrusting anyone outside his inner circle; he tells lies that the people believe; he plants spies in their midst to ferret out critics and dissidents; he withholds information and practices censorship; he divides the people among themselves by "sowing dissensions" and "creating quarrels" over real or imaginary issues of little or no importance, thereby turning the people against each other so that they wrongly see their fellow citizens as enemies and don't pay attention to what the tyrant is doing. The tyrant also implicates as many people as possible in his crimes, so that they too are guilty; he subverts the administration of justice by "altering the constitution" and putting innocent people on trial and letting guilty men go unpunished if they are willing to serve him; he uses the courts and other agencies of government to help his friends and harm his enemies; he distracts the people with spectacles and entertainments; he makes some people beholden and loyal to him by enriching them at public expense. And, above all, the tyrant maintains the *appearance* of being a good man and a just ruler: he *pretends* to be a "guardian of the public treasury" even as he plunders it by spending recklessly; he will *seem* to be a "steward of the public rather than a tyrant"; and—not least—he will "*appear* to be particularly devout in his worship of the gods." By these means, Aristotle notes, the tyrant lulls the people into a deep civic sleep. If and when they wake up it's likely to be too late to retrieve their rights and restore their liberties.

Another noteworthy feature of Aristotle's classification of constitutions or regime-types is the inclusion of **polity**, the good form of rule by the many. For Aristotle, polity differs from democracy because it mixes elements of rule by the few with elements of rule by the many. The virtue of this **mixed constitution** or **government** is that each group can keep an eye on the other—the well-to-do few on the many, the many on the well-to-do few—so that neither class can pursue its interest at the expense of the common interest. Aristotle also suggested that polity may differ from democracy in its distribution of wealth and property; in a democracy, that is, the many will be poor. This is simply the way things usually are, according to Aristotle, and there is little one can do about it. However, in those rare but fortunate circumstances where most of the people are neither rich nor poor but "have a moderate and sufficient property," one can expect the many to rule in a prudent manner.[5] This is because the many, when they are "middle class," will avoid the excesses of the envious poor and the arrogant rich. Seeing the good of the *polis* as their own good, the middling many will work to maintain moderation, peace, and stability in the city-state.

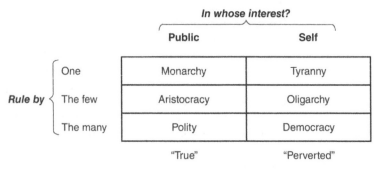

| | | In whose interest? | |
		Public	Self
Rule by	One	Monarchy	Tyranny
	The few	Aristocracy	Oligarchy
	The many	Polity	Democracy
		"True"	"Perverted"

FIGURE 2.1 Aristotle's classification of regimes.

Erich Lessing/Art Resource, NY

Aristotle (384–322 BCE)

In the final analysis, Aristotle believed polity to be good—he even suggested that it is the best of the six regimes—while democracy is bad. But he also argued that democracy is better than tyranny and oligarchy because many heads are better judges than one or a few. Even if none of the common people is an especially good judge of what is right or wrong, good or bad, their collective judgment is still better than that of any individual or small group, including a group of experts. This is true, Aristotle said, in the same way that "a feast to which many contribute is better than a dinner provided out of a single income."[6] Besides, democracy gives more men the chance to participate in the active life of the citizen—to rule and be ruled in turn, as he put it.

Yet even as Aristotle was celebrating the citizen and the *polis*, this way of life was falling victim to a much larger political unit—**empire.** First under the leadership of Philip of Macedon (382–336 BCE), and then under his son (and Aristotle's student), Alexander the Great (356–323 BCE), the Hellenic Empire spread across Greece, throughout the Middle East, and all the way to India and Egypt. As the empire concentrated all power in the hands of the emperor, the self-governing city-state died, and rule by the many, whether in the form of democracy or polity, perished with it.

DEMOCRACY AND REPUBLIC

Popular government survived in the ancient world, but in the form of a **republic** rather than a democracy. "Republic" derives from the Latin *res publica*, which literally means "the public thing," or "public business." It took on a more specific meaning, however, in the hands of the Greek historian Polybius (c. 200–c. 118 BCE).

The Republic and Mixed Government

Polybius spent some seventeen years in Rome as a hostage. This experience inspired his interest in the growth of Roman power, which Polybius saw as part of a cycle of the rise and fall of great powers. Every powerful empire or country is doomed to decline, Polybius said, for both history and nature tell us that no human creation lasts forever. Still, some hold their power far longer than others, and Polybius thought the example of Rome helped to explain why this is so.

The key to Rome's success, Polybius argued in his *Histories*, was its mixed government. This was not an entirely new idea—Plato had hinted at it, as had Aristotle in his discussion of the polity—but Polybius developed it more clearly than his predecessors. The Roman Republic was a mixed government, he said, because neither one person (monarchy), nor the few (aristocracy), nor the many (democracy), held all the power. Instead, the republic mixed or balanced these three regimes in a way that provided the benefits of each form while avoiding its defects. Rather than give all power to one person, or a few people, or the common people, in other words, the Roman Republic divided power among the three. Thus, the people as a whole exercised some control over policy-making through their assemblies—at least the free, adult males did—but so, too, did the aristocrats, who controlled the Senate. Then, in place of a monarch, the republic relied on consuls to put the policies into effect. In this way, Polybius said, no group was able to pursue its own interest at the expense of the common good. Each kept watch over the others, and the result was a form of government that was free, stable, and long-lasting. Like an alloy that is stronger than any one of the metals that make it up, a mixed government, Polybius believed, will prove more durable than any "pure" or unmixed form of rule.

A republic, then, was a form of popular government, but its defenders insisted that it not be confused with a democracy. Democracy promoted vice—the self-interested rule of the common people—while a republic promoted virtue. Republican virtue (in Latin, *virtus*) was the ability of an individual to rise above personal or class interest to place the good of the whole community above one's own. Only active citizens could achieve and exercise this virtue, republicans argued. Such citizens would be eager to exercise their liberty, yet wary of any person or group who might try to seize power. Mixed government served both these purposes by encouraging some degree of popular participation in government while making it difficult for anyone to acquire enough power to threaten liberty and the common good.

Within 100 years of Polybius's death, however, the Roman Republic had given way to the Roman Empire. Beginning with Julius Caesar (100–44 BCE), a series of emperors drained the power from Rome's republican institutions and concentrated it in their own hands. Almost 1500 years would pass before the republican ideal was fully revived in the city-states of northern Italy during the **Renaissance**. Another 400 years would pass before the democratic ideal itself was revived.

Christianity and Democracy

There were, of course, many significant developments in the intervening years, perhaps the most significant being the rise of Christianity. In some respects Christianity seems a natural ally of democracy, for it proclaims that every person, regardless of gender, nationality, or status, is a child of God. By the standards of the ancient world, certainly, Christianity stood for radical equality. Rich or poor, slave or free, citizen or alien, Greek, Jew, or Roman, woman or man—none of these differences really mattered, the Christians preached, because all are equal in the eyes of God.

We might expect, then, that the early Christians would argue that everyone should have an equal voice in government. But they did not. This was not because the early Christians were antidemocratic but because they were antipolitical. Christians believed that life on earth is a preparation for the coming kingdom of God, an often painful pilgrimage to the Christian's true home in heaven; so by themselves the affairs of this world have no true value or lasting significance. Many early Christians also believed that the end of the world was near. These beliefs led some to take a lawless attitude. The common or orthodox position with regard to the law, however, was that Christians are obligated to obey human laws and earthly rulers. As St. Paul stated, "Let every person be subject to the governing authorities. For there is no authority except from God, and those that exist have been instituted by God. Therefore he who resists the authorities resists what God has appointed, and those who resist will incur judgment."[7] Where politics was concerned, in other words, the Christian message was simply to obey those in power and seek no power yourself.

Matters could not remain so simple, however, particularly when various Roman emperors sought to destroy this new and (to their eyes) dangerous religion. Matters became even more complicated when, in the fourth century AD, Christianity survived the persecutions to become the official religion of the Roman Empire. Then, following the collapse of the Roman Empire around CE 500, the Christian Church became the dominant institution in Europe. It remained so throughout the period we know as the Middle Ages—roughly CE 500 to CE 1400. With the disintegration of the empire, the church itself gradually divided into two wings: the Eastern Orthodox Church, led by the Byzantine Emperor, who ruled from Constantinople (now Istanbul); and the Roman Catholic Church, headed by the Bishop of Rome, who came to be known as the Pope. The rise and rapid spread of the Islamic faith throughout the Middle East, across Northern Africa, and into Spain in the seventh and eighth centuries also meant that much of the Mediterranean world was lost to Christianity. Yet the Roman Church saw itself as the one true church—"catholic" means "universal"—and it preached its message and enforced its doctrines wherever possible.

The Roman Church provided the spiritual bond that united most of Western and Central Europe throughout the Middle Ages. Yet there was no comparable political bond. The collapse of the Roman Empire had brought a return to localism, although not of the Greek city-state variety. There were some independent city-states in the Middle Ages—Rome, for instance, where the Pope ruled—but more common varieties of local rule developed around tribal loyalties or the old military regions of the fallen empire. This happened, in the latter case, as some regional commanders of the Roman army managed to keep their forces together and their regions secure even as the empire crumbled. From these *duces* and *comites*, who found themselves governing their territories as best they could, came the "dukes" and "counts" of the Middle Ages.

There were occasional attempts to revive a more nearly universal political bond in the form of a new empire, the most notable beginning on Christmas Day in the year 800, when Pope Leo III placed a crown on Charlemagne, king of the Franks, and proclaimed him emperor. Despite repeated efforts over the centuries, however, the new Holy Roman Empire never achieved the power and stature of the old; as the philosopher Voltaire later quipped, it was "neither holy, nor Roman, nor an empire." Local ties and loyalties simply proved stronger than the desire for a politically united Christendom.

These local ties and loyalties also encouraged **feudalism**. This form of social organization, rooted in the need for protection from marauding Vikings and Magyars, led to a great emphasis on "status," that is, one's station or position in society. A few people were aristocrats or nobles, some were free, and a great many more were serfs (peasants who lived and worked in bondage to an aristocrat in exchange for protection). According to the medieval ideal, every person occupied a rank or station in society and was expected to perform the duties and enjoy the privileges of that rank or station. In this way everyone supposedly contributed to the common good, just as every bee in a hive does what is best for all by performing its own strictly defined duties.

In such a society, there was little room for the democratic ideal. The outlook began to shift with the Renaissance, however, as a renewed concern for human achievement led to a revival of republicanism.

Renaissance and Republicanism

In the late Middle Ages, particularly in the thirteenth century, several developments prepared the way for the Renaissance (or "rebirth"). One of these was Western civilization's renewed contact with the East. This contact came about partly through the Crusades—that is, the attempts to recapture the Christian holy land of the Middle East from the "infidel" Muslims—and partly through dealings with Islamic Spain, which Muslims had conquered in the early 700s. As so often happens, contact with strangers from different cultures stimulated many in the West to examine their own customs and beliefs. The discovery that other people live quite satisfactorily in ways very different from what one has always assumed to be the natural and only reasonable way to live is often unsettling and disturbing. But it can also encourage creativity, as people begin to see that it is possible to live in different, and perhaps better, ways. This happened most directly as Christian scholars rediscovered, through Spain, many works of ancient scholarship that had been lost to the West since the collapse of the Roman Empire. The most significant of these in political terms was Aristotle's *Politics*, which was translated into Latin in 1260—but only after the Church convened a committee of scholars to determine whether the "pagan" philosopher's ideas were compatible with Christianity.

A second development preparing the way for the Renaissance was the revival of the self-governing city-state in Italy.[8] Many Italian cities enjoyed a measure of independence before the thirteenth century, but they remained subject to the Germanic head of the Holy Roman Empire. After years of struggle, they seized the opportunity presented by the death of Emperor Frederick II in 1250 to become self-governing city-states. Even as empire and monarchy were the predominant forms of rule, the citizens of these city-states looked for a way to justify their "new" form of government. They found this justification in the ancient theorists of republicanism.

These and other developments led to the flowering of Western culture in the fourteenth through sixteenth centuries that scholars of that time took to be a renaissance—a rebirth or revival that began in the Italian city-states. Under the inspiration of the ancient philosophers, they concluded that life on earth is not simply a vale of tears, a wearisome journey that the Christian must take on his or her way to the kingdom of God in heaven. On the contrary, life on earth, so rich and diverse, is not only worth living but worth living freely and fully. For human beings are capable of many wondrous things—not the least of which is self-government.

Drawing on the writings of Aristotle and Polybius and the examples of the ancient republics of Rome and Sparta, the Renaissance republicans argued for a revival of civic life in which public-spirited citizens could take an active part in the governance of their independent city or country. The key concepts in this republican discourse were *liberty, virtue,* and *corruption.* Nowhere were these concepts deployed more sharply and effectively than in the writings of Niccolò Machiavelli.

Machiavelli (1469–1527) was a prominent official in the republic of Florence in 1512 when the Medici family overthrew the republican government and installed themselves as rulers of the city-state. Implicated in a plot to overthrow the Medici and restore the republic, Machiavelli was arrested, tortured, and banished to his family estate in the countryside. While in exile, he wrote two books. The better known of the two is *The Prince,* the small book in which Machiavelli apparently instructs princes and petty tyrants to put conscience aside and do whatever it takes—lie, steal, even murder—to stay in power. Indeed, Machiavelli became so notorious that Shakespeare later referred to him as "the murderous Machiavel."[9] Even today we sometimes call a cunning and unscrupulous person "machiavellian."

Whether this is a fair reading of Machiavelli's purposes in *The Prince* is something scholars continue to debate.[10] But it definitely does *not* capture Machiavelli's purposes in his second, longer book, the *Discourses*. In this book Machiavelli makes clear his distrust of princes as he analyzes the factors that promote the longevity of a vital, virtuous, and free form of government—the republic.

For Machiavelli, a republic is a mixed government in which no single class rules. Instead, all classes share power as each checks the potential excesses of the others. It is a system of government in which vigilant citizens jealously guard their liberties against the threat of domination by would-be tyrants in their midst. For liberty, as Machiavelli understands it, *is* self-government; it is something found not in private life but in public action. But why must citizens be vigilant? Because as soon as they become complacent and indifferent to public affairs they will find a tyrant waiting to relieve them of the burden of self-government and deprive them of their liberty. Thus, Machiavelli insists that the greatest enemies of free government are complacent and self-interested citizens.

akg-images/Rabatti - Domingie/Newscom

Niccolò Machiavelli (1469–1527)

Such citizens care more for money and luxury than for the commonwealth. The love of wealth, luxury, and ease, together with a corresponding indifference to public affairs, is what Machiavelli calls "corruption." To keep corruption at bay, citizens must possess and exercise "civic virtue." That is, they must be attentive and alert to public affairs, always striving to do what is best not for themselves as private persons but as public-spirited *citizens* acting in the best interest of their republic. If citizens are to be "virtuous," then, they must be free—free to assemble, to argue among themselves, to expose corruption, and to criticize their leaders and one another. If citizens neither enjoy nor exercise these essential liberties, their republic is doomed to an early death and to be replaced by a tyranny.

According to Machiavelli, the greatest danger a republic faces is that it will be destroyed from within by corruption. But because foreign enemies are also likely to threaten republics, a genuinely free republic must also require all able-bodied males—and only males could be citizens—to be members of a citizen militia, prepared to take up arms against any external threat to their liberty.

Above all, Machiavelli maintained that a free government must be ruled not by the whim or caprice of any person or persons, or even of the majority of citizens, but by law. A truly free government is a government of laws, not of men. A government of laws is more consistent, more concerned with fairness, than a government of men. More important, laws are impersonal. We can depend on the laws without losing our independence. When we depend upon individual people or even a majority of men, we are subject to their will—and this can hardly be called liberty. This is why Machiavelli, like Aristotle long before him, considered pure democracy a bad form of government while regarding a mixed constitutional republic as the best form.

A mixed government, a virtuous citizenry, the rule of law—these were the republican ideals of Machiavelli's *Discourses*. If much of this sounds familiar, it is because this vision inspired the Atlantic republican tradition—a way of thinking about politics that spread from Italy to Great Britain in the seventeenth century—and from there to Britain's American colonies in the eighteenth.[11]

The Atlantic Republican Tradition

In Britain the turmoil of the 1600s sparked interest in both republicanism and democracy. Civil war broke out in 1642 as King Charles I and the English Parliament each claimed to be the sovereign or highest authority in the land. The war ended with the parliamentary forces victorious under the leadership of Oliver Cromwell, and in January 1649 Charles I was beheaded. An attempt to establish a republic followed, but it failed as Cromwell assumed the powers, if not quite the title, of monarch. (His official title was Lord Protector.) After Cromwell's death in 1658, another attempt to establish a republic also failed.

In these turbulent times, many Englishmen turned their thoughts to public matters. Among them was James Harrington (1611–1677), who published his *Oceana* (1656) apparently in hopes of persuading Cromwell to create a republic with a mixed or "balanced" system of government. More than a mixture of rule by one, the few, and the many, Harrington's "balance" included an effort to distribute land in a more nearly equal fashion so that no citizen would be dependent on another for his livelihood. This would help to ensure liberty under a government of laws, not of men. Harrington also advocated regular and frequent elections and a system of representation in which representatives would be rotated in and out of office. Like recurrent calls for term limits in American politics, this "rota" would presumably protect liberty by preventing anyone from acquiring too much power by winning reelection to office term after term. It would also promote virtue by enabling more citizens to take an active and responsible part in the government of the commonwealth.

In England, Harrington's ideas and those of other republican thinkers were aborted by the Restoration of 1660, when the Parliament recalled Charles II, son of the beheaded king, to the throne. But if republican ideas were eclipsed in England, they exercised great influence across the Atlantic in the colonies of British North America. Other influences were also at work, however, including the influence of men who had begun to speak favorably, for virtually the first time in 2000 years, of democracy. We shall see shortly how these influences intertwined to produce a "democratic republic" in the United States. But first we need to trace the reclamation of democracy.

THE RETURN OF DEMOCRACY

During the English Civil War of the 1640s, some supporters of the parliamentary cause took the radical position of advocating democracy. They reached this position in part because of their religious convictions. Like most of Northern Europe, Great Britain had legally forsaken Catholicism in the sixteenth century as the Protestant Reformation shattered the religious unity of Christendom. The new Protestant forms of Christianity emphasized a direct, immediate relationship between the individual and God. According to Martin Luther, the German priest who initiated the Reformation in 1517, what truly mattered was not strict conformity to church doctrine but faith and faith alone. Salvation did not come through priests, bishops, popes, and an elaborate church organization. All one needed was belief. Thus, the true Christian church was simply the congregation of the faithful or, as Luther put it, "the priesthood of all believers."

Seventeenth-Century Democrats

Although Luther did not conclude that this emphasis on individual conscience and faith made democracy desirable, others did. One was Roger Williams (1604–1683), a Protestant minister who left England for Massachusetts in 1631. In Massachusetts, Williams continually ran afoul of the colony's Puritan authorities. He insisted that the colonists should pay the American Indians for the land taken from them, for instance, and he advocated a sharp separation of religious and civil leadership—a radical step in a colony where church and government were nearly one and the same. The authorities banished Williams from the colony in 1636, whereupon he and his followers moved south, bought land from the Indians, and established the colony of Rhode Island. Rhode Island became known for its defense of religious liberty, but it is also noteworthy that the government of the colony, according to its constitution of 1641, was a

Democratical or Popular Government; that is to say, It is in the Power of the Body of Freemen, orderly assembled, or the major part of them, to make or constitute just Lawes, by which they will be regulated, and to depute from among themselves such Ministers [i.e., police officers, judges] as shall see them fairly executed between Man and Man.

The constitution of 1647 reaffirmed this commitment, proclaiming Rhode Island's form of government to be "Democraticall; that is to say, a Government held by ye free and voluntary consent of all, or the greater parte [i.e., majority] of the free inhabitants."[12]

Across the Atlantic in England, a group called the Levellers advanced similar ideas during the Civil War of the 1640s. The Levellers claimed that political authority could be founded only on the consent of the people. For the Levellers, this meant that the franchise—the right to vote—had to be extended to all adult males except for those who had surrendered this right either by committing crimes or by putting themselves, like servants and recipients of public charity, into dependence upon others. Such was the birthright of all men, the Levellers claimed, regardless of how much—or how little—property they owned. The most famous statement of this position came from Colonel Thomas Rainsborough, an officer in Oliver Cromwell's New Model Army:

> For really I think that the poorest he that is in England hath a life to live as the greatest he; and therefore truly, sir, I think it's clear, that every man that is to live under a government ought first by his own consent to put himself under that government; and I do think that the poorest man in England is not at all bound in a strict sense to that government that he hath not had a voice to put himself under...[13]

The radically democratic doctrine of that day became the conventional view of later times. But the Levellers failed to convince Cromwell and others in power of the wisdom of their arguments. For the most part, those engaged in political activity and debates continued to regard democracy as a dangerously unstable form of government. Still, the efforts of the Levellers and the example of Rhode Island mark the beginning of a remarkable, although gradual, shift in attitude toward democracy.

The United States as Democratic Republic

Democratic ideas and arguments played a part in the American War of Independence against Great Britain, but there were few favorable references to democracy either then or during the drafting of the Constitution of the United States in 1787. In general, "democracy" continued to stand for a form of class or even mob rule. It was, as Aristotle observed long ago, the bad form of popular government; the good form was the republic.

Throughout the quarrel with Great Britain that led to the Declaration of Independence in 1776, the American colonists typically couched their arguments in republican terms. They had no complaint against the form of British government, for the most part, because they believed it to be republican. With the Crown, the House of Lords, and the House of Commons sharing the powers of government, the British constitution was a mixture or balance of rule by one, the few, and the many, just as republican theory prescribed. The problem, as the colonists saw it, was corruption. Corrupt British officials were working to upset the balanced constitution so that they could concentrate all power in their own hands. Spurred by ambition and avarice, they aimed to replace a government of laws with a government of men, and their first target in this corrupt enterprise was the rights of Britain's American colonists.[14]

The war that the colonists fought at first to defend their rights as Englishmen soon became a war to secure their independence from England. Once they began to think about independence, however, the colonists also had to think about how best to organize the governments of the thirteen states. Faced with this problem, they drew again on the resources of republicanism. This fact is especially clear in John Adams's (1735–1826) *Thoughts on Government*, written early in 1776. Reading the works of republican writers, Adams said,

> will convince any candid [i.e., open] mind that there is no good government but what is republican. That the only valuable part of the British constitution is so because the very definition of a republic is "an empire of laws, and not of men." That, as a republic is the best of governments, so that particular arrangement of the powers of society ... which is best contrived to secure an impartial and exact execution of the laws is the best of republics.[15]

In the beginning, then, the favored form of government in the United States was not democratic but republican. The U.S. Constitution itself testifies to this, for it makes no mention of democracy. But it does guarantee to each state "a Republican Form of Government..." (Article 4, Section 4). Nor do we have far to look for signs that the Founders—the men who drafted the Constitution—intended the government of the United States as a whole to be a republic.

The first sign is the separation of the government's powers into three branches—the legislative, executive, and judicial—with each branch put into position to "check and balance" the other two. This is a modification of the old idea of mixed or balanced government. The executive branch corresponds to the monarchical element, rule by one; the judicial to the aristocratic, rule by the few; and the legislative to the popular, rule by the many. The correspondence is not quite this neat, however, as the legislative branch is itself a mixture of "aristocratic" and "democratic" elements. According to the original plan, the House of Representatives was to be a democratic body, closely responsive to the wishes of the people. Members of the House serve a two-year term of office, therefore, in the belief that the need to stand for reelection frequently will require them to stay in close contact with the voters. Members of the U.S. Senate, on the other hand, serve a six-year term precisely so that they may follow their own judgment rather than the voters' wishes. The "aristocratic" nature of the Senate was even clearer under the original Constitution, which placed election to the Senate in the hands of the state legislatures, not of the ordinary voters. This mode of election did not change until the Seventeenth Amendment (1913) established the direct election of senators.[16]

This system of checks and balances also reflects the republican fear of corruption. Checks and balances are necessary, James Madison (1751–1836) observed in his defense of the new Constitution, because men are not angels. They are, on the contrary, ambitious and competitive, and the key to good government is to keep ambitious men from destroying the liberty of the rest. In Madison's words,

> Ambition must be made to counteract ambition... It may be a reflection on human nature, that such devices should be necessary to control the abuses of government. But what is government itself, but the greatest of all reflections upon human nature? If men were angels, no government would be necessary. If angels were to govern men, neither external nor internal controls on government would be necessary. In framing a government which is to be administered by men over men, the great difficulty lies in this: you must first enable the government to control the governed; and in the next place oblige it to control itself.[17]

Other republican features of the Constitution appear in the Bill of Rights (1791)—the first ten amendments to the Constitution. The First Amendment, for instance, guarantees that Congress shall make no law depriving people of freedom of speech and assembly—two freedoms that republican writers saw as absolutely essential to the preservation of free government. In the Second Amendment, the republican emphasis on a civil militia also appears: "A well-regulated militia being necessary to the security of a free state, the right of the people to keep and bear arms shall not be infringed."

Thus, the Constitution created a government in which the popular element was checked and controlled by the Senate, the courts, and the president. Not everyone was entirely pleased with this arrangement. Alexander Hamilton (1755–1804) supported the proposed Constitution, but thought it too democratic. Others, like Patrick Henry (1736–1799), opposed it because it was not democratic enough. He and other "Antifederalist" critics of the Constitution objected that it took power from the state governments—which were closely connected to the wishes of the people—and concentrated it in the remote and dangerous federal government. It was largely in response to the Antifederalists' objections that Congress in 1791 added the Bill of Rights to the original Constitution.

In the course of the debate over the ratification of the Constitution, the term "democracy" began to play a prominent part in political disputes. The Federalists, as those who favored the new Constitution were called, attacked their opponents as reckless democrats. The Antifederalists responded by blasting the "aristocratic" bias and pretensions of the Federalists. Once the Constitution was ratified, this dispute persisted in a new form as two political parties gradually emerged to challenge each other for political power. One party, the Federalists, followed Hamilton's lead in trying to strengthen the national government. In response, a second party joined former Antifederalists with some prominent supporters of the Constitution, notably Thomas Jefferson (1743–1826) and James Madison. This party, which won a great victory in 1800 with Jefferson's election to the presidency, was known first as the Republican Party, then as the Democratic-Republican Party, and finally, under the leadership of Andrew Jackson, president from 1829 to 1837, simply as the Democratic Party.

Upon Jackson's election in 1828, the United States entered into a period heralded as "the age of the common man." The various state governments had abolished most property qualifications for voting, thus extending voting rights to almost all adult white males—but not to women, slaves, and Native Americans. In this era of Jacksonian democracy, Americans celebrated not only the glories of liberty but those of equality as well. While many found this new emphasis on democracy and equality exhilarating, others found it alarming. One observer, Alexis de Tocqueville, thought it a bit of both.

Tocqueville on Democracy

Tocqueville (1805–1859) was a French aristocrat who traveled throughout the United States in the early 1830s. Upon his return to France, he wrote *Democracy in America*, a two-volume work in which he analyzed democracy in the United States largely in order to foresee what the coming of democracy implied for France and the rest of Europe. Tocqueville saw democracy as an irresistible force that was overwhelming the ranks, orders, and aristocratic privileges of the old way of life. In many ways, Tocqueville took this to be a change for the better. Democracy frees the common people, for example, and gives them a chance to make their way in the world. But Tocqueville also warned that democracy, with its overbearing emphasis on equality, threatens to produce mediocrity or despotism—or both.

Democracy promotes mediocrity, Tocqueville claimed, precisely because it celebrates equality. When everyone is supposed to be equal, there will be tremendous pressure to conform—to act and think as everyone else acts and thinks. No one will want to stand out, to rise above the crowd, for fear of being accused of putting on airs and trying to be better than everyone else. Rather than risk this, Tocqueville warned, people will conform. The result will be a society in which those who have something original or outstanding to contribute will remain silent because of the social pressure toward equality. Tocqueville called this pressure to conform "the tyranny of the majority."

Democracy also presents the threat of despotism, a more old-fashioned kind of tyranny. Like Plato and Aristotle more than 2000 years earlier, Tocqueville warned that the common people are easily swayed by demagogues who flatter and mislead them in order to win power. An aristocracy helps to prevent this, he argued, because a class of people with inherited property and privileges will be on guard to protect its position against demagogues and despots. Once democracy and equality overwhelm this aristocratic barrier, however, there is little to prevent despotism from destroying liberty.

But Tocqueville did see a positive possibility in democracy, one that joined republicanism to the democratic ideal. He believed that civic virtue could be promoted through participation in public affairs. The people who join with their neighbors to settle common problems and disputes will learn the importance of cooperation, feel a strong attachment to their community, and develop those "habits of the heart" that lead them to identify their own welfare with the welfare of the community as a whole.[18] By offering all citizens the opportunity to participate, democracy promises to cultivate a widespread and deeply rooted devotion to the common good. For this reason Tocqueville was particularly impressed by two institutions of American democracy: the New England town meetings, where all citizens could participate directly in local government, and the shared responsibility of jury duty.

Alexis de Tocqueville (1805–1859)

THE GROWTH OF DEMOCRACY

Despite Tocqueville's concerns about the tendencies of democracies to degenerate into mediocrity and despotism, democracy became ever more popular. This popularity stemmed from a number of social and economic developments during the Industrial Revolution of the late eighteenth and nineteenth centuries. The most important of these were the growth of cities, the spread of public education, and improvements in communication and transportation such as the telegraph and railroad. Each of these developments helped to spread literacy, information, and interest in political matters among the populations of Europe and America, thereby contributing to the growing faith in the common people's ability to participate knowledgeably in public affairs.

In nineteenth-century England, the arguments for democracy tended to center on two concerns: self-protection and civic and self-development. According to the "philosophic radicals" or **Utilitarians**, the duty of government is "to promote the greatest happiness of the greatest number." The best way to do this, they concluded, is through representative democracy, which will enable every man to vote for representatives who will protect his interests. One Utilitarian, John Stuart Mill, went on to argue in *The Subjection of Women* (1869) that this chance at self-protection through voting ought to extend to women as well.

Mill also maintained that political participation is valuable because of the opportunity it provides for self-development. Like Tocqueville, Mill believed that democracy strengthens civic virtue among the common people through "the invigorating effect of freedom upon the character." Political participation—not merely voting for representatives, but also direct participation at the local level—will educate and improve people by teaching them discipline, sharpening their intelligence, and even shaping their morality. Thus Mill drew attention to

> the moral part of the instruction afforded by the participation of the private citizen, if even rarely, in public functions. He is called upon, while so engaged, to weigh interests not his own; to be guided, in case of conflicting claims, by another rule than his private partialities; to apply, at every turn, principles and maxims which have for their reason of existence the common good: and he usually finds associated with him in the same work minds more familiarised than his own with these ideas and operations... He is made to feel himself one of the public, and whatever is for their benefit will be for his benefit.[19]

Such arguments have helped to bring about a gradual extension of the franchise in the past 150 years. The right to vote was at first restricted to property-owning white males and later extended to all adult males—although this was not fully accomplished in Great Britain until 1885—then to male ex-slaves (at least technically) after the Civil War in the United States, and finally to women in the early 1900s in both countries. These extensions did not come easily or swiftly. Every extension of the franchise was resisted by many of those who already had the vote. Warnings and dire predictions of mayhem and mob rule were issued by defenders of the status quo—for example, on the eve of Britain's Reform Acts of 1832, 1867, and 1884; in the United States, before granting male ex-slaves the right to vote (Fifteenth Amendment) and enfranchising women (Nineteenth Amendment); in the run-up to the Seventeenth Amendment (1913), which allowed for the direct election of U.S. senators (who under the original Constitution were elected by state legislatures); and before Congress passed the Voting Rights Act (1965), which ensured African-Americans' right to vote. Switzerland, sometimes called the world's oldest continuous democracy, did not grant full voting rights to women until 1971.[20] Often, these changes came only after heated debate, protests, and violence. Some critics contend that even now women, people of color, and other minority groups are denied full membership in the United States, Canada, Britain, and other Western "democracies."

This is a matter of some dispute, of course. What is beyond dispute is that almost everyone in the so-called Western democracies accepts democracy as the best form of government. But so, too, do the leaders and peoples of many countries that are far from democratic by Western standards. How can we account for this?

DEMOCRACY AS AN IDEAL—AND IN PRACTICE

As we noted at the beginning of this chapter, democracy is now so popular that most political ideologies claim to favor it. Yet these supposedly democratic ideologies are in constant competition and occasional conflict with one another. The best explanation for this oddity is to say that different ideologies do indeed pursue and promote democracy, but they do so in different ways because they disagree about what democracy is. They can do this because democracy is not a single thing, as our brief history of democracy makes clear. Rather than a specific kind of government that must take a definite form, democracy is, instead, an ideal.

To say that democracy is an ideal means that it is something toward which people aim or aspire. In this respect it is like true love, inner peace, a perfect performance, or the surfer's perfect wave. Each is an ideal that inspires people to search or strive for it, but none is easy to find, or even to define. What one person takes to be true love, for instance, is likely to be quite different from another person's romantic ideal. So it is with democracy. Everyone agrees that democracy is government or rule by the people, but exactly what that means is subject to sharp disagreement. Who are "the people" who are supposed to rule? Only the "common" people? Only those who own substantial property? Only adult males? Or should everyone who lives in a country—including resident foreigners, children, and convicted felons have a formal voice in its government?

How, moreover, are "the people" to rule? Should every citizen vote directly on proposed policies, as the Athenians did, or should citizens vote for representatives, who will then make policy? If they elect representatives, do the people then cease to govern themselves? With or without representatives, should we follow majority rule? If we do, how can we protect the rights and interests of individuals or minorities, especially those who say and do things that anger or offend the majority? But if we take steps to limit the power of the majority—as a system of constitutional checks and balances does, for instance—are we not restricting or even retreating from democracy? The long-standing debate in the United States over term limits for members of Congress poses this problem in a particularly acute form. If we limit the number of terms for which an elected official can hold office, are we making the government more responsive to the people, and therefore more democratic? Or are we making it less democratic by denying a potential majority of voters the chance to reelect a representative they like time and time again?[21]

All this is by way of asking a recurring question about democracy: How far should majority rule extend? What, if any, limits may legitimately be placed on majority rule? Should voters be able to decide almost any and every issue by majority vote? The American Founders thought not, and Abraham Lincoln agreed with them. In 1854 Congress passed the Kansas-Nebraska Act into which its chief author, Senator Stephen A. Douglas of Illinois, had inserted his doctrine of popular sovereignty. According to Douglas's doctrine, a majority of voters (i.e., enfranchised white males) would decide whether their territory would enter the Union as a free or a slave state. How is it, Lincoln asked in one of the fiercest speeches of his career, that some men should be able to decide, democratically, to enslave others? There are, Lincoln thundered, some issues that should not be decided by majority vote.[22]

The same question arises from time to time, in different forms. For example, before they were repealed by the Supreme Court in 1967, thirty states had majority-approved statutes outlawing marriages between blacks and whites. That these laws were quite popular can be seen in a 1958 Gallup poll that reported that 96 percent of white Americans believed that interracial marriage should be illegal. But in the case of *Loving v. Virginia*, the Supreme Court, in a rare unanimous decision, declared that all such "anti-miscegenation" laws were unconstitutional. And before 2003—when the Court overturned them in *Lawrence v. Texas*—thirteen states had laws making engaging in same-sex relations a criminal act punishable by imprisonment. As of 2014, twenty-eight states had majority-approved laws or constitutional amendments outlawing same-sex marriage. In the following year the Court struck down these democratically passed laws. Critics claimed that in so doing the Court was being "undemocratic" by denying the will of the majority.

In these and many other instances, the Court and the Constitution thwart the will of the majority. Thus there is a continuing and oft-times troubling tension between majority will and minority rights.

Another troubling aspect of American democracy concerns the indirect—and, some critics claim, undemocratic—election of the president. Instead of electing the president directly, American voters elect electors—members of the Electoral College—who are pledged to vote for particular candidates. This system of indirect election effectively disenfranchises many Americans. For example, Democratic voters in a "red" state like Wyoming will be heavily outnumbered by Republican voters, and all three of Wyoming's electoral votes will therefore be cast for the Republican presidential candidate. Likewise, Republican voters in a "blue" state like New York are effectively disenfranchised in presidential elections. Thus, Democrats in Wyoming and Republicans in New York might as well not even bother to vote in presidential elections, since their states' electoral votes will not reflect their preferences. Moreover, as sometimes happens, the candidate with more popular votes can lose to the one with more electoral votes. This is what happened in the election of 2000 when Al Gore, who received half a million more votes than his opponent, lost the presidential election to George W. Bush, who received more electoral votes. This and other violations of the principle of "one person, one vote" have led some to call for direct election of the president, which would of course require a constitutional amendment. By way of precedent they point to the provision in the original Constitution (Article I, Section 3) requiring that senators be elected indirectly, by state legislatures. This provision was revoked by the Seventeenth Amendment (1913), which mandates direct popular election of senators. Whether the president should likewise be elected directly by the people remains a controversial question.

Yet another controversial question concerns the limits of the legitimate power of majorities to restrict the alleged rights of minorities. Particularly pointed instances of such majority power can be seen in recent elections in which majorities have voted to amend state constitutions so as to outlaw same-sex marriage. In 2008 California joined other states that had earlier defined marriage as a legal union of "one man and one woman." Defenders said that they had acted democratically in deciding the issue by majority vote. Critics claimed that no majority may legally and legitimately deprive anyone of the "equal protection" guaranteed by the U.S.

Constitution—and afforded by the institution of marriage. In 2015 the U.S. Supreme Court agreed, in the landmark decision discussed in Chapter 8.

And, not least, in modern representative democracies like that of the United States, money is a major factor in electoral politics. To run for public office—or, before that, to even be *nominated* to run—is enormously expensive. The vast majority of Americans cannot afford to run for any but the most local of offices, such as the school board or the library board. And those who do run for higher office must either be wealthy or rely heavily or even exclusively on financial donors. These donors—especially the wealthiest and most generous ones—typically expect something in return for their largesse; and what they expect is access to the office holder once he or she is elected. Senators, representatives—and presidents—are expected to "return the favor" by supporting legislation, policies, and pet programs that further the donors' financial or other interests. And this, say critics, is clearly undemocratic since, in a democracy, all citizens' interests ought to be given equal consideration. Critics contend that, as things now stand, matters are quite otherwise, as can be seen in the Supreme Court's decisions in several landmark cases, including *Citizens United* (2010). In that case the Court ruled that campaign contributions are a form of free speech and are therefore protected under the First Amendment, and that corporations are persons with full free-speech rights, including the right to donate unlimited amounts of money to candidates whose campaigns they choose to support. And, extending the reach of its *Citizens United* decision, the Court in 2014 abolished limits on total individual donations.[23] Critics contend that the likely result will be to replace democracy—rule by the majority of citizens—with plutocracy, i.e., rule by a wealthy minority. There are already signs that this may be happening.[24] In the most recent national elections, it cost approximately $1 billion to be elected president, $10 million to be elected to the Senate, and $1 million to win a seat in the House of Representatives. If one is to have any chance at all to hold higher office, one must turn to wealthy donors—either individual or corporate—for financial support; and these donors in turn expect what is euphemistically called "access," i.e., the sympathetic ear of office holders to whose campaigns they contributed.[25] As one prominent political theorist has observed, present-day American democracy deserves to be called "Democracy, Incorporated."[26]

Beginning in 2011 an increasing number of Republican-controlled state legislatures began passing laws requiring voters to show photo IDs at the polls, outlawing early voting and same-day voter registration, and other legislation to effectively restrict the right to vote. The justification offered for these laws is that they would curtail allegedly widespread voting fraud. Critics responded by noting that such fraud is rare and that the intended effect of these laws is to discourage or even disenfranchise voters who are poor, black, and/or Hispanic and who tend to vote Democratic.[27] Another long-standing barrier to blacks voting is the number of state laws that permanently bar convicted felons from voting, even after serving their sentences. Because African-Americans are disproportionately represented in the nation's prison population, such "felon disenfranchisement" laws hit them particularly hard. One in thirteen black Americans is barred for life from voting, for this reason alone—fully four times the number for whites. These laws are especially common in the American South.[28]

What are the likely effects of these developments on American democracy? Will they be benign, beneficial, or—as critics contend—harmful? Several effects became evident in the course of the 2012 elections. Some voters, especially in poorer precincts, stood in long lines for up to eight hours. Those without required voter IDs were made to cast provisional ballots, which would be counted only if the voter returned days later with proof of identification. Another evident effect is the record amounts spent on the presidential and congressional campaigns. For the first time ever, secretive "Super PACs" (political action committees) were allowed to contribute so-called "dark money" without disclosing the identities of the contributors. This set off the electoral equivalent of an arms race: when one side raises large amounts of money, the other side tries to match or exceed that amount, to which the first responds by raising even more money, and spending spirals ever upward. Not surprisingly, the 2012 election campaigns were the costliest ever. Nearly $6 billion were spent, with almost one-third—$1.75 billion—going to the presidential race alone. Many millions more were spent on campaigns at the state and local level, and on ballot initiatives regarding gay or same-sex marriage, genetically modified food labeling, and a host of other issues placed before the voters.

How does "big money" affect American politics? And what are the likely long-term effects of these and other developments on American democracy? These are troubling questions for anyone who claims to be a small-d democrat. As our brief history of democracy suggests, questions about the vitality and even the viability of democracy have been raised repeatedly and answered in very different ways over the centuries. Such questions have also led a number of political thinkers to worry about the instability of democracy, with a particular concern for its supposed tendency to degenerate into anarchy and despotism. This concern has been largely responsible for the creation of an alternative form of popular government: the republic. But the popularity of republicanism has waned as democracy has gained acceptance; where republicanism survives, it is mostly in the hybrid form of democratic republicanism.[29] This is especially evident in the United States, where a democratic commitment to universal suffrage is carried out within the republican institutional framework devised by the Founding Fathers and enshrined in the Constitution.

Despite the difficulties of defining it, the democratic ideal of "rule by the people" remains attractive to those who seek to promote freedom and equality, because democracy implies that in some sense every citizen will be both free and equal to every other. But exactly what freedom and equality are, or what form they should take and how the two relate to each other, is open to interpretation.

This is where political ideologies enter the picture. Whether they accept or reject it, all ideologies must come to terms with the democratic ideal. "Coming to terms" in this case means that political ideologies have to provide more definite notions of what democracy involves. They do this by drawing on their underlying conceptions of human nature and freedom to determine whether democracy is possible and desirable and, if so, what form it should take.

To put the point in terms of our functional definition of ideology, we can say that an ideology's explanation of why things are the way they are largely shapes its attitude toward democracy. If an ideology holds, as fascism does, that society is often in turmoil because most people are incapable of governing themselves, it is hardly likely to advocate democracy. But if an ideology holds, as liberalism and socialism do, that most people have the capacity for freedom and self-government, then the ideology will embrace the democratic ideal—as most of them have done in one way or another. The ideology that does so will then evaluate existing social arrangements and provide a sense of orientation for individuals based largely on how democratic it takes these arrangements to be. If the individual seems to be an equal partner in a society where the people rule in some suitable sense, then all is well; but if he or she seems to be merely the pawn of those who hold the real power, then the ideology will encourage people to take action to reform or perhaps to overthrow the social and political order. This, finally, will require a program for change in what the ideology takes to be a democratic direction.

Every political ideology, then, offers its own interpretation of the democratic ideal. This ideal it interprets or defines according to its particular vision. In turn, the men and women who promote political ideologies will use their vision of democracy to try to inspire others to join their cause.

THREE CONCEPTIONS OF DEMOCRACY

To clarify the connection between political ideologies and the democratic ideal, let us examine briefly the three principal versions of democracy in the modern world. Although all three share several features, their differences are sharp enough to make them distinctive and competing conceptions of democracy.

Liberal Democracy. As the name suggests, liberal democracy emerged from liberalism—the ideology examined in our next chapter. As with liberalism in general, liberal democracy stresses the rights and liberty of the individual, and it is this form of democracy that characterizes most Western democracies. For liberals, democracy is certainly rule by the people, but an essential part of this rule includes the protection of individual rights and liberties. This means that majority rule must be limited. Democracy is rule by the majority of the people, in this view, but only as long as those in the majority do not try to deprive individuals or minorities of their basic civil rights. The right to speak and worship freely, the right to run for public office, the right to own property—these are among the rights and liberties that liberals have generally taken to be necessary to realize the democratic ideal as they interpret it.

Social Democracy. Within the Western democracies, especially in Europe, the main challenge to the liberal conception is social democracy. This view is linked to the ideology of socialism. From a "social democratic" or "democratic socialist" perspective, the key to democracy is equality, especially equal power in society and government. Social democrats argue that liberal democracy puts poor and working-class people at the mercy of the rich. In the modern world, they say, money is a major source of power, and those who have wealth have power over those who do not. Wealth makes it possible to run for office and to influence government policies, so the rich exercise much greater influence when public policies are made. Yet this advantage, social democrats insist, is hardly democratic. Democracy is rule by the people, and such rule requires that every person have a roughly equal influence over the government, in keeping with the principle "one person, one vote." But we will not really have this equal influence, social democrats say, unless we take steps to distribute power—including *economic* power—in a more nearly equal fashion. That is why the program of social democrats typically calls for the redistribution of wealth to promote equality, public rather than private control of natural resources and major industries, and workers' control of the workplace. Like liberals, then, social democrats want to preserve civil liberties and promote fair competition for political office. Unlike liberals, however, they deny that most people can be truly free or political competition fair when great inequalities of wealth and power prevail.

People's Democracy. In communist countries, the prevailing version of the democratic ideal has been **people's democracy.** In some ways people's democracy is theoretically closer to the original Greek idea of democracy—rule by and in the interests of the *demos*, the common people—than liberal or social democracy. From a communist perspective, the common people are the proletariat, or the working class, and democracy will not be achieved until government rules in their interest. This does not necessarily mean that the proletariat must itself directly control the government. As we shall see in Chapter 5, communists once called for the **dictatorship of the proletariat**, a form of dictatorship that Karl Marx described as ruling in the interests of the working class. The immediate purpose of this dictatorship would be to suppress the capitalists or bourgeoisie who have previously used their power and wealth to exploit the working class. By suppressing them, the dictatorship of the proletariat supposedly prepares the common people for the classless society of the communist future, when the state itself will "wither away." In the meantime, people's democracy is to consist of rule by the Communist Party for the benefit of the working majority. This is the sense in which Mao Zedong spoke of a "people's democratic dictatorship" in the People's Republic of China.

When the Soviet Union and its communist regime disintegrated in the early 1990s, the idea of people's democracy suffered a serious blow. But in China, the world's most populous country, this vision of the democratic ideal persists, if perhaps only in the pronouncements of the communist leadership. In the summer of 1989, after ordering an attack on students protesting in Beijing's Tiananmen Square—ironically, for the sake of greater democracy—the leaders of the Chinese Communist Party dogmatically continued to insist on the need for a "people's democratic dictatorship." The alternative, they said, was "bourgeois liberalization"—otherwise known as liberal democracy—and this they found completely unacceptable, even if this meant maintaining their iron-fisted hold on power and information until some vague and unspecified future point. In the early twenty-first century, however, they share this view only with the communist leaders of Vietnam, Cuba, and North Korea. It also bears mentioning that none of these regimes, nor any others committed to "people's democracy," has ever seen fit to move beyond rule by a single authoritarian and allegedly all-wise Communist party. As critics contend, this raises serious and troubling questions about the authenticity and depth of their dedication to this or any other version of the democratic ideal.

CONCLUSION

We have spoken so far of democracy as an ideal that different ideologies envision in their own ways. But we must also recognize that ideologies try to put these ideals into effect—to *implement* them in the form of constitutions and institutions—and that is no easy matter, as we see quite clearly in recent and ongoing attempts to introduce liberal democracy into formerly undemocratic countries, such as Iraq, or the "people's democracies" of the former Soviet Union. Following in the footsteps of Aristotle, modern political scientists and democratic theorists argue that democracy cannot be transplanted easily, if at all, in culturally alien or barren soil. Liberal and social democracy require a history of tolerance; of live-and-let-live; of fair play, trust, mutual respect, and a willingness to compromise; of disagreements aired openly; of defeats borne gracefully by the losers and generously by the winners. Where these preconditions are absent, neither liberal nor social democracy can flourish or perhaps even survive for very long.[30]

We see this truism being played out particularly in the new democracies of the Middle East and elsewhere. Once in office, members of the majority party too often tend to ride roughshod over the rights and interests of the minority. Case in point: In elections in Egypt, after the overthrow of Hosni Mubarak in 2011, the Islamist Muslim Brotherhood won the presidency and a plurality of seats in the parliament. The new president, Mohamed Morsi, saw the election results as a mandate to impose the Brotherhood's vision of an Islamist state in Egypt. His high-handedness frightened and offended many Egyptians, who took to the streets in protest. To restore "order," the military declared a state of emergency, during which President Morsi and his fellow Islamists were forcibly removed from office, put on trial, convicted of treason, and sentenced to death. The commander of the military, General Abdel Fattah el-Sisi, became president in 2014 and has since ruled with an iron fist. And in Iraq, the victorious Shi'ite government of President Nouri Al-Malaki systematically excluded the Sunni minority, with the disastrous results—the rise of ISIS—we describe in Chapter 10. In short, the current conditions of self-professed democracies around the world often seem to leave much to be desired.

Some contemporary commentators have wondered whether democracy in America might be undermined by ideologically polarized and polarizing "talk radio" and by hyperpartisan television commentators who hurl insults and innuendos at members of the other political party, sowing the seeds of distrust and disrespect among the citizenry.[31] Other commentators and critics claim that Americans are increasingly sorting themselves into their own "lifestyle enclaves" of like-minded neighbors, friends, and associates. In his book *The Big Sort: Why the Clustering of Like-Minded America Is Tearing Us Apart* (2008), Bill Bishop writes:

> We have built a country where everyone can choose the neighborhood (and church and news shows) most compatible with his or her lifestyle and beliefs. And we are living with the consequences of this segregation by way of life: pockets of like-minded citizens that have become so ideologically inbred that we don't know, can't understand, and can barely conceive of "those people" who live just a few miles away.[32]

Still other observers, by contrast, claim that empirical evidence from opinion surveys strongly suggests that the specter of a self-sorted and badly "polarized America" is a "myth" created and maintained by political partisans and abetted by television and talk radio to boost ratings (and advertising revenue), and that Americans of almost all political persuasions agree on far more than they disagree about. The same cannot be said, however, for political leaders in Congress and many state legislatures, who often tend to be much more deeply divided along partisan and ideological lines than their constituents are.[33]

To conclude: liberal democracy, social democracy, and people's democracy are the main visions of the democratic ideal in the modern world. In this democratic age, it is important to understand these visions and how they relate to various political ideologies. With this point in mind, we shall explore in the next eight chapters the major ideologies of the modern world—liberalism, conservatism, socialism, and fascism—and some of their recently emerging rivals. Each discussion will conclude with an assessment of the connection between the particular ideology and its interpretation of the democratic ideal.

Discussion Questions

1   Why were the ancient philosophers Plato and Aristotle convinced that democracy is a bad form of government? Do you find their arguments persuasive? Explain why you do or do not.
2   What have Machiavelli and other political theorists meant by the term "republic"? How, if at all, is a republic different from a democracy?
3   Is the United States best described as a democracy, a republic, or a hybrid democratic republic? Explain and defend your position.
4   What were the three principal conceptions of democracy in the twentieth century? How do they differ from one another, and which, in your view, is the best way of thinking about democracy?
5   Ball, Dagger, and O'Neill maintain that democracy is not an ideology but an ideal. Why do they say this? Are they right or wrong about this? Hint: In answering, ask yourself how or whether democracy can perform the four functions that every ideology must perform.

NOTES

1   Pericles's Funeral Oration, from Thucydides, *History of the Peloponnesian War*, vol. I, 2nd ed., trans. Benjamin Jowett (Oxford: Clarendon Press, 1900), pp. 126–135. Also in Terence Ball, Richard Dagger, and Daniel O'Neill, eds., *Ideals and Ideologies: A Reader*, 10th ed. (New York and London: Routledge, 2016), selection 2.3.
2   Ibid., p. 129.
3   Plato, *Apology*, 31, in *The Trial and Death of Socrates*, trans. G. M. A. Grube (Indianapolis, IN: Hackett Publishing Co., 1983), p. 33.
4   For Plato's account of democracy, see Book VIII of his *Republic*.
5   *The Politics of Aristotle*, ed. and trans. Benjamin Jowett (New York: Modern Library, 1943), p. 192; also in Ball, Dagger, and O'Neill, eds., *Ideals and Ideologies*, selection 2.4.
6   Ibid., p. 146; *Ideals and Ideologies*, selection 2.4.
7   The New Testament, Romans 13:1–2.

8 See Quentin Skinner, "The Italian City-Republics," in John Dunn, ed., *Democracy: The Unfinished Journey* (Oxford: Oxford University Press, 1992), pp. 57–69.

9 William Shakespeare, *King Henry the Sixth*, Third Part, Act III, Scene 2.

10 See, for example, Mary Dietz, "Trapping the Prince: Machiavelli and the Politics of Deception," *American Political Science Review* 80 (September 1986): 777–799, along with the response by John Langton and rejoinder by Dietz in *American Political Science Review* 81 (December 1987): 1277–1288. "For Machiavelli's own critique of princely rule, see Ball, Dagger, and O'Neill, eds., *Ideals and Ideologies*, 10th ed., selection 2.5."

11 See J. G. A. Pocock, *The Machiavellian Moment: Florentine Political Thought and the Atlantic Republican Tradition* (Princeton, NJ: Princeton University Press, 1975).

12 Quotations from the Rhode Island constitutions are from Russell Hanson, "Democracy," in Terence Ball, James Farr, and Russell L. Hanson, eds., *Political Innovation and Conceptual Change* (Cambridge: Cambridge University Press, 1989), pp. 72–73.

13 Rainsborough's remarks are from David Wootton, ed., *Divine Right and Democracy* (Harmondsworth, U.K.: Penguin, 1986), p. 286.

14 For an elaboration of this analysis, see Bernard Bailyn, *The Ideological Origins of the American Revolution* (Cambridge, MA: Harvard University Press, 1967).

15 John Adams, *Thoughts on Government* (1776), in Charles Francis Adams, ed., *The Works of John Adams*, vol. IV (Boston: Little, Brown, 1851), p. 194; also in Ball, Dagger, and O'Neill, eds., *Ideals and Ideologies*, selection 2.6.

16 For criticism of the Senate and other "undemocratic" features of the Constitution, see Robert Dahl, *How Democratic Is the American Constitution?* (New Haven, CT: Yale University Press, 2001).

17 *The Federalist*, ed. Terence Ball (Cambridge: Cambridge University Press, 2003), No. 51, p. 252.

18 For two analyses of contemporary American life that owe much to Tocqueville, see Robert Bellah et al., *Habits of the Heart: Individualism and Commitment in American Life* (New York: Harper & Row, 1986); and Robert D. Putnam, *Bowling Alone: The Collapse and Revival of American Community* (New York: Simon & Schuster, 2000).

19 Both quotations are from Mill's *Considerations on Representative Government*, in Mill, *Utilitarianism, Liberty, and Representative Government* (New York: E. P. Dutton, 1951), pp. 289, 291; also in Ball, Dagger, and O'Neill, eds., *Ideals and Ideologies*, selection 2.9. For further discussion of "economic" versus "educative" theories of democracy, see Terence Ball, *Transforming Political Discourse* (Oxford: Blackwell, 1988), Chapter 6.

20 For a discussion of democracy and liberty in Switzerland, see Benjamin Barber, *The Death of Communal Liberty* (Princeton, NJ: Princeton University Press, 1974).

21 Advocates of term limits in the United States primarily have Congress in mind; the president is already limited to two terms in office. For the case for term limits, see George Will, *Restoration: Congress, Term Limits and the Recovery of Deliberative Democracy* (New York: The Free Press, 1992); for the opposing view, see Garry Wills, "Undemocratic Vistas," *New York Review of Books* 39 (November 19, 1992): 28–34.

22 See Abraham Lincoln, "Speech on the Kansas-Nebraska Act" (October 16, 1854), in Terence Ball, ed., *Abraham Lincoln: Political Writings and Speeches* (Cambridge: Cambridge University Press, 2013), pp. 22–35.

23 Adam Liptak, "Justices, 5-4, Kill Key Spending Cap in Political Races: Ruling Ends Limit on Individual's Total Donations to Federal Candidates," *New York Times*, April 3, 2014, pp. A1, A16.

24 Nicholas Confessore, Sarah Cohen and Karen Yourish, "Small Pool of Rich Donors Dominates Election Giving—Fewer than 400 Families Have Contributed Nearly Half of Money to Campaigns," *New York Times*, August 2, 2015, pp. A1, A13.

25 See Timothy K. Kuhner, *Capitalism v. Democracy: Money in Politics and the Free Market Constitution* (Stanford: Stanford University Press, 2014).

26 Sheldon S. Wolin, *Democracy, Incorporated: Managed Democracy and the Specter of Inverted Totalitarianism* (Princeton: Princeton University Press, 2008).

27 For a brief history of voter suppression in the United States, see Alexander Keyssar, "The Strange Career of Voter Suppression," *New York Times*, February 13, 2012, p. A19; reprinted in Ball, Dagger, and O'Neill, eds., *Ideals and Ideologies*, selection 2.10.

28 Brent Staples, "The Racist Origins of Felon Disenfranchisement," *New York Times*, November 19, 2014, p. A22.

29 For a discussion of the development of "democratic republicanism" in the United States, see Russell L. Hanson, "'Commons' and 'Commonwealth' at the American Founding: Democratic Republicanism as the New American Hybrid," in Terence Ball and J. G. A. Pocock, eds., *Conceptual Change and the Constitution* (Lawrence, KS: University Press of Kansas, 1988), pp. 165–193.

30 For a collection of essays on the importance of the cultural preconditions of democracy, see Charles Cnudde and Deane Neubauer, eds., *Empirical Democratic Theory* (Chicago: Markham, 1969).

31 See Ronald Dworkin, *Is Democracy Possible Here? Principles for a New Political Debate* (Princeton, NJ: Princeton University Press, 2006). Dworkin answers the question posed in his title in the affirmative.

32 Bill Bishop, *The Big Sort: Why the Clustering of Like-Minded America Is Tearing Us Apart* (Boston: Houghton Mifflin, 2008), p. 40.

33 See Morris P. Fiorina, with Samuel J. Abrams and Jeremy C. Pope, *Culture War? The Myth of a Polarized America*, 3rd ed. (New York: Longman, 2011). See also the careful critique of Bishop's method, argument, evidence, and conclusions in Samuel J. Abrams and Morris P. Fiorina, "'The Big Sort' That Wasn't: A Skeptical Reexamination," *PS: Political Science & Politics*, 45:2 (April 2012): 203–210.

FOR FURTHER READING

Dagger, Richard. *Civic Virtues: Rights, Citizenship, and Republican Liberalism*. New York: Oxford University Press, 1997.

——. "Republican Citizenship," in E. F. Isin and B. S. Turner, eds., *Handbook of Citizenship Studies*. London: SAGE, 2002.

Dahl, Robert. *Democracy and Its Critics*. New Haven, CT: Yale University Press, 1989.

——. *On Democracy*. New Haven, CT: Yale University Press, 1998.

——. *How Democratic Is the American Constitution?* New Haven, CT: Yale University Press, 2001.

Dunn, John, ed. *Democracy: The Unfinished Journey*. Oxford: Oxford University Press, 1992.

Farrar, Cynthia. *The Origins of Democratic Thinking*. Cambridge: Cambridge University Press, 1988.

Gooch, G. P. *English Democratic Ideas in the Seventeenth Century*, 2nd ed. New York: Harper & Brothers, 1959.

Gould, Carol C. *Rethinking Democracy*. Cambridge: Cambridge University Press, 1988.

Hanson, Russell L. *The Democratic Imagination in America: Conversations with Our Past*. Princeton, NJ: Princeton University Press, 1985.

Held, David. *Models of Democracy*. Stanford, CA: Stanford University Press, 1986.

Honohan, Iseult. *Civic Republicanism*. London: Routledge, 2002.

Macpherson, C. B. *The Life and Times of Liberal Democracy*. Oxford: Oxford University Press, 1977.

——. *The Real World of Democracy*. Oxford: Oxford University Press, 1966.

Mansbridge, Jane. *Beyond Adversary Democracy*. Chicago: University of Chicago Press, 1983.

Pateman, Carole. *Participation and Democratic Theory*. Cambridge: Cambridge University Press, 1970.

Pettit, Philip. *Republicanism: A Theory of Freedom and Government.* Oxford: Clarendon Press, 1997.

Pocock, J. G. A. *The Machiavellian Moment: Florentine Political Thought and the Atlantic Republican Tradition.* Princeton, NJ: Princeton University Press, 1975.

Rahe, Paul. *Republics Ancient and Modern: Classical Republicanism and the American Revolution.* Chapel Hill: University of North Carolina Press, 1992.

Sandel, Michael. *Democracy's Discontent: America in Search of a Public Philosophy.* New York: Basic Books, 1996.

Skinner, Quentin. *The Foundations of Modern Political Thought,* 2 vols. Cambridge: Cambridge University Press, 1978.

Walzer, Michael. *Radical Principles.* New York: Basic Books, 1980.

Wood, Gordon. *The Creation of the American Republic, 1776–1787.* Chapel Hill: University of North Carolina Press, 1969.

From the Ball, Dagger, and O'Neill Reader *Ideals and Ideologies,* Tenth Edition

Part II: The Democratic Ideal

Historical and Philosophical Foundations

CHAPTER 3

LIBERALISM

Over himself, over his own body and mind, the individual is sovereign.

John Stuart Mill, *On Liberty*

In contemporary political discourse, the words "liberal" and "liberalism" are sometimes contentious, even provocative. Here we try to trace the complex history of this particular ideology. What are its origins? What are its key features? And how has it changed? For more than three centuries, the hallmark of liberalism has been the attempt to promote individual liberty. But this very broad goal leaves room for liberals to disagree among themselves as to what exactly liberty is and how best to promote it. Indeed, this disagreement is now so sharp that liberalism is split into two rival camps of "neoclassical" and "welfare" liberals. Later in this chapter we shall see how this split occurred. But first we need to look at that broad area of common ground on which all liberals meet—the desire to promote individual liberty.

The words "liberal" and "liberty" both derive from the Latin *liber*, meaning "free." "Liberal" did not enter the vocabulary of politics until early in the nineteenth century, however, long after "liberty" was widely used as a political term—and at least a century after ideas now regarded as liberal were in the air. Before the nineteenth century, "liberal" was commonly used to mean "generous" or "tolerant"—an attitude that supposedly befit a "gentleman," just as a "liberal education" was meant to prepare a young gentleman for life. "Liberal" still means generous or tolerant, of course, as when someone says that a teacher follows a liberal grading policy or a child has liberal parents. But nowadays, through an extension of this common use, "liberal" more often refers to a political position or point of view.

The first clear sign of this political use occurred in the early nineteenth century when a faction of the Spanish legislature adopted the name *Liberales*. From there the term traveled to France and Great Britain, where the party known as the Whigs evolved by the 1840s into the Liberal Party. These early liberals shared a desire for a more open and tolerant society—one in which people would be free to pursue their own ideas and interests with as little interference as possible. A liberal society was to be, in short, a "free" society. But what makes a society "free"? What *is* freedom and how can we best promote it? These questions have occupied liberals for more than three centuries now, providing the grounds not only for arguments among liberals but also for disputes between liberalism and other ideologies.

LIBERALISM, HUMAN NATURE, AND FREEDOM

In Chapter 1 we noted that some conception of human nature provides the underpinnings for every political ideology. In the case of liberalism, the emphasis on individual liberty rests on a conception of human beings as fundamentally rational individuals. There are, we shall see, significant differences among liberals on this point. But in general liberals stress individual liberty largely because they believe that most people are capable of living freely. This belief sets them apart from those who believe that human beings are at the mercy of uncontrollable passions and desires, first pushing in one direction, then pulling in another. Liberals acknowledge that people do have passions and desires, but they maintain that people also have the ability, through reason, to control and direct their desires. Most women and men, they insist, are rational beings who know what is in their own interests and, given the opportunity, are capable of acting to promote those interests.

Liberals generally agree that self-interest is the primary motive for most people. Some argue that self-interest should be given free rein, while others respond that it should be carefully directed to promote the good of all; but most hold that it is wisest to think of people as beings who are more interested in their own good than in the well-being of others. This implies, in turn, that all these rational, self-interested men and women will find themselves competing with one another in their attempts to promote their personal interests. This is healthy, liberals say, as long as the competition remains fair and stays within proper bounds. Exactly what is fair and where these proper bounds lie is a subject of sharp disagreement among liberals, as is the question of how best to promote competition. For the most part, though, liberals are inclined to regard competition as a natural part of the human condition.

On the liberal view, then, human beings are typically rational, self-interested, and competitive. This implies that they are capable of living freely. But what does it mean to live in this way? How, that is, do liberals conceive of freedom? To answer this question, let us employ the model introduced in Chapter 1 depicting freedom as a triadic relationship involving an *agent* who is free from some *obstacle* to pursue some *goal*. In the case of liberalism, the agent is the individual. Liberals want to promote the freedom not of a particular group or class of people but of each person as an individual. To do this, they have sought to free people from a variety of restrictions or obstacles. In the beginning liberals were most concerned with removing social and legal barriers to individual liberty, especially social customs, ties of feudal dependence, and religious conformity. Since then other liberals have claimed that poverty, racial and sexual prejudice, ignorance, and illness are also obstacles to individual liberty. But in spite of these differences, liberals agree that the individual must be free to decide for himself—and, more recently, herself— what goals to pursue in life. Most liberals have believed, that is, that the individual is the best judge of what is in his or her interest, so each person ought to be free to live as he or she sees fit—as long as the person does not choose to interfere with others' freedom to live as they see fit (see Figure 3.1).

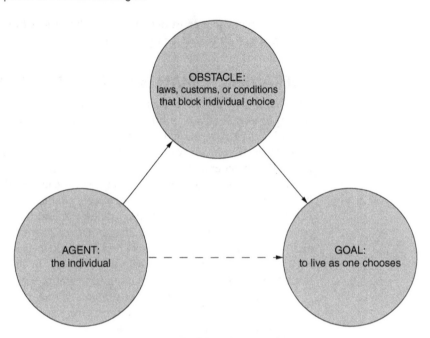

FIGURE 3.1 The liberal view of freedom.

That is to say that equality is also an important element in the liberal conception of freedom. In the liberal view each person is to have an equal opportunity to enjoy liberty. No person's liberty is more important or valuable than any other's. This does not mean that everyone is to be equally successful or to have an equal share of the good things of life, whatever they may be. Liberals do not believe that everyone can or should be equally successful—only that everyone should have an *equal opportunity to succeed*. Liberalism thus stresses competition, for it wants individuals to be free to compete on an equal footing for whatever they count as success. Anything that prevents a person from having an equal opportunity—whether it be privileges for the aristocracy, monopolies that block economic competition, or discrimination based on race, religion, or gender—can be an obstacle to a person's freedom that ought to be removed.

Liberalism, in short, promotes individual liberty by trying to guarantee equality of opportunity within a tolerant society. In the English-speaking world, these ideas are so much a part of our lives and our thinking that they seem natural. But that is because these liberal ideas are so much a part of our heritage throughout Western civilization in general. These ideas were not always taken for granted, however, not even in England and Europe. To appreciate their full significance we need to see how liberalism began as a reaction against the European society of the Middle Ages.

HISTORICAL BACKGROUND

Medieval Origins

The origins of liberalism can be traced to a reaction against two of the characteristic features of medieval society in Europe: **religious conformity** and **ascribed status**. This reaction, which developed over the course of centuries, took different forms in different times and places. By the time *liberal* entered the political vocabulary in the early nineteenth century, however, a distinctive political viewpoint had clearly emerged.

Religious Conformity. Liberals called for freedom of religion and separation of church and state. These ideas ran counter to the dominant ways of thinking in the Middle Ages, when church and state were supposed to be partners in the defense of Christendom. Indeed, there was no clear distinction between church and state in medieval Europe. For its part, the Christian Church saw its mission as saving souls for the Kingdom of God—something that could best be done by teaching and upholding orthodoxy, or "correct belief." Those who took an unorthodox view of Christianity or rejected it altogether thus threatened the Church's attempts to do what it saw as the work and will of God. In response to these threats, the Church used its powers, and called on the kings and other secular authorities to use theirs, to enforce conformity to Church doctrine. For their part, the secular rulers were usually willing—out of either religious conviction or a desire to maintain order in their domains—to suppress those whom the Church considered heretics or infidels. Throughout medieval Europe, then, religious and political authorities joined forces to ensure conformity to the doctrines of the Roman Church, which they believed to be the true and universal path to the Kingdom of God.

Ascribed Status. The other feature of medieval society to which early liberals objected was *ascribed status*. In a society based on ascribed status, a person's social standing is fixed, or ascribed, at birth, and there is little that he or she can do to change it. This stands in contrast to a society based on **achieved status**, in which everyone is supposed to have an equal opportunity to work his or her way to the top—or, for that matter, to the bottom—of society. But equality of opportunity was by no means the ideal of medieval society. To be sure, Christians in the Middle Ages professed that all people are born equal in the eyes of God, but this kind of equality was compatible in their eyes with great inequalities in life here on earth. What counted was the state of one's soul, not one's status in society.

Yet status mattered very much in earthly life, for one's position and prospects were fixed by his or her social "rank," "order," or "estate." This was especially true under **feudalism**, which became the main form of social and economic organization in Europe after the disintegration of Charlemagne's empire in the ninth century. Under feudalism, an intricate web of relationships developed in which one knight, the lord, would give the use of land to a lesser knight, the vassal, in return for military service. The vassal might then divide the land into parcels to be offered to others, who then, in exchange for various services, became *his* vassals. In the beginning the original lord retained ownership of the land, with the vassal receiving only the right to use it and enjoy its fruits. These relationships gradually became hereditary, however, leading to a complicated network of ranks, statuses, and loyalties.

In one respect, though, feudalism simplified matters by reinforcing the existing tendency to divide society into two broad classes of people: nobles and commoners. As feudal relationships were passed down the generations, a distinct class of landowning nobles or aristocrats took shape. These nobles thought themselves naturally superior to the commoners, who were the great majority of the people. They also believed that their noble birth entitled them to exercise authority over the commoners and to enjoy privileges and liberties unavailable to common men and women.

This emphasis on social "rank" or "estate" was reflected in the parliaments or estates-general that began to appear in the late Middle Ages. These political bodies, usually summoned by kings, spoke for the different orders of society. The Estates-General of France, for instance, which first convened in 1302, comprised representatives of the clergy (the First Estate), the nobility (the Second Estate), and the commoners (the Third Estate). Because the members of this last group lived mostly in the cities and towns—*bourgs* in French—they were called the **bourgeoisie**. There were no representatives for those who were not free, such as the serfs.

Serfs (from the Latin *servus*, meaning "slave") were commoners, but they were not free. They were peasants, or agricultural laborers. Unlike free peasants, the serfs owned no land. Instead, they farmed small plots of land owned by the lord of the manor, and from their plots they had to provide for their families and pay rent to the lord, typically in the form of crops.

The most distinctive feature of serfdom, however, was the serfs' lack of freedom to choose where to live and what work to do. Serfs were often legally "attached" to the land or the person of the lord. By custom and law they were bound—hence the term "bondsman"—either to remain on and work the land where they were born or, if attached to a person, to serve the lord wherever required. In exchange, serfs received from the lord protection. If the serfs thought this a poor bargain, there was nothing they could do, as a rule, to earn release from serfdom. Some tried to win their freedom by force of arms; others ran away to the towns and cities; and still others accepted their condition as part of the natural course of life, although perhaps cherishing a hope that their lord might one day free them.

Everyone—whether a serf, a noble, or a free commoner—was born into a certain rank or estate in medieval Europe and could do little to change it. The Church provided an exception to this rule, for people from all ranks of society could hope to find a place among the clergy. In other respects, though, medieval society was firmly rooted in ascribed status. Nobles were those born into the nobility, for the most part, while the children of free commoners and serfs were virtually locked into the social position of their parents. No amount of effort or ability could significantly improve their stations in life. Even freedom was a matter of social position, with different liberties attached to different levels of status in society. For example, in the Magna Carta, the Great Charter of rights that the feudal barons of England forced King John to accept in 1215, the king agreed that "No free man shall be taken, or imprisoned… or outlawed, or exiled, or in any way destroyed … except by lawful judgment of his peers or by the laws of the land."

But in this case "free man" (*liber homo*) referred only to the barons and other nobles. Those of lesser rank could still be taken, imprisoned, or killed without the lawful judgment of their peers—without, that is, a trial by a jury.

Against this society rooted in ascribed status and religious conformity, liberalism emerged as the first distinctive political ideology. But this reaction did not take definite shape until a number of social, economic, and cultural changes disturbed the medieval order. Many of these changes were directly related to the outburst of creativity in the fourteenth and fifteenth centuries known as the **Renaissance**. But there was also the Black Death, an epidemic that devastated Europe between 1347 and 1351, killing about one of every three people. This epidemic opened new opportunities for survivors from the lower ranks of society and loosened the rigid medieval social structure. The expansion of trade and commerce in the late Middle Ages played a part in the breakdown of the medieval order too, as did the wave of exploration set in motion by this expansion. Christopher Columbus's attempt to find a new trade route to Asia is noteworthy in this regard, for he discovered what was, for Europeans, an entirely new world—a New World that became a symbol of great new possibilities. But of all the historical developments that contributed to the decline of the medieval order and the rise of liberalism, the most important was the Protestant Reformation.

The Protestant Reformation

The Protestant Reformation can be dated from 1521, the year in which the Roman Catholic Church excommunicated Martin Luther. Luther (1483–1546) was a priest and professor of theology at the University of Wittenberg when he posted his famous Ninety-five Theses on the door of the church at Wittenberg in 1517. By themselves, the Ninety-five Theses were not a direct threat to the authority of the Church. Their immediate purpose was to call for a debate on the sale of "indulgences," which were issued on the authority of the Pope to raise money for Church projects—in 1517, the rebuilding of St. Peter's Basilica in Rome. Although the purchase of an indulgence was only supposed to release a sinner from some acts of penance, eager salesmen sometimes led people to believe that an indulgence could secure a place in heaven. This provoked Luther to issue his challenge to a debate.

With the aid of a relatively new invention, the printing press, Luther's theses circulated quickly through the German principalities and found a receptive audience among Christians disturbed by the corruption of the Church. They also caught the attention of the German nobles, many of whom regarded the Church as their main rival for earthly power. The resulting furor led Luther's superiors in the Church to command him to admit that he was mistaken and to submit to the authority of the Pope. But Luther refused, saying, as legend has it, "Here I stand. I can do no other." Thus began the Reformation.

The Church, in Luther's view, had vested too much authority in priests and too little in the Bible. In place of the Church's emphasis on tradition, rituals, and sacraments, Luther favored strict attention to scripture, the word of God. And in place of the Church's emphasis on the authority of priests, bishops, and the Pope, Luther favored the "priesthood of all believers." All that matters is faith, he declared, and the only way to nurture faith is to read the Bible and do as God there commands us to do. With that in mind, Luther and his colleagues translated the Bible into German to make it accessible to those who could not read Latin.

Despite some early remarks defending freedom of conscience, Luther never meant to encourage people to believe and worship in whatever way they chose. Apparently, he expected that everyone who read the scriptures could not help but understand them as he did. But that did not happen. To the contrary, Luther's proclamation of the "priesthood of all believers," with its stress on individual conscience, opened the floodgates for a variety of interpretations of the Bible and a profusion of Protestant sects. Luther neither foresaw nor welcomed this development. Nor did he intend to separate church from state. Indeed, one reason that Luther's challenge to the supremacy of the Church succeeded where earlier challenges had failed is that Luther was able to win the protection of the German princes, many of whom saw in the controversy a welcome opportunity to gain wealth and power at the Church's expense. In any case, in Germany and elsewhere the immediate effect of the Reformation was the forging of an alliance between a king or prince, on the one hand, and the leaders of a reformed or Protestant church, on the other. In this way various local or national churches began to challenge the authority of the universal church.

England soon provided the clearest example of a national church. There King Henry VIII (r. 1509–1547), angered by the Pope's refusal to grant him permission to divorce his first wife, declared the Church of England separate from Rome and, with the approval of the English Parliament, made himself its head. A church of a different sort emerged in Geneva. Now part of Switzerland, Geneva was an independent city-state when Jean (or John) Calvin (1509–1564), a French Protestant, became its leader in political as well as in religious matters. Like most of the other Protestants or reformers, in fact, Calvin was no more inclined to distinguish politics from religion, or church from state, than his Roman Catholic opponents were. The point of the Reformation was not to enable people to believe as they saw fit, but literally to *reform* the Church so that people could believe as reformers thought they should. Under Calvin's leadership, Geneva became a **theocracy**. The law of the city was to be a direct reflection of God's will, to the extent that a pastor could enter a house at any hour of the day or night to make sure that no one was violating God's commandments.

Where the political authorities remained loyal to the Catholic Church, they often tried to suppress the Protestants. In such cases Luther and Calvin usually counseled their followers not to resist their rulers, since God gave rulers their power to do His will. Later, however, some of Calvin's followers concluded not only that resistance is sometimes justified but also that the people have a right to overthrow any ruler who denies them the free exercise of their religion. By this they meant the exercise of their form of Calvinism, to be sure, because few of them wanted to allow the free exercise of other religions. Yet their arguments for freedom of conscience, which rested in part on the claim that government receives its authority from the consent of the people, planted the seeds of the argument in favor of religious toleration.

Before these seeds could sprout, however, people had to be convinced that it was either wrong or simply impossible to replace enforced conformity to the

Roman Church with enforced conformity to one or another of the Protestant churches. This conviction did not begin to develop until the seventeenth century, and then only after a series of bloody religious wars persuaded some, such as John Locke, that it was better to tolerate some differences of religion than to try to win converts at the point of a sword.

Quite unintentionally, then, the Protestant reformers prepared the way for liberalism. By teaching that salvation comes through faith alone, Luther and the other reformers encouraged people to value individual conscience more than the preservation of unity and orthodoxy. Moving from individual conscience to individual liberty was still a radical step for the time, but it was a step that the early liberals took. Thus liberalism began as an attempt to free individuals from the constraints of religious conformity and ascribed status. It also began, as most ideologies have begun, as an attempt to bring about a fundamental transformation of society. It was, in short, revolutionary. To see this more clearly, we need to look at the great revolutions of the seventeenth and eighteenth centuries.

LIBERALISM AND REVOLUTION

England

After defeating the Spanish Armada in 1588, England entered the seventeenth century more secure and powerful than it had ever been. Queen Elizabeth I was on the throne, and William Shakespeare was writing plays. Then came contributions to literature by John Donne and John Milton, to philosophy by Thomas Hobbes and John Locke, and to science by Isaac Newton and William Harvey, the physician who discovered the circulation of blood. Meanwhile, commerce and exploration flourished as English colonies sprang up in North America and India.

But the seventeenth century was also a time of turmoil for England. Elizabeth was succeeded in 1603 by a distant cousin, James Stuart, King of Scotland. The new king soon found himself engaged in a power struggle with Parliament, a struggle that grew more heated during the reign of his son, Charles I. Money was often at the root of the conflict, with Charles insisting that he had a divine right, as king, to gather revenue through taxes, while Parliament insisted that this was its right as the body representing the people of England. In 1642 the conflict erupted into civil war.

The war between Crown and Parliament was further fueled by religious, social, and economic elements. For many people the war was primarily a religious conflict. As king, Charles I was the official head of the Church of England, and all the English were expected to conform to the beliefs and practices of that Church. Those loyal to the Church of England tended to support the king, then, while the dissenting Puritans took the side of Parliament. The Puritans often disagreed with one another—some were Presbyterians, some Independents or Congregationalists, some Separatists—but all wanted to "purify" the Church of England of the traces of Catholicism they thought it had retained. Their hope, in general, was to enforce conformity to their religion, just as those who supported the established church sought to enforce conformity to theirs. The social and economic divisions are less clear, but it seems that the landowning aristocracy supported the king while the middle class—the "gentlemen" landowners and the merchants—generally sided with Parliament.

In the English Civil War pen and ink played as great a part as bullets and swords. From every side came a vast outpouring of pamphlets, treatises, sermons, and even major works of political theory. In the previous chapter we noted the efforts of James Harrington, who argued for a republican form of government, and of the Levellers, who pressed the case for a more democratic form. Now we must take note of the first major work of political philosophy to bear the distinctive stamp of liberalism, Thomas Hobbes's *Leviathan*.

Hobbes (1588–1679) wrote *Leviathan* in France, where he had fled to avoid the war, and published it in 1651, two years after the beheading of Charles I brought the war to an end. There was nothing new in the conclusion he reached in *Leviathan*. Like St. Paul and many others, Hobbes maintained that the people of a country should obey those who have power over them. But he refused to base this

North Wind Picture Archives/Alamy

Thomas Hobbes (1588–1679)

conclusion on the simple claim that this was God's will. Even though Hobbes cited scripture, his argument was fundamentally secular—and, he thought, "scientific"—as it was based on self-interest rather than divine commands.

According to Hobbes, the individual should obey whoever is in power, as long as the person or persons in power protect the individual. The first "law of nature" requires us to preserve ourselves. Self-preservation is greatly aided by government and greatly degraded by its absence. To provide protection or security is the only reason for government in the first place. To prove his point, Hobbes asked his readers to imagine that they were in a **state of nature**, a condition of perfect freedom in which there was no government and no one had any authority over them. In such a state, he said, all individuals are equal—no one is born to hold a higher rank or status than anyone else—and have a **natural right** to do as they wish. Since in the state of nature their freedom is absolute, they should be happy; what problem could possibly arise? The problem is human nature: "I put for a general inclination of all mankind, a perpetuall and restlesse desire of Power after power, that ceaseth onely in Death."[1] This "restlesse desire" for power leads individuals into conflict with one another and turns the state of nature into a "warre of every man against every man" where life can be nothing but "solitary, poore, nasty, brutish, and short."[2] Hobbes's state of nature thus inevitably became a state of war.

Nothing, in Hobbes's view, could be worse than this. So the fearful, self-interested, and rational individuals in the state of nature enter into an agreement or **social contract** to establish political authority. To provide for their security, they surrender all but one of their rights—the right to defend themselves—to those to whom they grant authority. On Hobbes's argument, then, government is founded in the consent of the people. But by their consent, the people authorize the sovereign—the person or persons in power—to do anything necessary to maintain order and peace. This includes the power to force everyone to worship as the sovereign requires, for Hobbes saw religious differences as one of the leading sources of conflict. For the sake of security, then, the people grant the sovereign absolute, unlimited power, retaining only the right to defend themselves when the sovereign directly threatens them.

Given this conclusion, the claim that *Leviathan* bears the distinctive stamp of liberalism may seem odd. Liberals certainly have not made a habit of supportingabsolute rulers or enforcing religious conformity. What gives Hobbes's theory a distinctly liberal tinge is not his conclusion, however, but his premises. Individuals are equals, on Hobbes's account, and everyone has a natural right to be free. They create government through their consent in order to protect their interests. In these respects, Hobbes's position is very much that of a liberal or, as some prefer to say, a "protoliberal"—that is, one who articulated the main premises of an emerging liberal ideology. It remained for John Locke to use these premises to reach conclusions that were definitely liberal.

Locke (1632–1704) was sixteen years old when Charles I was beheaded and Parliament abolished the monarchy. Yet only eleven years later, Parliament invited the son of the late king to return from his exile in France—where Hobbes had been one of his tutors—to restore the monarchy. This Restoration brought relief from political turmoil, but it proved to be only temporary. As Charles II grew older, it became clear that he would leave no legitimate heir to the throne. This situation placed his brother James in position to be the next king and aroused the suspicion that James, a Catholic, would try to take England back into the Catholic camp—and to become, like his cousin Louis XIV of France, an absolute ruler. To prevent this from happening, an effort was mounted to exclude James from the throne. During the Exclusion Crisis of 1680–1683, Charles II suspended Parliament and his opponents responded with plots and uprisings against him. The effort failed—James became King James II upon Charles's death in 1685—but it did lead John Locke to begin writing his *Two Treatises of Government*.

Locke completed the *Two Treatises* while in exile in Holland, where he had fled for his life in 1683. In Holland, then the most tolerant country in Europe, Locke also wrote his *Letter Concerning Toleration*. Both works were published in England after the Glorious Revolution of 1688 forced James II to flee to France. James's daughter Mary and her husband William, Prince of Orange (in the Netherlands), became England's new monarchs. In assuming the throne, however, William and Mary accepted the Bill of Rights, which recognized the "true, ancient, and indubitable rights of the people of this realm,"[3] and the supremacy of Parliament.

John Locke (1632–1704)

From this time forward England would be a constitutional monarchy, with the king or queen clearly subject to the law of the land. In the Toleration Act (1689), furthermore, Parliament granted freedom of worship to "dissenters," that is, those Protestants who refused to join the established Church of England.

These developments were very much to Locke's liking. In the *Letter Concerning Toleration* he argued that it is wrong for governments to force their subjects to conform to a particular religion. Drawing a distinction between private belief and public behavior, Locke said that religious belief is normally a private concern and not a proper subject for government interference. Any attempt to coerce or compel belief will only produce hypocrites who publicly profess one thing while inwardly believing something else entirely. Governments should tolerate diverse religious beliefs unless the practice of those beliefs directly threatens the public order. But Catholicism should *not* be tolerated for exactly this reason. Catholics owe their first loyalty to a foreign monarch, the Pope, so they cannot be trustworthy members of a commonwealth. Locke also refused toleration to atheists for a similar reason, claiming that anyone who denied the existence of God, salvation, and damnation could not be trusted at all. If these seem severe restrictions by current standards, they were nonetheless quite liberal, even radical, by the standards of Locke's time.

In addition to religious toleration, Locke articulated another key tenet of liberalism: equality under the law. He wrote:

> They [rulers] are to govern by *promulgated establish'd Laws*, not to be varied in particular Cases, but to have one Rule for Rich and Poor, for the Favourite at [the king's] Court, and the Country Man at Plough.[4]

Or, to put Locke's point another way, justice is blind: it cannot see or take into account differences of social status, wealth, or political power. That, after all, is why statues depicting the goddess Justice always show her wearing a blindfold.

Important as his arguments for religious toleration and legal equality were, Locke's theory of political authority in the second of his *Two Treatises of Government* (1690) marked an even more important milestone in the development of liberalism. Locke's purpose in the *Second Treatise* was much the same as Hobbes's in *Leviathan*—to establish the true basis for political authority or government—and in several crucial respects his premises resemble Hobbes's. He agrees with Hobbes that self-preservation is the first law of nature. "Every one," Locke writes, "is bound to *preserve himself*," but then Locke immediately adds—from an explicitly Christian standpoint that Hobbes did not share—"and as much as he can *to preserve the rest of mankind*."[5] He also imagines, as Hobbes did, a state of nature, in which everyone is free and equal. There is no ascribed status in this state of nature, "there being nothing more evident, than that Creatures of the same species and rank promiscuously born to all the same advantages of Nature, and the use of the same faculties, should also be equal one amongst another without Subordination or Subjection..."[6] There are natural rights, though, which Locke usually referred to as "life, liberty, and property." These rights a person may surrender or forfeit—by attacking others, for instance, a person may forfeit his right to life or liberty—but no one can simply take them away.

Unlike Hobbes's state of nature, Locke's is *not* a state of war. It is "inconvenient," however, largely because so many people are unwilling to respect the rights of others. Recognizing this difficulty, people in the state of nature enter into a social contract to establish a political society with laws and a government to make, interpret, and enforce them. But we should remember, Locke said, that people create government to do a job—to protect their natural rights. The government has authority, therefore, only insofar as it does what it needs to do to preserve the lives, liberty, and property of its subjects. If the government begins to violate these rights by depriving its subjects of life, liberty, and property, then the people have the right to overthrow the government and establish a new one in its place.

Although he began with premises very similar to Hobbes's, Locke reached a very different conclusion. Both denied that social status was somehow fixed or ascribed by nature, and both believed that government is founded on the consent of the people; but Locke believed that people can consent to create and obey only a limited or constitutional government. To give anyone total and absolute power over people's lives would be both irrational and contrary to the will of God as expressed through natural law. Both also believed that people have natural rights; but for Locke this included a right to worship as one chose, within limits, and *a right of revolution*—a right that would be invoked four score and six years after the publication of the *Two Treatises of Government*, in the American Declaration of Independence.

The American Revolution

Neither the American Revolution nor the French Revolution was the direct result of Locke's writings, of course. In both cases a variety of social, economic, and religious factors combined with philosophical and political issues to lead to revolution.

The thirteen British colonies that eventually became the United States were settled during the seventeenth century—a turbulent time for England. During the 1600s, perhaps because it was preoccupied with problems at home, the British government generally left the colonists to look after their own affairs. This situation continued throughout the first half of the eighteenth century, a relatively stable period in English politics. The colonies had governors appointed by the Crown, but they also had their own legislatures and raised their own taxes. The colonists consequently took it for granted that they enjoyed all the rights of Englishmen, including the right to constitutional self-government through elected representatives.

But in 1763, at the end of the French and Indian (or Seven Years) War, the British government began to levy taxes on the colonists in order to pay for the war and the defense of the colonies. The colonists objected that this violated their rights as Englishmen. Parliament had no right to tax the American colonists, they argued, as long as the colonists elected no representatives to Parliament. For Parliament to tax them when they had no voice in the matter was tantamount to taking their property without their consent. Indeed, the colonists' position was quite simple: "No taxation without representation!"

Parliament's response was to point out that the colonists were in exactly the same situation as most of the people of England itself, where only a small minority enjoyed the right to vote at that time. Because of corruption and outdated electoral rules, whole cities were without representatives; yet all British subjects were "virtually represented" by the members of Parliament, who looked after the interests of the entire commonwealth. To this argument the colonists replied by saying, in effect, that if the people of England were foolish enough to settle for "virtual" representation, so much the worse for them. As the colonists saw it, if representation is not "actual," it is not representation at all.

This, in brief, was the quarrel that led to armed revolt in 1775. In the beginning the colonists maintained that they were loyal subjects of the Crown who fought only to restore their rights—rights that the British government was supposed to protect but had instead violated. Yet in little more than a year the colonists abandoned this position to take the radical step of declaring themselves independent of Great Britain.

They took this step in part because of the arguments set out in *Common Sense*, a pamphlet written and published in February 1776 by Thomas Paine (1737–1809). The arguments of *Common Sense* are quite similar to Locke's in the *Second Treatise*, but Paine expressed them in a vivid and memorable way. Society, Paine said, is always a blessing; but government, even the best government, is a "necessary evil." It is evil because it coerces us and controls our lives; but it is necessary because most of us, fallen creatures that we are, cannot be trusted to respect the natural rights of others. To protect our natural rights, then, we create government. If the government does its job, it deserves our obedience. But if it fails to protect our natural rights—if it turns against us and violates our rights—the government ceases to be a necessary evil and becomes an intolerable one. When this happens, Paine concluded, the people have every right to overthrow their government and replace it with one that will respect their rights.

The American colonies, said Paine, should sever their ties with Great Britain and establish themselves as an independent, self-governing state. If it is to be truly self-governing, though, the new state must be a republic. Paine took this to mean that there must be no king, for he believed monarchy to be absolutely incompatible with individual liberty. In this respect he went beyond Locke—who may have preferred to abolish monarchy but did not say so in the *Second Treatise*.

Within six months of the publication of *Common Sense*, the Continental Congress declared, on July 2, 1776, that "These United Colonies are, and of right ought to be, free and independent states." Two days later the Congress adopted the Declaration of Independence, a document written principally by Thomas Jefferson (1743–1826). The exact character of Jefferson's justification of the separation from Great Britain is a matter of some dispute among scholars, but there is no doubt that the argument of the Declaration, as well as some of its striking phrases, closely resembles Locke's.[7] (Jefferson's fellow Virginian, Richard Henry Lee, exaggerated only slightly when he said that Jefferson had merely "copied [the Declaration] from Locke's treatise on government."[8]) Thus we are told that certain "truths" are "self-evident":

that all men are created equal, that they are endowed by their Creator with certain unalienable Rights, that among these are Life, Liberty, and the pursuit of Happiness.— That to secure these rights, Governments are instituted among Men, deriving their just powers from the consent of the governed.—That whenever any Form of Government becomes destructive of these ends, it is the Right of the People to alter or to abolish it, and to institute new Government, laying its foundation on such principles, and organizing its powers in such form, as to them shall seem most likely to effect their Safety and Happiness.[9]

Following this preamble comes a long list of specific grievances submitted as evidence that the British government had indeed become "destructive of these ends" for which government is created, thereby entitling the colonists "to alter or to abolish it, and to institute new Government..."

The Declaration of Independence, then, employs a compressed version of the argument advanced by Locke and other early liberals. Two features of this argument deserve particular attention. The first is the claim that "all men are created equal" This phrase caused some embarrassment when the Declaration was issued, for a number of colonists, American "patriots" as well as pro-British "tories," pointed out that it was hypocritical for a slaveholding country to proclaim the equality of all mankind. In England Dr. Samuel Johnson criticized Washington, Jefferson, and other slaveholding colonists for their hypocrisy: "How is it that we hear the loudest *yelps* for liberty among the drivers of Negroes?"[10] In fact, Jefferson, a slave-owner himself, included a sharp attack on the slave trade in his original draft of the Declaration. This section was removed by other members of Congress, however, while the claim that all men are created equal remained.

This embarrassment reveals a more general problem in the position of the early liberals. They spoke a democratic language when they proclaimed that all men are naturally free and equal and that government rests on the consent of the people; yet they never explained whom they counted as "men" or "the people." For instance, Locke's references to "men" and "the people" make him seem to be a democrat. But Locke did not clearly advocate an extension of voting rights beyond the property-holders who were allowed to vote in his day; he also held shares in a company engaged in the slave trade.[11] Locke and other early liberals simply took it for granted, moreover, that natural equality and the right to self-government did not include women.[12] By making these claims, however, early liberals provided an opening for those who could say, "If all men are created equal, why isn't this or that group of men or women being treated as equals?" By speaking the language of equality, in other words, they contributed, perhaps unwittingly, to the growth of democracy and the expansion of the franchise.

A second feature of the Declaration that deserves particular attention is its defense of the rights and liberties of individuals against government. This defense is typical of early liberals, who saw government as a continuing threat to individual liberty; but it also shows the influence of classical republicanism, with its constant warnings about the danger of corruption. Indeed, the republican and liberal traditions were so closely entwined at this point that it is difficult to separate them. But there were differences of emphasis. Republicans worried about the corruption of the people as much as the corruption of the government, while early liberals were concerned almost exclusively with the abuse of power by government. Freedom, as republicans saw it, was largely a matter of governing oneself through political participation, and therefore closely connected with civic virtue; in the liberal view, freedom was more a matter of being free from interference by the government, and virtue something to be learned and practiced in private life.

Out of this combination came the Constitution of the United States. The Constitution provides for a strong central government, but it also limits the government's powers in a number of ways. In this respect it is a republican as well as a liberal framework for government. But it also makes no direct provision for the promotion of civic virtue. Some of the Founding Fathers, including George Washington and James Madison, urged the creation of a national university partly for this purpose, but their efforts failed. In this respect, the lack of concern for civic virtue suggests the specifically liberal element of the Constitution—the attempt to prevent the government from meddling in those areas of life, such as religion and the cultivation of character, that belong to the private domain.

Drafted in 1787 and ratified in 1788, the Constitution took effect in 1789. Two years later the Bill of Rights was added. These were momentous years for the United States, yet every bit as momentous elsewhere for the development of political ideologies. For in these years a revolution began in France that was to prove at least as important in world affairs as the events taking shape in the United States.

The French Revolution

To understand the French Revolution and liberalism's role in it, we need to know something about the *ancien régime*—the "old order" of French society in the years before the Revolution. Three features of this old order are particularly important: its religious conformity, its aristocratic privilege, and its political absolutism. In all three respects, the condition of France before its revolution differed significantly from that of the American colonies before theirs.

First, **religious conformity**. In the years following the Reformation, France suffered a series of bloody civil wars between Huguenots (French Protestants) and Catholics. Most of the violence ended in 1598 with the Edict of Nantes, a compromise that granted freedom of worship to the Huguenots while acknowledging Catholicism as the official religion. This lasted until 1685, when Louis XIV, the so-called "Sun King," revoked the edict and required all his subjects to conform to Catholic doctrine. From then until the eve of the Revolution, religious conformity remained government policy. This favored status, together with its wealth from its extensive landholdings, made the Catholic Church a bulwark of the *ancien régime*—and a major obstacle for those who desired a more open society. Chief among these were the thinkers of the **Enlightenment**, such as Voltaire (1694–1778), who believed that the light of reason would lead to a better understanding of the world and a freer, more rational society. For that to happen, however, reason would first have to overcome the forces of superstition—forces led, as they saw it, by the Catholic Church.

Aristocratic privilege, the second leading feature of the old order, was a vestige of feudalism. In this respect France differed markedly from the American colonies, where hereditary aristocracy had never taken root. In France the roots of the aristocracy were very deep indeed, and most aristocrats were anxious to preserve the special rights they enjoyed as nobles. One of these privileges was exemption from most taxes. This exemption troubled the French government, which was constantly in need of funds, and was greatly resented by those who bore the burden of taxation—the middle class (*bourgeoisie*) and the peasants. Another important privilege the nobles enjoyed was the almost exclusive right to high positions in the government, military, and Church. Louis XVI, who was king when the Revolution began, chose almost all his advisers and administrators from the nobility and required all candidates for officer's rank in the army to have at least four generations of noble blood.[13] Aristocratic privilege meant, then, that in the *ancien régime* ascribed status counted far more than ability or effort—something else the bourgeoisie greatly resented.

Political absolutism, finally, placed the king above the law and concentrated political power in the throne. This was the legacy of Louis XIV, whose long reign (1643–1715) set the pattern for absolute monarchy. According to tradition, the king of France was responsible to the Estates-General, which consisted of representatives of the three orders or "estates" of the country: the clergy, the nobility, and the bourgeoisie. But Louis XIV never convened the Estates-General—it had last met in 1614—and found ways of appeasing and weakening the three estates. He secured the Church's support by suppressing the Huguenots; he drew the nobility to his extravagant court at Versailles, where they became dependent upon his favor; and he flattered the bourgeoisie by choosing some of his government ministers from their ranks. With no effective opposition to limit his power, Louis XIV was able to govern as he saw fit. As he supposedly said, *"L'état, c'est moi"* ("I am the state").

Neither of his successors, Louis XV (r. 1715–1774) nor Louis XVI (r. 1774–1792), was as adept as the Sun King at exercising absolute authority, but both followed his example. Neither summoned the Estates-General, for instance, until a financial crisis finally forced Louis XVI to do so in 1788. This event sparked the Revolution.

When Louis XVI called for elections to the Estates-General in the winter of 1788–1789, he and the nobles expected the representatives of the First and Second Estates—the clergy and the nobility—to prevent any drastic action by the Third Estate, or "the people." But the Third Estate insisted on double representation to more accurately reflect its percentage of the population, and public pressure forced the king to concede. Then, with the support of some liberal nobles and parish priests, the deputies of the Third Estate declared themselves the National Assembly and began to draft a constitution for France. The French Revolution had begun.

Although the Revolution ended ten bloody years later with a new form of absolutism, the revolutionaries' original aim was to establish a limited government that would protect the natural rights of French citizens—rights that the French kings had refused to acknowledge. The revolutionaries wanted to overthrow the old order, replacing religious conformity with tolerance, aristocratic privilege with equality of opportunity, and absolute monarchy with constitutional government. These aims are evident in their Declaration of the Rights of Man and of the Citizen of 1789. In the first of the Declaration's seventeen articles, the National Assembly attacked aristocratic privilege and ascribed status: "Men are born, and always continue, free and equal in respect of their rights. Civil distinctions [i.e., ranks or estates], therefore, can be founded only on public utility." The second and third articles attacked political absolutism, proclaiming that government rests on the consent of the governed:

> II. The end [i.e., goal] of all political associations is the preservation of the natural and imprescriptible rights of man; and these rights are liberty, property, security, and resistance of oppression.
>
> III. The nation is essentially the source of all sovereignty; nor can any individual, or any body of men, be entitled to any authority which is not expressly derived from it.

Nor did the National Assembly overlook religious conformity. In the tenth article of the Declaration it declared, "No man ought to be molested on account of his opinions, not even on account of his *religious* opinions, provided his avowal of them does not disturb the public order established by the law."[14] This and the other "rights of man," it should be noted, were rights for males only. Females were not accorded political and civil rights, as Olympe de Gouges pointed out with some bitterness in her "Declaration of the Rights of Woman and the Female Citizen" (1791).[15]

Liberalism was not the only current of thought in the French Revolution; republicanism, with its emphasis on civic virtue, also played a part. "Liberty, Equality, Fraternity"—the famous slogan of the Revolution—suggests how liberalism and republicanism were entwined, as they had been in the American Revolution. Every man has a right to be free, the argument went, because all are born equal, and each should have an equal opportunity to succeed. Yet liberty and equality were also prized, in republican terms, as the chief ingredients in an active public life directed toward virtue. The cry for "fraternity" also evoked republican themes, suggesting that the divisive civil distinctions be replaced with a sense of common citizenship. With this in mind, the revolutionaries abandoned the traditional titles or salutations of *monsieur* and *madame* and began to address everyone as *citoyen* or *citoyenne* ("citizen"). "Fraternity" suggested that there is more to life than being free to pursue one's private interests; indeed, a citizen has a responsibility to participate actively in public life.[16] "Fraternity" implied an interest in solidarity, in putting the common good ahead of one's private desires. It also took on nationalistic overtones as the French thought of themselves less as subjects of a monarch than as citizens of a single nation.

As the Revolution continued, Church lands were "secularized" and sold, and, in 1791, the National Assembly drafted a constitution that limited the powers of the king, abolished the three estates, and granted the right to vote to more than half of the adult males. France thus became a constitutional monarchy, with a government more limited and a franchise more democratic than Great Britain's.

Once begun, however, the Revolution could not be stopped. The more radical revolutionaries demanded greater democracy, help for the poor, and less concern for the protection of property. War broke out when Prussia and Austria sent armies to the French borders to check the spread of revolution and restore the *ancien régime.* One economic crisis followed another. Under the pressure of these circumstances, the revolutionaries abolished the monarchy and established the Republic of France on September 22, 1792; later revolutionaries proclaimed this the first day of the first month of the Year I, the beginning of a new era of history that required a new calendar. The events of the next year were no less dramatic. The execution of Louis XVI in January was followed by a new constitution granting universal manhood suffrage. Then, from June 1793 until July 1794, came the Reign of Terror. During this period the guillotine became the chief symbol of the Revolution. Some 300,000 people were arrested on suspicion of betraying the Republic, and more than 17,000 were executed in view of cheering crowds. The Terror ended when its principal leader, Maximilien Robespierre, was himself beheaded, and in 1795 a measure of calm was restored under another constitution. Less democratic than its predecessor, the Constitution of 1795 restricted the vote to the property-owning bourgeoisie and created a five-member Directory to head the government. This arrangement survived until 1799, when Napoleon Bonaparte seized power, turning France into a military dictatorship and later a monarchy with himself as emperor.

LIBERALISM AND CAPITALISM

In both the Old World and the New, then, liberalism was a vigorous revolutionary force. In the name of "natural rights" and "the rights of man," liberals struggled for individual liberty against the social, political, and religious arrangements that lingered from the Middle Ages. A central aspect of this struggle was the quest for *economic liberty.*

By opposing ascribed status, early liberals sought wider opportunities for more people, not just the privileged few born into the nobility. Economic opportunity was particularly important to the merchants, bankers, and lawyers who made up the middle class, or bourgeoisie. For them, acquiring wealth was the main avenue of social advancement. But in early modern Europe, this avenue was blocked by numerous church- and government-imposed restrictions on manufacturing and commerce. These restrictions included the traditional Christian limits on usury—the practice of charging interest on loans—and various local regulations concerning working conditions and the production, distribution, and sale of goods. In the seventeenth and eighteenth centuries, still other restrictions stemmed from the economic theory of **mercantilism.**

Mercantilism. According to mercantilist theory, one country could improve its economic strength only at the expense of others. Acting on this theory, European nation-states engaged in economic warfare that frequently led to real combat. One tactic was to establish colonies, extract their resources, and forbid the colonists to buy from or sell to anyone but the "mother country." Another was to set high tariffs, or taxes on imported goods, to discourage the sale of foreign goods and encourage the growth of domestic industries. A third tactic involved **monopoly,** the practice of granting exclusive control over a market to a single firm on the grounds that this was the most efficient way to handle the risks of trade between the far-flung colonies and the European homeland. Two leading examples of monopolies were the Dutch East India and the British East India companies, each of which received from its own government (but not from the native peoples) the exclusive right to govern as well as to trade with vast colonial territories.

Mercantilism, then, attempted to promote the national interest directly through the use of restraints and monopolistic privileges. These attempts worked to the advantage of some—especially those who were able to secure the privileges— and to the disadvantage of others. The middle class, which generally fell into this second camp, pressed for a wider and more nearly equal opportunity to compete for profits. Anything less, they believed, was an unjust obstacle in the way of individual liberty. This liberal belief found expression in the economic theory of **capitalism**.

Capitalism. Under capitalism, economic exchanges are essentially a private matter between persons pursuing profits. This emphasis on private profit ran against the grain of much of the Christian and republican traditions, neither of which assigned great value to either privacy or profits. Indeed, Christianity had long regarded usury (lending money at interest) and the attempt to maximize profit as sinful. But the 1700s produced some forceful statements of the argument that people ought to be free to pursue their private interests, including their economic interests. One of the first was *The Fable of the Bees,* published in 1714 by Bernard Mandeville (1670–1733). Mandeville's fable is the story of a hive in which the bees, shocked by their own selfishness, decide to reform and act with the good of others in mind. But reform proves disastrous. Soldier, servant, merchant, and most of the other bees are thrown out of work because there is no demand for their services. The richness and variety of life are gone. Indeed, Mandeville suggests, the hive was much better off in the old, selfish days when the bees acted out of vanity and greed—a time when

> … every Part was full of Vice,
> Yet the whole Mass a Paradise;
> Such were the Blessings of that state;
> Their Crimes conspir'd to make them Great.

The moral of the story, captured in the subtitle of the *Fable,* is *Private Vices, Publick Benefits.* In other words, selfish behavior produces publicly beneficial results.

This idea—that the best way to promote the good of society as a whole is to let people pursue their private interests—became the cornerstone of liberal economic thought in the eighteenth century. In the middle of the century a group of French thinkers, the **Physiocrats**, developed this idea into an economic theory. Arguing against mercantilism, the Physiocrats maintained that the true basis of wealth is neither trade nor manufactures but agriculture. Furthermore, they claimed, the best way to cultivate wealth is not through regulations and restrictions but through unrestrained or free enterprise. Their advice to governments—remove regulations and leave people alone to compete in the marketplace—was captured in the phrase, *laissez faire, laissez passer* ("let it be, leave it alone").

Adam Smith

The most thorough and influential defense of *laissez faire* was Adam Smith's *Inquiry into the Nature and Causes of the Wealth of Nations* (1776). Smith (1723–1790), a Scottish moral philosopher and economist, agreed with the Physiocrats' attack on mercantilism and monopoly. Far from serving the public interest, Smith said, restraints on economic competition serve only the interests of those few people who are able to take advantage of them. For most people, lack of competition simply means higher prices and scarcer goods.

As a remedy, Smith recommended an economic policy that would allow individuals to compete freely in the marketplace. Not only is this the fairest policy, because it gives everyone an equal opportunity, but it will also be the most efficient. For there is nothing like self-interest—in this case, the desire for profits—to motivate people to provide the goods and services that others want. As Smith put it, "It is not from the benevolence of the butcher, the brewer, or the baker that we expect our dinner, but from their regard to their own interest. We address ourselves, not to their humanity but to their self-love, and never talk to them of our own necessities but of their advantage."[17] Smith reasoned that removing economic restrictions and privileges will encourage people to produce and sell goods for a profit. In order to turn a profit, producers have to produce either a better or a cheaper good than their competitors; otherwise, people will not buy their products. Private interest, set free, will thus indirectly promote the public good by making available more and better and cheaper goods. It is, Smith said, as if an **"invisible hand"** were directing all these self-interested competitors to serve the common interest of the whole society:

> He [the merchant or trader] generally ... neither intends to promote the publick interest, nor knows how much he is promoting it ... [H]e intends only his own gain, and he is in this, as in many other cases, led by an invisible hand to promote an end which was no part of his intention... By pursuing his own interest he frequently promotes that of the society more effectually than when he really intends to promote it.[18]

Although the invisible hand of the market often promotes the public interest, it does not always do so, Smith says. Sometimes, the more visible hand of the state (or government) is required to serve the interest of the public at large. To this end Smith advocated limited government regulation in some areas, even though such restrictions curtail our "natural liberty" to do as we like. He was in favor, for example, of regulating banks to prevent bankers from taking undue risks with depositors' money:

> Such regulations may, no doubt, be considered as in some respect a violation of natural liberty. But those exertions of the natural liberty of a few individuals, which might endanger the security of the whole society, are, and ought to be, restrained by the laws of all governments ... The obligation of building party walls [i.e., fireproof walls separating adjoining apartments] in order to prevent the communication [i.e., spread] of fire, is a violation of natural liberty, exactly of the same kind with the regulations of the banking trade which are here proposed.[19]

Just as government is justified in imposing building and fire codes in the interest of public safety, so it is justified in regulating banking and finance to protect the interests not only of depositors and investors but of the public at large.

Smith also advocated tax-supported "publick works"—his term for what we now call "infrastructure"—which included roads, bridges, canals, harbors, and other things that serve to facilitate commerce. In Smith's day most roads were toll roads, supported not by taxes but by tolls paid by travelers to those who owned the roads. These travelers included farmers taking their produce to town and merchants their goods. The tolls they paid, Smith reasoned, amounted to a tax that was much more onerous and burdensome—and costly—than a tax paid to the government to build and maintain public roads. These roads facilitated commerce and in so doing benefited not only farmers and merchants but consumers as well. What is true of public roads, bridges, and canals is also true of tax-funded free public education for all: a better educated workforce is a more productive workforce; and a better educated citizenry is a more enlightened and virtuous citizenry.

Smith also argued, against the mercantilists, for free trade between countries. If people in some foreign land can sell us something we want for less than it costs to produce it ourselves, then let them do it. High taxes on foreign imports may encourage industry at home, Smith said, but they do so at great cost to the consumer, who has fewer and more expensive goods available. And because consumers seek to purchase goods at the lowest price, an illegal or "black" market in smuggled goods is the almost inevitable result. In the long run, peaceful and unrestricted trade between countries benefits everyone.

Smith was a staunch advocate of self-interest in economic matters. But humans, he says, are not only "traders and barterers"—that is, economic creatures—but social and sociable creatures as well. He was appalled by Mandeville's "selfish system," to which he counterposed his own system in *The Theory of Moral Sentiments*, which begins with these words:

> How selfish soever man may be supposed to be, there are evidently some principles in his nature, which interest him in the fortunes of others, and render their happiness necessary to him, though he derives nothing from it except the pleasure of seeing it. Of this kind is pity or compassion, the emotion which we feel for the misery of others … That we often derive sorrow from the sorrow of others, is a matter of fact... The greatest ruffian, the most hardened violator of the laws of society, is not altogether without it.[20]

The "moral sentiments" of pity or compassion, sympathy (or what we would call empathy), benevolence, and the like are deeply ingrained in humans, and make civilized society possible.

At first sight this seems to contradict Smith's advocacy of self-interest. Some scholars, finding it difficult to square the message of *The Wealth of Nations* with that of *The Theory of Moral Sentiments*, refer to this alleged difficulty as "the Adam Smith problem." But the "problem" is really no problem at all, for in the former Smith was chiefly attempting to describe and explain the behavior of humans acting as economic creatures and in the latter he was more concerned with how and why we act as social and sociable creatures. *Homo economicus* is only half a man. To be a whole human being requires that *homo economicus* be supplemented by *homo socialis*, who seeks the company and comfort of others. However, in *The Theory of Moral Sentiments*, Smith argues that our self-interested economic decisions and actions should be moderated in order for individuals to exhibit and exercise moral virtue. Far from arguing that greed is good, Smith consistently maintained that unmitigated greed is a form of moral corruption.[21]

From Smith's point of view, however, virtue was a matter for each individual to develop, and government should with some exceptions have as little as possible to do with *economic* exchanges insofar as they do not adversely affect society at large. Government has only three proper functions, he said. First, it must defend the country against invasion. Second, it must promote justice and maintain order. Finally, it must provide certain "public works." All other matters are best left to the private business of self-interested individuals, who should be free to make their way in the world as they see fit. In this respect, Smith and other advocates of capitalism have taken a liberal position.

Adam Smith (1723–1790)

North Wind Picture Archives/Alamy

LIBERALISM IN THE NINETEENTH CENTURY

In the early 1800s liberalism remained a revolutionary force. In South America liberal ideas helped to inspire struggles for independence in the Spanish colonies. Even in France, the dictatorship of Napoleon did not mean a return to the *ancien régime*. In his revision of the French laws, the Napoleonic Code, Napoleon gave lasting approval to the principle of civil equality: the aristocrats kept their titles but lost most of their economic and political privileges. While he reestablished Catholicism as the official religion of France, Napoleon also guaranteed freedom of worship to Protestants and Jews. Some Europeans even welcomed Napoleon's conquests of their countries as liberation from the old aristocratic social order. Napoleon's defeat of the Prussian army in 1806, for instance, led Prussia (later part of Germany) to undertake many reforms, including the abolition of serfdom.

On the European continent, however, Napoleon's defeat at Waterloo in 1815 marked the beginning of thirty years of reaction against these revolutionary changes. Monarchs and aristocrats reasserted their hereditary rights. Ironically, the country most responsible for Napoleon's defeat, England, was also the country in which liberalism had made its greatest gains.

At the beginning of the 1800s, the British Empire was still expanding. The thirteen American colonies had gained their independence, but Britain continued to control India, Canada, and Australia, and it was soon to acquire vast territories in Africa as well. The Industrial Revolution was also making England the world's first great industrial power. Beginning about 1750, the invention of new machinery, the discovery of steam power, and the development of assembly lines and other mass-production techniques brought about a remarkable increase in productive power. English merchants thus were able to import raw materials, such as cotton, and to manufacture goods to be sold at home and abroad for handsome profits. With its combination of empire and industry, Great Britain became "the workshop of the world"—and the world's greatest imperial power—in the nineteenth century.

But power comes at a price, and in Britain the price was a society more sharply divided along class lines. Although the landed aristocracy was still the dominant force in the early 1800s, middle-class merchants and professionals made enormous political and economic gains during the first half of the century. The same cannot be said of the men, women, and children of the working class. Poor and numerous, they toiled in the mines, mills, and factories that sprang up during the Industrial Revolution, and their situation was bleak indeed. Without unemployment compensation, or regulation of working hours or safety conditions, or the legal right to form trade or labor unions, they worked for very low wages under extremely harsh and insecure conditions. Just how harsh is suggested by a bill proposed in Parliament early in the century to *improve* the workers' position. The bill forbade factories to employ children under the age of ten, to put anyone under eighteen on night work (i.e., 9 P.M. through 5 A.M.), or to require anyone under eighteen to work more than ten and one-half hours a day. Even this bill did not pass until, after years of debate, it had been so weakened as to be ineffective.[22]

In economic status and in political power, too, the working class fell far behind the middle class in the first half of the nineteenth century. The Reform Bill of 1832 lowered property qualifications enough to give middle-class males the right to vote, but most adult males and all women were still denied suffrage. This situation was a matter of some concern to the leading liberal writers of the day, a group known then as the Philosophic Radicals and later as the Utilitarians.

Utilitarianism

Jeremy Bentham. The original leader of the Utilitarians (or Philosophic Radicals) was the English philosopher Jeremy Bentham (1748–1832). Society must be made more rational, he insisted, and the first step in this direction is to recognize that

Bettmann/Getty Images

Jeremy Bentham (1748–1832)

people act out of self-interest. Moreover, everyone has an interest in experiencing pleasure and avoiding pain. As Bentham put it, "Nature has placed mankind under the governance of two sovereign masters, *pain* and *pleasure*. It is for them alone to point out what we ought to do, as well as to determine what we shall do."[23] This is simply a fact of human nature, he thought, and there is nothing we can do to change it. But once we understand that all people seek pleasure and avoid pain in everything they do, we can take steps to be better pleasure-seekers and pain-avoiders.

Bentham did not mean that we should seek pleasure in immediate gratification—in getting drunk, for example—because the pain we experience during a hangover or others suffer from our obnoxious drunken behavior later will probably outweigh the short-term pleasure. He meant, rather, that we should seek **utility**. Something has utility—a hammer for a carpenter, for instance, or money for almost everyone—if it helps someone do what he or she wants. Because people want to be happy, utility promotes happiness.

Bentham recognized that people will sometimes fail to see what does and does not have utility for them—someone who drops out of school may not appreciate the utility of education, for example. He also admitted that, in pursuing our own pleasures, we may bring pain to others. But the purpose of government is to solve these problems. In Bentham's words, "The business of government is to promote the happiness of society, by punishing and rewarding."[24] By punishing those who cause pain to others and by rewarding those who give pleasure, in other words, government can and should act to promote the greatest happiness of the greatest number.

From this Bentham drew two general conclusions about government. The first was that government could often, though not always, promote the greatest happiness of the greatest number simply by leaving people alone. Individuals are usually the best judges of their own interests, so government should usually let people act as they see fit. For this reason Bentham accepted the *laissez faire* arguments of Adam Smith. His second conclusion was that government is not likely to promote the greatest happiness of the greatest number if it is controlled by a small segment of society. In the pursuit of utility, Bentham declared, everyone is to count equally. In calculating the greatest happiness of the greatest number, "each [individual person is] to count for one, and none for more than one."[25] Thus government cannot favor the rich over the poor, men over women, or be partial to any particular individual or group. Government must weigh everyone's interests equally, and this requires that almost everyone be allowed to vote. Although Bentham's views on voting are not altogether clear, he did support universal male suffrage and, with certain reservations, the vote for women as well.[26]

In retrospect it is scarcely surprising that what has been called the age of democratic revolution[27]—the late eighteenth century—produced a democratic revolution in moral and political philosophy. Utilitarianism, democratic inasmuch as it is majoritarian ("the greatest happiness of the greatest number") and revolutionary inasmuch as its egalitarian ethos ("each to count for one and none for more than one"), challenges the older aristocratic ethos of inequality. But it remained for followers of Bentham to iron out the kinks and work out the details. Foremost among these was James Mill.

James Mill. Bentham's chief disciple and propagandist was James Mill (1773–1836), a dour Scotsman who had been educated for the Presbyterian ministry, lost his faith, and moved to London. There he met Bentham and became his most ardent ally and spokesman. Bentham the wealthy and eccentric bachelor and Mill the harried and hard-working father of eight made an odd but effective team. When the critic William Hazlitt heard that one of Bentham's books had been translated into French, he asked jokingly, "But when will someone translate Mr. Bentham into English?" That, in effect, is what James Mill did: he turned Bentham's wordy and prolix prose into his own clear and plain English. His brief essay *Government* (1820) is the most succinct statement of Benthamite political theory.[28] Mill maintains that the aim of government is to promote the greatest happiness of the entire community and of the individuals composing it. All those individuals are motivated by self-interest, and in particular the interest in experiencing pleasure and avoiding pain. It is the nature of humans to not only desire happiness but to expend as little effort as possible in obtaining it. Labor being the means of obtaining happiness, and our own labor being painful to us, we will, unless prevented, try to live off the labor of others. It is the job of government to prevent this outcome by protecting the fruits of our labor from the predations of others. Mill's essay is the classic statement of the **protectionist theory of democracy**.

James Mill was the father, and Bentham the godfather, of another and even more eminent philosopher, John Stuart Mill.

John Stuart Mill. The views of John Stuart Mill (1806–1873) in some respects resembled and in others repudiated those of Bentham and his father. Like them, he professed to be a Utilitarian; but he believed that the protectionist theory of democracy was incomplete and insufficient, and that his father's and godfather's version of Utilitarianism did not go far enough in protecting and promoting the liberty of all individuals, including women, to live their own lives as they see fit. The most influential Utilitarian of his day, the younger Mill championed a number of controversial causes. Whether supporting women's rights or arguing that government should set minimum educational standards for all, Mill's greatest concern was to defend and extend individual liberty. This concern is most evident in his essay *On Liberty*.

When Mill published *On Liberty* in 1859, liberalism seemed to have triumphed, at least in England and the United States. The old enemies—ascribed status, religious conformity, and absolute government—were no longer the obstacles to individual liberty they once had been. Yet Mill was alarmed by what he took to be a new threat to liberty in the growing power of public opinion. In the old days, Mill said, the chief enemy of freedom was the government; but now that we elect representatives, the government is more responsive to the desires of the people. It is responsive, however, to the majority of the people, or at least the majority of those who vote, and this allows them to use the government to restrict or take away the liberty of those who do not share the majority's views. Moreover, the majority can bring social pressure to bear on those who do not conform to the ordinary, conventional ways of life. Without going through the government or the law, the "moral coercion of public opinion" can stifle freedom of thought and action by making social outcasts of individuals who do not conform to social customs and conventional beliefs. Like Alexis de Tocqueville, whose *Democracy in America* he greatly admired, Mill was worried about "the tyranny of the majority."

Unfortunately, Utilitarianism, in its original Benthamite formulation, not only includes no adequate safeguards against this new kind of tyranny, it could conceivably aid and abet it. The problem arises in this way. Suppose that a majority of the members of a community decide that what would make them happy is to torment or even torture an unpopular individual or minority. What, on Utilitarian grounds, is to stop them and thereby protect the liberty and promote the happiness of the unpopular individual or minority? To this question Bentham had no adequate answer. Mill set out to rectify what he saw as a defect in democracy and Utilitarianism: the possibility in both of majoritarian tyranny.

On Liberty was Mill's attempt to deal with this new form of tyranny. There he advanced "one very simple principle": "The only purpose for which power can

John Stuart Mill (1806–1873)

be rightfully exercised over any member of a civilized community, against his will, is to prevent harm to others. His own good, either physical or moral, is not a sufficient warrant."[29] According to this principle—sometimes called the **harm principle**—every sane adult should be free to do whatever he or she wants so long as his or her actions do not harm or threaten to harm others. Government and society, then, should not interfere with an individual's activities unless that individual is somehow harming or threatening to harm others. Government has no business prohibiting the sale of alcohol, for instance, on the grounds that drinking harms the drinker; but government should certainly prohibit drunken driving on the grounds that this poses a serious threat of harm to others.

In formulating the harm principle Mill in effect formalizes an idea expressed by Thomas Jefferson some seventy-five years earlier. "The legitimate powers of government," Jefferson wrote, "extend to such acts only as are injurious to others. But it does me no injury for my neighbor to say there are twenty gods, or no god. It neither picks my pocket nor breaks my leg."[30] I might find my neighbor's opinion offensive or upsetting; but unless its expression causes demonstrable *harm* to me or to someone else, government has no legitimate role in outlawing its expression, however offended or upset some people might be.

Mill defended his principle by appealing not to natural rights, as most of the early liberals had done, but to utility. Freedom is a good thing, he argued, because it promotes "the permanent interests of man as a progressive being."[31] By this he meant that both individuals and society as a whole will benefit if people are encouraged to think and act freely. For the individual, freedom is vital to personal development. Our mental and moral faculties are like muscles, Mill said. Without regular and rigorous exercise, they will weaken and shrivel. But people cannot exercise their minds and their powers of judgment when they are constantly told what they can and cannot do. To be fully human, then, individuals must be free to think and speak for themselves—as long as they neither harm nor threaten harm to others.

Critics were quick to point out that it is often difficult, if not impossible, to draw a clear and sharp distinction between being *offended* and being *harmed*. Imagine a black child who is called the "n-word" and other racist insults. Isn't that child's moral, emotional, and intellectual development being stunted? Is she not therefore being *harmed*? If so, certain sorts of speech may be legitimately outlawed, at least where children are present. And Mill agrees:

> It is ... hardly necessary to say that [the harm principle] is meant to apply only to human beings in the maturity of their faculties [i.e., to adults]. We are not speaking of children, or of young persons below the age which the law may fix that of manhood or womanhood. Those who are still in a state to require being taken care of by others, must be protected against their own actions as well as against external injury.[32]

But what of (say) young adults of college age who are subjected to racist taunts and insults? They are—of course and quite rightly—*offended* by such speech; but are they actually and demonstrably *harmed* by it? Should they be protected by campus codes which make "hate speech" a punishable offense? Or should they subscribe to the old adage, "Sticks and stones may break my bones, but names will never hurt me"? This leaves advocates and defenders of Mill's harm principle in a problematic position, to say the least. If nothing else, this raises anew the age-old question of how one is to distinguish offense from harm.

It is always possible, of course, that people who speak and act freely will make others, perhaps even the majority of society, uncomfortable and unhappy. But in the long run, Mill argued, the ideas of outspoken nonconformists such as Socrates, Jesus, and Galileo—however upsetting or offensive their views were at the time—work to the benefit of society. Progress is possible only when there is open competition between different ideas, opinions, and beliefs. As in economics, a free marketplace of competing ideas yields a greater variety to choose from and allows people to distinguish good ideas from bad. Without freedom of thought and action, society will remain stuck in the rut of conformity and will never progress. But, as critics note, insults and name-calling contribute nothing to the progress of society, and might actually retard or impede it. Therefore, by Mill's own lights, there may be good grounds for restricting or outlawing certain kinds of speech. And the debate continues.

Mill's desire to promote individual liberty also led him to recommend representative democracy as the best possible form of government. In *Considerations on Representative Government* (1861) he maintained that political participation is one of the best forms of exercise for the mental and moral faculties. Only in a democracy, he argued, is this kind of exercise available to *all* citizens. In this respect Mill's argument for democracy differed from Bentham's, who thought that democracy is valuable as a means of protecting individuals' material interests. That is, insofar as everyone has an equal vote in a democracy, then every voter has an equal say when voting for or against proposed policies or candidates for office an equal say that Bentham believed that voters would use to protect their personal interests. Mill agreed that "self-protection" is a valuable feature of democracy, but he held that "self-development" is even more valuable, as democratic participation can promote the civic education of citizens by broadening their horizons and sympathies through discussion, debate, and public service, such as jury duty. In this way Mill stressed the **educative theory of democracy** rather than the *protectionist theory* that his father and Bentham espoused.[33] Even so, Mill's fear of "the tyranny of the majority" kept him from embracing democracy wholeheartedly, in an era when most voters were ill- or uneducated and many were even illiterate. Among other things, he favored a form of plural voting in which every literate man and woman will have a vote, but some—those with higher levels of education, for instance—will have two, three, or more. Plural voting thus would enable everyone to enjoy the benefits of political participation, yet allow more enlightened and better-informed citizens to protect individual liberty. Such a system was necessary, Mill believed, at least until the overall level of education was high enough to remove the threat of majority tyranny. Like his father, Mill was a lifelong employee of the British East India Company and, with some qualifications and limitations, a defender of British imperialism. As such, he argued that neither liberty nor democracy would be appropriate outside "civilized" Western societies for some time to come. "Despotism," he wrote, "is a legitimate mode of government in dealing with barbarians, provided the end be their improvement, and the means justified by actually effecting that end."[34] We must remember that in the context of

Mill's own time, this seemingly illiberal and even shocking statement was markedly more liberal than the views expressed by many if not most of Mill's contemporaries.

As for economic matters, Mill began his career as a staunch defender of *laissez faire* capitalism. Toward the end of his life, however, he called himself a socialist.[35] This shift in his thinking was one of the first signs of an even greater shift on the part of many liberals in the latter part of the nineteenth century—a shift that divided liberalism into rival camps.

LIBERALISM DIVIDED

The division among liberals stemmed from their different reactions to the social effects of the Industrial Revolution. The misery of much of the English working class became increasingly obvious, in part through the depiction of their plight in the popular novels of Charles Dickens (who, as a child, had worked in a boot-blacking factory under harsh and unhealthy conditions). Reform movements were under way, and socialism was gaining support, especially on the European continent. Some liberals began to argue that government should rescue people from poverty, ignorance, and illness. Because of their concern for the well-being, or "well-faring," of the individual, this group has come to be called welfare or welfare-state liberals. Conservative critics like to label these liberals as "big-government liberals." To this charge welfare liberals reply that big government is needed to restrain and regulate big business. The wealth of large corporations, big banks, and other businesses translates quickly into undue and disproportionate political power and influence, thus endangering democracy. Other liberals maintain that welfare-state liberals would invest too much power in the government, which they continued to regard as a necessary evil and one of the main obstacles to individual liberty. Because their position is in some respects close to that of early liberalism, this second school of thought has come to be called neoclassical (or "new classical") liberalism.

Neoclassical Liberalism

Since the second half of the nineteenth century, neoclassical liberals have consistently argued that government should be as small as possible in order to leave room for the exercise of individual freedom. The state or government should be nothing more than a "night-watchman" whose only legitimate business is to protect the person and property of individuals against force and fraud. Some neoclassical liberals have based this argument on an appeal to natural rights, others on an appeal to utility. In the late 1800s, however, the most influential among them based their arguments on Darwin's theory of evolution.[36]

In his *Origin of Species* (1859), Charles Darwin used the idea of "natural selection" to account for the evolution of life-forms. Darwin held that individual creatures within every species experience random mutations, or accidental changes, in their biological makeup. Some mutations enhance a creature's ability to find food and survive, while others do not. Those lucky enough to have beneficial mutations are more likely to survive—and to pass these biological changes along to their offspring—than less fortunate members of their species. Thus nature "selected" certain creatures with certain mutations and thereby "directed" the path of evolution. But all this was accidental and unintentional. This biological good fortune also gives the members of some species an adaptive advantage over others in competition for food—for instance, giraffes are able to eat the leaves on the higher branches of trees, which is a distinct advantage when food is scarce. Mutations thus account not only for the evolution of species but also for their survival or extinction.

Although Darwin did not derive any social and political implications from his theory, others were quick to do so. Many who had stressed the importance of economic competition seized upon Darwin's theory of natural selection as "proof" that the struggle for survival was natural to human life and that government should not "interfere" in that struggle. Two of the most important of these **Social Darwinists** were Herbert Spencer and William Graham Sumner.

Social Darwinism. Herbert Spencer (1820–1903), an English philosopher, had begun to think in evolutionary terms even before Darwin's *Origin of Species* appeared, and he took Darwin's work to confirm the main lines of his own thought. In particular, Spencer claimed that there is a natural struggle for survival within the human species. Nature means for individuals to be free to compete with one another. Those who are strongest, smartest, and most fit for this competition will succeed and prosper; those who are unfit will fail and suffer. But this is simply nature's way, Spencer said. Helping the poor and the weak impedes individual freedom and retards social progress by holding back the strong. Indeed, it was Spencer who coined the phrase, "survival of the fittest." Such views made Spencer a leading advocate of the minimalist "night-watchman state."

William Graham Sumner (1840–1910) was the leading American advocate of Social Darwinism. A professor of sociology at Yale University, Sumner proclaimed that "there are two chief things with which government has to deal. They are, the property of men and the honor of women."[37] These are, Sumner says, the *only* matters with which government should concern itself. In the competition for survival, government should simply see to it that everyone competes fairly and freely. Freedom, for Sumner, meant the freedom to compete, including the freedom of the victors to keep and enjoy the fruits of their victory without having to share them with anyone else—certainly not with the poor, who were poor precisely because they had lost in this life-and-death competition. In fact, Sumner and the Social Darwinists insisted that neither government nor even private charity should try to help anyone, no matter how weak or desperate he or she might be, except by providing protection against force and fraud. As Sumner put it, "A drunkard in the gutter is just where he ought to be, according to the fitness and tendency of things. Nature has set up on him the process of decline and dissolution by which she removes things which have [outlived] their usefulness."[38] When a policeman picks the man up to prevent him from drowning face-down in the gutter, he is not performing a noble and charitable act; he is instead helping to secure the survival of the unfittest and burdening the honest law-abiding taxpayer who pays the policeman's salary and for the upkeep of the jail.

Most neoclassical liberals have not been as extreme in their views as the Social Darwinists; few neoclassical liberals today base their arguments on Darwinian-evolutionary premises. But in the latter part of the nineteenth century, the Social

Darwinists were quite influential in England and the United States, especially among wealthy businessmen who sought "scientific" support for *laissez faire* capitalism.

Welfare Liberalism

Like classical and neoclassical liberals, reformist or welfare liberals believe in the value of individual liberty. But welfare liberals maintain that government is not just a necessary evil. On the contrary, properly directed, government can be a positive force for promoting individual liberty by ensuring that everyone enjoys an equal opportunity in life.

T. H. Green. One of the first to make the case for reformist or welfare liberalism was Thomas Hill Green (1836–1882), a professor of philosophy at Oxford University. The heart of liberalism, Green said, has always been the desire to remove obstacles that block the free growth and development of individuals. In the past that meant

Thomas Hill Green (1836–1882)

limiting the powers of government so that people can be free to live, worship, and compete in the marketplace as they see fit. By the mid- to late 1800s these aims had largely been accomplished in countries like England, and it was time to recognize and overcome still other obstacles to freedom—obstacles such as poverty and illness, prejudice and ignorance. To overcome *these* obstacles, Green argued, it was necessary to enlist the power of the state.

Green based his argument on a distinction between two different ways of thinking about freedom, ways that he called **negative** and **positive freedom**. The early liberals regarded freedom as a negative thing, he said, for they thought of freedom as the *absence* of some obvious obstacle or restraint. Someone who was restrained—tied up and locked in jail, for instance—was not free, while someone who was unrestrained was. But Green believed that there is more to freedom than this. Freedom is not merely a matter of being left alone; it is also—and no less importantly—the positive power or ability to *do* something that is worth doing. Thus we may say that a child born into poverty, with no real opportunity to escape, is not truly free to grow and develop to the full extent of his or her abilities. Even if no one is intentionally restraining that child by keeping him or her in poverty, the child is still not free. But if we admit this, Green argued, anyone who values individual liberty will want to take steps to overcome those circumstances—poverty, ill-health, ignorance—that are such formidable obstacles to freedom.[39]

Green and other welfare liberals believed that society, acting through government, should establish public schools and hospitals, aid the needy, and regulate working conditions to promote workers' health and well-being. Only through such public support would the poor and powerless members of society become truly free. Neoclassical liberals complained that these policies simply robbed some individuals of their freedom by forcing them to transfer their property, through taxes, to others. Green responded that everyone gained freedom when he or she served the common good. For *positive* freedom is the ability to realize or achieve our ideal or "higher" selves in cooperation with others. Contrary to Bentham and the Utilitarians, human beings are not merely pleasure-seekers and pain-avoiders. We have higher ideals, including ideals of what we can and ought to be as persons. The laws and programs that help the unfortunate, smooth social relations, and restrict all-out competition are positive *aids* to liberty, not restraints that limit our freedom. They may restrict our selfish or "lower" selves, but laws and programs of this sort encourage our "higher" selves to realize our nobler and more generous ideals through social cooperation.[40] Thus the welfare liberal view of freedom relies on what is sometimes called the "dual self" or "two selves" doctrine, according to which the self is not singular or united, but consists of a "lower" and a "higher" self. This is a very old idea, one that goes all the way back to Plato, who held that the mind or soul (*psyche*) has a lower or "appetitive" side and a higher or "rational" side. These two are often in tension and sometimes in conflict, leading Plato to speak of a "civil war within the soul."[41] This is similar to the Judeo-Christian view that humans are both "flesh" and "spirit"; in the former respect we resemble the lower animals, and in the latter our Creator. "True" freedom is, accordingly, the freedom of the higher self from the snares and temptations of the lower self.[42] This, in a nutshell, is Green's conception of "positive" liberty.[43] The positive or welfare liberal conception of freedom is pictured in Figure 3.2.

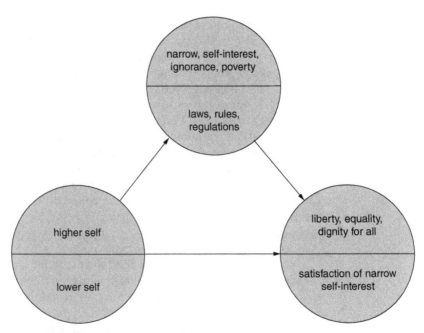

FIGURE 3.2 The welfare liberal or "positive" view of freedom.

Or, to put Green's point another way, the lower or selfish self has an unduly narrow conception of self-interest, one that does not take the interests of others into account. The higher or social self, by contrast, takes the interests, safety and well-being of others into account via the harm principle. But, unlike Mill, Green believes that "harm" involves much more than injuries intentionally inflicted by other human beings. People can, for example, be harmed by poverty that is no one's fault. You are not legitimately free to act—or fail to act—in ways that endanger or infringe the interests of others, including their interest in leading free and dignified lives. There is nothing wrong with pursuing our self-interest, so long as we have a sufficiently expansive (or "higher") view of the self. We are not isolated, solitary selves but social and sociable selves who need the presence and help of others to develop our abilities and talents to their fullest. Some people need more help than others—the poor, the young, the ill, the aged and infirm—and those who are able to provide such help should do so. If it is within our power to (say) alleviate other people's poverty, we who are more fortunate are obligated to do so. "The lottery of life" or "the wheel of fortune" favors some more than others. Some are fortunate enough to be born of wealthy and well-educated parents; others are born to poor, uneducated, perhaps even drug-addicted parents. The latter's lot in life should not be determined by sheer dumb luck. If he or she is to compete on an equal footing, chances and opportunities should be equalized by leveling the playing field. This is the justification offered for Head Start and other programs of the modern welfare state.

In the late nineteenth and early twentieth centuries, many scholars and political figures—Leonard Hobhouse and the young Winston Churchill among them—adopted views similar to Green's. These other welfare liberals saw an active government as a useful, even necessary tool in the campaign to expand individual liberty. Like Green, they also insisted that human beings are social creatures, not solitary, self-sufficient, or isolated individuals who owe nothing to anyone else. Gradually, their ideas and arguments prevailed among liberals. By the middle of the twentieth century, in fact, welfare liberals were usually known simply as "liberals," while their neoclassical rivals were often called "conservatives"—a piece of terminological confusion that we shall try to clarify in Chapter 4.

The Welfare State. As we shall see in later chapters, socialists also advanced plans and programs for social reform. But it is important to distinguish welfare or welfare-state liberalism from socialism. Socialists want to do more than tame or reform capitalism; they want to replace it with a system of publicly owned and democratically controlled enterprises. Welfare liberals, by contrast, prefer private ownership and generally take a competitive capitalist system for granted. From the perspective of the welfare liberal, the role of government is to regulate economic competition in order to cure the social ills and redress individual injuries wrought by capitalist competition. Unlike socialists, in short, welfare liberals regard economic competition as a good thing—but only up to the point where it comes at the expense of individual welfare.

It is also important to note that the grandfather of the modern welfare state was neither a socialist nor a liberal of any sort. Otto von Bismarck (1815–1898), the staunchly conservative and ardently antisocialist "Iron Chancellor" who united Germany in the latter part of the nineteenth century, believed that the welfare state was the best way to oppose socialism. Through a state-sponsored system of taxing employers and employees to support ill, injured, and unemployed workers, the German state stole the thunder of the socialists, who had played upon the fears and anxieties of workers subject to the up-and-down cycles of a capitalist economy. To accomplish this, Bismarck first pushed anti-socialist legislation through the Reichstag (the German parliament) in 1878, forcing many leading socialists to leave the country or go underground and remain silent. Second, there soon followed legislation that created the first "social insurance state," or welfare state. These included the Health Insurance bill of 1883, the Accident Insurance bill of 1884, and the Old Age and Disability Insurance bill of 1889.

But why would a conservative create the first welfare state? To understand Bismarck's reasoning, imagine yourself a German worker in the late nineteenth century, before Bismarck's reforms. Socialism appeals to you because you agree with the socialist critique of capitalism's "boom and bust" economy that periodically throws conscientious and hard-working laborers out of work. If you are injured or ill, you lose your job. Whatever the cause, unemployed workers are out of luck. They can't feed, house, or clothe themselves and their families. Little wonder, then, that the socialists, with their plans for "full employment" in a post-capitalist socialist economy, capture the attention and allegiance of many workers in Germany and elsewhere. But Bismarck's reforms, once enacted, allay workers' worries. If you are ill or injured, your hospital bills will be paid by the German government from the "social insurance" fund that workers and employers pay into. If you lose your job through no fault of your own, you will receive unemployment compensation. When you retire you will receive a monthly check drawn from a fund you paid into while working (something like the Social Security system later adopted by the United States). Thus in Bismarck's Germany socialism loses its allure and attractiveness to workers who, instead of becoming socialists and turning to revolution to overthrow the German state, become even more loyal and patriotic Germans. And capitalism remains intact. Although Bismarck's means were those of a welfare liberal, the ends he sought to achieve were conservative ones. And that explains why an ardent conservative, combining ingenuity with irony, created the first welfare state.

The birth of the welfare state also coincided roughly with the expansion of voting rights throughout much of Europe. In England the reforms of 1867 and 1885 brought the franchise to almost all adult males and thus made the working class a more powerful political force. The political representatives of this class contributed not only to the growth of the welfare state but also to the prominence of welfare liberalism in the twentieth century.[44]

LIBERALISM IN THE TWENTIETH CENTURY

Another factor also contributed to the dominance of welfare over neoclassical liberalism. By the beginning of the 1900s, capitalist competition looked quite different from what it had been a century before. In the industrialized world the lone entrepreneur who ran his (or her) own business had largely given way to the corporation, the trust, the syndicate, and the conglomerate. Business was now "big business," and many people began to call for government intervention in the marketplace, not to restrict competition, but to keep the large corporations from stifling it.

Historical Developments

In one form or another, however, the neoclassical liberals' faith in individual competition and achievement survived into the twentieth century, most notably in the United States. This faith was severely tested by the Great Depression of the 1930s. Individuals, no matter how rugged, seemed no match for this devastating economic collapse. The effects, political as well as economic, were felt throughout the world, as ideologues of every stripe sought to explain and exploit the situation. Many blamed the Depression on capitalism and turned either to socialism or communism, on the one hand, or to fascism, on the other. In the English-speaking countries, by contrast, the main response was to turn to the welfare state.

The liberal case for active government gained further support from the theory advanced by the English economist John Maynard Keynes (1883–1946). In his *General Theory of Employment, Interest and Money* (1936), Keynes argued that governments should use their taxing and spending powers to prevent depressions and maintain a healthy economy. Put simply, Keynes's theory holds that governments should try to manage the economy to damp down disruptive cycles of "boom and bust." When prices are rising, the government should raise taxes to reduce consumer spending and prevent inflation. When inflation is no longer a threat, government should lower taxes, increase spending on social programs, or both, in order to stimulate the economy and maintain high levels of employment.

Whatever the strategy at any particular time, Keynes's "contra-cyclical" approach calls for active government management of economic matters—an approach welcomed by welfare liberals and now practiced by all advanced capitalist countries, including the United States.

Such governmental regulation of the economy began in earnest during the Great Depression of the 1930s. President Franklin D. Roosevelt's New Deal regulated financial markets, banks, and other economic institutions, protected depositors from bank failures, provided public sector employment for unemployed Americans, and stimulated the economy by "priming the pump" with government spending on public works and other projects. Conservative critics cried "socialism." But Roosevelt was no socialist. Like Bismarck before him, he was attempting to oppose socialism by reforming capitalism and saving it from its own excesses. Moreover, massive expenditures for infrastructure—roads, bridges, dams that prevented floods and produced hydroelectric power, and the like—not only alleviated suffering in the present but was actually a form of investment that would pay large dividends in the future.

The even more massive governmental expenditures of World War II finally brought an end to the Great Depression, but the welfare state remained. Welfare liberalism became the dominant ideology of the Western world. Welfare liberals usually reached some sort of accommodation with their socialist and conservative rivals, as most parties accepted the desirability of the welfare state. Indeed, this consensus seemed so broad and firm that some political observers began to speak in the late 1950s of "the end of ideology." That hope was soon dashed in the political turmoil of the 1960s and early 1970s and the resurgent conservatism of the 1980s.

For one thing, there were controversies within liberalism. In the United States, Martin Luther King, Jr., and other leaders of the civil rights movement pointed out that liberal promises of liberty and equality were still unfulfilled for African-Americans. This was a painful truth that all liberals had to acknowledge, however reluctantly. When King and others protested against the segregation laws that made black people second-class citizens, neoclassical and welfare liberals alike could join in support. But King went on to call for government action not only to eliminate legal discrimination against African-Americans and other minorities but also to provide social and economic opportunities.[45] This was acceptable to welfare liberals, but not to their neoclassical cousins. The neoclassical wing formed a distinct minority among liberals, however, as their losing battle against President Lyndon Johnson's "Great Society" programs of the 1960s testifies. These programs, which sought to end discrimination against racial minorities, to fight a "War on Poverty," and to use the powers of government to provide equality of opportunity, sprang from the welfare liberals' belief that government can and should be used to foster individual liberty. The War on Poverty was undercut by another war—the war in Vietnam—which cost the country dearly in blood and treasure, and provoked protests all across the nation.

The turmoil of the 1960s also presented another challenge to welfare liberalism—the New Left. Vaguely socialist in its orientation, the New Left rejected both the "obsolete communism" of the Soviet Union and the reformist welfare liberalism and "consumer capitalism" of the Western liberal democracies. Most

New Leftists accepted the liberal emphasis on individual rights and liberties, and most also supported government programs to promote equality of opportunity. But they complained that liberal governments worked first and foremost to protect the economic interests of wealthy capitalist corporations. Although they agreed that these governments did take steps to improve the material circumstances of their people, the New Leftists charged that most people were reduced to the status of mere consumers when they ought to be encouraged to be engaged and active *citizens*. This led to the call for "participatory democracy," a society in which average people would be able to exercise greater control over the decisions that most closely affected their lives.[46]

If welfare liberalism remains the dominant ideology and the dominant form of liberalism in the Western world—and during the second decade of the twenty-first century it seems that it does—it has clearly not gone unchallenged. A particularly strong challenge, in the form of a mixture of neoclassical liberalism and conservatism, appeared in the 1970s and 1980s as first Margaret Thatcher in Great Britain and then Ronald Reagan in the United States became heads of government. Neither leader dismantled the welfare state, although both moved some distance in that direction. But dismantle it we must, the neoclassical liberals continue to insist. So the contest within liberalism continues, with neoclassical and welfare liberals engaging in ongoing disputes at the philosophical as well as the political level.

Philosophical Considerations

The ongoing debate within liberalism is captured nicely in books by two influential philosophers: John Rawls's *A Theory of Justice* (1971) and Robert Nozick's *Anarchy, State, and Utopia* (1974).[47]

Rawls and Justice. According to Rawls (1921–2002), the classical liberal device of the social contract can help us to discover the principles of social justice. Rawls begins by asking the reader to imagine a group of people who enter into a contract that will set out the rules under which they will all have to live as members of the same society. Imagine, too, that all of these people are behind a "veil of ignorance" that prevents anyone from knowing his or her identity, age, gender, race, or abilities or disabilities. Although all act out of self-interest, no one will be able to "stack the deck" by fashioning rules that promote his or her personal advantage, because no one will know what is to his or her personal advantage. Thus the veil of ignorance ensures impartiality.

What rules will emerge from such an impartial situation? Rawls believes that the people behind the veil of ignorance will unanimously choose two fundamental principles to govern their society—the two principles of justice. According to the first principle, everyone is to be *equally* free. Everyone is to have as much liberty as possible, provided that every person in society has the same amount. According to the second principle, everyone is to enjoy equality of opportunity. To help ensure this, each person is to have an equal share of wealth and power *unless* it can be shown that an unequal distribution will work to the benefit of the worst-off persons. If an equal distribution means that each gets $10, say, it is more just than a distribution where half the people get $18 and the other half only $2. But if an unequal distribution would give everyone, even the worst-off person, *at least* $11, perhaps because of incentives that encourage people to work harder and produce more, then justice requires the unequal distribution, not the strictly equal distribution in which each receives only $10.

Why does justice require this? Isn't it just to pay or reward people according to their efforts and abilities, not their position at the bottom of the social scale? Rawls's response is that the people who make the greatest efforts and display the highest abilities do not really *deserve* a larger reward than anyone else. Effort and ability are generally characteristics that people come by through heredity and environment. Someone may be an outstanding surgeon because she was born with superior mental and physical potential that she then worked hard to develop. But this person cannot take credit for talent she was born with, nor even for her hard work if her family instilled in her the desire to work and achieve. If justice requires us to give greater rewards to some people than to others, Rawls concludes, it is not because they deserve more but because this is the best way to promote the interests of the worst-off people in society. If justice requires us to pay physicians more than coal miners or barbers or secretaries, then it can only be because this is the best way to provide good medical care and thus promote everyone's vital interest in health—including the vital interests of society's worst-off members.

The significance of Rawls's second principle is that it takes welfare liberalism in a more egalitarian direction. An equal distribution of wealth and resources is Rawls's starting point, and an unequal distribution is justified only if it is better for those at the bottom of society. If the wealth and power of those at the top of the social scale do not indirectly benefit those at the bottom, then Rawls's theory calls for a redistribution of that wealth and power in a more nearly equal manner and argues that under blind or impartial conditions this is what any rational self-interested individual committed to liberty and democracy would want. For people can enjoy neither equal liberty nor equal opportunity when there are great and unjustified inequalities of wealth.

Nozick and the Minimal State.   Three years after Rawls's *Theory of Justice* appeared, Robert Nozick (1938–2002) published *Anarchy, State, and Utopia*. There Nozick asserts that all individuals have rights that it is wrong to violate. But if this is true, he asks, can there ever be a government or state that does not violate the rights of its people? Nozick answers by drawing on another old liberal idea—the state of nature. Like Hobbes and Locke, Nozick wants the reader to imagine a condition in which there is no government, no state, no political or legal authority of any kind. In this state of nature, individuals have rights, but they lack protection. Some sharp-eyed entrepreneurs will notice this and go into the business of providing protection, much as private security guards and insurance agencies do. Those who want protection may sign on with a private protective agency—for a fee, of course—and those who do not must fend for themselves. Either way the choice is strictly theirs—a choice denied, Nozick says, to people who live under governments that make them pay for protection whether they want it or not.

When people subscribe to a private protective agency, in other words, no one violates their rights by forcing them to do something they do not want to do. But out of a large number of competing protective agencies, Nozick argues, one will grow and prosper until it absorbs the rest. This single protective agency, so large that it serves almost everyone in an area the size of a modern nation-state, will become for all practical purposes a state itself. And it will do so, Nozick claims, without violating anyone's rights.

This new state, however, performs only the functions of a protective agency. Nozick claims that this "minimal state" is legitimate or just because no one's rights are violated by its creation. But it is also the *only* legitimate state. Any state or government that does more than merely protect the people *must* violate someone's rights and therefore must be unjust. The policy of using taxation to take money from some people for the benefit of others, for instance, is "on a par with forced labor."[48] Someone who earns $100 and has $20 taken in taxes probably has no complaint if that $20 goes to provide him or her with protection; but if, say, $10 goes to provide benefits for others—health care, education, unemployment compensation then the worker is effectively forced to spend 10 percent of his or her working time working for others. This is the equivalent of forced labor, according to Nozick, and therefore a violation of individual rights.

Like other neoclassical liberals, Nozick holds that government should protect us against force and fraud, but otherwise should leave us alone to compete in an unrestricted free-market economy. Government should not forbid capitalist acts between consenting adults, as he puts it. Like other neoclassical liberals, Nozick defends the individual's right to think, say, and do whatever he or she pleases—as long as no one else's rights are violated. But the individual can enjoy these rights only if the state is a "minimal" one.

Nozick's philosophical defense of neoclassical liberalism extends the arguments of several contemporary theorists, notably Friedrich Hayek (1899–1992) and Milton Friedman (1912–2006). Ayn Rand (1905–1982) also gave fictional form to similar ideas in such popular novels as *The Fountainhead* (1943) and *Atlas Shrugged* (1957). In the last forty years or so, in fact, neoclassical liberalism has enjoyed a revival in both philosophy and politics under the name of **libertarianism**, playing an important part, as we have seen, in the "conservative" economic policies of Margaret Thatcher and Ronald Reagan. Hayek and other neoclassical liberals, however, insist that they are not conservatives who want to preserve society's traditional arrangements, but true liberals who are committed to protecting and extending individual liberty, even if that means upsetting customs and traditions.[49] Inspired by Hayek, Friedman, Rand, and others, neoclassical liberalism in the United States has given rise to the Libertarian Party, which sponsors candidates who want to move the country in the direction of the minimal state. But for some libertarians, even the minimal state is too much government. In their view, true devotion to liberty demands that government be abolished altogether.

Libertarian Anarchism. In many respects libertarian anarchism is simply the most extreme extension of liberalism. Libertarian anarchists share the liberal belief in the value of individual liberty and equal opportunity. They also agree with classical and neoclassical liberals that the state is the major threat to individual freedom. But libertarian anarchists go beyond other liberals to argue that the state is an altogether *un*necessary evil. Because it is both evil and unnecessary, they conclude, government ought to be eliminated entirely. In their view, true liberalism leads to anarchy (from the Greek *an archos*, meaning "no government"). In other words, anarchism is the logical culmination of liberal individualism.

Although this position has never enjoyed broad popular support, it has had some articulate defenders, such as the American economist Murray Rothbard (1926–1995). Rothbard and other libertarian anarchists maintain that free-market anarchism is both desirable and practical. It is desirable because when there is no coercion from government every individual will be free to live as he or she chooses. And it is practical, they claim, because anything governments do, private enterprise can do better. Education, fire and police protection, defense, traffic regulation—these and all other public functions can be performed more efficiently by private companies competing for customers. Someone who wants police protection can "shop around" to find the company that provides the right level of protection at the best price, just as consumers nowadays can shop for a car, house, or insurance policy. Roads can be privately owned and operated, just as parking lots are now; all schools can be private, just as some are now; even currency can be provided by private enterprise, just as credit cards are now. There is, in short, no good reason to retain the state. Once enough people recognize this, the libertarian anarchists say, we will be on the way to a truly free and truly liberal society.[50]

THE LIBERTARIAN VISION

Most libertarians are not anarchists. In their view, government is necessary to a secure an orderly society, but it should be a government that does little or nothing more than protect people against threats to their property and safety. But what would their libertarian society look like? There would be many fewer, and perhaps no, "public" things—libraries, schools, beaches, parks, and roads—and many more private ones as the result of "deregulation" and "privatization." "Deregulation" means that government regulations in a variety of areas would be phased out entirely. For example, governmental rules regulating prescription drugs, workplace safety, health inspections at restaurants, and the like would be taken off the books. People are rational enough to look out for their own interests, the libertarians say, and diners would gravitate toward restaurants that have a reputation for cleanliness, and away from those that do not, just as they now gravitate toward those that have a reputation for serving good food. "Privatization" means turning public entities into private, and usually for-profit, enterprises. Thus public parks would be sold to developers who would determine whether it is more profitable to keep them as private parks or turn them into housing subdivisions, office parks, or shopping centers; all roads would become toll roads; libraries would be private, fee-charging businesses; all schools and universities would be private, some on a for-profit basis and others, such as church schools, as nonprofit institutions. Beaches and waterways would be privately owned, and swimmers and surfers would have to pay to use them. Government subsidies to support schools, hospitals, airports, subways, railways, docks and harbors, and so on, would be eliminated. Police protection might be provided, but probably not fire protection or emergency-medical services. In short, libertarians envision and work toward a market-driven society in which formerly public services would be bought and sold in presumably competitive markets.[51]

Advocates of privatization say that goods and services would be delivered more cheaply, abundantly, and efficiently under competitive market conditions. Critics contend that actual practice does not square with the theory. For example, formerly public utilities and services have been privatized in Great Britain and the United States, with mixed results. After California chose to get out of the business of generating and distributing electricity, prices actually went up, in some part because of Enron and other corporate traders manipulating the market and inflating prices, but also because of other factors.[52] Libertarians reply that manipulated markets are not the free and competitive ones that they champion. Critics respond that competitive markets are open to the machinations of manipulators like Enron and that public ownership or oversight of some goods and services is both desirable and necessary to keep costs down and quality up by preventing manipulation.

LIBERALISM TODAY: DIVISIONS AND DIFFERENCES

Now that we have traced liberalism from its beginnings to the present, what can we say about its current condition? Three points deserve special mention here. The first is that liberalism is no longer the revolutionary force it once was—at least not in the West. But in other parts of the world the liberal attack on ascribed status, religious conformity, or political absolutism still strikes at the foundations of society. This is most evident in Iran and other countries of the Middle East and North Africa, where liberalism has provoked a radical response from radical Islamists (see Chapter 10). Elsewhere, champions of change in communist and formerly communist countries have often claimed "liberalization" as their goal. In the Western world, however, the aims of early liberals are now deeply entrenched in public policy and public opinion. Here, liberalism is no longer a revolutionary ideology but an ideology defending a revolution already won.

The second point is that liberals remain divided among themselves. Despite their agreement on fundamental ends, especially the importance of individual liberty, liberals disagree sharply over means—over how best to define and promote these ends. Welfare liberals believe that we need an active government to give everyone an equal chance to be free; neoclassical liberals (or libertarians) believe that we need to limit government to keep it from robbing us of freedom; libertarian anarchists believe that we should abolish government altogether.

The third point is that liberals are now wrestling with a set of very difficult problems that stem from their basic commitments to individual liberty and equality of opportunity. The first problem is, How far should individuals be able to go in exercising their freedom? Most liberals, welfare and neoclassical alike, accept something like Mill's harm principle—people should be free to do as they wish unless they harm (or violate the rights of) others. When it comes to applying this principle, however, the difficulty of defining "harm" becomes clear. Many liberals say that "victimless crimes" like prostitution, gambling, and the sale of drugs and pornography should not be considered crimes at all. If one adult wants to be a prostitute and another wants to pay for his or her services, no one is harmed, except perhaps those who enter into this exchange. If no one else is harmed, government has no business outlawing prostitution. To this argument other liberals respond that "victimless crimes" are not as victimless as they appear.

Pimps force women into prostitution and "loan sharks" take unfair advantage of people who borrow money at very high interest rates. Those who favor abolishing "victimless crimes" counter by arguing that the government can carefully regulate these activities if they are legal—as prostitution is in the Netherlands and parts of Nevada, for example. But the argument continues without a resolution. Despite their desire to separate the sphere of private freedom from that of public control, liberals have found the boundary between private and public difficult to draw with any precision.

Part of the reason for this boundary problem is that liberals disagree about the proper role of government in helping people to lead a good or decent life. According to some, such as John Rawls, the job of government in a liberal society is to preserve justice and to protect the individual's right to live as he or she sees fit. It is not the government's business to promote one way of life or conception of the good—say, the life of the devout Christian—at the expense of others—say, the life of the devout Jew or of the atheist who thinks all religions are merely forms of superstition. Government should remain neutral with respect to these and other competing conceptions of the good life, according to Rawls, who refers to his position as *political liberalism*—that is, the belief that liberal governments should confine themselves, like a referee at a sports match, to limiting and settling conflicts without taking sides in disputes about how people ought to live.[53] But other liberals insist that government neither can nor should be completely neutral in this way. Liberal societies depend upon citizens who are rational, tolerant, far-sighted, and committed to the common good, they argue, and a good government will necessarily encourage people to develop and display these desirable traits. As they see it, political liberalism betrays the liberal tradition by depriving liberalism of its concern for character and virtue.[54]

The second problem grows out of the liberal commitment to equal opportunity. For libertarians, this means simply that everyone ought to be free to make his or her way in the world without unfair discrimination. Only discrimination on the basis of ability and effort is justified. The liberal state should then outlaw discrimination on the basis of race, religion, gender, or any other irrelevant factor. By contrast, most welfare liberals maintain that government ought to help disadvantaged people enjoy equal opportunity. Thus they support public schools, medical care, and even financial assistance for those in need. But how far should this go? Should we try to distribute wealth and resources in a more nearly equal way, as Rawls suggests? Will that promote true equality of opportunity? And is it fair to those who have earned their wealth without violating the rights of others?

To overcome a legacy of discrimination against women and racial minorities, many welfare liberals advocate **affirmative action** programs. Such programs give special consideration in education and employment to members of groups that have historically suffered from discrimination. But how is this to be done? By providing special training? By setting aside a certain number of jobs or places in colleges and professional schools for women and minorities? But aren't these efforts actually ways of discriminating *against* some people—white males—by discriminating in favor of others? Can this be justified in the name of equality of opportunity?

Another problem arises from the liberal commitment to individual liberty and individual rights. In the next chapters we shall see how conservatives, socialists, and fascists have often maintained that liberals give too much attention to the individual and too little to the community or society of which the individual is a part. In recent years this complaint has arisen within the ranks of liberalism as well. In this case the complaint is that liberals are so concerned with protecting individual rights and interests that they ignore the common good and the value of community. According to these **communitarian** critics, rights must be balanced by responsibilities. Individuals may have rights against others, such as the right to speak or to worship in ways that others do not like, but individuals must also recognize that they owe something to the community that enables them to exercise these rights. The danger today, communitarians contend, is that countries like the United States are degenerating into a condition in which everyone is jealously guarding his or her rights against everyone else, which leads to a hostile, suspicious, "me first" atmosphere that makes it impossible to act for the common good. People will no longer be willing to make the small sacrifices—paying taxes, obeying burdensome laws—that are necessary to hold society together and secure individual rights.

To counteract this overemphasis on individual rights, communitarians want to place more stress on individuals' responsibility to promote the good of the community. As one leading communitarian has said, "communitarians see a need for a social order that contains a set of shared values, to which individuals are taught they are obligated. Individuals may later question, challenge, rebel against, or even transform a given social order, but their starting point is a shared set of definitions of what is right versus what is wrong."[55]

This emphasis on community was one of the themes of Bill Clinton's successful campaign for the presidency of the United States in 1992 and of Barack Obama's in 2008. In Clinton's case, the communitarian slant is especially clear in the national service program that his administration implemented. By offering financial aid for college expenses to young people who agree to serve in various public service groups, this program aims to encourage the sense of civic responsibility among the volunteers. On a smaller scale, many colleges and universities are now offering academic credits to students who engage in community "service-learning" projects. A former community organizer, President Obama proposed to continue and even to enlarge such programs.

To this point these public service programs have enjoyed widespread support among liberals. Such support may shrink, however, if national service becomes mandatory, as it is in some countries. Other attempts to strengthen community have already led to disagreement among liberals, largely because they raise the fear of the "tyranny of the majority." Should cities or public schools be able to sponsor Christmas pageants or display nativity scenes? Do the members of a community, or a majority of them, have the right to limit freedom of speech by outlawing or regulating the distribution of pornography? Should the police be allowed to stop cars at random in order to detect drunken drivers? Or do these attempts to promote the public well-being amount to intolerable infringements of individual rights?

These and other questions of individual liberty and equality of opportunity are especially troublesome for liberals because their creed forces them to confront such issues head-on. There is, as yet, no obvious or agreed-upon "liberal" answer to these questions. Some critics see this as a serious or even fatal weakness—a sign that liberalism is near the end of its rope. A more sympathetic response might be that liberalism is still doing what it has always done—searching for ways to advance the cause of individual liberty and opportunity. Certainly anyone who agrees with Mill's claim that flexing our mental and moral muscles is vital to individual growth will find plenty of room for exercise in contemporary liberalism—which is just as Mill would want it.

CONCLUSION
Liberalism as an Ideology

What can we conclude, then, about liberalism as an ideology? In light of liberalism's long history it is scarcely surprising that differences and discontinuities have developed over time. But the oft-noted and alleged "break" between old or classical liberalism and modern welfare liberalism might not be such a radical rupture after all. Recall that Locke, for one, said that the law of nature requires that we not only preserve ourselves but also that we "*preserve the rest of mankind*" insofar as we are able to do so. And Adam Smith observed that our actions are not only motivated by self-interest but by such "moral sentiments" as compassion, pity, and benevolence. Smith also favored the visible hand of the state when the "invisible hand" of the market does not work well, or at all, and he favored a program of tax-supported public works to build and maintain infrastructure and to educate the young.

Even so, given the often-acrimonious rift between welfare liberals and libertarians, or neoclassical liberals, does it even make sense to speak of liberalism as a single ideology? We think it does, although the division between the two camps is deep and may be widening. At present, however, their differences are largely matters of emphasis and disagreement about means, not ends. A quick look at how liberalism performs the four functions that all ideologies perform should make this point clearer.

Explanation. First, all ideologies purport to explain why things are the way they are, with particular attention to social, economic, and political conditions. For liberals, these explanations are typically individualistic. Social conditions are the result of individual choices and actions. Liberals recognize that the choices open to individuals are often limited and frequently have consequences that no one intended or desired. Yet despite the limits on their foresight and understanding, individuals still make choices that, taken together, explain why social conditions are as they are.

Why, for example, do economic depressions occur? Liberals generally believe that they are the wholly unintended results of decisions made by rational individuals responding to the circumstances in which they compete—or in some cases are prevented from competing—in the marketplace. Welfare liberals generally follow Keynes's economic views and argue that the job of the government is to shape these choices, perhaps by lowering or raising taxes to give people more or less disposable income, in order to prevent or lessen economic distress. The neoclassical position is that the competitive marketplace will correct itself if left alone and it is wrong for government to interfere. Despite these different views of what should be done, however, both sides share the fundamental premise that individual choices ultimately explain why things are as they are.

Evaluation. When it comes to *evaluating* conditions, liberalism again turns to the individual. Conditions are good, as a rule, if the individual is free to do as he or she wishes without harming or violating the rights of others. The more freedom people have, liberals say, the better; the less freedom, the worse. What freedom there is must be enjoyed as equally as possible. Thus the liberal view of freedom requires that individuals have an equal opportunity to succeed. On this point all liberals agree. But they disagree, with welfare liberals going in one direction and libertarians in another, on how best to provide equality of opportunity. For both, however, a society in which individuals enjoy an equal opportunity to choose freely is clearly better than one in which freedom is restricted and opportunity unequal.

Orientation. Political ideologies also provide people with some sense of identity and orientation—of who they are and where and how they fit into the great scheme of things. Liberalism pictures people as rational individuals who have interests to pursue and choices to make. Liberals thus direct our attention to the characteristics that they believe all people share, not toward the differences that separate people from one another. Some liberals push this point much further than others, and Bentham and the Social Darwinists perhaps furthest of all, but there is a tendency among liberals to believe that deep down all women and men are fundamentally the same. Differences of culture, race, religion, gender, or nationality are ultimately superficial. Our identity is an individual—not a group—identity. At bottom, most people are rational, self-interested individuals who want to be free to choose how to live. Once we understand this, liberals believe, we will respect the right of others to live freely and will expect them to respect ours in return.

Program. As regards the programmatic function, liberals espouse programs for promoting individual liberty and opportunity. Historically, this has meant that liberals have opposed religious conformity, ascribed status, economic privileges, political absolutism, and the tyranny of majority opinion. With these obstacles removed, individuals are free to worship (or not) as they see fit; to rise or fall in society according to their efforts and ability; to compete on an equal footing in the marketplace; to exercise some control over government; and to think, speak, and live in unconventional ways. On these points liberals seldom disagree. When some liberals began to say that freedom is not merely a matter of being left alone but a positive power or ability to do what one chooses, disagreements emerged. Welfare liberals insist that the government must be enlisted in the struggle against illness, ignorance, prejudice, poverty, and any other condition that threatens liberty and equality of opportunity, while neoclassical liberals complain that government "meddling" is itself the chief threat to liberty and equality.

These two schools of liberalism now offer rival political programs, not because their goals are different but because they disagree on how best to achieve those goals. The dispute is over means, not ends. That is why we believe that liberalism, divided as it is by the intramural dispute between its neoclassical and welfare camps, remains a single, albeit fragmented, ideology.

Liberalism and the Democratic Ideal

At the outset of the twenty-first century, liberals are firmly committed to democracy, but that has not always been the case. Throughout most of its history, in fact, liberalism has been more concerned with protecting people from their rulers than with establishing rule by the people. From its inception, as we have seen, liberalism has fought to remove obstacles that stand in the way of the individual's freedom to live as he or she sees fit, and in the beginning most of those obstacles—religious conformity, ascribed status, political absolutism, monopolies, and other restraints on economic competition—were either provided or supported by government. Rather than strive to enable people to rule themselves *through* government, then, the classical liberals struggled to free people *from* government. They tried, in other words, to reduce the areas of life that were considered public in order to expand the private sphere.

From the beginning, however, liberalism also displayed several democratic tendencies, the most notable being its premise of basic equality among human beings. Whether couched in terms of natural rights or the Utilitarians' claim that everybody is to count for one and nobody for more than one, liberals have always argued from the premise that every person's rights or interests should count as much as everyone else's. Early liberals defined "person" in such narrow terms that the only true "person" was a free adult male who owned substantial property. But as they spoke and argued in terms of natural equality, liberals opened the door for those—including later liberals—who demanded that slavery be abolished and that women and the propertyless should be extended the right to vote, to run for public office, and generally be politically equal to property-owning males.

This liberal tendency did not lead in an openly democratic direction until the 1800s, when Bentham and the Utilitarians began to argue that democracy gave every citizen the chance to protect his—and later her—interests. If the business of government is to promote the greatest good of the greatest number, they reasoned, then the only way to determine the greatest good is to allow every citizen to say what is good for him or her. Earlier liberals had proclaimed that government must rest on the consent of the people, and they had devised constitutions and bills of rights in order to limit the powers of government, but it was not until the 1800s that liberals began to regard the vote as a way to give everyone an equal chance to protect and promote his or her interests. This is the protectionist theory of democracy.

For the most part, liberals favor democracy because it enables citizens to hold their government accountable, thereby protecting their personal interests. Some, including John Stuart Mill, have gone further, arguing that democracy is good because it encourages widespread political participation, which in turn enriches people's lives by developing their intellectual and moral capacities. Yet most liberals have attached no particular value to political activity, seeing it as simply one possible good among many. The state should be neutral, they say, leaving people free to pursue whatever they consider good—as long as they respect others' freedom to do the same. If people find pleasure or satisfaction in public life, well and good; but if they derive more pleasure from private pursuits, then they should be free to follow that path.

As a rule, liberal democracy emphasizes the importance of individual rights and liberty. Everyone is supposed to be free to participate in public life; but the primary concern is to protect people from undue interference in their private affairs. Consequently, deciding what counts as "private" and how far an individual's "right to privacy" extends are matters of debate (as in the abortion controversy). For the liberal, democracy is good so long as it protects these rights and interests in privacy and free action. It does this primarily by making the government responsive to the needs and interests of the people, thus preventing arbitrary and tyrannical government. But if rule by the people begins to threaten individual rights and liberties, then one can expect liberals to demand that it be curbed. In liberal democracy, in short, democracy is defined mainly in terms of the individual's right to be free from outside interference to do as he or she thinks best.

Coda 1: The Limits of Liberal Toleration

As we have seen, liberals have historically prided themselves on their tolerance of those whose tastes, preferences, identities, beliefs, and behavior are unorthodox and perhaps shocking to many people in the so-called mainstream of society. Thus today's liberals favor the decriminalization of same-sex relations between consenting adults, of pornography (except when it involves children), and in some cases of drug use and other activities that cause no demonstrable harm to others. But how far should such tolerance extend? Should it, for example, be extended to illiberal individuals or groups who scorn or even seek to overthrow liberal societies?

This question has often been asked both by liberals and their conservative critics, especially when confronting fascists, Nazis, communists, radical Islamists, and others who will trample on individual rights and liberties and destroy liberal societies in the name of some supposedly higher good. Some liberal democracies have answered by banning political parties with such totalitarian aims. In recent years, however, the question of whether to tolerate those who seem to be intolerant has been asked with renewed urgency in Denmark, the Netherlands, and other European nations known for their tolerance of other cultures and ways of life. Middle Eastern immigrants, most of them Muslims, have immigrated into Europe but have retained beliefs and customs that people in their host countries deem sexist, homophobic, and generally intolerant of liberal toleration. The resulting clash of cultures has produced some dramatic confrontations, such as the murder of Dutch filmmaker Theo van Gogh in 2005 by a Dutch-born Muslim of Moroccan descent. Van Gogh had recently released a film, *Submission* (which is what "Islam" means in Arabic), which exposed and criticized the mistreatment of women in some conservative Islamic communities. The murderer used a knife in van Gogh's chest to pin a note threatening death to Ayaan Hirsi Ali, the Somali-born Muslim woman and member of the Dutch Parliament who had collaborated with van Gogh on the film.[56] In another event, the publication in Denmark in 2006 of newspaper cartoons depicting the Prophet Mohammed in satirical and unflattering ways sparked riots and the firebombing of Danish embassies and businesses in several Middle Eastern countries. These scenes were repeated on an even larger scale in 2012 after a crudely made film deriding the Prophet set off a firestorm of protests around the world. American embassies and consulates were attacked and firebombed, and in another, apparently unrelated incident, the American ambassador and three aides were killed in Benghazi.

These events testify to the importance of the question, Should liberals tolerate those who are not themselves tolerant? Liberals typically answer by drawing a distinction between belief and behavior. Following John Stuart Mill, they say that liberal societies should tolerate almost any attitude or belief or opinion, however abhorrent others may find it. If, however, someone *acts* on such a belief *and* if that action produces *harm* to someone other than the actor, then the action—but not the belief, or public expressions of the belief—can be forbidden by law and punished accordingly.

Conservative critics (and some liberals) object that there is no hard-and-fast distinction between belief and behavior, pointing out that—as Mill himself wrote—"It is what men *think* that determines how they *act*..."[57] People who think illiberal thoughts or hold illiberal opinions and intolerant beliefs are apt to act in illiberal and intolerant ways. Therefore, critics contend, there are good grounds for a liberal society to censor public expressions of illiberal views and to outlaw or exclude anti-liberal individuals or groups (for example, Nazi parties). The Danes and the Dutch have not gone this far—yet. But the Dutch government has begun to tell prospective immigrants that they must be tolerant if they are themselves to be tolerated in turn. As the *New York Times* reported from the Netherlands:

> So strong is the fear that Dutch values of tolerance are under siege that the government [in 2006] introduced a primer on those values for prospective newcomers to Dutch life: a DVD briefly showing topless women and two men kissing. The film does not explicitly mention Muslims, but its target audience is as clear as its message: embrace our culture or leave.[58]

Intolerance in the form of terrorism raises the same question in a different form. In the United States, liberals, long committed to fair play and the rule of law, are now divided over how to deal with the threat of terrorism. Should the right of privacy be protected or compromised in the face of potential terrorist threats? Are secret searches without warrants justified in some circumstances? Should the security of the wider society take precedence over the civil rights of individuals? Should federal government agencies such as the NSA (National Security Administration) be allowed to use drone aircraft, massive data collections of telephone calls, and other means to monitor the actions of American civilians under some circumstances? Many, perhaps most, liberals answer negatively; but some answer in the affirmative, claiming that al-Qaeda, ISIS, and other radical Islamist groups are not only terrorist but totalitarian organizations prepared to turn American civil liberties against liberty itself.[59] And the libertarian-leaning judge and legal scholar Richard Posner contends that during a "national emergency" the U.S. Constitution is "not a suicide pact" that protects the civil liberties of the possibly guilty few at the cost of the liberty and even the lives of the innocent many.[60] Shortly before leaving office in 2007, moreover, British Prime Minister

Tony Blair issued a similar warning. It is, he said, a "dangerous judgement" to put the rights of suspected terrorists ahead of the safety of the public, and he promised to give British police sweeping powers to stop and question anyone without a warrant.[61]

By contrast, liberals like Ronald Dworkin (1925–2013) hold that liberties protected only when the state finds it convenient or costless to do so are not really liberties at all. All governments will, if they can, extend their powers into the lives and liberties of individuals, using any reason or excuse, including "national security" or "the global war on terror." No government should ever be given a free hand to bypass the Constitution and curtail the freedom of its citizens or to engage in torture and other violations of human rights.[62] If we are to remain citizens of a free and open society dedicated to the rule of law, there are strict ethical and legal limits on what the government can do in our name.

Such tensions divide liberals, now perhaps more than ever. As we shall see in the chapter following, conservatives—like liberals—agree about many issues, but do not speak with a single voice on every issue. Senator John McCain (Republican, Arizona), for example, is generally considered quite conservative, especially where national security is concerned, but he has taken a stand against torture that is similar to the liberal Dworkin's. As McCain has argued, the question is not who "they" (terrorists or suspected terrorists) are, but who *we* are as a nation and what we will become if we allow suspects to be tortured in our name and supposedly for our sake.[63] Neither liberalism nor conservatism is so sharply defined and coherent as to have one and only one position for a liberal or a conservative to take on every possible issue. In fact, as the following chapters will show, *no* ideology is so clear-cut that its adherents never disagree among themselves. If the lack of agreement on such an important question as whether to tolerate the intolerant is a problem for liberals, in short, it is not a problem that they alone must face.

Coda 2: A New New Deal?

Since the election of Ronald Reagan in 1980 there has been a concerted and partially successful effort to roll back or repeal the reforms of the New Deal era. Regulations on banks and other financial institutions were eased or eliminated, allowing them to expand into areas of the economy that had previously been off limits. Deregulation and privatization—long the watchwords of neoliberalism—became the new currency of political debate and public policy during the presidencies of Reagan, George H. W. Bush, Bill Clinton, and George W. Bush. Then in 2007, the last year of the younger Bush's administration, the unthinkable happened: economies around the globe, including the American economy, began to contract and even to collapse in the greatest recession since the Great Depression. Major banks and other large financial institutions—Bear Stearns, Lehman Brothers, and others—collapsed like a house of cards. Credit dried up almost overnight. Undercapitalized and overleveraged, unregulated or under-regulated to a remarkable degree, and hoping to reap enormous profits, these institutions had taken huge gambles—largely though not exclusively in the subprime mortgage market—and had lost almost everything.

The ensuing financial firestorm prompted the outgoing Bush administration and the incoming Obama administration to take drastic measures to prop up failed or fast-failing financial institutions deemed "too big to fail." The "bailout" of these institutions was quickly followed by a rescue of the American automobile giants, General Motors (GM) and Chrysler (Ford took no government money). In exchange for federal loans, GM and Chrysler issued stock certificates as collateral to secure those very large loans. In 2009 the federal government oversaw the sale of Chrysler to the Italian automaker Fiat and took ownership of 60 percent of GM, with the Canadian government and the United Autoworkers Union owning another 12.5 percent. In the case of the auto industry, as with the financial sector, the justification offered for the bailout was that the failure of these large and iconic institutions would be catastrophic for the rest of the economy. Jobs lost in the auto industry would mean jobs lost in plants and factories that manufacture the thousands of parts that go into every car, from pistons and camshafts to axles and tires, dashboards and windshields. The resulting "ripple effect" of failure at one end would produce a cascade of catastrophes in communities all across the country. Having taken such a huge stake in the financial and auto industries, the federal government became the "stakeholder of last resort"—a move that outraged conservatives and troubled many liberals, especially those who protested that the government seemed prepared to rescue large banks and mortgage companies while leaving small mortgage holders to fend for themselves, which often meant facing foreclosure and the loss of their homes to the very banks that had taken taxpayer money.

The Obama administration's controversial bailout of big banks and two of the three major auto companies not only saved both industries but, in the end, returned a profit for taxpayers. The federal government's TARP (Troubled Assets Relief Program) and other relief efforts, begun under Bush and continued under Obama, injected more than $426 billion into banks and auto companies. Interest payments and stock sales yielded nearly $442 billion—a net profit of more than $15 billion for U.S. taxpayers—and saved an estimated 1 million jobs.[64] The bailout of Wall Street proved more profitable than the rescue of General Motors. While GM managed to pay back roughly three-quarters of what it owed—$37.5 billion of the $49.5 billion it borrowed—in 2012, the government decided to sell its remaining stock in the company at a loss. This move ensured that American taxpayers would never be repaid fully for the GM bailout, a point which critics of the move lamented and supporters insisted was always secondary to saving an industry so central to the nation's economic health.[65]

Some—critics and supporters alike—dubbed the Obama administration's policies a "new New Deal" that emulated and in some respects even exceeded the original New Deal. To be sure, there are some similarities. For one, both were prompted by a dire financial emergency. For another, both were experimental attempts to save capitalism from its own excesses. It merits mentioning and underscoring that both FDR and Obama regarded their efforts as attempts to stimulate and *reform*—rather than replace—a capitalist economy in crisis. Liberal defenders of both say that conservative critics who cried "socialism" seem neither to appreciate nor to understand the crucial distinction between reforming capitalism and replacing it outright. Under the previous system profits had been privatized and risks socialized—that is, if a large firm (bank, insurance company, hedge fund, etc.) took risks that led to its failure, the American taxpayer would come to the rescue. Such a system was rife with **moral hazard**, that is, the danger that people who don't have to experience the consequences of their bad behavior will behave more recklessly and irresponsibly than those who do.

FDR once quipped that he felt like someone who had saved a drowning man only to be criticized for not saving the man's hat as well. His point was that the drowning man—capitalism, or rather its agents and avatars (bankers, hedge fund managers, and others)—can be saved only if that man agrees (or is required) to wear the life preserver of financial regulation. Without those regulations and restrictions, he will take undue and even reckless risks with other people's money, swimming without protection in the roiling waters of financial danger and opportunity. This might be well and good, if only his own life and livelihood were in danger; but, liberals from Roosevelt to Obama note, other people's lives and livelihoods are at stake here—workers, homeowners, investors, depositors, retirees, pension funds, and of course taxpayers—and so the harm principle requires that government intervene to prevent harm to those endangered others: taking risks with other people's money, homes, and jobs is quite clearly an other-regarding act. For liberals, then, the harm principle undergirds and justifies a "new New Deal" in America and, indeed, in any society with a capitalist economy.[66]

It has since become clear that President Obama's plans for economic recovery have produced mixed results. They may well have prevented the Great Depression 2.0, but they have not succeeded as fully as hoped. Some economists, including Paul Krugman, predicted this outcome, saying that the President's stimulus package was not nearly large enough to provide sufficient stimulus. Other economists disagree. But it is at least clear that Obama's program for economic recovery was not nearly as ambitious as Roosevelt's New Deal. For one, Roosevelt, unlike Obama, made the federal government the employer of last resort. Roosevelt created the Works Progress Administration and the Civilian Conservation Corps to hire unemployed workers to build dams, roads, and trails in national parks and other facilities. His was an early version of "workfare," in which recipients had to work for their federal paychecks. By contrast, President Obama's stimulus program subsidized private employers to hire workers to do such work. In this sense, Obama's recovery program was much less ambitious and government-centered than Roosevelt's. In short, his was no "new New Deal."

President Obama did, however, achieve something that no previous progressive or liberal president has achieved—passage of the Affordable Care Act (ACA), or, as conservative critics call it, "Obamacare"—which provides near-universal access to health care. The criticism that the ACA was unconstitutional was made moot by 2012 and 2015 Supreme Court decisions declaring it constitutional. The ACA, or something like it, has been proposed by presidents from Theodore Roosevelt to Richard Nixon to Bill Clinton. Ironically, it is less extensive than the plan proposed by President Nixon, a Republican, and is modeled on a 1993 proposal by the conservative Heritage Foundation, which was subsequently implemented in Massachusetts by Republican governor Mitt Romney. More ironically still, the Affordable Care Act is a distant descendant of Bismarck's Health Insurance Act of the mid-1880s and a markedly more conservative cousin of the single-payer health care coverage long available in the United Kingdom, Canada, and other Western democracies. In short, the idea of universally accessible health care—now often viewed as a "liberal" or even by some as a "socialist" idea—also has strong conservative credentials. Why many American conservatives now oppose this idea will be considered in Chapter 4.

Coda 3: The "Occupy" Movement

The "Arab Spring" that began in 2011 helped to inspire the so-called "American Autumn" of protests against the excesses of Wall Street, the big banks, "corporate greed," and the power of "big money" in American politics. In late September 2011 a movement calling itself Occupy Wall Street took over Zuccotti Park in New York's financial district. Despite some police harassment, including the unprovoked pepper-spraying of peaceful protesters, the occupation continued to grow. It also inspired similar "Occupy" movements in cities all across the country and even beyond the borders of the United States. Their slogan—"We are the 99 percent"—referred to glaring and still-growing inequalities in American society. In 2005, the top 300,000 Americans made roughly as much income as the bottom 150 million of their fellow citizens, with the top one-hundredth of 1 percent (.01 percent) having an average income of $25.7 million. The average income of the top 1 percent of individual earners grew 275 percent between 1979 and 2007. By 2010, the top 1 percent of households owned 35.4 percent of all privately held wealth, and the next 19 percent had 53.5 percent, which means that just one-fifth (20 percent) of the people owned 89 percent of the wealth, leaving 11 percent for the bottom 80 percent.[67]

The problem, as protesters pointed out, is not that wealth is a bad thing—far from it—but that economic wealth translates very quickly and readily into political power. And that power enables the very wealthy to pay lobbyists to influence legislators to pass laws and promote policies that favor the wealthy few while ignoring the interests of the less affluent majority who have no lobbyists. These legislators, the Occupy movement argues, are increasingly beholden to wealthy individuals and corporations for campaign contributions. In a series of sweeping decisions, including *Citizens United* (2010), the U.S. Supreme Court ruled that campaign contributions constitute a form of free speech and are therefore protected under the First Amendment; reaffirmed that corporations are, legally speaking, artificial "persons" with many of the same rights and privileges as real persons, including the right to donate as much money as they wish to candidates of their choosing; and held that the candidates they choose to support are those who will promote policies and pass laws favorable to their interests. Taken together, say the Occupy Wall Street protesters, these interconnected developments are contributing to the demise of democracy in the United States.

Critics—and some supporters—of the Occupy movement note that it has had little if any actual impact on legislation and public policy, perhaps because it is so localized and decentralized, and its members wary of organization, hierarchy, and leadership. It has, however, succeeded in calling attention to the large and still-widening wealth gap in the United States.

Discussion Questions

1 What is the "Adam Smith problem," how does it arise, and how might it be solved?
2 What is the protectionist theory of democracy, who propounds it, and for what purpose(s)?
3 What is the harm principle, who formulated it, and for what purpose(s)?
4 Who created the first welfare state and where? What was his ideological affiliation, and what were his reasons for creating it?
5 Why do many/most modern liberals believe that "big government" is both necessary and justifiable?
6 What particular tensions have arisen within liberalism in the wake of 9/11 and the subsequent "war on terror"?
7 What are the basic differences between Neoclassical and Welfare Liberals?
8 What is the theoretical relationship between liberalism and libertarianism?

NOTES

1 Thomas Hobbes, *Leviathan*, Chapter 11; see Terence Ball, Richard Dagger, and Daniel O'Neill, eds., *Ideals and Ideologies: A Reader*, 10th ed. (New York and London: Routledge, 2016), selection 3.11.
2 Hobbes, *Leviathan*, Chapter 13.
3 Quoted in Herbert Muller, *Freedom in the Western World: From the Dark Ages to the Rise of Democracy* (New York: Harper & Row, 1963), p. 307. The English Bill of Rights (1689) should not be confused with the U.S. Bill of Rights (1791), which comprises the first ten amendments to the U.S. Constitution.
4 John Locke, *Second Treatise of Government*, in *Two Treatises of Government*, Peter Laslett, ed. (Cambridge: Cambridge University Press, 1988 [1690]), paragraph 142.
5 Locke, *Second Treatise of Government*, paragraph 6, p. 271; Locke's italics.
6 Locke, *Second Treatise of Government*, paragraph 4; Ball, Dagger, and O'Neill, *Ideals and Ideologies*, selection 3.12.
7 For a systematic comparison of the Declaration of Independence and Locke's arguments, see Garrett Ward Sheldon, *The Political Philosophy of Thomas Jefferson* (Baltimore, MD: Johns Hopkins University Press, 1991), pp. 42–49. On the background and meaning of the Declaration, see Carl Becker, *The Declaration of Independence* (New York: Random House, 1942); Garry Wills, *Inventing America: Jefferson's Declaration of Independence* (Garden City, NY: Doubleday, 1978); Morton White, *The Philosophy of the American Revolution* (New York: Oxford University Press, 1978); and Pauline Maier, *American Scripture: Making the Declaration of Independence* (New York: Alfred A. Knopf, 1997).
8 Thomas Jefferson to James Madison, August 30, 1823, in *Thomas Jefferson: Political Writings*, Joyce Appleby and Terence Ball, eds. (Cambridge: Cambridge University Press, 1999), p. 146.
9 The full text of the Declaration is printed in Ball, Dagger, and O'Neill, *Ideals and Ideologies*, selection 3.14. For Jefferson's original draft, see Appleby and Ball, eds., *Thomas Jefferson: Political Writings*, pp. 96–102.
10 Samuel Johnson, *Taxation No Tyranny* (London, 1775); quoted in James Boswell, *Life of Johnson* (Oxford: Oxford University Press, 1960 [1791]), p. 876.
11 See James Farr, "'So Vile and Miserable an Estate': The Problem of Slavery in Locke's Political Thought," *Political Theory* 14 (1986): 263–289.
12 For a debate on Locke's purported "feminism," see Melissa Butler, "Early Liberal Roots of Feminism: John Locke and the Attack on Patriarchy," *American Political Science Review* 72 (1978): 135–150, and Terence Ball, "Comment on Butler," ibid. 73 (1979): 549–550, followed by Butler's "Reply," ibid.: 550–551.

13   Muller, *Freedom in the Western World*, p. 382.
14   As translated in Thomas Paine, *The Rights of Man* (1792); emphasis in original. For the full text of the *Declaration of Rights of Man and the Citizen*, see Ball, Dagger, and O'Neill, Ideals and Ideologies, selection 3.15.
15   Included in Ball, Dagger, and O'Neill, *Ideals and Ideologies*, as selection 8.55.
16   Michael Walzer, "Citizenship," in Terence Ball, James Farr, and Russell L. Hanson, eds., *Political Innovation and Conceptual Change* (Cambridge: Cambridge University Press, 1989), pp. 211–219, provides an insightful account of the notion of citizenship in the French Revolution.
17   Adam Smith, *An Inquiry into the Nature and Causes of the Wealth of Nations* (1776), R. H. Campbell and A. S. Skinner, eds. (Oxford: Oxford University Press, 1976), 2 vols., vol. I, Book I, Chapter 2, pp. 26–27; see Ball, Dagger, and O'Neill, *Ideals and Ideologies*, selection 3.16.
18   Smith, *The Wealth of Nations*, vol. I, Book IV, Chapter 2, p. 456.
19   Smith, *The Wealth of Nations*, vol. I, Book II, Chapter 2, p. 324.
20   Adam Smith, *The Theory of Moral Sentiments* (1759), D. D. Raphael and A. L. Macfie, eds. (Oxford: Oxford University Press, 1976), p. 1.
21   Smith, *The Theory of Moral Sentiments*, pp. 25, 61–62.
22   J. Bronowski and Bruce Mazlish, *The Western Intellectual Tradition: Leonardo to Hegel* (New York: Harper & Row, 1960), p. 455.
23   Jeremy Bentham, *Introduction to the Principles of Morals and Legislation* (New York: Hafner, 1948), p. 1.
24   Ibid., p. 70.
25   Bentham, *The Rationale of Judicial Evidence*, J. S. Mill, ed. (1827), in *The Works of Jeremy Bentham*, John Bowring, ed. (Edinburgh: W. Tait, 1843), vol. VII, p. 334.
26   For Bentham's views on voting, see Terence Ball, "Utilitarianism, Feminism and the Franchise," *History of Political Thought* 1 (1980): 91–115.
27   See R. R. Palmer, *The Age of Democratic Revolution: A Political History of Europe and America, 1760–1800* (Princeton: Princeton University Press, 1964), 2 vols.
28   James Mill, *Government*, in *James Mill: Political Writings*, Terence Ball, ed. (Cambridge: Cambridge University Press, 1992), pp. 3–42.
29   John Stuart Mill, *On Liberty*, in *J. S. Mill: On Liberty and Other Writings*, Stefan Collini, ed. (Cambridge: Cambridge University Press, 1989), p. 13; see Ball, Dagger, and O'Neill, *Ideals and Ideologies*, selection 3.18.
30   Thomas Jefferson, *Notes on the State of Virginia* (Chapel Hill: University of North Carolina Press, 1982 [1785]), p. 159.
31   Mill, *On Liberty*, p. 14.
32   Ibid., p. 13.
33   See the excerpt from Mill's *Representative Government* in Ball, Dagger, and O'Neill, *Ideals and Ideologies*, selection 2.9. For further discussion of "protective" (or "economic") versus "educative" theories of democracy, see Terence Ball, *Transforming Political Discourse* (Oxford: Blackwell, 1988), Chapter 6.
34   Mill, *On Liberty*, pp. 13–14.
35   See J. S. Mill's posthumously published "Chapters on Socialism" (1879) in *The Collected Works of John Stuart Mill*, John M. Robson, ed. (Toronto: University of Toronto Press, 1963–1991), 33 vols., vol. V: *Essays on Economics and Society—Part II* (1967); also in *On Liberty and Other Writings*, Collini, ed., pp. 221–279.
36   We accede here to a popular if not altogether accurate description of Darwin's theory. In actuality that theory holds that the "evolution" of a particular species is a demonstrable fact which the theory of natural selection serves to explain. Thus for example, the fact that some bacteria evolve so as to become resistant to antibiotics is due to their having an accidental genetic or other "adaptive advantage" that most other bacteria lack; hence their survival and subsequent capacity to reproduce antibiotic-resistant progeny.
37   William Graham Sumner, *What Social Classes Owe to Each Other* (Caldwell, ID: Caxton, 1970), p. 88; see Ball, Dagger, and O'Neill, *Ideals and Ideologies*, selection 3.19.
38   Ibid., p. 114.

39 See Green's essay, "Liberal Legislation and Freedom of Contract," part of which appears as "Liberalism and Positive Freedom," in Ball, Dagger, and O'Neill, *Ideals and Ideologies*, selection 3.20.

40 For an important and influential critique of positive liberty, see Isaiah Berlin, "Two Concepts of Liberty," in Berlin, *Liberty*, ed. Henry Hardy (Oxford: Oxford University Press, 2002).

41 Plato, *Republic*, Book IV, p. 444b.

42 For one prominent modern liberal's deep reservations about "positive" liberty and its distinction between a "higher" and a "lower" self, see Isaiah Berlin, "Two Concepts of Liberty" and "Final Retrospect," both in Berlin, *Liberty*, op. cit. (n.40 above), pp. 166–217 and 327–328, respectively. For a critique of Berlin's defense of negative liberty, see Charles Taylor, "What's Wrong with Negative Liberty," in Taylor, *Philosophical Papers* (Cambridge: Cambridge University Press, 1985), 2 vols., vol. II, pp. 211–229.

43 Here we follow the lead of Isaiah Berlin, who held that Green subscribed, at least implicitly, to "the metaphysical doctrine of the two selves ..."—a doctrine with which Berlin disagreed wholeheartedly: Berlin, *Liberty*, p. 41 n. Berlin's contention is disputed by Avital Simhony, "On Forcing Individuals to be Free: T. H. Green's Liberal Theory of Positive Freedom," *Political Studies* 39:2 (1991): 303–320.

44 For an overview, see Michael Freeden, "The Coming of the Welfare State," in Terence Ball and Richard Bellamy, eds., *The Cambridge History of Twentieth-Century Political Thought* (Cambridge: Cambridge University Press, 2003). See, further, Robert E. Goodin, *Reasons for Welfare: The Political Theory of the Welfare State* (Princeton, NJ: Princeton University Press, 1988).

45 See Martin Luther King, Jr., *Where Do We Go from Here: Chaos or Community?* (Boston: Beacon Press, 1968).

46 See, for example, "The Port Huron Statement" of the Students for a Democratic Society; reprinted in James Miller, *Democracy Is in the Streets: From Port Huron to the Siege of Chicago* (New York: Simon & Schuster, 1987), pp. 329–374.

47 John Rawls, *A Theory of Justice* (Cambridge, MA: Harvard University Press, 1971); Robert Nozick, *Anarchy, State, and Utopia* (New York: Basic Books, 1974).

48 Nozick, *Anarchy, State, and Utopia*, p. 169.

49 See Hayek, "Why I Am Not a Conservative," printed as the Appendix to his *The Constitution of Liberty* (Chicago: University of Chicago Press, 1960). See, further, James M. Buchanan, *Why I, Too, Am Not a Conservative: The Normative Vision of Classical Liberalism* (Cheltenham, U.K.: Edward Elgar, 2005).

50 For an elaboration of the libertarian anarchist position, see Murray Rothbard, *For a New Liberty* (New York: Macmillan, 1973); also Ball, Dagger, and O'Neill, *Ideals and Ideologies*, selection 3.26.

51 See Terence Ball, "Imagining Marketopia," *Dissent* 48 (2001): 74–80; reprinted in a slightly revised and updated version as "A Libertarian Utopia" in Ball, Dagger, and O'Neill, *Ideals and Ideologies*, selection 3.27.

52 Edison Electric Institute report, "Why Are Electricity Prices Increasing?" (Washington, D.C.: The Edison Foundation, Summer 2006); David Cay Johnston, "Competitive Era Fails to Shrink Electric Bills," *New York Times*, October 15, 2006, pp. A1, A27; and "Flaws Seen in Markets for Utilities," *New York Times*, November 21, 2006, pp. C1, C4.

53 John Rawls, *Political Liberalism* (New York: Columbia University Press, 1993).

54 See, for example, William Galston, *Liberal Purposes* (Cambridge: Cambridge University Press, 1991); George Sher, *Beyond Neutrality: Perfectionism and Politics* (Cambridge: Cambridge University Press, 1997); and Thomas A. Spragens, Jr., *Civic Liberalism: Reflections on Our Democratic Ideals* (Lanham, MD: Rowman & Littlefield, 1999).

55 Amitai Etzioni, *The New Golden Rule: Community and Morality in a Democratic Society* (New York: Basic Books, 1996), p. 12.

56 Ayaan Hirsi Ali has since sought political asylum in the United States and published an autobiography, *Infidel* (New York: Free Press, 2007).

57 Mill, *Considerations on Representative Government* in Mill, *Utilitarianism, Liberty, and Representative Government*, A. D. Lindsay, ed. (New York: E. P. Dutton, 1951), p. 247.

58 "Across Europe, Worries on Islam Spread to the Center," *New York Times*, October 11, 2006, pp. A1, A12.

59 Paul Berman, *Terror and Liberalism* (New York: W. W. Norton & Co., 2003).

60 Richard Posner, *Not a Suicide Pact: The Constitution in a Time of National Emergency* (New York: Oxford University Press, 2006).

61 "Police to Get Tough New Terror Powers," *The Sunday Times*, May 27, 2007; available at www.timesonline.co.uk/tol/news/uk/crime/article1845196.ece as of August 19, 2007.

62 Ronald Dworkin, "Terror and the Attack on Civil Liberties," *New York Review of Books* 50 (November 6, 2003): 37–41.

63 John McCain, "Torture's Terrible Toll," *Newsweek*, November 21, 2005; available at www.newsweek.com/id/51200 as of July 22, 2009.

64 Jonathan Weisman, "U.S. Declares Bank and Auto Bailouts Over, and Profitable," *New York Times*, December 20, 2014, pp. B1, B2.

65 Brent Snavely, "Final Tally: Taxpayer Auto Bailout Loss $9.3 B," *USA Today*, December 30, 2014, p. 1.

66 Many free-market libertarians, including Ayn Rand follower and former Federal Reserve Chairman Alan Greenspan, were by their own admission caught completely off-guard by the Great Recession that threatened to turn into the Great Depression 2.0. For one libertarian-leaning thinker's rethinking of unregulated free-market capitalism, see Richard A. Posner, *A Failure of Capitalism: The Crisis of '08 and the Descent into Depression* (Cambridge, MA: Harvard University Press, 2009). Note that Posner writes of "a failure," and not (as a socialist might) of "the failure" of capitalism. His point is that this is a particular failure from which we can learn lessons about what reforms and regulations are needed, and why. But he regards "recession" as a euphemism and insists that "depression" better describes "the crisis of '08." So too does the economist Paul Krugman in *End This Depression Now!* (New York: W. W. Norton & Co., 2012). See, further, Krugman, "The Conscience of a Liberal," in Ball, Dagger, and O'Neill, eds., *Ideals and Ideologies: A Reader*, selection 3.24.

67 David Cay Johnston, "Income Gap Is Widening, Data Shows," *New York Times*, March 29, 2007; Robert Pear, "Top Earners Doubled Share of Nation's Income, Study Finds," *New York Times*, October 25, 2011; G. William Domhoff, "Wealth, Income, and Power," cited at www2.ucsc.edu/whorulesamerica/power/wealth.html. Domhoff is a sociologist at the University of California, Santa Cruz.

FOR FURTHER READING

Ashcraft, Richard. *Revolutionary Politics and Locke's Two Treatises of Government*. Princeton, NJ: Princeton University Press, 1986.

Berlin, Isaiah. *Liberty*. Oxford: Oxford University Press, 2002.

Boaz, David. *Libertarianism: A Primer*. New York: The Free Press, 1997.

Dagger, Richard. "Communitarianism and Republicanism," in G. Gaus and C. Kukathas, eds., *Handbook of Political Theory*. London: SAGE, 2004.

Dworkin, Ronald. *Taking Rights Seriously*. Cambridge, MA: Harvard University Press, 1977.

Elton, G. R. *Reformation Europe, 1517–1559*. New York: Harper & Row, 1963.

Etzioni, Amitai, ed. *New Communitarian Thinking: Persons, Virtues, Institutions, and Communities*. Charlottesville: University of Virginia Press, 1995.

Friedman, Milton, and Rose Friedman. *Free to Choose*. New York: Avon Books, 1981.

Goodin, Robert E. *Reasons for Welfare: The Political Theory of the Welfare State*. Princeton, NJ: Princeton University Press. 1988.

Gray, John. *Liberalism*. Milton Keynes, U.K.: Open University Press, 1986.

Halévy, Elie. *The Growth of Philosophic Radicalism*. London: Faber & Faber, 1928.

Hayek, Friedrich. *The Road to Serfdom*. Chicago: University of Chicago Press, 1976.

Krugman, Paul. *The Conscience of a Liberal*. New York: W. W. Norton, 2007.

Manning, D. J. *Liberalism*. New York: St. Martin's Press, 1976.

Miller, James. *Democracy Is in the Streets: From the Port Huron Statement to the Siege of Chicago*. New York: Simon & Schuster, 1987.

Moon, J. Donald. *Constructing Community: Moral Pluralism and Tragic Conflicts*. Princeton, NJ: Princeton University Press, 1993.

Raz, Joseph. *The Morality of Freedom*. Oxford: Oxford University Press, 1986.

Ruggiero, Guido de. *The History of European Liberalism*, trans., R. G. Collingwood. Boston: Beacon Press, 1959.

Ryan, Alan. *The Making of Modern Liberalism*. Princeton: Princeton University Press, 2012.

Sandel, Michael. *Liberalism and the Limits of Justice*. Cambridge: Cambridge University Press, 1982.

Selznick, Philip. *The Communitarian Persuasion*. Washington, D.C.: Woodrow Wilson Center Press, 2002.

Skinner, Quentin. *The Foundations of Modern Political Thought*, 2 vols. Cambridge: Cambridge University Press, 1978.

Spragens, Thomas A., Jr. *The Irony of Liberal Reason*. Chicago: University of Chicago Press, 1981.

Terchek, Ronald. *Republican Paradoxes and Liberal Anxieties*. Lanham, MD: Rowman & Littlefield, 1997.

Wolfe, Alan. *The Future of Liberalism*. New York: Random House, 2009.

From the Ball, Dagger, and O'Neill Reader *Ideals and Ideologies*, Tenth Edition

USEFUL WEBSITES

Americans for Democratic Action: www.adaction.org
Move On: www.moveon.org
People for the American Way: www.pfaw.org
The American Prospect: www.prospect.org
The Ayn Rand Institute: www.aynrand.org
The Cato Institute: www.cato.org

CHAPTER 4

CONSERVATISM

What is conservatism? Is it not adherence to the old and tried against the new and untried?

Abraham Lincoln, *Cooper Union Address* (1860)

As Abraham Lincoln noted in the passage quoted above, there is a persistent and recurring difficulty in defining "conservatism." In one sense conservatism is easy to define; in another, quite difficult. It is easy because all conservatives share a desire to "conserve" or preserve something—usually the traditional or customary way of life of their societies. But these traditions or customs are likely to vary considerably from one society to another. Even where they do not, different conservatives are likely to have different ideas about what elements or parts of their established way of life are worth preserving. Conservatives may all want to conserve something, then, but they do not all want to conserve the same things. That is what makes conservatism so difficult to define.

This difficulty is evident in two ways. First, the word "conservative" is often applied to anyone who resists change. There is nothing wrong with this use of the term, except that it means that two people who bitterly oppose each other's position can both be described as conservative. As Russia and the other republics of the former Soviet Union moved toward free-market economies, for instance, the hard-line communists who resisted this change were sometimes called conservatives. Yet these "conservative" communists are the old and bitter enemies of those who are known as conservatives in the English-speaking world. Indeed, *anti*-communism has been one of the defining marks of conservatism in the West since at least the Russian Revolution of 1917, and most American-style conservatives advocate a free-market economy. If a conservative is simply anyone who wants to preserve some important feature of his or her society, however, then we must conclude that the hardline communist in Russia and the die-hard anti-communist in the United States are both conservatives. And that seems plainly absurd.

If conservatism is a distinctive political position, on the other hand, it must entail more than the simple desire to resist change. There must be some underlying principles or ideals that conservatives share—some general agreement on what is worth preserving. But here we encounter the second difficulty in defining "conservative." This difficulty is evident in the contrast between the early conservatives and the most prominent self-proclaimed conservatives of recent years. As we shall see, early or **classical or traditional conservatives** were in large part trying to preserve or restore an aristocratic society under attack from liberalism in general and the French Revolution in particular. They defended the traditional social hierarchy; they insisted on the need for a government strong enough to restrain the passions of the people; and they were often skeptical of attempts to promote individual freedom and equality of opportunity in a competitive society. By contrast, the best-known conservatives of the late twentieth century—former British Prime Minister Margaret Thatcher (1925–2013) and former U.S. President Ronald Reagan (1911–2004)—were individualist conservatives who advocated reducing the size and scope of government in order to free individuals to compete for profits.[1] With its enthusiasm for *laissez-faire* capitalism, in fact, their brand of conservatism is remarkably similar to classical and neoclassical liberalism. What early conservatives resisted, many self-described conservatives now embrace.

Many, but not all. Conservatism nowadays is a house of many mansions—and a house often divided against itself. Certainly, the divisions run deep enough for one conservative to complain that "what popularly passes for 'conservative' in America is often only a petrified right-wing of atomistic *laisser-faire* [*sic*] liberalism."[2] Later in this chapter we will explore the different kinds of conservatism. But first we need to begin with a point on which the house of conservatism was built and upon which it still stands—a shared conception of human nature.

THE POLITICS OF IMPERFECTION

In Chapter 1 we noted that every political ideology rests on a conception of human nature, including some notion of human potential—of what men and women have it in them to do and to be. In the case of conservatism, the fundamental conviction is that human beings are, and always will be, deeply flawed. This is why some scholars call conservatism "the political philosophy of imperfection."[3]

But what does it mean to say that human beings are imperfect? According to conservatives, it means that we are neither as intelligent nor as good as we like to think we are. We may believe ourselves capable of governing solely by the light of reason, but we are wrong. The light of reason does not shine far enough or bright enough to enable most of us to see and avoid all of the problems that beset people and societies, conservatives say, and even the smartest among us can never foresee all of the consequences of our actions and policies. The so-called "law of unintended consequences" holds that, however noble our intentions, our actions often backfire and produce ignoble and undesirable consequences. That is why the boldest attempts to do good often do the greatest harm.

In the face of our passions and desires, moreover, human reason is weak, even impotent. When we want something that we know is not good for us, or when we want to do something that we know may harm others, we often find ways to rationalize our conduct—to invent "reasons" for following our desires. Human beings are not only intellectually imperfect, then, but morally imperfect, too. We tend to be selfish, to put our desires and interests above others', and to reach for more power and wealth than is good either for us or for social peace and stability. Indeed, most conservatives have believed that in some sense, either theological or psychological, human beings are marked by **original sin**. They believe, that is, that the story of Adam and Eve's defiance of God in the Old Testament Book of Genesis conveys a basic truth, whether literal or symbolic, about human nature. Just as Adam and Eve in the Garden of Eden could not resist the temptation to reach for something more—something they knew they were not meant to have—so men and women continue in their pride and greed to risk the destruction of all they have in their desire for something more.

This, conservatives say, is how it always has been and always will be. To hope for some radical change in human nature—to hope that our intellectual and moral imperfections can be removed—is vain and foolish. More than that, it is dangerous. Any attempt to remake human beings by remaking their societies is likely to end in disaster. The best we can do, as they see it, is to restrain the passions and instincts that lead to conflict. This we can do through government, which imposes restraints on us, or through education—whether in schools, churches, families, or other groups—which teaches us self-restraint. As one conservative puts it,

> The function of education is conservative: not to deify the child's "glorious self-expression," but to limit his instincts and behavior by unbreakable ethical habits. In his natural instincts, every modern baby is still born a caveman baby. What prevents today's baby from remaining a caveman is the conservative force of law and tradition, that slow accumulation of civilized habits separating us from the cave.[4]

Or, as another conservative has said, "Every new generation constitutes a wave of savages who must be civilized by their families, schools, and churches."[5]

This view of human nature leads directly to the conservative warning against bold attempts to improve society. Radical proponents of other ideologies hold out visions of utopian societies; they call for revolutions to create perfect societies; or they promise at least to bring about great progress. Conservatives are skeptical of these ideological claims—so skeptical, indeed, that conservatism has been called an "anti-ideology."[6] In their view, these grandiose attempts to transform human life and society are doomed to end not only in failure but in catastrophe. We do much better, conservatives argue, to proceed slowly and cautiously in our attempts to improve society; and we are much wiser to cherish a peaceful and stable society than to risk its loss in the futile quest for perfection. This has been the fundamental conviction of conservatism from its beginning over 200 years ago in the writings of Edmund Burke.

THE CONSERVATISM OF EDMUND BURKE

Because conservatism is largely a matter of temperament, of a disposition to preserve the tried-and-true ways of life, it is easy to find people at any period in history who might reasonably be called conservatives. Yet there is widespread agreement that the true founder of conservatism was Edmund Burke (1729/30–1797), an Irishman who moved to England and served for nearly thirty years in the House of Commons of the British Parliament. Burke never called himself a conservative—neither "conservatism" nor "liberalism" entered the vocabulary of politics until the 1800s—but in his speeches and writings he defined a distinctively "conservative" political position.

Edmund Burke (1729/30–1797)

A fiery and eloquent orator, Burke developed and expounded his views in the heat of political controversies, particularly in reaction to the French Revolution. When the Revolution began in 1788–1789, many observers in England hailed it as a great step forward for both France and the cause of liberty. But Burke saw the French Revolution, from the beginning, as a foolhardy attempt to create a new society from the ground up. Nearly three years before the Revolution's Reign of Terror, Burke issued his condemnation and warning in his *Reflections on the Revolution in France* (1790). In particular, Burke took exception to the revolutionaries' view of human nature and government, which he thought mistaken, and their conception of freedom, which he thought misguided.

Human Nature and Society

Burke's objection to the French Revolution rests largely on the claim that the revolutionaries misunderstood human nature. By concentrating on the rights, interests, and choices of the individual, he charged, the revolutionaries had come to think of society as nothing more than a loose collection of self-contained atoms that are no more connected to one another than marbles on a tray. From Burke's point of view this **atomistic conception** of humans and society, as later conservatives called it, is simply wrong. It loses sight of the many important ways in which individuals are connected to and depend upon one another. Political society is no mere heap of individuals, but a living and changing organism, a whole that is greater than the sum of its parts. On this **organic conception of society**, individuals are related to one another and to the society in the same way that the heart and eyes and arms are related to the body—not as separate and isolated units but as interdependent members of a living organism. Or, to use one of Burke's favorite metaphors, society is like a fabric—the "social fabric"—and its individual members are like the interwoven threads of a richly textured tapestry. Although the tapestry as a whole is beautiful, the individual threads are not. Taken separately they are nothing special. But when woven together, threads of different colors and textures take on a beauty that far surpasses that of any single thread. Likewise, when humans come together to form a society, that society surpasses any single member of it. Far from being artificial institutions that individuals choose to create, then, society and government are outgrowths of human nature that are necessary to human life.

This organic view explains why Burke rejected the claim that civil society is brought into existence—and can just as easily be dissolved—by consenting individuals who enter into a **social contract**. If civil or political society rests on a contract, he said, it is no ordinary contract between individuals but a sacred covenant that binds whole generations together. To recognize that "society is indeed a contract" does not mean that it is

> nothing better than a partnership agreement in a trade of pepper and coffee, calico or tobacco, or some other such low concern, to be taken up for a little temporary interest, and to be dissolved by the fancy of the parties [to the contract]... It is a partnership in all science; a partnership in all art; a partnership in every virtue, and in all perfection. As the ends of such a partnership cannot be obtained in many generations, it becomes a partnership not only between those who are living but between those who are living, those who are dead, and those who are to be born.[7]

To preserve this partnership, Burke believed that both government and long-standing customs and traditions are indispensable. People tend to be self-interested (a view Burke shared with the early liberals) and short-sighted, which is precisely why they need the power of government to restrain them and keep their passions in check. But government is not a machine that can be taken apart and reassembled whenever and however people want. It is a complex and delicate organism that must be rooted in the customs and traditions of the people, who must acquire the habit of obeying, respecting, and even revering it.

Freedom

Burke also believed that the French revolutionaries' conception of freedom was misguided. From his point of view, freedom is not necessarily good. It *can* be, but it does not *have* to be. To ask whether freedom is a good thing is like asking whether fire is a good thing. Fire confined to the stove or fireplace is a good and useful thing; but if unconfined and out of control, fire is among the most dangerous and destructive of forces. Like fire, freedom is good if it is kept under control and put to good use. When used wisely and with restraint, freedom is very valuable indeed. But the destructive power of people freed from all legal and traditional restraints is truly terrifying. In Burke's words, "The effect of liberty to individuals is, that they may do what they please; we ought to see what it will please them to do, before we risk congratulations, which may be soon turned into complaints."[8]

For Burke and classical conservatives, liberty is worthwhile only when it is properly ordered. Individuals should be free from obstacles to pursue their goals, but only when their goals do not threaten the social order; if they do, then individual freedom must be restricted (see Figure 4.1).

Unlike the early liberals, furthermore, Burke did not regard government as a major obstacle to freedom, and therefore as a necessary evil. In Burke's eyes, the very fact that government prevents people from acting on every whim or impulse is what makes ordered liberty possible. "Liberty," wrote Burke, "must be limited in order to be possessed."[9] Without government restraints, more people would do more things that endanger both themselves and social peace. Burke would surely agree with the observation of a more recent conservative:

> Freedom is comprehensible as a social goal only when subordinate to something else, to an organization or arrangement which defines the individual aim. Hence the aim of freedom is at the same time to aim at the constraint which is its precondition... One major difference between conservatism and liberalism consists, therefore, in the fact that, for the conservative, the value of individual liberty is not absolute, but stands subject to another and higher value, the authority of established government.[10]

Without government there could be no civilized society, only anarchy and the rule of the mob. That is what Burke saw when he looked across the English Channel to France, where a violent revolution was raging. And, closer to home and on a smaller scale, that is what he saw in the practice of the pillory. Burke came to the public defense of two men accused of sodomy or same-sex sexual relations who were sentenced to stand in the pillory as a form of public shaming. While defenseless and unable to move, the men were attacked by a mob, leading to the death of one and the severe beating of the other. Addressing the House of Commons Burke argued that it would be better to abolish the pillory altogether as a means of legal punishment rather than allow it to become a spectacle for "popular fury, assault and cruelty," which included "torment" or torture, and could culminate in the "death and murder" of people who engaged in particular sexual practices. For taking this stand Burke was quickly attacked in the London newspapers, which insinuated that he was sympathetic to "sodomites" who engaged in same-sex relations and called upon him to explain why the "crime" these men committed "deserved a milder chastisement than ignominious death" at the hands of the mob.[11] Burke's point, of course, was that the rule of law is infinitely preferable to that of the lawless mob. Passion should not overrule reason, however passionate some people may feel.

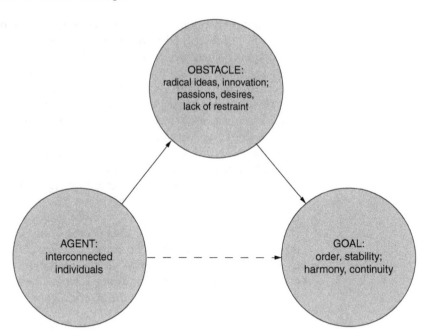

FIGURE 4.1 The classical conservative conception of freedom.

Revolution and Reform

Burke was not opposed to all **revolutions**. He looked back with approval to England's Glorious Revolution of 1688, and as a member of Parliament he was sympathetic to the American colonies in their struggle with the British government. But in Burke's view these were revolutions in the old-fashioned sense. As we saw in Chapter 1, "revolution" referred originally to a return or restoration—a "revolving" or coming full circle. According to Burke, then, the English and Americans had fought to restore their rights, to return to a condition they had previously enjoyed. But the French were engaged in a revolution of a new and much more radical sort. They sought to uproot the settled order of their society and government in order to replace it with something new and untried—and therefore certain, Burke believed, to end in disaster.

Burke never claimed that French government and society were perfect, nor did he flatly oppose all attempts at change. On the contrary, he regarded change as a necessary feature of human life and society. But change should be brought about carefully and gradually—the kind of change that Burke called **reform**—and not through **innovation**. As he saw it, innovation is the attempt to do something entirely new or novel on the grounds that the new must be better than the old. Innovation is therefore change for the sake of change, based on abstract reason. It abandons the old ways, the habits that have stood the test of time, in order to launch drastic and dangerous experiments.

Burke believed that the French revolutionaries were like people who lived in a house with a leaky roof and broken windows. Rather than make the necessary repairs, they decided that the house that had sheltered them all their lives must be torn down to make way for a new, glorious, rational structure. Drawing their plans with no experience of architecture or carpentry, they would soon find themselves homeless and unprotected. The revolutionaries had forsaken the tried-and-true way of gradual reform for the path of rapid and radical *innovation* and were now following it to their ruin.

So Burke preferred reform to innovation because it was safer and surer. After all, a successful reform will do some good, and an unsuccessful one will do little harm. He also claimed that reform grew out of **prejudice**, which he thought superior to abstract reason. But prejudice for Burke is not so much a matter of prejudging people as it is a disposition to prefer the familiar habits and traditions of one's own society. In this sense, Burke claimed, prejudice is stored-up or "latent" wisdom. Customs and traditions have gradually evolved over the generations, so they reflect the lessons that people and societies have learned, bit by bit, in the course of their lives. The fact that traditions have lasted so long is evidence that they have literally stood the test of time. They embody the wisdom not just of one or two people but of generations—a wisdom that we seldom appreciate because we simply take our customs for granted as they become second nature.

Burke on Government

With prejudice as our guide, then, we can reform government and preserve society without exposing ourselves to the dangers of innovation. But what sort of government and society did Burke have in mind? What was his idea of a sound body politic? To questions of this sort, Burke's response was to say that there is no one best form of government. Government must reflect the history, habits, and prejudices of a people, so that a form of government that ably serves the needs of one country could fail utterly in another. Even so, Burke's speeches and writings suggest that there were certain features of government and society that he thought especially desirable, at least in countries like Great Britain. These features include representative government; a "true natural aristocracy"; private property; and the distribution of power among the families, churches, and voluntary associations that form the "little platoons" of society.

Representative Government. It is scarcely surprising that Burke, a member of Parliament, should favor representative government. But we should not take this to mean that he also favored democracy. In Burke's day only a small minority of the British population, principally the large landholders, could vote or stand for election, and Burke saw no need to expand the electorate. The interests of the people should be represented in government, according to Burke, but one did not have to vote to have his or her interests well represented. What matters more than the right to vote is having the right kind of person in office—a wise, prudent, and well-informed person to whom we can entrust our interests. In his "Speech to the Electors of Bristol" in 1774, Burke stated his case in this way:

> Certainly, Gentlemen, it ought to be the happiness and glory of a representative to live in the strictest union, the closest correspondence, and the most unreserved communication with his constituents. Their wishes ought to have great weight with

him; their opinions high respect; their business unremitted attention. It is his duty to sacrifice his repose, his pleasure, his satisfactions, to theirs—and above all ... to prefer their interest to his own.

But his unbiased opinion, his mature judgment, his enlightened conscience, he ought not to sacrifice to you, to any man, or to any set of men living... Your representative owes you not his industry only, but his *judgment*; and he betrays, instead of serving you, if he sacrifices it to your opinion.[12]

Like many conservatives, Burke believed that democracy would seriously threaten the health of representative government. As the masses of people gain the franchise, they will vote for candidates who pander to their passions and desires, electing representatives who will respond to their momentary wishes instead of promoting the society's long-term interests. So it is best, Burke thought, not to broaden the franchise—at least not until the people as a whole have given some sign that they are ready and willing to cast their votes responsibly. That is why Burke actually suggested reducing rather than expanding the number of eligible voters in his own day.

The Natural Aristocracy. But even under a restricted franchise, where are these unbiased, mature, and enlightened trustees to be found? Burke's answer is to look to what he called a "true natural aristocracy." These are the rare few who have the ability, the experience, and the inclination to govern wisely in the interest of the whole society. These are the people who are natural leaders; who learn from an early age that others look to them for direction. These are the people who have the leisure as children to study, to gain knowledge of politics and society, and to develop their abilities. These are the people, Burke thought, who are most likely to come from the hereditary aristocracy.

Burke did not say that the "true natural aristocracy" and the hereditary aristocracy are one and the same. But he did believe that a person could not achieve a place in the **natural aristocracy** without both the ability *and* the necessary opportunity to learn the art of governing wisely and well. In Burke's day the people who were most likely to have the opportunity were those who came from the hereditary aristocracy. Society was accustomed to looking to the nobility for leadership, and the nobles were accustomed to providing it. Perhaps even more important was the opportunity the hereditary aristocracy enjoyed as the largest landholders in a society where wealth came primarily from the land. Because they had wealth, the sons of the aristocracy enjoyed leisure; because they enjoyed leisure, they had time for education; because they were educated, they could gain the knowledge and develop the abilities necessary to play a leading part in politics. For all of these reasons, Burke thought that they were bound to form the core of the "true natural aristocracy." There was room for others—such as himself—but a society deprived of its hereditary aristocracy was deprived of many of its best and brightest members. The French revolutionaries and others who attacked **aristocratic privilege** in the name of freedom were guilty of the worst kind of folly, for the destruction of the hereditary aristocracy will surely set off a mad scramble for power among men whose only claim to leadership was their ability to rouse the rabble.

Private Property. Burke's own respect for aristocratic privilege was due in part to the connection he saw between aristocracy and property. In general, he took inequality in private property to be natural, and to act as a stabilizing and conservative force in society. People who own property, especially property in land, will identify their interests, and even themselves, with their property, which will give them a stake in and strengthen their attachment to the society and government that surround and protect their property. This is especially likely to happen, according to Burke, when property is passed down, generation after generation, within a family, so that attachment to land, family, and country become practically indistinguishable from one another. This attachment is most likely to be found among the hereditary aristocracy.[13]

The Little Platoons. Burke's notion of a good government is one that will enlist enlightened representatives, drawn from the natural aristocracy, in the defense of private property and the common good. To do its job properly, the government must be strong. Yet its strength should not be concentrated in one person or in one place, lest this concentration tempt those in power to abuse it. This is why Burke stressed the importance of the "little platoons," those intermediate or secondary associations of "civil society" that stand between an individual and the government. Burke argued that power should be spread throughout society. Local concerns should be addressed at the local level, not the national; and instead of placing all power in the government itself, the traditional authority of churches, families, and other groups should be respected. In this way government will be strong enough to protect society, but not so strong as to smother the "little platoons" that make ordered liberty possible.

Taking a cue from a prominent student of Burke's political philosophy, we may say that society, for Burke, is like a large choir in which every voice blends with every other to create sounds that no single person could create.[14] Each singer may have a pleasant voice, but some—the soloists—are more melodious and impressive than others. Ordinary members of society are like the ordinary singers, and the members of the "natural aristocracy" correspond to the soloists. Moreover, the sections of the choir—the basses, baritones, altos, and sopranos—are like the "little platoons" that make up and give vibrancy to the society as a whole by expressing their distinctiveness. Like a choir, finally, a society will need discipline and direction if it is to perform in a way that enriches the lives of its members. For that discipline and direction, the members of society must look to and respect their government, just as the members of a choir must look to their conductor or choir director.

Burke's Legacy

In all four of these respects, many conservatives continue to share Burke's views on society and government. Although most have come to accept democracy, they still prefer a representative government that is not directly responsive to the will of the people. Few conservatives now defend hereditary aristocracy, but most still believe that some form of "true natural aristocracy" is necessary if society is to be stable, strong, and healthy. All contemporary conservatives, moreover, share Burke's faith in the value of private property and his desire to defeat the concentration of power by maintaining the strength of society's "little platoons." Despite the differences that divide them, conservatives of the twenty-first century owe enough to Burke to make it clear why he is often called the father of conservatism.

CONSERVATISM IN THE NINETEENTH CENTURY

Edmund Burke died in 1797, two years before Napoleon Bonaparte seized power and halted the French Revolution that Burke so feared and despised. Yet in some respects the Revolution continued until Napoleon's final defeat at the battle of Waterloo in 1815. Napoleon's regime preserved many of the changes the revolutionaries had fought for—including the abolition of **feudalism** with its aristocratic powers and privileges. Many aristocrats resisted these changes throughout the Revolution and the Napoleonic era that followed. Some even saw the Revolution as the enemy of all that was good and worthwhile in life. Their reaction against it was so fierce and uncompromising that they became known as reactionaries.

Conservatism and Reaction

To say that someone is a **reactionary** is to say that he or she not only reacts against the present but wants to return to an earlier form of society. Unlike Burkean or classical conservatives, whose concern is to preserve the traditional features of existing society through cautious reform, reactionaries want to turn back the clock, to restore society as it used to be. Their aim, then, is to overthrow the current social and political arrangements in order to return to the ways of the past. That is precisely what the European reactionaries proposed to do.

Among the most important of the reactionaries was Count Joseph de Maistre (1753–1821). De Maistre was born in Savoy, now a part of France but then a French-speaking province of the Kingdom of Piedmont-Sardinia. De Maistre reacted vehemently against the revolutionaries' attacks on monarchy, aristocracy, and religion. As he saw it, the French Revolution was primarily an assault on "throne and altar," king and church. But without these two institutions to provide the subjects with a sense of majesty and unity, no society could long survive. Once throne and altar are gone and people are left with nothing to respect and nothing to rely on but their own wits and reason, chaos and catastrophe are sure to follow. That, de Maistre said, is precisely what happened during the French Revolution. How could people be surprised at the bloodshed of the Reign of Terror when the revolutionaries had uprooted the old society, the majestic work of God, to replace it with the work of mere man? Indeed, de Maistre went so far as to reject the notion that a people is capable of drafting and establishing a suitable constitution for its society. A written constitution is downright dangerous, he declared, because it exposes the weakness of government:

> The more that is written, the weaker is the institution, the reason being clear. Laws are only declarations of rights, and rights are not declared except when they are attacked, so that the multiplicity of written constitutional laws shows only the multiplicity of conflicts and the danger of destruction.[15]

De Maistre's quarrel with the French Revolution was part of his larger struggle against the spirit of the eighteenth century. The French *philosophes* had proclaimed this the time of **Enlightenment**, the period when human reason was beginning at last to rout the forces of superstition, prejudice, and ignorance. But de Maistre saw the Enlightenment as an age of arrogance that led to the downfall of the most sacred and necessary social institutions—throne and altar. So not only the Revolution but also the eighteenth century's rationalist mentality must be defeated in order to return society and government to their proper conditions. As we shall see in Chapter 7, de Maistre was an important contributor to the reactionary movement that came to be called the **Counter-Enlightenment**.

De Maistre lived long enough to see the Reaction, as it was called, take effect in the years after Napoleon's defeat. The chief architect of this attempt to restore the old aristocratic order was a German aristocrat, Clemens von Metternich (1773–1859). As foreign minister of the Hapsburg (or Austrian) Empire, Metternich presided over the Congress of Vienna in 1815. This Congress brought together representatives of the forces at war with Napoleonic France—chiefly Britain, Russia, and Austria—in order to find some basis for preserving peace and stability in Europe. With Metternich's guidance, the Congress settled on hereditary monarchy as the only legitimate form of rule and aimed to restore their thrones to the European kings who had been ousted from power after 1789. Metternich's reactionary work endured for more than thirty years. In 1848, however, a series of liberal uprisings swept through Europe, and Metternich himself was forced from office, a victim of the forces he had sought to repel.

Throughout this period and well into the second half of the nineteenth century, the leadership of the Catholic Church also played a conservative, and often reactionary, role in Europe. Given the Church's privileged position in the old aristocratic order—being the First Estate in France's Estates-General, for instance—this fact is hardly surprising. When early liberals attacked the Church as an enemy of reason and freedom, the Church counterattacked at every opportunity. Thus in 1864 Pope Pius IX issued his *Syllabus of Errors*, in which he sharply criticized liberalism for undermining religion and the traditional order. Among the grievous errors of liberalism, Pius IX included the following beliefs he considered mistaken:

3   Human reason, without any regard to God, is the sole arbiter of truth and falsehood, of good and evil; it is a law to itself, and by its natural force it suffices to secure the welfare of men and nations.

77   In the present day, it is no longer expedient that the Catholic religion shall be held as the only religion of the State, to the exclusion of all other modes of worship.[16]

But reaction was not the only form that conservatism took in the nineteenth century. There were more moderate forms too, particularly those that emerged in Great Britain: **cultural conservatism** and **Tory democracy**.

Cultural Conservatism. When the French Revolution began many people in England greeted it as the dawn of a glorious new age. As William Wordsworth (1770–1850) put it in his poem "French Revolution as It Appeared to Enthusiasts at Its Commencement,"

> Bliss was it in that dawn to be alive,
> But to be young was very heaven.

But Burke's *Reflections on the Revolution in France* and subsequent events—especially the Reign of Terror—soon quelled this early enthusiasm for the Revolution. War between England and France began in 1793 and continued almost without interruption until 1815. Compared to the countries of the European continent, England survived the revolutionary era with relatively little social upheaval, leaving English conservatives little reason to become reactionary.

To be sure, English conservatives did oppose the French Revolution and the changes it wrought. Even Wordsworth turned against it, arguing that the revolutionaries placed too much faith in reason and too little in people's emotional or spiritual tie to nature. But for Wordsworth, his friend and fellow poet Samuel Taylor Coleridge (1772–1834), and other English conservatives of the early 1800s, the greatest threat to English society came not from the French Revolution but from another, very different kind of revolution—the Industrial Revolution that was reshaping English society from top to bottom. In particular, after Burke, English conservatism defended the traditional agricultural society against the ravages of industry and commerce. Commerce and capitalism were the enemies of spirituality and culture, they argued. The new creed of production in pursuit of profit simply fostered crass materialism. All of the old virtues, all loyalties, all ties to persons and places were vanishing in the pursuit of money—a pursuit that would end with men and women out of touch with themselves, with one another, and with nature. As Wordsworth complained in 1806,

> The world is too much with us; late and soon,
> Getting and spending, we lay waste our powers:
> Little we see in Nature that is ours;
> We have given our hearts away, a sordid boon!

With its suspicion of commerce and its hatred of materialism, cultural conservatism has proven to be an enduring theme, not only in England but also in the United States and elsewhere. In England more than other countries, however, cultural conservatism found an ally in a political party that made conservatism an effective political force.

Tory Democracy

Throughout the eighteenth century the Tory and Whig parties in England had vied for power. This competition continued into the 1800s, with the Tories generally defending the interests of the landowning aristocracy and the Whigs favoring a more commercial and competitive society. The differences between the two gradually focused on their attitudes toward the expansion of the electorate. Tories typically opposed any expansion of voting rights beyond the small minority who already held them. But the Whigs campaigned to win the vote for middle-class males—merchants, industrialists, and professional men for the most part—until they succeeded in 1832 in passing the Great Reform Bill. With the influx of new voters eager to support their cause, the Whigs looked forward to a long period of political dominance.

The Tories, on the other hand, could look forward only to losing elections unless they could find some way to attract new voters to their cause. The Tory leader who found the way was Benjamin Disraeli (1804–1881). Disraeli's solution was to form an alliance between the aristocratic upper class and the working class. This would enable his party, which he called the Conservative Party, to compete against the Liberals, as the Whigs had come to be known. To accomplish this, Disraeli pursued the policies of Tory democracy.

Tory democracy attempted to address the needs of the working class while instilling in the workers a respect for the traditional order of English life—including a respect for the monarchy, the aristocracy, and the established Church of England. In Disraeli's words,

> Instead of falling under ... the thraldom [spell] of capital—under those who, while they boast of their intelligence, are more proud of their wealth—if we must find a new force to maintain the ancient throne and monarchy of England, I, for one, hope that we may find that novel power in the invigorating energies of an educated and enfranchised people.[17]

So Disraeli set out both to include the workers in the electorate and to improve their condition in life. His support of the Reform Bill of 1867 helped to bring the vote to the working-class males of the cities, and in his second term as prime minister (1874–1880) he made trade unions legal and recognized the workers' right to strike against their employers. With these and other measures, Disraeli extended the cultural conservatives' dislike of the commercial middle class into a political alliance between the conservative aristocracy and the potentially revolutionary working class. Hence the term, "Tory democracy." This was to be the dominant form of British conservatism, under the leadership of Winston Churchill (1874–1964) and others, until Margaret Thatcher became prime minister in 1979.

But Tory democracy remained a distinctly British form of conservatism. The Prussian Prime Minister Otto von Bismarck (1815–1898) accomplished something similar in Germany with his provision of state-supported insurance and benefits for workers, but Bismarck was no democrat. He was a Prussian militarist and German nationalist who consolidated the various provinces of Germany into a powerful and united nation-state, and viewed the "social insurance state" (or welfare state) as a means to that end. Elsewhere, especially in the United States, what came to be called "conservatism" was a far cry from Tory democracy.

Conservatism in the United States

American conservatism followed a different course in the nineteenth century. When the Constitution was drafted in 1787, the free population of the United States comprised about three million people, almost all of whom were Protestants of European descent. Lacking experience of feudalism and hereditary aristocracy, having no monarch, no aristocracy, and no established national church, American conservatives were hardly likely to follow the path either of Burke, of de Maistre's reactionary appeal to throne and altar, or of Tory democracy. In a country founded on the principles of liberalism—or perhaps more accurately, as we noted in Chapter 3, on a mixture of liberal and republican principles—American conservatives were chiefly concerned with preserving an essentially liberal society and way of life.

Two of the American Founders, John Adams (1735–1826) and Alexander Hamilton (1757–1804), are sometimes taken to be conservatives in the Burkean mold. But the differences between them and Burke are more telling than the similarities. Like Burke, Adams often spoke favorably of the "natural aristocracy," but Adams could not look to a hereditary nobility, as Burke did, to provide the core of this group of natural leaders, for there was no such class in the United States. The closest Adams could come was "men of property," and this was a much broader group in the United States than in Burke's England. As for Hamilton, his claim to the credentials of a classical conservative rests largely on his defense of constitutional monarchy at the time of the founding. But the plan he drafted as secretary of the treasury—a plan to make the United States a great commercial power—hardly displayed a classical conservative's suspicion of commerce and reverence for the settled forms of social life.

In the early and middle 1800s, there were several figures in the United States whose views could be linked to cultural conservatism. Perhaps the most important of these, at least in retrospect, were two friends who became giants of American literature—Nathaniel Hawthorne (1804–1864) and Herman Melville (1819–1891). In various stories and novels both authors criticized what they saw as the foolishly optimistic temper of their times. Hawthorne depicted the vanity and futility of the quest for perfection in his story "Earth's Holocaust," for instance, and then portrayed the tragic consequences of such a quest in stories like "The Birthmark." For his part, Melville heaped scorn on those who preached the doctrine of faith in human nature in his bitterly ironic novel, *The Confidence Man;* and his "Bartleby the Scrivener: A Story of Wall Street" can be read as an attack on the dehumanizing consequences of capitalism.

As in England, cultural conservatism has remained an important thread in the fabric of American conservatism. More characteristic, however, was the shift in the direction of *laissez-faire* capitalism that took place in the late nineteenth century. This was the period when the name "conservative" began to be applied to the businessmen and industrialists who had previously been seen as the enemies of tradition. What was called liberalism in other countries was called conservatism in the United States. How did this happen? Two principal factors seem to have been at work.

First, businessmen and industrialists stressed the importance of private property—a point on which conservatives and liberals agree—and individualism. Both these ideals had long been important in the United States, so the captains of industry could in a sense appeal to traditional values of their country when they defended *laissez-faire* capitalism. The United States had been founded on the belief in the individual's natural rights to life, liberty, and the pursuit of happiness, after all. Once American business leaders interpreted these rights to mean that every individual should be free to pursue profits in the competitive marketplace, they could then be regarded as conservatives.

The second factor was the development of **welfare liberalism** in the late nineteenth century. The rise of this new form of liberalism, with its call for government action to promote individual liberty and equality of opportunity, meant that those who clung to the views of early or classical liberalism were now in danger of being left behind. As we saw in Chapter 3, this change produced a split between welfare and neoclassical liberalism. Because the neoclassical liberals remained true to the faith of the early liberals—especially the faith in what men and women can do when they are freed from the restraints of that "necessary evil," government—the neoclassical liberals came to seem old-fashioned. By sticking to the older form of liberalism, there was a sense in which they were surely conservatives.

For both of these reasons, classical liberalism came to be called "conservatism" in the United States. Even the **Social Darwinists**, whom we described in Chapter 3 as neoclassical liberals, were included. Thinkers such as Herbert Spencer and William Graham Sumner advanced an atomistic conception of society, with people locked in a struggle for survival with one another. No classical or cultural conservative could accept such an atomistic and anti-organic vision. But in the United States the Social Darwinists' defense of private property and competitive individualism, coupled with their attack on government regulations, placed them squarely, if a bit uncomfortably, in the conservative camp.

For the past century, conservatism in the United States has suffered from the continuing tension between traditional conservatives, on the one hand, and those who see conservatism as primarily the defense of *laissez-faire* capitalism, on the other. There are points on which the two sides agree, of course, such as the value of private property and the folly of abstract social planning—especially in the form of socialism or **communism**. But there are so many points on which they disagree that the two sides seem to be enemies as often as allies. Certainly it is difficult to see how anyone with a Burkean distrust of innovation can join comfortably with someone who, in the name of competition and progress, is constantly seeking new products to sell to more people in hopes of a better, and more affluent, life.

CONSERVATISM IN THE TWENTIETH CENTURY

In recent years this tension between these two kinds of conservatism has spread beyond the United States, leading most notably to a division in the ranks of conservatives in Great Britain. In the early years of the twentieth century, however, conservatives in Europe and traditional conservatives in the United States were united in their attacks on what they called **mass society**.

Conservatism versus Mass Society

The nineteenth century had been the age of democracy. The franchise had been greatly extended throughout the Western world. The power of the old aristocracy had been broken, and the spread of public education meant that many of the barriers to social mobility and advancement were falling. At the beginning of the twentieth century, moreover, the rapid development of industrial mass production made it seem as if economic barriers were collapsing as well. Items that once would have been available only to the wealthy few—the automobile, for instance—were now being built for and sold to the masses.

Some welcomed these developments, but not the traditional or classical conservatives. From their point of view, this new mass society posed the same threat that democracy had always posed—the threat that the masses would throw society first into chaos, then into despotism. In arguments similar to those of Plato, Aristotle, and more recently Alexis de Tocqueville, traditional conservatives maintained that the common people were too weak and too ignorant to take charge of government. Too weak to curb their appetites or restrain their desires, the people will want more wealth, more property, and more power, like gluttons who ruin their health because they cannot stop eating. And they are too ignorant, too short-sighted, to see the disaster they are bringing upon their society and themselves. Once their unchecked demands have taken society to the brink of anarchy, the masses will then cry out for a strong and decisive leader who will restore law and order—even at the expense of liberty.

This conservative argument against mass society gained credence in the 1920s and 1930s as fascists and Nazis came to power in Italy, Spain, and Germany. To the conservative eye, these brutal movements were the logical result of the democratic excesses of mass society. All the hard-won accomplishments of European civilization, particularly representative government in parliaments, were in danger of being ground under the boot-heels of Fascist "blackshirts" and Nazi "stormtroopers" and their dictatorial leaders. Even defenders of **liberal democracy** like the Spanish philosopher José Ortega y Gasset (1883–1955) adopted a conservative stance in the face of fascism. In *The Revolt of the Masses*, Ortega asserted that

> nothing indicates more clearly the characteristics of the day than the fact that there are so few countries where an opposition exists. In almost all, a homogeneous mass weighs on public authority and crushes down, annihilates every opposing group. The mass ... does not wish to share life with those who are not of it. It has a deadly hatred of all that is not itself.[18]

In response to this threat, conservative critics of mass society maintained that the masses need to be taught self-restraint. This meant that the masses must learn either to curb their appetites and respect the traditional ways or, more likely, to recognize that it is better to entrust their government to the aristocracy or elite—to those, that is, with superior wisdom, experience, and foresight. This view is, of course, similar to the argument Burke made on behalf of his "true natural aristocracy." The difference is that, by the twentieth century, few conservatives looked to the hereditary aristocracy to form the core of this natural governing elite. Still, conservatives believed—and classical conservatives continue to believe—that in every society there will be some small number of men and women who are suited by ability, experience, and temperament to govern, while the great majority are utterly unsuited in one or more of these respects. If we must live in mass society, conservatives say, we should at least be prudent enough to put a substantial share of power in the hands of those who rise above the mass.

Levelling

An abiding fear of mass society explains why so many conservatives, from Burke to the present, have opposed what they call **levelling**. Conservatives have typically been suspicious of attempts to achieve greater democracy or equality because they believe these will "level" society. One can presumably promote equality either by improving the condition of people at the bottom of society or by worsening the condition of those at the top. As conservatives point out, attempts to make the people at the bottom better off usually involve taking something away from the top—as in "soak the rich" tax policies. The problem with such schemes, according to the conservative argument, is that they raise the people at the bottom very little, lower the people at the top a great deal, and in the long run reduce everyone in society to the same low level. In the name of equality, conservatives claim, levelling programs simply promote economic and social stagnation.

Levelling is also culturally pernicious, according to conservatives. In this age of equality everyone is taught that his or her opinions or beliefs are just as good as anyone else's. Thus we find ourselves in an age of fads and fancies, with fashions changing constantly and the only standards of worth being novelty and popularity. Serious literature, music, and art are overwhelmed by the levelling tendencies of mass society. The quantity of sales counts for more than the quality of the work in this age of "best-selling" books and "blockbuster" movies, all produced according to formulae that appeal to a mass audience. Even in colleges and universities, students forsake philosophy, literature, and history to study advertising and marketing—two "disciplines" that are concerned not with truth but with increasing the sales of products of dubious value.

Conservatives have often seen levelling as a threat to society in another way as well. In addition to its harmful effects in economic and cultural matters, they see levelling as the enemy of social variety and diversity. Drawing on arguments similar to Burke's praise of the "little platoons" of society, conservatives frequently defend the neighborhood, the town, or the region as centers of local variety and diversity—centers that are always in danger of being squashed by the levelling forces of mass society. Within a society, conservatives say, it is healthy to have diverse communities. Diversity, in fact, is a sign of health, for it shows that people at the local level are able to muster the resources they need to meet the challenges of life—challenges that will vary considerably from one community to another. We should especially hope to preserve communities where people are disposed to follow the customs and habits of their ancestors. Such a disposition, or prejudice in Burke's sense, inclines people not only to follow the time-tested ways but also to remain loyal to a community that they see themselves sharing with their ancestors, their children, and generations yet to come.

This is the kind of argument offered in *I'll Take My Stand*, a collection of essays published in 1930 by a group of writers known as the Southern Agrarians.[19] The Agrarians defended the traditional agricultural society of the southern United States against the invasion of industrialism from the northern states. An agricultural society will necessarily be traditional, they argued, for it will necessarily be concerned with property and family. Both literally and figuratively, an agricultural society is concerned with roots. Industrial society, however, is rootless, and all traditional loyalties and affections give way in face of the demands for production and consumption that characterize mass society.

From early in the twentieth century, then, conservatives have issued warnings against the excesses of mass society. Mass society threatens to degenerate into anarchy and despotism, or at least to level society into a rootless crowd of consumers who relentlessly seek new name-brand commodities to consume.

Conservatives and Communism

One of the pervasive themes of twentieth-century conservatism is its fear and hatred of communism. This, indeed, is one of the few points on which all conservatives agree. There are some, like the historian and journalist Garry Wills, who think that conservatives have been so obsessively anti-communist that they have mistakenly seen everything as part of a fight to the death between communism and Western civilization.[20] But even those who share Wills's concern believe that communism and conservatism are incompatible, and most conservatives will go further and say that the two ideologies are implacable enemies. From the Russian Revolution of 1917 to the present, conservatives have been among the most outspoken opponents of communism.

Why are conservatives so united, and so vehement, in their opposition to communism? The answer lies in two contrasting views of human nature and freedom. For conservatives, human beings are fundamentally imperfect creatures who are likely to abuse freedom through their selfishness and short-sightedness. But communists, as we shall see in Chapters 5 and 6, take a more optimistic view. Communists typically argue that the source of social problems is not human nature but social conditions—especially the division of society into social and economic classes based on the ownership and control of property. Once people are freed from these crippling conditions, communists say, they will grow and flourish. This belief, of course, is directly contrary to the conservative view.

Out of this general opposition emerge three more particular respects in which conservatives are fundamentally at odds with communism: progress, perfectibility, and planning. In all three respects conservatives reject the communist position. First, following Burke, most conservatives continue to argue that faith in progress is unwarranted. Social change is not necessarily change for the better. Every change carries with it certain risks, and the kind of revolutionary changes communists call for are far too risky—and unrealistic—to be taken by prudent persons.

Second, the communists' faith in progress rests on their utterly unjustified faith in the perfectibility of human nature and society. This faith, according to conservatives, runs counter to all human experience. Indeed, some conservatives suggest that belief in perfectibility is a heresy—a view, that is, that contradicts certain religious truths. When communists claim that men and women must free themselves from oppressive social conditions in order to live rich and full lives, they deny original sin and human imperfection. The fact that many communists, including Karl Marx, have been atheists has only fueled the hostility of conservatives of a religious orientation. Those conservatives who are not themselves religious attack the communist belief in perfectibility as a dangerous illusion, if not a heresy.

Third, most conservatives dislike the communists' emphasis on centralized state planning. Like neoclassical liberals, some conservatives believe that such planning is always inefficient; we should instead, they say, leave matters to competition on the open market. Burkean or classical conservatives believe that some planning is necessary and desirable, but only planning on a small scale for gradual, piecemeal social change. But communists have often called for social planning of the broadest, most comprehensive sort. They want to survey all aspects of society, according to their conservative critics, in order to anticipate all social needs, to estimate the resources available to meet those needs, and to take action to solve all social problems. Planning on such a grand scale, conservatives claim, places entirely too much faith in human reason. It encourages grandiose social schemes that are almost certain to collapse in failure, thereby sinking people deeper in the misery from which the communists had planned to rescue them.

Moreover, planning of this sort requires that power be concentrated in the hands of a few at the center of society. There is no room for diversity or variety—no room for freedom—at the local level. The "little platoons" of society are absorbed into the homogeneous mass as everyone in society is "levelled" to a similar condition—everyone, that is, but the few who hold power. The result of grand social planning, in short, is neither progress nor perfection but misery, brutality, and despotism. Instead of freeing people from oppressive social conditions, conservatives charge, Soviet-style central planning sacrifices freedom to the oppression of communist central planners.

In view of the differences between them, it is hardly surprising that conservatives have been so bitterly opposed to communism. This opposition was particularly strong in the years following the end of World War II in 1945. As communist regimes came to power in Eastern Europe, Asia, and elsewhere, communism became the chief focus of conservative concern.

Anti-communism (and opposition to the supposedly "socialistic" reforms of President Franklin D. Roosevelt's New Deal) became a central pillar of conservatism in the United States in the post-World War II era. Whereas earlier conservatism tended to be distrustful of ideas and of the intellectuals who espoused them, the new post-war conservatism took ideas and intellectual debate seriously. This intellectual engagement is especially evident in the writings of Richard M. Weaver (1910–1963), Russell Kirk (1918–1994), Peter Viereck (1916–2006), and William F. Buckley, Jr. (1925–2008). Weaver, Kirk,[21] and Viereck were traditionalist conservatives in the Burkean mold. Viereck went so far as to defend the New Deal, which he believed had helped repair the social fabric torn by the Great Depression, and was a strong supporter of labor unions, which he believed belonged to Burke's "little platoons." A more eclectic thinker, Buckley attempted to combine Burkean conservatism and an anti-authoritarian libertarianism. Buckley used a portion of his personal wealth to establish *The National Review* in 1955. And, wanting to make conservatism a respectable and mainstream movement, Buckley heaped scorn on far-right groups such as the John Birch Society, whose founder, Robert Welch, harbored various conspiracy theories claiming that the entire federal government had been taken over by Communists and had even called President Eisenhower "a dedicated and conscious agent of the Communist Conspiracy." Although himself a staunch anti-communist, Buckley, believing that those who knew the most about communism were communists who had turned against their former ideology, included on *The National Review*'s editorial board the ex-communists-turned-conservatives Whittaker Chambers (1901–1961) and Frank S. Meyer (1909–1972), who is credited with developing the position known as "fusionism" that has come to characterize the eclectic conservatism of *The National Review*. That magazine has since been followed by many others representing a variety of viewpoints within American conservatism.

Despite differences within the broad-based conservative movement, the one issue that united conservatives of all kinds was their shared opposition to communism. As the principal representative of international communism, the Soviet Union appeared to many conservatives to be an "evil empire," as President Ronald Reagan later called it. But with the sudden collapse of communism in Eastern Europe in 1989 and the disintegration of the Soviet Union itself two years later, conservatives have subsequently found themselves in an odd position. They remain very much united in their opposition to communist ideology, but that ideology no longer seems to be a serious threat. Now that their common enemy apparently is vanquished, the question facing conservatives is whether they will find a new reason to make common cause with one another or, failing that, split into quarreling factions.

CONSERVATISM TODAY: A HOUSE DIVIDED

Even before the demise of Soviet communism, conservatism seemed to be giving way to a variety of conservatisms. There are points on which conservatives continue to agree, of course, such as a general respect for private property and an opposition to communism. But there are so many differences of opinion and emphasis that we can now identify four distinct strands of thought in contemporary conservatism. Two of these, **traditional** and **individualist conservatism**, would by now be familiar to you from our discussion of the split in conservatism in the United States in the 1800s. The remaining two, **neoconservatism** and the **religious right**, have become prominent in the last three decades or so. Each of these four deserves a closer look, with special attention to the two most recent forms of conservatism.

Traditional Conservatism

The heirs of Edmund Burke—those who adhere to the positions of the classical and cultural conservatives—are now often called "traditional" (or Burkean) conservatives. Like Burke, they think of society as a delicate fabric in which individual lives are woven together. On this view, a society of self-seeking individuals, each of whom is essentially independent of the others and therefore free to pursue his or her own self-interest, is deranged and disordered—a threadbare fabric that hardly deserves to be called a society. Society should promote freedom, to be sure, but traditional conservatives share Burke's conviction that this must be ordered liberty. Society does not consist of isolated or atomistic individuals but of people involved in a complex web or network of interdependent and mutual relationships. Each person has a particular station or status and a stake in the larger society into which he or she is born, lives, and dies. The purpose of political activity, then, is to preserve the social fabric within which these vital human activities are carried on from generation to generation. Because this fabric is easily torn, it requires our constant care and respect. Hence politics, as the British conservative philosopher Michael Oakeshott (1901–1990) put it, is nothing more than attending to the arrangements of one's society.[22]

Like Burke again, traditional conservatives see private property as essential to social stability. They do not equate private property with unbridled capitalism, however, which they continue to regard with some suspicion. According to conservative columnist and author George Will, capitalism at its worst is a "solvent" that can dissolve the web of traditional relationships.[23] Government must therefore take care to see that the economic competition of capitalism is kept within bounds—a point on which traditional conservatives sharply disagree with individualist conservatives.

Individualist Conservatism

In the nineteenth century, as we have seen, businessmen, industrialists, and others who held to the views of the early liberals came to be called conservatives in the United States. This trend has continued into the present century, and in recent years especially it has spread beyond the United States. For these "individualist" or "free-market" conservatives, society is not Burke's delicate fabric but a rough-and-tumble, competitive marketplace. Rather than talk about how individuals are inevitably situated in a web of interdependency and connected across generations with their ancestors and their unborn successors, as traditional conservatives do, individualist conservatives prefer to talk about "rugged individualists" pulling themselves up by their bootstraps. For the individualist, furthermore, freedom is not ordered liberty but the freedom of individuals to compete with one another, particularly in the economic arena of the free market. What these modern individualist conservatives propose to conserve, then, is this now well-established freedom. In this respect, as we saw in Chapter 3, they have more in common with neoliberals—and more especially libertarians—than with traditional conservatives. The conservative columnist and author David Brooks underscored the difference between Burkean or classical conservatism and modern libertarianism when he wrote, in defense of the former: "People are not better off when they are given maximum personal freedom to do what they want. They're better off when they are enshrouded in commitments that transcend personal choice—commitments to family, God, craft and country."[24]

Modern market-oriented individualist conservatives place property rights that is, the right to own property and to do with it as one pleases without government interference—at the top of their list of rights. This explains why Senator Barry Goldwater and Ronald Reagan opposed the 1964 Civil Rights Act. They believed that the owner of a hotel or restaurant or other business has the right to refuse service to anyone, including African-Americans, Hispanics, or others of whom the property owner may disapprove. Since it forbids such exclusion, the Civil Rights Act, according to Goldwater and Reagan, constitutes an improper and illegitimate infringement on property rights. Many if not most modern individualist conservatives have not gone this far, if only for fear of alienating African-American and other minority voters. But some, like the libertarian-leaning Republican congressman and former presidential candidate Ron Paul, have done, and proudly so. In 2004 he said that he would have voted against the Civil Rights Act if he had been in office in 1964 because it was "a massive violation of the rights of private property and contract, which are the bedrocks of free society."[25]

Individualist conservatism is the conservatism of Goldwater and Reagan in the United States and of Margaret Thatcher in Great Britain. Contrary to traditional or classical conservatives, who stress the intricacy of society and the complexity of its problems, modern individualist conservatives are inclined to claim that social problems and their solutions are simple. Most problems stem mainly from "too much government," as they see it, by which they usually mean too much taxation and government interference in the operations of the free market. The solution then is correspondingly simple: "Get government off our backs!" Cut taxes, eliminate or reduce regulations, and reduce government spending, particularly for social welfare, and give the free market a free rein, in economic if not in moral matters. Some traditional conservatives have criticized these individualist schemes to cut spending for health services, education, and social welfare, complaining that these amount to cuts or tears in the social fabric of civility and stability. When she was prime minister of Great Britain, Thatcher and her followers responded by dubbing these critics "wet hanky" conservatives, or "wets" for short. Let the free market do its work, individualist conservatives say, and everyone will eventually benefit. So the tension between traditionalists and individualists continues within conservatism.

In the era of the communist threat—the so-called Cold War—this tension was often checked by the common desire for a strong military to defend against communist aggression. For even individualist conservatives believed that government ought to be strong and active in the area of military defense. More than anything else, in fact, this belief distinguished individualist conservatives from neoclassical liberals. Now that communism no longer poses so grave a threat to the security of capitalist countries, individualist conservatives may move increasingly in the libertarian direction of the neoclassical liberals. This, however, is a move that other conservatives are unlikely to make.

Neoconservatism

To complicate matters further, other forms of conservatism have emerged from the political turmoil of the 1960s. One of these, "neoconservatism," occupies a position somewhere between traditional and individualist conservatism. Neoconservatism takes its bearings from a group of prominent academics and public figures, including one former vice president of the United States—Dick Cheney—and others who have held important positions in recent Republican administrations, including Lynne Cheney, who chaired the National Endowment for the Humanities from 1986 to 1993, before her husband became vice president.

Other prominent neoconservatives have included Senator Daniel Patrick Moynihan (Democrat, New York), the author Irving Kristol (and his son, William, editor of *The Weekly Standard*), UN Ambassador Jeanne Kirkpatrick, former *Commentary* editor Norman Podhoretz, the political scientist James Q. Wilson, the sociologist Nathan Glazer, and—until their recent disavowal of neoconservatism—authors Francis Fukuyama and Michael Lind.

Many neoconservatives can be described as disenchanted welfare liberals. Once enthusiastic supporters of President Lyndon Johnson's "Great Society" programs in the 1960s, these neoconservatives became disillusioned with these programs and with the general direction of welfare liberalism. Government is trying to do too much, they concluded, and it is making things worse, not better. The time has come for government to do less for people so that they may be encouraged to do more for themselves. Senator Moynihan called this policy "benign neglect."

Like traditional conservatives, neoconservatives warn that well-intended policies and programs can and often do produce unintended harmful consequences. Since such consequences are not only unforeseen but are unforeseeable in principle, we should be wary of any plan, program, or policy that promises only good results. Such schemes of "social engineering" tend to go awry and to backfire, harming those they were meant to help.[26] Also like traditional conservatives, neoconservatives regard capitalism with a mixture of admiration and suspicion. They acknowledge its merits as an economic system capable of generating great wealth, but they also are aware of the social disruption and dislocations brought about by a freewheeling market economy—including labor unrest, unemployment, periods of economic boom and bust, and an apparently permanent "underclass" of the uneducated and unemployed. As one neoconservative, Irving Kristol, once said, capitalism deserves two cheers, but not three.[27] According to Daniel Bell, capitalism harbors a number of "cultural contradictions" through which it undermines its own moral and intellectual foundations.[28] On the one hand, capitalism rests on people's willingness to defer pleasures and gratifications—to save and invest in the present in order to receive a greater return in the future. On the other hand, capitalism in the age of the credit card creates an illusion of abundance that leads people to think that there are no limits—that anything is possible—and that one can have it all, here and now. So capitalism is, in a sense, at odds with itself. It praises the virtues of thrift, saving, and hard work, on the one hand, while on the other its advertising agencies and marketing experts encourage people to buy now, pay later, and aspire to a life of luxury and ease.

Nor is this attitude confined to economic matters. It spills over into other areas as well, neoconservatives say. This "buy now, pay later" attitude is especially dangerous insofar as it shapes attitudes about government. Neoconservatives complain that too many people now expect too much, too quickly from all of their institutions, including government. They want lower taxes and at the same time increased government spending for their pet projects. They want to live on their lines of credit in politics as they do in their personal finances. These attitudes, on which contemporary capitalism relies, have potentially disastrous social and political consequences. This is particularly true in modern democracies, where every interest group clamors for an ever-larger share of the public pie. The consequences, neoconservatives say, are too obvious to miss—runaway debt, budget deficits too large to comprehend, and worst of all, a citizenry incapable of checking its appetites and demands. As these problems mount, demands on government increase—and government loses its capacity to govern.

In domestic matters, then, neoconservatives tend to be skeptical liberals. They support government-sponsored welfare programs, but they insist that these programs should help people become independent, not make them ever more dependent upon the government. In foreign affairs, they have taken a hard-line anti-communist stance, generally calling for economic and military assistance for anti-communist regimes and rebel movements around the world. More recently they have been strong proponents of the "war on terrorism" and "regime change" in Iraq and other countries that allegedly harbor terrorists. Neoconservatives believe that power—military power in particular—is no good unless it is used to achieve ends they deem to be in the national interest. Acting on this belief, Vice President Cheney and other "neocons" in President George W. Bush's administration led the United States to invade Iraq and overthrow Saddam Hussein's regime in 2003. The subsequent attempt to establish stability and democracy there has produced mixed results, ranging from provoking a bloody and costly civil war among religious sects and ethnic groups within Iraq, and drawing radical Islamists from other countries into Iraq, to an unstable and uncertain peace in the aftermath of American withdrawal—all contrary to neoconservative hopes and expectations. The result has been a widespread condemnation of neoconservatism, and some who were once proud to call themselves neoconservatives now disavow the movement.[29]

Neoconservatives also take a strong interest in the political implications of art, literature, education, and other broadly cultural matters. Like all cultural conservatives, neoconservatives believe that a people defines who it is, or who it aspires to be, through its culture. In too many aspects of our culture—in our music, our literature, our theater, our movies, our art, our schools—we are defining ourselves, neoconservatives argue, as ill-mannered, amoral drifters and degenerates who are undermining or discarding what remains of a once great and vibrant Western culture. Indeed, neoconservatives sometimes suggest that an "adversary culture" of left-leaning intellectuals, feminists, and assorted malcontents poses a greater threat to our values and way of life than do any real or imagined threats to the free market. So the political struggle that "true" conservatives wage must be, in their view, a cultural and intellectual struggle against this "adversary culture." For while "highbrow" culture and university education may initially influence the outlooks and attitudes of only a relatively small segment of society, these attitudes and values eventually trickle down to the masses—just as the long hair and drug dabbling of college radicals in the 1960s gradually spread throughout American society. One of the projects undertaken by neoconservatives, consequently, is the attempt to remind people of the value of work, discipline, and virtue.[30]

Like other cultural conservatives, neoconservatives see politics and culture as two sides of the same coin. Whether expressed by the intellectuals of the adversary culture or the stars of popular music, movies, and television, the attitudes of too many cultural leaders have set the tone for the rest of society—and with disastrous effects. Rock and rap music lyrics feature four-letter words that have lost their capacity to shock and disgust many people. This change amounts to "defining deviancy down," according to Daniel Patrick Moynihan.[31] That is, actions once regarded as aberrant, shocking, and shameful are now accepted as normal. For example, men and women who live together without being married and have children out of wedlock are no longer viewed as shameful and abnormal but as normal and acceptable. Illegitimacy has lost its stigma. Thus it comes as no surprise, according to another leading neoconservative, that

> the percentage of illegitimate births has increased to a startling percentage since World War II… Girls today are far more "sexually active" … than was formerly the case. Why this increase in sexual activity? Well, the popular culture surely encourages it. You can't expect modesty (to say nothing of chastity) from girls who worship Madonna.[32]

The reference to Madonna may be dated, but the neoconservative message is clear: to preserve or to restore the discipline and self-restraint necessary to any decent society, we must attend to cultural changes—and strive to stem the cultural tide. On this point neoconservatives agree with the conservatives of the religious right.

The Religious Right

In the years after World War II, a number of evangelical Protestant ministers led campaigns against the dangers of what they called "Godless, atheistic communism." In the 1970s these campaigns grew into a larger movement known as the "religious right." This movement marked a reaction against the changes many saw, and deplored, in the American society during the 1960s. High divorce and crime rates, urban decay and riots, growing welfare rolls, the decline of patriotism, widespread drug use, and legalized abortion—all were signs that the United States had lost its way. The time was ripe for a movement that would restore the country to its traditional ways. The time had come, according to the religious right, for a return to morality in government and in the wider society.

As defined by the leaders of the religious right, "morality" is the moral code of Christian fundamentalism. Christian fundamentalists believe that the Bible is to be read literally, not symbolically, with every word taken to express and reveal the will of God. That is why they protest against the teaching of Darwin's theory of evolution in public schools, for instance, and why they generally decry the growth of liberal or secular humanism. In their view the United States was founded and has prospered as a "Christian nation," and it must now return to its roots. It comes as no surprise that the leaders of the religious right have often been ministers of evangelical churches such as the Reverends Jerry Falwell (1933–2007) of the Moral Majority and Pat Robertson of the Christian Coalition.

The religious right also claims to be democratic, by which it means that society should follow the lead of a righteous or "moral" majority of Christians. Where will this moral majority lead? To less government intervention in the economy, as the individualist conservatives wish, but also to a larger and more active government in other respects. In the past the religious right has campaigned for a strong defense to check and turn back the threat of communism, and now it supports an aggressive "war on terrorism." It also wants increased government intervention in activities and areas of life that others, including many other conservatives, deem to be private. They want the government to ban abortions, to permit prayer in public schools, to restrict or outlaw certain sexual activities, and to purge schools and public libraries of materials that they regard as morally offensive. On these and other points the religious right would greatly expand the powers of government.

In that respect their views stand in sharp contrast to the professed views of other conservatives.

In their broad vision of what they hope to accomplish, however, the conservatives of the religious right agree with other conservatives. According to Ralph Reed, the former director of the Christian Coalition, the members of this coalition pray and work for a spiritual awakening that will lead to a political and cultural restoration. If this were to happen, he writes,

> America would look much as it did for most of the first two centuries of its existence, before the social dislocation caused by Vietnam, the sexual revolution, Watergate, and the explosion of the welfare state. Our nation would once again be ascendant, self-confident, proud, and morally strong. Government would be small, the citizenry virtuous, and mediating institutions such as churches and volunteer organizations would carry out many of the functions currently relegated to the bureaucracy. Instead of turning to Washington to solve problems, Americans would turn to each other.[33]

In their efforts to bring about the political and cultural restoration that Reed calls for, conservatives of the religious right sometimes take steps or give voice to opinions that definitely distinguish them from other conservatives. One way in which they do this is by calling for the legal recognition of the United States as a Christian (or Judeo-Christian) nation. In 2003, for example, Judge Roy Moore of Alabama insisted on displaying the Ten Commandments in his courtroom, which led to his suspension from his post. Judge Moore and his supporters maintain that the Ten Commandments belong in courtrooms and other public buildings because the U.S. Constitution is "based on" the commandments. Critics were quick to point out that this claim is both historically and textually dubious. The Constitution says nothing at all about God—whose name was intentionally excluded by the Founders—or about having no other gods before Him or coveting thy neighbor's wife or honoring one's parents and so on for all ten of the commandments. In fact, the only mention of religion in the Constitution is a negative one, which prohibits any religious test for holding public office (Article VI). Furthermore, critics note, the Bill of Rights only mentions religion in the First Amendment, and it too is in the negative voice: "Congress shall make no law respecting an establishment of religion, or prohibiting the free exercise thereof."[34] Some religious right conservatives concede these points, and advocate amending the Constitution to designate the United States as a "Christian nation" that constitutionally outlaws same-sex marriage and abortion, among other actions and activities they consider to be contrary to Christianity. Not surprisingly, the religious right was outraged by the U.S. Supreme Court's 2015 decision making same-sex marriage legal throughout the United States. This, they say, is all the more reason to amend the American Constitution to accord more closely with Christianity as they understand it.

Another way in which the religious right has distinguished itself from other kinds of conservatism is in the tendency of some of its leaders to claim that disasters befalling the United States are signs of God's displeasure. In an appearance on Pat Robertson's television show, for example, the late Reverend Jerry Falwell once blamed the terrorist attacks of September 11, 2001, on America's toleration of "the pagans, and the abortionists, and the feminists, and the gays and the lesbians..., the ACLU [American Civil Liberties Union], People for the American Way, all of them who have tried to secularize America." Falwell subsequently apologized for this remark, but he did so while continuing to hold that God may have lifted "the veil of protection which has allowed no one to attack America on our soil since 1812."[35] On this interpretation of events, God was punishing the United States for its moral laxity, and the terrorists were doing God's work—which is exactly what the terrorists themselves thought they were doing. On this point, at least, Robertson's and Falwell's fundamentalist Christianity and fundamentalist or radical Islamism appear to agree.

To be sure, not all religious right conservatives share Falwell's and Robertson's tendency to view political and natural events, such as 9/11 or Hurricane Katrina, as God's judgment on a wicked people. Nor do all religious conservatives identify themselves with the religious right. For example, John Danforth, an ordained Episcopal priest and three-term Republican senator from Missouri, published a book in 2006 in which he chides religious right conservatives for invoking God for political purposes.[36] Danforth's book is itself testimony to the significance of the religious right, however, for he surely would not have thought it worthwhile to write the book unless he regarded the religious right as a potent force in American politics—and especially within American conservatism.

"FUSIONIST" CONSERVATISM

In the late 1950s the ex-communist turned anti-communist conservative Frank Meyer (1909–1972) advocated a "third way" between religious-traditionalist conservatism, on the one hand, and a more libertarian-leaning conservatism, on the other. The former seeks to promote and uphold "order," the latter, "liberty." Instead of opting for one over the other, Meyer argued, the two should be held in a kind of dynamic tension. He thought that this enduring tension—found throughout the Western tradition—is most adequately and admirably represented in the "shimmering tension" achieved in the constitutional republic of the United States, in which "order" is upheld and "liberty" protected. In practical political terms, Meyer advocated a "fusion" of various kinds of conservatism. Instead of quarreling among themselves and emphasizing their differences, Meyer argued, conservatives should recognize and appreciate their common intellectual roots and shared aims and aspirations. By forming an alliance or coalition, conservatives of different persuasions could create a united front for opposing their common enemies—communism, socialism, and liberalism—in a more effective way. Meyer made his case primarily in the pages of *The National Review* (of which he was co-editor) and in his book *In Defense of Freedom* (1962). One of Meyer's most ardent admirers and readers was the Hollywood-actor-turned-television-host Ronald Reagan. As governor of California, and later as president, Reagan both preached and practiced what had come to be called "fusionism."

The four aforementioned kinds of conservatism were cobbled together in a powerful but uneasy coalition by President Ronald Reagan in the 1980s that was renewed, twenty years later, by George W. Bush's chief strategist, Karl Rove. Holding the coalition together, however, proved increasingly difficult. Religious right conservatives emphasize "traditional" or "family" values, want prayer in public schools, and the prohibition of abortion, pornography, and same-sex marriage—

all of which would greatly expand the size, scope, and reach of government. Individualist conservatives want to reduce government spending, balance the budget, and generally shrink the size of the government, leaving individuals to live as they please as long as they respect the rights of others. Neoconservatives want a militant and muscular foreign policy that makes maximum use of American power—political, economic, and especially military—in Iraq, Iran, and elsewhere. Traditional or Burkean conservatives, by contrast, prefer a cautious foreign policy and insist that there is nothing "conservative" about engaging in risky "foreign adventures" whose outcomes are uncertain; good intentions, they say, do not guarantee good results.

In the run-up to the 2006 congressional elections—and, even more, after the 2008 and 2012 presidential and congressional elections—this strained coalition threatened to come apart. Religious right conservatives—and Protestant fundamentalists in particular—complained that the Bush administration and the Republican-controlled Congress had not done nearly enough to advance Christian conservative causes such as initiating constitutional amendments banning abortion and same-sex marriage or to affirm that the United States is a "Christian nation." As Dr. James Dobson, the founder and former head of Focus on the Family, lamented that he and other conservative Christians were "extremely disappointed with what the Republicans have done with the power they were given."[37] Individualist conservatives, by contrast, complained that the Bush administration had kowtowed to the religious right while running up record deficits even as it cut taxes, enlarged the federal government's role in education and elsewhere, increased government spending, and launched expensive wars in Iraq and Afghanistan. The prominent conservative columnist and author Andrew Sullivan argues that "the conservative soul" has been lost, or hijacked, by the religious right. "The conservatism I grew up around," Sullivan says, "was a combination of lower taxes, less government spending, freer trade, freer markets, individual liberty, personal responsibility and a strong anti-Communist foreign policy."[38] The conservative Christian "base" of the Republican Party cares much less about these issues than about reinstating God and prayer in the classroom and in outlawing abortion and gay or same-sex marriage. These fundamentalist Christians, Sullivan contends, are the Christian counterpart to radical Islamists: both are absolutely certain that they are right, that God (or Allah) is on their side, and that almost any means are justifiable in attempting to achieve righteous ends. For their part, neoconservatives complain that the Bush administration did not commit nearly enough troops to fight in Iraq and Afghanistan or stand up to nuclear threats from Iran and North Korea. (They have subsequently leveled the same criticisms at President Obama, also chiding him for ruling out torture—or, as they call it, "enhanced interrogation"—as a means of dealing with suspected terrorists, and for even considering closing the American prison at Guantanamo Bay, which he has not yet done.) Traditional conservatives complain that neoconservatives are incautious, imprudent, and arrogant. According to David Keene, former chair of the American Conservative Union and president of the American Rifle Association, "The principal sin of the neoconservatives is overbearing arrogance," inasmuch as they make mistake after mistake and never admit to being wrong.[39]

Besides tensions and disagreements among several kinds of conservatism, there are emerging disagreements within each type. These disagreements are especially sharp within the religious right, where some say, for example, that being "pro-life" means not only opposing abortion but also capital punishment ("Thou shalt not kill" and "'Vengeance is mine,' sayeth the Lord"). Being consistently pro-life, according to some evangelical Christians, also requires "caring for creation" as stewards or caretakers of the natural environment (see the extended discussion of evangelical environmentalism or "creation care" in Chapter 9). Moreover, a small but growing number of evangelical Christians have "come out of the closet" and publicly acknowledged their same-sex orientation. They want to be accepted by and admitted into mainstream evangelical Christian churches; but such acceptance is relatively rare, and most gay evangelicals worship together in their own congregations, meeting mostly in members' homes. They have also created several organizations, such as Soulforce (www.soulforce.org), founded by Reverend Jerry Falwell's former assistant, Reverend Mel White, and they maintain such websites as gaychristian.net.

As these rifts within the religious right indicate, modern conservatism—at least in the United States—is increasingly a house divided. The Reagan-Rove coalition that once proved so powerful is now under considerable strain, and the question facing American conservatives is whether the issues that divide them are stronger than those that bring them together.[40] And, as if this were not division enough, the conservative house became even further divided in the wake of the worldwide economic meltdown that began in 2007 and the 2008 presidential and congressional elections which installed a center-left Democratic president, Barack Obama, and clear Democratic majorities in the Senate and House of Representatives. Invited by the new president to join a bipartisan partnership—particularly for the purpose of stimulating the ailing American economy, aiding automobile manufacturing, and reforming health care and the financial system—most conservative Republican legislators opted for an oppositional role. Many conservative Republican state governors, by contrast, eagerly embraced the president's economic "stimulus package" as providing a positive way forward for their states' sagging economies. Whether, or to what extent, these and other rifts within conservative ranks may be healed remains an open question.

A more recent question concerns the emergence of a militant "Tea Party" movement and its effect on American conservatism. The 2010 congressional elections swept a number of Tea Party Republicans into office, at both the state and national level, and gave the Republican Party control over the House of Representatives. (The 2012 election saw the defeat of several high-profile Tea Party representatives, thereby reducing but not rolling back the Republican majority.) Tea Party conservative candidates claimed to be fiscal conservatives who insisted on deep cuts in the federal budget (except for the military), fiscal austerity, and balanced budgets. Once in office, however, many adopted a more militant social or religious-right agenda to outlaw abortion and even contraception. They are especially incensed by "Obamacare"—President Obama's Affordable Care Act guaranteeing near-universal access to health care—which they view as an unwarranted and unconstitutional "power grab" by the federal government and its "individual mandate" to buy health insurance as an unjustifiable intrusion into individuals' freedom of choice. Interestingly, it was the Heritage Foundation, a leading conservative "Think Tank," that first proposed the individual mandate as a way to ensure individual responsibility to buy health insurance—an idea strongly supported by Republican Speaker of the House Newt Gingrich and subsequently implemented in Massachusetts by Republican Governor Mitt Romney. By the time of the 2012 presidential election, Gingrich, Romney, and all the Republican candidates were outspoken in their opposition to this and other features of "Obamacare," which they and the Tea Party claimed was unconstitutional. But their constitutional claim was dealt a decisive blow by the Supreme Court's 2012 decision declaring the individual mandate to be constitutional—a decision made all the more galling because the decisive vote was cast by the conservative Chief Justice John Roberts. Something similar happened in 2015 when the Supreme Court upheld the constitutionality of providing federal tax subsidies to help poor people to buy health insurance. These decisions and other setbacks, however, have not deterred Tea Party activists from pursuing an agenda that they call "truly conservative." In pursuit of these ends they pride themselves on their ideological purity and their intransigence and unwillingness to compromise—not only with the Democratic Party and the president, but with fellow Republicans whom they consider insufficiently conservative "RINOs" (Republicans in Name Only)— and this has driven yet another divisive wedge within the ranks of American conservatives. These internal divisions and differences became even more evident in the wake of President Obama's reelection in 2012. Tea Party militants claimed that Governor Romney lost the election because he was not "conservative enough." The lesson to be learned from the 2012 election, they say, is to nominate much more conservative candidates in the future.

In the 2016 presidential nomination contest, each of the Republican candidates claimed to be the "real" or "true" conservative, or to be "more conservative" than the others. If nothing else, this serves to show that the meaning of "conservative" and "conservatism" is hotly disputed among conservatives themselves. Two of the leading contenders, Donald Trump and Senator Ted Cruz (Republican, Texas), claimed to be running against the "Republican Establishment" represented by other contenders, Jeb Bush in particular, who, they say, are not "real" conservatives. Other self-described conservatives contended that Trump, in particular, is an "authoritarian populist" and "big-government liberal" in conservative clothing. So claimed *The National Review* in an unprecedented edition (February 15, 2016) titled "Against Trump," consisting entirely of articles by authors who claimed that Trump's nomination would be a disaster for the conservative movement and for the Republican Party, since it would almost certainly ensure the election of a Democratic president.

CONCLUSION

What, then, can we say of the condition of conservatism today? Two points stand out. The first, as we have just seen, is that the different kinds of conservatives coexist in uneasy tension with one another. They can agree and cooperate on some matters, but on others they are deeply divided. Perhaps the most marked division is between the libertarian and religious-right wings of the Republican Party. This is in part a generational difference, pitting young against old. On social issues such as abortion and same-sex marriage, younger libertarian-leaning Republicans disagree, sometimes vehemently, with their elders on the religious right.[41] Such differences have led some to call themselves "conservatarians." They are "conservative" in fiscal matters—favoring free markets, small government, and balanced budgets—and "libertarian" on social issues such as abortion and same-sex marriage.[42] Let us look a little more closely at these contentious issues.

Foremost among these divisive issues are those involving same-sex marriage and **gays** in the military. On these matters the conservative gays of the Log Cabin Republicans are at odds with the religious right. So, too, are individualist or libertarian-leaning conservatives who defend abortion rights and quote the late Arizona Senator and one-time Republican presidential candidate Barry Goldwater, who held that gays should be allowed to serve in the military because "you don't have to be straight to shoot straight!" The issue of same-sex marriage has, if anything, been even more divisive. Those in the more libertarian wing of the party see the decision to marry someone of the same sex simply as a matter of individual choice in which government at any level—local, state, or federal—should have no say. Some traditionalist or Burkean conservatives have constructed a different kind of case for same-sex marriage. The conservative columnist and author David Brooks, for one, holds that the institution of marriage constrains sexual promiscuity and creates a "culture of fidelity" that encourages mutual respect and sacrifice for the sake of one's spouse. "The conservative course," Brooks writes, "is not to banish gay people from making such commitments. It is to *expect* them to make such commitments... We [conservatives] should regard it as scandalous that two people could claim to love each other and not want to sanctify their love with marriage and fidelity."[43] Another prominent conservative, Theodore B. Olson, later made an even more sweeping "conservative case for Gay Marriage."[44] Roundly condemned by religious right conservatives, Brooks and Olson were nevertheless making a classical conservative argument that all human beings, gay or straight, need constraining institutions that will, in Burke's words, "bridle and subdue" our passions.[45] Marriage is certainly such an institution. If society is to be stable and reasonably harmonious, as conservatives agree it should be, then Brooks's and Olson's point—that gay men and lesbians need to be woven into the "social fabric" of American society—has as valid a claim to being "conservative" as the position of their religious right opponents.

The second point to be made about the condition of contemporary conservatism is that such internal quarrels may well be a sign of conservatism's vitality. That people find it worthwhile to argue about what "true" conservatism is and what direction "proper" conservatism should take suggests that conservatism remains a powerful force in the politics of the English-speaking world. For many people who are unhappy with the fruits of liberalism and unsympathetic to the aims of socialism, conservatism remains an attractive ideology.

Conservatism as an Ideology

With all the division and diversity within the conservative camp, does it still make sense to speak of conservatism as a single ideology? In our view it does. For one thing, conservatives are no more divided among themselves than the followers of other ideologies, including liberalism. For another, the differences that distinguish the several varieties of conservatism from one another should not obscure certain "family resemblances" that they all share. These resemblances can be clarified by considering how conservatism performs the four functions of all ideologies: the explanatory, evaluative, orientative, and programmatic functions.

Explanation. For most conservatives, the basis for explaining why social conditions are the way they are is human imperfection. Conservatives do refer to other factors—historical circumstances and economic conditions, for instance, and certainly government policies and cultural trends—but they ultimately trace all these to the frailty of imperfect human nature. If things have gone wrong, it is probably because fallible men and women, acting through government, have tried to do more than humans are capable of doing. If things have gone well, it is because they have kept their hopes and expectations low and proceeded with caution.

Evaluation. But how do we know when things have gone well or poorly? Conservatives usually evaluate social conditions by appealing to social peace and stability. If the relations between the different classes or levels of society are harmonious, so that the leaders display a sense of responsibility to the followers and the followers a sense of loyalty to the leaders, then the social fabric is in good condition. If it is torn by conflict, strife, and bitterness, however, then action must be taken to repair the fraying social fabric.

Orientation. Conservatism tells the individual that he or she is not simply an individual. Each of us is part of a greater whole, and each should realize that he or she must act with the good of the whole society in mind. The best way to do this is usually to play our part in society—to be a good parent or teacher or engineer or plumber and to recognize how each part must blend with all of the others to provide social harmony. Individualist conservatives differ sharply from the others on this point, for they favor competitive individualism. But in this respect, they are much closer to the liberal tradition than the classical conservative tradition of Burke and his heirs.

Program. The political program that conservatives pursue varies from one time and place to another. But the general message of conservatives is to take things slowly and proceed carefully, on the grounds that it is better to do a little good than a lot of harm. In gazing toward the possibilities of a glorious future, conservatives point out, it is all too easy to lose sight of the good things we already enjoy. We should take our eyes off distant horizons in order to appreciate what we have here and now. Once we see this clearly, conservatives say, we will cherish and conserve what we have.

Conservatism and the Democratic Ideal

This desire to preserve the good things a society presently enjoys helps us to see how conservatism, which began with a distinctly antidemocratic attitude, has in the past century come to terms with the democratic ideal. In societies where democracy has become an integral part of the social fabric, of the traditional and customary way of life, conservatives will support democracy. But it will always be a chastened or modest form of representative democracy.

The conservative view of human nature, then, leads to a modest view of what is possible in any political society, including a democracy. Given the weakness of human reason and the strong tendency toward selfishness, conservatives will expect any pure democracy to degenerate into anarchy, followed shortly by dictatorship or despotism. Democracy is acceptable to conservatives, therefore, only when the people generally have limited power and make limited demands. The people must learn self-restraint, or learn at least to place sufficient power to restrain themselves in the hands of those prudent and virtuous women and men who form the natural aristocracy of any society. Instead of turning to demagogues and rabble-rousers, the people must elect cautious, conservative leaders who will exercise their duties with great care for the needs of the people and the delicacy of the social fabric. To do more might be democratic, but it could not be conservative.

Discussion Questions

1 Who uses the imagery of the social fabric, and for what purpose(s)?
2 In the United States, conservatives are usually taken to be people who want less government. Is this an adequate understanding of conservatism in general? Why or why not?
3 Some say that conservatives are so divided among themselves nowadays that it makes no sense of think of conservatism as a single ideology. Are they right to say this? Why or why not?
4 What is "fusionist" conservatism, who formulated it, and for what purpose(s)?
5 What are the major kinds of conservatism in the United States today? Which of them do you find most and least satisfactory? Refer to specific policies and positions as you explain your choices.
6 Some contemporary conservatives call themselves "conservatarians." What do they mean by this? And why do they think it necessary and/or desirable to invent a new category or classification within conservatism?

NOTES

1 Given the growth in government spending, tax cuts, and the resulting deficits during their administrations, due largely to increased military expenditures, neither Thatcher nor Reagan actually achieved this aim.
2 Peter Viereck, *Conservatism: From John Adams to Churchill* (New York: Van Nostrand Reinhold, 1956), p. 19.
3 Anthony Quinton, *The Politics of Imperfection* (London: Faber & Faber, 1978), and N. K. O'Sullivan, *Conservatism* (New York: St. Martin's Press, 1976), Chapter 1.
4 Peter Viereck, *Conservatism Revisited* (New York: Collier Books, 1962), p. 35. See also William Golding's novel, *Lord of the Flies* (1954).
5 Robert Bork, *Slouching Towards Gomorrah: Modern Liberalism and American Decline* (New York: HarperCollins, 1996), p. 21.
6 Isaac Kramnick and Frederick Watkins, *The Age of Ideology: 1750 to the Present*, 2nd ed. (Englewood Cliffs, NJ: Prentice-Hall, 1979), p. 27.

7 Edmund Burke, *Reflections on the Revolution in France*, Conor Cruise O'Brien, ed. (Harmondsworth, U.K.: Penguin, 1968), pp. 194–195; see also Terence Ball, Richard Dagger, and Daniel O'Neill, eds., *Ideals and Ideologies*, 10th ed. (New York and London: Routledge, 2016), selection 4.28.

8 Ibid., p. 91.

9 Burke, "Letter to the Sheriffs of Bristol" (1777) in *Works of the Right Honourable Edmund Burke*, 12 vols. (London: John C. Nimmo, 1899), vol. II, p. 229.

10 Roger Scruton, *The Meaning of Conservatism* (London: Macmillan, 1984), p. 19.

11 Edmund Burke, "Speech on Pillory" (1780), in *The Writings and Speeches of Edmund Burke*, 9 vols. to date (Oxford: Oxford University Press, 1981–2015), vol. III, pp. 583–586, at p. 585. See also *The Correspondence of Edmund Burke*, ed. Thomas W. Copeland, 10 vols. (Chicago: University of Chicago Press, 1958–1978), vol. III, pp. 230–231 and pp. 350–351 (for the quotation from *The Morning Post* newspaper).

12 Edmund Burke, "Speech to the Electors of Bristol" (1774), *Works*, vol. II, p. 95.

13 For an ironic commentary by a twentieth-century conservative on this claim, see Evelyn Waugh's novel, *A Handful of Dust* (1934).

14 Conor Cruise O'Brien, *The Great Melody: A Thematic Biography and Commented Anthology of Edmund Burke* (Chicago: University of Chicago Press, 1992).

15 *Considerations on France*, in Jack Lively, ed., *The Works of Joseph de Maistre* (New York: Macmillan, 1965), p. 78; for a selection from de Maistre's writings, see Ball, Dagger, and O'Neill, *Ideals and Ideologies*, selection 4.29.

16 Quoted in Viereck, *Conservatism*, pp. 165–166.

17 Ibid., p. 44.

18 José Ortega y Gasset, *The Revolt of the Masses* (New York: W. W. Norton, 1932), p. 77. The twin themes of "mass society" and "mass politics" have been sounded by sociologists and social theorists since the nineteenth-century studies of Gustav Le Bon (see Chapter 7) and others. See, for example, William Kornhauser, *The Politics of Mass Society* (Glencoe, IL: The Free Press, 1959), and the historical overview and critical reassessment by Richard Bellamy, "The Advent of the Masses and the Making of the Modern Theory of Democracy," in Terence Ball and Richard Bellamy, eds., *The Cambridge History of Twentieth-Century Political Thought* (Cambridge: Cambridge University Press, 2003).

19 *I'll Take My Stand*, by Twelve Southerners (New York: Harper & Brothers, 1930).

20 Garry Wills, *Confessions of a Conservative* (Garden City, NY: Doubleday, 1979).

21 See Russell Kirk, "Ten Conservative Principles," in Ball, Dagger, and O'Neill, *Ideals and Ideologies*, selection 4.31.

22 See the essays in Oakeshott's *Rationalism in Politics* (London: Methuen, 1962), especially "Political Education" and "On Being Conservative." Most of the latter essay is included in Ball, Dagger, and O'Neill, *Ideals and Ideologies*, selection 4.30.

23 George Will, *Statecraft as Soulcraft: What Government Does* (New York: Simon & Schuster, 1983), pp. 119–120.

24 David Brooks, "The Age of Possibility," *New York Times*, November 16, 2012, p. A29.

25 See www.ronpaul.com/on-the-issues/civil-rights-act.

26 For a historical sketch of the sources and consequences of this and other conservative complaints and warnings, see Albert O. Hirschman, *The Rhetoric of Reaction* (Cambridge: Harvard University Press, 1991).

27 Irving Kristol, *Two Cheers for Capitalism* (New York: Basic Books, 1978).

28 Daniel Bell, *The Cultural Contradictions of Capitalism* (New York: Basic Books, 1976).

29 See, for example, Francis Fukuyama, *America at the Crossroads: Democracy, Power, and the Neoconservative Legacy* (New Haven: Yale University Press, 2006); and Michael Lind, "A Tragedy of Errors," *The Nation*, February 23, 2004, pp. 23–32.

30 William Bennett, ed., *The Book of Virtues: A Treasury of Great Moral Stories* (New York: Simon & Schuster, 1993); James Q. Wilson, *On Character*, 2nd ed. (Washington, D.C.: AEI Press, 1995).

31 Moynihan, "Defining Deviancy Down," in Mark Gerson, ed., *The Essential Neoconservative Reader* (New York: Addison Wesley, 1996), pp. 356–371.

32 Irving Kristol, " 'Family Values'—Not a Political Issue," *Wall Street Journal*, December 7, 1992, p. 14; quoted in Mark Gerson, *The Neoconservative Vision: From the Cold War to the Culture Wars* (Lanham, MD: Madison Books, 1996), p. 270.

33 Ralph Reed, *Politically Incorrect: The Emerging Faith Factor in American Politics* (Dallas, TX: Word Publishing, 1994), pp. 35–36. For more on these themes, see Ronald Reagan, "Modern American Conservatism," in Ball, Dagger, and O'Neill, *Ideals and Ideologies*, selection 4.32; and Robert George et al., "Manhattan Declaration: A Call of Christian Conscience), ibid., selection 4.34.

34 For these and other criticisms, see Isaac Kramnick and R. Laurence Moore, *The Godless Constitution* (New York: W. W. Norton, 2005). See, further, Frank Lambert, *The Founding Fathers and the Place of Religion* in America (Princeton, NJ: Princeton University Press, 2003).

35 For Falwell's remarks, see archives.CNN.com/2001/US/09/14/Falwell.apology, as of August 24, 2012. Apparently, Falwell did not believe that the 1941 Japanese attack on Pearl Harbor and the subsequent invasion and occupation of Alaska's Aleutian Islands of Attu and Kiska (1942–1943) merited mention.

36 John C. Danforth, *Faith and Politics: How the "Moral Values" Debate Divides America and How to Move Forward Together* (New York: Viking Penguin, 2006).

37 David D. Kirkpatrick, "Republican Woes Lead to Feuding by Conservatives," *New York Times*, October 20, 2006, pp. A1, A16.

38 Andrew Sullivan, *The Conservative Soul: How We Lost It, How to Get It Back* (New York: HarperCollins, 2006), p. 2. See also Sullivan's blog at www.andrewsullivan.com.

39 David D. Kirkpatrick, "Republican Woes Lead to Feuding by Conservatives," *New York Times*, October 20, 2006, pp. A1, A16.

40 W. James Antle, III, "The Conservative Crack-up," *The American Conservative* (November 17, 2003).

41 Jonathan Martin, "Young Republicans Find fault with Elders on Social Issues," *New York Times*, March 11, 2014, p. A11.

42 See Charles C. W. Cooke, *The Conservatarian Manifesto* (New York: Crown, 2015).

43 David Brooks, "The Power of Marriage," *New York Times*, November 22, 2003, p. A29.

44 Theodore B. Olson, "The Conservative Case for Gay Marriage," *Newsweek*, January 8, 2010.

45 Edmund Burke, *Reflections on the Revolution in France*, as excerpted in Ball, Dagger, and O'Neill, *Ideals and Ideologies*, selection 4.28.

FOR FURTHER READING

Allitt, Patrick, *The Conservatives*. New Haven: Yale University Press, 2009.

Berlin, Isaiah. "Joseph de Maistre and the Origins of Fascism." In Berlin, *The Crooked Timber of Humanity: Chapters in the History of Ideas*. New York: Vintage Books, 1992.

Buckley, William F., Jr., *Up From Liberalism*. New York: Hillman, 1961.

——, and Charles R. Kesler, eds. *Keeping the Tablets: Modern American Conservative Thought*. New York: Harper & Row, 1987.

Dunn, Charles W., and J. David Woodard. *The Conservative Tradition in America*. Lanham, MD: Rowman & Littlefield, 1996.

Easton, Nina. *Gang of Five: Leaders at the Center of the Conservative Crusade*. New York: Simon & Schuster, 2000.

Gerson, Mark. *The Neoconservative Vision*. Lanham, MD: Madison Books, 1996.

——, ed. *The Essential Neoconservative Reader*. New York: Addison Wesley, 1996.

Goldwater, Barry, *The Conscience of a Conservative*. Shepherdsville, KY: Victor Publishing Co., 1960.

Hayek, Friedrich, *The Road to Serfdom*. Chicago: University of Chicago Press, 1994 [1944].

Hodgson, Godfrey. *The World Turned Rightside Up: A History of the Conservative Ascendancy in America*. New York: Houghton Mifflin, 1996.

Hogg, Quintin. *The Case for Conservatism*. Harmondsworth, U.K.: Penguin, 1947.

Kekes, John. *A Case for Conservatism*. Ithaca, NY: Cornell University Press, 1998.

——. "Conservative Theories." In G. Gaus and C. Kukathas, eds., *Handbook of Political Theory*. London: SAGE, 2004.

Kirk, Russell. *The Conservative Mind: From Burke to Eliot*, 4th ed. New York: Avon Books, 1968.

——, ed. *The Portable Conservative Reader*. Harmondsworth, U.K.: Penguin, 1982.

Kuo, David. *Tempting Faith: An Inside Story of Political Seduction*. New York: Free Press, 2006.

Meyer, Frank S. *In Defense of Freedom*. Indianapolis, IN: Liberty Fund, 1996 [1962].

Nash, George H. *The Conservative Intellectual Movement in America: Since 1945*. New York: Basic Books, 1979.

O'Gorman, Frank. *Edmund Burke: His Political Philosophy*. London: Allen & Unwin, 1973.

O'Neill, Daniel I. *The Burke-Wollstonecraft Debate: Savagery, Civilization, and Democracy*. University Park: Pennsylvania State University Press, 2007.

Rossiter, Clinton. *Conservatism in America: The Thankless Persuasion*, 2nd ed. New York: Random House, 1962.

Sager, Ryan. *The Elephant in the Room: Evangelicals, Libertarians, and the Battle to Control the Republican Party*. New York: John Wiley and Sons, 2006.

Scarborough, Joe. *The Last Best Hope: Restoring Conservatism and America's Promise*. New York: Crown Forum, 2009.

Skocpol, Theda, and Vanessa Williamson, *The Tea Party and the Remaking of Republican Conservatism*. New York: Oxford University Press, 2012.

Steinfels, Peter. *The Neoconservatives*. New York: Simon & Schuster, 1979.

Wills, Garry. *Confessions of a Conservative*. New York: Doubleday, 1979.

USEFUL WEBSITES

American Conservative Union: www.conservative.org

American Enterprise Institute: www.aei.org

Focus on the Family: www.family.org

The Heritage Foundation: www.heritage.org

Project for the New American Century: https://web.archive.org/web/20130609154959/http://www.newamericancentury.org

CHAPTER 5

SOCIALISM AND COMMUNISM: FROM MORE TO MARX

Wherever men have private property and money is the measure of everything, there it is hardly possible for the commonwealth to be governed justly or to flourish in prosperity.

Thomas More, *Utopia*

We cannot improve upon Sir Isaiah Berlin's brief definition of socialism:

> Socialism is a body of Western teaching and practice resting upon the belief that most social evils are due to unequal, or excessively unequal, distribution of material resources; and that these evils can be cured only by the transference, gradual or immediate, total or partial, of the ownership of property and of the means of production, exchange and distribution from private to public control.[1]

Although easily defined, socialism, as we shall see, takes many forms and has a long and rather complex history. So long and complex a history—and socialism's strangeness for many Americans, at least—requires that we devote two chapters to this ideology.

Modern socialism, like **classical conservatism**, began in part as a critique of the liberalism of the late eighteenth and early nineteenth centuries. Like the conservatives, socialists objected to the liberal emphasis on self-interest, competition, and individual liberty. For socialists believed then, as now, that human beings are by nature social or communal creatures. Individuals do not live or work in isolation, but in cooperation with one another. It is cooperation among individuals, not competition between them, that socialists see as the foundation of a society in which everyone can enjoy a decent measure of liberty, justice, and prosperity.

But socialists, unlike classical conservatives, assign no particular value to tradition or custom. Nor do they share the conservative's fondness for private property. From the socialist viewpoint, in fact, private property is the source of the class divisions that place some people in positions of power and privilege while condemning others to poverty and powerlessness. Indeed, socialists usually call for programs that will distribute wealth and power more evenly throughout society—programs that conservatives typically deplore as **levelling**. Everything that people produce, socialists say, is in some sense a social product, and everyone who participates in producing a good is entitled to a share in it. This means that society as a whole, and not private individuals, should own and control property for the benefit of all. That is the fundamental conviction that all socialists share.

But what exactly does this mean? How much property and what kind(s) is society to own and control? To this question different socialists have responded in very different ways. Some suggest that most goods should be regarded as public property; others maintain that only the major means of production—such as large factories and mines should be publicly owned and controlled. Most socialists fall somewhere between these two positions, with no clear point of agreement except on the general principle that anything that contributes significantly to the production, distribution, and delivery of socially necessary goods must be publicly controlled for the benefit of all.

This raises a second question: how is society to exercise this control? It is one thing to say that society as a whole should own and control a power plant but quite another to say just *how* society is to operate this plant. Is *everyone* to take a turn working in the plant, or to have a say in its daily operations? No socialist goes that far. Instead, socialists have generally argued for either **centralized** or **decentralized control** of public property. Those who favor centralized control want to see the state or government assume the responsibility for managing property and resources in the name of the whole society. This was the approach followed in the Soviet Union. This approach promotes efficiency, centralists say, because it gives the state the power to plan, coordinate, and manage the whole economy in the interests of every member of society. Other socialists dispute this claim by pointing to the top-heavy and sluggish bureaucracies that dominate centrally planned economies. As they see it, the best way to exercise control over public property is to decentralize to vest this control in groups at the local level, especially groups of the workers who labor in the factories, fields, and shops and of the consumers who purchase and use the workers' products. These people are the ones who feel most directly the effects of the use of social property, so they should decide how the property is to be used.

Like conservatives and liberals, in short, socialists differ among themselves on important issues. But socialists are united in their opposition to unrestricted **capitalism**, which they believe determines the distribution of power in every society in which it is the dominant form of economic exchange. Poor people have a good deal less power than the rich—less power because they have less ability to control and direct their own lives and to choose where and how to live. In a capitalist society, socialists charge, terms like "freedom" and slogans such as "equality of opportunity" ring hollow for many working people. To see why socialists object to capitalism, then, we need to examine their conceptions of human nature and freedom. With that as background, we shall then explore the history of socialism.

HUMAN NATURE AND FREEDOM

It is often said, especially in the United States, that socialism is contrary to human nature and "opposed to freedom." Socialists dispute both of these claims. They deny, first, that people are by nature competitive and self-interested. If people *appear* to be selfish and competitive, they argue, it is because social circumstances encourage and reward these traits—not because human nature makes us that way. Socialists conceive of human nature as a set of possibilities or potentialities waiting to be realized and perhaps perfected under the right conditions—namely, those prevailing in a post-capitalist socialist society. People are by nature potentially caring and cooperative, and able to take the interests of the entire community as their own. They will readily recognize and attempt to relieve the suffering or oppression of others. And they will work for the common good instead of (or in addition to) their own individual interests. Under capitalism, however, these potentials are not only unrealized, but discouraged, perverted, and distorted beyond all recognition. Capitalist society supplies incentives to encourage—and sometimes to richly reward—selfish and competitive behavior, and to punish or prevent (or at least not reward) selfless and cooperative behavior. In capitalist society selfishness, competition, and the pursuit of individual interests are lauded as "natural," and selfless public-spiritedness as "unnatural." Under capitalism, as the libertarian guru Ayn Rand put it, selfishness is a virtue.[2]

With regard to freedom, socialists are certainly opposed to the liberal-individualist understanding of freedom that we discussed in Chapter 3 and to the conservative's notion of "ordered liberty" described in Chapter 4. But this is because socialists propose an alternative conception of freedom, not because they consider freedom undesirable or unimportant.

The socialist view of freedom can be readily understood by referring once again to our triadic model. For socialists, the *agent* who is to be free is not the abstract or isolated individual, but "individuals in relations." Human beings are by nature and inclination social or communal creatures, socialists say, so we should think of an agent as someone who is connected to and dependent upon other people in various ways. In particular, we should think of agents as individuals engaged in relations of production, distribution, and exchange with others. The agent, in other words, is the producer, or worker, viewed not as an isolated individual, but as a member of a **class**—the working class. Members of the working class share several common *goals*, furthermore, including but not restricted to the following: fulfilling work, a fair share of the product they produce (or the profits thereof), a voice in the management of their affairs, and an equal opportunity for everyone to develop and use his or her talents to their full extent. In pursuing these goals, finally, workers find that the system of capitalist production thwarts their aspirations by throwing various *obstacles* in their way.

These obstacles or barriers can be either material or mental. They include the division of society into a wealthy class of owners and a poorer class of producers who are forced to sell their labor to eke out a subsistence living. People who must devote most of their time and energy merely to making a living can scarcely hope to develop their talents to the fullest. The division of society into classes of unequal political power and economic wealth also results in the sharpening and hardening of class differences that perpetuate these inequalities from one generation to the next. "The rich get richer," the old saying goes, "and the poor get poorer." To the extent that the rich own, or at any rate control, the system of education and information (radio and television stations, newspapers, and so on), they are able to raise and maintain still other obstacles. They can, for example, erect and maintain

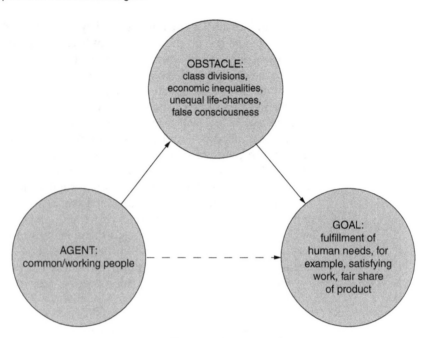

FIGURE 5.1　The socialist view of freedom.

mental barriers by seeing to it that the poor remain ignorant of radical alternatives to the status quo. In this way the members of the poorer classes may be kept in ignorance of their "true" or "real" interests and of the alternative political visions and economic arrangements that might better serve those interests.

To be truly free, then, is to be free from such obstacles and to be free to pursue one's aims and aspirations—so long, that is, as they are not detrimental or harmful to others. Thus one should not be free to make a private profit off the labor of another. Because we are social or communal creatures, it makes no sense to speak of one person's being free and another's not. Either all are free or none is. Karl Marx and Friedrich Engels made this point in *The Manifesto of the Communist Party* when they proclaimed that in a socialist society, "the free development of each is the condition for the free development of all."[3] This conception of freedom, quite different from the liberal view examined earlier, is summarized in Figure 5.1.

SOCIALISM: THE PRECURSORS

The first name likely to be associated with the ideology of socialism, or at least with its communist variant, is that of Karl Marx. Yet socialism predated Marx by many centuries.[4] Plato's *Republic* (circa 380 BCE) presents one early version, although Plato restricted the communal sharing of goods and spouses in his ideal society to a particular class, the Guardians.[5] Early Christians espoused a rather different version of socialism in the first and second centuries AD in the belief that Christians had a duty to share their labor and their worldly goods with one another. This simple form of communism continued in the practices of certain monastic orders up through the Middle Ages and still survives in some monasteries today.

Utopian thinkers such as Sir Thomas More (1478–1535), the Catholic saint and martyr of the early sixteenth century, advocated communal ownership as an antidote to the sins of pride, envy, and greed. Policies that encouraged competition for profits also encouraged these sins, More charged. As a result, most people were poor and powerless, while a few became rich and powerful. Even those few who gained material wealth paid a price, as their pursuit of money and position left them morally and spiritually impoverished. "Wherever men have private property and money is the measure of everything," the principal character of More's *Utopia* (1516) says, "there it is hardly possible for the commonwealth to be governed justly or to flourish in prosperity… I am fully persuaded that no equal and just distribution of goods can be made, and that there can be no true well-being in human affairs, unless private property is outlawed and banished."[6] In Utopia—the ideal but fictional society More depicts in his book—it is. Money is abolished. Every household contributes some good or service to the community and is entitled to withdraw what it needs, free of charge, from common storehouses of grains and other staples. Once the fears of poverty and hunger and homelessness are banished, the foundations of greed and envy disappear.[7] The society that results is indeed, as the punning name **utopia** (from the Greek *eu-topos* or *ou-topos*) suggests, either a "good place" or "no place."

Utopias like More's remained, of course, literary constructs—tributes to the fertile imagination that conceived them, but castles in the air nonetheless. In the aftermath of the English Civil War of the 1640s, however, the real world seemed for a time to be a more hospitable place for radical dreams and utopian schemes. Several communist or socialist sects sprang up during this period. One of them, the Diggers, claimed that God had created the earth for all people to share in common; private property was therefore forbidden by Him and ought to be abolished. "The earth," wrote Gerrard Winstanley, is "a common treasury" from which all are entitled to draw what they need.[8] Proceeding from that premise, the Diggers established communes and began digging the earth to plant crops. But because some of them dug land that was not legally theirs, they soon ran afoul of the law and their communes were forcibly disbanded by the authorities.

These and other views of communist or socialist society were, in the main, agrarian visions. The workers were to be agricultural laborers tilling the land together and sharing in the harvest. But this older agrarian vision was rendered quaint by the coming of the Industrial Revolution. In the late eighteenth and early nineteenth centuries, peasant farmers by the tens of thousands left the land, or in many cases were forced off it, to work in factories, mills, and mines. Steam power replaced horse power; the steamship, the sailing ship; the locomotive, the stagecoach; and the power loom, the spinning jenny. Workers were no longer tied to the seasonal rhythms of the land but to the harsher and more insistent rhythms of the factory. Entire families—fathers, mothers, and small children—worked seventy to eighty hours a week in dirty and dangerous conditions. Ill-housed, often hungry, and sometimes homeless, they led lives of misery and squalor.

Some accepted as inevitable the social disruptions and dislocations brought about by early capitalism, but others rejected them as inhumane and unnecessary evils. Some of the earliest and most vociferous critics of capitalism were political and cultural conservatives such as Thomas Carlyle (1795–1881) and Robert

Southey (1774–1843). The English poet William Blake lamented the "dark satanic mills" that blighted the once-green countryside and polluted the air and poisoned the workers within them. And in *A Christmas Carol* the novelist Charles Dickens embodied in the character of Ebenezer Scrooge the evils of a system that rewarded greed and selfishness. Moral outrage over the excesses of early capitalism led some to become reformers and others to become radicals and revolutionaries. Reform-minded liberals wished to improve working conditions and, if possible, to raise wages. More radical critics of capitalism, by contrast, advocated abolishing a system that produced such vast inequalities of opportunity, freedom, and wealth.

Many, though not all, of these critics were socialists of one stripe or another. In their assault on capitalism, they sounded one or both of two basic themes. One, already noted, was sheer moral outrage; the other was an appeal to science and history, with some socialists claiming that there were half-hidden historical processes at work that were undermining capitalism and paving the way for a future socialist society.

Saint-Simon

One of the first to try to set socialism on a "scientific" basis was the French aristocrat Count Claude-Henri de Saint-Simon (1760–1825). Human history, he held, is divided into successive stages or periods. As an older form of society disappears, a new one necessarily arises to take its place. Each is marked by the presence of particular classes and depends upon certain beliefs. As these beliefs lose credibility, so too does the social and economic system that rests upon them. Thus, said Saint-Simon, **feudalism** was marked by the presence of a landed nobility and a clergy who articulated the religious assumptions and beliefs upon which feudalism rested. These were in turn undermined and eventually replaced by the **Enlightenment** and the coming of industrial society, with its emphasis on science and technology. A new class of scientists, engineers, and industrialists was becoming increasingly important, said Saint-Simon, because without them, there could be no industrial society. This new form of society was enormously complex, depending as it did on the coordinated knowledge and skills of many different types of technicians and experts. In such a society it made no sense to speak, as liberals did, of "the individual." The isolated individual is a fiction. In the real world of the industrial society, individuals are reduced to their social roles and productive functions. In Saint-Simon's version, socialism involves the recognition and appreciation of the fact of social complexity and interdependence, which leads to the application of "positive" scientific knowledge to social and economic planning by an elite of experts.[9]

Saint-Simon did not expressly call for the transfer of property from private to public control, but he did argue that *laissez-faire* capitalism was inefficient because it led to gluts and waste, as people competing for profits produced too much of one good and too little of another. Through planning, Saint-Simon believed, experts could anticipate and thus meet social needs, providing an economic system that was both more efficient and more just than capitalism.

Carrying this idea further still, Saint-Simon's disciple Auguste Comte (1798–1857) called himself a "positivist" and emphasized the importance of scientific planning, prediction, and social control. "From science," he said, "comes prevision; from prevision comes control."[10] With its emphasis on social control, Comte's positivist version of socialism was characterized by a deep aversion to democracy and a fondness for technocracy, or rule by experts. Like Saint-Simon, Comte equated socialism with systematic "scientific" social planning, which was in turn to be justified by a new "religion of humanity" in which scientists were to be the high priests and Comte the pope.[11]

Although Saint-Simon and Comte favored centralized control of social production, other socialists in the early 1800s took the opposite position. Two prominent proponents of a decentralist version of socialism were Charles Fourier and Robert Owen, both of whom inspired disciples to establish short-lived utopian communities in the United States. Fourier and Owen devised schemes for a socialist society that were as visionary as Saint-Simon's and Comte's, but their visions were of small, self-sufficient, self-governing communities in which decisions were made not by experts but by all adult members of the community.

Fourier

Charles Fourier (1772–1837) was a French socialist whose vision of utopia derived from a mixture of mysticism, numerology, and a crude psychological theory. Modern society, he said, is not so far from barbarism as its inhabitants are inclined to believe. It is afflicted with the evils of commerce, selfishness, and deception, among many others (144 of them, to be exact). We not only deceive others, we also deceive ourselves by holding false or mistaken beliefs—especially the belief that wealth will bring happiness. The evils of commercial society, with its mad pursuit of wealth, are embodied in its institutions. The institutions of marriage, the male-dominated family, and the competitive market prevent the satisfaction of the passions, which are twelve in number. These include the passions of the five senses, along with those of familism, friendship, love, and ambition; to these are added the "butterfly" passion that leads us to look for variety, the "cabalistic" passion for plotting and intrigue, and the "composite" passion for combining physical and mental pleasures. There is also a thirteenth, the passion for "harmony" that comes from the proper balance of the twelve basic passions. But a competitive commercial society frustrates our desire for harmony, Fourier insisted. We can never satisfy this passion when we are divided against one another—and against ourselves—by competition for jobs and profits. Only when the evils of this society are overcome will humanity reach its highest stage, "harmonism," in which human beings will cooperate freely for the common good.

Fourier's vision of a harmonious society was captured in his account of the "phalanstery," a community of about 1600—the ideal population, he said, is 1610—in which the residents would produce all they needed and all the passions would be fully satisfied. The phalanstery was based on the principle of "attractive labor," which held that people will work voluntarily if only they find an occupation that engages their talents and interests. Those who like to grow things will be the gardeners. Those who like children will provide day care. And children, who like to play in the dirt, will sweep the streets and collect the garbage. Because people will work freely and spontaneously in these circumstances, the coercive apparatus of the state—laws, police, courts, prisons—will not be needed. Socialist society, as Fourier envisioned it, will be productive, prosperous, and free.

Owen

Robert Owen (1771–1858) was a British capitalist who, appalled by the effects of early capitalism, became an ardent socialist. Drunkenness, debauchery, theft, and other evils were, he held, the result not of **original sin** or of individual character defects but of a deformed social system. By rewarding the greed and selfishness of the capitalist, the capitalist system sent the wrong message to young people. Little wonder, then, that so many people try to advance themselves at other people's expense. The cure for the evils of capitalism can be found not only in a new system of production—cooperative production for public profit—but also in a new system of education. Owen believed that deformed character was the result of defective education—where "education" is understood in the broadest possible sense as the sum of all the formative influences in one's life.

In 1800 in New Lanark, Scotland, Owen established a model textile factory that was radical by the standards of the day. The factory was clean, and working conditions were relatively safe. The workweek was reduced. Children younger than ten not only were not allowed to work but also were educated at the owner's expense. Besides learning the three R's, children learned the value and necessity of cooperation in all aspects of life.

These and other practices Owen described and defended in *A New View of Society* (1813).[12] Over the next ten years he labored tirelessly to persuade his fellow capitalists to see the merits of his proposed system. He also appealed to workers to share his vision of a network of small, self-sufficient communities that would spread around the globe. Owen was more successful with the latter than with the former, who were understandably worried by his attacks on private property and religion and by his growing popularity among the working class. In 1824 Owen took his ideas to North America. On 30,000 acres he had purchased in southwest Indiana, he established the socialist community of New Harmony, which he intended as a model of social organization. Within four years, however, New Harmony had failed, and Owen lost most of his fortune in the venture. He spent the remainder of his life promoting trade unionism and advocating the establishment of worker-owned cooperatives as the nucleus from which a larger and more comprehensive socialist society might grow.

Many other thinkers also dreamed dreams and fashioned schemes for a socialist society. Important though these proponents of **utopian socialism** were, however, none of their efforts proved to be as long-lived and influential as those of Karl Marx. By the middle of the twentieth century, in fact, roughly one-third of the world's population lived under regimes that claimed to be Marxist. It is safe to say, then, that Marx is not only the most important thinker in the history of socialism but one of the most important in all history. That is reason enough to study his views closely and carefully.

Before beginning, we need to note that Marx was in effect two thinkers. The first and more familiar figure is Marx the political activist, arch-foe and critic of capitalism, and revolutionary firebrand. The second and less familiar thinker is

Marx the sociologist and economist, who still occupies a prominent place in the history of those social-scientific disciplines.[13] Marx himself, however, would not recognize this now-common distinction, because he believed that he was the first to put social science in the service of revolution and the coming communist society.

THE SOCIALISM OF KARL MARX

The Young Marx

Karl Marx was born in Trier, in the German Rhineland, in 1818, the son of a lawyer who had abandoned the Jewish faith and converted to Christianity because the government had decreed that no Jew could practice law. Comfortable though not wealthy, the Marx family was able to send their son Karl to the University of Bonn. There he studied law and engaged in the pursuits common to university students, including drinking at the local beer hall, talking politics, and fighting a duel with another student. Alarmed by their son's "wild rampagings" and lack of scholarly seriousness, Marx's parents made him transfer to the more demanding University of Berlin. Marx went on to earn his doctorate in philosophy in 1841, expecting to take up an academic post. But, being a political liberal of Jewish descent in a conservative and anti-Semitic society, Marx's academic aspirations went unfulfilled. He turned to journalism, first as a reporter and then as editor of the liberal *Rheinische Zeitung* (*Rhenish Times*) in 1842. In the following year Marx married his childhood sweetheart and moved to Paris to edit the *Deutsch-Französische Jahrbücher* (*German-French Yearbook*). While in Paris, Marx and Friedrich Engels became friends and collaborators, forming a philosophical and political partnership that lasted almost forty years.

Marx's early career as a muckraking journalist brought about two important changes in his outlook. First, he came to appreciate the central social and political importance of economic matters—of property ownership, of market forces, of the state's systematically favoring the rich over the poor. Second, he ceased to be a liberal and became a radical who believed that the political and economic system of his day was so rotten that it could not be reformed from within. Marx's move toward political radicalism was further hastened by his experience with the police, who censored, confiscated, and finally closed both publications for which he worked and issued a warrant for his arrest. Unable to return to Germany for fear of imprisonment, Marx went into a "temporary" exile that was to last until his death in 1883.[14]

Joking that the German authorities had "given me back my freedom," Marx returned to his philosophical pursuits, plunging into a serious and systematic study of the philosophy of G. W. F. Hegel (1770–1831). The result of these labors, the *Economic and Philosophical Manuscripts* of 1844, remained unpublished during Marx's lifetime. But they reveal quite clearly the enduring influence of Hegel on the main outline and themes of Marx's later work. Because it is nearly impossible to understand Marx's economic and political theory without knowing something about Hegel's philosophy, we need to consider briefly several of its main features.

Karl Marx (1818–1883)

The Influence of Hegel

During his lifetime and for some two decades after his death, Hegel had a virtual monopoly on the German philosophical imagination. It was largely within the framework of his philosophy that educated Germans, especially the young, discussed history, politics, and culture. Hegel's philosophy of history proved to be particularly influential. Human history, Hegel maintained, moves in a particular direction and according to a pattern that can be discerned, at least in hindsight. History is the story of the unfolding or evolution of mind or "spirit" (*Geist*). There is nothing necessarily mystical or spiritual about spirit—any more than there is in our expression "the human spirit" (as, for example, when we say that the first ascent of Mount Everest represented "a triumph of the human spirit"). Spirit, one might say, is a set of potentials waiting to be actualized or developed. The most important of these potentials is the human capacity for freedom. As Hegel saw it, history is the story of spirit's struggle to overcome obstacles in its search for freedom or self-emancipation. In the course of these struggles, spirit itself changes, becoming ever more mature and expansive.

At this point another key concept in Hegel's philosophy—estrangement or **alienation** (*Entfremdung*)—comes into play. Spirit evolves into its higher and more inclusive forms through a succession of separations or alienations. Spirit undertakes a journey, in other words, that resembles the spiritual or psychological development of individual human beings. A newborn baby is at first unable to distinguish itself from its mother. Over time, however, it becomes aware of itself as a separate creature with wants and needs distinct from those of its parents. This transition from infancy to childhood is the first of several alienations through which the individual develops his or her own distinctive personality. And, as with individual biography, so, too, with human history: the human species develops its distinctive characteristics through a series of struggles and successive alienations. Although wrenching and sometimes acutely painful, these changes are necessary if spirit is to grow and develop into new and higher forms.

The various stages through which spirit passes reveal what Hegel called the **cunning of reason** (*List der Vernunft*) and the operation of the **dialectic**. Individual human beings, and even entire nations, are characters in a vast unfolding drama whose plot—the progress of spirit and the growth of freedom—is unknown to them. Each plays his or her part, unaware of how that part fits into the greater whole. The story unfolds "dialectically," through the clash of opposing ideas and ideals. Out of this conflict emerge new and more comprehensive ideas and ideals. Foremost among these is the idea of freedom. In ancient and medieval times, to be "free" was to enjoy a particular legal status, that of free man, from which most people, including slaves and women, were excluded. Through the dialectic of reason, however, freedom becomes, over time, an ever more inclusive idea that old institutions and customs can no longer contain. In its quest for freedom and self-realization, spirit breaks down old social forms and helps to create new ones.

To show how this dialectical process works to promote human freedom, Hegel invites us to imagine the kind of conflict that might develop between a master and slave, the **master-slave dialectic**.[15] According to Hegel's account, the master becomes master by physically conquering another, whom he then enslaves. At first the slave is grateful for having his life spared and fearful that the master might yet take it from him. He sees himself through his master's eyes as inferior, degraded, and dependent. The master, likewise, sees himself through the slave's eyes as superior, ennobled, and independent. Yet each needs the other in order to be what he is: the master must have a slave if he is to be master; and the slave must have a master in order to be a slave. But their relationship is unstable. The slave chafes under his chains and dreams of freedom. He longs to lose his identity as slave and to take on (or to recover) his identity as a free human being. The slave, in other words, wants the master to recognize and acknowledge his humanity, which would in turn require the master to treat the slave as an equal—that is, to free him. Yet the master cannot free the slave without ceasing to be who he is, socially speaking—namely, a master. The master wants the slave to recognize and affirm his identity as master; the slave wants the master to recognize him as an equally worthy human being. Clearly their wants are contradictory in that they are incompatible and cannot both be satisfied. The stage is set for a showdown.

The master at first appears to have the upper hand. He has all the power. He holds the keys to all the locks. He has a monopoly on the means of coercion—the chains, the whips, and other instruments of torture. And yet, when the slave refuses to recognize the master's moral or social superiority, *he* gains the upper hand. In withholding this recognition the slave withholds from the master the one thing that the master wants but cannot compel. From the moment of the slave's refusal their positions are effectively reversed. The master is shown to have been dependent upon the slave all along. Not only did he depend for his livelihood on the slave's labor, but his very identity depended upon the presence and continued subservience of the slave—since, without a slave, he could not even *be* master. So, appearances aside, the master was in fact no more "free" than the slave, because his social role was in its own way restrictive and confining, keeping the master morally stunted and cut off from the humanity that he shares with the slave. Once they both recognize this fact, they cease to be master and slave and the institution of slavery is superseded or surpassed. Stripped at last of their "particularity" (their historically specific social roles), the former master and the former slave confront each other in their "universality" or common humanity as free and equal human beings. In freeing himself, the slave has freed his master as well.

Hegel tells this story to show how the dialectic operates so as to allow the idea of freedom to burst through the confines of a seemingly invulnerable institution. Marx, as we shall see shortly, changes the characters and modifies the story, but the essential story line—the dialectical logic of Hegel's tale—remains unchanged.

Marx's Theory of History

After Hegel's death, his followers split into two main camps. On one side were the conservative Right Hegelians, who interpreted Hegel's philosophy of history in theological terms. For them, "spirit" meant God or the Holy Spirit, and human history meant the unfolding of God's plan. On the other side were the Young or Left Hegelians, Karl Marx among them. They held that Hegel's philosophy was open to a more radical interpretation than Hegel had perhaps realized. So with the hope of revealing "the rational kernel within the mystical shell" of Hegel's philosophy, Marx renewed his study of Hegel in 1843–1844.[16]

Like Hegel, Marx saw history as the story of human labor and struggle. But history, for Marx, is the story not of the struggle of disembodied spirit but of the human species' struggles in and against a hostile world. Humans have had to struggle to survive heat and cold and the ever-present threat of starvation in order to wrest a living from a recalcitrant nature. But human beings have also struggled against each other. Historically, the most important of these conflicts is to be found in the struggle of one class against another. "The history of all hitherto existing society," write Marx and Engels in the *Communist Manifesto*, "is the history of class struggles."[17] Different classes—masters and slaves in slave societies, lords and serfs in feudal society, and later capitalists and workers in capitalist society—have different, if not diametrically opposed, interests, aims, and aspirations. So long as societies are divided into different classes, class conflict is inevitable.

To understand Marx's position here, we need to examine what Marx means by class, how he thought different classes come into being and into conflict, and how he expected a classless communist society to arise. We need, in short, to look closely at Marx's **materialist conception** (or **interpretation**) **of history**, which he called the "leading thread in my studies."[18]

Marx called his interpretation of history "materialist" to distinguish it from Hegel's "idealist" interpretation. Where Hegel had seen history as the story of spirit's self-realization, Marx saw history as the story of class struggles over opposing material, or economic, interests and resources. This does not mean that Marx was, as has sometimes been charged, an "economic determinist" who wished to "reduce everything to economics." He did, however, emphasize the primary importance of material production. "Before men do anything else," he said, "they must first produce the means of their subsistence"—the food they eat, the clothing they wear, the houses they live in, and so on. Everything else, Marx held, follows from the necessity to produce the material means of our subsistence.[19]

Material production requires two things. First, it requires what Marx called the **material forces of production**. These will vary from one kind of society to another. In a primitive hunting society, for example, the forces of production include the wild game and the hunter's bow, arrows, knives, and other tools. In a somewhat more sophisticated agrarian society, the forces of production include the seeds to be planted, the plows, hoes, and other implements used in planting and harvesting the crops, and the tools employed in separating the wheat from the chaff, milling the grain, and baking the bread. In a still more sophisticated industrial society, the productive forces include raw materials (metallic ores, coal, wood, petroleum, and so on), machinery for extracting these materials from their natural state, the factories in which these materials are turned into commodities, and the freight cars and trucks for transporting raw materials to the factories and finished products to market.

In addition to raw materials and machinery—the forces of production—material production requires a second factor that Marx called "the **social relations of production**." Human beings organize themselves in order to extract the raw materials; to invent, make, operate, and repair the machinery; to build and staff the factories; and so on. However primitive or sophisticated, material production requires a degree of specialization—what Adam Smith called the "division of labor" and Marx the social relations of production (or sometimes, for short, "social relations"). Different kinds of societies—or "social formations," as Marx sometimes says—have very different social relations of production. A hunting society, for example, will have hunters—almost always the younger males—who are organized into hunting parties; the females who bear and raise the children and transform the hides into clothing, blankets, and other useful items; and others with still other tasks to perform. In an agricultural society, the social relations of production include those who make the tools, who shoe and harness the horses, who plant the seeds and harvest the crop, who winnow the grain, who grind or mill it, and who bake the bread. The social relations of production in an industrial society are even more complex. They include the miners who extract the ore; the lumberjacks who fell the trees; the railway workers who transport raw materials to the factory; the people who invent, build, operate, and repair the machines;

the bankers and brokers who raise the capital and the investors who invest it; and many others.

Out of these social relations of production the different classes arise. Marx suggests that for purposes of "scientific" social analysis, we can simplify somewhat by imagining any society to contain two antagonistic classes, one of which dominates the other. A slave society has a dominant class of masters and a subservient class of slaves. In feudal society the two contending classes are the feudal lords and their serfs. And in an industrial capitalist society these classes are the capitalists—the **bourgeoisie**, Marx calls them—and the wage-laborers, or **proletariat**. Which class you belong to depends upon your relation to the forces of production. Very roughly, you belong to the subservient class if you are yourself merely a means or a force of production, much as a pit pony or a piece of machinery is. If you own or control the forces of production—including the human forces—then you belong to the dominant class. Less roughly and more precisely, you belong to the subservient or working class if you do not own but are in fact forced to transfer your labor or "labor power" to another for his or her pleasure or profit.

In every class-divided society, Marx notes, the dominant class tends to be much smaller than the dominated class. Slaves outnumber masters, serfs outnumber feudal lords, and workers outnumber capitalists. What the ruling class lacks in numbers, however, it more than makes up for in two other ways. First, the ruling class controls the agents and agencies of coercion—the police, courts, prisons, and other institutions of the state. The modern state in capitalist society is, as Marx puts it, merely the executive "committee for managing the common affairs of the bourgeoisie."[20]

Marx emphasizes, however, that the ruling class does not rule by brute force alone. If it did, it would not rule for long. The longevity and stability of the ruling class's dominance is due to a second and arguably more important factor: it controls the thoughts, the beliefs and ideas—the "consciousness"—of the working class. The material-economic **base** of every society is capped by an **"ideological superstructure"**—a set of ideas, ideals, and beliefs that legitimizes and justifies the arrangements and institutions of that society. These ideas characteristically take a number of forms—political, theological, legal, economic—but their function, in the final analysis, is the same: to explain, justify, and legitimize the division of labor, class differences, and vast disparities of wealth, status, and power that exist within a particular society. In a class-divided society, says Marx, we will always see "ideology" operating for the benefit of the dominant class and to the detriment of the subservient class (see Figure 5.2).

"The ideas of the ruling class," wrote Marx, "are in every epoch the ruling ideas."[21] By this Marx meant that the acceptable "mainstream" ideas in any society tend to serve the interests of the ruling class. Individual members of the ruling class may have their personal and political differences, but as a class they share an overriding interest in maintaining the social and economic dominance of their class. In order to do this they must be able to portray their dominance as normal, natural, and perhaps even necessary. So in ancient Greek society, for example, Aristotle and others said that some people are "slaves by nature"—that is, naturally fitted for no other role than that of slave or servant. Similarly, in the pre-Civil War American South, slaves and potential critics of slavery were taught from the pulpit

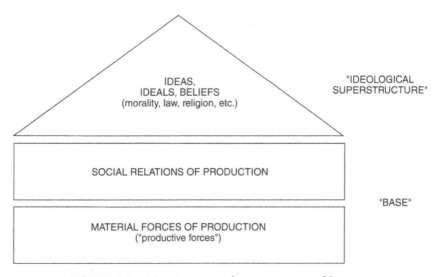

FIGURE 5.2 Marx's materialist conception of history.

that the institution of slavery had been ordained and blessed by God and should not be questioned or criticized. In modern capitalist societies, Marx claims, people internalize the ideas that serve the interests of the ruling capitalist class. These include religious ideas, such as that this world is a "vale of tears," that God loves the poor and the meek, who, if they walk humbly with their God in this life, will go to heaven in the next. Marx called religion **"the opium of the people"** because it dulls their minds and makes them uncritical of the wretched conditions in which they live. People living in capitalist society are also taught that it is "human nature" to be self-interested, acquisitive, and competitive. Moreover, Marx says, they learn to equate "freedom" with "the only unconscionable freedom—free trade"—the freedom to compete, to make a profit without "interference" from the government, and to enjoy the unequal blessings bestowed by the "free enterprise" system. The entire educational system, from kindergarten through college, hammers these lessons home. College professors, no less than lawyers and priests, are unwitting participants in this process of ideological indoctrination. Finally, the mainstream and mass-circulation media in capitalist societies portray capitalist relations of production as normal, natural, and necessary, and noncapitalist alternatives, such as socialism or communism, as unnatural, abnormal, aberrant, and unworkable.

In all of these ways, Marx maintained, the working class is kept from forming a true picture of its real situation. It mistakenly takes the ideas of the ruling class as its own. The working class suffers, in short, from **false consciousness**. As long as it does so, it will be a class "in itself"—that is, a class as yet unaware of its own interests and revolutionary political possibilities—but not yet "for itself." To see how the working class might overcome its false consciousness, and in the process become a class for itself ready to make a revolution against the ruling class, we need to examine Marx's critique of capitalism and his theory of revolution.

Marx's Critique of Capitalism

Although an outspoken critic of capitalism, Marx conceded that capitalism was at one time a progressive and even radical force: "The bourgeoisie, historically, has played a most revolutionary part."[22] In its early phase, he said, capitalism had performed three important and historically progressive functions.

First, in the late feudal period merchant capitalists hastened the demise of feudalism by breaking down trade barriers and opening new trade routes to Africa and the Orient. They were also instrumental in the European discovery of the New World: Columbus, after all, was looking not for America but for a shorter trade route by which to bring back tea, silk, and spices from the East Indies. Kings and aristocrats often found themselves in debt to newly wealthy merchant capitalists, who frequently forced legal and political concessions from them. In short,

> The bourgeoisie, wherever it has got the upper hand, has put an end to all feudal, patriarchal, idyllic relations. It has pitilessly torn asunder the motley feudal ties that bound man to his "natural superiors," and has left remaining no other nexus [i.e., connection] between man and man than naked self-interest, than callous "cash payment." It has drowned the most heavenly ecstasies of religious fervor, of chivalrous enthusiasm, of Philistine sentimentalism in the icy water of egotistical calculation. It has resolved personal worth into exchange value, and in place of the numberless indefeasible chartered freedoms [of feudalism], has set up that single, unconscionable freedom—free trade. In one word, for exploitation, veiled by religious and political illusions, it has substituted naked, shameless, direct, brutal exploitation.[23]

Strange as it may seem, Marx views these as progressive moves—painful but necessary steps that will lead eventually to a more just and nonexploitative society.

Capitalism has been a progressive force in a second respect. It has made human beings masters over nature. Capitalism "has been the first [economic system] to show what man's activity can bring about. It has accomplished wonders far surpassing Egyptian pyramids, Roman aqueducts, and Gothic cathedrals; it has conducted expeditions that put in the shade all former exoduses of nations and crusades." In sum,

> The bourgeoisie, during its rule of scarce one hundred years, has created more massive and more colossal productive forces than have all preceding generations together. Subjection of nature's forces to man, machinery, application of chemistry to industry and agriculture, steam navigation, railways, electric telegraphs, clearing of whole continents for cultivation, canalization of rivers, whole populations conjured out of the ground—what earlier century had even a presentiment that such productive forces slumbered in the lap of social labor?[24]

A third and closely related respect in which capitalism has proved to be a progressive force resides in its need for innovation and change. To remain profitable, industry must have new and more efficient machinery. These changes in the material forces of production bring about changes in the social relations of production, and thereby in the wider society:

> The bourgeoisie cannot exist without constantly revolutionizing the forces of production, and thereby the relations of production, and with them the whole relations

of society… Constant revolutionizing of production, uninterrupted disturbance of all social conditions, everlasting uncertainty and agitation distinguish the bourgeois epoch from all earlier ones. All fixed, fast-frozen relations, with their train of ancient and venerable prejudices and opinions, are swept away, all new-formed ones become antiquated before they can ossify. All that is solid melts into air, all that is holy is profaned, and man is at last compelled to face with sober senses his real conditions of life and his relations with his kind.[25]

In all of these respects, Marx contends, capitalism has been a progressive force for the good.

But if capitalism has been beneficial, why is Marx so critical of it? And why does he think that capitalism should be overthrown and replaced? Of the many reasons Marx gives for doing so, the following three are of special importance.

First, Marx claims that capitalism is outmoded. Although it was once progressive, capitalism has outlived its usefulness and now needs to be superseded. Just because capitalism represents an improvement over feudalism does not mean that no further advance is possible, desirable, or necessary. Just as adolescence prepares the way for adulthood, so, Marx maintains, capitalism has prepared the way for an even higher and freer form of society—communist society.

Second, Marx contends that capitalism creates alienation. As we noted earlier, the concept of alienation or estrangement loomed large in Hegel's philosophy of history. Marx also makes "alienation" central to his critique of capitalism. But Marx has a somewhat different understanding of alienation. In his view, it is not "spirit" that is alienated from itself, but people who are alienated from their work and from one another. The sense of alienation felt by the working class will eventually help to bring about the downfall of capitalism and the coming of communism.

Under capitalism, Marx maintains, workers are alienated in four distinct but related ways. (1) Because they are forced to sell their labor and do not own either the means of production (machinery, factories, etc.) or what they produce, they are alienated from the product of their labor. (2) Because the capitalist system of mass production kills the creative spirit, workers cannot find satisfaction in their labor and are therefore alienated from the activity of production itself. The worker becomes "an appendage of the machine."[26] (3) Workers are alienated from their distinctively and uniquely human potentials or "powers"—particularly the power to create and enjoy beauty—which are dulled or remain undeveloped in capitalist society. More specifically, humans have the ability to create objects that they have imagined beforehand, under circumstances of their own choosing. For Marx, what distinguishes humans from other animals is that humans do not necessarily have to produce driven blindly by an unthinking instinct for survival, but can produce freely as a means of self-expression and self-realization. Sadly, capitalism reduces work to mere necessity, robbing it of freedom and beauty, and thereby diminishes human life to a lower form of animal life. (4) Capitalism alienates workers from one another, inasmuch as it makes them compete for jobs and this competition in turn drives down wages.

But the workers are not the only ones who are alienated. Marx suggests that the capitalists, like the master in Hegel's tale of the master and slave, also suffer from alienation. With all their material comforts, they think themselves free and fulfilled; but in fact they are not. They are, according to Marx, mere "appendages" to capital. They are not its master but its slave. The capitalists bow to *their* master, the almighty market, and tailor their actions accordingly. Far from being free, their actions are determined by forces outside their control. A capitalist, as an individual and a citizen, might wish to invest capital in her or his own country; but if more money can be made by investing abroad and moving jobs there, that is what a rational capitalist will do. And, Marx reasoned, since capital has no fatherland, capitalists have no fatherland; and workers should realize that they don't either.

Third, Marx maintains that capitalism is self-subverting. The operation of the capitalist system has an iron logic that holds everyone—even the capitalist—in its grip. It keeps the capitalist from being a fully developed, kind, and caring human being and makes him or her instead a cold and callous calculating machine. Yet Marx insists repeatedly that he is not criticizing capitalism on moral grounds, nor is he questioning the moral character of capitalists as individuals or even as a class. His supposedly "scientific" critique of capitalism aims to show how the logic of capitalism constrains the actions of everyone, including the capitalists themselves. This constraint is especially evident in the way in which the system operates to keep workers' wages to a minimum subsistence level. "The average price of wage labor is the minimum wage, i.e., that quantum of the means of subsistence which is absolutely requisite to keep the laborer in bare existence as a laborer."[27] Capitalists keep wages low not because they are immoral or cruel, but because the logic of the system requires them to do so.

We can illustrate Marx's point by imagining two factories owned by competing capitalists. Both produce the same product—steel, say. One day, one of the capitalists takes pity on his workers. He raises their wages, shortens the working day, improves working conditions, installs safety equipment, adds a clinic and a day-care center. His competitor does none of these things. The result? The kindly capitalist goes out of business, his workers lose their jobs, and his heartless competitor flourishes. Why? Because to pay for these improvements he must either raise the cost of his product, which drives away consumers, or he must reduce his profit margin, which drives away investors, who want the largest possible return on their investment. The kindly capitalist, now bankrupt, is forced into the ranks of the workers. His competitor, by contrast, grows even richer. He and others like him corner ever-larger shares of their respective markets, resulting in reduced competition and a tendency toward **monopoly**. Such, according to Marx, is the logic of capitalism.

The point of this imaginary tale is that, under capitalism, worker and capitalist alike are alienated from the full and free development of their human powers. Yet they are prevented from seeing this because, under capitalism, nothing is what it appears to be; everything is "inverted."[28] Fair seems foul and foul seems fair. In this topsy-turvy world the market is free, but individuals are not. "In bourgeois society," says Marx, "capital is independent and has individuality, while the living person is dependent and has no individuality."[29] The workers *appear* to exchange their labor voluntarily for a daily wage. In reality, however, they are forced by fear of unemployment and eventual starvation to work for a subsistence wage. Capitalists *appear* to be free to act as they please. But in fact they are in the grip of forces beyond their control. Like the Sorcerer's Apprentice, the capitalists have grabbed hold of a broom that will soon sweep them away.[30]

Marx contends that capitalism has created conditions and unleashed forces that will one day destroy it. In particular, capitalism has created its own "grave diggers" by creating a class—the proletariat—with interests implacably opposed to its own, a class with everything to gain and nothing to lose by revolting against the ruling bourgeoisie. Yet, ironically, it is the bourgeoisie who are responsible for their own downfall, for they brought the workers together in the first place and then taught them to combine their labor and cooperate in the production of commodities. The workers eventually come to think of themselves as a unified class with common interests and a common class enemy, the bourgeoisie. They will then make the revolution that will overthrow capitalism and lead eventually to the creation of a classless communist society.

Before examining the goal—the coming of a communist society—we need to look more closely at the process by which Marx believed that it would be achieved. Let us look first at the bare essentials of Marx's "dialectical" story line, and then, second, fill in the more concrete social, economic, and political factors that lead to the revolutionary sequence in which capitalism is abolished and society radically transformed.

The Dialectic of Change

How, exactly, did Marx view the process that would bring about the momentous change from a competitive capitalist society to a cooperative communist society? Here we need to remember Marx's debt to Hegel, and particularly to Hegel's notion that history, in moving dialectically, exhibits the "cunning of reason." Capitalists and proletarians are characters enmeshed in a drama whose plot and ending they do not know. As we noted earlier, the plot of this drama resembles that of Hegel's parable of the master and the slave. Once again, of course, the actors are not individuals but two great contending classes—the bourgeoisie and the proletariat.

In Marx's retelling of Hegel's parable, the capitalist replaces the master and the worker the slave. The worker is in fact enslaved, though at first he or she does not know that. Grateful to the capitalist for a job, and fearful of losing it, the worker feels indebted to, and dependent upon, the capitalist. The worker also accepts the capitalist's view of the world and their respective places in it. In this view, the capitalist is credited with "creating" a job that he then "gives" to the lucky worker. Because the capitalist pays a wage in exchange for the worker's labor, the relationship *looks* like a reciprocal one. But the appearance is misleading. The capitalist exploits the worker by paying less than his or her labor is worth. By "extracting surplus value"—Marx's phrase for paying workers less than their labor is worth—the capitalist is able to live luxuriously, while the worker barely ekes out a living. Their relationship, though ostensibly reciprocal, is far from equal. The worker is impoverished, even as the capitalist is enriched. The poorer the proletariat, the richer the capitalist class, the bourgeoisie.

Under these conditions the worker feels a sense of unease. Often hungry and always insecure, the laborer begins to ask why his or her lot in life is so inferior to the capitalist's. The capitalists' stock answer—that they are rich because they have worked harder and saved more, and anyone who does so can become a capitalist, too—begins to ring hollow. After all, it would be impossible—logically impossible—for everyone to become a capitalist, no matter how hard he or she worked or how much he or she saved. Some people (most, in fact) must be workers if capitalism is to survive as a system. Reflecting on this idea, the worker eventually realizes that the fault lies not in him- or herself, not in the "stars" or "nature" or "fate," but in capitalism itself—a system that enriches the capitalist even as it stunts the mental and moral development of the worker. The worker, who had begun by believing that he or she needed the capitalist, now realizes, on reflection, that capitalists need the workers, without whose labor no wealth can be created—and without which they would lose their very identity as capitalists. The capitalist is therefore dependent upon the worker.

The obverse is of course equally true: without the capitalist class there would be no working class. The capitalist, understandably, wishes to maintain this state of affairs. The worker, by contrast, comes to realize that gaining freedom and overcoming alienation require the abolition of the two contending classes—bourgeoisie and proletariat. Abolition does not mean that their members must be killed but that the conditions that create and maintain class differences must be eliminated. One class must cease to exploit and profit from the labor of the other. But this, Marx notes, means that classes will cease to exist. Class divisions are by their very nature exploitative; eliminate exploitation and you eliminate classes, and vice versa.

The proletariat is unique, Marx says, because it is the only class in modern society that has an interest in abolishing itself. Instead of seeking to preserve itself as a class—as the bourgeoisie does—the proletariat seeks to abolish class rule by abolishing all class distinctions. The proletariat is, in Marx's view, the "universal class" because, in serving its interests, it serves the interests of all humanity.[31] It is in the workers' interest to abolish the working class—a class that is impoverished, despised, and degraded—and to become free and equal human beings. In freeing themselves, moreover, they free their former masters as well. They achieve at last "the free development of all."[32]

For Marx, then, true freedom—freedom from exploitation and alienation, the freedom to develop one's human powers to their fullest—can flourish only in a classless society. It is just this kind of society that workers have an interest in bringing about. But how, according to Marx's account, are they able to overcome false consciousness and to discover what their "true" interests are? How does the proletariat come to be a class "for itself," equipped with a revolutionary class consciousness? What, in short, are the actual steps or stages in the revolutionary sequence that leads to the overthrow of capitalism and the creation of a classless communist society? And, not least, what will communist society look like?

The Revolutionary Sequence

Marx predicted that proletarian revolution, though eventually worldwide, would begin in the more advanced capitalist countries and proceed in a fairly definite order. The stages in the revolutionary sequence can be outlined as follows (see Figure 5.3).

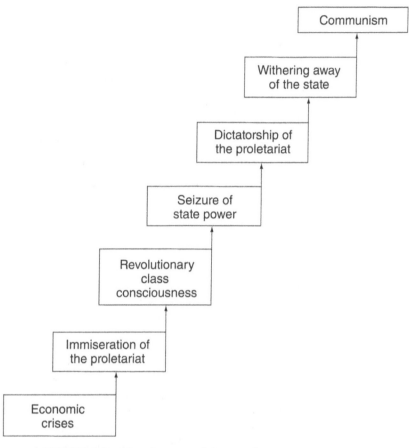

FIGURE 5.3 Marx's view of the revolutionary sequence.

Economic Crises. Capitalism, as Marx was by no means the first to observe, is plagued by periodic economic downturns—recessions and depressions. "Bourgeois" economists call these "fluctuations" in "the business cycle" that will, in time, correct themselves. Marx, by contrast, believed that these crises were due to the "anarchy of production" that characterizes capitalist society.[33] The more mature or advanced a capitalist society becomes, the more frequent and severe these crises will be—and the less likely they are to correct themselves.

Immiseration of the Proletariat. The bourgeoisie, being wealthier, is better able to weather these crises than are the workers. Recessions and depressions deprive workers of their jobs, their income, and finally their food and shelter. Unable through no fault of their own to find work, some resort to begging, others to petty thievery for which they risk imprisonment or even death, and still others die of starvation. However miserable their lot as workers, they become even more miserable when they lose their jobs. This process, the **immiseration of the proletariat**, is inescapable in capitalist society, according to Marx.

Revolutionary Class Consciousness. The workers in their misery begin to realize that the fault lies not with them but with the system—a system beset by "contradictions" too glaring to pass unnoticed. They are willing to work, but there are not enough jobs to go around. The bourgeois "coupon clippers" who do not work are nevertheless comfortable and affluent. Their children, well fed and warmly clothed, go to school; the workers' children—malnourished, hungry, and ill-clad—beg in the streets and dig through garbage for scraps of food. Seeing these contradictions leads workers to reflect critically on the causes of their misery. In this process, moreover, Marx's theory intervenes to make a contribution of its own: it supplies an explanation of how things came to be this way. It also proposes a solution: the overthrow of the ruling bourgeoisie. Because Marx believed that the workers would sooner or later arrive at this conclusion on their own, he saw himself as merely a "midwife" reducing the "birth pangs" by hastening the revolutionary process along the most direct and least painful course.

Seizure of State Power. Marx predicted that "objective" economic conditions (the economic crises resulting in the immiseration of the proletariat) and "subjective" conditions (revolutionary class consciousness) would combine to form a politically explosive mixture. Beginning with apparently unrelated, small, spontaneous strikes, boycotts, demonstrations, and riots, the revolutionary movement quickly coalesces into a more militant, organized, and unified force for the overthrow of the ruling class. Marx believed that this situation could come about in a number of ways. One possibility is that a nationwide "general strike" will cripple the economy and bankrupt the capitalists almost overnight. Another possibility is a bloody civil war pitting capitalists, soldiers, and police against armed proletarians. A third possibility, albeit an unlikely one (except perhaps in England, Holland, and the United States, Marx said), is that the bourgeoisie will be overthrown not by bullets but by ballots in a free and fair election.[34] In any case, the workers have the advantage of solidarity and sheer force of numbers. The struggle will be protracted, difficult, and probably violent. But, by whatever means, the proletariat will at last take state power out of the hands of the bourgeoisie and into their own.

Dictatorship of the Proletariat. Having seized state power, the proletariat proceeds to establish what Marx called the **revolutionary dictatorship of the proletariat**. By this inflammatory phrase, Marx meant merely this: the bourgeois state, being a system of class rule, amounts to the dictatorship of the bourgeoisie over the proletariat. When the workers take state power into their hands, they become the new ruling class. The workers, in other words, will rule in their own interest. Their most pressing interest would be to preserve the gains of the revolution and prevent the defeated bourgeoisie from regrouping and mounting (possibly with outside assistance) a counterrevolution to regain power. The working class must, accordingly, use the apparatus of the state—the schools, courts, prisons, and police—in as "dictatorial" a manner as necessary to prevent this counterrevolution. Marx expects the victorious workers to be democratic and open in their dealings with one another. Theirs is to be a dictatorship of and by, not over, the proletariat.

Withering Away of the State. In one of his later writings, *Critique of the Gotha Program*, Marx states that the proletariat's defeat of the bourgeoisie will inaugurate a transitional period that will take society from capitalism to full-fledged communism. Because the old competitive ways of thinking typical of bourgeois society will not disappear immediately, this first or transitional form of communism will include not only the dictatorship of the proletariat but also continued use of wage incentives to encourage people to work hard. In this first phase of communism, according to Marx, the rule should be "from each according to his ability, to each according to his labor." But the abiding interest of the proletariat, the "universal class," is in abolishing classes and class distinctions. This abolition will begin once the workers take control of the workplace and transform the conditions of labor, ending exploitation and alienation. As the bourgeoisie die out, or see the errors of their ways, the need for coercion will gradually fade. Marx expects, then, that "the dictatorship of the proletariat" will lose its reason for existing and simply "wither away" as communism achieves its full or mature form.

Communism. Marx said remarkably little about the specific features of this future communist society. One reason for this is that he—unlike earlier utopian socialists, with their detailed blueprints—refused to write "recipes for the kitchens of the future."[35] The shape of any future society, Marx thought, could only be decided by the people who would inhabit it. Even so, Marx did hint at several features that he thought such a society will have. For one, it will be open and democratic, with all citizens taking an equal and active part in governing it. For another, the major means of production—mills, mines, factories, and so on—will be publicly owned. Economic production will be planned and orderly. And distribution of goods and services will be based not on privilege or wealth, but on ability and need. Under **communism**, then, the rule will be "from each according to his ability, to each according to his need." People living in a communist society will at last be truly free. Having overcome the obstacles of exploitation, alienation, and ideological illusions, that is, they will be free to develop their many-sided personalities. Marx thus envisioned a future society in which every human being, not just a fortunate few, will be free to become well-rounded Renaissance men and women:

> In communist society, where nobody has one exclusive sphere of activity but each can become accomplished in any branch he wishes, society regulates the general production and thus makes it possible for me to do one thing today and another tomorrow, to hunt in the morning, fish in the afternoon, rear cattle in the evening, criticize after dinner, just as I please, without ever becoming hunter, fisherman, shepherd or critic.[36]

Marx died in 1883—too early to witness attempts to put his ideas into political practice. Others, however, calling themselves Marxists and claiming to speak in his name, were soon busy interpreting, reinterpreting, and adapting his ideas in ways that would almost certainly have astonished, and in some cases appalled, Karl Marx. Whether Marx would have liked it or not, he gave rise to Marxism. And Marxism after Marx, as we shall now see, has had an interesting career of its own.

Discussion Questions

1   Who spoke of "the cunning of history," and what did he or she mean by this phrase?
2   What is the materialist conception of history? Who formulated it and for what purpose(s)?
3   By what sequence of events did Marx believe that communism would come about?
4   Who called religion "the opiate of the masses," and why? Be specific.
5   What did Marx and Hegel mean by alienation? How and why is this concept important to Marx's theory?
6   What does Marx mean by consciousness (class consciousness, false consciousness, etc.), and how is this concept important to Marx's theory?

NOTES

1   Isaiah Berlin, "Socialism and Socialist Theories," in Berlin, *The Sense of Reality: Studies in Ideas and Their History* (New York: Farrar, Straus and Giroux, 1996), p. 77.
2   See Ayn Rand et al., *The Virtue of Selfishness* (New York: Signet Books, 1964).
3   As printed in Lewis Feuer, ed., *Marx and Engels: Basic Writings on Politics and Philosophy* (Garden City, NY: Doubleday Anchor, 1959), p. 29; also in Terence Ball, Richard Dagger, and Daniel O'Neill, eds., *Ideals and Ideologies: A Reader*, 10th ed. (New York and London: Routledge, 2016), selection 5.37.
4   For two histories of socialism with very different emphases, see Alexander Gray, *The Socialist Tradition: Moses to Lenin* (London: Longman, 1947) and George Lichtheim, *A Short History of Socialism* (New York: Praeger, 1970).
5   Plato, *The Republic* (Books III and IV, 412 b–421 c).
6   Thomas More, *Utopia*, J. Churlton Collins, ed. (Oxford: Clarendon Press, 1904), pp. 43–44. More wrote *Utopia* in Latin, and Collins reprints Ralph Robynson's translation of 1551. We have altered this translation, especially the spelling, to bring it up to date, as we do in the selection from *Utopia* in Ball, Dagger, and O'Neill, *Ideals and Ideologies*, selection 5.35.
7   Ibid., p. 68.
8   Gerrard Winstanley, *A New Yeers Gift for the Parliament and Armie* (1650); reprinted in David Wootton, ed., *Divine Right and Democracy* (Harmondsworth, U.K.: Penguin Books, 1986), pp. 317–333, 318. See also Winstanley, *The Law of Freedom* ([1652] New York: Schocken Books, 1973).
9   Saint-Simon, *Social Organization, The Sciences of Man, and Other Writings*, Felix Markham, ed. (New York: Harper Torchbooks, 1964).
10   Auguste Comte, *Auguste Comte and Positivism: Selections from His Writings*, Gertrude Linzer, ed. (New York: Harper & Row, 1975), p. 88.
11   See Frank E. Manuel, *The Prophets of Paris* (Cambridge, MA: Harvard University Press, 1962). For a scathing liberal-individualist critique of Comte, see John Stuart Mill, *Auguste Comte and Positivism* (Ann Arbor: University of Michigan Press, 1961). Karl Marx was no less critical of Comte's *"Scheiss positivismus"* (shit positivism): Marx to Engels, July 7, 1866, in Karl Marx and Friedrich Engels, *Werke* (Berlin: Dietz Verlag, 1968), vol. 31, p. 234.
12   Robert Owen, *A New View of Society and Other Writings*, G. D. H. Cole, ed. (London: E. P. Dent, 1927); for an excerpt, see Ball, Dagger, and O'Neill, *Ideals and Ideologies*, selection 5.36.
13   See Raymond Aron, *Main Currents in Sociological Thought*, 2nd ed. (New Brunswick: Transaction Publishers, 1999), 2 vols., vol. I.
14   David McLellan, *Marx: His Life and Thought* (London: Macmillan, 1973).

15 G. W. F. Hegel, *Phenomenology of Mind*, trans. J. B. Baillie (New York: Harper & Row, 1967), pp. 228–240.

16 Karl Marx, *Capital* (New York: International Publishers, 1967), vol. I, "Afterword to the Second German Edition," p. 20.

17 Marx and Engels, *The Manifesto of the Communist Party*, in Lewis Feuer, ed., *Marx and Engels: Basic Writings on Politics and Philosophy* (Garden City, NY: Doubleday Anchor, 1959), p. 7; also in Ball, Dagger, and O'Neill, *Ideals and Ideologies*, selection 5.37.

18 From the Preface to Marx's *Contribution to the Critique of Political Economy* in Ball, Dagger, and O'Neill, *Ideals and Ideologies*, selection 5.38.

19 All quotations in this paragraph are from Marx and Engels, *The German Ideology*, Part I (New York: International Publishers, 1947).

20 *Manifesto*, p. 9.

21 *The German Ideology*, p. 39; *Manifesto*, p. 26.

22 *Manifesto*, p. 9.

23 Ibid., pp. 9–10.

24 Ibid., p. 12.

25 Ibid., p. 10.

26 Ibid., p. 14.

27 Ibid., p. 22.

28 *The German Ideology*, p. 14.

29 *Manifesto*, p. 22.

30 Ibid., pp. 12–13.

31 "Critique of Hegel's Philosophy of Right," in Feuer, ed., *Marx and Engels*, pp. 141–142.

32 *Manifesto*, p. 29.

33 Ibid., p. 32.

34 Karl Marx, "Speech on the Hague Congress," September 8, 1872, in Karl Marx, *Political Writings*, vol. III: *The First International and After*, David Fehrnbach, ed. (New York: Vintage Books, 1972), p. 324.

35 Marx, *Capital*, vol. I, p. 17.

36 *The German Ideology*, p. 22.

FOR FURTHER READING

Ackroyd, Peter. *The Life of Thomas More*. New York: Doubleday, 1998.

Avineri, Shlomo. *The Social and Political Thought of Karl Marx*. Cambridge: Cambridge University Press, 1968.

Ball, Terence, and James Farr, eds. *After Marx*. Cambridge: Cambridge University Press, 1984.

Berlin, Isaiah. *Karl Marx: His Life and Environment*, 4th ed. Oxford: Oxford University Press, 1978.

Carver, Terrell. *Marx's Social Theory*. Oxford: Oxford University Press, 1982.

Cohen, G. A. *Karl Marx's Theory of History: A Defense*. Princeton, NJ: Princeton University Press, 1978.

Cohen, G. A. *Why Not Socialism?* Princeton, NJ: Princeton University Press,, 2011.

Eagleton, Terry. *Why Marx Was Right*. New Haven, CT: Yale University Press, 2011.

Gilbert, Alan. *Marx's Politics: Communists and Citizens*. New Brunswick, NJ: Rutgers University Press, 1981.

Kolakowski, Leszek. *Main Currents of Marxism*. 3 vols., trans. P. S. Falla. Oxford: Clarendon Press, 1978.

Manuel, Frank E. *The Prophets of Paris*. Cambridge, MA: Harvard University Press, 1962.

McLellan, David. *Karl Marx: His Life and Thought*. London: Macmillan, 1973.

Singer, Peter. *Marx*. Oxford: Oxford University Press, 1980.

Taylor, Keith. *The Political Ideas of the Utopian Socialists*. London: Cass, 1982.
Wilson, Edmund. *To the Finland Station*. New York: Doubleday Anchor, 1953.

From the Ball, Dagger, and O'Neill Reader *Ideals and Ideologies*, Tenth Edition

Part V: Socialism and Communism: More to Marx

5.35 Thomas More—Utopia
5.36 Robert Owen—Address to the Inhabitants of New Lanark
5.37 Karl Marx and Friedrich Engels—The Communist Manifesto
5.38 Karl Marx—On the Materialist Conception of History

USEFUL WEBSITES

Hegel, Stanford Encyclopedia of Philosophy: http://plato.stanford.edu/entries/hegel
Marx, Stanford Encyclopedia of Philosophy: http://plato.stanford.edu/entries/marx

CHAPTER 6

SOCIALISM AND COMMUNISM AFTER MARX

The Marxist doctrine is omnipotent because it is true. It is comprehensive and harmonious, and provides men with an integral world outlook irreconcilable with any form of superstition, reaction, or defense of bourgeois oppression.

V. I. Lenin, *Three Sources and Components of Marxism*

In the early twenty-first century, socialism—especially of the top-down, authoritarian, central-planning variety—seems to be an idea whose time has passed. In the early twentieth century, by contrast, socialism seemed to many in Europe and North America to be an idea whose time had come. The period from Marx's death in 1883 until the outbreak of World War I in 1914 was a time of intense political and theoretical ferment—and growing popular support for socialism and socialist parties. One observer has called this the "golden age" of socialism, and of Marxian socialism in particular.[1]

It was an age of Marxian socialism, to be sure, but it was also an age of Christian socialism, Fabian socialism, anarcho-communism, and other non-Marxian variants. While some socialists considered themselves Marxists, others were highly critical of various aspects of Marx's theory. Even those who called themselves Marxists often subscribed to different interpretations of what Marx meant and what Marxism was. Engels advanced his own distinctive interpretation of Marxism, as later did Lenin and the Bolsheviks, who thought of themselves as "scientific socialists" remaking the world in the fiery forge of revolution. Others were skeptical or critical, or both. The **revisionists**, for example, criticized the "revolutionary" thrust of Marx's theory. They thought that socialism, and later communism, would (and should) come about gradually and peacefully, by "evolutionary" means. Other critics, such as the anarcho-communist Mikhail Bakunin, suspected that Marxism harbored authoritarian or even totalitarian tendencies and should therefore be rejected as a guide to political practice.

Such faction and ferment characterized socialism throughout the twentieth century. As we shall see, there have been many voices in the socialist chorus—not all singing in the same key, and some marching to different drummers and singing

FIGURE 6.1 Major forms of socialist thought.

altogether different songs. Even so, Marx's voice has until recently boomed louder than anyone else's. Virtually every socialist since his time has thought it necessary to come to terms with Marx's theory, either to accept it, to revise it, to reject it outright, or to modify it almost beyond recognition. Something of the variety of Marxisms and of other forms of socialism can be seen in Figure 6.1.

MARXISM AFTER MARX

Several years before his death, Marx learned that a group of admiring French working men were calling themselves "Marxists." The idea that anyone would reduce his complex and supposedly "scientific" theory to a simplistic "ism" appalled the old man. As Marx told his son-in-law, "What is certain is that I am not a Marxist."[2] But if Marx did not regard himself as a Marxist, many others were happy to claim the title. Chief among these was Marx's old friend and coauthor, Friedrich Engels.

Engels's Marxism

Although a fierce critic of capitalism, Engels was himself a capitalist. His father, co-owner of the German textile firm of Ermen and Engels, had sent the young Engels to England in 1842 to manage the firm's factory in Manchester. Always a reluctant capitalist, Engels nevertheless enjoyed the good life. He was a connoisseur of fine wines and good cigars, and he kept a mistress, an Irish woman named Mary Burns who worked in his factory. She showed Engels the appalling conditions in which workers lived in Manchester. In Manchester and other mill, mining, and factory towns, Engels spent two years interviewing factory and mill workers, miners, and other working people about their wages, working hours and conditions, and other facets of their lives. These he then described memorably and in grisly detail in *The Condition of the English Working Class* (1845), a work that greatly impressed Marx and has since become a minor sociological classic.

In the mid-1840s Marx, the radical philosopher, teamed up with Engels, the wealthy capitalist. The serious and scholarly Marx, married to his childhood sweetheart and the doting father of four daughters, and Engels, the wealthy lifelong bachelor and *bon vivant*, were the original "odd couple" of modern socialism. Their partnership was in many ways unique. Each was strong where the other was weak. Marx quickly came to depend on Engels, not least for financial assistance during the early years of his exile in England, where the Marx family had moved in 1849, living for years in dire poverty. For his part, Engels depended on Marx for political inspiration and intellectual stimulation. Marx, as Engels readily acknowledged, was the deeper and more original thinker. But Engels was the better writer, with a knack for turning memorable phrases and writing with ease

Friedrich Engels (1820–1895)

and speed in several languages. In the works they wrote together—including the *Communist Manifesto* (1848)—the ideas were mainly Marx's, but much of the prose was Engels's. During Marx's lifetime, then, Engels did much to simplify and popularize his friend's ideas.

In the years immediately following Marx's death, however, Engels added his own ideas to Marx's. Engels adapted and interpreted—one might even say radically reinterpreted—Marx's theory in ways that Marx might not have recognized or approved of. Indeed, some scholars have suggested that it was Engels, not Marx, who invented "Marxism" so that later Soviet Marxism ("Marxism-Leninism") owes more to Engels than to Marx.[3] We will examine the latter claim shortly. But first we need to look more closely at Engels's political situation and his contribution to Marxism.

The political situation in which Engels found himself in the 1880s was peculiar. After Marx's death in 1883 he claimed to speak for Marx on a wide variety of subjects, including the direction in which the German Social Democratic Party (SPD) should be heading. The SPD had been formed in 1875 by an alliance of two rival German socialist parties—the United German Labor Party, founded in 1863 and led by Ferdinand Lassalle (1825–1864), and the Social Democratic Workers' Party, established in 1869 by Marx's disciples August Bebel and Wilhelm Liebknecht. Lassalle had been Marx's main rival for the theoretical and intellectual leadership of the German socialist movement, and each devoted considerable energy and effort to criticizing the other. Their contrasting visions of socialism were matched only by differences in their respective appearances and personalities. Marx—short, stout, and every inch the thorough and studious scholar—distrusted the tall, handsome, popular, and flamboyant Lassalle. A dashing and romantic figure, Lassalle was a spellbinding orator and a gifted writer of plays, poems, and political tracts of which Marx heartily disapproved.

Unlike Marx, an internationalist who held that the working class has no homeland, Lassalle was an ardent proponent of **nationalism**, who believed that workers of every nation should seek their own different and distinctive paths to socialism. The political tactics that will work for German socialists, for example, will not necessarily work for the French. Moreover, Lassalle believed, working people tend to be deeply patriotic and protective of their respective countries. To try to weld them into a unified international movement would therefore be ill-conceived and bound to fail. Also unlike Marx, Lassalle held that the state could not, should not, and would not "wither away." It must instead be captured electorally and controlled democratically by workers and their elected representatives. Socialism was to be imposed from above by a beneficent and all-powerful state.

Even after Lassalle's premature death in 1864—he was killed at the age of thirty-nine in a duel over his love affair with a seventeen-year-old girl—the Lassallean wing of the SPD continued to be a thorn in Marx's side. Its reformist tendencies, its eclecticism and romanticism, its German nationalism—all ran counter to Marx's vision of a broad, unified, and international workers' movement.

From Marx's death in 1883 until his own in 1895, Engels was the guardian of Marxian orthodoxy to whom Marxists in Germany and elsewhere looked not only for theoretical inspiration and clarification but also for practical advice. In addition to offering advice about political tactics, Engels supplied a simplified version

Classic Image/Alamy

Ferdinand Lassalle (1825–1864)

of Marx's theory that is in several respects difficult to square with Marx's own views. In particular, Engels made two very important moves. First, he claimed for Marxism the honorific title of "scientific socialism." Second, Engels reinterpreted what Marx meant by **materialism**.

Scientific Socialism. In his speech at Marx's graveside, Engels called Marx "the man of science," comparing his achievement to that of Charles Darwin. "Just as Darwin discovered the law of development of organic nature, so Marx discovered the law of development of human history."[4] There is at first sight an air of plausibility about the comparison. After all, Marx did believe that his inquiries were scientific. By "science" (the German word is *Wissenschaft*) Marx meant a body of organized knowledge that can be tested and found to be true or false. Scientific knowledge, he held, is not static and closed, but open to criticism and refutation. Marx was highly critical of earlier thinkers—including Adam Smith and many others—for being insufficiently "scientific." But he could also be quite critical of himself, and he repeatedly revised and amended his theory in the light of new evidence.

Marx's open and self-critical conception of science contrasts sharply with Engels's closed and uncritical view. Consider, for example, their respective views of the nature and function of scientific generalizations, or "laws." Some nineteenth-century thinkers maintained that, just as there are immutable laws of gravity, thermodynamics, and other natural phenomena, so too are there unchangeable laws governing history and human society. Marx agreed that there are social and historical laws, but he believed that these were historically changeable artifacts—mutable features characteristic of particular social formations rather than fixed features of all past, present, or possible societies. The so-called "law of supply and demand," for example, is not a timelessly true law, but merely an artifact of capitalist market society. When capitalist society is superseded, that "law" will no longer be valid. In this respect, the "laws" social scientists seek are quite unlike the timeless and universal laws discovered by physicists, chemists, and other natural scientists.[5]

Engels, by contrast, believed that the new "science" of **dialectics** showed that the laws governing nature and society were one and the same. According to dialectics, everything—nature, history, even human thought—is nothing more than matter moving in accordance with the timeless "laws" of dialectics. And dialectics, he wrote, is "the science of the most general laws of all motion. Therein is included that their laws must be equally valid for motion in nature and human history and for the motion of thought." Just as "all true knowledge of nature is knowledge of the eternal, the infinite, and hence essentially absolute," so, too, Engels claimed, is all true knowledge of human beings and their history absolute and unchanging.[6]

On this dogmatic and rigid "science of dialectics," Engels erected his claims for "scientific socialism." Engels maintained that scientific socialism—that is, his (and, he claimed, Marx's) version of socialism—was not simply one political ideology among many competitors, but an unchallengeable scientific account of how things were and must be. Any socialist who argued otherwise was merely a "utopian" whose views rested more on sentiment or opinion than on science.[7] Such dogmatic self-certitude represented a dramatic departure from Marx's call for a "relentless critique of all that exists"—including existing conceptions of "science."

Materialism. As we saw in the preceding chapter, Marx called himself a "materialist," largely in order to distinguish his views from those of Hegel and other philosophical idealists of whom he was highly critical. But he was no less critical of earlier "crude" materialists like Thomas Hobbes, who believed that the world and everything (and everyone) in it consisted of nothing but physical matter in motion. According to this view, human thoughts and actions are merely the effects of physical forces beyond human control. In the "Theses on Feuerbach," Marx heaped ridicule upon this kind of crude materialism:

The materialist doctrine that men are products of circumstances and upbringing, and that, therefore, changed men are products of other circumstances and changed upbringing, forgets that it is men that change circumstances and that the educator himself needs educating...[8]

Marx was a materialist in another and altogether different sense. He was not concerned with "matter" *per se* but with the ways in which human beings organize themselves in order to survive and flourish by using their labor to transform raw materials into humanly useful objects, artifacts, and commodities. These ways, in their turn, "influence" or "condition" (*bedingen*) the way in which people think about themselves and their world.

Engels's version of materialism has more in common with the materialism of Hobbes than with that of Marx. Everything, Engels asserts, is reducible to matter and its motions. However extensive the changes, matter remains eternally the same, its "motions" governed by timeless "iron laws":

We have the certainty that matter remains eternally the same in all its transformations, that none of its attributes can ever be lost, and therefore, also, that with the same iron necessity that it will exterminate on the earth its highest creation, the thinking mind, it must somewhere else and at another time again produce it.[9]

Thus Engels's materialism, with its emphasis on matter in motion, stands in curious contrast to Marx's materialism, with its emphasis on human beings in motion, making and remaking their world into an ever more humanly habitable place.

The Revisionists

At the end of the nineteenth century some Marxists favored revising Marxian theory in light of economic and political developments that had occurred since Marx's death. The leading theorist among this group, which came to be known as the revisionists, was Eduard Bernstein (1850–1932). A prominent member of the German Social Democratic Party (SPD), Bernstein believed that some aspects of Marx's theory were either false or out of date and should, accordingly, be rejected or revised; hence the name "revisionist."

An early and active member of the SPD, Bernstein had fled Germany to avoid imprisonment under Bismarck's antisocialist laws in effect from 1878 to 1890. Bernstein's "temporary" exile in Switzerland and England was to last thirteen years. He had previously met Marx and Engels, whom he found to be a good deal less dogmatic than many "Marxists" were. While in England, Bernstein also came under the influence of the **Fabian socialists**, who favored a strategy of gradual reform as the best way of creating a socialist society in Britain. Bernstein, too, came to believe that an "evolutionary" path to socialism was morally and politically preferable to a violent revolutionary one—as the title of his *Evolutionary Socialism* (1899) implies.

Bernstein regarded himself as a Marxist, in spirit if not always in letter. To reject those aspects of Marx's theory that were false and to revise those that were outmoded was, he thought, in the best critical "scientific" spirit of Marx himself, for the mark of a genuinely scientific theory is that its truth is open to question and

The Image Works

Eduard Bernstein (1850–1932)

criticism. Just as Marx had criticized his predecessors, so Bernstein did not flinch from criticizing Marx. His criticisms fall into three categories: moral, political, and economic.

Moral Criticism. Bernstein believed, first of all, that Marx and later Marxists had been too little concerned with ethics or morality. This omission had two aspects. For one thing, Marx had maintained that ethical values and beliefs belong to the **ideological superstructure** of society and therefore depend upon the economic **base**. From this idea it follows that ethical views and values are dependent upon nonethical factors; they can be effects, but never causes, of social actions and institutions. On this point, however, Bernstein disagreed and followed the German philosopher Immanuel Kant (1724–1804), who held that one's will is free of outside influences or causes. People are free, in short, to choose (or "will") as they please, and this means that they have a duty to make morally responsible choices. For Bernstein as for Kant, morally responsible choices start from the conviction that human beings belong to the "kingdom of ends." That is, individuals are "ends in themselves," and it is wrong to treat anyone as if he or she were merely an instrument or means for the fulfillment of some other person's desires or purposes. Thus capitalists are immoral in using workers as human machines and communists are immoral in proposing to use them as cannon fodder in the coming revolution.

A second and even more worrying aspect is that Marxian socialists had focused on the ultimate goal or end—the coming of a communist society—without worrying about the morality or immorality of the means used to arrive at that end. "To me," Bernstein wrote, "that which is generally called the ultimate aim of socialism is nothing, but the movement is everything."[10] By this Bernstein meant that socialists should think about the morality of the means by which they propose to bring about a socialist society. A society born in blood and violence is unlikely to be as peaceful and democratic as one that evolves by nonviolent means. Because ends and means are inextricably bound together, a just society cannot be created by unjust means. Nor can a democratic society come about by undemocratic means. And socialism without democracy is not worth having—indeed, without democracy socialism cannot exist.[11] Moreover, Bernstein believed that Marxists who focus upon distant aims rather than on shorter-term goals were being naively and dangerously utopian. To the extent that Marxists—including Marx himself—fix their gaze exclusively on the final victory of socialism, there "remains a real residue of Utopianism in the Marxist system."[12] His own brand of "practical political socialism," by contrast, "places near aims in front of distant ones."[13] In these respects, then, Bernstein was echoing what Lassalle had said earlier about the relation between ends and means:

> Show us not the aim without the way.
> For ends and means on earth are so entangled
> That changing one, you change the other too;
> Each different path brings different ends in view.[14]

Political Criticism. Besides these ethical reservations, Bernstein expressed doubts about some of Marx's political predictions. He pointed to a number of remarkable developments since Marx's death—developments that ran counter to Marx's expectations. For one, the labor movement in Germany and elsewhere had grown larger and stronger, partly because working-class males in most industrial countries could now vote. The socialist parties that maintained close ties with trade unions and other working-class organizations had also grown larger and stronger. Bismarck's antisocialist laws of 1878 had been repealed in 1890, making it possible for socialist parties to organize, to recruit members openly, and to send representatives to the Reichstag (the German parliament), where they could propose legislation favoring working-class interests, including the graduated income tax and a shorter work week. For the first time it appeared that the state, instead of suppressing the workers, could—as Lassalle had insisted—be their ally and guardian. These, in Bernstein's view, were hopeful developments pointing toward the possibility of a peaceful transition to socialism.

Economic Criticism. No less important, Bernstein claimed, were certain newly emergent economic facts and trends that tended to undermine Marx's theory. Indeed, he charged, "certain statements in *Capital* ... are falsified by facts."[15] For example, Marx had predicted that wealth would be concentrated in fewer and fewer hands until the few were very rich and the many were very poor. But, Bernstein noted, this had not happened in the advanced capitalist countries. Far from growing poorer and more miserable, the workers had, on the whole, become better off. Citing statistics, Bernstein showed that the real income of workers had risen in the latter part of the nineteenth century. Consequently, more workers were able to afford decent housing, better food and clothing, and other of life's amenities. These developments were not due to the generosity of the bourgeoisie but to the success of trade unions and socialist political parties in raising wages and improving working conditions.

To critics who complained that comfortable workers suffer from **false consciousness** and are apt to lose sight of socialist goals and aspirations, Bernstein replied:

> One has not overcome Utopianism if one assumes that there is in the present, or ascribes to the present, what is to be in the future. We [socialists] have to take working men as they are. And they are neither so universally pauperized as [Marx and Engels had predicted] in the *Communist Manifesto,* nor so free from prejudices and weaknesses as their courtiers wish to make us believe. They have the virtues and failings of the economic and social conditions under which they live.[16]

For his part, Bernstein had no doubt that these conditions were gradually improving and would continue to improve so long as workers continued to organize themselves into trade unions and political parties that would promote their interests.

When Bernstein brought these ideas back to Germany in the late 1890s, they proved to be both influential and controversial. The German Social Democratic Party did, in the end, come to favor a peaceful parliamentary path to socialism, but not without a good deal of fighting and feuding within party ranks. Former friends and allies, including Karl Kautsky (1854–1938), broke with Bernstein over the issue. Some years later, Kautsky, who initially maintained that revolution remained a viable possibility for socialists, finally came to share Bernstein's view.[17] Other breakaway socialist factions, such as the Spartacists, led by Rosa Luxemburg and Karl Liebknecht, remained revolutionists who were adamantly opposed to Bernstein's revised version of Marxism. And Russian Marxists, as we shall now see, branded Bernstein a traitor to Marxism.[18] For while "revisionist" Marxism carried the day in Germany and other advanced capitalist countries, a very different variant was taking shape to the east.

Soviet Marxism-Leninism

The Russian Context. Compared with North America and most of the countries of Western Europe, Russia in the late nineteenth century was economically and politically backward. Its economy was mainly agricultural, its industrial base relatively small, and its factories few and inefficient. The vast majority of its people were not proletarian wage-laborers working in factories, but peasants who tilled the land in exchange for a portion of the produce. Russia was as politically primitive as it was economically backward. Its institutions were undemocratic, its tsar an autocratic ruler, and its hereditary nobility oppressive and largely indifferent to the suffering of the common people.

Such a semifeudal society seemed singularly unlikely to spawn the kind of revolution that Marx had expected. Proletarian revolution, after all, required a large proletarian class, not a class of peasants afflicted with what Marx and Engels called "the idiocy of rural life."[19] Largely illiterate, deeply religious, and often strongly superstitious, such people seemed unlikely to make a revolution. Yet there was discontent—not only among peasants in the countryside but also among workers and intellectuals in the cities. Many Russian intellectuals, particularly the more radical among them, saw themselves as the conscience and voice of a vast and still-sleeping majority who would one day wake up, feel their power, and remake Russian society from the ground up. Until then the task of intellectuals was to try to rouse that sleeping giant and to prepare it for its destiny.[20]

Different groups of intellectuals had different visions of what that destiny was to be. Some saw the Russian people, particularly the Slavs, as the most spiritual of the world's people, destined to live—and to show others how to live—spiritually rich and meaningful lives. Others saw Russians as future Europeans, destined to be united with other Western European peoples. Still others saw Russia as a land ripe for a revolution that would shake the world and usher in a new era of equality, freedom, and communal harmony.

Tsarist Russia permitted virtually no freedom of debate or discussion. Opposition parties were outlawed. Police spies and informers were everywhere, and the jails and prisons were full of dissidents and political prisoners. Political discussions were generally confined to small groups of people who met in secret and at considerable risk to themselves, their friends, and their families. Their views reached a wider audience through illicit pamphlets and newspapers that were published secretly and passed from hand to hand. This atmosphere of secrecy and intrigue produced plots and conspiracies aplenty. Some became terrorists and tried to strike at the heart of the tsarist system itself by killing the tsar. One of these was a young student named Alexander Ulyanov, who paid with his life for his part in an unsuccessful attempt to assassinate Tsar Alexander III.

Alexander Ulyanov had an adoring younger brother, Vladimir, who wanted to be a lawyer and live a quiet and respectable life. But Alexander's execution changed all that. Vladimir Ilyich Ulyanov (1870–1924) became a revolutionary opponent of the tsarist regime, going underground and taking a new identity and a new name: Lenin.

Lenin's Contributions. With the help of the Russian Marxist philosopher Georgi Plekhanov (1856–1918), Lenin plunged into an intensive study of the few works of Marx and Engels then available.[21] These included *Capital* and the *Communist Manifesto*, but not *The German Ideology*, the *Economic and Philosophical Manuscripts* of 1844, and other important works. The main lesson that Lenin learned from his studies, and subsequently sought to apply in practice, is that class

V. I. (Ulyanov) Lenin (1870–1924)

struggle is the chief driving force of historical development. For the revolutionary, rational political action consists of following strategies for intensifying and taking advantage of class divisions and differences. Anything that helps to accomplish that end is justifiable. For the sake of the political struggle, one may lie, cheat, steal, embrace enemies, betray friends—all is acceptable if it furthers the cause of the class struggle.

The revolutionary, for Lenin, must be hardened against "softness" and "sentimentality," ready to reject the most elementary imperatives of "bourgeois" ethics if they interfere with the political struggle. Lenin heaped scorn on Bernstein and others who tried to supplement Marx's theory of history with Kant's theory of ethics. For Kantian moral imperatives—to keep one's promises and to treat others as ends and never as means—Lenin had nothing but contempt. "Promises,"

Lenin said, "are like pie crusts—made to be broken." To the objection that Lenin's "revolutionary" morality permitted people to be treated as mere means to some supposedly greater end, Lenin replied, "You cannot make an omelet without breaking eggs"—the implication being that you cannot make a revolution without breaking heads. Revolution is a tough, dirty, mean, and bloody undertaking, and revolutionaries must face that fact. They must be hardened not only against the influence of bourgeois morality but also against anything that might sap their revolutionary will—even art and music. Lenin loved music but, as his friend the playwright Maxim Gorky recalled,

> One evening in Moscow, when Lenin was listening to Beethoven sonatas ... he said: "I know nothing greater than the Appassionata; I'd like to listen to it every day. It's beautiful, superhuman music. I always think proudly—it may be naive—what marvelous things people can do...
>
> "But I can't listen to music too often, it ... makes you want to say kind, silly things, to stroke the heads of the people who, living in a terrible hell, can create such beauty. Nowadays you mustn't stroke anyone's head, you'd get your hand bitten off, you've got to hit them over their heads, without mercy, although, ideally, we're against the use of force. H'm, H'm, our duty is infernally hard."[22]

Lenin's view of the hardened revolutionary personality carried over to his vision of the Communist Party. Marx had viewed the communist movement as a large, inclusive, and broadly based organization of working people from many countries. But Lenin believed that the Communist Party should be small, exclusive, highly organized, tightly disciplined, and conspiratorial. No other party, he argued, could succeed in overthrowing the Russian police state. Lenin's view was put to the test in 1903. A rival wing of the Russian Communist Party wanted a less exclusive and more open party. Through some adroit maneuvering in this internal party struggle, Lenin's wing of the Communist Party gained control and began to call themselves Bolsheviks (meaning "majority"—that is, the majority within the Russian Communist Party).

In Lenin's view, the party's role is to agitate, organize, and educate the workers, teaching them where their "true" interests lie. The "function of the proletarian vanguard," Lenin wrote, "consists in training, educating, enlightening and drawing into the new life the most backward strata and masses of the working class and the peasantry."[23] This was necessary, Lenin believed, because most working people suffer from false consciousness, the most pernicious form of which is **trade union consciousness**:

> The working class, exclusively by its own effort, is able to develop only trade-union consciousness, i.e., the conviction that it is necessary to combine in unions, fight the employers, and strive to compel the government to pass necessary labor legislation, etc.[24]

Workers afflicted with trade union consciousness believe that nothing is wrong with capitalism that a few reforms can't fix. These reforms include the freedom to organize and join labor unions, to strike, to be guaranteed a minimum wage, the outlawing of child labor, a shortened work day and work week, and the like. In short, Lenin contended that trade union consciousness brings with it a mentality that is receptive to the welfare state that protects workers' well-being and takes for granted a (regulated) capitalist economic system. Workers with health-care coverage and the other amenities of the welfare state will not revolt against that state. That is why Lenin loathed liberal reformers, with their gradualist, non-revolutionary half-measures and piecemeal reforms—reforms that appeal to workers afflicted with trade union consciousness and would abort the revolution before it could even begin.

The alternative to trade union consciousness is *revolutionary class consciousness*, that is, the mindset that makes the proletariat aware that its interest as a class is implacably opposed to capitalism and the ruling bourgeoisie. But revolutionary class consciousness cannot, or should not be allowed to, come about spontaneously and by itself. It must instead be imported into the working class from outside, by a **vanguard party**, whose leadership was to consist primarily of revolutionary intellectuals drawn from the ranks of the bourgeoisie. "The theory of socialism," Lenin wrote, "grew out of the philosophic, historical, and economic theories elaborated by educated representatives of the propertied classes, by intellectuals. By their social status the founders of modern scientific socialism, Marx and Engels, themselves belonged to the bourgeois intelligentsia."[25] And so, of course, did Lenin and the leaders of the Bolshevik "vanguard party."

Without such a vanguard, Lenin feared, the working class would not only fail to become a revolutionary force but could become downright reactionary. Yet this vanguard party was supposed to be democratic in two rather restricted respects. First, it claimed to represent the real or true interests of the modern *demos*, the proletariat and the peasantry. Second, the party was meant to be, in itself, a microcosm of the democratic society that was to come. Inside the party, free discussion was to be permitted. But once a vote was taken and an issue decided, discussion was to cease and everyone was to follow the "party line." This notion of internal party democracy Lenin called **democratic centralism**. Democracy throughout society was not yet feasible, Lenin believed, because the masses could not yet be trusted to know their own real interests. Left to their own devices, without a vanguard party to tutor and guide them, the workers would make wrong or even reactionary decisions.

Lenin's low opinion of the working-class mentality was even further confirmed in 1914 with the outbreak of World War I. Marx had argued that the proletariat was an international class without a fatherland. And yet, in 1914, workers—many of whom called themselves socialists—volunteered in droves to fight workers, including socialist workers, from other countries. Why? What had happened? Was Marx wrong? Or were other factors at work that Marx had not taken into sufficient account?

What had happened, Lenin argued in *Imperialism, the Highest Stage of Capitalism* (1916), was this: the workers in the advanced capitalist countries— England, Germany, Italy, France, Belgium, and eventually the United States— were willing to go to war against their fellow proletarians because they had come to have a stake in their respective countries' colonization and exploitation of peoples in Africa, Asia, and South America. Each country had carved out "spheres of influence"—a polite phrase they used to mask brutal exploitation that exceeded even that of early capitalism in the West. World War I was a war for cheap labor, cheap raw materials, and foreign markets. The scene of the most brutal capitalist oppression and exploitation had shifted from Europe and North America to the countries on the capitalist periphery—the "Third World," as we say nowadays. Diamond miners in South Africa, tin miners in Bolivia, copper miners in Chile— these and many millions of other Third World laborers were being oppressed, exploited, and eventually worked to death for subsistence wages. Any attempt to organize unions or to strike for higher wages and improved working conditions was harshly suppressed by the armed forces of the occupying imperial power. That was why the U.S. Marines were in Latin America and the Caribbean, the British Army in India, and the French Foreign Legion in North Africa.

Meanwhile, according to Lenin, European and American workers were being allowed to organize into trade unions to demand a larger share of an ever-expanding economic pie—an expansion made possible by the "super-profits" that their countries' capitalists were extracting from the land, labor, and resources of these poorer nations. The capitalists were thus able to "bribe" their "own" workers and trade unionists with higher wages, shorter hours, better working conditions, health insurance plans, and other benefits of the welfare state. These super-profits, said Lenin, are the real source of the rising wages and ever-higher standard of living touted by Bernstein and the revisionists.[26]

Four important and far-reaching conclusions followed from Lenin's analysis of **imperialism**. First, it reconfirmed Lenin's suspicion of, and hostility toward, the revisionists, whom he saw as the allies of, and apologists for, the capitalist class that they claimed to oppose. Second, he concluded that members of the working class in the advanced capitalist countries have been infected with "trade-union consciousness"; they have, in effect, become "bourgeois" and cannot be counted on to make the revolution that Marx had predicted—at least not without the help of a vanguard party to show them the way. Which brings us to the third conclusion: the Communist Party plays the important, indeed indispensable, role of raising the consciousness and promoting the objective interests of the working class. A fourth—and, as we shall see, especially significant—conclusion is that the revolution will come first to those areas in which the proletariat is both "immiserated" and led by an active vanguard party. Instead of occurring first in the most advanced capitalist countries, as Marx predicted, proletarian revolutions will begin in the more backward nations of the world—in Russia and China, for example.

The Russian Revolution. In 1917 revolution came to Russia. Afraid he would miss it altogether, Lenin returned from his Swiss exile barely in time to take an active and leading part. The Russian Revolution of 1917 did not correspond to anyone's predictions—certainly not Marx's, and not even to Lenin's. The tsar had committed the Russian army to join the English and French in fighting against Germany in World War I. Ill-trained, ill-equipped, and badly led, the Russian army suffered one defeat after another. Morale in the army was low and the casualty rate high. Meanwhile, the Russian people—the peasants in particular—were suffering from shortages of food and fuel, high taxes, and the loss of their sons and brothers in an apparently endless and pointless war. They wanted an end to it. In March 1917, riots broke out in St. Petersburg and other Russian cities. Tsar Nicholas ordered his soldiers to stop the revolt, but they refused. Less than two weeks later, the tsar stepped down, to be replaced by a provisional government headed by Alexander Kerensky, a non-Bolshevik socialist committed to continuing the war against Germany. In October 1917 the Bolsheviks stormed the Winter Palace, seat of Kerensky's government, and seized state power. Lenin was named premier, and a government based on "soviets" (workers' councils) was set up.

The Bolshevik government attempted to restructure Russian society from the ground up. It seized mines, mills, factories, and other large manufacturing facilities and put them in the hands of the soviets. The new government also confiscated large tracts of land and gave small parcels to the peasants. While such measures were popular among peasants and workers, they were viewed with alarm by wealthy landowners and other privileged groups, who soon started a civil war or counterrevolution to regain state power. From 1918 to 1920, the "Red," or revolutionary, forces fought the "White," or reactionary, forces, who were helped by troops and supplies from England, the United States, and other capitalist countries. By 1920 the Whites were defeated, but there was dissension within the ranks of peasants and workers. There were revolts and strikes and even a sailors' mutiny at the massive Kronstadt naval base. Lenin realized that the new government could not consolidate its power without rebuilding an economy wrecked by war, revolution, and counterrevolution. His solution was the "New Economic Policy" (NEP) of 1921, which replaced the more radical socialist measures (known as "war communism," because of the shortages brought about by World War I) instituted earlier. Under the NEP (1921–1928) the government retained control of the major manufacturing concerns but permitted peasants to farm their own land and to sell their produce for a profit. The NEP gave the Bolshevik government breathing space and bought it time to consolidate state power. It was during this period that the Soviet secret police—which later became the infamous KGB—was established to keep an eye on potential counterrevolutionaries. During this period also, Lenin's health began to decline. In 1924 he died.

Stalin's Contribution. Shortly before he died, the ailing Lenin began preparing a final testament in which he demanded that Stalin be expelled from the Communist Party.[27] Lenin had long warned his fellow Bolsheviks to beware of Stalin. The warning proved prophetic. From 1929 until his death in 1953, Stalin ruled the Soviet Union and its Communist Party with a ruthlessness virtually unmatched in history, leaving a legacy of political repression that lingers to this day. He also left his mark on Marxism-Leninism, the ideology by which he justified his actions and policies for nearly one-quarter of a century. A closer look at Stalin's career and his additions to Marxism-Leninism is revealing.

Joseph Stalin (1879–1953) was born Iosif Djugashvili in Russian Georgia. The son of pious parents, he was sent in 1894 to the Tbilisi Seminary to be educated for the priesthood in the Russian Orthodox Church. Djugashvili was eventually expelled from the seminary, but not before learning several valuable lessons that he never forgot. One was to put the best face on a convoluted or even logically invalid argument so as to make it appear straightforward and logically valid. Another was that, if logical argument does not convince, simplification and ritualistic repetition will. All "lessons" must be hammered home with an air of infallibility and a certain repetitive intensity. And, not least, young Djugashvili took away the lesson that

Joseph (Djugashvili) Stalin (1879–1953)

texts—even sacred texts—are open to interpretation and sometimes, even, to radical reinterpretation. To have one's own interpretation of a sacred text accepted as authoritative can itself be a source of considerable power.

After being expelled from the seminary in 1899, Djugashvili drifted into politics, joining the Russian Social Democratic Labor Party in 1901. When that party split into two factions in 1903, he sided with Lenin and the Bolsheviks. Like many of his fellow party members, he, too, took on a new name—Stalin (meaning "man of steel"). The name was well chosen. Stalin had an appetite for danger and intrigue. He organized and participated in several bank robberies to fatten the coffers of the fledgling party, for instance, and soon developed a reputation for undertaking dirty and difficult tasks for the party.[28] His stature within the party grew apace. Partly because Stalin was so ruthless and cunning, Lenin came to distrust his Georgian comrade, whom he nicknamed "the priest." But with Lenin's death in 1924, the main obstacle to Stalin's advancement was removed.

In the late 1920s Stalin began consolidating his own power within the party and the country by discrediting and eventually eliminating all remaining opposition, whether personal, political, or theoretical. Although no match for theorists like Lenin or Leon Trotsky (1879–1940), Stalin nevertheless thought it necessary to portray himself as the party's preeminent theorist. What he lacked in subtlety he more than made up for in simplicity. As the Russian historian Roy Medvedev observes,

> In philosophy Stalin was at best a dilettante. He lacked both systematic training and genuine self-education. He never made a real study of Hegel, Kant ... or, judging by his pronouncements, the philosophical works of Marx, Engels, and Lenin. All his philosophical writings are marked by primitivism, oversimplification, superficiality, and a penchant for dogmatic schematization.[29]

In Stalin's writings, Medvedev adds, "originality is notable by its absence. Propositions that were hailed as great discoveries by propagandists of the [Stalin] cult were actually trivial platitudes. But it must be granted that Stalin was a master at making these platitudes seem important."[30]

To ensure that his interpretation of Marxism-Leninism was beyond question and above criticism, Stalin proceeded to eliminate questioners and critics—particularly those who had some knowledge of Marxian theory. This serves to explain why Stalin's emergence as the preeminent Marxist-Leninist theoretician coincided with the political purges and show trials of the mid-1930s. Leading Bolsheviks—many of them heroes of the October Revolution that brought the Communists to power—were "purged" from the party, imprisoned, tortured and put on public trial to "confess" to crimes they had not committed, and shot or sent to Siberia to starve or freeze to death. Nikolai Bukharin, a brilliant theorist and architect of the NEP, was tried on trumped-up charges and shot (he appears as the ill-fated character Rubashov in Arthur Koestler's novel *Darkness at Noon*). Leon Trotsky, living in exile in Mexico, was hunted down and murdered on Stalin's orders. Thousands of other old Bolsheviks met similar fates. By these brutal means, Stalin sought to eliminate not only real or potential political opponents but theoretical or ideological rivals as well. Ironically, the purge extended even to the writings of Marx and Engels themselves. Stalin suppressed publication of the authoritative edition of Marx and Engels's collected works, the *MEGA* (*Marx-Engels Gesamtausgabe*), and ordered its learned editor, David Riazanov, shot. He also saw to it that several of Lenin's writings were excluded from his *Collected Works*.[31] At the same time he oversaw the rewriting of Russian history, portraying himself—quite falsely, in fact—as Lenin's closest confidant, adviser, ally, and natural heir.

During the Stalinist era education, art and literature, and even science were turned to propagandistic use. Writers and artists were required to incorporate the tenets of "socialist realism," portraying proletarians as noble and selfless heroes with hearts of gold and nerves and muscles of steel. Scientists were required to think and theorize along "Marxist-Leninist" lines. Among the most notorious instances of the latter were the policies pursued by Stalin's chief commissar of science, Trofim Lysenko (1898–1976). Lysenko rejected the newly emerging science of genetics as "bourgeois" science, substituting his own Marxist-Leninist "proletarian" theory concerning the heritability of acquired characteristics in plants and animals. Applying this "theory" to the practice of Soviet agriculture, he made preposterous predictions about increasing crop yields. Contrary to Lysenko's predictions, crop production failed miserably and massively. But this failure was attributed to "scheming, counter-revolutionary peasants" who sought to sabotage Soviet agriculture. The result? "Confirmation" of Lysenko's theory, widespread crop failures and food shortages, mass starvation, a massive purge of peasants, and the execution of geneticists pursuing "bourgeois" science.[32] In Stalin's Soviet Union ideology trumped science, with disastrous results.

What, then, are the distinguishing features of Stalinism as a variant of (some would say a departure from) Marxism-Leninism? Three features are especially noteworthy. One concerns the role of the party and party leadership. Lenin had held that the working class suffers from false consciousness and needs a vanguard party to guide it. Stalin held that the party itself is afflicted with false consciousness and needs a vanguard—a single, all-wise, all-knowing genius—to guide it. That all-knowing guide was, of course, Stalin himself. This is the theoretical foundation for the cult of personality that Stalin built around himself.

A second feature of Stalinism is its notion of "socialism in one country." Socialism, said Stalin, must be created and consolidated in one country—the Soviet Union—before it can be constructed anywhere else. This is at odds with what Marx and Engels had to say about the international character of the socialist movement. Proceeding from this premise, Stalin's rival Leon Trotsky not only denied that it was possible to build socialism in a single country but also advocated "permanent revolution"—by which he meant that the revolution, even in the Soviet Union, can realize its aims only if the party remains vigorous, vital, and alert to the dangers of despotism within its own ranks. Trotsky, living in exile in Mexico, ceased saying such things after one of Stalin's secret agents buried an ice axe in the back of his head.

A third feature of Stalinism is to be found in Stalin's strategy of justification and legitimation. Stalin employed dialectics and **dialectical materialism (DiaMat)** to justify virtually every plan, policy, and result. According to Stalin's version of dialectical materialism—a phrase, incidentally, that Marx never used—there are no accidents or coincidences; all is determined by the movement of matter, and everything that happens had to happen as it did.[33] That this doctrine of "historical inevitability" commits the elementary logical fallacy of *post hoc, ergo propter hoc*—roughly, if one event occurred before another, the first must have caused the second—did not trouble Stalin.[34] His brand of logic was itself "dialectical." With it, even the most brazen contradiction could be reconciled "dialectically." Consider the following example:

> We stand [Stalin said] for the withering away of the state. At the same time we stand for the strengthening of the dictatorship of the proletariat, which is the mightiest and strongest state power that has ever existed... Is this "contradictory"? Yes, it is contradictory. But this contradiction is bound up with life, and it fully reflects Marx's dialectics.[35]

What Stalin omits to note, of course, is that Marx believed that the purpose of criticism was to expose contradictions as a prelude to overcoming them, and not—as Stalin would have it—to accept or acquiesce in them. By means of such casuistry, Stalin offered "dialectical" justifications for any position or action, however heinous.

Stalin's reign of terror came to an end with his death in 1953. Three years later the new leader of the Soviet Union, Nikita Khrushchev (1894–1971), denounced Stalin's crimes before the Twentieth Party Congress. His anti-Stalinist successors, including Mikhail Gorbachev (1931–), continued to do so, despite opposition from a small but vocal pro-Stalinist faction within the party.

Post-Soviet Communism. The Soviet Union no longer exists, but Stalin's ghost continues to haunt Russia and the other countries that once made up the Union of Soviet Socialist Republics. The twin transitions to liberal democracy and a capitalist market economy are proving painful and difficult, and some older Russians long for a return to the harsh certainties of the Stalinist era. In the mid-1990s the pace of political and economic reform began to slow, and some communists, sensing widespread discontent with reforms initiated by Russian President Boris Yeltsin (1931–2007), made a brief political comeback. Strident nationalists and neofascists, such as Vladimir Zhirinovsky, have also exploited ethnic divisions and promised to restore Russian power and prestige.

Under the leadership of Gennady Zyuganov, a reorganized Russian Communist Party—now known as the Communist Party of the Russian Federation (CPRF)—has proved to be a persistent and in some quarters popular critic of the reformist policies of Yeltsin's, and subsequently of Vladimir Putin's, government. (Putin's protégé, Dmitri Medvedev, who succeeded Putin as president in 2008, served as a placeholder for the former KGB agent, who continued to call the shots behind the scenes until his reelection in 2012.) These policies have led to high rates of inflation, the devaluation of the ruble (Russia's basic monetary unit), and the impoverishment of old-age pensioners and other people on fixed incomes. Putin's communist critics point to growing disparities of wealth, and thus of power, within Russian society as reasons for a return to communism. They also raise objections to the harsh and authoritarian tactics of Putin, who has invaded and annexed the Crimea (part of Ukraine) and eastern Ukraine, taken steps to sharply limit freedom of speech and press, and suppressed political opponents. A number of Putin's critics have died under mysterious circumstances, and others have been imprisoned. In 2012, for example, members of the all-female punk rock band Pussy Riot were sent to prison for two years for singing songs critical of Putin and his harshly authoritarian rule.[36] As for the Russian Communist Party, it is a shadow of its former self. The CPRF is one of the largest of Russia's many political parties, but in the 2003 elections its 13 percent of the total votes cast gave it only about one-fifth of the seats in the Duma (parliament)—not enough to mount an effective challenge to Putin. In the 2007 parliamentary elections the party received only 11.6 percent of all votes cast. In the 2012 presidential election, amid widespread reports of voting fraud perpetrated by Putin's United Russia Party, the CPRF candidate, Gennady Zyuganov, received 17 percent of the vote. Today the CPRF no longer speaks of revolution and class struggle, nor does it promise the utopia of a classless communist society. Instead, it promises only a transition to a competitive capitalist society that will protect the weak and poor along the way. This has led some commentators to describe the party's watered-down ideology as "Marxism-Leninism Lite." Whether this lighter and less militant version of communism might someday prove appealing remains to be seen. At present, its prospects in Putin's Russia appear to be unpromising.

Chinese Communism

The only remaining major global power whose ruling party calls itself communist is the People's Republic of China. With its increasing industrial might and a population of more than a billion—one out of five people alive today is Chinese—China plays an increasingly important role on the world's stage. If we are to understand current Chinese thinking and actions, we need to know something about China's past and its revolutionary path to the present.

The Chinese Context. The ideological thread of Chinese history over the past century consists of several complex strands. The oldest is Confucianism, a body of doctrine drawn from the teachings of Confucius (551–479 BCE). From a political perspective, Confucianism stresses order, hierarchy, respect for the monarchy and one's parents, and a bureaucracy managed by a learned elite, the mandarins. A second strand, Chinese nationalism, was born of a reaction against nineteenth-century European, American, and Japanese colonialism and foreign occupation. For a proud and ancient people to be economically dominated by "barbarians" was especially galling. Repeated attempts by the Chinese to drive the foreigners out—as in the Boxer Rebellion of 1899, for example—were suppressed by better-armed foreign forces. In 1912 the Nationalists under Sun Yat-sen (1866–1925) established a nominally independent Chinese Republic. After a series of setbacks, China was unified under the Nationalist leader, Generalissimo Chiang Kai-shek (1887–1975), in 1928.

But Chiang's Nationalist Party was not without rivals. The then still-new Chinese Communist Party (CCP), founded in 1921, represents a third strand in China's ideological configuration. While a young library assistant at Beijing University, Mao Zedong (1893–1976) was among the first to join the newly formed CCP. Mao had been electrified by the news of the 1917 Russian Revolution and had set about studying the works of Marx, Engels, and Lenin to see what lessons they might contain for China. Unable to read any language other than Chinese, however, Mao's choice of readings was severely restricted. Most of the works of Marx and Engels—with the exception of the *Communist Manifesto* and several other short works—had not yet been translated into Chinese. But a number of Lenin's essays were beginning to appear in translation. One of these, Lenin's *Imperialism*, was to have a decisive influence on Mao's thinking. Mao was drawn to Lenin's theory of imperialism for several reasons. First, it seemed especially well suited to Chinese conditions. For one thing, China had no sizable industrial proletariat; the vast majority of its people were peasants who tilled the soil on large farms owned by wealthy landlords. For another, the imperialist powers found in China vast resources—abundant raw materials and cheap labor—and a large foreign market for their own manufactured goods. Little wonder, Mao reasoned, that the advanced capitalist countries sought "super-profits" in China. But Lenin's analysis not only served to explain several puzzling features of modern Chinese history but also offered a prescription—revolution not as the internal class war that Marx had predicted, but as an anti-imperialist "war of national liberation" waged by the people of an economically "backward" nation against their foreign capitalist oppressors.

Corbis Historical/Getty Images

Mao Zedong (1893–1976)

Certainly China in the 1920s was neither prosperous nor powerful. Most of its people were pitifully poor. Nearly three out of four were poor peasants who owned little or no land and survived by working for the landlords of vast estates. There was little heavy industry. Only about 1 of every 200 Chinese could be classified as proletarians in Marx's sense. Those who were not poor peasants or industrial workers were mostly so-called "rich" peasants who, like Mao's parents, owned and farmed small plots. Mao's most original contribution to—or perhaps departure from—Marxian theory was his proposal to make a revolution that would downplay the importance of the urban proletariat and concentrate instead on harnessing the pent-up resentments of rural peasants.

The Rural "Proletariat." Mao's reliance on the Chinese peasantry rested on several factors. First, and most obviously, poor peasants constituted an overwhelming majority of the Chinese population. Once organized and mobilized, they would be an almost irresistible force. Second, they were not only the poorest but also the most oppressed sector of the populace. They therefore had everything to gain and little to lose by waging an all-out struggle against their landlord oppressors. Finally, Mao believed that the peasants were endowed with a kind of practical wisdom or common sense that comes not from books or theories, but from experience. If a revolution was to be made in China, it must be made by peasants led by a party whose leaders spoke their language and thought as they thought. Many of Mao's speeches and writings were, accordingly, directed against abstract theorizing and couched in a folksy style calculated to appeal to peasants:

> Marxism-Leninism has no decorative value, nor has it mystical value. It is only extremely useful. It seems that, right up to the present, quite a few have regarded Marxism-Leninism as a ready-made panacea: once you have it, you can cure all your ills with little effort. This is… childish… Those who regard Marxism-Leninism as religious dogma show this type of blind ignorance. We must tell them openly, "Your dogma is of no use," or to use an impolite phrase, "Your dogma is less useful than shit." We see that dog shit can fertilize the fields, and man's can feed the dog. And dogmas? They can't fertilize the fields, nor can they feed a dog. Of what use are they?[37]

Mao's Contribution. Although many of Mao's writings are concerned with "practice"—particularly with ways in which to mobilize the peasantry and the appropriate military strategy and tactics to use in different situations—he did amend Marxian theory in several significant ways. The first, as we have noted already, was to downplay the importance of the urban proletariat and to mold the peasantry into a revolutionary force. Revolution was to begin in the countryside. As the rural revolutionary forces gained strength, they could then encircle the cities and force them into submission. A second significant amendment was to downplay the importance of "objective" conditions, such as the size of the industrial working class, and to stress instead the central role of "subjective" factors. Especially in Mao's later life his revision of Marxian theory placed "consciousness" or political "will" above material or objective conditions. A third distinctive contribution was Mao's recasting of the concepts of class and class struggle. In Mao's hands the concept of class, which was of course central to classical Marxism, was largely replaced by the concept of nation or **nation-state**. Specifically, Mao redescribed national and international relations in "class" terms. China, he claimed, was a poor and oppressed "proletarian" nation that needed to throw off the yoke of the wealthy, "bourgeois" oppressor nations. Far from being a purely internal struggle, then, the Chinese Revolution pitted "proletarian" nationalist forces against the representatives of international capitalism. The Nationalist Party, some of whose leaders had encouraged and profited from foreign investment, was merely the Chinese agent or representative of the bourgeois nations. The CCP's struggle within China against Chiang and the Nationalists was therefore a surrogate struggle against the United States and other capitalist nations, which supported Chiang. Once the CCP took power, moreover, Mao began to argue that the Chinese Revolution was to be the prototype for revolutionary activity in Asia and Africa.[38] In a series of "wars of national liberation," the proletarian nations of the Third World would surround and starve the wealthy capitalist nations into submission. In short, Mao advocated that national liberation movements in the Third World employ the tactics that had proved so successful in the CCP revolutionary victory of 1948–1949.

All of these amendments are a far cry from anything that Marx had anticipated. But, on reflection, this is not entirely surprising. Mao had initially viewed Marx and Marxian theory through Leninist lenses. He adopted Lenin's notion that the Communist Party must be the vanguard that leads the people to revolution, for instance, and must then serve as the dictator in the name of the proletariat. Even his Leninist views were later filtered through Stalin's supposedly authoritative interpretations of what Lenin said or meant. Mao's was therefore Marxism-Leninism seen as through a glass darkly, and even suspiciously. Yet, while Mao maintained that one should not be an uncritical worshiper at the shrine of Marx or any other Marxist, he nevertheless proclaimed the purity and sanctity of his own version of Marxism. As he and the Chinese Revolution grew older, Mao became more and more a cult figure and object of veneration. The hero of the Chinese Revolution was transformed into a larger-than-life figure, "The Great Helmsman," whose every thought and deed was magnified to mythic proportions.

Reds and Experts. Mao had a greatly inflated sense of self-confidence and a penchant for performing large-scale experiments in social and economic transformation. The largest and most disastrous of these was the so-called "Great Leap Forward" of 1958–1961. Small private plots of farmland were taken out of peasants' hands and combined into huge collective farms run by CCP overseers who (in many peasants' eyes) looked a lot like the hated landlords of old. At the same time China underwent a process of rapid forced industrialization, one feature of which was the building of backyard furnaces to make steel that proved to be of poor and unusable quality. To stoke these furnaces, entire forests were cut down, denuding the land and leading to floods and erosion and the ensuing loss of fertile farmland. In "the Great Sparrow Campaign" peasants were ordered to kill sparrows and other birds that ate valuable grain. The result, predictably, was plagues of locusts and other insects that ate much more grain than their predators, the birds, ever did. This and other policies of the Great Leap Forward resulted in ecological devastation and mass starvation on a scale unprecedented in human history.[39] By a conservative estimate more than 36 million Chinese died and the natural environment was deeply damaged for generations to come.[40]

By the mid-1960s, Mao's cult of personality was building toward a disruptive and in many ways disastrous conclusion—the so-called "Cultural Revolution." To understand the theoretical roots of the Cultural Revolution, we must take note of Mao's distinction between being "red" and being "expert." To be "red" was to be ideologically pure and correct; to be "expert" was to emphasize technical proficiency instead of ideological correctness. Mao, who favored the former over the latter, believed that by the mid-1960s the pendulum had swung too far in the direction of the expert. Ideological purity was in danger. So he called for a Cultural Revolution that would oust the experts and restore the "reds" to their rightful role. Workers were encouraged to humiliate managers and engineers, and students to humble their professors. Many "experts" were killed or imprisoned or removed from their posts and sent to work in the fields. What had been up was now down, and vice versa. In this topsy-turvy situation, industrial and agricultural production fell drastically, with widespread suffering the result. So disruptive was the Cultural Revolution that Mao finally agreed to call in the People's Liberation Army to restore order in factories, in universities, and throughout society.

The Cultural Revolution left many of China's institutions and its economy in a shambles. It also tarnished Mao's reputation among the Chinese. The radicals, including Mao's wife, were discredited, and pragmatists such as Deng Xiaoping (1904–1997) gained the upper hand after Mao's death in 1976. Since then China has concentrated its energies on building its economic infrastructure. Under Deng's leadership, China began to reintroduce some features of a free-market economy, including extensive commerce with capitalist countries. Some steps were also taken in the direction of freedom of speech, especially the freedom to criticize the Communist Party leadership; but these were halted when the tanks and troops of the People's Liberation Army crushed the peaceful pro-democracy demonstration of Chinese students and their supporters in Beijing's Tiananmen Square in June 1989. In 1993, on what would have been Mao's 100th birthday, the Chinese authorities paid particular homage to Mao's thought and advocated its close and careful study by young people—a clear signal that the government would no more tolerate dissent or liberal-democratic ideas than Mao did during his lifetime.

But even as the Chinese Communist Party continues to suppress political opposition, it continues to relax its grip economically. It openly courts foreign investors and encourages Chinese entrepreneurs to build their own businesses. The government has emphasized, however, that economic liberalization is not to be linked to liberalization in political matters. During his state visit in 1997 to the United States, in fact, Chinese President Jiang Zemin defended his government's bloody suppression of the Tiananmen Square protestors as the "correct conclusion" to the affair.[41] The current president of China, Xi Jinping, shows no sign of departing from the views and policies of his predecessors. Whether the CCP's attempt to "decouple" economic and political liberty can or will succeed in the long term, however, is unclear.

What will become of communism in China? With Deng's death in 1997, the last of the older revolutionary generation passed from the scene, and younger party members are appearing in important posts. Some of these new leaders almost certainly hold beliefs and ideas with which their elders disagree. But exactly what those ideas may be—and how they may change the character of Chinese communism—remains to be seen.

Far from being dead, Mao Zedong thought appears to be undergoing a revival. China's current president, Xi Jinping, who took office in 2012, has cracked down on dissent and dissenters. Since then hard-line Maoists, who in the first decade of the twenty-first century were eclipsed by more moderate elements in the CCP, have acquired more power and prominence. Xi and the Maoists are attempting to root out "Western ideas," such as liberalism and liberal democracy, freedom of the press and assembly, and the right to question and even to criticize government leaders and their policies. A semi-secret policy directive, "Document No. 30," demands that such ideas be "cleansed" from colleges and universities, the media, and other institutions.[42]

Although the status of "Mao Zedong thought" seems uncertain in China, it nevertheless retains its attractions for guerrilla movements in several Third World countries. In Peru, the *Sendero Luminoso* or "Shining Path" movement has attempted to emulate the strategy and tactics of Mao Zedong, whom it claims as its ideological guide. In Nepal a small but powerful Maoist guerrilla movement threatens to further destabilize an already unstable government. And Maoist rebels effectively rule parts of eastern India.[43] These may be rather marginal movements in the Third World—so marginal that the Peruvian government almost destroyed *Sendero Luminoso* in the 1990s and early 2000s—but they continue to pose dangers at a local level. Globally speaking, however, they are more a nuisance than a genuine threat. One allegedly communist country that does pose a real threat, militarily speaking, is North Korea, about which we will say more in a moment.

It is often said that after the fall of the Soviet Union and its Eastern European satellite states, the only remaining communist regimes were those in China, Vietnam, North Korea, and Cuba. All these contentions are questionable, but the largest question mark hangs over the claim that North Korea is a communist regime. That nation's official ideology is called *Juche* (pronounced "joosh"), which means something like "national self-sufficiency." It is sometimes called "Kimilsungism" after its originator Kim Il Sung (1912–1994), who claimed that it was "uniquely Korean" and owed nothing to Western thinkers such as Marx, Engels, or Lenin. This is only partially true. Insofar as it insists on the need for a "Great Leader" who has absolute power and presides over a totalitarian police-state, there is a thread of Stalinism in Juche. And insofar as it emphasizes the primacy of revolutionary political "will" over objective material conditions, it bears more than a passing resemblance to Maoism or Mao Zedong thought. Juche is uniquely Korean inasmuch as it grew out of Korea's long history of being invaded, occupied, and colonized by China, Japan, Mongolia, and larger nations. Kim Il Sung saw the Soviet Union and communist China as threats to North Korean independence, and Marxism-Leninism and Maoism as ideological threats. All these experiences produced a kind of national inferiority complex to which Juche is offered as an antidote and corrective. That, at least, is the justification offered by Kim Il Sung, his son Kim Jong Il, and his son Kim Jong Un, the current "Great Leader." Skeptical scholars, East and West, view Juche as an opportunistic ideological rationale for keeping all power in the hands of the Kim family.[44] In any event, Juche is invoked to explain and justify North Korea's self-imposed isolation. It doesn't want to join the world of nations but to remain separate, distinct, and independent. Thus diplomatic overtures premised on the assumption that rogue nations long to join other nations are misplaced, resting as they do upon a failure to understand this unique—indeed idiosyncratic—ideology.

CRITICAL WESTERN MARXISM

Finally, a non-revolutionary strand of Marxian theory can be found in what is loosely called **critical Western Marxism**. From this perspective Marxian theory is best understood as a body of critical theory that affords a perspective or vantage point from which modern society can be critically comprehended. In the aftermath of World War I and the Russian Revolution, two things had become increasingly clear. One was that capitalism, at least in the advanced capitalist countries, was far more adaptive and resilient than Marx had recognized. The welfare state, labor unions, and socialist parties in Western Europe had to some extent tamed and taken the hard edges off of capitalist competition and production. This meant that communism (though not socialism) had lost its appeal among workers who had the vote, had political representation in parliaments or other political bodies, and enjoyed a measure of affluence (through minimum-wage legislation) and job security (through unemployment insurance). Henceforth, communism would appeal primarily to workers in Russia and China and other economically less-developed nations. And in those countries communism in practice was repressive and oppressive, and more closely akin to a dictatorship *over* the proletariat than a dictatorship *of*, by, and for the proletariat. According to the critical Western Marxists, then, communist rule has been worse—less productive and more repressive—than the capitalist disease it was meant to cure. Marxian theory, reinterpreted and put into practice as Marxism-Leninism in the Soviet Union or Maoism in China, provided no model for Western workers.

Does this then mean that Marxian theory is of little or no value in the West and perhaps elsewhere? By no means, say the critical Marxists. For Marx was not only a theorist of proletarian revolution but a social theorist or social scientist as well. In the latter role Marx supplied an astute and wide-ranging analysis of the inner workings of modern capitalist society. The critical Marxian theorists aim to build upon and develop Marx's insights.

One group of such theorists organized the *Institut für Soziadforschung* (Institute for Social Research) at Germany's University of Frankfurt am Main, better known as the Frankfurt School of Critical Theory.[45] These theorists—including Max Horkheimer, Theodor Adorno, Herbert Marcuse, Walter Benjamin, Erich Fromm, and others—believed that Marx had overemphasized material or economic factors and had underestimated the influence of cultural or ideological factors in explaining social change (or the lack thereof). These latter factors became ever more important in the age of mass media—radio, movies, and later television—which turns art, music, and other cultural forms into commodities that not only enrich corporations but that create a form of **false consciousness** in the minds of ordinary men and women. Under the guise of "entertainment" people are actually indoctrinated to become passive workers and inert consumers instead of active and critical democratic citizens.[46] Such indoctrination is not overt but covert and unconscious. Frankfurt School theorists borrowed heavily from Sigmund Freud, who had emphasized the important role of irrational motivations and subconscious desires in shaping people's perceptions and behavior. By means of systematic and sustained "ideology critique" the critical theorists hoped to free people from such indoctrination, making them critical of the conditions that keep them from being active participants in shaping their own lives, individually and collectively. The project of the Frankfurt School continues today in somewhat altered form in the work of Jürgen Habermas (1929–) and other contemporary critical theorists.

NON-MARXIST SOCIALISM

Marx and his followers have been the most influential of all socialists. For much of the twentieth century, in fact, roughly one-third of the world's population lived in countries governed by regimes that claimed to be Marxist. But Marx and the Marxists have by no means been the only founts of socialist or communist theory and practice. As we noted at the beginning of this chapter, there have been, and continue to be, many non-Marxian voices in the socialist chorus. Indeed, there are so many varieties of non-Marxian socialism that we can scarcely list them, much less describe them in any detail. Nevertheless, we can conclude our history of socialism with brief discussions of several of the more important and influential varieties of non-Marxist socialism.

Anarcho-Communism

Marx's main rivals within the ranks of the European socialist movement were the anarchists.[47] We have already seen, in Chapter 1, that anarchists agree only on one key point: that the state is an evil coercive institution that ought to be abolished and replaced by a system of noncoercive voluntary cooperation. But there the agreement ends. Some anarchists are radical individualists, others are communalists. Some advocate the violent overthrow of the state, others are pacifists who advocate a more peaceful path to a cooperative society. With the exception of the libertarian or individualist anarchists discussed in Chapter 3, however, all have played a part in the socialist tradition.

One of the earliest attempts to articulate and defend anarchism was William Godwin's *Enquiry Concerning Political Justice* (1793). Godwin, an Englishman, maintained that the state was by its very nature oppressive, and likely to become more so unless somehow stopped. One way to do this, he thought, was by making communities small enough to be governed directly by their members so as not to need the coercive control of the state. So far as property ownership was concerned, however, Godwin was not a consistent communist.[48] In this respect he differs from many later anarchists who held that the state is necessary as long as property is privately owned. For these socialist anarchists, or **anarcho-communists**, the abolition of the state and the abolition of private property are two sides of the same coin.

In contrast to the popular image of the bomb-throwing anarchist, many anarcho-communists have also made a strong moral case for pacifism and nonviolence. One of these, the Russian Count Leo Tolstoy (1828–1910)—author of *War and Peace* and other great novels—held fast to the principle that violence in any form is always wrong. A devout Christian, Tolstoy believed that this principle applies to the violence that the state does or is prepared to do to its own citizens. Why else, he asks, does it maintain a system of police, courts, tax collectors, and prisons? Why else does it employ an executioner? Without these means, whereby one human being does violence to another, the state would not exist. The state is, by its very nature, a violent institution. Violence being categorically wrong, the only moral thing to do is to get rid of the state, replacing it with a system of voluntary cooperation in which every person assists others and is in turn assisted by them.

How can such a society be brought into being? Peacefully, Tolstoy believed. The transition to anarchy can and should be accomplished by the power of persuasion—by persuading the rich to part with their wealth (as Tolstoy had with his) and by persuading everyone to withdraw support from the state and its institutions. But on this point there has been considerable disagreement among anarchists. Some, such as Tolstoy's countrymen Peter Kropotkin (1842–1921) and Mikhail Bakunin (1814–1876), have held that violent means may be required to eliminate the main source of violence, the state. For Bakunin, destruction can even be creative, as it is when people rise up to destroy the state—the master that enslaves them—and liberate themselves.[49]

It is easy to see why Marx regarded the anarchists with contempt, and why they viewed him with such suspicion. Marx, as we saw in Chapter 5, believed that the transition from capitalism to communism required that the victorious revolutionaries seize state power in order to prevent the defeated bourgeoisie from mounting a counterrevolution. When it was no longer needed, Marx predicted, this transitional state, or "dictatorship of the proletariat," would finally "wither away." This prediction was regarded with particular scorn by Bakunin, a Russian nobleman turned radical anarchist. A huge heavily bearded bear of a man with a booming voice and an acid-tipped pen, Bakunin turned both against Marx. In *Statism and Anarchy* (1874) Bakunin mounted a prophetic and withering criticism of Marx's claim that the state would, or could, spontaneously self-destruct. The state, said Bakunin, is not like that; its natural tendency is not to disappear but to acquire more and more power, to grow ever more oppressive and violent, and to subject its citizens to increasingly stringent scrutiny and control. This is as true of a so-called "workers' state" as of the state controlled by the bourgeoisie. In fact, Bakunin added, the workers' state is likely to be even more oppressive, for it—unlike the bourgeois state—has no militant and organized working class to oppose it and to check its growth.[50]

A rather different defense of anarchism was advanced by Kropotkin, particularly in *Mutual Aid* (1902). Because he was a Russian prince who had renounced his title in order to express a sense of solidarity with the common people, the Russian police kept a close watch on Kropotkin. In 1874 he was arrested for illegal political activities and sent to Siberia. After serving two years of his sentence, he made a daring escape and, like many political refugees, made his way to England—and an exile that was to last forty-two years. Much influenced by the writings of Charles Darwin and other prominent nineteenth-century scientists, Kropotkin accepted the view that all species evolve according to inexorable laws of development. He took this to mean that the human species is steadily evolving and that society will eventually become more peaceful and cooperative. By means of concerted political action, he thought, these processes of change can be speeded up and the state abolished and replaced by a noncoercive anarchist society. Indeed, he argued that the political lesson of Darwin's theory—contrary to the **Social Darwinists'** emphasis on competition between individuals—is that survival is likely to be the reward of those who learn to engage in "mutual aid" and cooperate for the common good.[51] When in 1917, after long years in exile, Kropotkin finally

T. Kajiwara/Library of Congress Prints and Photographs Division [LC-USZ62-48793]

Emma Goldman (1869–1940)

returned to Russia, he was pleased to see the tsar's and the nobility's demise, but deeply disappointed by their Bolshevik replacements.

Another Russian-born anarcho-communist, Emma Goldman (1869–1940), came to prominence in the United States, where she became known as "Red Emma." Like the other anarcho-communists, Goldman thought of anarchism as "the great liberator of man from the phantoms that have held him captive"— phantoms such as God, the state, and property. Anarchism, she declared, "really stands for the liberation of the human mind from the dominion of religion; the liberation of the human body from the dominion of property; liberation from the shackles and restraints of government."[52] To these concerns she added the feminist theme of liberation of women from the exploitation of men. Just as capitalism oppresses working men (and women), she argued, so marriage oppresses women. Capitalism, Goldman declared,

> robs man of his birthright, stunts his growth, poisons his body, keeps him in ignorance, in poverty, and dependence, and then institutes charities that thrive on the last vestige of man's self-respect.
>
> The institution of marriage makes a parasite of woman, an absolute dependent. It incapacitates her for life's struggle, annihilates her social consciousness, paralyzes her imagination, and then imposes its gracious protection, which is in reality a snare, a travesty on human character.[53]

As an advocate of "free love," Goldman also championed the cause of birth control—and, as a result, served a prison term. In 1919 the U.S. government deported her to her native Russia, where she became an outspoken critic of the new Bolshevik regime.

CHRISTIAN SOCIALISM

Another variant of socialism is Christian socialism. As the adjective suggests, Christian socialism is based on the Bible, and on the teachings of Jesus of Nazareth more particularly. The Old Testament (also known as the Hebrew Bible) says for example that if you "cast your bread upon the water"—that is, share your wealth with others—then you will be richly repaid (Ecclesiastes 11:1). Several passages appear to outlaw the practices that are the very foundations of capitalism. The book of Leviticus, for example, says that debts are to be forgiven every fifty years, during the year of Jubilee (Leviticus 25:9) and that money should not be lent at interest (Leviticus 25:36–37). And in the New Testament Jesus teaches that material rewards are of infinitely less value than spiritual rewards; that we are to love one another (John 13:31–35); that "it is easier for a camel to pass through the eye of a needle than it is for a rich man to enter the kingdom of heaven" (Matthew 19:16–30); and so on. Among the most important biblical texts for Christian socialists are Jesus' Sermon on the Mount (Matthew 5–7) and his final sermon, preached shortly before his crucifixion. In the Sermon on the Mount Jesus admonishes his audience to forgo earthly riches, to love their neighbors and not to judge them. And in his final sermon Jesus says that he is present in the lowliest of humans and as we treat them, so we treat him: "For I was hungry and you gave me food, was thirsty and you gave me drink, a stranger and you welcomed me, naked and you clothed me, ill and you cared for me, in prison and you visited me … whatever you did for the least of these my brothers, so have you done unto me" (Matthew 25:35–40).

These and other teachings were taken by late nineteenth- and early twentieth-century Christian thinkers such as F. D. Maurice (1805–1872), Henry Scott Holland (1847–1918), and R. H. Tawney (1880–1962) to entail or imply a certain sort of nonviolent and non-revolutionary socialism that puts the teachings of Jesus into political practice. There are today Christian socialists in many countries. One of the most active, the Christian Socialist Movement (CSM) in Great Britain (thecsm.org.uk), holds public meetings and publishes *The Common Good*, a quarterly magazine promoting and publicizing its aims and programs. The CSM is affiliated with the Labour Party and has more than forty members in the House of Commons and the House of Lords. Former British Prime Minister Gordon Brown is a member, as was his predecessor Tony Blair. The membership of Brown, the son of a Methodist minister, may attest to the truth of the adage that the gradualist socialism of the Labour Party owes much more to Methodism than to Marxism. In reality, however, Christian socialists come from almost all Christian denominations.[54]

Fabian Socialism

The Fabian Society, founded in London in 1884, took its name from the Roman general Quintus Fabius Maximus (d. 203 BCE), who refused to fight pitched battles, favoring instead a strategy of retreating and wearing down the enemy, finally getting them to surrender without major loss of life. It was in this spirit and by peaceful parliamentary means that the **Fabian socialists** sought to nudge England in an ever more markedly socialist direction.[55] Its leading members— including George Bernard Shaw, H. G. Wells, Graham Wallas, and Sidney and Beatrice Webb—were mostly middle-class writers and social reformers. They put their considerable talents to political use in the socialist cause, mainly by writing popular essays, plays, and books. Shaw's play *Pygmalion* (which, minus the socialist message, later became the Broadway musical and then the movie *My Fair Lady*) pokes fun at the English class system, and his *The Intelligent Woman's Guide to Socialism and Capitalism* (1928) explains socialist economic and political principles in a clear and witty way.

The Fabian philosophy of a peaceful parliamentary path to a socialist society was incorporated into the British Labour Party, founded in 1900. The Labour Party first won control of the British government in the election of 1924, when Ramsay MacDonald became Britain's first socialist prime minister. Since then, the Labour Party has been in and out of office many times and has succeeded in implementing such policies as the nationalization (that is, government ownership and operation) of certain services and industries, such as coal and steel, railroads and airlines, and telecommunications. The Labour Party also instituted a comprehensive social welfare system that includes a national health program providing free medical care for everyone. In the 1980s the Conservative Party, under the leadership of Prime Minister Margaret Thatcher, curtailed many social services and "privatized" (that is, sold to private investors) some public housing and a number of industries that had been nationalized by the Labour Party. Unable to agree about the best way of opposing the Conservatives, the opposition Labour Party was for a time rent by internal disagreements and differences. That situation began to change in the 1990s under the moderate leadership of Tony Blair. According to the more ardent socialists within his party, Blair changed the party's ideology into "Labour Lite." At the polls, however, Blair's blend of Christian socialism and **communitarianism** led to a resounding victory that returned the Labour Party to power in 1997 and made him prime minister of the United Kingdom—a position he held through two subsequent elections. His successor as prime minister and former leader of the Labour Party, Gordon Brown, shared these views. The current Labour Party leader, Jeremy Corbyn, advocates a return to the more militant "real socialism" of "Old Labour."

American Socialism

The United States has a long, but not very strong, socialist tradition. Exactly why socialism has not proved appealing to most Americans is a question that we will address in a moment. First, though, let us look briefly at the thought of one of the few original socialist thinkers that the United States has produced.

Edward Bellamy (1850–1898) was the author of a best-selling utopian novel *Looking Backward*, published in 1888. The novel's hero, Julian West, falls into a deep coma-like sleep and awakens in the year 2000 to find an America vastly different from the one he knew at the end of the nineteenth century. The United States, he discovers, has become a cooperative socialist society. When he tells his newfound friends about life in the old competitive capitalist society, they can hardly believe their ears. Why, they want to know, would anyone willingly live in a dog-eat-dog society? Julian West replies by

> compar[ing] society as it then was to a prodigious [stage-]coach which the masses of humanity were harnessed to and dragged toilsomely along a very hilly and sandy road. The driver was hunger, and permitted no lagging... Despite the difficulty of drawing the coach at all along so hard a road, the top was covered with passengers who never got down, even at the steepest ascents. These seats on top were very breezy and comfortable. Well up out of the dust, their occupants could enjoy the scenery at their leisure, or critically discuss the merits of the straining team. Naturally such places were in great demand and the competition for them was keen, every one seeking ... to secure a seat on the coach for himself and to leave it to his child after him... [Yet the seats at the top] were very insecure, and at every sudden jolt... persons were slipping out of them and falling to the ground, where they were instantly compelled to take hold of the rope and help to drag the coach... It was naturally regarded as a terrible misfortune to lose one's seat, and the apprehension that this might happen to them ... was a constant cloud upon the happiness of those who rode.[56]

The people on top, West continues, would express sympathy for and shout words of encouragement to those dragging the coach, and would sometimes send down salves and bandages for their bleeding hands and feet; but none of them ever got down to help. Such, says Bellamy, is the nature of competitive capitalist society.

Against this bleak picture Bellamy, speaking through his fictional hero, counterposes a socialist vision of mutual assistance and cooperation. The United

States in the year 2000 has no poverty and no unemployment. All able-bodied people work willingly, and all are compensated equally for their labors. Those who work at arduous or dirty jobs, such as coal mining, work fewer hours per week than those with easier or more pleasant jobs. There are no wages, for there is no money. Instead, everyone has a debit card (remarkably prophetic, that!) with which one "buys" from state-owned stores what is required to satisfy one's basic needs. Through these and other ingenious arrangements, people live in equality, harmony, and freedom.

This vision apparently appealed to many Americans, thousands of whom formed "Bellamy Clubs" to discuss how best to put these ideas into practice. Bellamy's popularity proved to be short-lived, but his influence is evident in subsequent socialist theorizing. His version of socialism became one of several strands in the socialist tradition, and its main themes were incorporated into the thinking of various populists and progressives at the turn of the century. Much has happened since then. But the year 2000 did not find the United States converted to socialism. Indeed, today in the United States, unlike most other countries, many people consider "socialism" a dirty word, even though (as several public opinion surveys suggest) most are unable to define it. One of the first questions that many foreigners ask is, Why do so many Americans find socialism so unappealing?

Several explanations are possible. One is that the United States is essentially a two-party political system in which third parties have little chance of significant electoral success. (Even so, Socialist Party presidential candidate Eugene V. Debs received nearly a million votes—more than 3 percent of the votes cast—in the 1920 presidential election while he was in federal prison for having spoken out against American participation in World War I.) Another explanation is that socialism is a working-class movement and ideology, and surveys show that most Americans—whether blue- or white-collar—think of themselves as belonging to the "middle class." A third and closely related explanation is that the purported fluidity of class distinctions, and a corresponding possibility of "moving up" socially and economically, renders socialism unappealing to people who think of themselves as upwardly mobile. Such people supposedly vote according to their aspirations instead of their actual situation. A fourth explanation is that the long and still-strong tradition of liberal individualism in the United States makes "collectivist" or "statist" ideologies unappealing. The idea of "rugged individualists" who "pull themselves up by their bootstraps" retains a powerful rhetorical appeal among many Americans. This idea typically loses much of its appeal in times of severe economic crisis when workers lose their jobs through no fault of their own.

For all of these reasons, many Americans have thought that socialism goes against the American grain or that it is "un-American." Many are therefore surprised to learn that the Pledge of Allegiance was composed in 1892 by Francis Bellamy, an American socialist, Baptist minister, and cousin of Edward Bellamy, author of *Looking Backward*. By "one nation, indivisible," Bellamy expressed an aspiration for a nation undivided by race, class, sex, or vast disparities of wealth and life-chances. America in the late nineteenth century did not fit this description. Segregationist "Jim Crow" laws oppressed African-Americans, as did the "night riders" of the Ku Klux Klan with their beatings and lynchings. In most states women could not vote or hold public office. Laborers, including young children, worked up to seventy hours per week in unsafe and unsanitary mines, factories, and "sweat shops," and their attempts to organize unions and recruit members were thwarted by both legal and illegal means. In the "Gilded Age," as Mark Twain called the 1890s, the rich "robber barons" bought and paid for politicians, who in turn passed laws favorable to the interests of the wealthy and contrary to the interests of the poor. "One nation, indivisible, with liberty and justice for all" was, in Bellamy's day, an aspiration, not a description of things as they actually were. (The words "under God" were not added until 1954, during the "Red scare" of the McCarthy era. By invoking the deity, Congress meant to rebuke "godless, atheistic Communism.") And so, socialists say, socialism is as American as apple pie—and the Pledge of Allegiance.

The difference between the way Americans like to think of their society and the way things really are is a continuing theme of American socialists. Some of them, such as Michael Harrington (1928–1989), have maintained that the picture of the rugged and self-reliant individual is an ideological fantasy that is out of touch with contemporary American realities. America has great wealth and abundant opportunities, they say, but these are unjustly distributed. A genuinely just society would not permit any of its citizens to go hungry, to be homeless, or to be willing to work but remain unemployed for long periods. The root of the problem lies not with these poor people, but with the system of profit and privilege that rewards "winners" and punishes "losers" and—worse yet—their children, who are themselves caught up in a cycle of poverty and despair perpetuated from one generation to the next. The only truly free society would be one in which opportunities to develop one's talents and abilities to their fullest would be equally distributed. Such a society, say the socialists, would necessarily be socialist.[57] That this message no longer seems as far-fetched as it once was is suggested by the surprisingly strong presidential candidacy of Senator Bernie Sanders of Vermont. A self-described democratic socialist, Sanders mounted a vigorous but ultimately unsuccessful campaign for the 2016 Democratic presidential nomination.

SOCIALISM TODAY

If the late nineteenth century was the "golden age" of Marxism, as Leszek Kolakowski has claimed, then how should we regard the end of the twentieth and the early twenty-first century, a time of dramatic and astonishingly swift change in the socialist world? From one point of view, these decades seem to signal the end of socialism as a compelling political ideology; from another, the turbulence of these years may mark a revival of socialism. As old institutions and dogmas are discredited and overturned, socialists confront new opportunities and challenges—especially the challenge of deciding what forms and directions socialism should take.

At this point it seems clear that the Marxist-Leninist version of communism is dying, if not already dead. In 1989, a year that future historians may consider as significant as 1789, the Soviet Union and Poland began to allow non-Communists to compete for political office, which resulted in an overwhelming electoral defeat for the Communists in Poland; the ruling Communist Party in Hungary, the Hungarian Socialist Workers' Party, dissolved itself; the communist government of East Germany, under the pressure of massive demonstrations and emigration, opened the Berlin Wall and promised its people free elections; the communist regime in Czechoslovakia collapsed, and a dissident playwright, Vaclav Havel, was elected president; and Communist Party rule was openly challenged in Bulgaria and Romania, which overthrew and executed its dictatorial leader. Not all signs pointed in the same direction in 1989, of course, for this was also the year in which the communist government of China violently suppressed the reform movement led by students. Yet even in China, Marxism-Leninism was under challenge—a challenge that began with the economic reforms initiated when Deng Xiaoping became head of the Chinese Communist Party in 1978. In some respects, the Chinese students who gathered in Tiananmen Square to call for an end to corruption in government and respect for human rights were seeking only to extend Deng's reforms from the economic to the political arena.

The movement toward economic competition continued throughout the 1990s and received a boost in 1997 when Hong Kong, with its powerful capitalist economy, rejoined the mainland. Whether China can sustain a competitive market economy and still retain a closed, noncompetitive political system is open to doubt. But even if it can, the political and economic system that results will be very different from the Marxist-Leninist-Maoist ideal. Until recently, the successor to (and in fact replacement of) "Mao Zedong thought" was euphemistically called "socialism with Chinese characteristics," which actually appeared to be more capitalist than socialist, and more internationalist or global than distinctly or uniquely Chinese. At present it is difficult to tell whether President Xi's attempt to revive Mao Zedong thought amounts to a repudiation of that more moderate and pro-Western ideology. One thing that is clear is that the Chinese regime faces a continuing crisis of legitimacy. During the boom years of the last decade of the twentieth century and the first eight years of the twenty-first, China shredded its social safety net, assuming—wrongly—that widespread unemployment was a thing of the past. The worldwide economic recession that began in 2007 and intensified in the years following hit the Chinese economy—and Chinese workers—very hard indeed. Whether, or to what extent, that downturn delegitimized communism and the CCP is difficult to discern; but it cannot have helped. The gap between the very wealthy and the very poor continues to grow, as does unrest in the cities and the countryside.

The reform movement in the Soviet Union also encountered resistance from hard-line communists, but there the outcome was vastly different from that in China. When a group of communist leaders tried to halt the drift away from communism in 1991 by seizing control of the government, they were unable to secure enough support from the military and the people to hold power for even a week. Instead, the failure of their *coup d'état* led swiftly to the disintegration of the Soviet Union itself. To many observers, this remarkable chain of events seemed to spell the death of communism as an ideology.

But what does it mean to say that communism is dead or dying? Although this question could be answered in many ways, two points are especially worth noting. The first is that the Communist Party has lost its claim to speak for and in the name of the proletariat. Instead of leading the way to the new world of communist society, the party became a stodgy, rigid, bureaucratic institution, more interested in maintaining the power and privileges of its leaders than in bringing an end to exploitation and alienation. Whether this was inevitable or avoidable is open to debate. But it is clear that, wherever the Communist Party has held power, democratic centralism has been far more centralist than democratic.

The second point follows from the first. Communists have typically taken democratic centralism to mean that political power *and* economic planning are to be under the control of the Communist Party. This means that communists have adopted the view that the economy must be centrally controlled and planned. In particular, communists have instituted a **command economy**, a "top-down," authoritarian system in which wages, prices, production, and distribution are determined not by the competitive market's law of supply and demand but by the decisions and commands of the government. By the 1980s, however, many communists had concluded that centralized control of property and resources was too cumbersome and inefficient. The most prominent spokesman for this disaffection was Mikhail Gorbachev, then head of the Communist Party of the Soviet Union, who announced his policy of **perestroika** (restructuring) shortly after taking office in 1985. Like Deng Xiaoping in China, Gorbachev sought to decentralize control of the economy and introduce elements of a competitive market economy into the Soviet Union. Now that the Soviet Union has fallen apart, Russia and most of the other formerly communist countries have moved, painfully and haltingly, toward a full market economy.

For both of these reasons, communism seems no longer to have the ability to inspire heroic sacrifices by dedicated and loyal followers. In this sense, it is dying. But this does not mean that all elements of Marxism-Leninism, much less socialism in general, are breathing their last. To many people in Asia, Africa, and Latin America, for instance, Lenin's account of imperialism still supplies the most powerful explanation of the plight of the countries of the Third World, which they see as dominated economically and politically by the capitalist powers of Europe, North America, and Japan. If communism is not the solution to their problems it once seemed, these people are still not likely to concede that capitalism is, either.

Indeed, it would be a great mistake to conclude that the death of communism will automatically mark the triumph of capitalism. In many cases, the people who are abandoning communism are not necessarily abandoning socialism. They continue to believe that *in some way* the major means of production in a society ought to be in the hands not of private persons, but of the public at large. They may have given up on the ideas of the one-party state and the command economy, but not on socialism in some form or other. In fact, non-Marxist socialist parties won elections that gave them control of the government in several European countries in the early 2000s, including Spain, Portugal, Austria, and Italy. Moreover, these parties have formed a partnership, the Party of European Socialists, through which they attempt to coordinate the activities and increase the effectiveness of the many socialists who have been elected to the parliament of the European Union. If electoral results are any guide, in short, socialism is still very much alive.

As we noted at the beginning of our discussion of socialism in Chapter 5, socialists have long been divided over two questions: How much and what kind of property is to be in public hands? And how is society to exercise control over this property? (See Figure 6.2 for a graph illustrating the positions various socialists have taken in their responses to these questions.) From Saint-Simon to the Soviet communists, some socialists have responded by calling for centralized control of most forms of property—factories and farms, mills and mines, and other means of production. But from the beginning, other socialists have responded to one or both of these questions in a more modest fashion. Owen and Fourier, with their visions of societies divided into small, self-sufficient, self-governing communities, called for highly decentralized forms of socialism. In the twentieth century, a growing number of socialists have advocated **market socialism**.[58] As the name implies, market socialism attempts to blend elements of a free-market economy with social ownership and public control of property. Although different socialists propose to blend these elements in different ways, the basic idea is that the major resources— large factories, mines, power plants, forests, mineral reserves, and so on—will be owned and operated directly for the public good, while private individuals will be free to own small businesses, farms, houses, cars, and so on. Middle-sized firms will be owned by those who work in them. All businesses, even the publicly owned firms, will compete in the marketplace for profits. If there are four or five steel factories in a country, for example, the workers in each factory will choose their supervisors, control their working conditions, and set the price of the finished steel, which they will then try to sell in competition with the other factories— and perhaps foreign competitors, too. Any profits will then be shared among the factory's workers as they see fit. If the factory loses money, it will be up to the workers to decide how to cope with the losses and become more competitive.

Some form of market socialism may well be the future of socialism. It promises neither the utopia of the early socialists nor the brave new world that Marx and his followers envisioned as the ultimate result of historical development. But it does promise to promote cooperation and solidarity rather than competition and individualism, even as it aims at reducing, if not completely eliminating, the class divisions that spawn exploitation and alienation. In these respects, the modest, decentralized version of socialism that seems to be emerging continues to draw on themes that have long inspired people to seize the socialist banner. If communism is dying, in short, it need not take socialism to the grave with it. On the contrary, communism's death could conceivably breathe new life into other forms of socialism.

To sum up: if "socialism" were identical with "Marxism-Leninism," then socialism would be dead or dying. But socialism comes in several varieties, some of which are Marxist, but many of which are not. Some socialists have heartily welcomed the end of communism, claiming that "real" or "true" socialism can now be given a chance to succeed. Critics, by contrast, say that socialism of any sort bears a stigma that it will not soon shed—and that will prevent it from being a credible contender in the ideological conflicts of the twenty-first century.

Such a conclusion is, depending on your own ideology, either too optimistic or too pessimistic. As we have seen, ideologies are adaptable, and after periods of decline they often reappear with renewed energy and appeal. Such may now be the case with fascism, especially in its neo-Nazi variant. A similar comeback may yet prove possible for socialism. So long as some people see market mechanisms as exploiting workers and distributing necessary goods and services in ways that are systematically unfair or unjust, so long as they are wary of concentrations of economic power in relatively few private hands and see such power reflected in political power or influence—so long, in short, as there is dissent, distrust, and

FIGURE 6.2 Differences among socialists on public ownership and control of property.

discontent within a capitalist system—then there are likely to be socialist critics of capitalism as an economic system and of democratic liberalism as its ruling ideology.

The globalization of capitalism and the Great Recession that began in 2007 have created renewed interest in socialist critiques of and alternatives to unregulated capitalism, not only among self-identified socialists but—more surprisingly still—among some mainstream economists. In an interview with the *Wall Street Journal* the (non-Marxian) eminent economist Nouriel Roubini said, "Karl Marx had it right. At some point, capitalism can destroy itself. You cannot keep on shifting income from labor to capital without having an excess capacity and a lack of aggregate demand. That's what has happened. We thought that markets worked. They're not working."[59] And the (non-Marxian) political theorist John Gray writes that while Marx was wrong about communism, he was quite correct in his critique and appraisal of capitalism as a self-destructive economic system.[60] Others disagree, of course; but such comments and conversations, which were all but inconceivable among mainstream thinkers before "The Crisis of '08," are now commonplace.[61]

CONCLUSION

Socialism as an Ideology

Like liberalism and conservatism, socialism comes in so many varieties that it sometimes seems to be not one but many different ideologies. Socialists do share certain core assumptions or beliefs, however, just as liberals and conservatives do. To see what these are, we must note how socialism performs the four functions that all political ideologies perform.

Explanation. To begin with, how do socialists try to explain social conditions? In general, they explain them in terms of economic and class relations. Rather than appeal to the choices of individuals, as liberals typically do, socialists are inclined to say that individuals are always caught up in social relations that shape and structure the choices available to them. Individuals may make choices, but they cannot choose to do just anything they wish. As Marx put it, "Men make their own history, but they do not make it just as they please..."[62] Some will have more to choose from than others. In particular, capitalists will have more options than workers, and the choices that capitalists make will sharply limit the choices available to the workers. A capitalist faced with declining profits can decide to expand or reinvest in his or her business, for instance, or move it to a different region or country, or simply sell or close it. Within the limits of his or her resources, the capitalist can do as he or she sees fit. But the worker can usually do nothing more than react to the choice the capitalist makes. Should the capitalist decide to close the business, the worker has little choice but to look elsewhere for work.

For these reasons, socialists maintain that social conditions must be explained by referring to economic or class relations. Because so much of what happens in society depends upon the way people organize themselves to work and produce goods and services, beginning with the food they need to live, then much of what happens in society can be accounted for only in terms of the division of society into classes. To explain the problem of crime, for example, socialists are not likely to point to the weakness of human nature, as conservatives do. Instead, they are inclined to say that much criminal activity is the result of the exploitation and alienation of working-class people who lack the power to improve their condition in a class-divided society.

Evaluation. This emphasis on social class carries over to the second function of ideologies, that of evaluating social conditions. In this case the key factor is the sharpness of class divisions in a society. If one class of people clearly has firm control of the wealth so that it is able to limit sharply the choices open to the working class, then conditions are, from the socialist point of view, exploitative and unjust. If class divisions are slight, or if there are no apparent classes at all, then conditions will be much better. But this can only happen, socialists say, when all members of society somehow share control of the major means of production.

Orientation. As regards orientation, socialists tell people that they should think of themselves mainly in terms of their position in the class structure. Some socialists have taken this to the extreme of saying that class differences are the only differences that matter. When Marx said that the workers have no fatherland, for instance, he seemed to say that nationality or citizenship should play no real role in one's identity. Not race or religion or nationality, but only class position really makes a difference in the world. Although most socialists do not go this far, all believe that our position in the class structure is an important factor in shaping our identities. We see things as we do and we are who we are largely because of our class position.

If the preceding claim is true, then what is the point of telling people that they should see themselves as members of this or that class? The point, according to socialists, is that class consciousness is a necessary step on the path to a classless society. Before a capitalist can see the error of his or her ways, the capitalist must first understand that he or she is a member of the class that exploits and oppresses the workers. Only then is there any chance that the capitalist will surrender control of wealth and resources to their rightful owner—society at large. More important, it is only when the workers see that they form a large and oppressed class that they will be able to take action to free themselves. If they fail to develop this awareness of their social position, they will have no more chance of liberating themselves than the slave who thinks that his or her slavery is altogether natural and proper.

Program. For most socialists, then, orientation is necessary to the programmatic function of their ideology. The socialist goal is simple: to bring about a society that is as nearly classless as possible. Exactly how they propose to do this will vary from one time and place to another, of course. Some look for an almost spontaneous revolution, as we have seen, while others believe that a single highly disciplined party must lead the way; some rely on persuasion and the force of example, while others favor violent revolution and the force of arms. But in all cases socialists maintain that steps must be taken to promote equality and cooperation among all members of society in order to give everyone greater control over his or her own life.

Socialism and the Democratic Ideal

In its pursuit of equality, socialism is an ideology committed to democracy in one or another sense of that contested term. As most socialists will quickly admit, leaders like Stalin have been more interested in acquiring personal power than in promoting democracy; but these leaders, they say, were not true socialists. True socialism requires government of, by, and for the people. It aims to give everyone an equal voice in the decisions that affect his or her life in direct and important ways. But this can only happen, socialists say, if no one person or class controls most of the wealth and resources—and thus most of the power—within a society. Wealth must be shared equitably if not equally, and resources must be owned and controlled for the benefit of the whole society if true democracy is ever to take shape. Otherwise, they insist, we shall have nothing but government of the wealthy, by the wealthy, and for the wealthy.

Discussion Questions

1   In what way(s) does Engels's version of Marxian theory differ from Marx's?
2   What were Eduard Bernstein's main criticisms of Marx and Marxian theory, and how did he propose to revise that theory?
3   Who spoke of "trade union consciousness" and what did he or she mean by this phrase? Is such consciousness in his or her judgment a good or a bad thing? What did he or she believe is the alternative to trade union consciousness?
4   What reason(s) did Lenin (and later Mao Zedong) have for believing that proletarian revolution would come first to economically backward countries such as Russia and China? Be specific.
5   What is Lenin's theory of imperialism and why did he devise it?
6   To what use(s) did Mao Zedong put Lenin's theory of imperialism? Be specific.
7   On what biblical passages and teachings do Christian socialists base their brand of socialism?

8   Why have anarchists, and Mikhail Bakunin in particular, objected to Marxian theory?

NOTES

1   Leszek Kolakowski, *Main Currents of Marxism*, vol. II, *The Golden Age* (Oxford: Clarendon Press, 1978).

2   Quoted in David McLellan, *Karl Marx: His Life and Work* (London: Macmillan, 1973), p. 443.

3   See Terrell Carver, *Engels* (Oxford: Oxford University Press, 1981); and *Marx and Engels: The Intellectual Relationship* (Brighton, U.K.: Harvester Press, 1983); Terence Ball, "Marxian Science and Positivist Politics," in Terence Ball and James Farr, eds., *After Marx* (Cambridge: Cambridge University Press, 1984), Chapter 11.

4   Friedrich Engels, "Speech at Marx's Graveside," in Karl Marx and Friedrich Engels, *Selected Works*, one-volume edition (New York: International Publishers, 1968), p. 435. For an inquiry into the "Marx-Darwin myth," see Terence Ball, *Reappraising Political Theory* (Oxford: Clarendon Press, 1995), Chapter 10.

5   See James Farr, "Marx's Laws," *Political Studies* 34 (1986): 202–222; and "Marx and Positivism," in Ball and Farr, eds., *After Marx*, Chapter 10.

6   Friedrich Engels, *Dialectics of Nature* (New York: International Publishers, 1963), p. 314.

7   Engels, *Socialism, Utopian and Scientific*, in Marx and Engels, *Selected Works*, pp. 399–434.

8   Marx, "Theses on Feuerbach," in *Selected Works*, p. 28.

9   Engels, *Dialectics of Nature*, p. 25.

10   Eduard Bernstein, *Evolutionary Socialism* (New York: Schocken Books, 1961), p. 202. See, further, Kolakowski, *Main Currents of Marxism*, vol. 2, Chapter 4; and Peter Gay, *The Dilemma of Democratic Socialism*, 2nd ed. (New York: Collier Books, 1962).

11   Bernstein, *Evolutionary Socialism*, p. 106.

12   Ibid., p. 210; also in Terence Ball, Richard Dagger, and Daniel O'Neill, eds., *Ideals and Ideologies: A Reader*, 10th ed. (New York and London: Routledge, 2016), selection 6.39.

13   Ibid., p. 202.

14   Ferdinand Lassalle, *Franz von Sickingen* (1859), Act III, scene 5; quoted from Arthur Koestler, *Darkness at Noon*, trans. Daphne Hardy (New York: Bantam Books, 1968 [1941]), p. 196.

15   Bernstein, *Evolutionary Socialism*, p. 211.

16   Ibid., p. 219.

17   See Gary P. Steenson, *Karl Kautsky, 1854–1938: Marxism in the Classical Years* (Pittsburgh, PA: University of Pittsburgh Press, 1978), esp. pp. 116–131, 186.

18   See, for example, V. I. Lenin, "Marxism and Revisionism," in Lenin, *Selected Works*, one-volume edition (Moscow: Progress Publishers, 1968), pp. 25–32; also in Ball, Dagger, and O'Neill, *Ideals and Ideologies*, selection 6.40.

19   Karl Marx and Friedrich Engels, *The Manifesto of the Communist Party*, in Lewis Feuer, ed., *Marx and Engels: Basic Writings on Politics and Philosophy* (Garden City, NY: Doubleday Anchor, 1959), p. 11; also in Ball, Dagger, and O'Neill, *Ideals and Ideologies*, selection 5.37.

20   For an engaging and insightful inquiry into the thought of these nineteenth-century intellectuals see Isaiah Berlin, *Russian Thinkers* (New York: Viking Press, 1978) and Tom Stoppard's lively, witty, and long (eight-hour) trilogy of plays, "The Coast of Utopia" (2007), much of which is based on Berlin's book.

21   Contrary to a popular misconception it was Plekhanov, not Lenin, who earned the title "the father of Russian Marxism." See Samuel H. Baron, *Plekhanov: The Father of Russian Marxism* (Stanford: Stanford University Press, 1963); and Isaiah Berlin's

essay, "The Father of Russian Marxism," in Berlin, *The Power of Ideas* (Princeton: Princeton University Press, 2000), pp. 126–133.

22   Quoted in Bruce Mazlish, *The Revolutionary Ascetic: Evolution of a Political Type* (New York: Basic Books, 1976), p. 140.

23   Lenin, "'Left Wing' Communism—An Infantile Disorder," in *Selected Works*, p. 535.

24   Lenin, "What Is to Be Done?" *Selected Works*, 3 vols. (Moscow: Progress Publishers, 1963), I, p. 114.

25   Ibid., p. 114.

26   Lenin, *Imperialism, The Highest Stage of Capitalism*, in Lenin, *Selected Works*, pp. 171–175, 240–247.

27   See Simon Sebag Montefiore, *Stalin: The Court of the Red Tsar* (New York: Knopf, 2003), pp. 36–37.

28   For a vivid account of one of the more ambitious and violent of Stalin's bank robberies, see the chilling "Prologue: The Bank Robbery," in Simon Sebag Montefiore, *Young Stalin* (New York: Random House, 2007), pp. 3–16.

29   Roy A. Medvedev, *Let History Judge: The Origins and Consequences of Stalinism*, trans. Colleen Taylor (New York: Knopf, 1972), p. 519. See also Robert C. Tucker, ed., *Stalinism* (New York: Norton, 1977); and Adam B. Ulam, *Stalin: The Man and His Era* (New York: Viking Press, 1973).

30   Medvedev, *Let History Judge*, p. 510.

31   Ibid., Chapter 14.

32   For a broad overview see David Joravsky, *The Lysenko Affair* (Chicago: University of Chicago Press, 1970); and, for a focus on the impact of Stalinist ideology on Soviet science, see Loren R. Graham, "Stalinist Ideology and the Lysenko Affair," in his *Science in Russia and the Soviet Union: A Short History* (New York and Cambridge: Cambridge University Press, 1994), Chapter 6.

33   Here, as elsewhere, Stalin's views stand in sharp contrast with those of Marx. On the role of chance and accident in history, see Marx's letter to Ludwig Kugelmann (April 17, 1871) in Marx and Engels, *Selected Correspondence* (Moscow: Progress Publishers, 1975), p. 248: "World history ... would ... be of a very mystical nature, if 'accidents' played no part."

34   For an examination and critique of claims about "historical inevitability," see Isaiah Berlin, "Historical Inevitability," in his *Liberty*, ed. Henry Hardy (Oxford and New York: Oxford University Press, 2002), essay 2, pp. 94–165.

35   Joseph Stalin, "Political Report of the Central Committee to the Sixteenth Congress," in Stalin, *Selected Works* (Moscow: Foreign Languages Publishing House, 1952–1955), vol. 12, p. 381.

36   See Masha Gessen, *Words Will Break Cement: The Passion of Pussy Riot* (New York: Penguin, 2014).

37   Mao Zedong, "The Chen-Feng Movement," in Conrad Brandt, Benjamin Schwartz, and John King Fairbank, eds., *A Documentary History of Chinese Communism* (New York: Atheneum, 1966), pp. 384–385. We have modified the sanitized translation to reflect Mao's earthy prose. "For more from Mao, see Ball, Dagger, and O'Neill, *Ideals and Ideologies*, selection 6.42."

38   See Bruce D. Larkin, *China and Africa, 1949–1970: The Foreign Policy of the People's Republic of China* (Berkeley and Los Angeles: University of California Press, 1971).

39   See Yang Jisheng, *Tombstone: The Great Chinese Famine, 1958–1962* (New York: Farrar, Straus and Giroux, 2012).

40   See Judith Shapiro, *Mao's War Against Nature: Politics and the Environment in Revolutionary China* (Cambridge: Cambridge University Press, 2001).

41   Terence Hunt, "Clinton, China Leader Spar Over Human Rights," *Arizona Republic*, October 30, 1997, p. A1.

42   Chris Buckley and Andrew Jacobs, "Maoists in China, Given New Life, Attack Dissent," *New York Times*, January 5, 2015, pp. A1, A6. See also Evan Osnos, "Born Red: How Xi Jinping became China's most authoritarian leader since Mao," *The New Yorker*, April 6, 2015, pp. 42–55.

43 See, for example, "Maoist Rebellion Shifts Balance of Power in Rural Nepal," *New York Times*, February 5, 2004, p. A3; "Maoist Rebels, Once Dismissed as Ragtag Band, Widen Reach in India," *New York Times*, November 1, 2009, pp. A1, A16.

44 Grace Lee, "The Political Philosophy of *Juche*," *Stanford Journal of East Asian Affairs*, 3:1 (Spring 2003), pp. 105–112.

45 See Martin Jay, *The Dialectical Imagination: A History of the Frankfurt School and the Institute of Social Research, 1923–1950*, 2nd ed. (Berkeley and Los Angeles: University of California Press, 1996).

46 For a readable and readily accessible argument along these lines, see Benjamin R. Barber, *Consumed: How Markets Corrupt Children, Infantilize Adults, and Swallow Citizens Whole* (New York: W. W. Norton, 2007).

47 See Paul Thomas, *Karl Marx and the Anarchists* (London: Routledge & Kegan Paul, 1980).

48 William Godwin, *An Enquiry Concerning Political Justice*, Isaac Kramnick, ed. (Harmondsworth, U.K.: Penguin, 1976). Also see Mark Philp, *Godwin's "Political Justice"* (London: Duckworth, 1984).

49 See n. 20, above.

50 See Mikhail Bakunin, "Anarcho-Communism vs. Marxism," in Ball, Dagger, and O'Neill, *Ideals and Ideologies*, selection 6.43.

51 Peter Kropotkin, *Mutual Aid* (London: Heinemann, 1902).

52 Emma Goldman, "Anarchism: What It Really Stands For," in Goldman, *Anarchism and Other Essays* (New York: Mother Earth Association, 1910), pp. 58, 68; also in Ball, Dagger, and O'Neill, *Ideals and Ideologies*, selection 6.44.

53 Emma Goldman, "Marriage and Love," in *Anarchism and Other Essays*, p. 241.

54 See Alan Wilkinson, *Christian Socialism: Scott Holland to Tony Blair* (London: SCM Press, 1998).

55 See Norman MacKenzie and Jean MacKenzie, *The First Fabians* (London: Weidenfeld & Nicholson, 1977); and A. M. McBriar, *Fabian Socialism and English Politics, 1884–1914* (Cambridge: Cambridge University Press, 1966); Margaret Cole, *The Story of Fabian Socialism* (Stanford, CA: Stanford University Press, 1961).

56 Edward Bellamy, *Looking Backward* (New York: New American Library, 1960), pp. 26–27; also in Ball, Dagger, and O'Neill, *Ideals and Ideologies*, selection 6.45.

57 See Michael Harrington, *Socialism: Past and Future* (New York: Penguin Books USA, 1990).

58 See, for example, Alec Nove, *The Economics of Feasible Socialism* (London: Allen & Unwin, 1983); and David Miller, *Market, State, and Community* (Oxford: Clarendon Press, 1989).

59 See the video interview at http://live.wsj.com/video/nouriel-roubini-karl-marx-was-right/68EE8F89-EC24-42F8-9B9D-47B510E473B0.html#!68EE8F89-EC24-42F8-9B9D-47B510E473B0.

60 See John Gray, *False Dawn: The Delusions of Global Capitalism*; and Gray's summary in "A Point of View: The Revolution of Capitalism" at www.bbc.co.uk/news/magazine-14764357.

61 As you will discover online if you google "Marx was right."

62 Karl Marx, "The Eighteenth Brumaire of Louis Bonaparte," in Marx and Engels, *Selected Works*, p. 97.

FOR FURTHER READING

Ball, Terence, and James Farr, eds. *After Marx*. Cambridge: Cambridge University Press, 1984.

Carr, E. H. *Michael Bakunin*. London: Macmillan, 1937.

Carver, Terrell. *Engels*. Oxford: Oxford University Press, 1981.

Cohen, G. A. *Why Not Socialism?* Princeton, NJ: Princeton University Press, 2009.

Cole, Margaret. *The Story of Fabian Socialism.* Stanford, CA: Stanford University Press, 1961.

Conquest, Robert. *Lenin.* New York: Viking Press, 1972

Crick, Bernard. *Socialism.* Minneapolis: University of Minnesota Press, 1987.

Garton Ash, Timothy. *The Magic Lantern: The Revolution Witnessed in Warsaw, Budapest, Berlin, and Prague.* New York: Random House, 1990.

Gay, Peter. *The Dilemma of Democratic Socialism: Eduard Bernstein's Challenge to Marx.* New York: Collier Books, 1962.

Gray, Alexander. *The Socialist Tradition: Moses to Lenin.* London: Longmans, Green, 1947.

Harrington, Michael. *Socialism: Past and Future.* New York: Penguin Books, 1990.

King, Preston, ed. *Socialism and the Common Good: New Fabian Essays.* London: Frank Cass, 1996.

Knei-Paz, Baruch. *The Social and Political Thought of Leon Trotsky.* Oxford: Oxford University Press, 1978.

Kolakowski, Leszek. *Main Currents of Marxism*, 3 vols., trans. P. S. Falla. Oxford: Clarendon Press, 1978.

Lichtheim, George. *A Short History of Socialism.* New York: Praeger, 1970.

Lukes, Steven. *Marxism and Morality.* Oxford: Oxford University Press, 1985.

Medvedev, Roy A. *Let History Judge: The Origins and Consequences of Stalinism*, trans. Colleen Taylor. New York: Knopf, 1972.

Meisner, Maurice. *Mao Zedong: A Political and Intellectual Portrait.* Cambridge, U.K.: Polity Press, 2007.

Miller, David. *Anarchism.* London: Dent, 1984.

Montefiore, Simon Sebag. *Stalin: In the Court of the Red Tsar.* New York: Knopf, 2004.

Patenaude, Bertrand M. *Trotsky: Downfall of a Revolutionary.* New York: Harper Collins, 2010.

Pierson, Christopher. *Socialism After Communism: The New Market Socialism.* University Park: Pennsylvania State University Press, 1995.

Roemer, John. *A Future for Socialism.* Cambridge, MA: Harvard University Press, 1994.

Spence, Jonathan. *Mao Zedong.* New York: Viking Penguin, 1999.

Starr, John B. *Continuing the Revolution: The Political Thought of Mao.* Princeton, NJ: Princeton University Press, 1979.

Tucker, Robert C., ed. *Stalinism.* New York: Norton, 1977.

Wolfe, Bertram D. *Three Who Made a Revolution.* New York: Dell, 1964.

Woodcock, George. *Anarchism.* Harmondsworth, U.K.: Penguin, 1963.

From the Ball, Dagger, and O'Neill Reader *Ideals and Ideologies*, Tenth Edition

Part VI: Socialism and Communism After Marx

USEFUL WEBSITES

Anarchy Archives: http://dwardmac.pitzer.edu/anarchist_archives/
Communist Party USA: www.cpusa.org
The Fabian Society: www.fabians.org.uk
The Monthly Review: www.monthlyreview.org
New Democratic Party (Canada): www.ndp.ca
Party of European Socialists: www.pes.org
Progressive Labor Party: www.plp.org
Socialist Party USA: http://socialistparty-usa.net
Socialist Workers Party: www.themilitant.com; www.swp.org.uk

CHAPTER 7

FASCISM

The sleep of reason brings forth monsters.

Francisco Goya

The words "fascist" and "fascism" are often invoked more in an emotional than in a cognitively meaningful way. Here we try to avoid the former and make use of the latter. The first thing to note about fascism—or perhaps we should say fascisms, in the plural—is that it (or they) is self-consciously and proudly "totalitarian." Historians may well remember the twentieth century as the age of world wars, nuclear weapons, and a new kind of political regime—**totalitarianism**. All of these developments are connected to political ideologies in one way or another, but to none more closely than totalitarianism. For totalitarianism is the attempt to take complete control of a society—not just its government but all of its social, cultural, and economic institutions—in order to fulfill an ideological vision of how society ought to be organized and life ought to be lived. This is what happened in the Soviet Union when Stalin imposed his version of Marxist socialism on that country. It is also what happened in Italy and Germany when Benito Mussolini and Adolf Hitler introduced varieties of a new and openly totalitarian ideology called fascism.

In fact, Mussolini and the Italian Fascists coined the word "totalitarian." They did this to define their revolutionary aims and to distinguish their ideology from liberalism and socialism, which they saw as defenders of democracy. Democracy requires equality of some sort, whether it be in the liberals' insistence on equal opportunity for individuals or the socialists' insistence on equal power for all in a classless society. Mussolini and his followers regarded these ideals with contempt, as did Hitler and the Nazis. They did appeal to the masses for support, to be sure, but in their view the masses were to exercise power not by thinking, speaking, or voting for themselves, but by blindly following their leaders to glory. As one of Mussolini's many slogans put it, *Credere, obbedire, combattere*—"Believe, obey, fight!"[1] Nothing more was asked, nothing more was desired of the people. By embracing totalitarianism, then, fascists also rejected democracy.

In this respect, fascism is a **reactionary** ideology. It took shape in the years following World War I as a reaction against the two leading ideologies of the time, liberalism and socialism. Unhappy with the liberal emphasis on the individual and with the socialist emphasis on contending social classes, the fascists provided a view of the world in which individuals and classes were to be absorbed into an all-embracing whole—a mighty nation under the control of a single party and a supreme leader. Like the reactionaries of the early 1800s, they also rejected the faith in reason that they thought formed the foundation for both liberalism and socialism. Reason is less reliable, both Mussolini and Hitler declared, than intuitions and emotions—what we sometimes call "gut instincts."

To say that fascism is in some ways a reactionary ideology is not to say, however, that fascists are simply reactionaries or extreme conservatives. In many ways they are quite different. Unlike Joseph de Maistre and the other reactionaries discussed in Chapter 4, for instance, fascists do not reject democracy, liberalism, and socialism in order to turn the clock back to a time when society was rooted in **ascribed status**, with church, king, and aristocracy firmly in power; on the contrary, many fascists have been openly hostile to religion, and few of them have had any respect for hereditary monarchs and aristocrats. Nor have they sought to return to the old, established ways of life; on the contrary, fascism in its most distinctive forms has been openly revolutionary, eager not only to change society but to change it root and branch. This revolutionary fervor by itself sets fascists apart from traditional or classical conservatives, who cannot abide rapid and radical change. So, too, does the fascist plan to concentrate power in the hands of a totalitarian state led by a single party and a supreme leader. Nothing could be further from the conservatives' desire to disperse power among various levels of government and the other "little platoons" that make up what they take to be a healthy society than the fascist vision of a unified state bending to the will of a single, all-powerful leader.

Fascism, then, is neither conservative nor simply reactionary. It is, as the original fascists boasted, a new and distinctive ideology. To appreciate how distinctive it is, we need to explore its background in the **Counter-Enlightenment**, in **nationalism**, and in other intellectual currents of the nineteenth century. We shall then examine fascism in its purest form in Mussolini's Italy, following that with a look at other varieties of fascism in Nazi Germany and elsewhere.

FASCISM: THE BACKGROUND

Although fascism did not emerge as a political ideology until the 1920s, its roots reach back two centuries to the reaction against the intellectual and cultural movement that dominated European thought in the eighteenth century—the **Enlightenment**. The thinkers of the Enlightenment dreamed a dream of reason. Taking the scientific discoveries of the seventeenth and eighteenth centuries as their model and inspiration, the Enlightenment philosophers claimed that the application of reason could remove all the social and political evils that stood in the way of happiness and progress. Reason can light the minds of men and women, they proclaimed, freeing them from ignorance and error and superstition.[2] The two great political currents that flow from the Enlightenment are liberalism and socialism. Different as they are in other respects, these two ideologies are alike in sharing the fundamental premises of the Enlightenment. These premises include the following:

1   *Humanism*—the idea that human beings are the source and measure of value, with human life valuable in and of itself. As Immanuel Kant (1724–1804) put it, human beings belong to the "kingdom of ends." Each person is an "end-in-himself," not something that others may use, like a tool, as a means of accomplishing their own selfish ends.

2   *Rationalism*—the idea that human beings are rational creatures and that human reason, epitomized in scientific inquiry, can solve all mysteries and reveal solutions to all the problems that men and women face.

3   *Secularism*—the idea that religion may be a source of comfort and insight but not of absolute and unquestionable truths for guiding public life. The Enlightenment thinkers differed from one another in their religious views. Some, like John Locke and Kant, remained Christians, although unorthodox in their views; others, like Voltaire (1694–1778) and the American revolutionary Thomas Paine (1737–1809), rejected Christianity but believed in a God who had created a world as well-ordered as a watch, which the "divine watchmaker" had wound and left to run; still others were atheists. But even those who took their religion seriously regarded it as something to be confined largely to private life, and therefore out of place in politics. The irreligious among the Enlightenment philosophers simply dismissed religion as an outmoded superstition that must give way to rational and scientific ideas.

4   *Progressivism*—the idea that human history is the story of progress, or improvement—perhaps even inevitable improvement—in the human condition. Once the shackles of ignorance and superstition have been broken, human reason will be free to order society in a rational way, and life will steadily and rapidly become better for all.

5   *Universalism*—the idea that there is a single, universal human nature that binds all human beings together, despite differences of race, culture, or religious creed. Human beings are all equal members of Kant's "kingdom of ends," who—regardless of race, religion, nationality, or ethnicity—share the same essential nature, including preeminently the capacity for reason.

These Enlightenment views are often linked to liberalism, but they provided much of the inspiration for socialism as well. Indeed, modern socialism arose in part from the complaint that liberalism was not going far enough in its attempt to remake society in the image of Enlightenment ideals. Fascism, however, grows out of the very different conviction that the ideals of the Enlightenment are not worth pursuing—a claim first put forward in the late eighteenth and early nineteenth centuries.

THE COUNTER-ENLIGHTENMENT

A diverse group of thinkers that some call the **Counter-Enlightenment** mounted an all-out attack on the Enlightenment.[3] Among them were the linguist Johan Gottfried von Herder (1744–1803); the royalists and reactionaries Joseph de Maistre (1753–1821) and Louis Gabriel de Bonald (1754–1840); the Marquis de Sade (1740–1814), now notorious as a libertine and pornographer; and racial theorists like Joseph-Arthur de Gobineau (1816–1882). None of them rejected every premise of the Enlightenment; each had particular concerns and complaints that the others did not share, but they were alike in dismissing the major premises of the Enlightenment as fanciful, false, and politically dangerous.

These Counter-Enlightenment thinkers were united, for instance, in denouncing "universalism" as a myth. Human beings are not all alike, they said; the differences that distinguish groups of people from one another run very deep. Indeed, these differences—of sex, race, language, culture, creed, and nationality—actually *define* who and what people are, shaping how they think of themselves and other people. Some of the Counter-Enlightenment thinkers stressed differences of one kind, while others focused on other kinds. For Herder, linguistic and cultural differences mattered most; for Gobineau, it was race; and for de Sade, it was gender. Men, de Sade observed, do not admit women to the "kingdom of ends." They treat them as means, as objects to be used, abused, and humiliated—and this is as it should be. Fittingly, our words "sadist" and "sadistic" come from the name de Sade.

These Counter-Enlightenment critics brought similar complaints against the Enlightenment's faith in reason and science. The problem with rationalism, they said, is that it flies in the face of all human experience. The prevalence of *un*reason, of superstition and prejudice, shows that reason itself is too weak to be relied on. Most people, most of the time, use reason not to examine matters critically and dispassionately but to rationalize and excuse their desires and deepen their prejudices. With this in mind, the Counter-Enlightenment writers often deplored the Enlightenment's assault on religion. Some of them wrote from sincere religious conviction, but others simply held that religious beliefs are socially necessary fictions. The belief in heaven and hell, they maintained, may be all that keeps most people behaving as well as they do; to lose that belief may be to lose all hope of a civilized and orderly society. If this means that government must support an established church and persecute or even execute dissenters, then so be it.

In different ways, each of these critics challenged the fundamental premises of the Enlightenment. Out of their challenge a different picture of human beings emerged. According to this picture, humans are fundamentally nonrational, even irrational, beings; they are defined by their differences—of race, sex, religion, language, and nationality; and they are usually locked in conflict with one another, a conflict sparked by their deep-seated and probably permanent differences. Taken one by one, there is nothing necessarily "fascist" about any element of this picture. Combining the elements, however, produces a picture of human capacities and characteristics that prepared the way for the emergence of fascism.[4] This picture should become clearer as we look at another feature of fascism—nationalism.

NATIONALISM

Nationalism, as we noted in Chapter 1, is the belief that the people of the world fall into distinct groups, or nations, with each nation forming the natural basis for a separate political unit, the **nation-state**. This sovereign, self-governing political unit is supposed to draw together and express the needs and desires of a single nation. Without such a state, a nation or people will be frustrated, unable either to govern or to express itself.

Although nationalistic sentiments are quite old, nationalism itself emerged as a political force only in the wake of the Napoleonic Wars of the early 1800s. As they swept across Europe, Napoleon's armies—the armies of the French *nation*—created a backlash of sorts, inspiring people in the various kingdoms and duchies of Germany, Italy, and elsewhere to recognize their respective nationalities and to struggle for unified nation-states of their own.

This first stage of nationalism is apparent in the works of the linguist Herder and of the philosopher Johann Gottlieb Fichte (1762–1814). Both appealed to the sense of German nationality, with Fichte laying particular stress on the distinctiveness of the German language—the only truly original European language, he said, for Latin had smothered the originality in the others.[5] In the winter of 1807–1808, still smarting from Napoleon's defeat in 1806 of the army of Prussia, the largest of the Germanic kingdoms, Fichte delivered his *Addresses to the German Nation* in Berlin. In the *Addresses* he maintained that the individual finds much of the meaning and value of life in being connected to the nation into which he or she was born. Rather than think of ourselves merely as individuals, in other words, we must think of ourselves as members of the larger and lasting community of the nation. Hence, Fichte said,

> The noble-minded man will be active and effective, and will sacrifice himself for his people. Life merely as such, the mere continuance of changing existence, has in any case never had any value for him; he has wished for it only as the source of what is permanent. But this permanence is promised to him only by the continuous and independent existence of his nation. In order to save his nation he must be ready even to die that it may live, and that he may live in it the only life for which he has ever wished.[6]

Longing for membership and meaning, the individual lives, according to Fichte, in and through the nation. The German nation was especially worth defending, Fichte thought, but neither he nor Herder was simply a German nationalist. All nations have value, they said, for all nations give shape and significance to the lives of their people. Against the universalism of the Enlightenment, then, Herder and Fichte argued that every nation brings something distinctive or unique to the world—something for which it deserves to be recognized and respected.

Yet neither Herder nor Fichte called for every nation to be embodied politically in its own distinct state. That development came later, most notably in the words and deeds of an Italian nationalist, Giuseppe Mazzini (1805–1872), and the German nationalist "Iron Chancellor" Otto von Bismarck (1815–1898).

In the early 1800s, Italy was as fragmented as Germany. Since the fall of the Roman Empire around AD 500, the word "Italy" had referred to a geographical and cultural region but never to a politically united country. Divided into kingdoms, duchies, and warring city-states, and often overrun by French and Spanish armies, Italy became the center of commerce and culture during the **Renaissance**, but it was far from the center of European political power. Niccolò Machiavelli called attention to this in the sixteenth century when he concluded his infamous book, *The Prince*, with "An Exhortation to Liberate Italy from the Barbarians"—but to no avail. Italy remained divided until the 1800s, when Mazzini and others made it their mission to unify the country. Other nations had found statehood—England, for instance, and France and Spain—and now, Mazzini said, it was time for Italy to join their ranks as a nation-state. Italy must be united not only geographically and culturally but politically as well. A nation cannot truly be a nation unless it can take its place among the powers of the earth. So Italians must be brought together, Mazzini argued, as citizens under a common government. Only then could they achieve freedom and fulfill their destiny as a people.

But Mazzini did not confine his nationalism to his native country. Like Herder and Fichte, he supported nationalism as an ideal for all nations, not just his own. Mazzini sometimes suggested that geography testified to God's intention of creating a world of distinct nations. Why else, he asked, did rivers, mountain ranges, and seas separate groups of people from one another and foster the development of separate languages, cultures, and customs? Mazzini even envisioned a world in which each nation had its own state and every nation-state lived in harmony with all the others—all following the example of a politically united Italy.

The nineteenth-century nationalists used the press, diplomacy, and occasionally the force of arms to achieve their goal, and by 1871 both Italy and Germany had finally become nation-states. The nationalistic impulse persisted too, and it continues to figure in the politics not only of Europe but also of Africa, Asia, and the American continents. It led to Zionism—the movement to establish a homeland, or nation-state, for Jews in Israel—and has taken a liberal direction in some cases, and a communist or socialist direction in others. That is a story for another chapter, however. In this chapter we shall concentrate on the nationalistic elements in fascism. But first, it is necessary to examine two intellectual currents of the late 1800s: **elitism** and **irrationalism**.

ELITISM

As we pointed out in earlier chapters, many nineteenth-century social thinkers regarded theirs as the age of democracy and "the common man." Many applauded this development, others abhorred it, and some, like Alexis de Tocqueville and John Stuart Mill, greeted it with mixed emotions. Democracy did expand opportunities and possibilities for the common people, they said, and to that extent it was good; but it also posed a threat to individuality—the threat of unthinking conformity and the "tyranny of the majority." Marx and the socialists largely dismissed or ignored this threat. For them, democracy—or socialist democracy, at any rate—would afford everyone an equal chance to live a creative, fruitful, and self-directed life. Such a life is possible, they said, only in a classless egalitarian society. But could a classless society ever be created? The socialists assumed that it could, with sufficient effort. But this assumption came under sharp attack in the late nineteenth and early twentieth centuries by thinkers who emphasized the importance—indeed, indispensability—of "elites" in society.

These "elite theorists," as they came to be called, were, broadly speaking, social scientists from different disciplines. They included Gaetano Mosca (1858–1941), Vilfredo Pareto (1848–1923), and Roberto Michels (1876–1936). In one way or another, each contributed to the idea of elitism by concluding that a classless society of equals was impossible. On the basis of historical studies, for instance, Mosca concluded that societies always have been, and always will be, ruled by a small group of leaders, even when it appears that the majority is ruling. Pareto, an Italian economist and sociologist, reached a similar conclusion. Perhaps most strikingly, so did Michels, a German-born Italian sociologist who undertook a study of the socialist parties and trade unions of Europe, which professed to be working to achieve a classless society. Yet Michels's study revealed that even these parties and unions, despite their proclaimed faith in democracy and equality, were controlled not by the majority of members but by a relatively small group of leaders.[7]

This discovery led Michels to formulate his **Iron Law of Oligarchy**. In large organizations, he said, power cannot be shared equally among all of the members. For the organization to be effective, real power must be concentrated in the hands of a small group—an elite, or oligarchy. This is simply the nature of large organizations—and by implication of entire societies—and there is nothing that can change it. According to Michels, no matter how equal people might be to begin with, this "iron law" is destined to defeat the well-meaning designs of democrats and egalitarians. Like Mosca and Pareto, he concluded that elites rule the world; they always have, and they always will.

The views of these elite theorists reinforced arguments advanced earlier by the German philosopher Friedrich Nietzsche and others. According to Nietzsche (1844–1900), all outstanding accomplishments were the work of one or another great man—the kind of person he called the *übermensch* ("overman" or "superman"). Yet, he complained, all the tendencies of the age are toward a mass society in which such outstanding individuals will find it ever harder to act in bold and creative ways. Powerful social pressures push people away from individual creativity and toward conformity. (This was a worry he shared with John Stuart Mill, among others; but Nietzsche was no liberal.) Elitism *should* be the rule, Nietzsche suggested; Mosca, Pareto, and Michels concluded that it *was*. Their notion of the elite may have been different from Nietzsche's, but the two views in combination helped to prepare the way for the explicitly elitist ideology of fascism. This is not to say, however, that any of these thinkers would have approved of the way in which their ideas were subsequently interpreted and put to murderous use by Italian Fascists and German Nazis.

IRRATIONALISM

The final element in the cultural and intellectual background of fascism was **irrationalism**. This term captures the conclusions of a variety of very different thinkers who all came to agree with the thinkers of the Counter-Enlightenment that emotion and desire play a larger part in the actions of people than reason does.[8] Among these thinkers was Sigmund Freud (1856–1939), the founder of psychoanalysis, whose observations of his patients—and even of himself—led him to detect the power of instinctive drives and "the unconscious" in human conduct.[9] In a similar vein, the American philosopher and psychologist William James (1842–1910) held that most people have a "will to believe."[10] Exactly what they believe is less important to them, James said, than that they believe in *something*. Psychologically speaking, people need something—almost anything, in fact—in which to believe. For the one thing that human beings cannot endure is a life devoid of some larger purpose or meaning.

Another social theorist who contributed to the development of irrationalism—and one who seems to have had a special influence on Mussolini—was the French social psychologist Gustav Le Bon (1841–1931). In his classic work, *The Crowd* (1895), Le Bon argued that human behavior in crowds is different from their behavior as individuals. Acting collectively and therefore anonymously, people will participate in acts of barbarism that they would never engage in as lone individuals. The psychology of lynch mobs, for example, is quite different from the psychology of the individuals who compose that mob. People acting *en masse* and in mobs are not restrained by individual conscience or moral scruple. A mob psychology, or a "herd instinct," takes over and shuts down individual judgments regarding right and wrong.

In a similar spirit, Pareto examined the social factors influencing individual judgment and behavior, concluding that emotions, symbols, and what he called "sentiments" are more important than material or economic factors.[11] And Mosca suggested that people are moved more by slogans and symbols, flags and anthems—by "political formulae," as he called them—than by reasoned argument and rational debate.[12]

All of these thinkers—Freud and James, Le Bon, Pareto, and Mosca—were more immediately concerned with explaining how people acted than in leading people to action. Not so Georges Sorel (1847–1922), a French engineer turned social theorist and political activist. In his *Reflections on Violence* (1908), Sorel insisted that people are more often moved to action by political "myths" than by appeals to reason. To bring about major social changes, it is necessary to find—or even create—a powerful myth that can inspire people to act in selfless or self-sacrificing ways. Looking at the longevity of the Catholic Church, Sorel saw the power and persistence of myth. A widely shared belief in such myths as the virgin birth, the resurrection and return of Jesus, and an afterlife spent either in heaven or in hell proved to be powerful sources of motivation for Christians from the first century to the present. Socialism and other modern ideologies, Sorel believed, were excessively rationalistic. What they lack, but sorely need, are motivating myths. For Sorel, the idea of a nationwide "general strike" could prove to be such a myth. The general strike was a myth, in other words, in that there was no guarantee that it would really lead to the revolutionary overthrow of the bourgeoisie and capitalism. If enough people could be brought to *believe* in the myth of the general strike, however, their efforts, inspired by this belief, would indeed lead to a successful revolution. What matters most, Sorel concluded, is not the reasonableness of a myth but its emotional power, for it is not reason but emotion that leads most people to act. And when the people act *en masse*, they can smash almost any obstacle in their path.

This was advice that Mussolini, Hitler, and other fascist leaders quite obviously took to heart. The slogans, the flags and banners, the mass demonstrations, the torchlight parades—all were designed to stir the people at their most basic emotional and instinctive levels. It is important to note that, in glorifying irrationality and intuition, fascism was not necessarily irrational; rather, it made instrumentally rational use of (most) people's irrational instincts and prejudices, harnessing these forces and motivating men and women to march together in conformist lockstep to achieve great things. These things include the creation of powerful nation-states, and then mighty empires, all under the leadership of the fascist elite. So it was not only irrationalism but elitism and nationalism and the attitudes of the

Counter-Enlightenment, too, that came together in the early twentieth century in the totalitarian ideology of fascism.

Another source of fascism, and of Italian fascism in particular, can be found in several late-nineteenth and early twentieth-century movements in art and literature. Perhaps the most important of these was Futurism. In Filippo Tommaso Marinetti's *Futurist Manifesto* (1909), he said that art and literature should depict and glorify speed and technology, violence and war, self-sacrifice and death. In a similar spirit the proto-fascist Italian poet and firebrand Gabrielle D'Annunzio (1863–1938) equated manliness and militarism. For D'Annunzio, war, like sexual seduction, is the best test of one's manhood. There is an erotic aspect to war, and a warlike aspect to seduction, as can be seen, he said, in the language men use to describe a successful seduction: they call it a victory or a "sexual conquest."[13] To see how fascism combined these elements, we shall turn now to the clearest case of fascism—that of Italy under Mussolini.

FASCISM IN ITALY

Because the rise and fall of Italian fascism is so closely associated with one man, Benito Mussolini, it will be convenient to chart its course through an account of Mussolini's life. Some historians even suggest that Italian fascism was little more than a vehicle for Mussolini's ambitions—a loose and largely incoherent set of ideas that he cobbled together to help him achieve and keep power. There is surely some truth to that view. Mussolini was an **ideologue**, but he was also an opportunist who trimmed and shifted his ideological position to suit his current political needs. Yet, even his shifts and inconsistencies reveal a certain coherence to his views, for they emphasize his faith in his own intuition and his conviction that the most important form of power is will power.

Mussolini and Italian Fascism

Benito Mussolini was born in a village in rural Italy in 1883, the year that Karl Marx died. Mussolini's father was a blacksmith and an atheist, his mother a schoolteacher and a Catholic. As a young man, Mussolini himself was a schoolteacher, but he soon took up political journalism and Marxist socialism. In 1912 he became editor of *Avanti!* (*Forward!*), the largest of Italy's socialist journals. As editor he remained a revolutionary socialist, proclaiming that capitalism would fall only after a violent proletarian uprising. Even at this point, however, Mussolini placed more emphasis on the *will* to engage in revolutionary struggle than on economic factors and the internal contradictions of capitalism.

Mussolini's break with socialism came during World War I. Before the war, socialists across Europe had agreed that they would take no part in any "capitalist" war. If the bourgeoisie of France and England and Germany wanted to slaughter one another, so be it; the socialists would urge the working classes of all countries to stay out of the war and wait for the opportunity to create socialist societies once the capitalist powers had destroyed one another. But when World War I erupted in August 1914, almost all of the socialist representatives in the legislatures of the warring countries voted to support the war efforts of their countries. Even more remarkably, hundreds of thousands of workers—many of them staunch socialists—volunteered to join the military and fight workers (including socialist workers) from other nations. This support was a sign, according to some observers, that nationalism—the love of flag and fatherland—was a far stronger force in human life than loyalty to one's social class.

Mussolini agreed and began urging Italy to join the war—a stance that cost him his position as editor, because the official socialist policy in Italy was to stay out of the war. Italy did enter the war on the side of England and France, though, and Mussolini was eventually drafted into the army, where he served until a mortar he was loading exploded, wounding him seriously.

For Mussolini, World War I proved once and for all that Marx was wrong when he asserted that the workers have no fatherland. Workers *do* have a fatherland—at least they want to *believe* that they do. Any political party or movement that denies this is doomed to failure. Socialists, he said, "have never examined the problems of *nations* [but only of classes. Contrary to Marx], the nation represents a stage in human [history] that has not yet been transcended... The 'sentiment' of nationality exists; it cannot be denied."[14] So Mussolini set out to affirm and take political advantage of the widely shared sentiment of nationalism.

He did this first by founding and editing the fascist newspaper *Il Popolo d'Italia* (*The People of Italy*) and then by forming the *fasci di combattimento*, or "combat groups," that consisted largely of World War I veterans, and then the Fascist Party itself. The party espoused a program that sometimes seemed revolutionary, sometimes conservative, but always nationalistic. Italy had been a unified nation for less than fifty years when World War I ended, and many Italians felt that their country, unlike France and England, had not received its fair share of the spoils when Germany and Austria surrendered. Playing upon this resentment, the fascists

Benito Mussolini (1883–1945)

Hulton Archive/Getty Images

promised action to end the "bickering" between the various Italian political parties. There has been too much talk, too much debate, they declared; the time has come for forceful action, even violence, if Italy is to take her rightful place among the major powers of Europe.

This emphasis on national unity was apparent in the word "fascism" itself, which derives from the Italian *fasciare*, "to fasten or bind." The aim of the Fascist Party was to bind the Italian people tightly together, to overcome the divisions that weakened their country. Fascism also appealed to the glories of the ancient Roman Empire by invoking one of the old Roman symbols of authority, the *fasces*—an axe in the center of a bundle of rods, all fastened together as a symbol of the strength that comes from unity. To achieve this unity, the Italian Fascists said, it is necessary to overcome certain obstacles. According to the *Manifesto of the Fascist Intellectuals* (1925), written by the fascist philosopher Giovanni Gentile (pronounced "Gentee-lay") and signed by 250 prominent writers and activists, there are two main obstacles to be overcome. One of these is liberalism, with its emphasis on individual rights and interests. No nation can be strong, according to the fascists, if its members think of themselves first and foremost as individuals who are concerned with protecting their own rights and interests. The main mistake of liberalism is to pit the interests of individuals against those of the state instead of subsuming individual interests under those of the state. Another obstacle to the unity of the nation is socialism, with its emphasis on opposing and antagonistic social classes. Mussolini, the former Marxist, particularly attacked Marxian beliefs about class divisions and class struggle, which he regarded as divisive and therefore as enemies of national unity. Italians must not think of themselves either as individuals or as members of social classes, he said; they must think of themselves as Italians first, foremost, and forever.

Mussolini and his followers adopted black shirts as their uniform and set out to seize power. They ran candidates for public office, they used the press to spread propaganda, and they sometimes simply beat up or intimidated their opponents. In October 1922 Mussolini—now known to the fascists as *Il Duce*, "the leader"—announced that the Fascists would march on Rome, the seat of the Italian government, and seize power if it were not given to them. The march began on October 27. It seems clear that the Italian army could have sent the blackshirts scurrying, but the Italian king overestimated the strength of the fascists and overruled the prime minister's declaration of martial law. On October 29, 1922, he invited Mussolini to form a government and serve as the new prime minister of Italy.

Once in office, Mussolini moved to entrench himself and his Fascist Party in power. He ignored the Italian Parliament, outlawed all parties but the Fascist Party, struck a compromise with the Catholic Church, gained control of the mass media, and stifled freedom of speech, press, and assembly. He also set out to make Italy a military and industrial power so that it would again be the center of a great empire. Indeed, Mussolini made no secret of his ambitions for Italy—ambitions that included war and conquest. In his speeches and writings, Mussolini praised toughness and masculinity. He often spoke of war as the true test of manly virtue, and he had warlike slogans stenciled on walls and buildings throughout Italy. "War," one of them proclaimed, "is to the male what childbearing is to the female!" "A minute on the battlefield," according to another, "is worth a lifetime of peace!"[15]

Mussolini made good his threats by engaging in a number of military adventures, notably the conquest of Ethiopia in 1935–1936. His ambitious aim was to resurrect the Roman Empire in all its strength, splendor, and glory. His imperial ambitions soon led him into an alliance with Adolf Hitler and Nazi Germany, and from there into World War II, which Italy was woefully unprepared to fight. In July 1943 the king, with the support of the Grand Council of Fascists, relieved Mussolini of his dictatorial powers and placed him under house arrest. That September, German troops rescued Mussolini and established him as head of a pro-Nazi puppet government in northern Italy. But in April 1945, as the war was ending, Mussolini and his mistress were captured and shot by anti-fascist Italian partisans. Their bodies were taken to Milan, stripped naked, and strung upside down over one of the city's squares. Thus ended the career of *Il Duce*.

Fascism in Theory and Practice

While Mussolini was in power, he encouraged the belief that Italian fascism rested on a philosophical or ideological basis. The fascists had a plan for transforming Italy, he said, a plan that grew out of a coherent view of the world. Included in that view were distinctively fascist conceptions of human nature and freedom.

For the fascist, an individual human life only has meaning insofar as it is rooted in and realized through the life of the society or the nation as a whole. Fascists reject **atomism** and individualism, in other words, and subscribe to an **organic conception of society**. The individual on his or her own can accomplish nothing of great significance, they said. It is only when the individual dedicates his or her life to the nation-state, sacrificing everything to its glory, that the individual finds true fulfillment.

The Italian Fascists also stressed the value of the state, which they saw as the legal and institutional embodiment of the power, the unity, and the majesty of the nation. To be dedicated to the service of the nation was thus to be dedicated to the state—and to its great and glorious leader, *Il Duce*. The state was to control everything, and everyone was to serve the state. For the fascist, Mussolini proclaimed, "everything is in the State, and nothing human or spiritual exists, much less has value, outside the State."[16]

Thus, *freedom* for the fascists was not, and is not, individual liberty but the freedom of the *nation*, the integrated, organic whole that unites all individuals, groups, and classes behind the iron shield of the all-powerful state. Individual liberty, in fact, is an obstacle to freedom because it distracts people from their true mission to "believe, obey, fight." Freedom of speech, freedom of assembly, freedom to live as one chooses—these are all "useless liberties," according to the fascists. The only freedom that truly matters is the freedom to serve the state. In terms of our triadic definition of freedom, then, the Italian Fascists conceived of liberty as shown in Figure 7.1.

True freedom, in the fascist view, is found in serving the state, and there is nothing more fulfilling than doing one's part, however small, to promote its power and glory. But how was the glory of the state to be achieved? Through military

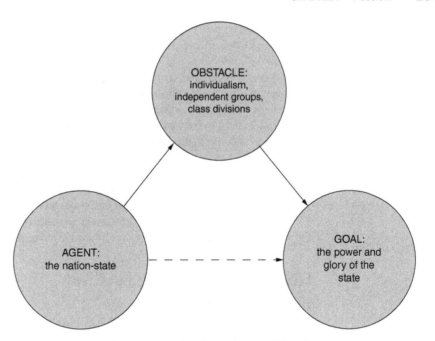

FIGURE 7.1 The fascist view of freedom.

conquest, Mussolini said, and conquest required the discipline and loyalty of the Italian people. This Mussolini and the fascists attempted to win through massive propaganda efforts, always designed to appeal to the emotions and instincts of the people. The people were a mass, a "herd" incapable of leading themselves. They needed an elite to guide them, and they especially needed a dictator with an almost mystical ability to know where their "true" interests lay. Hence the people were told, in schools and in speeches and in slogans emblazoned on walls, that "Mussolini is always right!" Everything—newspapers, radio, schools—was to be used to instill this conviction in the people. In 1936, for instance, the compulsory reader for eight-year-olds in Italian schools contained the following:

> The eyes of the *Duce* are on every one of you. No one can say what is the meaning of that look on his face. It is an eagle opening its wings and rising into space. It is a flame that searches out your heart to light there a vermillion fire. Who can resist that burning eye, darting out its arrows? But do not be afraid; for you those arrows will change into rays of joy.
>
> A child, who, even while not refusing to obey, asks "Why?" is like a bayonet made of milk… "You must obey because you must," said Mussolini, when explaining the reasons for obedience.[17]

But indoctrination and propaganda are not enough to convert a people into a modern military machine; they also need weapons, fuel, and food. To this end, Mussolini tried to encourage industrial production in Italy. He did this through the policy of **corporativism**, according to which property was to remain in private hands even as it was put to public use. To prevent disputes between owners and workers from disrupting business and production, the Ministry of Corporations was supposed to supervise economic affairs. The economy was divided into twenty-two sectors, or corporations, each of which was administered by representatives of ownership, labor, and the Ministry of Corporations. The representatives of the ministry were supposed to look after the interests of the public as a whole, and the three groups were supposed to work together in harmony for the good of all Italians. In practice, however, the fascist representatives of the ministry could do pretty much as they pleased. They were often pleased to accept bribes and to do as those who paid the bribes—usually the owners—suggested.

Partly for this reason Mussolini was unable to realize his military ambitions. Nor, despite all the talk about totalitarianism, was Mussolini able to convert Italy into a society in which the Fascist Party and state truly controlled all aspects of life. That was his aim, however, and that is surely the important point.

To the north of Italy, another variety of fascism appeared in the 1920s with the same totalitarian aim—and came much closer to succeeding.

FASCISM IN GERMANY: NAZISM

Hitler and Nazism

Just as Italian fascism was closely associated with Benito Mussolini, so its German counterpart, Nazism, was inextricably linked with Adolf Hitler. Hitler was born in Austria, near the German border, in 1889. Moving to Vienna when he was eighteen, Hitler tried, unsuccessfully, to establish himself as an artist. He remained there for several years, living practically as a vagrant, until World War I began. Hitler then joined the German army and served with distinction, twice winning the Iron Cross for bravery. He was in the hospital when the war ended in 1918, and shortly thereafter his political career began.[18]

When Germany surrendered to end World War I, German troops were still on French soil, and many Germans believed that surrender was unnecessary. Germany had not been defeated on the battlefield, they charged, but betrayed by traitorous politicians. Hitler shared these sentiments. He was hardly alone in his hatred of Jews, socialists, and communists, and in his resentment of the punitive postwar reparations that the Allies had forced Germany to pay. After his release from the hospital, Hitler remained with the army as a spy. In this role he attended the meetings in Munich of a tiny group that called itself the German Workers' Party. Somehow Hitler saw an opportunity in this group, which he joined in 1920. He soon became the leader of the party under its new name, the National Socialist German Workers' Party—or the Nazi Party in its abbreviated form.

The party grew quickly under Hitler's direction. To give an impression of discipline and strength, the Nazis established a paramilitary organization, the brownshirted "storm troopers," which they used to break up meetings of the Socialist and Communist parties. In 1923, perhaps hoping for the same luck Mussolini had enjoyed with his march on Rome the year before, Hitler launched the "Beer Hall *Putsch*." This was an attempt to overthrow the government of the German province of Bavaria in the hope that doing so would topple the whole German government and bring the Nazis to power. The *Putsch* (or *coup d'état*) failed, however, and Hitler was arrested and tried for treason. Yet, for his part

Adolf Hitler (1889–1945)

in this armed uprising against the government, Hitler received a mere five-year prison sentence, of which he served only nine months. During his imprisonment, he wrote the first part of his autobiography, *Mein Kampf*, or "My Battle."

In that book Hitler made clear the basic outlines of his ideology. Germany has a great destiny, he wrote, if only the German *Volk* ("folk" or "people") can join forces and throw off those enemies who divide and betray them—particularly the communists and the Jews. But the German people will not be able to do this without a single party and supreme leader to forge them into a united and invincible force. As he said in *Mein Kampf*,

The psyche of the great masses is not receptive to anything that is half-hearted and weak.

> Like the woman, whose psychic state is determined less by abstract reason than by an indefinable emotional longing for a force which will complement her nature, and who, consequently, would rather bow to a strong man than dominate a weakling, so likewise the masses love a commander more than a petitioner and feel inwardly more satisfied by a doctrine tolerating no other beside itself, than by the granting of liberal freedom with which ... they can do little...[19]

This was Hitler's notion of the *Führerprinzip*, the "leadership principle," according to which the masses and the *Führer*, or "leader," were bound tightly together. The relationship, as Hitler's words indicate, is erotic and even "sadistic" in the original Sadean sense. Like the Italian Fascists' slogan, "war is to the male what childbearing is to the female," Hitler's words also reveal the fascist preoccupation with masculinity, which the Nazis and fascists associated with strength, action, and dominance.

Once out of prison, Hitler returned to his political agitation, relying on a combination of ordinary political campaigning and strong-arm tactics. By 1933 the Nazis were the largest of several parties in the German *Reichstag*, or parliament, although they did not control a majority of the seats. When Hitler was appointed Chancellor, he quickly proved even more adept than Mussolini at converting his position as head of government into an outright dictatorship. He then moved to create a Third *Reich* (empire) in Germany, one that would surpass the first two—the Holy Roman Empire and the German Empire that Bismarck had consolidated by 1871. This would be a "Thousand-Year *Reich*," and throughout this millennium Germany would be the preeminent political, cultural, and military leader of Europe.

To accomplish this, Hitler planned to do three things. The first was—in clear and blatant violation of the hated Treaty of Versailles—to rearm Germany and end reparations payments to the Allies. Germany had been hit hard by the Great Depression, and continued payment only made matters worse. To stimulate the ailing German economy, Hitler undertook a massive program of public works, including the building of *autobahns* (freeways) crisscrossing Germany and—not least—an accelerated program to rearm Germany by building tanks, airplanes, battleships, submarines, and other weapons of war.

Hitler's second task was to provide Germany with *Lebensraum*, the "living space" it needed to become a great empire. With this in mind, Hitler looked to the east—to Poland, and to the Soviet Ukraine in particular—for land that would become the "breadbasket" and oil reserves of Germany. These lands were to be conquered, and their people—who were inferior, the Nazis declared, to the Germans—were to be enslaved. Hitler set this part of his plan in motion when he invaded Poland on September 1, 1939, thus beginning World War II.

The third of Hitler's plans was to eliminate all enemies standing in the way of the Thousand-Year *Reich*. These included the communists, both in Germany and elsewhere, and the Jews. In attempting to fulfill this plan, Hitler in 1941 invaded the Soviet Union, with which he had signed a nonaggression pact, and undertook the "Final Solution" to the "Jewish Problem." This led, before and during World War II, to the formation of *Einsatzgruppen*—mobile death squads—which rounded up and shot or gassed victims before dumping their bodies into mass graves. This was followed by the construction of concentration camps in which "enemies of the state" were brought together or "concentrated" and either killed outright (as were the old, the ill and infirm, the young, and most women) or worked to death (healthy younger men), following the Nazi policy of "extermination through labor." The concentration camp was made possible by two technological innovations—the invention of barbed wire and the machine gun—which allowed a relatively small group of guards to surveil and control large numbers of prisoners.[20] By these brutal means some 6 million Jews, along with Slavs, Gypsies, and other supposedly "inferior" peoples, were systematically murdered.

World War II ended for Germany in the spring of 1945 with English and American armies moving toward Berlin from the west and the Soviet army entering it from the east. In the last days of April, while confined to his underground bunker in Berlin, Hitler married his mistress, bade farewell to his staff, and, with his new bride, committed suicide. To avoid meeting the same humiliating fate as Mussolini and his mistress, Hitler left orders that their bodies be doused with gasoline and burned beyond recognition. Thus ended the career of *der Führer*.

Nazism in Theory and Practice

In most respects Nazism in Germany closely resembled fascism in Italy. There was the same hatred of liberalism and communism, for instance; the same attitude toward the masses, who were to be molded to the will of the great leader through propaganda and indoctrination; the same reliance on an organic conception of society; the same appeal to military might and the need for discipline and sacrifice; the same stress on manliness and masculinity; the same emphasis on nationalism; and the same totalitarian ethos. Neither Hitler nor Mussolini had much interest in economic matters, moreover, at least not as long as they thought that their countries were producing enough weapons and other war materiel. The inclusion of the word "socialist" in the name of the National Socialist (or Nazi) Party has led to some confusion on this point, but Hitler certainly was not a socialist in any ordinary sense of the term. As he explained in a speech,

> Every truly national idea is in the last resort social, that he who is prepared so completely to adopt the cause of his people [*Volk*] that he really knows no higher ideal than the prosperity of this—his own—people, he who has so taken to heart the meaning of our great song *"Deutschland, Deutschland über alles,"* that nothing in this world stands for him higher than this Germany, people and land, land and people, he is a socialist... [He] is not merely a socialist but he is also national in the highest sense of that word.[21]

After proclaiming himself "a German nationalist" Hitler went on to say, "This means that I proclaim my nationality. My whole thought and action belongs to it. I am a socialist. I see no class and no social estate before me, but that community of people [*Volksgemeinschaft*] who are linked by blood, unified by language, and subject to the same general fate."[22]

For Hitler, then, "socialism" was merely another name for nationalism. The "nation," however, did not include everyone born within the borders of Germany but only those born into the racial group to which the German *Volk* belonged. Thus, long-assimilated German Jews were categorically excluded from the privileged and racially superior *Volk*.

Moreover, despite the "socialist" in the name of the National Socialist German Workers' Party, the economy of Nazi Germany was not socialist but may be best described as *state-assisted capitalism*. The ownership of Germany's largest corporations—including Krupp (steel and arms manufacturing), Bayer (chemicals), Mercedes-Benz and BMW (automobiles and trucks), and others—remained in private hands. The Nazi state assisted these corporations in various ways, including allowing and even encouraging them to establish factories in or near state-run concentration camps and employing slave laborers from those camps. And those slave laborers were drawn primarily from members of supposedly "inferior" races. In this way, the German state subsidized privately owned enterprises which in turn reaped enormous profits from that mutually beneficial arrangement, a policy which can scarcely be described as "socialist" in any meaningful sense of that term.

Race and racial "purity" was at the center of all legislation and all Nazi public policy—education, health care, family policy, and many other areas as well. As Hitler wrote,

> The folkish state [*Volkstaat*] ... *must set race at the center of all life. It must take care to keep it pure. It must declare the [Aryan] child to be the most precious treasure of the people [Volk]... [I]t must be considered reprehensible to withhold healthy [Aryan] children from the nation.*[23]

For that reason the Nazi government outlawed abortion for Aryan women, making it a crime punishable by death (before the "Final Solution" there were no similar restrictions on abortions for Jewish women; afterward Jewish mothers and their children, born and unborn, were murdered in their millions). The state provided substantial subsidies to families giving more Aryan children "to the nation"; similar subsidies were not available to non-Aryan families.[24] And under the *Lebsensborn* ("life spring") program, S.S. officers impregnated Aryan women at state-run "breeding centers" in order to produce "perfect" blond-haired and blue-eyed Aryan offspring.

This ideal of racial purity was to be expressed especially in the arts. Hitler, who fancied himself as an artist and art critic, personally directed a purge of "degenerate art" (*entarete kunst*), which included most modern art in every imaginable style—cubist, Dadaist, pointillist, fauvist, and others—and sculptures and paintings by Picasso, Gaugin, Cezanne, Duchamp, Braque, Toulouse-Lautrec, Van Gogh, and many others. In their place Hitler proposed a politically and racially pure "Aryan art" depicting blond, blue-eyed, strong, square-jawed Aryan men and blond, blue-eyed, supine Aryan women and smiling, obedient children. According to Hitler and the Nazis, all art and artists—painters, sculptors, musicians—should selflessly serve the state and the Aryan *Volk*.

In Nazi Germany race remained paramount, extending even to the natural sciences. Albert Einstein's theory of relativity, which made possible the development of nuclear weapons, was derided and dismissed as "Jewish science." And toward the end of World War II locomotives and other railroad rolling stock were diverted from the German war effort to transport Jews and members of other "inferior" races to the death camps at Auschwitz and elsewhere. Militarily, this was a huge mistake; but ideologically, militant Nazi officials believed, it was the correct course of action.

From the beginning Nazism relied, and continues to rely, on the idea that *race* is the fundamental characteristic of human beings. Race was not important for the Italian Fascists—not, that is, until pressure from Hitler led Mussolini to take action against Jews in Italy. Fascism was not, and need not be, a racist ideology, in other words; Nazism was and is. Indeed, racial theory is at the core of Nazism— so much so that we can define Nazism in terms of the simple formula, *fascism + racism = Nazism*. This belief is especially clear in the Nazi views of human nature and freedom.

HUMAN NATURE AND FREEDOM

For Hitler and his followers, the fundamental fact of human life is that human beings belong to different races. Contrary to Kant and other thinkers of the Enlightenment, there is no such thing as a universal human nature shared by all human beings. The differences that distinguish one race from another are deep, innate, and indelible. Nazis accordingly have an *exclusionist* rather than an inclusive or universalist view of human nature. Each race allegedly has its own unique nature. It is the "nature" of the Oriental races to be crafty, cunning, and sly, and of black Africans to be stupid and slavish. It is the nature of Jews to be scheming, greedy, and selfish, and to seek to suborn and corrupt other races, and the Aryan "master race" above all. It is the nature of the Aryans to be the noblest, most creative, cultured, and dominant of all the races. The Aryans' destiny is to subordinate and subjugate all "inferior" races—and the Jews in particular—to their "superior" will. There was nothing really new in any of these ideas, for Hitler was not an original thinker. The themes in *Mein Kampf* are recycled from earlier racial theorists, such as Joseph-Arthur de Gobineau, Houston Stewart Chamberlain, and Ludwig Woltmann.

According to Gobineau's *Essay on the Inequality of the Human Races* (1855), race was the key to the rise and fall of great civilizations. Like many other people over the centuries, Gobineau (1816–1882) wondered why once-mighty empires such as Rome lost their power and collapsed. The answer he hit upon was miscegenation, the mixture of races. A people rose to power, Gobineau concluded, when its racial composition was pure and vigorous. But as it expanded its control over conquered peoples—as it became an empire—the original racial stock was weakened by interbreeding with other races. The result was an inferior people that was incapable of maintaining its identity and power. The loss of empire followed. Furthermore, the races were not created equal. The white race is superior to the yellow, Gobineau said, and the yellow is superior to the black. This is the pattern of nature, as he saw it, and it ought to be observed in society as well. The ideas of Gobineau and other so-called "racial theorists" soon seeped into otherwise respectable mainstream magazines and books—even the supposedly authoritative eleventh edition of the *Encyclopedia Britannica* (1910–1911). Its entry "Negro," for example, states that "mentally, the negro is inferior to the white."[25]

Ideas like Gobineau's were much in the air in the late nineteenth century, as were the ideas of the **Social Darwinists**. As advanced by Herbert Spencer and William Graham Sumner, Social Darwinism was not a racist doctrine. But its emphasis on the struggle for survival lent itself to a racist interpretation. All one had to do was to say that the struggle for survival was not a struggle between individuals, as Spencer and Sumner said, but a broader struggle between entire *races* of people. Nazism, then, was an outgrowth of just this sort of "racial Darwinism."

This was, in fact, the position that Ludwig Woltmann took. In two books—*Historical Materialism: A Critique of the Marxist World-View* (1900) and *Political Anthropology* (1903)[26]—Woltmann (1871–1907) argued that what is missing from Marxist theory is the most central concept of all: *race*. Why, Woltmann asks, have the greatest achievements in art, music, literature, philosophy, and industry been concentrated in Western Europe? It is because the superior Germanic or **Aryan** race resides there. This race has evolved further and faster than "lesser" races because the European climate is neither as harsh and unyielding as the Arctic nor as lush as the tropics. Eskimos cannot create philosophy or great music because they must spend most of their time and energy in wresting a livelihood from a frigid and infertile environment. Polynesians and Africans, by contrast, live in a lush and fertile climate in which fish are plentiful and fruit falls from the trees. They have no incentive to invent technology to transform nature or to create culture. Only in Western Europe is the climate neither excessively harsh nor extraordinarily fecund. This climate has produced a race that, over millennia, has developed technologies to transform nature, has created a rich culture, and has in turn exhibited its intellectual, artistic, and scientific superiority to the rest of the world. To this race belong Beethoven, Goethe, and other giants of German culture.

But now, Woltmann warned, this race faces several threats. Chief among these is the population crisis. Woltmann believed that **Malthus's law**—that population grows at an ever-increasing geometric rate while food supplies grow only at a steady arithmetical rate—portends a racial war for increasingly scarce resources and *Lebensraum*. The world is rapidly reaching the point at which population will outstrip the resources available to support human life (as illustrated in Figure 7.2). The competition for scarce resources will not pit one individual against another but one race or *Volk*—the Aryans—against all others. According to Woltmann's "racial Darwinism," the Darwinian struggle for survival will be along racial lines, and the Aryans had better brace themselves for the coming competition. They must toughen themselves by repudiating "soft" or "sentimental" ideas of racial equality, interracial harmony, the "brotherhood of man," and other liberal and socialist claptrap. These "Jewish" ideas weaken the resolve and sap the strength of Aryans, and those who hold and teach these ideas must be censored—or silenced forever.

Hitler also borrowed ideas from English and American sources. Among the authors he admired was Houston Stewart Chamberlain (1855–1927), an English aristocrat who moved to Germany, married the daughter of the ardently anti-Semitic composer Richard Wagner, and wrote *The Foundations of the Nineteenth Century* (1899), a book that praises "Germanism" and criticizes Jews as an alien force that has debased European culture. Another influence was Madison Grant (1865–1937), an American racial theorist and author of *The Passing of the Great Race; or, The Racial Basis of European History* (1916), which Hitler read in German translation in the early 1920s. Perhaps most influential of all, however, was the American automobile magnate Henry Ford (1863–1947), founder of the Ford Motor Company, whose anti-Semitic articles in *The Dearborn Independent* were published as *The International Jew: The World's Foremost Problem* (1922)

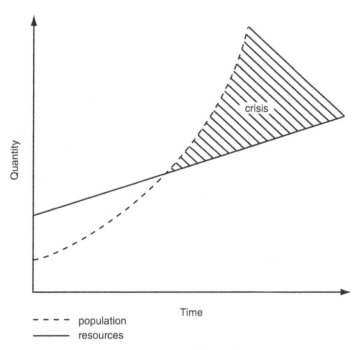

FIGURE 7.2 Malthus's law.

and subsequently translated into German and several other languages. Hitler read and was greatly impressed by Ford's anti-Semitic book, which was made required reading for Nazi Party members.[27] Visitors to his headquarters in Berlin were often startled to see that the largest picture in Hitler's office was a portrait of Henry Ford. In 1938, on Ford's seventy-fifth birthday, Hitler awarded Ford the Grand Cross of the Order of the German Eagle, the highest honor that Germany could bestow on a foreigner, for "meritorious service" to the *Volk* and the Fatherland.[28]

Chamberlain, Grant, and Ford sounded similar warnings: The rising tide of inferior "colored races" threatens to swamp the morally and intellectually superior "white race"; whites must therefore take protective measures by restricting immigration, outlawing miscegenation, and sterilizing "subhumans" (this last was the particular goal of the eugenics movement of the late nineteenth and early twentieth centuries). Hitler's first foray into Nazi racial engineering was the mass sterilization of mentally retarded and physically handicapped children. From there it was a short step to the "Final Solution"—the systematic extermination of Jews, Gypsies, Slavs, and other "inferior" peoples. Jews were especially dangerous, in Hitler's view, as they were responsible not only for encouraging "race mixing" and the consequent "mongrelization" of the white race (and the Aryans in particular) but also for the spread of communism, which divided the white race along class lines and joined together white and colored workers in a worldwide class struggle. By these and other means the Jews supposedly aimed to achieve "world domination." This assertion—that Jews were bent on conquering the world—was advanced in the *Protocols of the Learned Elders of Zion* (1905), a document that purported to be the minutes of a secret meeting of chief rabbis in the 1880s. Although the *Protocols* was in fact a forgery produced by agents of the Russian tsar's secret police to justify pogroms (state-sponsored attacks on Jews), many people—including Ford and Hitler—believed it to be authentic.[29]

All of these ideas reappear in Hitler's *Mein Kampf,* in Nazi theorist Alfred Rosenberg's *Der Mythus des XX Jahrhunderts* (*The Myth of the Twentieth Century*)— and in Nazi military and political practice. These ideas supplied the rationale for the German invasion of Poland and the Soviet Union, which extended Aryan *Lebensraum* into the oil and wheat fields of Russia and the Ukraine. These theories justified censorship and book burnings, the banning of "Jewish" ideas from German classrooms and libraries, and the silencing of critics. Most notoriously of all, these ideas rationalized the systematic enslavement and murder of millions of Jews and other "inferior" peoples, including Slavs, Gypsies, homosexuals, the handicapped, and other *"lebens unwertes Leben"* ("lives unworthy of life").

The only people whose lives truly were worth living, according to Nazi doctrine, were the racially pure Aryans. But what is this Aryan race? Hitler was notoriously vague on this point. He took the idea of an Aryan race from Woltmann and others, who themselves drew on the studies of a number of nineteenth-century scholars, especially linguists. In studying various languages, these scholars had found evidence that not only the European languages but also those of the Middle East and some of India shared a common source. Some scholars concluded that these languages, and all of the civilizations of India, Europe, and the Middle East, must have emerged from a single group of people, which they referred to as "the Aryans."[30] Gradually, the belief grew that the Aryans were an extraordinary race, the fountain of most of what was civilized and worthwhile in the world. On the basis of this speculation, the Nazis decided that it was the destiny of Aryans to rule others, to subjugate the inferior races so that culture could advance and reach new and glorious heights.

Hitler claimed that the Aryan race was the source—the "culture-creating" source—of European civilization, and the Germanic people were the highest or purest remnant of the Aryan race. Thus, the destiny of the German *Volk* was clear: to dominate or even exterminate "lesser" peoples and thus establish the glorious Thousand-Year *Reich.*

The Nazis also drew upon this racial view of human nature in developing their conception of freedom. Like the Italian Fascists, they opposed the liberal view that freedom is a matter of individual liberty, favoring instead the idea that freedom, properly understood, is the freedom of the nation or *Volk.* But the Nazis gave this idea their characteristic racial twist. The only freedom that counts, they said, is the freedom of the people who belong to the "master race." Freedom should be the freedom of Aryans because that is nature's plan. But there are obstacles in the way of the Aryan race's realizing its destiny. There is the obstacle, first, of the members of "inferior" races who are doing what they can to drag the Aryans down to their own level. There is also the obstacle presented by certain ideas and ideals— specifically, the humanist ideas of the Enlightenment. These were "Jewish" ideas, according to Hitler, ideas that made even Aryans soft and squeamish. Because these ideas of universal brotherhood and equality are embedded in liberalism and Marxism, it followed for Hitler that these ideologies are not merely obstacles but enemies to be rooted out and destroyed. This was the rationale for censorship, for book burnings, and for toughening the minds of the young to make them into willing servants of the *Führer* and the *Volk*.

Every individual, in the Nazi view, is merely a cell in the larger *völkisch* organism. The destiny of the organism is also the individual's destiny. Gottfried Neese, a Nazi Party ideologist, illustrates this reliance on organic metaphors when he says that the people (*Volk*)

> form a true organism—a being which leads its own life and follows its own laws, which possesses powers peculiar to itself, and which develops its own nature… This living unity of the people [*Volk*] has its cells in its individual members, and just as in every body there are certain cells to perform certain tasks, this is likewise the case in the body of the people. The individual is bound to his people not only physically but mentally and spiritually…[31]

Outside the *Volksgemeinschaft*—the racially pure "folk community"—nothing worthwhile exists. In seeking to create and sustain such a community, therefore, one must not be distracted by softness or compassion or pity. "Inferior" peoples must be regarded as subhuman animals or "vermin" to be destroyed without a moment's thought or hesitation. Only in that way can the Aryan people be free to achieve their great destiny. For Nazis, then, "freedom" takes the form shown in Figure 7.3.

The Nazi view of freedom differed markedly from that of the people they conquered, subjugated, and killed. Although resistance was rare—many, probably most, Germans supported Hitler—there were notable exceptions, both inside and outside of Nazi Germany.[32] Inside, a small number of writers and pastors

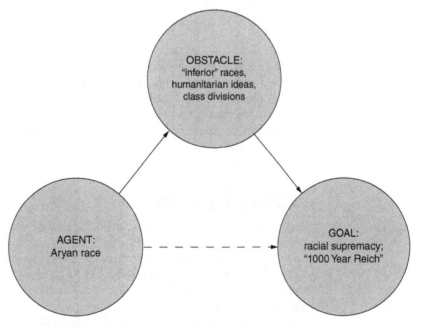

FIGURE 7.3 The German fascist (Nazi) view of freedom.

were outspoken in their opposition to Hitler's regime. The open opposition of Reverend Dietrich Bonhoeffer (1906–1945) led first to prison and then to death by hanging. He was allegedly associated with a small group of German army officers led by Colonel Claus von Stauffenberg, who plotted to kill Hitler in 1944. Stauffenberg placed a briefcase containing a powerful bomb under a heavy wooden table at which Hitler was seated. The bomb exploded, wounding but not killing Hitler. The plotters were rounded up, tortured, and their deaths filmed for Hitler's viewing pleasure. Another, nonviolent form of opposition came from a group of university students calling themselves *die Weiss Rose* (The White Rose), whose members painted anti-Nazi graffiti, printed and distributed pamphlets detailing Nazi atrocities inside and outside of Germany, and tried to disrupt the regime in various ways. Almost all were arrested and summarily executed. Another way that some civilians impeded the regime was to hide Jews in attics or basements to prevent their deportation to the death camps. When discovered, as they often were, both rescued and rescuer were sent to the camps. Some are still alive today to tell their stories.[33] Their actions and their bravery are remembered and celebrated at Yad Veshem in Israel, where they are called "The Righteous Among Nations." They were determined to act, so as not to behave as the imaginary German does in a famous poem by Pastor Martin Niemoller:

> First they came for the Socialists, and I did not speak out—
>   Because I was not a Socialist.
> Then they came for the Trade Unionists, and I did not speak out—
>   Because I was not a Trade Unionist.
> Then they came for the Jews, and I did not speak out—
>   Because I was not a Jew.
> Then they came for me—
>   And there was no one left to speak for me.

Outside Germany, in the "Occupied Territories"—that is, countries conquered by the German military—various resistance groups sprang up. One of these was a group of young Danes who called themselves the Churchill Club. They engaged in acts of violent and nonviolent sabotage of trains and communications channels. Another, much larger group was the French *Résistance*, which consisted of communists, socialists, and other anti-Nazi activists. They blew up bridges and rail lines, infiltrated spies and saboteurs into the German military, and sheltered Allied airmen who had been shot down over occupied France.

FASCISM ELSEWHERE

Although fascism has been most closely identified with Italy and Germany in the period from World War I to World War II, it was not confined to those two countries. Fascist parties and movements spread throughout Europe in the 1920s and 1930s, from Romania to France and England, and made a brief appearance in the United States in the 1930s. Aside from Italy and Germany, however, the only European country in which fascism came to power was Spain under the regime of General Francisco Franco. With aid from both Germany and Italy, Franco's forces won the Spanish Civil War (1936–1939) that overthrew the Spanish Republic.

Once the Civil War was over, though, and especially when World War II began to go against the fascist powers, Franco (1892–1975) ousted the more ardent fascists from his government and moved in the direction of a conservative, even reactionary, dictatorship. Franco was more concerned, that is, with maintaining firm authority in a quiet Spain than in mobilizing mass support in order to win glory and a new empire for his country.

Fascism also enjoyed some success outside Europe, notably in Argentina in the 1940s and 1950s under the leadership of Juan Perón, an army officer who won a large following among the Argentine working class. There have been elements of fascism in South Africa too. In that country the official policy of **apartheid**, or racial separation, was often justified by invoking ideas about the organic unity of a racially superior Afrikaner *Volk*.

"Apartheid" literally means "apartness," and there are two senses in which the South African government pursued a policy of "apartness" until recent years. The first was segregation of the races. Beginning in 1948, when the Afrikaner Nationalist Party first won control of the government, the people of South Africa were officially divided into four racial groups: African, Asian, colored (that is, of mixed descent), and white. Although the Africans were easily the largest part of the population—more than 72 percent of the total, according to the 1980 census— the ruling Nationalist Party denied them voting rights and virtually shut them out of the country's regular political process until President F. W. de Klerk began to dismantle apartheid in the early 1990s. Until then, marriage between whites and nonwhites had been prohibited, "pass laws" had required black Africans to obtain permission to enter white urban areas, and the government had attempted to confine black Africans to ten territorial *bantustans* or "homelands"—modeled in part on the American system of Indian reservations—located in some of the poorest and most barren areas of South Africa.

White South Africans, especially descendants of Dutch and German colonists known as "Afrikaners," tried to justify this policy by appealing to the belief that racial differences are fixed and unchanging features of life. According to this view, each race has its own distinct characteristics and no good can come from attempts to bring the races together. Each race can best develop along the lines nature intends only if it remains separate from the others—hence the notion that the different races of South Africa were pursuing "separate development." Separate, but not equal. For one race, the white, is supposedly superior to the others. Not only must whites keep apart from other races, but they must also exercise the leadership necessary to make separate development possible for all.

This brings us to the second sense in which "apartheid" has meant "apartness" in South Africa. Many Afrikaners have believed that they are a special people, chosen by God to carry out His plan in their country. One Afrikaner leader stated this view in 1944:

> In every People in the world is embodied a Divine Idea and the task of each People is to build upon that Idea and to perfect it. So God created the Afrikaner People with a unique language, a unique philosophy of life, and their own history and tradition in order that they might fulfill a particular calling and destiny here in the southern corner

of Africa. We must stand guard on all that is peculiar to us and build upon it. We must believe that God has called us to be servants of his righteousness in this place.[34]

So the Afrikaner *Volk*, who compose the majority of the minority white population, are a special people with a special calling. Militantly racist Afrikaners believe themselves to be a breed apart from others, and hold that if they are to accomplish their mission they must remain apart.[35]

To their sense of the racial superiority of whites in general, then, white Afrikaners added a belief in their national destiny as a distinctive people or *Volk*. These, as we have seen, were among the key ingredients of Nazism in Germany and, except for the racism, of fascism in Italy. Even after apartheid ended and black Africans headed the government of South Africa, groups like the Afrikaner Resistance Movement defended their attempts to restore the old system by appeals to racism and nationalism. In these respects their views—and the system of apartheid in general—bear more than a passing resemblance to fascist and Nazi doctrine.

Nor are fascist ideas influential only in white racist circles. In India, the militant Hindu organizations which later gave birth to today's right-wing Bharatiya Janata Party (BJP) were deeply influenced by Italian fascism and Nazism. Hindu nationalist leaders during the 1930s greatly admired Hitler's ideas about scapegoating minority populations such as Jews in Germany and Muslims in India, and even visited Mussolini to learn how to reorder Indian society along fascist lines. The current leader of the BJP, Narendra Modi, stands accused by Human Rights Watch of inciting Hindus to large-scale violence against Muslims in the Indian state of Gujarat in 2002, where the history textbooks still speak glowingly of Hitler.[36] In 2014 Modi was elected prime minister of India. Hindu extremists, espousing the neofascist ideology of Hindutva, or "Hinduness," seek to "cleanse" India of non-Hindus—Muslims, most particularly—and to make it a "Hindu nation." To that end they have murdered Muslim (and secular) writers and intellectuals, as well as Muslims suspected of eating beef (because the cow is holy according to Hindu scripture). About these actions Modi has maintained a stony silence.[37]

FASCISM TODAY

Although it is difficult to gauge the strength or popularity of fascism today, it is clear that fascism is not altogether dead and gone—not even in the two countries in which it seemed so thoroughly defeated. The Fascist Party is outlawed in Italy, as is the Nazi Party in Germany, but neofascists and neo-Nazis manage to run for office, and occasionally stir up trouble, under different names. In Italy in 1992, for example, Allesandra Mussolini, granddaughter of *Il Duce*, won election to a seat in the Italian Parliament as a member of the neofascist Italian Social Movement (later renamed the National Alliance). In Germany neo-Nazi organizations—most notably the NPD (*Nationaldemokratische Partei Deutschlands*)—have operated openly and in apparent defiance of the German constitution which outlaws such parties. The NPD is at least loosely affiliated with the National Socialist Underground, which has claimed responsibility for firebombing attacks and other assaults that have killed Vietnamese, Turkish "guest workers," and others.

Attempts to outlaw the NPD have so far failed.[38] These attacks and the revival of fascism in general seem to be the result of a renewed nationalism that has been brought to the fore by resentment of foreign workers, refugees, and immigrants.

In France more than a decade ago, the neofascist National Front, led by Jean-Marie Le Pen, won control of some municipal governments with campaigns that blamed immigrants for high rates of unemployment, crime, and welfare costs. Le Pen himself finished a stunning second in the first round of the French presidential election of 2002. He lost by an overwhelming margin in the run-off election, but Le Pen's surprisingly strong showing in the first round suggests that a sizeable portion of the French electorate is prepared to blame immigrants for various social ills. More recently, the leadership of the National Front has passed to Le Pen's daughter, Marine Le Pen, who followed in her father's footsteps and ran as a candidate for the French presidency in 2012, finishing in third place, although with a higher percentage and nearly a million more votes than her father had received ten years earlier. Like her father, she is an ultra-nationalist who is deeply skeptical of globalization and European economic and political integration, and hostile to immigration, even going so far as to compare Muslims praying *en masse* in French public streets to the Nazi occupation of France during World War II. Yet, in contrast with her father, as leader of France's National Front Party the younger Le Pen has dialed down the overtly racist rhetoric and now seeks to present a more moderate, reasonable public face with greater middle-class appeal. This strategy has also worked for other far-right parties in Europe, many of whose once shaven-headed members have traded jackboots for Gucci loafers and black leather jackets for Armani suits and silk ties in an attempt to create a more polished, presentable image—while still retaining their extreme nationalist ideology. Le Pen is now forming alliances with many of those parties to promote and encourage the election of representatives to the European Parliament. Once inside, they hope to upset the Parliament's proceedings and obstruct legislation. Her party, like all of Europe's neofascist parties, despise the European Union and seek to restore their respective nations' sovereignty and to replace the euro with their old currencies. About the prospects for a united Europe, Ms. Le Pen said, "I am just waiting for one thing, which is that it break into pieces."[39] At present she appears to have a promising political career ahead of her in French—and, more broadly, European—neofascist politics. Her political career received a further boost from the ISIS terrorist attacks on Paris in November 2015. The reaction to these attacks increases the likelihood that she will run for president, and possibly win.[40]

In Britain the far-right United Kingdom Independence Party (UKIP)—once described and dismissed by Conservative Prime Minister David Cameron as "a bunch of fruitcakes, loonies, and closet racists"—won 25 percent of the local council elections it contested in 2013. Its increasingly popular platform calls for British withdrawal from the European Union and a crackdown on immigrants and immigration. UKIP has affinities with even more extreme neo-Nazi parties, including the English Defence League and the British National Party.[41]

Similar electoral challenges occurred elsewhere in Europe in the first two decades of the twenty-first century. Neofascist parties, capitalizing on anti-immigrant (and especially anti-Islamic) sentiments, captured 23 percent of the vote in parliamentary elections in Austria, 27 percent in Switzerland, and 12 percent in

Denmark. Even in the Netherlands, long a bastion of racial and religious tolerance, Pim Fortuyn's List, an anti-immigrant party led by the late Pim Fortuyn, came close to electoral victory in 2002. Had Fortuyn not been assassinated in May 2002, shortly before parliamentary elections, his party almost certainly would have won control of the Dutch Parliament, making Fortuyn the prime minister. Fortuyn's place has been taken by Geert Wilders, whose right-wing Party for Freedom is anti-immigrant and anti-Muslim. Wilders (1963–) asserts that Islam is an extremist ideology instead of a religion; that this "ideology," whose key text is the Qur'an, espouses terrorism; that the Qur'an ought to be banned in the Netherlands and elsewhere in Europe; and that Muslim immigrants should be repatriated to their countries of origin. These assertions appear in his speeches in the Dutch parliament and in his 2008 film *Fitna*. The Party for Freedom is increasingly popular in the Netherlands, and in future elections could conceivably win enough seats in parliament to make Wilders prime minister.

In local elections elsewhere in Europe, neofascist candidates for town councils have won some seats by sizable margins. In Belgium, for example, the Vlaams Blok (Flemish Bloc) made a strong showing in a number of regional and municipal elections before the Belgian Supreme Court outlawed it, in November 2004, for preaching racial and ethnic discrimination. The party has since reconstituted itself as Vlaams Belang (Flemish Interest).[42]

Neo-Nazis continue to take political and electoral advantage of the widespread backlash against Muslim immigrants in Europe. As one commentator observes, "[T]he primary threat to democracy in Europe is not 'Islamofascism' … but plain old fascism." He also notes that neofascists and neo-Nazis control several city councils and are members of national parliaments in several European countries. In Italy, France, Austria, Belgium, and Denmark, "hard-right national and anti-immigrant parties regularly receive more than 10 percent of the vote." Moreover, such parties have in earlier elections received 22 percent of the vote in Norway, and 19 percent in Switzerland. From 2000 to 2005 official reports of racist violence increased 21 percent in Ireland, 34 percent in France, and a stunning 71 percent in Denmark. "Far from being the principal purveyors of racial animus in Europe, Muslims are its principal targets."[43] (This began to change in 2015, with ISIS-inspired attacks on Jews and Jewish businesses.) The worldwide global economic meltdown that began in 2007, combined with continuing fear of terrorist attacks, has made matters much worse, and has led to calls for expelling Muslims from several European countries. In Greece, for example, the neo-Nazi Golden Dawn Party, long regarded as a ragged band of thugs and street fighters, is gaining increasing recognition and respectability for its radical anti-immigrant proposals and its call to roll back the Greek government's stringent austerity measures.[44]

In the summer of 2015, hundreds of thousands of refugees from Syria—almost all of them Muslims—began to flee their war-torn homeland and seek refuge in Europe. This has caused an anti-refugee backlash there, and has given a boost to far-right neo-Nazi parties. Syrian and other refugees face persecution from these groups, whose membership is on the rise. In Eastern Europe, far-right parties are growing in power, popularity, and legitimacy with their militant anti-migrant and anti-Roma proclamations and attacks. The Roma, a loose collection of peoples with ethnic origins in India who came to Europe during the Middle Ages, face systematic social prejudice and exclusion in housing, education, employment, and health care across the continent. They have faced eviction from their settlements in France, Italy, Hungary, and elsewhere, and some Slovak municipalities have built walls to separate Roma neighborhoods from the wider community. In Bulgaria, for example, Ataka ("Attack") has attacked Syrian refugees and members of the Roma minority. In the 2013 election Ataka received 7 percent of the popular vote and now holds 23 of 240 seats in parliament. And in Hungary the neo-Nazi Jobbik party won 20 percent of the vote in 2014 and has since become the second largest party in the country.[45]

Like-minded parties are gaining in popularity even in the otherwise progressive nations of Scandinavia. Denmark, Sweden, and Norway have seen the rise of anti-Muslim, anti-immigrant parties, which continue to attract adherents and sympathizers even from the liberal left. In Norway, the Progress Party attracts at least some Norwegians who view conservative religious Muslims as a threat to the tolerant, laid-back liberalism to which most Norwegians subscribe, and see immigrants as overburdening the highly popular programs of their welfare state.[46] The Progress Party has gained enough support to form a coalition government with the prime minister's Conservative Party. That party was, and apparently remains, a far-right extremist organization. Whether their newfound respectability is real or only skin-deep remains to be seen.

In the most infamous instance of right-wing extremism in Europe in recent years, a mentally unstable Norwegian neo-Nazi named Anders Behring Breivik murdered seventy-seven people in 2011, most of them defenseless teenagers at an island summer camp. Breivik's self-professed purpose for slaughtering his countrymen was to draw attention to his neo-Nazi cause and what he alleged to be the weakness of left-wing multicultural policies that he blamed for flooding Norway and other European countries with Muslim immigrants.

Nor has fascism revived only in Europe. In the Middle Eastern country of Iraq, the late Saddam Hussein's regime sought to build a society based on nationalism, militarism, and totalitarian control. The militaristic and totalitarian elements of that regime became well known during the Gulf War of 1990–1991, which followed the Iraqi invasion of Kuwait. The nationalistic element, however, received less attention in the West.

The nationalistic element of Saddam Hussein's now-deposed regime was most evident in his affiliation with a political party, the Ba'ath Party, which has been active in several Middle-Eastern countries. Since its founding in the 1950s the Ba'ath Party has preached *pan-Arabism*—the belief that all Arabs belong to a single nation, or people, destined to live in a single united state. In this way the Ba'ath Party has hoped to restore the strength and identity of an Arab people—*ba'ath* means "resurrection"—that finds itself divided into several different states and religions. The Ba'ath Party claims that this resurrection will benefit all Arabs, whether they are Muslim, Christian, or some other religion, because it gives them "a special mission in the world and a right to independence and unity."[47] This emphasis on nationality rather than religion explains why Osama bin Laden and other radical Islamists criticized Saddam Hussein's Ba'athist regime for being "secularist."

Arab nationalist sentiment is not enough by itself to produce fascism. But nationalism is a key ingredient in fascism, and when it is complemented by militarism and the attempt to establish totalitarian control, as in Iraq under Saddam Hussein, then fascism follows.[48]

But what of al-Qaeda, ISIS, and other radical or fundamentalist Islamist organizations? Some contemporary observers, including former president George W. Bush and some prominent neoconservatives, speak of radical Islamism as a form of fascism—as "Islamic fascism" or "Islamofascism." But radical Islamists are neither nationalists nor racists, although they are avowedly anti-Semitic. Their aim is to establish a kind of theocracy or religious state, not a state that unites and glorifies the people of a particular nation or race. The fascist label thus does not apply to them, as we shall see in Chapter 10.

In the United States the Nazi Party and other groups with fascist leanings—the Ku Klux Klan, Aryan Nation, World Church of the Creator, and assorted "skinheads"—sometimes make their presence felt. Such was clearly the case when in 2015 a 21-year-old white supremacist murdered nine African-American worshippers at a church in Charleston, South Carolina. His website included a 2,000-word racist manifesto and photographs of himself wearing a sweatshirt with "88"—neo-Nazi code for "Heil Hitler" (H being the eighth letter of the alphabet)—and posing with a pistol and a Confederate battle flag. His hope was to start a "race war" between blacks and whites. Instead, his actions brought them closer together in their shared grief, and resulted in the removal of the Confederate flag from state capitol grounds.

During the 2016 presidential nomination contest, the Republican front-runner, Donald Trump, caused a controversy by two actions in quick succession. In the first, he tweeted with approval a quotation from Benito Mussolini: "It is better to live one day as a lion than 100 years as a sheep." And then he was slow to disavow David Duke's declaration of support for Trump's candidacy. Duke, the former Grand Wizard of the Ku Klux Klan, enthusiastically endorsed Trump for his anti-Mexican, anti-Muslim, and anti-immigrant stances. Republican leaders were quick to condemn Trump's tardiness. For his part, Trump dismissed their condemnation as the "political correctness" of cowed politicians. Posts on white supremacist and neo-Nazi websites were effusive in their praise of Trump's "courageous" stance.[49]

Some, though certainly not all, of the "militia" movements in the United States have neo-Nazi leanings. Their members claim that the country has been taken over by Jews and the United Nations, which run the ZOG (Zionist Occupation Government) in Washington, D.C. This illegitimate government is bent on disarming white citizens, leaving them defenseless against blacks, Hispanics, and other nonwhites, and it is therefore the duty of patriotic whites to overthrow the ZOG. This is the thinking that has animated a number of militia-led bombings of federal facilities—most infamously and destructively, the 1995 bombing of the Murrah Federal Building in Oklahoma City. One of the convicted bombers, Timothy McVeigh, kept and often quoted from *The Turner Diaries*—a book whose contents provide a startling insight into the thinking of members of various radical-right, neo-Nazi militia groups.[50]

The Turner Diaries is a work of fiction. Written by William Pierce (1933–2002), founder of the neo-Nazi National Alliance, *The Turner Diaries* purports to be the diaries of Earl Turner, a militant member of a neo-Nazi group called the Organization that, in the "Great Revolution" of the late twentieth century, overthrew the Jewish-led "System"—the U.S. government—and in the twenty-first century inaugurated an all-white, racially pure New Era. During the Old Era, according to the *Diaries*, the System discriminated against patriotic white Americans by confiscating their guns; promoting policies of affirmative action; encouraging nonwhite foreign immigration and interracial marriage; and putting Jews, African-Americans, and other minorities in positions of authority in schools and universities, the mass media, and the FBI and other government agencies. This revolution pitted "patriotic" white Americans against an anti-white government bent on disarming and "mongrelizing" the white race by allowing interracial marriage and other forms of "race-mixing," such as integrated schools and churches. Opposing this anti-white system is the Organization—a group of right-wing, anti-liberal, white men and women who have not been "brainwashed" by the "liberal media." One of the characters in the *Diaries*, a white woman named Katherine, rejects her liberal leanings after being given

> some books on race and history and some Organization publications to read. For the first time in her life she began thinking seriously about the important racial, social and political issues at the root of the day's problems.
>
> She learned the truth about the System's "equality" hoax. She gained an understanding of the unique historical role of the Jews as the ferment of decomposition of races and civilizations. Most important, she began acquiring a sense of racial identity, overcoming a lifetime of brain washing aimed at reducing her to an isolated human atom in a cosmopolitan chaos.[51]

Here, in a nutshell, is the essence of Nazi, and now neo-Nazi, ideology: racial differences are innate and indelible; they lie at the root of all social and political problems; people of different races cannot live together in peace or harmony; the Jews, however, promote social and political chaos by preaching—and forcing people to practice—racial integration and "equality"; white people who are brainwashed by Jewish propaganda have no sense of "white" pride and identity, seeing themselves as the atomized individuals depicted by classical liberal and Enlightenment thought. "The key to the whole problem," Turner writes, is "the corruption of our people by the Jewish-liberal-democratic-equalitarian plague..."[52] This "plague" is first and foremost ideological, caused by white people accepting "Jewish" and "liberal" ideas, and it can be cured only by rejecting these ideas and replacing them with "correct" ideas about white identity and racial pride.

Putting her newfound ideology into practice, Katherine joins Turner and the other Organization members in fighting the System. They raise money to buy weapons by robbing Jewish-owned businesses and killing, with obvious enjoyment, the owners and employees. They make a fertilizer bomb and blow up the FBI's national headquarters, killing scores of agents and civilians alike. They also bomb the offices of the *Washington Post* and other "liberal" newspapers and television stations. They mount a mortar attack on the U.S. Capitol: "We saw beautiful blossoms of flame and steel sprouting everywhere ... erupting now inside and now outside the Capitol, wreaking their bloody toll in the ranks of tyranny and treason."[53] On the same day, "the Organization used a bazooka to shoot down an airliner which had just taken off for Tel Aviv with a load of vacationing dignitaries, mostly Jews. There were," Turner adds with evident satisfaction, "no survivors."[54] Later, during the "Day of the Rope," the Organization publicly hangs hundreds of thousands of black and white "race traitors" from trees, lampposts, and overpasses as a warning to those who might be tempted to "betray" the white race by befriending, defending, dating, or marrying members of other races.

Throughout *The Turner Diaries* the emphasis is on *difference*—not only between races, religions, and nations but also between the sexes. Liberalism and feminism are reviled for being effeminate and unmanly and for denying the importance of innate and deep-seated differences:

> Liberalism is an essentially feminine, submissive world view... "Women's lib" was a form of mass psychosis which broke out during the last three decades of the Old Era. Women affected by it denied their femininity and insisted that they were "people," not "women." This aberration was promoted and encouraged by the System as a means of dividing our [white] race against itself.[55]

And what of democracy? The *Diaries* condemns constitutional democracy: "The American people *voted themselves* into the mess they're in now," and "the Jews have taken over the country fair and square, according to the Constitution." The Constitution does not and cannot protect the integrity and identity of the "white race" and should therefore be scrapped. Elections aren't the answer: "Where [do you] think new elections can possibly lead now, with this generation of TV-conditioned voters, except right back into the same Jewish pigsty?"[56] In place of liberal democracy, *The Turner Diaries* advocates autocratic rule by a racially pure elite. This was finally achieved with the Organization's victory in the Great Revolution of "1999—just 110 years after the birth of the Great One." The unnamed Great One who was born in 1889 is, of course, Adolf Hitler.

Although Hitler died in his Berlin bunker in 1945, his ideas live on in the dreams and schemes and plans—and practices—of neo-Nazi groups in North America and Europe. These groups are especially eager to attract young recruits, boasting that "We don't just entertain racist kids ... we create them." In 2004, for example, Panzerfaust Records announced "Project Schoolyard," which aimed to distribute 100,000 sampler CDs—"70 minutes of pure White Power Rock and Roll"—to American students between the ages of thirteen and nineteen years.[57] Project Schoolyard was modeled on a similar National Socialist Movement Project in Germany. Panzerfaust Records subsequently disbanded, but its place was taken by Free Your Mind Productions, which sponsors Radio White on the Internet and groups such as H8Machine, the Midtown Boot Boys, and the Hammerskins. In August 2012 a gunman affiliated with the Hammerskins attacked worshipers at a Sikh temple in the Milwaukee suburb of Oak Creek, Wisconsin, killing six and seriously wounding four others. How powerful or threatening such groups as the Hammerskins are is difficult to tell, as their numbers are small, but apparently growing, among alienated and disaffected whites in America and elsewhere.

It would be a mistake, however, to conclude that all of the so-called militia groups in the United States take their inspiration from Hitler and the Nazis. According to one estimate, there were more than 850 militia groups in the United

States in the 1990s.[58] By 2007 their number had dropped to 148. But after the election of Barack Obama in 2008 their number increased to more than 1,200—an increase of 755 percent.[59] The members of these groups share a strong suspicion of the federal government and a fondness for firearms, but many of them are neither racists nor nationalists. Nor are they bent on establishing a totalitarian government. As the word "militia" suggests, the members of these groups often believe that they must remain vigilant, on guard against government attempts to seize more and more power. They typically insist that political power should be concentrated at the local level, not at the national, so that citizens acting in townships and counties can control their own affairs and live free from the meddling control of "big government." When power is concentrated in the hands of judges, representatives, and bureaucrats who are distant from the ordinary people, they argue, individual liberty is likely to be smothered. Comparing themselves to the minutemen and Sons of Liberty who took up arms in the American Revolution to defend the liberty of the American people against the oppressive designs of the British government, members of many militia groups claim to be fighting against a government that is too large, too remote, and too powerful for the good of the people.

In that respect, certainly, these militia groups are very different from Mussolini's fascists and Hitler's Nazis. Fascists celebrate power and seek to concentrate it in the state, in a single party, even in a single leader. For the true fascist, there must be nothing outside the state, nothing against the state, and everything for the state. That is a view that many militia members cannot accept. But others, such as the members of the Aryan Nation, can and do.

CONCLUSION

Fascism as an Ideology

One feature of fascism is clear. No matter what the form, fascists have always tried to win mass support by appealing to people in the simplest, most emotional terms. This feature becomes evident as we look at how fascism and Nazism perform the four functions of a political ideology.

Explanation. Why are social conditions the way they are? Fascists typically answer this question with some account of heroes and of villains engaged in massive conspiracies to undermine or even destroy the nation and its right-thinking citizens. Usually, they concentrate on the scoundrels or traitors—mostly Jews and their liberal lackeys—who conspire to keep the nation or the *Volk* weak in order to serve the interests of their own class, race, or ethnic group. They look for scapegoats, in other words, and blame all problems on them. This is what the Nazis did to the Jews, for instance, and what neo-Nazis or "white supremacists" do to blacks or Hispanics or other "inferior" and "foreign" groups.

Evaluation. Whether a situation is good or bad, according to fascists, will usually depend on some evaluation of a nation's or *Volk*'s unity and strength. If the people are fragmented, at odds with one another, then it is time to hunt down and punish—or preferably exterminate—the villains who are tearing the *Volk* or nation apart. If the people are united behind their party and their leader, on the other hand, then all is well.

Orientation. What is one's place in the world, one's primary source of belonging or identification? According to the Italian Fascists, it is the nation; to the Nazis, the nation defined in racial terms. In either case, the individual should recognize that he or she is of no significance as an individual but only as a member of the organic whole—the nation-state or the race—that gives meaning and purpose to his or her life.

Program. What is to be done? Again, the answer is simple—believe, obey, fight! Follow one's leaders in the struggle against the enemies of the nation or race, and do whatever is necessary to bring glory to one's people by helping to establish it as a leading power in the world. Give everything to the state, keep nothing from the state, and do nothing against the state. And ruthlessly and systematically murder Muslims, Jews, communists, and anyone else believed to be enemies of the state.

Fascism and the Democratic Ideal

In its strongest forms, then, whether in Italian Fascism, German Nazism, or neo-Nazism, fascism is a totalitarian ideology. Fascism does respond to the democratic ideal, to be sure, but it responds with contempt. For the fascist, democracy is merely another name for division and weakness in a world where unity and strength are what matter most.

DISCUSSION QUESTIONS

1 In what way(s) does Nazism resemble Mussolini's fascism? How does Nazism differ from fascism?
2 Who was Ludwig Woltmann and what was his contribution to Nazi ideology?
3 What reasons do Nazis give to explain their hatred of Jews, people of African descent, and other races and/or ethnic groups?
4 What does the German term *Lebensraum* mean? Why did the Nazis think this was an important term, and what were its practical political and military implications?
5 It has often been noted that, strictly speaking, the name "National Socialism" (Nazism) is misleading, since it was neither nationalist nor socialist. Is this true? Why or why not?
6 Mussolini and the Italian Fascists coined the word "totalitarian." What did they mean by that term, and why did they think it a good thing for a society to be totalitarian?
7 Where is fascism influential in today's global political landscape, and why?

NOTES

1 William S. Halperin, *Mussolini and Italian Fascism* (Princeton, NJ: Van Nostrand, 1964), p. 47.

2 For a clear statement of this view, see Immanuel Kant, "What Is Enlightenment?" in Terence Ball, Richard Dagger, and Daniel O'Neill, eds., *Ideals and Ideologies: A Reader*, 10th ed. (New York and London: Routledge, 2016), selection 3.17.

3 We take the term "Counter-Enlightenment" from Isaiah Berlin's essay, "The Counter-Enlightenment," in Berlin, *Against the Current: Essays in the History of Ideas* (Harmondsworth, U.K.: Penguin, 1982), pp. 1–24.

4 See Isaiah Berlin, "Joseph De Maistre and the Origins of Fascism," in Berlin, *The Crooked Timber of Humanity: Chapters in the History of Ideas*, 2nd ed., Henry Hardy, ed. (Princeton: Princeton University Press, 2013), pp. 95–177.

5 Hans Kohn, *Nationalism: Its Meaning and History* (Princeton, NJ: D. Van Nostrand, 1955), p. 36.

6 As reprinted in William Y. Elliot and Neil McDonald, eds., *Western Political Heritage* (New York: Prentice-Hall, 1949), p. 797.

7 Roberto Michels, *Political Parties: A Sociological Study of the Oligarchical Tendencies of Modern Democracy*, trans. Eden Paul and Cedar Paul (New York: Hearst's International Library, 1915).

8 See the synoptic survey in H. Stuart Hughes, *Consciousness and Society: The Reorientation of European Social Thought, 1890–1930*, rev. ed. (New York: Vintage Books, 1977).

9 See, for example, Sigmund Freud, *Civilization and Its Discontents*, trans. James Strachey (New York: W. W. Norton & Co., 1962).

10 William James, *The Will to Believe and Other Essays in Popular Philosophy* (Cambridge, MA: Harvard University Press, 1979 [1896]).

11 Vilfredo Pareto, *The Mind and Society*, trans. A. Livingston and A. Bongioro, 4 vols. (New York: Harcourt Brace, 1935).

12 Gaetano Mosca, *The Ruling Class*, trans. A. Livingston (New York: McGraw-Hill, 1939).

13 See Lucy Hughes-Hallett, *Gabrielle D'Annunzio: Poet, Seducer and Preacher of War* (New York: Anchor Books, 2014).

14 Quoted in A. James Gregor, *Contemporary Radical Ideologies* (New York: Random House, 1968), p. 131.

15 Quoted in Halperin, *Mussolini and Italian Fascism*, p. 47.

16 Benito Mussolini, "The Doctrine of Fascism," in Ball, Dagger, and O'Neill, eds., *Ideals and Ideologies*, selection 7.48.

17 Both passages quoted in Denis Mack Smith, "The Theory and Practice of Fascism," in Nathanael Greene, ed., *Fascism: An Anthology* (New York: Thomas Y. Crowell, 1968), pp. 109–110.

18 The following account owes a great deal to several histories of the period between 1918 and 1945, including especially Richard J. Evans's monumental *The Third Reich Trilogy: The Coming of the Third Reich* (New York: Penguin, 2003), vol. I; *The Third Reich in Power, 1933–1939* (New York: Penguin, 2005), vol. II; and *The Third Reich at War* (New York: Penguin, 2008), vol. III.

19 Adolf Hitler, *Mein Kampf*, trans. Ralph Manheim (Boston: Houghton Mifflin, 1943), p. 42; also in Ball, Dagger, and O'Neill, eds., *Ideals and Ideologies*, selection 7.50.

20 Richard J. Evans, "The Anatomy of Hell," *New York Review of Books*, July 9, 2015, pp. 52–54.

21 Quoted in Gregor, *Contemporary Radical Ideologies*, p. 197.

22 Quoted in ibid., p. 198.

23 Hitler, *Mein Kampf*, pp. 403–404; Hitler's italics.

24 See Lisa Pine, *Nazi Family Policy, 1933–1945* (Oxford, U.K.: Berg, 1997).

25 "Negro," *Encyclopedia Britannica*, 11th ed. (London, 1911), vol. 19, p. 344.

26 Woltmann, *Der historiche Materialismus: Darstellung und Kritik der Marxistischen Weltanschauung* (Dusseldorf: Michels, 1900); and *Politische Anthropologie: Eine*

Untersuchung über den Einfluss der Descendenztheorie auf die Lehre von der politischen Entwicklung der Völker (Weimar: Thüringische Verlags-Anstalt, 1903); 2nd ed. (Leipzig: Doerner, 1936).

27 A list of forty-one required books was printed on the back of membership cards issued to Nazi Party members. Ford's *International Jew* featured prominently on that list. See Timothy W. Ryback, *Hitler's Private Library: The Books That Shaped His Life* (New York: Knopf, 2008), p. 57.

28 See Neil Baldwin, *Henry Ford and the Jews* (New York: Public Affairs, 2001) and, more generally, Charles Higham, *American Swastika* (Garden City, NY: Doubleday, 1985).

29 For a history of the Protocols and its influence, see Stephen Eric Bronner, *A Rumor About the Jews: Antisemitism and the Protocols of the Learned Elders of Zion* (New York: St. Martin's Press, 2000).

30 According to Shlomo Avineri, "F. Von Schlegel's book, *The Language and Wisdom of the Indians*, appearing in the twenties [i.e., 1820s], first expounded the *Aryan* view in Germany, arguing for a national and racial affinity between the Germans and Indians on the basis of the linguistic relationship between Sanskrit and Old Gothic. Schlegel was the first to coin the phrase, 'the Aryan peoples.'" Avineri, "Hegel and Nationalism," in Walter Kaufmann, ed., *Hegel's Political Philosophy* (New York: Atherton Books, 1970), p. 111.

31 Quoted in Raymond E. Murphy et al., "National Socialism," in *Readings on Fascism and National Socialism* (Chicago: Swallow Press, 1952), p. 65.

32 On resistance inside Germany, see Hans Mommsen, *Germans Against Hitler: The Stauffenberg Plot and Resistance Under the Third Reich*, trans. Angus McGeoch (London: I. B. Tauris, 2009).

33 See the interviews with some of the rescuers in Kristin R. Monroe, *The Heart of Altruism: Perceptions of a Common Humanity* (Princeton: Princeton University Press, 1996), Part II.

34 Quoted in Leonard Thompson, *The Political Mythology of Apartheid* (New Haven: Yale University Press, 1985), p. 29.

35 See Saul Dubow, *Scientific Racism in Modern South Africa* (Cambridge: Cambridge University Press, 1995), esp. Chapter 7.

36 See Marzia Casolari, "Hindutva's Foreign Tie-Ups in the 1930s: Archival Evidence," *Economic and Political Weekly*, January 22, 2000, pp. 218–228; Parvis Gassem-Fachandi, *Pogrom in Gujarat: Hindu Nationalism and Anti-Muslim Violence in India* (Princeton: Princeton University Press, 2012); and Martha Nussbaum, *The Clash Within: Democracy, Religious Violence, and India's Future* (Cambridge, MA: Harvard University Press, 2009).

37 Gardener Harris, "India's Muslims Wary of Rising Political Star," *New York Times*, March 4, 2014, pp. A4, A7; Sonia Faleiro, "India's Attack on Free Speech," *New York Times*, October 4, 2015, p. SR7.

38 Melissa Eddy, "German Legislators Begin New Effort to Ban Extreme Right-Wing Party," *New York Times*, December 15, 2012, p. A8.

39 Alissa J. Rubin and Scott Sayare, "French Far-Right Leader Aims for E.U. Parliament," *New York Times*, January 10, 2014, p. A9.

40 See Adam Nossiter, "Party Chief's Sway Grows With Anti-Islam Message," *New York Times*, November 18, p. A13.

41 John F. Burns, "Insurgent Party in Britain Gains in Popular Support," *New York Times*, May 4, 2013, p. A8.

42 Craig S. Smith, "Fear of Islamists Drives Growth of the Far Right in Belgium," *New York Times*, February 12, 2005; available at www.nytimes.com/2005/02/12/world/europe/fear-of-islamists-drives-growth-of-far-right-in-belgium.html.

43 Gary Younge, "In Europe, Where's the Hate?," *The Nation*, January 7–14, 2008, p. 10.

44 Rachel Donadio and Dimitris Bounias, "Hard Times Lift Greece's Anti-Immigrant Fringe," *New York Times*, April 13, 2012, pp. A1, A12.

45 Andrew Higgins, "Far Right Gains as Syrians Reach Eastern Europe," *New York Times*, December 15, 2015, pp. A1, 18.

46 Steven Erlanger, "Amid Debate on Migrants, Norway Party Comes to Fore," *New York Times*, January 24, 2014, pp. A3, A8.

47 Albert Hourani, *A History of the Arab Peoples* (Cambridge, MA: Harvard University Press, 1991), p. 405.

48 See the discussion of Saddam Hussein's regime in Walter Laqueur, *Fascism: Past, Present, Future* (New York: Oxford University Press, 1996), pp. 161–163. Laqueur notes that "Saddam has even become a cult figure among German neo-Nazis, Le Pen's followers, and the Russian neofascists" (p. 163). Roger Griffin argues that Iraq's "official ideology" was "uncannily akin to Nazism in some ideological aspects," but cannot be considered truly fascist because "it rejects the notion of mass politics from below and represses genuine populism in a way quite unlike Nazism…" Griffin, *The Nature of Fascism* (London: Routledge, 1993), p. 178.

49 Jonathan Mahler, "Trump's Message Resonates with White Supremacists," *New York Times*, March 1, 2016, p. A19.

50 Andrew Macdonald (pseudonym for William L. Pierce), *The Turner Diaries*, 2nd ed. (Arlington, VA: National Vanguard Books, 1985). An excerpt is available in Ball, Dagger, and O'Neill, *Ideals and Ideologies*, selection 7.51.

51 Ibid., p. 29.

52 Ibid., p. 42.

53 Ibid., p. 61.

54 Ibid., p. 62.

55 Ibid., pp. 42, 45.

56 Ibid., p. 173.

57 See www.nsm88.com/project%20Schoolyard.html (as of May 2, 2005).

58 Estimate of the Southern Poverty Law Center (SPLC), reported in Mark Shaffer, "Militias Find Recruiting Easy," *Arizona Republic*, September 29, 1997, p. B1.

59 "As Election Season Heats Up, Extremist Groups at Record Levels," SPLC Report, March 8, 2012. For this and other reports, go to splcenter.org.

FOR FURTHER READING

Aho, James. *The Politics of Righteousness: Idaho Christian Patriotism*. Seattle: University of Washington Press, 1990.

Arendt, Hannah. *The Origins of Totalitarianism*. Cleveland, OH, and New York: Meridian Books, 1958.

Barkun, Michael. *Religion and the Racist Right: The Origins of the Christian Identity Movement*. Chapel Hill, NC: University of North Carolina Press, 1994.

Bosworth, R. J. B. *Mussolini*. Oxford: Oxford University Press, 2002.

Bullock, Alan. *Hitler: A Study in Tyranny*, rev. ed. New York: Harper & Row, 1964.

Eatwell, Roger. *Fascism: A History*. New York: Viking Penguin, 1997.

Farrell, Nicholas. *Mussolini: A New Life*. London: Weidenfeld & Nicholson, 2003.

Griffin, Roger. *The Nature of Fascism*. London: Routledge, 1993.

Kershaw, Ian. *Hitler*, 2 vols., New York: Norton, 1999, 2000.

Kohn, Hans. *The Idea of Nationalism: A Study in Its Origin and Background*. New York: Collier, 1967.

Laqueur, Walter. *Fascism: Past, Present, Future*. New York: Oxford University Press, 1996.

Mack Smith, Denis. *Mussolini*. New York: Alfred A. Knopf, 1982.

Miller, Judith, and Laurie Mylroie. *Saddam Hussein and the Crisis in the Gulf*. New York: Times Books, 1990.

Mosse, George. *The Crisis of German Ideology: Intellectual Origins of the Third Reich*. New York: Grosset & Dunlap, 1964.

Nolte, Ernst. *Three Faces of Fascism: Action Française, Italian Fascism, National Socialism,* trans. Leila Vennewitz. New York: Holt, Rinehart & Winston, 1965.

Paxton, Robert. *The Anatomy of Fascism.* New York: Knopf, 2004.

Payne, Stanley G. "Fascism and Racism." In Terence Ball and Richard Bellamy, eds., *The Cambridge History of Twentieth-Century Political Thought.* Cambridge: Cambridge University Press, 2003.

——. *A History of Fascism, 1914–1945.* Madison: University of Wisconsin Press, 1996.

Pfaff, William. *The Wrath of Nations: Civilization and the Furies of Nationalism.* New York: Simon & Schuster, 1993.

Southern Poverty Law Center. *False Patriots: The Threat of Anti-Government Extremists.* Montgomery, AL: Southern Poverty Law Center, 1996.

Stern, Kenneth. *A Force upon the Plain: The American Militia Movement and the Politics of Hate.* New York: Simon & Schuster, 1996.

Sternhell, Zeev, et al. *The Birth of Fascist Ideology: From Cultural Rebellion to Political Revolution,* trans. David Maisel. Princeton, NJ: Princeton University Press, 1993.

Thompson, Leonard. *The Political Mythology of Apartheid.* New Haven, CT: Yale University Press, 1985.

From the Ball, Dagger, and O'Neill Reader *Ideals and Ideologies,* **Tenth Edition**

Part VII: Fascism

7.47 Joseph-Arthur de Gobineau—Civilization and Race
7.48 Benito Mussolini—The Doctrine of Fascism
7.49 Alfredo Rocco—The Political Theory of Fascism
7.50 Adolf Hitler—Nation and Race
7.51 Andrew Macdonald (William L. Pierce)—The Turner Diaries

USEFUL WEBSITES

Ku Klux Klan: www.kkk.com
National Alliance (USA): www.natall.com
National Front (France): www.frontnational.com
National Socialist Movement: www.nsm88.org
Southern Poverty Law Center: www.splcenter.org
Stormfront: www.stormfront.org

CHAPTER 8

LIBERATION IDEOLOGIES AND THE POLITICS OF IDENTITY

Man is born free, yet everywhere he is in chains... The one who thinks himself the master of others is as much a slave as they.

Jean-Jacques Rousseau, *The Social Contract*

For more than half a century, several ideologies have affixed the word "liberation" to their names. The call for *black liberation* came out of the ferment of the 1960s, as did the *women's liberation* movement. These movements were followed by the *gay liberation* movement, *aboriginal* or *native peoples' liberation*, *liberation theology*, and even an increasingly influential *animal liberation* movement. In many respects, of course, these are very different movements with vastly different ideologies. Each has its distinctive arguments and each addresses a particular audience. However, despite their differences, all share common features that mark their respective ideologies as members of an extended family.

This "family resemblance" should become clear in this chapter as we examine the extent to which these liberation ideologies possess similar features. How does each ideology understand freedom or liberty? How does each fulfill the four functions of an ideology? And how does each define the democratic ideal?

LIBERATION IDEOLOGIES: COMMON CHARACTERISTICS

An interest in liberation is, of course, nothing new. All political ideologies have stressed the importance of liberty, although, as we have seen, they conceive of liberty in very different ways. In some respects, then, contemporary liberation ideologies simply extend or amend the views of earlier ideologies, especially liberalism and socialism. But these new ideologies seek liberation from forms of oppression and domination that earlier ideologies have, in the liberationists' view, wrongly neglected or overlooked. They also recommend new and distinctive strategies for overcoming or ending oppression.

Liberation ideologies share several core, or common, features. The first is that each addresses a particular audience—blacks or women or gays and lesbians, native or aboriginal people, poor peasants, or even people distressed by the mistreatment of animals. (As we shall see, the ideology of "animal liberation" runs into theoretical and conceptual difficulties faced by no other liberation ideology.) The members of each of these audiences are not people who chose to be in that audience, as the people attending a concert have done. Instead, liberation ideologies address themselves to groups of people who share certain characteristics, such as race or sex or sexual orientation, by the accident of birth. Liberation ideologies maintain that these characteristics, whether chosen or not, form a major part of the *identity* or self-identification of the people who share them. In other words, how others think of a person—and how that person thinks of him- or herself—depends largely upon given conditions, such as skin color, sex, and sexual orientation. It is not enough, therefore, to follow the liberal program of working to promote individual liberty. According to the various liberation ideologies, people are not only individuals, so they cannot be liberated simply as individuals. People identify with certain groups—and are identified by others as members of those groups—and they must be freed or liberated as members of those groups—as blacks or women or gays and lesbians or native people. Hence, these liberation ideologies are typically associated with what has come to be called "the politics of identity."

A second feature is that each of the groups addressed understands itself to be mistreated or oppressed by some dominant group. The term "oppression" refers to the many means—institutional, intellectual, legal, even linguistic—that some people use to "press down," or otherwise "deform" others.[1] It is in this sense, their adherents claim, that blacks have been and still are oppressed by a predominantly white power structure; women, by "patriarchy" or structures of masculine domination; gays and lesbians by heterosexism; native people, by the lingering legacy of colonial rule; poor peasants, by laws and institutions that favor wealthy landowners; and animals, by humans who hold and act upon "speciesist" beliefs and attitudes.

A third feature common to all liberation ideologies is that they aim to liberate an oppressed group not only from "external" restraints or restrictions, such as unjust or discriminatory laws, barriers to entry in education, housing, and employment, but also from "internal" restrictions. Internal restrictions are those beliefs and attitudes that oppressed people have come to accept—uncritically and unconsciously—as true, and that then serve to inhibit their quest for freedom or liberation. Liberation ideologies are addressed, then, to people who have in some sense acquiesced to or participated in their own oppression or victimization. On this view, for example, some black people have internalized "white" values and racist attitudes toward blacks;[2] some women have accepted men's diagnoses and explanations of their discontent;[3] some gays and lesbians have felt ashamed because they are not "straight";[4] Native Americans and other indigenous people may feel ashamed of their "savage" ancestry and "primitive" customs;[5] many Latin American peasants have accepted their "lot" in life as "fate" or as "the will of God";[6] and if not animals, then at least those humans who eat their flesh and wear their fur have accepted the claim that humans are a "higher" species with the right to eat or skin members of "lower" species.[7] The dominance of the ruling race, gender, sexual orientation, culture, class, or species depends on the oppressed group's continuing acceptance of their condition as natural, normal, or inevitable. To break the grip and the legitimacy of the dominant group requires a change of outlook and attitude on the part of the oppressed, who suffer from something like **false consciousness** in the Marxian sense.[8]

From the foregoing there follows a fourth feature common to all liberation ideologies: all aim to "raise the consciousness" and change the outlooks of people who have somehow participated—however unwillingly, unwittingly, or unconsciously—in their own oppression or victimization. Such participation may take many forms. For example, a black person might feel socially or intellectually inferior to whites; women might think themselves to be helpless, or at least less powerful than men; and homosexuals might feel ashamed of being **gay** rather than "straight." The aim of the various liberation ideologies is to confront and criticize the sources of these feelings of inadequacy, inferiority, or shame—and in so doing to "liberate" or "emancipate" members of oppressed groups by helping them to help themselves. A major part of this effort consists in promoting the identification of the individual with the group. For example, a woman who thinks of herself primarily or even exclusively as a wife or mother or member of a church will be less likely to think of herself as an oppressed *woman*. If she can be brought to think of herself as a woman whose opportunities and position in life are largely determined by her **gender** and constrained by a system of patriarchal power, then she will be much more likely to identify with the plight of other women and join with them to work for their mutual liberation.

Fifth and finally, liberation ideologies also aim to identify, criticize, and transform systems and structures of oppression and in so doing to liberate the oppressors—to free them from the illusion of their own superiority and to help them to recognize their former victims as fellow human beings (or, in the case of animal liberation, as fellow beings). The aim of all liberation ideologies, in short, is to break those "mind-forged manacles" about which William Blake wrote more than two centuries ago.[9]

Because each of these liberation ideologies addresses a specific audience or group, we can best understand their structure, arguments, and appeal by looking at the groups to which each is addressed.

BLACK LIBERATION

"Black liberation" encompasses a wide range of theories and movements that aim at overcoming the obstacles that stand in the way of freedom for black people. These obstacles are many and varied. One is widespread and pervasive racism, often buttressed and legitimized by "scientific" studies that purportedly "prove" the moral, cultural, and intellectual inferiority of black Africans (recall the racist treatises by Gobineau and others discussed in Chapter 7). A no less obvious obstacle was the institution of slavery itself. Captured in Africa and forcibly brought to the western hemisphere, black Africans endured the most brutal conditions imaginable, both *en route* and after their arrival on these shores. Three centuries of chattel slavery ended officially in the United States with the ratification of the Thirteenth Amendment in 1865, which abolished slavery, followed by the Fourteenth Amendment granting full citizenship (1868) and then the Fifteenth Amendment enfranchising black males (1870). But for blacks who remained in the South, life was hard and liberty merely a word. Harsh "Jim Crow" laws ensured the segregation of the races. This system of official and unofficial segregation separated the races and consigned blacks to an inferior position. For black people, the right to vote existed only on paper. Schools were segregated by race, with black children almost always receiving a substandard education; "white" restaurants, hotels, movie theaters, swimming pools, and other venues were strictly off-limits to Americans of African ancestry. Anyone who objected or tried to stand up to this system was likely to be beaten or lynched by the Ku Klux Klan. In the South, black men were effectively re-enslaved as convicts in a system of mass incarceration that continued until World War II and—as black liberationists contend—continues even today.[10] Once thought to guarantee equal rights to African-Americans, some provisions of the 1964 Civil Rights Act and the 1965 Voting Rights Act are currently under attack, although in less overt and more subtle forms such as "voter ID" laws. Although officially illegal, the practice of "redlining"—that is, denying mortgages to people living in "black" neighborhoods—has returned in a newer and more covert form.[11]

One of the more overt forms of oppression is the brutal treatment of blacks by police. With the advent of social media police brutality has become much more visible than before. The videotaped beating of Rodney King by four Los Angeles police officers in 1991 was merely the first in a long line of publicly documented beatings, shootings, and stranglings of black men by white officers. In that infamous instance the four policemen were acquitted by an all-white jury, which sparked the 1992 Los Angeles riots in which fifty-three people died and more than 2000 were injured. Since then the ownership and use of smart phones and other social media has skyrocketed, resulting in widespread documentation of instances of police violence. These include the police killings of Laquan McDonald, Eric Garner, Michael Brown, Walter Scott, Samuel Dubose, and Tamir Rice in 2014–2015, among others. Such killings, as well as events like the death of Freddie Gray while in police custody in Baltimore, led to the formation of the movement Black Lives Matter (blacklivesmatter.com), which publicizes African-American grievances and proposes placing "cop cams" on all patrolling police officers. Members of this movement can claim some success but by their own admission have a long way to go.

Black students at predominantly white colleges and universities have long suffered the sting of racist remarks and innuendoes which, when reported to campus authorities, too often come to nothing. In 2015, black students staged protests and sit-ins at several universities, resulting in the resignations or removal of several high-ranking administrators. Perhaps the most notable of these protests was at the University of Missouri, where the mostly black football team joined in, leading to the resignation of the university's president. So far such victories are few and far between, and individual and institutional racism persists. In these and many other ways, African-Americans continue to live out a long legacy of enslavement and racism.

It is this legacy that black liberationists address and attempt to overcome. Far from speaking with a single voice, however, black liberationists disagree among themselves about a wide range of issues, ends, means, and methods of liberating black people. The range is so wide, in fact, that one scholar has identified six "historically important black political ideologies" in the United States alone.[12] One of the major divisions, however, is between those advocates of black liberation who take an *integrationist* or *assimilationist* approach, on the one hand, and those who call for more radical *separatist* or *nationalist* policies, on the other. As so often happens with political ideologies, this division is not a sharp or rigid one. Some people who take a generally integrationist position, such as Reverend Martin Luther King, Jr. (1929–1968), have also agreed with some aspects of black separatism; and some who have been fiery nationalists, such as Malcolm X (1925–1965), later modified their views in an integrationist direction. Nevertheless, the division does represent the two main tendencies within the black struggle against **racism**.

As the name indicates, the principal aim of the integrationist approach is the full integration or assimilation of black people into society. In this view, black liberation is mostly a matter of removing the barriers to black people's full and free participation in the social, economic, and political life of their countries—barriers such as laws that deny them equal voting rights or equal opportunities for housing, employment, and education (see Figure 8.1). The point is that blacks ought to be treated first and foremost as *individuals*, with the same rights and liberties as theother individual members of society. If justice is blind, after all, it must also be

Martin Luther King, Jr. (1929–1968) and Malcolm X (1925–1965)

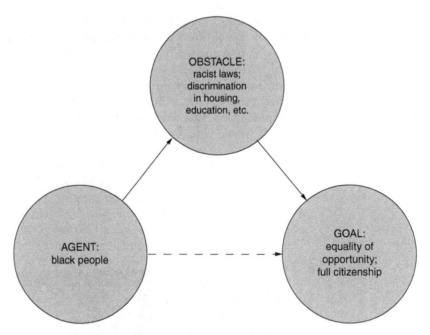

FIGURE 8.1 The "black integrationist" view of freedom.

color-blind. In this respect, the integrationist or assimilationist approach is essentially liberal in outlook. When white-dominated society has excluded blacks from full membership, the integrationist response has been to take legal and political action to overturn the laws and break down the prejudices that have enforced racial segregation and discrimination. The goal, as Martin Luther King said in his "I Have a Dream" speech (1963), is a society in which people "will not be judged by the color of their skin but by the content of their character."

For their part, black separatists or nationalists insist that integration is not the solution to the problems that confront black people in white-dominated societies. The first and most important task, in their view, is to build racial pride and economic self-sufficiency among black people—something that can be done only if blacks recognize that they are not merely individuals but members of a distinct community, nation, or people. Some black nationalists have literally campaigned for a separate territory or homeland for blacks. One of these was Marcus Garvey (1887–1940), a Jamaican immigrant to the United States who condemned interracial marriage and founded the United Negro Improvement Association with the eventual aim of establishing an independent, black-governed nation in Africa. Other black nationalists have called for a "nation-within-a-nation." This would mean, for example, converting part of the United States into a black-governed territory, as in one organization's plan for turning five southern states into a Republic of New Africa.[13] Like other nationalists, in short, some black separatists or nationalists hold that separate nations (or peoples) should each be united in its own self-governing nation-state.

Most black separatists, however, have not taken their nationalism that far. Instead, they have devoted themselves to promoting a stronger sense of identity, community, and pride among blacks. While Reverend King was leading marches and boycotts and the National Association for the Advancement of Colored People (NAACP) was filing lawsuits to bring an end to racial segregation in the 1960s, the Black Panthers and other black nationalists were calling for "Black Pride" and "Black Power." In South Africa, Steve Biko (1946–1977) led a movement for "Black Consciousness."[14] Black people must take charge of their own lives, these separatists argued, and they cannot do this as long as they are under the illusion that they can become free and equal members of societies that are in fact racist to the core. The first step toward liberation, they reasoned, must be liberation from the racist thinking that infects not only whites but all too often black people themselves.

A theme voiced eloquently by the novelists Richard Wright (1908–1960) and James Baldwin (1924–1987), by the poet Langston Hughes (1902–1967), the playwright August Wilson (1945–2005), and author and activist Malcolm X (1925–1965) is that the most pernicious form of racism may well be that which lodges inside, and warps, the psyche of blacks themselves. People of color, and perhaps black people in particular, have long felt the sting of prejudice and racial discrimination. Whether in the form of racial slurs, stereotypes, or jokes, such prejudice wounds the pride and undermines or even destroys the dignity and self-respect of racial minorities. However hard a black person may work to earn the respect of others, he or she is still likely to be viewed and assessed in racially stereotypical terms. To shed the burdens of the racist stereotype, he or she may try to "pass"—if not actually to pass as white, then at least to be accepted by whites by, for example, adopting "white" tastes in music, food, clothes, and friends, and taking care not to use "black" expressions or turns of phrase. Because such attempts are almost always unsuccessful, one might then turn one's anger inward, toward oneself, hating one's own blackness more than one hates white racists.

This double rage—hatred not only of one's oppressors but also of oneself and one's race—has often been noted by black writers. Having been suppressed and turned inward by black people, this anger sometimes comes to the surface in self-destructive ways. Psychoanalysts call this process "sublimation" and "the return of the repressed." It may take a skilled psychoanalyst to help someone delve deep inside his or her psyche to bring such long-suppressed anger to light. So perhaps it is not surprising that some of the most far-reaching analyses of black feelings have been made by psychoanalysts. Two of them, Dr. William Grier and Dr. Price Cobbs, call the syndrome "black rage"—an anger against whites that blacks vent on themselves and each other.[15] This rage, in conjunction with poverty, despair, lack of educational opportunities, and other social and economic inequalities, may help to explain the disturbingly high homicide and drug addiction rates among inner-city black people in the United States.

Nor are these conditions confined to North America. In *Black Skins, White Masks*, the Algerian psychoanalyst Frantz Fanon (1925–1961) describes the feelings of futility of black Africans who tried to adopt white European attitudes and values and, in the attempt, lost their identity and sense of self-worth. Their French might be exquisite and more eloquent than that of their colonial masters, their European suits of impeccable cut and quality, and their manners charming; but, try as they may, they never will be white Europeans. The result, as Fanon recounts it, is an unrequited love for white Europeans and all things European, on the one hand, and an abiding hatred of all things black and African, on the other. Such feelings give rise to self-destructive behavior.[16] The only way out of this impasse, says Fanon, is for black people to break out of their mental prisons, not to be freed by others but to free themselves from the false beliefs and illusions in which they have for too long been ensnared. The process of healing, of recovering from the massive psychic injury that whites have visited upon blacks (and blacks upon themselves), begins by calling white culture into question, by showing that "white" standards are not necessarily the true or the only standards of intelligence, beauty, and achievement. Fanon—and, more recently, scholars engaged in "whiteness studies"[17]—contend that blacks need to recognize that their alleged "inferiority" is a "mind-forged manacle," or, to change the metaphor, an illusory bubble that bursts as soon as it is seen for what it is.

Black liberationists try to burst this bubble by several means. One is to recover black history—the story of how blacks have, in the long history of their bondage, triumphed time and again against their white masters; how they have retained their dignity despite the indignities heaped upon them by slaveholders and other oppressors; and how they have developed an affirmative culture, including art, music, poetry, and literature, that has infused and influenced the dominant culture of today. (Think, for example, of blues, jazz, rock, and hip-hop.) Another means of bursting the bubble is to repudiate white views of blacks (and of some blacks' internalized views of themselves) by reclaiming and proclaiming "black" values and standards. This can be done, for example, by affirming that "black is beautiful," that curly or "nappy" hair is attractive, and that "black" English (or "Ebonics") and dress should be displayed proudly as badges of black identity and solidarity. In these and other ways, black nationalists have attempted to instill a sense of racial pride and black identity.

Pride and identity are necessary steps on the road to liberation, according to this view. This will be liberation not only for oppressed black people but for their oppressors as well. On this point the civil rights and liberationist variants of black liberation agree. Like the master in Hegel's parable of the master and slave (see pp. 157–58), whites cannot be free as long as they refuse to acknowledge that blacks are equally worthy as human beings. Martin Luther King, Jr., who had studied Hegel's philosophy in divinity school, gave eloquent statement to this view in a speech in 1962:

> Many [white] Southern leaders are pathetically trapped by their own devices. They know that the perpetuation of this archaic, dying order [of racial segregation] is hindering the rapid growth of the South. Yet they cannot speak this truth—they are imprisoned by their own lies. It is history's wry paradox that when Negroes win their struggle to be free, those who have held them down will themselves be freed for the first time.[18]

This Hegelian idea was reiterated by President Barack Obama, speaking in 2013 at Nelson Mandela's memorial service in South Africa: "It took a man like Madiba [Mandela's clan name] to free not just the prisoner but the jailer as well."[19] Although advocates of black liberation agree that Obama's election to the presidency marks a milestone in American race relations, they disagree that the struggle for racial justice and full equality has finally ended in the United States. Much has been achieved, but much remains to be done. Legal segregation of the races may have ended in schools and other institutions but informal segregation and racial discrimination are still practiced in hiring and promotion and in private clubs and other organizations. In other respects, however, conditions have improved to an extent that would astonish someone living in the mid-twentieth century. For example, in 1950, in thirty of the then forty-eight states, it was a crime for blacks and whites to marry. Only in its 1967 decision in *Loving v. Virginia* did the U.S. Supreme Court strike down so-called "anti-miscegenation" laws preventing interracial marriage, three years after passage of the 1964 Civil Rights Act and two years after the 1965 Voting Rights Act. Culturally and politically speaking, progress has been made, as these developments—and Obama's election in 2008 and his reelection in 2012—attest. But in economic terms, African-Americans on average continue to lag far behind their white fellow citizens. It was for this reason that, shortly before he was assassinated, Martin Luther King came to advocate that *civil* rights be supplemented by *economic* rights.[20] And in the 2008 presidential campaign Barack Obama chided black critics who hold the "static" view that little or no progress has been made and that nothing has been done to improve the lives of black Americans even as he acknowledged that much remains to be done if African-Americans are to enjoy economic and political parity with white Americans.[21]

Consider by way of example these continuing inequities: African-Americans have shorter life spans than white Americans; relative to their numbers in the general population, fewer graduate from high school and college; they are twice as likely to be unemployed; the practice of "redlining"—effectively denying home mortgages to blacks—is illegal, but continues to be practiced covertly; one in nine black men between the ages of twenty and thirty-four has served or is now serving prison sentences (largely though not exclusively because of drug laws and selective law enforcement that targets blacks); and many American states have "felon disenfranchisement" laws that bar former convicts from voting. That these are intolerable statistics is something on which all black liberationists agree wholeheartedly. In all these ways, they argue, America has yet to become a "post-racial" society.

Another point on which black nationalists and integrationists sometimes agree is on the demand for *reparations*. That is, they hold that one way to overcome the long history and lingering effects of slavery and racism in the United States would be for white Americans to make reparation by paying black Americans for the enslavement and exploitation of their ancestors.[22] Such reparations, amounting to several billions of dollars, would not be in the form of direct payment to individuals, but would instead take the form of scholarships for black students, financial aid to historically black colleges, low- or no-interest loans to black-owned businesses, and the like. By these means African-Americans would receive an apology for slavery and racism that is both material and symbolic. Not surprisingly, this proposal has prompted an intense and continuing debate. Opponents, including some African-Americans, claim that there is no such thing as "collective guilt"; responsibility rests always and only with individuals, and those individuals responsible for slavery—and those who were themselves slaves—are long dead. Present-day white Americans had nothing to do with slavery, nor were present-day black Americans ever enslaved; therefore, whites owe nothing to blacks except a level playing field and a game in which the umpire-state is color-blind. Proponents of reparations counter by pointing to the lingering legacy of slavery and legally sanctioned racial discrimination (the so-called "Jim Crow" laws). Whites profited from the unpaid labor of black slaves, they charge, and those immoral profits have been passed on through the generations in the form of inheritance. They also invoke the precedent of German reparations to Jewish survivors and descendants of victims of the Holocaust. The victims of slavery and racism, they insist, deserve no less.[23]

Despite the possibility of their agreement on reparations and other matters, the integrationist and nationalist approaches continue to represent two opposing tendencies among advocates of black liberation. For the integrationist, the objective is to remove those legal and other obstacles that deny black people an equal opportunity to live as free individuals and first-class citizens in a color-blind society. For the separatist or nationalist, however, the aim is still to promote identity, pride, and self-sufficiency among black people. These themes are often sounded in hip-hop and "rap" music, and they find expression also in the doctrines of the Nation of Islam (or Black Muslims). This group, until recently led by Reverend Louis Farrakhan (1933–), teaches that black people must take control of their own destiny through hard work, discipline, and abstinence from alcohol, drugs, and extramarital sex. Much of its work is done at the local level, but the Nation of Islam has also organized national demonstrations, notably the Million Man March on Washington, D.C., in 1995—a march followed in later years by Million Woman and Million Youth marches. The Million Man March produced a manifesto that states not only the purpose of the march but also the aspirations of black nationalists in general:

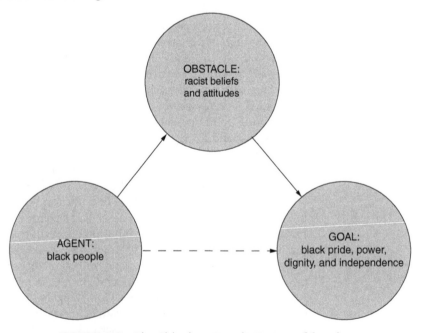

FIGURE 8.2 The "black nationalist" view of freedom.

An affirmation of self-determination and unified commitment to self-sufficiency through economic and human development; political empowerment; and international policy and development by African Americans in the interest of people of African descent throughout the African world community, our youth, and future generations.[24]

The conception of freedom (or liberty) at the core of the ideology of black nationalism is summarized in Figure 8.2.

WOMEN'S LIBERATION (FEMINISM)

Since women constitute fully half of the human race, feminism has proved to be a particularly important and influential liberation ideology. Still, misunderstandings remain. One is that feminism and feminists are somehow "anti-men." What feminism and feminists are opposed to, on the contrary, is a pervasive and persistent attitude to which many men (and some women) subscribe. Formerly called **patriarchy** (or patriarchalism) or "sexism," and now male (or masculine) domination, this attitude holds that men are intellectually and morally superior to women and have a legitimate claim to control their lives and their bodies, allegedly "for their own good" or the good of "the family" or of society at large. Feminists contend, by contrast, that women are men's equals and are quite capable of controlling their own lives and bodies.

The view that women are weak, irrational, and in need of guidance by men is very old indeed. Aristotle, long regarded as "the master of them that know," provides a particularly eminent case in point. "The male," he wrote, "is by nature more expert at leading than is the female." Thus it is "natural" for men to rule over women: "The relation of male to female is by nature a relation of superior to inferior and ruler to ruled."[25] A similar view is expressed by Saint Paul: "I do not permit a woman to teach or to assume authority over a man; she must be quiet" (I Timothy 2:12). It is perhaps not surprising that a male philosopher of the third century BCE or a first-century CE Christian would hold that women are inferior to men and should be subordinate to them. More surprising is that many modern men would hold such views. That American exemplar of the Enlightenment, Thomas Jefferson, believed that a woman's place is in the home, and most assuredly not in politics or public office. When his Treasury Secretary suggested that some government offices might be held by women, President Jefferson wrote a curt one-sentence reply: "The appointment of a woman to office is an innovation for which the public is not prepared, nor am I."[26] And Charles Darwin wrote that "the chief distinction in the intellectual powers of the two sexes is shown by man's attaining to a higher eminence, in whatever he takes up, than women can attain—whether requiring deep thought, reason, or imagination, or merely the use of the senses and hands."[27] Numerous "scientific" studies allegedly "proved" the intellectual inferiority of women and their need to be cosseted and controlled by men.[28] Well into the twentieth century even some of the most educated and enlightened of men held such views regarding women. And, considered globally, these views of women's abilities and proper "place" persist and predominate.

A traditional ballad succinctly summarizes the age-old plight of women:

Hard luck's the misfortune of all womankind.
They're always controlled, they're always confined.
Controlled by their fathers until they are wives.
Then slaves to their husbands the rest of their lives.

Feminism addresses and attempts to rectify this condition.

Contrary to the widely held view that the women's liberation movement and its ideology originated in the 1960s, feminism has a long history. Yet this history has until recently remained half-hidden, and women's voices have been submerged or ignored. Some few of these voices have come down to us, however. Writing to her husband, John Adams (1735–1826), who was attending the 1776 Continental Congress, Abigail Adams (1744–1818) asked him to "remember the ladies and be more generous and favorable to them than your ancestors. Do not put such unlimited power into the hands of the husbands. Remember, all men would be tyrants if they could. If particular care and attention is not paid to the ladies, we are determined to foment a rebellion, and will not hold ourselves bound by any laws in which we have no voice or representation."[29] In a similar spirit, Mary Wollstonecraft and Olympe de Gouges criticized the French revolutionaries for championing "the rights of man" while neglecting the rights of women.[30] The nineteenth century saw an increasing militancy on the part of women. Suffragists in England and the United States demanded that women be allowed to vote, while others lobbied for changes in the laws regulating marriage and divorce. Many in the early nineteenth-century American women's movement—Sarah and Angelina Grimké, Margaret Fuller, Lucy Stone, Sojourner Truth, Elizabeth Cady Stanton, and others—were also active in the antislavery movement. As they pointed out, the condition of women and of slaves was similar in many ways: both were without the right to vote, to run for public office, to own property in their own name, or to leave an abusive master or husband.[31] Others, such as Susan B. Anthony, were active in the temperance movement because many wives and children were sexually abused, beaten, neglected, and abandoned by alcoholic husbands and fathers. In 1848, representatives of the women's movement met in Seneca Falls, New York, to draft a statement of principles. The outcome—the Seneca Falls Declaration of Sentiments and Resolutions—was modeled on the Declaration of Independence, declaring that "all men and women are created equal." The delegates declared that women should have the right to own property, to divorce cruel or uncaring husbands, to vote, and to "an equal participation with men in the various trades, professions, and commerce."[32]

The response of many men was either to ignore or to ridicule women who dared to make such outlandish and radical demands. As it gained strength in the nineteenth century, the women's movement became an object of male scorn, of jokes and cartoons; newspaper editorials predicted that if these women had their way, husbands would look after the children while their wives worked and went to the saloon to drink whisky and smoke cigars. Not all men laughed, however; some risked ridicule by siding with the women. In England, William Thompson issued *An Appeal of One-Half of the Human Race* (1825), and John Stuart Mill decried *The Subjection of Women* (1869), as did Friedrich Engels in *Origins of the Family, Private Property and the State* (1884). In the United States the ex-slave Frederick Douglass

Mary Wollstonecraft, later Mary Wollstonecraft Godwin (1759–1797)

spoke and wrote on behalf of the fledgling women's movement, and the antislavery advocate William Lloyd Garrison editorialized in defense of women's rights.[33]

The twentieth century saw the publication of several pathbreaking books by feminist theorists. Among these was Simone de Beauvoir's *The Second Sex* (1949), in which she draws a sharp distinction between sex and gender. One's sex is biologically determined; one's gender is socially constructed. As Beauvoir famously put it, "One is not born, but rather becomes, a woman."[34] That is, the traits, attitudes, and behavior that lead one to think and to self-identify as a woman are not innate but are instilled or inculcated in biological females through a process of indoctrination. Another important work, Betty Friedan's *The Feminine Mystique* (1963), dealt with the malaise that many modern women feel but cannot name or identify. It is a feeling of emptiness or unfulfillment in one's life. The "happy housewife" of post-World War II affluent America was unhappy because her human potentials were being stifled by the very things that supposedly made her happy—marriage and motherhood. The problem, Friedan argued, was not with marriage and motherhood *per se* but with the expectation that a woman could be happy and find fulfillment by losing herself completely in those roles.

These important works were followed by a veritable outpouring of books, treatises, and articles on feminist theory and practice. Several variants within feminism soon emerged, often in combination with other ideologies such as socialism and anarchism. Socialist feminists, for example, have argued that women cannot be free until capitalism has been replaced by socialism.[35] Anarchist feminists claim that women will be oppressed as long as the state exists.[36] Lesbian separatist feminists claim that women will be oppressed as long as they associate with and are dependent upon men.[37]

Another approach to understanding developments in feminism is to conceive of its history in terms of successive "waves." In the nineteenth and early-to-mid-twentieth century "first wave" feminism focused on eliminating legal inequalities. In the 1960s and early 1970s this approach was sometimes referred to as "liberal feminism." Like the civil rights variant of the movement for black liberation, liberal feminism was motivated not only by a desire to overcome overt forms of discrimination—in marriage, educational opportunities, legal rights, and, above all, the right to vote—but to extend liberty and democracy in the United States and elsewhere. Women's right to vote was won in the United States in 1920, with the ratification of the Nineteenth Amendment to the Constitution, which states that "the right of citizens of the United States to vote shall not be denied or abridged by the United States or by any state on account of sex." The removal of these and other legal and institutional barriers has been the primary aim of liberal feminists. Their goal has been to give women the same rights and opportunities that men enjoy. The liberal or first-wave feminist conception of freedom is summarized in Figure 8.3.

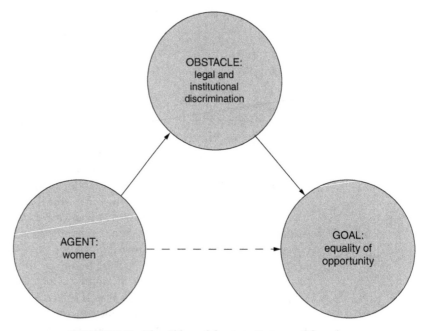

FIGURE 8.3 The "liberal feminist" view of freedom.

A second and more militant wave of feminist theory and practice first appeared in the late 1960s. This second wave, sometimes referred to as "radical feminism," was concerned not only with overt sexual discrimination (as liberal feminism is) but also with identifying, criticizing, and overcoming inequalities in the workplace, in marriage and the family, and with issues of sexuality and reproductive rights. Such second-wave feminists aimed to expose and overcome more subtle forms of **sexism.** A term coined in the 1960s, sexism refers to the belief or attitude that one sex (usually women) is inferior to or less able than another (usually men). It can also refer to stereotyping women in terms of "femininity" and men in terms of "masculinity." The belief that men are superior to women is a form of sexism that also exists in relations or institutions of power that constitute "male chauvinism" or "masculine domination." Both liberal and radical feminists attempt to expose, criticize, and overcome these sexist attitudes and beliefs, which are (or were in the 1960s) widely held by men and—no less importantly—by many women as well. To the degree that some women share these sexist views, they are afflicted with a lack of dignity and respect for themselves and for other women.

Such sexist attitudes and beliefs underlie and legitimize pervasive and persistent double standards, which include, but are not limited to, the following: it is "unfeminine" to be successful in scholarly, athletic, or other endeavors, particularly in competition with males; girls have no talent for math (or science or sports); the same actions that are "bold" and "assertive" when a man performs them are "bossy" and "aggressive" when undertaken by a woman; a man who makes a concession or a compromise is being "diplomatic," whereas a woman is showing "weakness"; men get "angry," while women become "bitchy"; a man who is sexually active or "sleeps around" is "masculine" or "macho," whereas a women who does so is "slutty"; and a woman who is raped probably provoked or invited the attack. These and many other sexist beliefs, attitudes, and stereotypes are or once were widely held by many men and some women as well. For the fact that these views are no longer as widely held as before, the women's movement takes a large measure of credit.

Feminists have pursued several strategies for fighting sexism. In the 1960s and early 1970s especially, "consciousness raising groups"—small groups of women who met to talk about their own experiences with and feelings about men, women, sex, love, marriage, children, parents, husbands, lovers, and friends—were formed for this purpose. "Take Back the Night" marches and demonstrations were held to publicize the crime of rape. Women's counseling centers and battered women's shelters were opened, and women were invited to talk and to do something about issues that concerned them. Women's studies programs were started in colleges and universities to enable students to study women's history (or "herstory") and other subjects from feminist perspectives. Through these and other means, women's liberationists have confronted and resisted the sexist stereotypes, beliefs, and attitudes.[38]

Unlike many liberal feminists, who tend to stress the legal and political equality of the two sexes—especially with regard to equal rights, equal opportunities, and equal pay for comparable work—some radical feminists tend to emphasize differences. Men and women not only have different biological makeups, they also have different attitudes, outlooks, and values. Women should be free to be different, they argue, and these differences should be respected and protected. Their humanity and dignity should also be respected, and protected from forces that would reduce them to objects or things. Consider, for example, the attitude toward women that is displayed in pornographic pictures and literature. There women are depicted as mere bodies or body parts—as "objects"—rather than as whole people; they are shown to enjoy pain, degradation, and humiliation; and they are always subservient to men, who are depicted as proud, cruel, and uncaring. Not surprisingly, then, radical feminists in the 1980s and 1990s often waged legal and political war against pornography and pornographers.[39]

The degrading depiction of women and women's bodies in the mass media is symptomatic, feminists believe, of a male *system* of power. Masculine power is both systematic and pervasive. It is not confined to legal and political institutions but suffuses the culture and outlook of most societies. For example, in Western societies pictures of naked or nearly naked women are used to sell everything from soap to automobiles. Older men divorce their wives to marry much younger women who are referred to as "trophy wives"—as though they were to be exhibited as big-game hunters exhibit their kills—and are regarded as symbols of masculine status and power. Hollywood movies offer few depictions of older women as attractive, desirable, or wise. In these and other ways women are systematically exploited and oppressed through cultural representations and images. Therefore, feminists say, it is not enough to eliminate or mitigate legal or institutional discrimination against women. Feminists must wage a broadly *cultural* struggle as well.

If feminism is now a well-established mainstream ideological perspective in the Western democracies, it is regarded as a radical and subversive ideology in many parts of the world. In traditional, male-dominated societies feminists face more than derision and ridicule; they may face death from (for example) radical Islamists who opposed educating girls and granting legal and political rights to women. In 2012, Malala Yousafzai, a fourteen-year-old Pakistani girl who had spoken publicly in favor of female education, was targeted by a team of Taliban assassins. Shot several times, she barely survived, though with serious and possibly permanent injuries. The Taliban have vowed to try again. Other outspoken women face similar threats. For example, feminist scholars, such as Amina Wadud, who reinterpret the *Qur'an* from a feminist perspective, face *fatwas* (decrees issued by Muslim clerics) calling for their death. And in Egypt in 2013, then-president Morsi and the Muslim Brotherhood issued a statement calling for the further subordination of women to strict *Sharia* law and wives to their husbands.[40] We will discuss this further in Chapter 10.

To be sure, women in the near and Middle East and in Asia face threats from non-Islamists as well. In India, for example, two especially horrific—though not at all unusual—cases of gang rape galvanized that nation of 1.4 billion people. Both rapes occurred in late 2012. The first involved a seventeen-year-old girl who was raped by a group of men. When she reported the rape to the police, they refused to investigate and told her that she should drop the charges and marry one of the rapists (a not-unusual "resolution" in India and elsewhere). Frustrated and humiliated, she committed suicide.[41] In the second instance a twenty-three-year-old medical student was beaten, gang-raped, and thrown off a moving bus on which she and her attackers were riding. She subsequently died of severe internal injuries.[42] And in Afghanistan and elsewhere in the Middle East, women who are raped are often arrested and charged with adultery.[43] Many rape victims are shunned by their communities and blamed for bringing shame to their families.

But it is not only women in foreign lands who face political oppression and personal danger. Feminists in the United States warn American women against believing that their victories in controlling their own lives and bodies are permanent and secure. They point to the 2010 mid-term elections that swept into office many self-described conservatives who have proposed—and in several states passed—legislation to roll back reproductive rights for women. These include laws that make it almost impossible for abortion clinics to operate, "personhood" amendments to state constitutions stipulating that human life begins at the moment of conception, and that using certain kinds of contraceptives therefore amounts to murder. In 2012 several state legislatures passed laws requiring that a woman wishing to undergo an abortion must, with or without her consent, have a "trans-vaginal probe" inserted in her vagina to take a sonogram of the fetus which she must then watch. Critics contend that this procedure is not only invasive and medically unnecessary but is tantamount to state-sponsored rape, in that in many states rape is defined as the insertion of anything into anyone's orifice without that person's consent. Not surprisingly, many American women—not all of whom describe themselves as feminists—were angered at these and other developments, which they viewed as an assault on their dignity amounting to a veritable "war on women."

When she was Secretary of State, Hillary Clinton, herself a prominent feminist, said,

> Why extremists always focus on women remains a mystery to me. But they all seem to. It doesn't matter what country they're in or what religion they claim. They want to control women. They want to control how we dress. They want to control how we act. They even want to control the decisions we make about our own health and bodies ... [It] is hard to believe that even here at home, we have to stand up for women's rights and reject efforts to marginalize any one of us.[44]

As another prominent feminist noted, "American women have suddenly realized that their emancipation in the 21st century is not as secure as they had assumed."[45] In light of these recent developments, women of various political parties and persuasions have reiterated their right to liberty and to live as they see fit.

We have already examined the liberal or first-wave feminists' conception of liberty (Figure 8.3). The view of liberty and liberation at the core of the ideology of the second-wave or radical feminist wing of the women's liberation movement is summarized in Figure 8.4. Although the distinction between liberal and radical feminism retains some slight semblance of validity, it is increasingly the case that the two variants look less different than they did a generation ago, and that this distinction no longer captures the variety and complexity of feminist theory and practice. A more recent "third wave" of the feminist movement, for example, complicates matters by introducing issues of identity, multiculturalism, race, and sexual orientation into the ongoing debate that is modern feminism. Third-wave feminism asks whether it is still useful to talk about a generic category called "women," whose members are all supposedly oppressed in the same way by men, or if it might be more useful to think about female identity as highly variable across culture, race, and sexual preference, among other attributes. If this is true, third-wave feminists argue, then we need to think carefully about how the oppression of women is as varied and multifaceted as their identities. For example, a poor black lesbian is actually or potentially oppressed in different ways and from different directions: as a woman, as a poor person, as a black person, and as a lesbian. Feminist theorists call this "intersectionality," inasmuch as each and every person is located in social space at the intersection of several sources of identity—gender, race, class, sexual orientation, and so on. Such intersectionality complicates and differentiates different forms of feminism.

For the most part, feminism has historically been a broadly based movement whose members work within already-existing political parties to achieve their goal of greater equality in pay and many other matters. Lately, however, some feminists have organized feminist parties to advance their aims. These relatively new political parties include the Women's Equality Party in the United Kingdom and the Swedish Feminist Initiative party, which in 2014 sent to the European Parliament the only woman yet elected on a feminist ticket. At present it seems unlikely that these parties will become mainstream parties in their own right; rather, their aim is to push and prod mainstream parties to pay closer attention to women's issues and to incorporate these smaller parties into theirs. As the leader of Britain's Women's Equality party put it, "In ten years' time, I hope we don't exist."[46] In the meantime, as she and others acknowledge, they have much work to do.

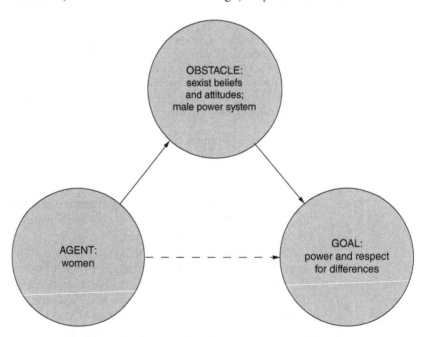

FIGURE 8.4 The "radical feminist" view of freedom.

GAY LIBERATION (LGBT)

The gay liberation movement has in recent years widened its focus and expanded its membership by joining forces with bisexual and transgender groups under the banner of LGBT—Lesbian, Gay, Bisexual, and Transgender. We begin, however, with a brief history of gay liberation in particular, before discussing its more recent, and broader, appeal.

The gay liberation movement and its ideology are relatively recent arrivals on the political scene. This fact might at first seem surprising, since "homosexuality"—the word itself was coined in the nineteenth century as a medical term to denote the alleged "pathology" of same-sex attraction—is as old as "heterosexuality." In the ancient Athens of Socrates, Plato, and Aristotle, for example, men acknowledged that sexual relations between men and women were necessary in order to produce children and continue the species; but they also pointed out that biologically necessary activities, like eating and sleeping, are not necessarily noble or beautiful. As they saw it, same-sex love could be considered superior to and more uplifting than heterosexual love because it represented an intimate relationship between equals (man to man or woman to woman) rather than between unequals (man to woman).[47] Similar attitudes often prevailed in ancient Rome.

If the classical world was hospitable to same-sex relations, however, the religions that emerged from the Middle East took a decidedly different view of the matter. Jewish, Christian, and Islamic doctrines, as traditionally interpreted, have all condemned same-sex attraction as perverted, unnatural, and sinful.[48] From these doctrines followed centuries of persecution of people who were attracted to others of the same sex. In medieval Europe such people were sometimes burned at the stake. Until the latter half of the twentieth century, to engage in same-sex relations was in most Western countries a crime punishable by imprisonment.

The case of Alan Turing (1912–1954) is as instructive as it is chilling. A brilliant British mathematician, cryptologist, and the father of the modern computer, Turing was instrumental in breaking the Nazis' supposedly unbreakable Enigma code during World War II, saving untold thousands of Allied soldiers', sailors', and civilian lives and shortening the war as well. In 1952 he was convicted for having same-sex relations with a consenting adult male. Sentenced to a choice between being castrated and going to prison, he chose castration. Publicly humiliated, demeaned, depressed, and stripped of his top-secret security clearance, Turing committed suicide by eating an apple soaked in cyanide.[49] The memory of a prominent war hero's shocking death was fresh in the minds of the newly formed Wolfenden Committee, headed by Sir John Wolfenden, which met three months later to consider the desirability and feasibility of decriminalizing homosexual acts between consenting adults. *The Wolfenden Report*, published in 1957, concluded that such acts "should no longer be a criminal offense."[50]

Decriminalization has come more slowly in several Western nations, including the United States. Into the twenty-first century several American states still had "sodomy" laws prohibiting sexual relations between persons of the same sex, but the U.S. Supreme Court decided in *Lawrence v. Texas* (June 2003) that all such laws are unconstitutional. Even where legal penalties have been repealed or unenforced, other forms of discrimination persist. In many communities gays and lesbians have faced difficulties in securing employment, housing, and medical care. Lesbian mothers and gay fathers have been denied legal custody of their children. Teachers who admit to being gay have sometimes lost their jobs, as have gays in the armed forces and in other public service occupations.

In the face of these and other obstacles, the gay liberation movement emerged slowly from several sources. One was the Daughters of Bilitis, organized in 1955 to protect and promote the interests of lesbians. Another, the Mattachine Society, was founded in 1950 to promote pride, solidarity, and self-respect among gay men. Both advocated legal and civil rights, psychological acceptance, self-help, and respectability. The Mattachine Society campaigned vigorously against the idea that same-sex attraction is a form of mental illness and therefore in need of a "cure." In 1973 the American Psychiatric Association agreed, and took "homosexuality" off its list of mental disorders.

The summer of 1969 was a defining moment for the gay liberation movement in the United States. Early in the morning of June 28, policemen burst into the Stonewall Inn, a gay bar in New York City, to intimidate its patrons and to arrest some of them. Such police raids were not at all unusual. On this occasion, however, the patrons resisted. Soon a full-scale riot was under way. Battered by bricks and bottles, the surprised policemen beat a hasty retreat. The rioting continued for three days, during which many gay men and lesbians discovered a newfound sense of power and pride. The 1969 Stonewall Riot may be said to mark the beginning of the modern gay liberation movement in America.[51]

Some gay men and lesbians object to the very label "homosexual" (since, as we noted earlier, it is a now-defunct and discredited medical term) and to what they regard as a self-imposed gay straitjacket. Some favor flamboyant forms of self-expression and gay identity. "Drag queens" openly parody "straight" sexuality, and black-clad "leather boys" and "bikers" and "butch" lesbians defy conventional stereotypes of gay "effeminacy." Such open expressions of gay sexuality and identity are sometimes met with official censure or violent repression, especially from the police and from young "gay-bashers."

The aim of the gay liberation movement has been twofold. Gays and lesbians have organized to repeal discriminatory laws and to gain access to opportunities previously denied them. In addition to opposing overt discrimination, gay liberationists have worked to overcome mistaken beliefs about, and attitudes toward, gay people. These **homophobic** beliefs include, but are not limited to, the following: all or most gays molest children; gay people generally seek to recruit children and young people into their ranks; all gays are sexually promiscuous; homosexuality is an abnormal or perverted sexual preference that can, and should, be "corrected" by religious, psychiatric, or other means; deep down, most gays really want to be straight; and gays can be straight if they try hard enough. These and other homophobic beliefs are widely shared not only by heterosexuals but even by some gays and lesbians who, by internalizing these attitudes, come to loathe themselves and other people like them. Gay liberation aims to overcome both overt discrimination and homophobic attitudes and beliefs.[52] The movement has provided encouragement and support for those who wish to "come out of the closet" and publicly acknowledge their sexual orientation. Their means of doing and affirming this include gay counseling centers, support groups, and "gay pride" marches and demonstrations. Gay liberationists also have adopted the inverted pink triangle as the symbol of their movement and as a reminder of the oppression gays suffered at the hands of the Nazis, who forced gays into concentration camps where some were castrated and all made to wear pink-triangle arm badges. There they were treated with a contempt and brutality second only to that accorded to Jews.[53]

Today the tactics, if not the ideology, of the gay liberation movement are quite diverse. Some gays are politically conservative, seeking acceptance and "a place at the table," as the conservative Log Cabin Republicans do.[54] Others are liberal reformers working for inclusion in mainstream institutions, including the military.[55] To be openly gay has long been grounds for dishonorable discharge in the American armed forces, and remained so under the Pentagon's "don't ask, don't tell" policy until that policy was repealed in 2011. Critics of the policy pointed out that, because of its application and enforcement, the military had lost several thousand highly (and expensively) trained soldiers, sailors, and pilots, along with translators and others with highly specialized skills. And this in turn undermined the military's ability to defend the United States. Even now, veterans who were dishonorably discharged simply for being gay receive no health or pension benefits.[56]

In recent years the institution of marriage has become a focus for gay and lesbian reformers who advocate legalizing same-sex marriage. Against conservative critics who claim that gays and lesbians seek "special rights," the reformers reply that allowing men to marry men and women to marry women is a matter of *equal* rights. The U.S. Congress disagreed, and both houses by large majorities passed the Defense of Marriage Act (DOMA), which President Bill Clinton signed into law in 1996. DOMA defined marriage as the legal union of one man and one woman, and stipulated that states that don't recognize same-sex marriage are not required to recognize marriages contracted in states that do. It also denied federal pension, health care, and medical leave benefits to same-sex spouses who have been legally married. And when a same-sex spouse dies, his or her surviving spouse is ineligible to receive the deceased spouse's Social Security payments, as other married couples can. DOMA was challenged in court, with ever-increasing success, on two grounds. The first is that it violated the "full faith and credit" clause of the U.S. Constitution (Article IV, Section 1), which requires that contracts and agreements made in one state be recognized as valid in all states. The second objection to DOMA was that it violated the "equal protection" clause of the Constitution, which provides that no state may "deny to any person within its jurisdiction the equal protection of the laws" (Fourteenth Amendment). The courts and legislatures of several states agreed, and legalized same-sex marriage.

And then, in 2015, the U.S. Supreme Court in the landmark decision *Obergefell v. Hodges* overturned all state laws banning same-sex marriage on the ground that they are unconstitutional. This decision presumably put an end to the controversy (although, as we shall see shortly, significant issues remain unresolved). Let us briefly retrace the route that led to this historic decision.

Even after the turning point of the Stonewall riot, few in the gay liberation movement spoke (or even thought) of the right of gays and lesbians to marry. Those in the movement were more concerned with removing more immediate and pressing obstacles to their liberation—the federal government's reluctance to fund research on HIV/AIDS, discrimination in housing, employment, and military service among them. And when, in the early 1990s, they did begin to address the issue of same-sex marriage, they met with immediate and widespread resistance. A spate of state and federal laws (including DOMA) were passed to prevent the possibility that people of the same sex could ever marry.

Although the issue of same-sex marriage remains a matter of fierce and sometimes shrill debate and continues to divide Americans, it is fast becoming a decreasingly divisive issue. Surveys showed that in 1996 some 26 percent of Americans were in favor of allowing same-sex couples to marry; by 2011 that had more than doubled to 53 percent. The issue still divides Americans along generational and geographic lines. In 2010, 70 percent of Americans between the ages of eighteen and thirty-four favored legalizing same-sex marriage; 53 percent between thirty-five and fifty-four; and for those fifty-five and older, 39 percent. No less significant was that support for same-sex marriage had increased within all age groups. Much but not all of the opposition comes from the South. Thirty-one states amended their constitutions to outlaw same-sex marriage; eight others had statutes barring it; and nine states and the District of Columbia legalized it.[57] In May 2012 President Barack Obama angered religious right conservatives by announcing his support for same-sex marriage. And in the 2012 election, voters in four states approved measures allowing same-sex couples to marry. As of 2014 sixteen states and Washington, D.C., had legalized same-sex marriage. One of these was Maine, which in 2009 outlawed same-sex marriage by 53–47 percent and in 2012 legalized it by exactly the same margin.[58]

What accounted for this seemingly sudden shift of attitude and outlook? Several things, apparently. For one, as more gay men and lesbians "came out of the closet," revealing their sexual orientation to family, friends, neighbors, and coworkers, the more readily could heterosexuals see them as "normal," sometimes even boringly so. Americans who are personally acquainted with a gay man or lesbian are much more likely to support gays' right to marry. Another, related factor is generational: younger Americans are much more likely than their parents and grandparents to have openly gay friends and to support same-sex marriage. Positive portrayals of gay men and lesbians have also become increasingly common in popular culture, particularly in movies and television shows.

The conflict over same-sex marriage does not necessarily pit liberals against conservatives. In 2010 two prominent lawyers—one liberal, the other conservative—joined forces to try to overturn the outcome of Proposition 8, the 2008 ballot initiative that proposed to amend California's state constitution to outlaw same-sex marriage. In a close contest California voters supported this constitutional ban. The liberal lawyer David Boies and his conservative counterpart, Theodore B. Olson, agreed that this ban violates the U.S. Constitution's guarantee of "equal protection under the law." But how can a conservative like Olson—who served as Assistant Attorney General in the Reagan Administration and as Solicitor General in the George W. Bush Administration—work with a liberal like Boies to support same-sex marriage? The answer is that Olson is not a religious right conservative but one who holds that the Constitution and the rule of law are sources of social stability and that all law-abiding citizens, regardless of race or sexual orientation, are equal in the eyes of the law and should, in traditional Burkean-conservative fashion, be welcomed and woven into the fabric of American society.[59] In February 2012 the U.S. Circuit Court of Appeals for the Ninth District agreed, and ruled that California's ban on same-sex marriage was unconstitutional. At that point it became clear that the legality or illegality of same-sex marriage would be decided by the Supreme Court. In 2013, the Court took a step toward legalizing same-sex marriage by striking down a provision of DOMA prohibiting the federal government from recognizing such unions as unconstitutional. In addition, for the first time a current president of the United States publicly advocated legalizing same-sex marriage, a move in keeping with a profound shift in public opinion on the issue.

This trend toward acceptance accelerated quickly and dramatically in June 2015 when the Supreme Court ruled that state bans on same-sex marriage are unconstitutional. That still-controversial decision concludes by saying:

> No union is more profound than marriage, for it embodies the highest ideals of love, fidelity, devotion, sacrifice, and family. In forming a marital union two people become something greater than they once were... It would misunderstand these men and women to say that they disrespect the idea of marriage. Their plea is that they do respect it, respect it so deeply that they seek to find its fulfillment for themselves. Their hope is not to be condemned to live in loneliness, excluded from one of civilization's oldest institutions. They ask for equal dignity in the eyes of the law. The Constitution grants them that right.

Gay men and lesbians are now free to marry in all fifty states.

Not all gays and lesbians want the right to marry and to be woven into a social fabric that they regard as rotten and threadbare. Some want to remain well outside the dominant heterosexual culture as militant critics of a homophobic society. Queer Nation, Lesbian Nation, ActUp, and other groups assume a militant stance to publicize gay grievances.[60] These and other differences within the gay liberation movement are, however, mainly about strategies and tactics, and less about fundamental principles and ideas, including freedom. Hence, the conception of freedom or liberty at the core of the gay liberation ideology can be summarized as in Figure 8.5.

In recent years many lesbians and gay men have joined forces with others who have been oppressed or discriminated against because of their sexual preference, orientation, and/or identity. These others include, most prominently, bisexuals (people attracted to both males and females) and transsexuals (males who identify themselves as female, and females who identify as males). Transgender people may be gay, straight, bisexual, or asexual. Originating in and deriving from the older and more narrowly focused gay liberation movement, the newer LGBT (Lesbian, Gay, Bisexual, and Transgender) movement aims to form a larger, broader, more diverse—and therefore culturally and politically more powerful—"united front" of people who have been persecuted and oppressed because of being different, or "queer." Once a term of opprobrium and insult, "queer" is now embraced by many in the LGBT movement as a badge of distinction and honor. "Queerness" has also become a subject for scholarly study. Many colleges and universities now offer courses in "queer studies" and "queer theory," and there is a growing scholarly literature on "queer" themes and topics in literature, philosophy, and other disciplines.[61]

Although the campaign for LGBT liberation has made remarkable strides in recent years, its proponents say that much remains to be done. They note that only twenty-two states have laws banning discrimination against gays in employment, housing, and other areas, while twenty-eight do not, thus allowing gay teachers to be fired, gay tenants to be evicted, and same-sex couples denied the right to adopt or even to foster children. In 2015, Indiana became the first of several states to pass a "Religious Freedom Restoration Act," which allows stores, restaurants, and other businesses to refuse service to anyone the owner disapproves of because of the owner's religious beliefs. So, for example, a wedding planner or caterer can refuse service to same-sex couples, simply by citing his or her religious beliefs. Although aimed at same-sex couples, such laws—as critics were quick to point out—have much wider ramifications. For example, a Muslim store owner could refuse to serve a woman wearing shorts or other "immodest" clothing because she offends his religious beliefs. Similarly, a neo-Nazi motel owner could claim exemption from the Civil Rights Act and refuse accommodation to African-Americans because he is a member of the World Church of the Creator and his religion requires racial discrimination and segregation. So far, such considerations have not deterred state legislatures from passing such legislation.[62]

If gays and lesbians are finding increasing acceptance in the United States and other Western democracies, the same is not true of their counterparts in other countries. In 2013 the Russian Parliament passed, and President Putin signed, laws making it a crime to be openly gay, or even to be a heterosexual speaking publicly in defense of gays. Laws and public policies in the Middle East and Africa are even

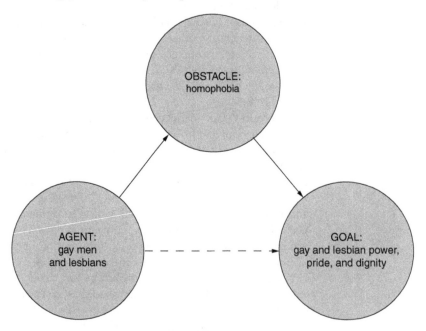

FIGURE 8.5 The "gay liberation" view of freedom.

more onerous. Of the fifty-four African nations, thirty-eight have laws making it illegal to be attracted to persons of the same sex. In Uganda, for example, the national legislature has made it a crime to even *be* gay or lesbian—a "crime" punishable by imprisonment or even death. Other African nations have already passed or are currently considering similar legislation, in spite of an international outcry and opposition from the United Nations Human Rights Commission, the U.S. State Department, and other organizations. U.S. Secretary of State Hillary Clinton's declaration that "gay rights are human rights" has so far fallen on deaf ears.[63]

As we noted in Chapter 2, democratically enacted bans on same-sex marriage raise once again a perennial problem in democratic theory and practice: Should majorities be able to decide any and every issue, or are there issues that should not be decided by majority vote? This is a question confronting every democracy. In Nigeria, for example, 98 percent of the populace favors harsh new—and democratically enacted—laws against homosexuality, making same-sex relations a capital crime. Nigerian democrats describe Western critics as hypocrites, since these critics praise democracy while condemning democratically passed legislation against gays and lesbians.[64]

All these difficulties notwithstanding, advocates contend that the struggle for gay and lesbian liberty, pride, and dignity must continue until it succeeds at home and abroad.

NATIVE PEOPLES' LIBERATION (INDIGENISM)

Over the past half-century or so, various native peoples' (or indigenist) movements have become more vocal and increasingly militant. These native (or indigenous) peoples include the Aborigines in Australia, the Maori in New Zealand, First Nations in Canada, and Native Americans in the United States. Despite the great geographic distance between them, the history and circumstances of these peoples share several striking similarities. First and most obviously, they live on lands of which their ancestors were the first known inhabitants. Second, their ancestral lands were subsequently taken from them and occupied by European colonizers. Third, these native peoples thus became aliens and outsiders in their own lands; their religions, their cultural practices and traditions, were ridiculed by Christian missionaries as "uncivilized," "savage," and "primitive"; in some instances they were forced to adopt beliefs and practices that they found alien and unfamiliar. Fourth, their land having been taken from them, their people deprived of pride and denied political power, their cultures demeaned or destroyed, these native peoples lost a sense of their identity—of who and what they are as a people. Fifth and finally, the destruction of their culture and identity has brought in its wake a host of social ills: high rates of unemployment, alcoholism, suicide, and other social problems unknown to their ancestors now plague native peoples. Guided by an ideology that some call **indigenism**, various native peoples' liberation groups aim to break this vicious cycle of poverty, social and economic subordination, and political powerlessness by reclaiming and restoring lost or long-eclipsed group identities.[65]

In the nineteenth and early twentieth centuries especially, white immigration into the territories of indigenous peoples in North America, Australia, New Zealand, Latin America, and elsewhere created competition for ever scarcer resources—

land, game, timber, and minerals. The increasing numbers of European settlers and their sophisticated technology—guns, railroads, steamships, and so on—gave them an advantage over the indigenous peoples they encountered. The result was not only the military defeat of native peoples but also their political, economic, and cultural conquest. Native peoples were forbidden to follow many of the customs and practices of their ancestors; their children were forced to attend schools where they were forbidden to speak the language of their parents and grandparents; they were made, by a variety of means, to feel inferior to "civilized" white settlers and to be ashamed of their ancestors' "savage" ways. Many native children were put up for adoption by white families, who often used them as a source of cheap labor. Taken together, these policies are tantamount to "cultural genocide"—the cultural, if not the physical, eradication of entire peoples.

Consider, for example, what happened to the Aborigines in Australia. Between 1910 and the early 1970s, some 100,000 Aboriginal children—fully one-third of the present Aboriginal population—were forcibly taken from their families on the ground that theirs was a "doomed race." The lighter-skinned children were handed over to white Australian families for adoption. The darker-skinned children were placed in orphanages but not made available for adoption. Children in both groups were forbidden to speak their native language or to follow the religious and other customs of their birth-parents. This policy of "saving" Aboriginal children from their parents resulted in a "stolen generation."

The phrase "stolen generation" was used by Australian Prime Minister John Howard in a personal apology to the Aborigines in May 1997. Speaking before the Australian Reconciliation Convention, Howard said, "I feel deep sorrow for those of my fellow Australians who suffered injustices under the practices of past generations toward indigenous people." Aboriginal leaders replied that a personal apology, although a good beginning, is not nearly enough. They wanted an official apology from the Australian government (the prime minister and the parliament) and monetary compensation for their individual and collective trauma. Australia's Federal Human Rights Commission agreed and recommended that a fund be established to compensate victims of earlier government policy, but the Australian government rejected the proposal on the ground that the present generation of white Australians should not be held accountable for what their parents' and grandparents' generations did to the Aborigines. When Kevin Rudd defeated Howard to become prime minister in the fall of 2007, however, Rudd promised to issue a formal apology early in his first parliamentary term.[66]

Early in 2008 and as the first act of his new administration Prime Minister Rudd offered a formal and public apology for the laws and policies that "inflicted profound grief, suffering and loss" on Australia's Aborigines. Rudd hoped his apology would "remove a great stain from the nation's soul, and in a true spirit of reconciliation" to heal the wounds inflicted upon its native people. Like his predecessor, however, Rudd refused to offer monetary compensation for the pain and suffering experienced by Aboriginal children and their parents.[67] That long legacy of mistreatment has taken a terrible toll. The average life span of Aborigines is seventeen years shorter than that of white and Asian Australians. Aborigines are also three times as likely to be unemployed as other Australians, and are much more likely to abuse alcohol, use illegal drugs, and to serve time in prison.

Australia is hardly alone in its mistreatment of indigenous people. Earlier generations of Canadians and Americans, among others, have treated native peoples no better. Some of this mistreatment resulted from well-meant, if misguided, attempts to "educate" and "civilize" supposedly "savage" peoples "for their own good." However well-intentioned some of these paternalistic policies may have been, they have produced deeply damaging results. The loss of identity, of power, of pride and dignity has produced a host of social ills, including high rates of unemployment, mental illness, alcoholism (and fetal alcohol syndrome), homicide, and suicide. To atone for this mistreatment, the Canadian government issued in 1998 a formal apology to Canada's native peoples for past acts of oppression. The government has also divided Canada's Northwest Territories in order to create a new territory—Nunavut, or "our land"—governed by aboriginal people.[68]

In the United States the director of the Bureau of Indian Affairs apologized in 2000 for the government's long history of mistreating Native Americans. "This agency," said BIA Director (and member of the Pawnee tribe) Kevin Gover, "participated in the ethnic cleansing that befell the Western tribes" and contributed to "the decimation of the mighty bison herds, the use of the poison alcohol to destroy mind and body, and the cowardly killing of women and children." He concluded his apology by pledging, "Never again will we attack your religions, your languages, your rituals or any of your tribal ways. Never again will we seize your children, nor teach them to be ashamed of who they are. Never again."[69]

Although welcome, such apologies are widely viewed by Native Americans as too little and too late. Long mistrustful of the U.S. government, many believe that Native Americans must reclaim their heritage and rebuild their culture. The militant American Indian Movement (AIM), for one, seeks to restore the sense of identity, power, pride, and dignity that have been stripped, they say, from Native Americans (aimovement.org). This they do in a variety of ways. One strategy is broadly cultural and aims at instilling a sense of identity and pride through tribal convocations and powwows, drumming ceremonies, medicine lodges, and, not least, "little red schoolhouses" to educate Indian children. AIM has exposed and criticized the stereotypes of Indians in the press, in movies, and on television. Historically, Hollywood has depicted Native Americans either as bloodthirsty killers or as noble savages. Both depictions are crude caricatures that oversimplify complex reality and distort the history of white–Indian relations in North America. AIM has also challenged the demeaning stereotypes of Native Americans in the names and symbols of several major sports organizations, including the Cleveland Indians, the Atlanta Braves, and the Washington Redskins. Imagine what an uproar there would be if there were teams called the Cleveland Kikes or the Washington Rednecks or the Houston Honkies or the Pittsburgh Palefaces. This difference, AIM says, shows that Native Americans are not accorded the respect given to other groups.

The reassertion of their treaty and other rights has led to legal battles between Native Americans and the federal, state, and local governments. In Wisconsin and Minnesota, for example, Native Americans have recently reclaimed the spearfishing rights guaranteed to them by nineteenth-century treaties. Their exercise of these rights has angered white fishermen, leading to clashes in court—and sometimes to physical confrontation at contested sites. So far federal and state courts have ruled that the treaties are still valid and have upheld tribal spearfishing rights. Even so,

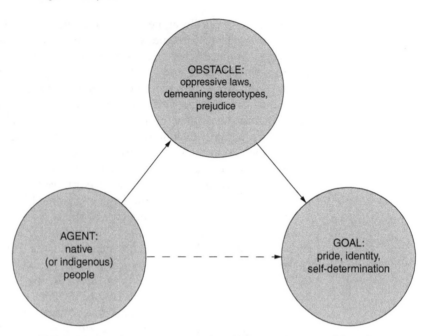

FIGURE 8.6 The "native peoples' liberation" view of freedom.

some Native Americans contend that they can receive justice only in their own tribal courts. Indians who break the law, they say, should not be tried in "white" courts. Instead, Indian offenders should be tried by courts of tribal elders and sentenced to traditional punishments—for example, being sent to live by themselves in the forest for a prescribed period so that they can reflect on their wrongdoings and their duties to society. (On rare occasions, U.S. courts have permitted such alternative punishments to be imposed on first-time juvenile offenders.)

Such indigenist beliefs and practices run counter to classical liberalism, with its emphasis on individualism, color-blind justice, and equality before the law. Critics contend that allowing Native Americans to be tried in tribal courts seems to give them special treatment as a group. And groups, unlike individuals, do not have rights. But Native Americans and other indigenous people insist that their rights and dignity as individuals require respect for their rights and dignity as a people. The identity of each and every member of a native people is—or ought to be— bound up with the identity of his or her people. For the individual to be free, then, it is first necessary that his or her people be free as a group from the obstacles imposed on them by the people who have colonized them and occupied their land. This indigenist conception of freedom is set out in Figure 8.6.

LIBERATION THEOLOGY

A liberation movement of a different kind emerged in the 1960s and 1970s in the form of liberation theology. This movement aims to call attention to the plight of the poor and the oppressed, not only in Third World countries but in affluent and developed ones as well, and to inspire people, including the poor themselves, to help bring an end to their poverty. Liberation theology is of two interrelated types. The first, which is usually referred to simply as "liberation theology," has developed primarily within the Roman Catholic Church. The center of its attention has been Latin America, where the population is overwhelmingly Catholic and many people are desperately poor; but liberation theology also has its advocates in Africa,[70] Asia, Europe, the Near and Middle East,[71] and North America. A second variant or type of liberation theology—Black Liberation Theology (BLT)—is primarily Protestant and African-American. As the adjective suggests, BLT is addressed primarily to black Americans and to those who have oppressed them. Otherwise its tenets are almost identical to the first type of liberation theology, and we will treat the two as virtually interchangeable despite minor differences between them.

Liberation theology goes beyond the traditional Christian concern for saving souls for an afterlife. In addition, and perhaps more emphatically, it calls for political—even revolutionary—action on behalf of the poor in this earthly life. Not surprisingly, then, it has been the focus of considerable controversy within the Catholic Church, particularly in Latin America, and in Baptist and other Protestant denominations in North America. Some see liberation theology as an attempt to blend the teachings of Jesus with those of Marx, with critics complaining that there is more Marx than Jesus in the mixture. One of liberation theology's leading critics, Cardinal Joseph Ratzinger, became Pope Benedict XVI.[72] It is true that liberation theology, especially in its Latin American version, draws some of its key concepts and categories from critical Western Marxian theory, and from "critical theory" in particular (discussed earlier, in Chapter 6).[73] As the liberation theologians see it, however, they are only following the example of Jesus in working for social justice. To do this work, they must draw on the insights of modern social theorists, including Marx, who reveal the human and structural sources of poverty and oppression. Thus, they believe, they act in the spirit of Jesus when they subject the church and the affluent parts of society to severe criticism.

Gustavo Gutierrez of Peru and other advocates of the Latin American variant of liberation theology have undertaken this "critique of the activity of the church and of Christians" by urging the Catholic Church and Christians in general to take a more active part in liberating the poor from poverty. The church, they say, should exercise its "preferential option for the poor." To do this, the church must move away from its traditional emphasis on rituals and sacraments. In helping people to reach and live in a "state of grace," the church has concentrated almost exclusively on orthodoxy—on teaching people the "correct beliefs." That is well and good, according to liberation theology, except that it has led to the neglect of the poor, who find each day a struggle with misery and despair. In addition to orthodoxy, then, the church should promote **orthopraxis**—that is, "right" or "correct" action in this world.

But what kind of action is "right" or "correct"? Liberation theology provides no single answer to this question and no systematic program for change. A few of its proponents have seemed willing to accept violent revolution as a necessary means of winning justice for the poor. For the most part, however, liberation theologians see their mission, like other liberation ideologies, in terms of "consciousness raising." We must follow the example of Jesus, they say, and go to live and teach among the poor. To this end, they have established "ecclesial base communities," where they instruct poor people not only in the Christian scriptures and faith but also in reading, writing, health care, and social action. The core idea is to help the poor to see that their poverty is not simply the way life must be but something that can and should be changed. Once they become aware of this, the poor will be able to take steps to free themselves from those sinful social structures that deny their human dignity and condemn them to poverty. In Gutierrez's words,

> we will have an authentic theology of liberation only when the oppressed themselves can freely raise their voice and express themselves directly and creatively in society and in the heart of the People of God, when they themselves "account for the hope," which they bear, when they are the protagonists of their own liberation.[74]

From the standpoint of liberation theology, in short, ending poverty is not simply a matter of growing more food and distributing it to more people. Poverty in Latin America and elsewhere is the result of systemic or structural oppression. Some people live in luxury and comfort while—and perhaps because—others barely survive. Ending poverty, then, is not just a matter of food and money but a matter of liberation—of freeing people, and helping them to free themselves, from injustice and oppression.

African-Americans have long been oppressed. Captured in Africa and brought by force to North America as slaves, their early experience, and its long legacy of racism and oppression, forms the backdrop and inspiration for Black Liberation Theology. As developed and articulated by James H. Cone and other prominent theologians,[75] BLT owes less to critical Western Marxian theory than does its Latin American counterpart, and more to scripture as interpreted through a "liberationist" lens. One of its key texts is the book of Exodus, which tells the story of the ancient Israelites' liberation from slavery in Egypt. This story shows that God is on the side of the poor and oppressed and will help enslaved peoples to liberate themselves.[76] Another key text is Luke 4:18: "Preach the Gospel to the poor, heal the brokenhearted, set the captives free, offer sight to the blind, and liberate those who are oppressed." And another is Matthew 25:40, in which Jesus says that "As you have done unto the least of these my brothers, you have done unto me." Oppression takes many forms. Cone has in recent years connected BLT to environmental concerns, noting that people of color suffer disproportionately from pollution and the siting of and emissions from chemical factories, refineries, and toxic waste disposal sites. Such practices constitute a relatively new form of exploitation and oppression—sometimes called "environmental racism"—that require new thinking and new alliances. Cone accordingly calls for a new political alliance between "black" and "green"—that is, between African-Americans and (mostly) white environmentalists—to rectify environmental injustices and to take care of God's Creation, given in common to people of all colors and creeds.[77]

Liberation theology thus combines religious inspiration with political action in a way that differs from the other liberation ideologies discussed in this chapter. Yet it clearly shares the five common features that, as we noted earlier, distinguish "liberation ideologies" from other ideologies. It is directed, first, to a particular audience—an audience composed of Christians. The poor are the principal subjects, of course, but liberation theology seeks to convert not only them but all Christians

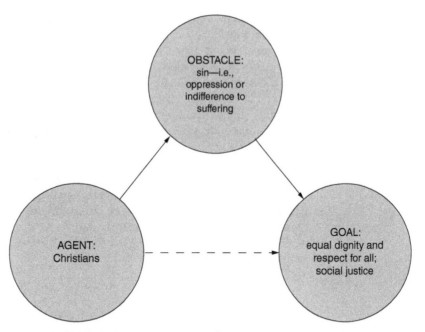

FIGURE 8.7 The "liberation theology" view of freedom.

to its interpretation of the Christian mission. Second, it also informs that audience about the ways in which the poor have been oppressed by a dominant group—the affluent elite in Latin America, in North America, and elsewhere. Third, this oppression is not only "external" but also "internalized" in the form of a tendency among poor people to accept poverty as a normal part of life. Liberation theology says that the poor suffer from this internal oppression because they have been taught to see their poverty as their inevitable "fate," as something that no one can control or change. In attempting to defeat this fatalistic attitude, liberation theology displays the fourth feature of liberation ideologies: it aims to raise the consciousness of the poor so that they will be able to emancipate themselves. Again, however, it is not only the poor to whom liberation theology speaks. It also speaks, fifth and finally, to oppressors who sin directly against the poor and to bystanders who sin by their inaction. Those whose concern for themselves blinds them to the needs of the poor can be wealthy in worldly terms—houses, cars, and cash—but suffer from a poverty of the spirit. Liberation theology thus addresses all Christians, rich and poor alike, for all need to be liberated from sin—including the sins of injustice, exploitation, and indifference to the sufferings of the poor.

The conception of freedom at the core of liberation theology is illustrated in Figure 8.7.

ANIMAL LIBERATION

We have left the ideology of animal liberation for last, not because it is unimportant or without influence—quite the contrary—but because it encounters a number of conceptual difficulties that other liberation ideologies do not face. Before examining these difficulties, however, let us begin by looking briefly at the history of this ideology.

Human beings have long used animals for many purposes—as beasts of burden, as sources of food and fur, and more recently as pets. But human beings have also subjected animals to other less necessary and arguably more insidious uses. In the name of pleasure and entertainment, humans have used roosters in cockfights, bulls in bullfights, foxes in foxhunts, and dogs in dogfights. These contests are bloody, gruesome, always painful, and often fatal to the animals forced to participate in them.

The forerunner of the ideology of animal liberation can be found in nineteenth-century England, particularly in the increasingly widespread revulsion against the wanton use and abuse of animals for spectator sports.[78] Such suffering, said Jeremy Bentham (1748–1832), offends—or rather should offend—the moral sensibilities of any reasonably sensitive human being. At a time when growing numbers of people were actively attempting to free black slaves in America and elsewhere, Bentham wrote,

> The day may come when the rest of the animal creation may acquire those rights which never could have been with[held] from them but by the hand of tyranny. [Some] have already discovered that the blackness of the skin is no reason why a human being should be abandoned without redress to the caprice of a tormentor.[79]

But why, Bentham asked, are animals different from human beings? Is it because they have four legs? Or do animals deserve different treatment because they lack the use of reason? Or is it because animals cannot speak? To argue in this way, Bentham goes on to say, is self-subverting. Surely, he says,

> A full-grown horse or dog is beyond comparison a more rational, as well as a more conversable animal, than an infant of a day, or a week, or even a month, old. But suppose they were otherwise, what would it avail? The question is not, Can they reason? nor Can they talk? but, Can they *suffer*?[80]

This increasing sensitivity to the suffering of sentient creatures—human and non-human alike—led not only to the formation of anti-slavery societies but to the Society for the Prevention of Cruelty to Animals (SPCA) in Great Britain, the United States, and elsewhere. In the nineteenth century many abolitionists (anti-slavery advocates) were also advocates of animal welfare. One particularly prominent abolitionist—William Wilberforce, who was instrumental in abolishing slavery throughout the British Empire—founded the Royal Society for the Prevention of Cruelty to Animals in 1824.

The animal liberation movement of the late twentieth and early twenty-first centuries traces its origins to such nineteenth-century figures as Wilberforce, Bentham, and Henry Salt (whose *Animal Rights*, first published in 1892, made the moral case for vegetarianism).[81] But to its moral argument it adds a certain militancy and a willingness to take personal and political risks to protect the rights of animals. Members of such groups as the Society for Animal Rights (SAR) and People for the Ethical Treatment of Animals (PETA) have not only lobbied their legislative representatives but have also picketed furriers' shops and animal laboratories. Some have freed caged animals, including mice, monkeys, and dolphins. The 1986 movie *Turtle Diary* is about three people who kidnap sea turtles from the London Zoo in order to release them into the ocean. In Britain, the Animal Liberation Front (ALF) has poured blood on expensive fur coats and set fire to furriers' warehouses. In 1988 animal liberationists in Sweden succeeded in their campaign to outlaw certain kinds of beef- and poultry-raising practices. In past years several supermodels and other celebrities have protested publicly against the manufacture, sale, and wearing of fur coats. Among the most expensive and desirable coats are those made from the fur of baby seals and mink. Baby seals, unlike adults, are prized for their soft, pure white fur. To take this fur, hunters club the babies to death since stabbing or shooting them would result in unsightly holes in the fur, which would reduce its value. So too with the fur of minks. Electrodes are inserted in the mouth and anus of the animal which is then electrocuted, leaving the fur intact and without blemishes. While there is no way to make fur coats without killing animals, it is possible to make cosmetics in a less hurtful and more humane way. The Body Shop, for example, has developed a highly successful retail business on the basis of selling perfumes and cosmetics that were manufactured without testing on animals. Under pressure from PETA and other groups, some manufacturers have followed suit.

Not content with purely voluntary compliance, animal rights groups have lately lobbied legislators and have put propositions on the ballot in several states. In 2008, for example, California voters approved a ballot initiative requiring that chickens and other farm animals be allowed room to move about, turn around, and lie down. "If animals are going to be killed for food," said the president of the Humane Society of the United States, "the least we can do is treat them with decency and give them a semblance of life." The measure was strongly supported by animal rights groups, veterinarians, and others, and equally strongly opposed by poultry producers and other factory farming interests.[82]

Animal liberationists take particular exception to experiments on animals that appear to have no medical or other value. As a particularly extreme example, they point to experiments conducted by the American psychologist Harry Harlow (1905–1981), who separated infant monkeys from their mothers to study the effects of maternal deprivation; not surprisingly, the infants cried and shivered and developed signs of severe mental illness. His next experiment was designed to test the effects that an "evil mother" might have on her offspring. To do this, he constructed a metal surrogate mother that he named "the Iron Maiden." When an infant monkey would try to embrace it, the metal surrogate shot out sharp spikes and blasts of cold air that sent the infant screaming in terror. These infants grew up (again unsurprisingly) to be neurotic, even psychotic, adults. Females who had been raised in this wretched way refused, when they became adults, to mate with males. Harlow then constructed what he called a "rape rack" to which these female monkeys were tied while males mated with them. One of his final experiments he called "the well of despair," in which monkeys were hung upside down in an isolation chamber for as long as two years, unable to move or view the outside world. Monkeys treated in this way became disoriented, even insane.[83]

Critics—not only animal liberationists but some animal experimenters as well—have argued that such experiments have more to do with sadism than with science.

One result of such excesses is that most respectable research laboratories now have committees to review and assess proposed experiments and to stop those that they deem cruel or inhumane. Animal liberationists typically want to go further, but they nevertheless regard such scrutiny of animal experiments as a step in the right direction. Animals are unable to free themselves, say animal liberationists, so human beings acting on their behalf should be prepared to do so. Animal liberationists, in short, view their actions as emancipatory and their ideology as a fully formed "liberation" ideology. Let us look more closely at that claim.

As we noted at the beginning of this chapter, liberation ideologies share several features in common. The first is that each is addressed to a particular audience—to women, or black people, or gays and lesbians, and so on. To whom is the ideology of animal liberation addressed? In one sense, of course, the audience—the group to be liberated—consists of animals; but, in another and more important sense, the ideology of animal liberation is addressed to human beings.

The second feature of any liberation ideology is that its audience must have been oppressed by some dominant group. In the case of animal liberation, however, human beings are both audience and oppressor. The ideology of animal liberation therefore directs its appeals to humans who (1) oppress or abuse animals, (2) derive some supposed benefit from such oppression, or (3) do not benefit but stand by and do nothing to prevent the further abuse and oppression of animals. An example of the first might be a hunter who clubs baby seals to death; of the second, a woman who wears a sealskin coat; of the third, those who take no action—such as writing letters of protest, making financial contributions, and so on—to protect baby seals.

The third feature of liberation ideologies is that they seek to liberate some group not only from external oppression but also from psychological barriers or inhibitions that members of oppressed groups have "internalized" and made part of their own outlook. Obviously, it is difficult, if not impossible, to talk about the psychological states of animals. But this difficulty is reduced considerably if we remember that the ideology of animal liberation is addressed primarily to human beings, who quite clearly do harbor certain beliefs and attitudes that have a bearing upon their treatment of animals. Many human beings subscribe to a set of ideas, beliefs, and attitudes that animal liberationists call **speciesism.** To put it simply, "speciesism" is the belief—or rather, the unexamined prejudice—that human beings are superior to animals; that we have all the rights and they have none; that we may treat them in any way that we believe will benefit us, either as individuals (the steak on my plate) or as a species (the use of monkeys in medical experiments). The German Nazis, as animal liberationists remind us, also subscribed to their own version of speciesism: before murdering or performing medical experiments on Jews, they first took great pains to reclassify them as subhumans, as "animals" or "vermin" without rights and thus undeserving of humane treatment. This fact alone, say the animal liberationists, should give us pause. It should at least lead us to reflect on our beliefs about, and attitudes toward, the "lower" animals whose flesh we eat and on whom we perform experiments of various and often vicious kinds. These experiments range from surgical removal of limbs and organs to testing the toxicity of detergents, bleaches, cosmetics, and other products by injecting them into the eyes of rabbits and other laboratory animals.

It is surely no coincidence that the rise of the animal liberation movement coincided with the growth, in the latter half of the twentieth century, of large, industrial-scale "factory farming." Cattle, hogs, and other animals that once grazed in open pastures are now typically kept in confined spaces so that they will not move around and become tough and muscular rather than tender and meaty. Veal calves are kept in cages and fed an all-milk diet so that their meat will be pink and tender. Chickens and turkeys are confined to small cages with wire floors through which their manure can drop. These and other creatures have become "units" whose diet and movement are carefully calculated, measured, and monitored to ensure their profitability. Modern science also plays a part as cattle are injected with Bovine Growth Hormone (BGH) to speed their growth. To prevent the spread of disease in their confined quarters, cattle and poultry are injected with large quantities of antibiotics, which remain in their flesh to be ingested by humans. In short, say critics of this system, "Old MacDonald's Farm" is now MacDonald's Factory Farm.[84]

Some animal welfare activists have gone undercover and taken jobs at factory farms, feed lots, and slaughterhouses, where they videotape grisly scenes of animal abuse, which they then post online at Mercy for Animals (mercyforanimals.org) and other websites. Large agribusiness corporations call these activists "terrorists" and have successfully lobbied legislatures in several states to pass "ag-gag" laws making it a felony to take a job with the intention of exposing animal abuse or other kinds of cruelty and then posting or otherwise publicizing photos or videos.[85]

In calling our attention to the abuse of animals, animal liberation fulfills the fourth function of a liberation ideology. It aims to "raise the consciousness" of a particular audience, leading its members to examine critically what they had previously taken for granted. Many human beings simply assume that animals exist to serve our purposes and our pleasures, and so see nothing wrong with electrocuting minks and other fur-bearing animals or clubbing baby seals to death to "harvest" their pelts. The existence of animals is justified, in other words, only insofar as they provide meat, fur, or entertainment, or serve as experimental subjects in laboratories, or in some other way contribute to the benefit of human beings. The ideology of animal liberation calls this attitude into question, and thus poses a radical challenge to the widely shared set of unexamined assumptions and prejudices that it calls speciesism.

These arguments are brought together in Peter Singer's *Animal Liberation.*[86] Singer (1946–), an Australian philosopher who now teaches at Princeton University, examines each of the arguments advanced in favor of speciesism and finds them either unwarranted, untenable, or incoherent. Consider, for example, the claim that humans are entitled to eat the flesh of "lower" animals such as cows. On what, Singer asks, is this claim based? It rests on the belief that humans are a "higher" species. On what, then, is this claim to superiority based? It is based on the unique qualities of human beings—qualities that they do not share with lower and lesser creatures. These qualities include, preeminently, the facts that human beings have the use of speech and reason. But this claim, says Singer, is singularly self-subverting. For by this logic we should be prepared to eat the flesh of severely retarded human beings, who lack the power of reason, and of humans who are unable to speak. That we are unwilling to do so only shows that the standard arguments in defense of human superiority are without rational and moral foundation.

Or consider what might be called the "ET argument." Suppose that an extraterrestrial species were to invade and occupy planet earth. Suppose further that even the most mediocre members of this species were vastly more intelligent than the greatest geniuses of the human species, and the Newtons and Einsteins and Hawkings of our species had the intelligence of chickens compared with that of these extraterrestrial invaders. Suppose still further that these ETs had a taste for human flesh and turned the earth into a gigantic factory farm. Would humans who believed themselves justified in eating the flesh of (relatively) unintelligent chickens then concede that these vastly more intelligent ETs would be justified in eating human flesh? Logical consistency would require us to answer yes, and agree to be eaten. But most likely we would not agree, and for good reason: eating the flesh of a sentient fellow creature is morally wrong, no matter how (un)intelligent that creature may be. And for equally good reason we should not think ourselves justified in eating the flesh of chickens, cows, or other nonhuman animals, however unintelligent we may believe them to be.

Intelligence aside, it has long been known that animals express emotions such as anger, anxiety, grief, fear, hope, joy, and sadness. One of the first studies of its kind, Charles Darwin's *The Expression of the Emotions in Man and Animals* (1872), documented these capacities in considerable detail. More recent and sophisticated studies by biologists and zoologists have shown that many animals— including elephants, whales, dolphins, dogs, and cats—have complex cognitive and emotional lives. MRI scans of dogs and cats, for example, show brain wave patterns similar to those of humans exposed to similar stimuli. Animals also have complex communication systems and can form friendships, some even crossing species boundaries (a sampling of these can be seen in videos posted on the website, thedodo.com). Having co-evolved with humans over many millennia, dogs are especially attuned to human moods and emotions, as can be seen in studies of dogs' eye-movements when watching and interacting with people.[87]

With the aid of scientific studies and logical and philosophical arguments, animal liberationists hope to raise the consciousness and critical self-awareness of human beings. Once humans come to see their relationship with animals in a new and different light, they will no longer exploit or oppress them. Humans will at last be freed of their false and self-demeaning sense of their own innate superiority. The aim of animal liberation, then, is not only to deliver animals from human oppression but also to deliver human beings from the cloying confines of speciesism.[88]

Although animal liberationists agree about this much, there are differences among them regarding emphasis and strategy. Some militant animal liberationists assert that animals have "rights," including legal rights to bodily safety and security.[89] Others deny that animals have rights, but hold that they do have "interests" that are worthy of moral consideration and deserving of respect and protection by human beings.[90] Rights-oriented animal liberationists such as Tom Regan argue that no medical experiments of any kind should ever be performed on or with the aid of animals, no matter how great the potential benefit to humans (or even to other animals). Others, including the interest-oriented utilitarian philosopher Peter Singer, argue that such experiments may be justified if the suffering of a relatively small number of animals is outweighed by the benefit to a large number of other sentient creatures, human or nonhuman. Some animal liberationists hold that the hunting of any and all animals is immoral and should be illegal. Yet others claim, on the contrary, that the killing of, say, a deer that has had a good "deer life" until the moment it is shot is much more humane than keeping a cow confined and condemned to live a short and unhappy "cow life" until it is taken, trembling, to a slaughterhouse. Hunters, they say, take responsibility for their actions, whereas the rest of us rely on others to do the killing and butchering for us. Consumers who buy their meat wrapped in Styrofoam and plastic are not somehow more "moral" than hunters, but are merely distancing themselves from the unpleasant tasks of killing and butchering that are a necessary part of the process of putting meat on the table. These and other issues remain the subject of lively and ongoing debate by and among animal liberationists.

In some cases, moreover, people who share a belief in the importance of protecting the rights or interests of animals find themselves at odds on many other matters. Peter Singer, for example, is an atheist who has defended legal abortion and harshly criticized former president George W. Bush; Matthew Scully is a conservative Christian who opposes abortion and served as a senior speechwriter in the second Bush administration. Yet both are vegetarians and animal liberationists, in Scully's case because he holds that humans should show mercy to other animals as part of the duty to care for God's creation and all of His creatures.[91] Nonhuman animals are God's creations and our fellow creatures. Accordingly, says Scully, we must not harm, kill, or eat them.

The human (mis)treatment of animals has long been addressed by different faith traditions. Judaism, for example, advocates the protection and minimizing the suffering of animals, based in part on the principle *tza'ar ba'alei chayim*, "the suffering of living creatures." The principle is spelled out in the Talmud's commentary on Exodus 23:5, which requires humans to assist in unloading burdens from animals. This is generalized and extended to other areas and activities involving animal and human interactions. For example, kosher butchers are commanded to kill an animal as quickly and painlessly as possible, and out of sight and earshot of other animals so as not to distress them. The laws of *Shabbat* (Sabbath) require that animals, like humans, rest every seventh day (Exodus 20:8). The Talmud allows humans to break the law of *Shabbat* to care for any ill or injured creature, be it man or beast. Islam has similar strictures regarding the treatment of animals (*Qur'an* 6:38, 24:41, 55:10).

The mistreatment of animals is also a current and growing concern among theologians and other religious scholars. The distinguished British theologian Dr. Andrew Lindzey was among the first to take up this topic, in his *Animal Rights: A Christian Assessment* (1976). Another British theologian, Dr. David Clough, authored a two-volume treatise on the topic, *On Animals* (1988). And an American Catholic theologian, Dr. Charles Camosy, has recently written *For Love of Animals: Christian Ethics, Consistent Action* (2013). The Catholic Camosy and the atheist Peter Singer have in recent years engaged in a dialogue that resulted in Camosy's book, *Peter Singer and Christian Ethics: Beyond Polarization* (2012), and the exchange has led Singer to soften his critique of religion, and Christianity in particular. All attest to the growing importance of the animal liberation movement

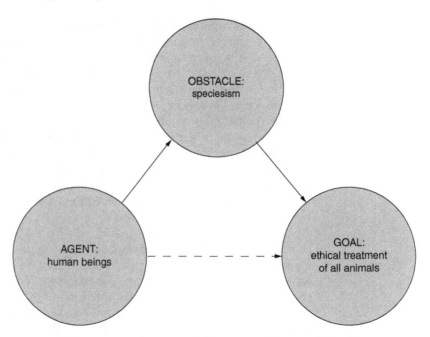

FIGURE 8.8 The "animal liberationist" view of freedom.

and its still-developing ideology.[92] By this point it should be clear that one need not be a "leftist" or liberal to advocate animal liberation, or at least the humane treatment of animals. If you doubt it, consider the case of Arizona. One of the most conservative of the Republican "red" states, Arizona has some of the strictest animal-protection laws in the nation. Among these is the Humane Treatment of Farm Animals Act, approved by 62 percent of Arizona voters in 2006. One prominent public official urging its passage was Maricopa County sheriff Joe Arpaio, who calls himself "the toughest cop in the country," saying, "I am a meat-eater, and I enjoy a good steak as much as the next guy. But I believe that even animals raised for food deserve a decent life and a merciful death."[93] Other states have since followed Arizona's lead.

We can conclude by noting that animal liberation, like other liberation ideologies, subscribes to its own distinctive conception of freedom or liberty, which is summarized in Figure 8.8.

CONCLUSION
Liberty, Identity, and Ideology

Each of these ideologies takes a particular group, which it sees as systematically abused or oppressed, as the subject of its concern. But these groups can and do overlap, as in the case of black women, for example, or of native people who live in poverty. They also share a "family resemblance," as we have seen. For these reasons, we can treat them as a unit—as the family of liberation ideologies—as we examine the ways they perform the four functions of ideologies.

Explanation. Liberation ideologies do not try to explain all social conditions and circumstances. They begin, instead, with the condition of the specific group with which they are concerned—black people, women, gays and lesbians, native peoples, the poor, and nonhuman animals. This condition they then explain in terms of certain beliefs—racist, sexist, homophobic, and so on—held by oppressors and internalized by the oppressed. These beliefs stem from the fact of domination and oppression. That is, the plight of their group is not simply a natural fact of life that must be accepted, like the need to eat, sleep, and breathe, but is the result of oppression—of blacks by whites, of women by men, and so on.

Evaluation. Just as oppression is the key word in the liberation ideologies' explanation of conditions, so, too, is it the key to their evaluations of these conditions. When oppression crushes or stifles people, and thus prevents them from living full and free lives, then things are not as they should be. Every liberation ideology teaches that things are not yet as they should be, since each of the groups they address continues to suffer (or sometimes to cause) oppression. Rather than saying that conditions are good or bad, then, they tend to evaluate them in terms of better or worse. In societies and times in which women are relatively free to speak and think for themselves, for instance, conditions are better—less oppressive—for them than they are in societies and times in which women are treated simply as the property of men. To say that conditions are better, however, is not to say that they are already as good as they can and should be.

Orientation. One of the central features of liberation ideologies is the attempt to make members of oppressed groups conscious or aware of their oppression—to see themselves as the victims of some dominant or powerful group. This is a matter of orientation and identity—of who or what one is. Far from being isolated individual atoms, people are apt to identify themselves—and be identified by others—with one or another race, gender, religion, sexual orientation, or other group affiliation. People must understand their location in the social world before they can do anything to change their circumstances. The victim of injustice must be brought to see that he or she is not responsible for the suffering he or she endures, nor is this suffering simply his or her inevitable fate. So, too, must the oppressor be brought to see the injustice that he or she is doing, wittingly or unwittingly, to other human beings or to animals.

Program. Orientation or understanding by itself, of course, is not enough to overcome oppression. It must be joined to action. But action of what kind? Here the liberation ideologies take many different courses, depending upon the challenges they confront in different circumstances. Here the differences between "liberal" and more "radical" variants of black liberation and feminism become most pronounced. The "liberal" or "civil rights" variants typically try to bring about change by legal actions, such as the court cases brought by the National Association for the Advancement of Colored People (NAACP) and the attempt to add to the U.S. Constitution an Equal Rights Amendment outlawing discrimination against women. The more radical variants tend to favor activities that either challenge or circumvent the established social and legal powers, such as the formation of self-help and self-protection groups by the Black Panthers and Nation of Islam. Liberation groups of all sorts often resort to boycotts, demonstrations, and civil disobedience—public and peaceful acts of lawbreaking—to call attention to their views. Some advocates of liberation ideologies have said that violence is justified, in some circumstances, as a form of self-defense against the oppressors who are doing violence to them.[94] But whatever their tactics, in general terms they all share the same program: to bring an end to the oppression of a group of people (or of nonhuman animals) so that they may live full and free lives.

Liberation, Identity, and the Democratic Ideal

One final question remains: how do liberation ideologies construe, or construct, the democratic ideal? The various liberationists typically think of democracy as self-rule, which is consistent with the conception of democracy found in other ideologies. But liberation ideologies also point out that self-rule is impossible unless people have a more or less well-developed sense of self-worth and self-respect. Thus, the various liberation ideologies aim to implant and reinforce that sense of dignity, self-worth, and identity in their respective audiences. This they do in the five ways that we listed at the beginning of this chapter. Each addresses a particular audience—black people, women, gays, native peoples, the poor—whose experiences are historically unique, although all have experienced oppression of some sort. Each liberation ideology recognizes these experiences as real and valid, and leads those whom it addresses to examine the origins, memory, and effects of such oppression. Typically, these include internalized inhibitions and barriers— feelings of inferiority or inadequacy, for example—that stand in the way of their being actively self-ruling agents who seek to achieve the goals they have set for themselves. Because these effects are not only physical but also psychological, an ideology of liberation helps people recognize and overcome the damage oppression has done to their psyches by affirming their identities and "raising their consciousness," that is, by making conscious and articulate what had previously remained unconscious and inarticulate. Finally, liberation ideologies intend to inform and educate not only victims but their oppressors as well. Oppressors suffer (usually without knowing it) from the stifling and stunting of their moral, intellectual, and civic capacities, just as the master in Hegel's parable (discussed in Chapter 5) oppressed not only his slave but also himself.

Current clashes over "multiculturalism" grow out of the efforts of the various liberation ideologies. Advocates of "identity politics" or "the politics of difference" view the new or renewed emphasis on cultural differences as a positive development. Every group that has been pushed to the margins of mainstream society has its own culture—gays, women, people of color, native peoples, and even the physically disabled, who sometimes speak, for example, of "deaf culture" or "the deaf way."[95] It is about time, these multiculturalists say, that these long-oppressed groups gain political respect and legal recognition. They should wear their respective badges of group identity with pride and a sense of solidarity. For only by joining forces with other members of one's identity group can the individual attain an effective voice in public affairs and therefore be free. Some advocates of "the politics of difference" argue that this kind of voice and freedom will be available to the members of oppressed groups only when they are guaranteed group representation in legislative bodies—that is, so many seats in Congress or Parliament set aside for women, so many for native peoples, for black people, for gays, and so on.[96]

Critics of "multiple sovereignties" and "multicultural citizenship" contend that such policies are socially and culturally divisive. The "politics of identity and/ or difference" is mistaken, they charge, when it views individuals as members of this or that group rather than simply as individuals or citizens. As citizens, individuals should be equal before the law. Courts of justice and other institutions should be blind to race, ethnicity, and other forms of group identification. No one should be given special treatment because of his or her race or ancestry or ethnic affiliation. Besides, these critics add, what begins innocently and with the best of intentions may end disastrously, as an emphasis on ethnic "difference" could lead to intergroup hostility and **ethnic cleansing.** Even if matters stop short of that, the emphasis on difference could still lead to the fragmentation of political systems. The national motto of the United States, for instance, is *e pluribus unum*—"out of many, one." But the multiculturalists emphasize the *pluribus*—that is, plurality and difference—at the expense of the *unum*—that is, national unity.[97]

Advocates of identity politics will often agree that the law should be blind to racial and ethnic and other differences—*in an ideal world*. But our world is not ideal; it is scarred by a long history of oppression visited upon the members of the groups that have achieved, at best, partial liberation.[98] That is why special efforts, such as **affirmative action** and group representation, are necessary to overcome the lingering effects of past oppression and to put an end to continuing discrimination. Moreover, they claim, there are some respects in which treating people as equals requires the recognition of their differences. Women can give birth and men cannot, for instance, and various laws and policies can treat women and men as equals only when this and other differences are taken into account.

In these and other ways, liberation ideologies try to make people strong enough to bear the burdens and experience the satisfaction of self-rule—of democracy, in other words. Now it might be thought that one of these ideologies—animal liberation—cannot achieve any such end, since it is concerned with the well-being of animals. But this objection, as we have seen, misses the point. The ideology of animal liberation is addressed to human beings with the aim of liberating them as well as other animals. For to the degree that we accept unquestioningly the assumptions of speciesism, animal liberationists say, we remain locked into a false picture of the world and our place in it. This, as we shall see in Chapter 9, is a theme shared—albeit in a quite different way—with another newly emerging ideology.

Discussion Questions

1   All liberation ideologies address a particular audience, whose members' freedom they try to promote. Choose one of these liberation ideologies, and use the triadic model of freedom to explain how and why it proposes to liberate its particular group.

2   Some say that the election of an African-American as president—and for two consecutive terms, no less—"proves" that black people have "made it" and

that racism and racial discrimination are no longer persistent problems in the United States. Discuss.

3   Give three contemporary examples of sexism and/or patriarchalism and try to explain their longevity or persistence.

4   What is "indigenism" and what is its conception of freedom?

5   What, in your view, accounts for the fairly rapid recent acceptance of same-sex relationships, extending even to marriage, by a majority of "straight" Americans?

6   What is the "ET argument," who uses it, and for what purpose(s)?

NOTES

1   See Marilyn Frye, "Oppression," in her *The Politics of Reality* (Trumansburg, NY: Crossing Press, 1983), pp. 1–16; also in Terence Ball, Richard Dagger, and Daniel O'Neill, eds., *Ideals and Ideologies: A Reader*, 10th ed. (New York and London: Routledge, 2016), selection 8.57.

2   See the works by Grier and Cobbs in n. 15 later, and by Fanon (n. 16).

3   See, for example, Frye, "Oppression."

4   This sense is captured in the ideas of "heteronormativity" (i.e., the unspoken assumption that heterosexuality is normal and same-sex attraction is not) and "compulsory heterosexuality" (all the educational and institutional pressures to be, or at least appear to be, "straight"). The term "heteronormativity" was coined by Michael Warner in "Introduction: Fear of a Queer Planet," *Social Text* 9 (1991): 3–17; and "compulsory heterosexuality" by Adrienne Rich in "Compulsory Heterosexuality and Lesbian Existence," *Signs: Journal of Women in Culture and Society*, 5:4 (1980): 631–660.

5   This was a view instilled in native peoples by government policies that took native children from their families to "educate" them in far-away boarding schools, where they were punished for speaking their native language, for following the customs of their culture, and other alleged "offenses."

6   See the work by Gustavo Gutierrez cited later, n. 74.

7   See the works by Peter Singer and Tom Regan, cited later, nn. 78, 81.

8   For a classic exposition of this view, see Paulo Freire, *Pedagogy of the Oppressed*, trans. Myra Bergman Ramos (New York: Continuum, 2007); and, more generally, Stephen T. Leonard, *Critical Theory in Political Practice* (Princeton, NJ: Princeton University Press, 1990).

9   This comes from Blake's poem "London," in his *Songs of Innocence and Experience* (1789), in David V. Erdman, ed., *The Poetry and Prose of William Blake* (New York: Doubleday, 1968), pp. 26–27.

10   Douglas A. Blackmon, *Slavery by Another Name: The Re-Enslavement of Black Americans from the Civil War to World War II* (New York: Knopf, 2009). The claim that such re-enslavement continues even today is defended by Ta-Nehisi Coates, "The Black Family in the Age of Mass Incarceration," *The Atlantic*, October 2015, pp. 60–84.

11   Rachel L. Swarns, "Long Banned, Mortgage Bias Is Back as Issue," *New York Times*, October 31, 2015, pp. A1, A3.

12   According to Michael Dawson, these are the ideologies of radical egalitarianism, disillusioned liberalism, black Marxism, black nationalism, black feminism, and black conservatism. See Dawson, *Black Visions: The Roots of Contemporary African-American Political Ideologies* (Chicago: University of Chicago Press, 2001), Chapter 1.

13   Ibid, p. 94.

14   See, for example, Steve Biko, "Black Consciousness and the Quest for a True Humanity," in Basil Moore, ed., *Black Theology: The South African Voice* (London: C. Hurst & Co., 1973).

15   William Grier and Price Cobbs, *Black Rage* (New York: Basic Books, 1969).

16   Frantz Fanon, *Black Skins, White Masks* (New York: Grove Press, 1982).

17 See, for example, David R. Roediger, *Towards the Abolition of Whiteness* (New York: Verso Books, 1994) and *Colored White: Transcending the Racial Past* (Berkeley and Los Angeles: University of California Press, 2002).

18 Quoted in Taylor Branch, *Parting the Waters: America in the King Years, 1954–1963* (New York: Simon & Schuster, 1988), p. 589.

19 Lydia Polgreen, Nicholas Kulish, and Alan Cowell, "World Bids Farewell in the Land Mandela Freed," *New York Times*, December 11, 2013, pp. A6, A8.

20 See Martin Luther King, Jr., "Where Do We Go from Here?" (1967) in King, *Where Do We Go from Here: Chaos or Community?* (Boston: Beacon Press, 1968).

21 See Barack Obama, "A More Perfect Union" (speech on race), Philadelphia, March 18, 2008; available at obamaspeeches.com/EO5-Barack-Obama-A-More-Perfect-Union as of August 2, 2009.

22 Randall Robinson, *The Debt: What America Owes to Blacks* (New York: Dutton, 2000); the case was made earlier and more systematically in Boris I. Bittker, *The Case for Black Reparations* (New York: Random House, 1973). Perhaps the clearest and most accessible argument for black reparations is Ta-Nehisi Coates, "The Case for Reparations," *The Atlantic*, June 2014, pp. 54–71.

23 For discussion of the arguments for and against reparations, with particular attention to black slavery, see: Roy L. Brooks, ed., *When Sorry Isn't Enough: The Controversies over Apologies and Reparations and Human Injustice* (New York: New York University Press, 1999), esp. Part 6; Janna Thompson, *Taking Responsibility for the Past: Reparation and Historical Injustice* (Cambridge: Polity Press, 2002); and John Torpey, *Making Whole What Has Been Smashed: On Reparations Politics* (Cambridge, MA: Harvard University Press, 2006), esp. Chapter 4.

24 Quoted in Dawson, *Black Visions*, p. 120.

25 Aristotle, *Politics*, Book I, 1259a41 and 1245b12.

26 Thomas Jefferson to Albert Gallatin, January 13, 1807, in Joyce Appleby and Terence Ball, eds., *Jefferson: Political Writings* (Cambridge: Cambridge University Press, 1999), p. 545.

27 Charles Darwin, *The Descent of Man* (London: John Murray, 1871), pp. 563–564. Numerous attempts to prove "scientifically" the alleged moral and intellectual "inferiority" of women are chronicled by Cynthia Eagle Russett, *Sexual Science: The Victorian Construction of Womanhood* (Cambridge: Harvard University Press, 1989).

28 See, e.g., Cynthia Eagle Russett, *Sexual Science: The Victorian Construction of Womanhood* (Cambridge: Harvard University Press, 1989).

29 Quoted in Miriam Schneir, ed., *Feminism: The Essential Historical Writings* (New York: Vintage Books, 1972), p. 3.

30 See Ball, Dagger, and O'Neill, *Ideals and Ideologies* for excerpts from de Gouges's "Declaration of the Rights of Woman and the Female Citizen," selection 8.55, and from Wollstonecraft's *Vindication of the Rights of Woman*, selection 8.54.

31 For Sarah Grimké's observations on the connection between slavery and the condition of women, see her *Letters on the Equality of the Sexes* (Boston: Isaac Knapp, 1838), Letter VIII.

32 "Seneca Falls Declaration of Sentiments and Resolutions," in Ball, Dagger, and O'Neill, *Ideals and Ideologies*, selection 8.56.

33 See Schneir, ed., *Feminism*, Part IV: "Men as Feminists."

34 See, for example, Sheila Rowbotham, *Women's Consciousness, Man's World* (Harmondsworth, U.K.: Pelican Books, 1973).

35 Ibid.

36 See, for example, Emma Goldman, *Anarchism and Other Essays* (New York: Mother Earth Association, 1910); two of her essays—"The Traffic in Women" and "Marriage and Love"—are included in Schneir, ed., *Feminism*, pp. 308–324.

37 See, for example, Shulamith Firestone, *The Dialectic of Sex: The Case for Feminist Revolution* (New York: Morrow, 1970).

38 See Vivien Gornick, *Essays in Feminism* (New York: Harper & Row, 1978).

39 For one radical feminist's case against pornography, see Catherine MacKinnon, *Only Words* (Cambridge, MA: Harvard University Press, 1993). For a liberal feminist's rejoinder, see Nadine Strossen, *Defending Pornography: Free Speech, Sex, and the Fight for Women's Rights* (New York: Scribner, 1995).

40 David Kirkpatrick and Mayy El-Sheikh, "Muslim Brotherhood's Statement on Women Stirs Liberals' Fears," *New York Times*, March 15, 2013, p. A4.

41 "India: A Rape Victim Commits Suicide," *New York Times*, December 28, 2012, p. A8.

42 "India: Victim Dies After Gang Rape That Galvanized India over the Dangers That Women Face," *New York Times*, December 29, 2012, p. A7.

43 "Afghan Prosecutor Faces Criticism for Her Pursuit of 'Moral Crimes'," *New York Times*, December 29, 2012, p. A8.

44 Hillary Clinton, remarks at the Women in the World Summit, Lincoln Center, Washington, D.C., March 10, 2012; quoted in Maureen Dowd, "Don't Tread on Us," *New York Times*, March 14, 2012, p. A25.

45 Maureen Dowd, "Don't Tread on Us," p. A25.

46 Saphora Smith, "New Political Party in Britain Seeks Faster Equality for Women," *New York Times*, November 28, 2015, p. A8.

47 For Greek attitudes toward sexuality and same-sex love (the term "homosexuality" was not coined until the late nineteenth century), see Plato, *The Symposium*; K. J. Dover, *Greek Homosexuality* (Cambridge, MA: Harvard University Press, 1978); and Michel Foucault, *The History of Sexuality*, vol. I, trans. Robert Hurley (New York: Pantheon, 1986).

48 Elaine Pagels, *Adam, Eve, and the Serpent* (New York: Random House, 1988), pp. 10–11; but note the statement of the National Conference of Catholic Bishops, *Always Our Children: A Pastoral Message to Parents of Homosexual Children and Suggestions for Pastoral Ministers* (Washington, D.C.: Office of Communications, National Conference of Catholic Bishops, U.S. Catholic Conference, 1997).

49 The story of Turing's life and death is told by Andrew Hodges, *Alan Turing: The Enigma* (Princeton: Princeton University Press, 1983), and dramatized in the 1986 play *Breaking the Code*, by Hugh Whitemore, on which the 1996 movie of the same title is based.

50 Committee on Homosexual Offences and Prostitution (London: Her Majesty's Stationery Office, 1957), p. 187.

51 Martin Duberman, *Stonewall* (New York: Dutton, 1993).

52 See, for example, Richard Mohr, *Gays/Justice* (New York: Columbia Press, 1988); and John Corvino, "Homosexuality—The Nature and Harm Arguments," in Ball, Dagger, and O'Neill, *Ideals and Ideologies*, selection 8.59.

53 Richard J. Evans, *The Third Reich in Power* (New York: Penguin, 2005), pp. 529–537, 543–545.

54 See Bruce Bawer, *A Place at the Table: The Gay Individual in American Society* (New York: Poseidon Press, 1993).

55 See Randy Shilts, *Conduct Unbecoming: Gays and Lesbians in the U.S. Military* (New York: St. Martin's Press, 1993).

56 Dave Philipps, "Ousted as Gay, Aging Veterans Battling Again—Pentagon Is Asked to Upgrade Discharges to 'Honorable'," *New York Times*, September 7, 2015, pp. A1, A12.

57 Dorothy Samuels, "A Long, Winding Road to Marriage Equality," *New York Times*, November 13, 2011, p. SR10.

58 See Erik Eckholm, "As Victories Pile Up, Gay Rights Advocates Cheer 'Milestone Year'," *New York Times*, November 8, 2012, p. P7; and "Push Expands for Gay Marriage," *New York Times*, November 13, 2012, pp. A1, A15.

59 See Theodore B. Olson, "The Conservative Case for Gay Marriage," *Newsweek*, January 8, 2010; available at www.newsweek.com/conservative-case-gay-marriage-70923.

60 For a wide-ranging "oral history" of the gay liberation movement, see Eric Marcus, *Making History: The Struggle for Gay and Lesbian Equal Rights, 1945–1990* (New York: HarperCollins, 1992).

61 See, for example, Annamarie Jagose, *Queer Theory: An Introduction* (New York: New York University Press, 1996); William B. Turner, *A Genealogy of Queer Theory* (Philadelphia: Temple University Press, 2000); and Nikki Sullivan, *A Critical Introduction to Queer Theory* (New York: New York University Press, 2003).

62 Erik Eckholm, "Next Fight for Gay Rights: Bias in Jobs and Housing," *New York Times*, June 28, 2015, pp. A1, A20.

63 Hillary Clinton, "Remarks in Recognition of International Human Rights Day," at the Palais des Nations, Geneva, Switzerland, December 6, 2011.

64 Adam Nossiter, "Wielding Whip and a Hard New Law, Nigeria Tries to 'Sanitize' Itself of Gays," *New York Times*, February 9, 2014, pp. A1, A14.

65 For the term "indigenism," see Ward Churchill, "I Am Indigenist: Notes on the Ideology of the Fourth World," in Churchill, *Acts of Rebellion: The Ward Churchill Reader* (New York: Routledge, 2003).

66 "Unofficial Apology Offered to Aborigines," AP dispatch, *Minneapolis Star-Tribune*, May 27, 1997; "Rudd to Apologize to Aborigines," www.news.bbc.co.uk/2/hi/asiapacific/7112773.stm, November 26, 2007.

67 Tim Johnston, "Aborigines Get Apology from Leader of Australia," *New York Times*, February 13, 2008, p. A8.

68 "Canada Apology to Native Peoples," *Arizona Republic*, January 8, 1998, p. A8; "Canada Will Form New Arctic Territory Ruled by Aboriginals," *Arizona Republic*, April 5, 1998, p. A28.

69 David Stout, "At Indian Bureau, a Milestone and an Apology," *New York Times*, September 9, 2000, p. A7.

70 Most especially in South Africa, where it is generally referred to as "black theology." See Basil Moore, ed., *Black Theology: The South African Voice* (London: C. Hurst and Co., 1973).

71 In Jerusalem, for example, a group of Palestinian Christians have maintained an "ecumenical liberation theology center" called Sabeel—Arabic for "the way"—since 1989. See www.sabeel.org.

72 When he was head of the official Congregation for the Doctrine of the Faith, the future pope wrote a document highly critical of liberation theology: Joseph Ratzinger, *Instruction on Certain Aspects of Liberation Theology* (Rome: Congregation for the Doctrine of the Faith, 1984). In 2013 Pope Benedict XVI was succeeded by Pope Francis, who is markedly more sympathetic to liberation theology.

73 See Leonard, *Critical Theory in Political Practice*.

74 Gustavo Gutierrez, *A Theology of Liberation: History, Politics, and Salvation*, trans. Sister Caridad Inda and John Eagleson (Maryknoll, NY: Orbis Books, 1973), p. 307; see excerpt in Ball, Dagger, and O'Neill, *Ideals and Ideologies*, selection 8.61.

75 See James H. Cone, *Black Theology and Black Power*, rev. ed. (New York: Orbis Books, 1997). For a wide range of reconsiderations and criticisms, see Dwight N. Hopkins, ed., *Black Faith and Public Talk: Critical Essays on James H. Cone's Black Theology and Black Power* (New York: Orbis Books, 2000).

76 This is a theme that runs through many revolutionary and emancipatory movements. See Michael Walzer, *Exodous and Revolution* (New York: Basic Books, 1985).

77 See Cone, "Whose Earth Is It, Anyway? Why the Environmental Movement and the Racial Justice Movement Need Each Other," in Cone, *Risks of Faith: The Emergence of a Black Theology of Liberation, 1968–1998* (Boston: Beacon Press, 1999), pp. 138–145; also reprinted in Ball, Dagger, and O'Neill, *Ideals and Ideologies*, selection 9.66.

78 Peter Singer and Tom Regan trace some of the sentiments and ideas of "animal liberation" back as far as Plutarch (c. 49–119) and St. Thomas Aquinas (1224–1274): Singer and Regan, eds., *Animal Rights and Human Obligations* (Englewood Cliffs, NJ: Prentice-Hall, 1976), pp. 111–121.

79   Jeremy Bentham, An Introduction to the Principles of Morals and Legislation in *Collected Works of Jeremy Bentham*, J. H. Burns and H. L. A. Hart, eds. (London: Athlone Press, 1970 [1789]), p. 283.

80   Ibid.

81   See the selections from Salt's works in Regan and Singer, *Animal Rights and Human Obligations*, pp. 173–178, 185–189. For a more substantial selection, see George Hendrick and Willene Hendrick, eds., *The Savour of Salt* (London: Centaur Press, 1989).

82   Jesse McKinley, "A California Ballot Measure Offers Rights for Farm Animals," *New York Times*, October 24, 2008, p. A12.

83   Lauren Slater, *Opening Skinner's Box: Great Psychological Experiments of the Twentieth Century* (New York: W. W. Norton & Co., 2004); see also Peter Singer's review, *New York Times Book Review*, March 28, 2004, p. 6.

84   C. David Coats, *Old MacDonald's Factory Farm* (New York: Continuum, 1989); and Eric Schlosser, *Fast Food Nation: The Dark Side of the All-American Meal* (Boston: Houghton Mifflin, 2001).

85   Ted Genoways, "Gagged by Big Ag," *Mother Jones*, July/August 2013; available at www.motherjones.com/environment/2013/06/ag-gag-laws-mowmar-farms.

86   Peter Singer, *Animal Liberation*, 2nd ed. (New York: Random House, 1990), and "All Animals Are Equal," in Ball, Dagger, and O'Neill, *Ideals and Ideologies*, selection 8.62. As a utilitarian, Singer is skeptical of the idea of the "intrinsic worth" of life and the language of "rights." He rests his case on the claim that animals, like humans, are sentient creatures capable of experiencing pain and pleasure.

87   See the studies summarized in Carl Safina, *Beyond Words: What Animals Think and Feel* (New York: Henry Holt, 2015).

88   Tom Regan's *The Case for Animal Rights* (Berkeley and Los Angeles: University of California Press, 1983). Like Singer, Regan argues that "animal liberation" entails the liberation of humans, freeing them from previously unexamined "speciesist" prejudices and practices.

89   In addition to Regan, *The Case for Animal Rights* (n. 88, earlier), see Steven M. Wise, *Rattling the Cage: Toward Legal Rights for Animals* (Cambridge, MA: Perseus Books, 2000), and Wise, *Drawing the Line: The Case for Animal Rights* (Cambridge, MA: Merloyd Lawrence Books, 2002).

90   Lawrence E. Johnson, *A Morally Deep World* (Cambridge: Cambridge University Press, 1991), Chapter 6.

91   Matthew Scully, Dominion: *The Power of Man, the Suffering of Animals, and the Call to Mercy* (New York: St. Martin's Press, 2002). For Singer's criticism of President Bush, see *The President of Good and Evil: The Ethics of George W. Bush* (New York: Dutton, 2004).

92   Mark Oppenheimer, "Scholars Explore Christian Perspectives on Animal Rights," *New York Times*, December 7, 2013, p. A17.

93   Quoted in "Take a Bow, Arizona" (editorial), *Arizona Republic*, December 11, 2012, p. B8.

94   See, for example, Malcolm X, "The Ballot or the Bullet" (1964), in *Malcolm X Speaks* (New York: Merit Publishers, 1965), pp. 23–44.

95   See C. J. Erting et al., *The Deaf Way: Perspectives from the International Conference on Deaf Culture* (Washington, D.C.: Gallaudet University Press, 1994).

96   For a clear and forceful statement of this position, see Iris Marion Young, *Justice and the Politics of Difference* (Princeton, NJ: Princeton University Press, 1990).

97   See, for example, Arthur M. Schlesinger, Jr., *The Disuniting of America* (New York: Norton, 1992).

98   For attempts to reconcile liberal egalitarianism with multiculturalism, see Will Kymlicka, *Multicultural Citizenship: A Liberal Theory of Minority Rights* (Oxford: Clarendon Press, 1995), and Kymlicka, *Politics in the Vernacular: Nationalism, Multiculturalism, and Citizenship* (Oxford: Oxford University Press, 2001); David Miller, *On Nationality* (Oxford: Clarendon Press, 1996); Jeff Spinner-Halev, *The Boundaries of Citizenship:*

Race, Ethnicity, and Nationality in the Liberal State (Baltimore, MD: Johns Hopkins University Press, 1994); Bhikhu Parekh, *Rethinking Multiculturalism: Cultural Diversity and Political Theory* (Cambridge, MA: Harvard University Press, 2000); and Jacob Levy, *The Multiculturalism of Fear* (Oxford: Oxford University Press, 2000). For an "egalitarian critique," see Brian Barry, *Culture and Equality: An Egalitarian Critique of Multiculturalism* (Cambridge, MA: Harvard University Press, 2001); also Michael Kenny, *The Politics of Identity: Liberal Political Theory and the Dilemmas of Difference* (Cambridge: Polity Press, 2004). For a useful overview, see Bernard Yack, "Multiculturalism and the Political Theorists," *European Journal of Political Theory* 1 (July 2002): 107–119.

FOR FURTHER READING
Black Liberation

Biko, Steve. *I Write What I Like*, Malusi and Thoko Mpumlwana, eds. London: Bowerdean Press, 1996.

Branch, Taylor. *Parting the Waters: America in the King Years, 1954–1963*. New York: Simon & Schuster, 1988.

——. *Pillar of Fire: America in the King Years, 1963–1965*. New York: Simon & Schuster, 1998.

Carmichael, Stokely, and Charles Hamilton. *Black Power*. New York: Vintage Books, 1967.

Fanon, Frantz. *Black Skin, White Masks*. New York: Grove Press, 1982.

Grier, William H., and Price N. Cobbs. *Black Rage*. New York: Bantam Books, 1969.

King, Martin Luther, Jr. *Why We Can't Wait*. New York: Harper & Row, 1964.

West, Cornel. *Race Matters*. New York: Vintage Press, 1994.

X, Malcolm. *The Autobiography of Malcolm X*. New York: Grove Press, 1965.

——. *Malcolm X Speaks*. New York: Grove Press, 1966.

Women's Liberation

Beauvoir, Simone de. *The Second Sex*. New York: Bantam Books, 1968.

Elshtain, Jean Bethke. *Public Man, Private Woman: Women in Social and Political Thought*. Princeton, NJ: Princeton University Press, 1981.

Evans, Sara M. *Born for Liberty: A History of Women in America*, 2nd ed. New York: Simon & Schuster, 1997.

Friedan, Betty. *The Feminine Mystique*. New York: Norton, 1963.

Grimké, Sarah. *Letters on the Equality of the Sexes*, Elizabeth Ann Bartlett, ed. New Haven, CT: Yale University Press, 1988.

hooks, bell. *Feminist Theory: Margin to Center*. Boston: South End Press, 1984.

Jaggar, Allison. *Feminist Politics and Human Nature*. Lanham, MD: Rowman & Littlefield, 1988.

Kristof, Nicholas D. and Sheryl WuDunn. *Half the Sky: Turning Oppression into Opportunity for Women Worldwide*. New York: Knopf, 2009.

Mill, John Stuart. *The Subjection of Women* [1869] in *John Stuart Mill: Three Essays*, ed. Richard Wollheim. Oxford: Oxford University Press, 1975.

Mitchell, Juliet. *Woman's Estate*. New York: Vintage Books, 1973.

Schneir, Miriam, ed. *Feminism: The Essential Historical Writings*. New York: Vintage Books, 1972.

Tong, Rosemarie. *Feminist Thought*, 2nd ed. Boulder, CO: Westview Press, 1998.

Gay Liberation

Bawer, Bruce. *A Place at the Table: The Gay Individual in American Society.* New York: Poseidon Press, 1993.

Corvino, John, ed. *Same Sex: Debating the Ethics, Science, and Culture of Homosexuality.* Lanham, MD: Rowman & Littlefield, 1997.

Crompton, Louis. *Homosexuality and Civilization.* Cambridge, MA: Harvard University Press, 2003.

Cruikshank, Margaret. *The Gay and Lesbian Movement.* London: Routledge, 1992.

Duberman, Martin. *Stonewall.* New York: Dutton, 1993.

Marcus, Eric. *Making History: The Struggle for Gay and Lesbian Equal Rights, 1945–1990.* New York: HarperCollins, 1992.

Mohr, Richard. *Gays/Justice.* New York: Columbia University Press, 1988.

Sullivan, Andrew. *Virtually Normal: An Argument About Homosexuality.* New York: Alfred A. Knopf, 1995.

Native Peoples' Liberation (Indigenism)

Alfred, Taiaiake. *Wasáse: Indigenous Pathways of Action and Freedom.* Peterborough, ON: Broadview Press, 2005.

Brown, Dee. *Bury My Heart at Wounded Knee: An Indian History of the American West.* New York: Holt, Rinehart & Winston, 1970.

Churchill, Ward. *Acts of Rebellion: The Ward Churchill Reader.* New York: Routledge, 2003.

Deloria, Vine, Jr., and Clifford Little. *The Nations Within: The Past and Future of American Indian Sovereignty.* New York: Pantheon, 1984.

Little Bear, Leroy, Menno Boldt, and J. Anthony Long, eds. *Pathways to Self-Determination.* Toronto: University of Toronto Press, 1984.

Monture-Angus, Patricia. *Thunder in My Soul: A Mohawk Woman Speaks.* Halifax, Nova Scotia: Fernwood Publishing, 1995.

Richardson, Boyce, ed. *Drumbeat: Anger and Renewal in Indian Country.* Assembly of First Nations: Summerhill Press; distributed by University of Toronto Press, 1989.

Wub-E-Ke-Niew. *We Have the Right to Exist.* New York: Black Thistle Press, 1995.

Liberation Theology

Berryman, Phillip. *Liberation Theology: Essential Facts About the Revolutionary Movement in Latin America—and Beyond.* Philadelphia: Temple University Press, 1987.

Cone, James H. *Black Theology and Black Power,* rev. ed. New York: Orbis Books, 1997.

Hopkins, Dwight N., ed. *Black Faith and Public Talk: Critical Essays on James H. Cone's Black Theology and Black Power.* New York: Orbis Books, 2000.

McGovern, Arthur F. "The Evolution of Liberation Theology." *New Oxford Review* 17 (June 1990): 5–8.

Pottenger, John. *The Political Theory of Liberation Theology.* Albany: State University Press of New York, 1989.

Ratzinger, Joseph. *Instruction on Certain Aspects of Liberation Theology.* Rome: Congregation for the Doctrine of the Faith, 1984.

Sigmund, Paul. *Liberation Theology at the Crossroads: Democracy or Revolution?* New York: Oxford University Press, 1990.

Animal Liberation

Amory, Cleveland. *Man Kind?* New York: Harper & Row, 1974.

Coats, C. David. *Old MacDonald's Factory Farm.* New York: Continuum Books, 1989.

Francione, Gary L., and Alan Watson. *Introduction to Animal Rights.* Philadelphia: Temple University Press, 2000.

Frey, R. G. *Interests and Rights: The Case Against Animals.* Oxford: Oxford University Press, 1980.

Regan, Tom. *The Case for Animal Rights.* Berkeley and Los Angeles: University of California Press, 1983.

Regan, Tom, and Peter Singer, eds. *Animal Rights and Human Obligations.* Englewood Cliffs, NJ: Prentice-Hall, 1976.

Scully, Matthew. *Dominion: The Power of Man, the Suffering of Animals, and the Call to Mercy.* New York: St. Martin's Press, 2002.

Singer, Peter. *Animal Liberation,* 2nd ed. New York: Random House, 1990.

USEFUL WEBSITES

Black Liberation

African National Congress: www.anc.org.za
Black Lives Matter: www.blacklivesmatter.com
Congress of Racial Equality: www.core-online.org
Nation of Islam: www.noi.org
National Association for the Advancement of Colored People: www.naacp.org
National Urban League: www.nul.org
New Black Panther Party: www.cbpm.org/nbpp.html
Southern Christian Leadership Conference: www.nationalsclc.org

Women's Liberation

Feminist Majority Foundation: www.feminist.org
Feminist.com Foundation: www.feminist.com
National Organization for Women: www.now.org
Radical Women: www.radicalwomen.org

Gay Liberation

ACT UP: www.actupny.org
GLBT Historical Society: www.glbthistory.org
Human Rights Campaign: www.hrc.org
Log Cabin Republicans: www.logcabin.org

Native Peoples' Liberation (Indigenism)

American Indian Movement: www.aimovement.org
First Nations: www.firstnations.org
Indigenous Waves: www.indigenouswaves.com
World Natives United: worldnativesunited.tribe.net
Zapatista Network: enlacezapatista.ezln.org.mx

Liberation Theology

Catholic Worker Movement: www.catholicworker.org
The Conviviality Project: www.krysallis.com
Liberation Theology Resources: www.liberationtheology.org
Sabeel Ecumenical Liberation Theology Center, Jerusalem: www.sabeel.org
Sojourners: www.sojo.net

Animal Liberation

Animal Liberation Front: www.animalliberationfront.com
People for the Ethical Treatment of Animals: www.peta.org
The Tom Regan Animal Rights Archive: www.lib.ncsu.edu/animalrights

CHAPTER 9

GREEN POLITICS: ECOLOGY AS IDEOLOGY

A thing is right when it tends to preserve the integrity, stability and beauty of the biotic community. It is wrong when it tends otherwise.

Aldo Leopold

As we have seen, ideologies are born of crisis. Starting from a shared sense that something is wrong, that the world is not as it should be, ideologies attempt to explain or account for puzzling or problematic features of people's lives. Then, on the basis of these explanations, they offer diagnoses and prescriptions for the ills of a troubled time. The ideology we examine in the present chapter is certainly no exception to this rule. Although many of its ideas are quite old, this ideology is quite new—so new, in fact, that it has, as yet, no generally agreed-upon name. The term "ecologism" has caught on and gained acceptance in Great Britain, as has "environmentalism" in the United States. But because many within this broad-based international movement call their perspective **green politics** and themselves "Greens," we will refer to them and their ideology in this way.[1]

The crisis out of which a broadly based green movement has emerged is the environmental crisis. Actually, this is not a single crisis but a series of crises arising in connection with the ecological and environmental damage wrought by population growth, pollution of air and water, the destruction of the tropical rain forests, the rapid extinction of entire species of plants and animals, the **greenhouse effect** (the warming of the earth's atmosphere), the destruction of forests and lakes by acid rain, the depletion of the earth's protective ozone layer, and other now-familiar instances of environmental damage and degradation.

These crises are interconnected. All, moreover, are the result of human actions and practices over the past two centuries. Many are by-products of technological innovations, such as the internal combustion engine. But the causes of these environmental crises, according to many environmentalists, are as much ideological as they are technological. They stem, that is, from ideas and ideologies that place human beings above or apart from nature. Against these, an emerging green movement proposes its own *counter-ideology*, which has two main aspects. This counter-ideology consists, first of all, of a critique of some of the key assumptions underlying the ideologies that have long dominated modern politics. Second, it attempts to offer a more positive and hopeful vision of human beings' relation with the natural environment and with one another.

It would be a mistake, however, to think of advocates of a green or environmental ideology as exclusively "liberal" or left-leaning. To be sure, some—such as former Vice President Al Gore—are decidedly liberal in their outlook. But some call themselves "conservative environmentalists" in the tradition of Edmund Burke, who wrote that each generation has a duty to leave to posterity "an habitation," not a "ruin."[2] (Until the election of Ronald Reagan in 1980 the Republican Party was the pro-environment or "conservation" party. A Republican president, Theodore Roosevelt, established the National Park system in the United States. Another Republican president, Richard Nixon, created the Environmental Protection Agency in 1970 to coincide with the first annual Earth Day.) Others call themselves free-market or libertarian environmentalists because they believe that free-market competition and private ownership of property are the best means of protecting the natural environment.[3] Still others proceed from the religious premise that the earth and its environment are to be treated with the reverence befitting God's creation. Human beings have a sacred duty to care for and be good stewards of nature, they contend, and not to exploit or despoil it for momentary pleasure or profit.[4]

Claiming to be "neither right nor left," environmentalism has adherents all along the ideological spectrum. A "new green ideology," writes one prominent commentator, "has the power to mobilize liberals and conservatives, evangelicals and atheists, big business and environmentalists around an agenda that can both pull us together and propel us forward."[5] For example, increasing numbers of evangelical Christians have come to believe that being conservative requires, as the word implies, "conserving" or caring for life: not only the life of the unborn but all of God's creation, including plants, animals, habitats, ecosystems—in short, the natural environment. The U.S. Conference of Catholic Bishops has called upon Catholics and their fellow Christians to be caretakers or "stewards" of the environment. That message has recently been conveyed even more forcefully in Pope Francis's far-reaching (critics say radical) encyclical *Laudato si': On Care for Our Common Home* (2015).[6] In a similar spirit such Protestant organizations as EarthCare and the Evangelical Environmental Network cite Genesis 2:15— "Then the Lord God put the man [Adam] in the Garden of Eden to cultivate it and take care of it"—and call upon Christians to engage in **"creation care."** As one evangelical Christian succinctly summarized their view, "If you worship the Creator, you take care of His creation."[7] This concern led eighty-six evangelical Christian leaders to sponsor the "Evangelical Climate Initiative" and in February 2006 to issue "An Evangelical Call to Action" against global warming.[8] Such actions have led to an increasingly bitter and public split within the ranks of American evangelical Christians.[9]

There are differences among Greens, then, just as there are differences among liberals, conservatives, socialists, and the adherents of other ideologies. But there is little disagreement about the urgency of the need to rethink our attitudes toward and actions within the natural environment.

THE GREEN CRITIQUE OF OTHER IDEOLOGIES

To devise and act upon an alternative environmental ideology, say the Greens, is not merely one option among many. It may be the only remaining chance that human beings have to save the planet's myriad species—including the human species itself, which is linked to, and deeply dependent upon, other species of plants and animals. All species are, in a word, interdependent. To see this interdependence in action, consider the tale of the tree. Trees are a source not only of shade and lumber but also of oxygen, which they exchange for the carbon dioxide (CO_2) that is a by-product of burning and other processes of oxidation, including our own breathing: approximately twenty times per minute we breathe in a mixture of oxygen and nitrogen, exhaling CO_2 with every breath. To clear-cut tropical rain forests or to destroy northern forests with acid rain is therefore to reduce the amount of oxygen available for us and other creatures to breathe. This in turn increases the amount of CO_2 in the atmosphere, which results in the further warming of the earth's atmosphere, known as "the greenhouse effect." This global warming in its turn brings drought, transforms formerly fertile land into deserts and dust bowls, and thereby reduces crop production, which means that humans and animals go hungry or perhaps even starve. Global warming is already bringing in its wake the gradual melting of the polar ice caps. This will raise sea levels and eventually flood, thereby raising sea levels and permanently flooding many low-lying coastal areas, including most of Florida and much of countries like Bangladesh.

The moral of the tale of the tree is simply this: all things are connected. Or, to put the point another way: what goes around, comes around. In one sense, of course, this is not an entirely new message. All of the world's great religions have said much the same thing in one way or another. "Whatsoever a man soweth, that shall he also reap" (Galatians 6:7). This is true not only of individuals but also of human beings from one generation to another. "The fathers have eaten sour grapes and their children's teeth are set on edge" (Ezekiel 18:2). In other words, what human beings do in one time and place will affect other human beings, and other species, in other times and places. All actions, however small, can have large and long-lasting consequences.

But while the world's major religions have taught that all things are interconnected, most of the major modern ideologies have not. It is for this reason that the Greens tend to be quite critical of other ideologies, **right** and **left** alike. They criticize not only the specific beliefs and doctrines of those other ideologies but, no less important, their unexamined assumptions as well.

Consider, for example, the assumptions about nature and human beings' relationship to nature shared by several modern ideologies. Liberals, socialists, and individualist conservatives have shared a similar attitude toward nature, one that celebrates the ever-increasing human "conquest" or "mastery" of nature. They tend to see nature as either a hostile force to be conquered or a resource base to be harnessed for such human purposes as "growth" and "economic development." Technological, scientific, and economic progress is therefore to be measured in terms of the human species' power over nature. Such an adversarial attitude was expressed early on by seventeenth-century thinkers, including Thomas Hobbes's friend Sir Francis Bacon. Indeed, Bacon speaks of nature much as the Marquis de

Sade was later to speak of women. Nature (always "her") is haughty and proud but must be subdued and humbled by "man," whose sense of power increases with his "conquest" of nature. Nature must be "interrogated," "subdued," and made to "yield up her secrets" to man, Bacon declared, so that man can then turn nature's secrets against her, "shaping nature as on an anvil." Through their technology men do not "merely exert a gentle guidance over nature's course; they have the power to conquer and subdue her, to shake her to her foundations." Finally, "by art and the hand of man she is forced out of her natural state, and squeezed and moulded" for human purposes.[10] Similarly, though less "sadistically," John Locke believed that nature in itself was without value. It is only when people put "waste" land and resources to human use that they acquire whatever "value" they have: "land that is left wholly to nature, that hath no improvement of pasturage, tillage, or planting, is called, as indeed it is, waste; and we shall find the benefit of it amount to little more than nothing."[11] Karl Marx, critical as he was of capitalism and the liberal ideology that justified it, nevertheless waxed enthusiastic about the increased power over nature that capitalism had brought about:

> The bourgeoisie, during its rule of scarce one hundred years, has created more massive and more colossal productive forces than have all preceding generations together. Subjection of nature's forces to man, machinery, application of chemistry to industry and agriculture, steam navigation, railways, electric telegraphs, clearing of whole continents for cultivation, canalization of rivers, whole populations conjured up out of the ground—what earlier century had even a presentiment that such productive forces slumbered in the lap of social labor?[12]

And Ayn Rand, in her novel *The Fountainhead*, has its hero Howard Roarke viewing a pristine mountain lake ringed by granite cliffs and pine trees:

> He looked at the granite. To be cut, he thought, and made into walls. He looked at a tree. To be split and made into rafters. He looked at a streak of rust on the stone and thought of iron ore under the ground. To be melted and to emerge as girders against the sky.
>
> These rocks, he thought, are here for me; waiting for the drill, the dynamite and my voice; waiting to be split, ripped, pounded, reborn; waiting for the shape my hands will give them.[13]

Rand's hero presents us with a near-perfect expression of the anthropocentric (human-centered) outlook that nature has no **intrinsic value**—that is, value in and of itself—but has value only as a "resource base" for human beings to draw upon and use for their own purposes.

In light of this view, Greens say that it is scarcely surprising that liberal capitalist and communist societies are alike in sharing an "anthropocentric" or "humanistic" bias.[14] Both tend to prefer economic "growth" and productivity to the protection of the natural environment. Nor is it surprising, they say, that rivers like the Volga and the Mississippi are little more than open sewers and that the lakes and fish and pine trees of Siberia and New England and Canada are being poisoned by acid rain. Although the Soviet Union was the scene of the world's worst nuclear accident to date—at Chernobyl in 1986—the United States came quite close to disaster at Three Mile Island in Pennsylvania in 1979, and Japan met catastrophe with the

Fukushima Daiichi nuclear disaster in 2011. Past and possible future accidents aside, the United States, Russia, China, and other countries are producing deadly nuclear and chemical wastes without any means of storing them safely for the tens of thousands of years that they will remain highly dangerous to the health of humans and other beings.

From a purely ecological point of view, Greens see little difference between communism and capitalism. The ideologies by means of which both systems justify themselves are largely heedless of the natural environment upon which we and all creatures ultimately rely. Therefore, say the Greens, we need to rethink the assumptions on which these influential ideologies are founded in the first place. More than that, we need to devise an alternative ideology that recognizes and respects nature's delicate system of checks and balances.

TOWARD AN ECOLOGICAL ETHIC

Many Greens prefer not to call their perspective an ideology but an "ethic." Earlier ecological thinkers, such as Aldo Leopold, spoke of a **land ethic**.[15] Others have spoken, more recently, of an ethic with earth itself at its center,[16] while others, in a similar spirit, speak of an emerging "planetary ethic."[17] Despite differences of accent and emphasis, however, all appear to be alike in several crucial respects.

An environmental or ecological ethic—which environmental thinkers sometimes call **biocentrism** (a life-centered ethic) or **ecocentrism** (an ecosystem-centered ethic)—these thinkers say, would at a minimum include the following features. First, such an ethic would emphasize the web of interconnections and mutual dependence within which we and other species live. People are connected both with one another and with other species of animals and plants. The latter include not only those that human beings eat—fish, cows, and corn, for example—but also the tiny plankton on which whales and ocean fish feed, the insects and minnows eaten by lake and river fish, and the worms that loosen and aerate the soil in which the corn grows. The corn feeds the cows that fertilize the fields, and the humans eat the fish, the corn, and the cows. All are interdependent participants in the cycle of birth, life, death, decay, and rebirth. All of the participants in this cycle depend upon the air and water, the sunlight and soil, without which life is impossible.

These, the Greens say, are elemental truths that we forget at our peril. Yet forget them we have. In separating ourselves from nature, we have divided our lives and experiences into separate compartments. We think of vegetables and meats as commodities that come from the grocery store wrapped in plastic and Styrofoam, for instance, and water as it comes from the faucet or bottle. We rarely pause to reflect upon what makes these things possible and available to us, or of how much we depend on them—and they on us. But this sense of disconnectedness, the Greens charge, is an illusion that, unless dispelled, will doom our species and many others to extinction.

But where do we go to learn about these interconnections? There are many available avenues. One is science, particularly the disciplines of biology, **ecology**, and geology, and also literature, music, and art. Philosophy and various religions also have much to contribute. But one neglected source, the Greens remind us, is to be found in the folk wisdom of native peoples, such as the Indians of North

America. The land and air and water belong to everybody and to nobody, according to this folk wisdom; nature is not for sale at any price, for it is not a commodity that exists apart from us. On the contrary, we are part of the earth and it is part of us. To fail to recognize this interconnectedness is to doom our own species and all others to increasing misery and even eventual extinction.

Several other features of an environmental, or green, ethic follow from the recognition of interconnectedness and interdependence. The first of these is a respect for life—not only human life but all life, from the tiniest microorganism to the largest whale. The fate of our species is tied to theirs, and theirs to ours. Because life requires certain conditions to sustain it, a second feature follows: we have an obligation to respect and care for the conditions that nurture and sustain life in its many forms. From the aquifers below to the soil and water and air above, nature nourishes its creatures within a complex web of interconnected conditions. To damage one is to damage the others, and to endanger the existence of any creatures that dwell within and depend upon the integrity of this delicate, life-sustaining web is to endanger all.

To acknowledge this interdependence is not, however, to overlook or deny the enormous power that humans have over nature. On the contrary, it requires that we recognize the extent of our power—and that we take full responsibility for restraining it and using it wisely and well. Greens point out that the fate of the earth and all its creatures now depends, for better or for worse, on human decisions and actions. Not only do we depend on nature, they say, but nature depends on us—on our care and restraint and forbearance. It is within our power to destroy the earth many times over. This we can do very quickly in the case of nuclear war (or rather—because the word "war" implies victors and vanquished, and nuclear war will have no winners—"nuclear omnicide," that is, the destruction of everything and everyone). Every local conflict, however small at first, could turn into a nuclear confrontation, with predictably deadly results. From this emerges a further feature of a "green" ethic: Greens must work for peace. This is not to say that Greens are to avoid all confrontation or conflict but that they are to employ the tactics of direct confrontation, of nonviolent protest and resistance, in the manner of Mahatma Gandhi (1869–1948), Martin Luther King, Jr. (1929–1968), and others. Many militant Greens have done this, not only in antiwar protests but also in attempts to slow or stop the clear-cutting of old-growth forests, the construction of nuclear power plants, and other activities they deem to be destructive of the natural environment.

Such a stance is now necessary, in their view, because the earth and all its inhabitants can be destroyed both by nuclear omnicide and by slower, though no less destructive, methods of environmental degradation, including the cumulative effects of small-scale, everyday acts. All actions, however small or seemingly insignificant, produce consequences or effects, sometimes out of all proportion to the actions that bring them about. (Consider, for example, the simple act of drinking coffee from a Styrofoam cup. That convenient but nonbiodegradable container will still be around for many hundreds of years after its user's body has been recycled into the soil.) In modern industrial society the old adage "Mighty oaks from tiny acorns grow" might well be amended to read, "Mighty disasters from tiny actions grow." It is from our everyday actions, however insignificant they might appear to be, that large-scale environmental consequences follow; hence the duty of **stewardship**.

Stewardship and Future Generations. To be a steward is to be responsible for the care of something, and Greens contend that we all must be stewards of the earth. This stewardship includes a duty to take into account the health and well-being of distant future generations. Humans now have the power to alter the natural environment permanently in ways that will affect the health, happiness, and well-being of people who will not be born until long after we are all dead. The radioactive wastes generated by nuclear power plants, for example, will be intensely "hot" and highly toxic far into the future. No one yet knows how to store such material safely for hundreds, much less the necessary tens of thousands, of years. Obviously it would be unjust for the present generation to enjoy the benefits of nuclear power while passing on to distant posterity the burdens and dangers brought about by our actions.

There are many other, less dramatic but no less serious, examples of intergenerational harm or hazard that Greens warn against: global warming, loss of precious topsoil, disappearing rain forests, the emptying and/or polluting of underground aquifers, and the depletion of nonrenewable energy sources, such as fossil fuels. Reserves of oil and natural gas are finite and irreplaceable. Once burned as gasoline—or turned into plastic or some other petroleum-based product—a gallon of oil is gone forever; every drop or barrel used now is therefore unavailable for future people to use. As Wendell Berry observes, the oft-heard claim that fossil-fuel energy is "cheap" rests on a simplistic and morally doubtful assumption about the "rights" of the present generation:

> We were able to consider [fossil fuel] "cheap" only by a kind of moral simplicity: the assumption that we had a "right" to as much of it as we could use. This was a "right" made solely by might. Because fossil fuels, however abundant they once were, were nevertheless limited in quantity and not renewable, they obviously did not "belong" to one generation more than another. We ignored the claims of posterity simply because we could, the living being stronger than the unborn, and so worked the "miracle" of industrial progress by the theft of energy from (among others) our children.

And this, Berry adds,

> is the real foundation of our progress and our affluence. The reason that we [in the United States] are a rich nation is not that we have earned so much wealth—you cannot, by any honest means, earn or deserve so much. The reason is simply that we have learned, and become willing, to market and use up in our own time the birthright and livelihood of posterity.[18]

These and other considerations lead Greens to advocate limits on present-day consumption so as to save a fair share of scarce resources for future generations.

But why, skeptics ask, should we do anything for posterity? After all, what has posterity ever done for us?[19] What motivation might we have to act now for the sake and safety of future people? These questions raise the so-called *time-horizon* problem.

Time Horizons and Collective Action. "Time horizon" refers to how far ahead people think when they are deciding what to do. Horizons mark the limits of our vision—of how far we can see—so a *time* horizon marks the limit of how far into the future people can or will see. Those people who always seem to be planning years and even decades in advance have long time horizons; those who have trouble thinking beyond today have very short ones. But everyone faces the question of how to weigh the value of something near at hand against the value of something in the future. If someone offers to give you $20 today or $20 tomorrow, for instance, you would almost certainly take the money today. If you were offered a choice between $20 today or $22 tomorrow, you would have to decide whether the extra $2 was worth the wait. And if you had to choose between $20 now and $200 a year from now, what would you do? In general, the more distant the benefit, the greater the benefit must be to compensate for the delay in receiving it.

This time-horizon problem is especially troublesome for Greens. When they urge people to sacrifice now for the sake of the future—to cut back on driving and airplane travel in order to reduce current CO_2 emissions or to conserve fossil fuels for future generations, for example—Greens are asking people to adopt a time horizon that extends far beyond their own lives. Worse yet, persuading people to care about the well-being of future generations may not be enough to persuade them to make sacrifices for the sake of the future. Greens will also have to convince people that their individual sacrifices will actually do someone some good. For why should you, or anyone, make a sacrifice for the sake of the future unless you can be sure that many other people will make a similar sacrifice?

Thus Greens face a second problem—the problem of *collective action*—when they urge people to consume less and conserve more for the benefit of future generations. In this case, in fact, the problem applies to sacrifices made for the good of people who are now living as well as the good of those who may or will live in the future. To understand this collective-action problem, we must grasp the difference between *private* and *public* goods. A "private good" is anything, such as money or food, that can be divided and distributed. If Ann and Bob buy a cake, they can divide it between themselves as they see fit. They can also refuse to give any of it to anyone who did not help to pay for the cake. But a "public good" cannot be divided or distributed in this way. In technical terms, public goods are "indivisible" and "nonrival." In other words, a public good cannot be divided into portions, nor is there any competition or rivalry to possess it. Clean air is a standard example: it cannot be divided, and no one's enjoyment or use of it prevents anyone else from enjoying or using it equally.

Problems arise, though, when a public good requires the cooperation of many people, as it does in efforts to reduce pollution or conserve resources. In such cases individuals have little reason to cooperate by joining the effort, especially when cooperation is unpleasant. One person's contribution—using less gasoline or electricity, for example—will make no real difference to the success or failure of the effort, but it will be a hardship for that person. So a rational, self-interested person will try to be a "free rider"—that is, try to withhold cooperation while hoping that enough people will participate to make the effort a success. If that happens, then the free rider will eventually enjoy the public good of cleaner air even though he or she did nothing to help reduce air pollution. If too many people try to be free riders, of course, the attempt to produce the public good will fail for lack of cooperation (as Figure 9.1 illustrates). But every person who tried to be a free rider can always say, "My actions didn't make the difference. The effort would have failed whether I joined in or not."

This collective-action problem leads to many social and political difficulties, not the least of which are environmental. It may explain, for example, why voluntary campaigns to reduce automobile traffic and cut energy or water use so often fail. As formulated in the "tragedy of the commons," moreover, collective-action theory accounts for the tendency to overuse and exhaust common resources, such as grazing land, fishing banks, and perhaps the earth itself. The American ecologist Garrett Hardin developed this idea in an essay, "The Tragedy of the Commons," by using the history of the village commons in England as a model of the relationship between modern society and the natural environment.[20] English villagers once had the right to graze their livestock on common land that belonged to the whole village. If they grazed too many animals there, the grass would be depleted and no more grazing would be possible. Yet every villager had an incentive to add more and more animals to the common land, for the gain from raising another sheep or cow always outweighed, from the individual's point of view, the damage to the commons that one more animal would cause. One more sheep or cow would not ruin the commons by itself, so why not add it to the land? The commons was thus a public good, and every villager had an incentive to try to be a free rider—in this case, to put more animals on the land while hoping that others would reduce their herds or flocks. As long as the villagers thought and acted in this way, the result, sooner or later, would be the overgrazing of the commons and a disaster for the entire village.

Hardin's conclusion—and the conclusion reached by most Greens—is that society cannot rely on voluntary efforts or appeals to individual consciences to solve such environmental problems as overfishing, overgrazing, and pollution of the air and water. The earth's atmosphere and oceans are "commons" that are in grave danger, not because of some large anti-planetary conspiracy but because of a lack of coordinated regulation and the gradual accumulation of the effects of small and seemingly insignificant actions. The earth itself may be in danger of exhaustion, but no individual's action will be sufficient to prevent its collapse. Instead, Hardin's solution is "mutual coercion, mutually agreed upon by the

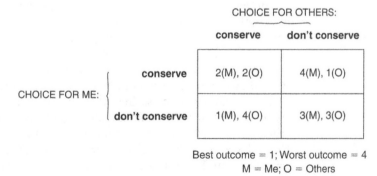

FIGURE 9.1 The collective-action problem illustrated: is it rational for the individual to try to conserve resources when he or she does not know whether others will conserve?

majority of the people affected." Just as the villagers need to arrive at a collective solution to the problem of overgrazing by setting a limit to the number of animals anyone may put out to graze on the commons—and by punishing those who exceed the limit—so people in modern industrial societies need to find ways to force themselves, through taxes and penalties, rules and regulations, to limit their use of fossil fuels and other natural resources. Otherwise, the destruction of the environment will proceed apace.

Together, the problems of collective action and time horizons explain why Greens must engage in politics. If they are to meet and overcome the environmental crises, Greens must be able to persuade people to change how they think about the world and their place in it. But that is not enough. Greens must also bring about changes in laws and policies so that people have an incentive, as individuals, to think about the effects of their actions on future generations and cooperate in the preservation of clean air, fresh water, and other natural resources. This means that Greens must take political action.

From the Greens' perspective, each of us is an actor—whether as producer, consumer, or in some other role—so each of us bears full responsibility for his or her actions and, in a democracy, partial responsibility for others' actions as well. Each of us has, or can have, a hand in making the laws and policies under which we live. For this reason Greens give equal emphasis to our collective and individual responsibility for protecting the environment that protects us. Greens are, in short, "small d" democrats whose "ethic" emphasizes the importance of informed and active democratic citizenship. But as to what that ethic consists of, and as regards the best way of informing oneself and others and of being an active citizen, Greens differ among themselves.

UNRESOLVED DIFFERENCES

Environmentalists come, so to speak, in several shades of green. "Light Green" reform-minded environmentalists favor laws and public policies that serve human needs and wants while minimizing damage to the natural environment. "Dark Green" environmentalists favor more radical measures to roll back development and to protect and even extend wilderness areas.[21] Another way of describing this difference is suggested by the Norwegian mountaineer and "ecosopher" (eco-philosopher) Arne Naess. Naess (1912–2009) draws a distinction between "shallow environmentalism" and **deep ecology**. The former perspective puts human beings at the center of concern and views environmental problems in "anthropocentric" and "instrumental" terms. Thus a shallow environmentalist might favor saving the spotted owl or some species of whale so that human owl- or whale-watchers might derive satisfaction from seeing such animals. The deep ecologist, by contrast, contends that owls and whales—indeed, all living creatures and the ecosystems that support them—are not instrumentally but *intrinsically* valuable. That is, they have value in and of themselves, quite apart from the value that human beings may place on them. Deep ecology is thus a *biocentric* (or life-centered) perspective that places other species and ecosystems on a par with human beings.[22]

Still another way of describing these differences among environmentalists is to say that some subscribe to a "garden" and others to a "wilderness" view.[23]

Defenders of the garden view, such as René Dubos and Wendell Berry, hold that human beings are part of nature and that part of *their* nature and their need is to cultivate the earth.[24] This humans must do if they are to feed, clothe, and shelter themselves. Such cultivation should be done carefully and reverently, but it must be done if human well-being is to be advanced. Defenders of the garden view tend to be critical of the wilderness perspective that puts the interests of nonhuman animals and their habitats ahead of legitimate human interests. Humans are animals too, with their own species-specific needs and their own ways of living in and transforming nature. As Berry puts it:

> People cannot live apart from nature; that is the first principle of the conservationists. And yet, people cannot live in nature without changing it. But this is true of *all* creatures; they depend upon nature, and they change it. What we call nature is, in a sense, the sum of the changes made by all the various creatures and natural forces in their intricate actions upon each other and upon their places.[25]

Defenders of the wilderness view, such as Edward Abbey and Dave Foreman (cofounder of Earth First!), see matters differently. Humans have taken over and despoiled too much of the earth, all in the name of "progress" or "development." They have clear-cut old-growth forests, strip-mined mountain ranges, destroyed animal habitats and entire ecosystems, dammed rivers, turned forested mountainsides into ski slopes—all the while heedless of the effects of their actions on animals and the long-term health of the ecosystems that sustain them. To take only two of many examples, wolves were until very recently nearly extinct in the lower forty-eight states of the United States (and even endangered in Alaska), and grizzly bears and mountain lions fared little better. These and other species are out of place in a "garden" and at home only in "wilderness"—or, as Foreman prefers to say, "the Big Outside." These and other species cannot disappear without taking something precious away from the human species. As Foreman notes:

> We retain these fearsome beasts as cultural icons—the University of New Mexico's football team, the Lobos [wolves], the Grizzly Bear on the state flag of California—but unless we share the land with them again, the [American] West will become as tame spiritually and ecologically as Britain.[26]

Bears and other wild animals have as much right as humans to live satisfying lives. We humans are not, or should not regard ourselves as, masters of nature. On the contrary, as Aldo Leopold puts it in *A Sand County Almanac*—which Foreman calls "the most important, the loveliest, the wisest book ever penned"[27]—an alternative "land ethic" requires that humans see themselves in a more humble role: "In short, a land ethic changes the role of *Homo sapiens* from conqueror of the land-community to plain member and citizen of it. It implies respect for his fellow-members, and also respect for the community as such."[28] As Leopold tells the story, he began to appreciate the need for this land ethic when, as a young employee of the U.S. Forest Service, he shot a she-wolf. Leopold had accepted the Forest Service's policy of exterminating predators, but he had an epiphany when he approached the wolf he had shot and saw "a fierce green fire dying in her eyes." Wolves and other predators, he came to realize, have their rightful place in the order

Courtesy of the Aldo Leopold Foundation, www.aldoleopold.org

Aldo Leopold (1887–1948)

of nature. Like their prey, they are indispensable parts of complexly interdependent ecosystems. Remove them, and the entire ecosystem is endangered.

For Leopold, then, the central precept of an environmental or land ethic is this: "A thing is right when it tends to preserve the integrity, stability, and beauty of the biotic community. It is wrong when it tends otherwise."[29] But what, exactly, are the bases of these moral and philosophical precepts? How are they to be translated into political action? Can the differences between the various "shades" of Greens be resolved? These are among the questions that the relatively new green or environmental movement has raised but has yet to answer in a clear and comprehensive manner.

Consider first the question: Do we need an entirely new ethic—a distinctly ecological ethic—to protect the planet, its people present and future, and its fragile ecosystems? Some radical or "Dark Green" environmentalists answer in the affirmative, claiming that the Western philosophical tradition is replete with subtle, systematic, and pervasive prejudices against the weak: women, minorities, animals, and, weakest of all, generations yet unborn. We are therefore in dire need of an entirely new ethic, if we are to respect and protect the health of the earth and the well-being of future people, species, and ecosystems. The proposed counter-discourse is almost always characterized by its adherents with the prefix "post" and the suffix "ism"—post-humanism, post-individualism, and the like. The concepts and categories and frameworks that belong to "Western culture" need to be obliterated and replaced root and branch by something new, non-Western, and not at all beholden to "dead white males" (mostly philosophers) whose works comprise the "canon" of Western political and philosophical thinking.[30]

Critics, by contrast, contend that the Western tradition (supplemented, to be sure, by Eastern and other traditions of thought) is rich and varied enough to supply the scaffolding of an environmental ethic. Some have suggested that Plato, that deadest of dead white males, and his pupil Aristotle have much to teach us.[31] This is *not* to say that they were environmentalists in our modern sense (how could they be?), only that their thought is open to a "green" interpretation and application. The same can be said of St. Francis of Assisi (the namesake of the present Pope), of Jean-Jacques Rousseau (about whom, more in a moment), Edmund Burke, John Stuart Mill, and many other contributors to the "canon" of Western thought.[32] To illustrate how this might be done, recall Mill's "harm principle," previously discussed (Chapter 3, pp. 77–79). When Mill says that "harm to others" is sufficient reason to place limitations on the freedom of individuals to act, he does not specify who those "others" are. They could conceivably include future people, or animals, or even ecosystems.

This has made for a lively and ongoing debate about the character and sources of an emerging environmental or land ethic. Is it sacred, as some Greens suggest, or is it secular and scientific, as others insist? A second question, or rather series of questions, concerns the strategies and tactics to be employed by the environmental movement. Should Greens act in new and different ways, or in ways that the various "interest groups" have traditionally acted? Should they, for example, form their own political party, or work within existing parties? Should they hire lobbyists to influence legislation, or work outside conventional interest-group politics? After all, as Greens often note, the earth and its human and nonhuman inhabitants are hardly one "special interest" among others. Let us consider each of these issues in turn.

An environmental ethic, according to some Greens, is in the final analysis religious or spiritual, resting as it does on the virtues of humility, respect, and reverence. An environmental ethic entails humility in the face of our individual mortality and our collective status not as solitary dwellers on or masters of our planet but as one species and generation among many. An environmental ethic also requires that we respect life in all its forms and the conditions, both animate and inanimate, that sustain and nurture it. Finally, such an ethic entails an attitude of reverence and awe. It requires that we revere, cherish, and care for other people and other species not only in our own time but also in the generations and ages to come. We have, to paraphrase Edmund Burke, a sacred obligation to leave to future generations a habitation instead of a ruin.

On this much, at least, most Greens agree. But beyond this point agreement ends and differences begin to appear, as some Greens take a spiritual or religious turn that other Greens find odd, or worse. Those who conceive of an environmental ethic grounded in spiritual or religious values say that we should look upon the earth as a benevolent and kindly deity—the goddess Gaia (from the Greek word for "earth")—to be worshipped in reverence and awe. A number of Greens, including some (but not all) of those who call themselves "deep ecologists," suggest this as a way of liberating ourselves from the confines of a purely materialistic or scientific perspective into another state of mind, one more attuned to "listening" to and learning from nature than to talking to and dictating for it.[33] Others, however, seem to speak of the goddess Gaia in a less metaphorical and more literal fashion.[34]

Some deep ecologists, particularly those affiliated with the Earth First! movement, are inclined to speak neither in humanistic nor in religious terms but in a more Malthusian idiom. Thomas Malthus was the nineteenth-century English cleric and economist who claimed—as we saw in Chapter 7—that human population increases geometrically (that is, at an ever-increasing rate) while the resources available to sustain that population increase at an arithmetic (that is, a steady) rate. Thus, according to **Malthus's law** (see Figure 7.2), the ever-growing human population increasingly outstrips available resources, with hunger and starvation the inevitable result. From widespread starvation comes a further result: a new equilibrium between population and resources. Unfortunately, this short-lived equilibrium ends as population increases, and the cycle begins all over again. Taking their cue from Malthus, the leading thinkers of Earth First!—including the late novelist Edward Abbey and Dave Foreman, former editor of the newsletter *Earth First!*—claim that nature is not without its own resources for countering human hubris and error. Widespread starvation, famine, floods, forest fires, drought, the AIDS epidemic, the Ebola virus—by these and other means, nature chastises the heedless human species and punishes at least some of its members for their species' pride, ignorance, and/or indifference. Although the language of Earth First! is not religious, its vision of dire punishments sometimes seems to come straight from the vengeful God of the Old Testament.

By contrast, ecologists of a more secular stripe are apt to regard any talk of religion and goddesses and deep ecology with deep suspicion, if not downright hostility. These critics include the "social ecologist" Murray Bookchin (1921–2006), among many others. They contend that talk about goddesses is mystical mumbo jumbo to be avoided at all costs. And they view Earth First! as an antihuman and inhumane organization that seeks to remove human beings from the ecological equation entirely. By contrast, **social ecologists** acknowledge humanity's dependency on and responsibility for the environment, but hold that human life has special status and importance. They also argue that human beings are not all equally responsible for the systematic and continuing pillaging of the planet. The chief culprits are the most powerful, privileged, and wealthiest humans who own and operate the large multinational corporations and who not only dominate the natural environment but subjugate human beings as well. The domination and resulting destruction of nature begins in the domination of some human beings by others.

Proponents of **ecofeminism** agree with social ecologists that environmental plunder and predation are practiced on a global scale by the most powerful, privileged, and wealthy human beings, but add that these humans are mostly male, Western, and white. And these men have an "androcentric" or male-centered outlook that leads them to regard nature as feminine ("Mother Nature") and therefore to regard nature's interests, like the interests of women, as rightfully subordinate to the interests of men. Such androcentric beliefs, when acted upon, result in the rampant destruction of ecosystems and the human and nonhuman creatures who depend on them. Western androcentrism is said by such ecofeminists as Vandana Shiva (1952–) to wreak particular havoc in the lives and livelihoods of women in the Third World.[35]

Other differences within the broadly based green movement are beginning to emerge. Although all agree about the importance of informing and educating the public, they are divided over how this might best be done. Some say that Greens should take an active part in electoral politics. This is the course favored by many European Greens, who have organized Green parties in Germany and other countries and have won seats in various national parliaments. In the United States, Green Party candidate Ralph Nader won 3 percent of the vote in the 2000 presidential election. However, most Greens, mindful of the difficulties facing minority third parties, have generally opted for other strategies. Social ecologists, for example, tend to favor local grassroots campaigns to involve neighbors and friends in efforts to protect the environment. Some, though not all, social ecologists are **anarchists**, who see the state and its "pro-growth" policies as the problem rather than the solution and seek its eventual replacement by a decentralized system of communes and cooperatives.[36]

Other Greens have chosen to pursue quite different strategies. Some groups, such as Greenpeace (greenpeace.org/international), favor dramatic direct action calculated to make headlines and capture public attention. Greenpeace activists have interposed their bodies between whalers' power harpoons and the whalers' prey, for instance. They have also confronted hunters in search of baby seals and tracked down and publicly exposed those who illegally dump toxic wastes. These and other tactics have been publicly condemned by the governments of Japan, Iceland, and France. In 1985 French agents in neutral New Zealand blew up and sank Greenpeace's oceangoing vessel, *The Rainbow Warrior*, killing a crew member. (After that attack, donations poured in, and a new and larger vessel, *Rainbow Warrior II*, was launched and commissioned to continue the work of its predecessor.) Even more militant groups, such as Earth First! (earthfirst.org), have advocated **ecotage** (ecological sabotage) or **monkey-wrenching** as morally justifiable means of protesting, if not always preventing, injuries and insults to the natural environment. Some members of Earth First! have "spiked"—that is, driven long metal spikes into—thousand-year-old redwood trees to prevent their being cut down by logging companies seeking short-term profits. The spike does no harm to the tree, although it poses a serious danger to any chainsaw or sawmill operator whose blade might strike it. These and other tactics are described, and even celebrated, in Edward Abbey's novel, *The Monkey-Wrench Gang* (1975), and described in detail in Dave Foreman's *Ecodefense: A Field Guide to Monkey Wrenching* (1985). Another group, the Sea Shepherd Society (seashepherd.org), takes direct action against human predators on the open ocean. Among other actions, they ram and disable whaling ships whose crews are hunting whales illegally in international waters. In so doing the Society says it is merely enforcing international laws and treaties regulating whaling—laws that are almost never enforced otherwise—and by videotaping and televising these "enforcement actions" they make the public aware of what happens on the high seas and out of their sight.[37]

The tactics of Greenpeace and the more militant measures advocated by Earth First! and the Sea Shepherd Society have been criticized and disowned by other environmental groups, especially those favoring more subtle, low-key efforts to influence legislation and inform the public on environmental matters. The Sierra Club, for example, actively lobbies Congress and state legislatures in hopes of passing laws to protect the natural environment. It also publishes books and produces films about a wide variety of environmental issues. Similar strategies are followed by other groups, such as the Environmental Defense Fund. Another group, the Nature Conservancy, solicits funds to buy land to turn into nature preserves.

Although quite new, the green movement is already beset by factional infighting. Anarchists are opposed to the tactics favored by environmental lobbyists; social ecologists are appalled by the political pronouncements of Earth First!; and the moderate and conservative members of the Nature Conservancy and Sierra Club are embarrassed by all the adverse publicity. Radical or "Dark Green" environmental groups are highly critical of these moderate or mainstream groups, which they regard as timid or ineffective, or both. Despite their disagreements, moderates and radicals criticize the federal Environmental Protection Agency, the U.S. Forest Service, and the Department of the Interior for being lax in enforcing existing environmental protection laws and for opposing stricter regulations on polluting industries, timber and mining companies, and other organizations. Critics charged that such laxity in environmental oversight characterized the eight years of the George W. Bush administration. Although President Obama's environmental record is mixed, he paid particular attention to the issue of climate change, over the strong objections of the Republican-controlled Congress. Only time will tell how effective his environmental efforts were. And of course future presidents will either build on his efforts or reverse them. He was a strong supporter of the international climate change accord signed in Paris in late 2015. At present, however, Greens disagree over whether President Obama's and other world leaders' means will be sufficient to the end of protecting the planet and its future inhabitants from climate change and its attendant maladies.

As Greens are quick to note, however, the important point is not that environmentalists sometimes disagree with others and among themselves about means but that they agree about fundamental assumptions and ends. They are alike in assuming that all things are connected—"ecology" is, after all, the study of interconnections—and they agree that the maintenance of complex ecosystems is not only a worthy goal but also a necessary one if the human race and other species are to survive.

And not only to survive physically but to flourish psychologically. That is the message of a newly emerging field within psychology. Ecopsychology studies the psychological relationship that humans have with nature and with animals and other humans in and through nature. Ecopsychology builds upon and extends the central insight in Edward O. Wilson's book, *Biophilia*.[38] As its title suggests, humans have an instinctive love of living things, not only their fellow human beings but all life-forms. As with any psychological condition, it can take either of two forms, healthy or unhealthy (or pathological). We humans are psychologically healthy when we feel a sense of kinship with and affection for the natural world. But when our love of nature is thwarted we experience psychological difficulties such as the mental stress and anxiety brought about by witnessing environmental degradation, the disappearance of entire species, and other modern maladies. According to a 2009 study by the American Psychological Association titled

"Interface Between Psychology and Global Climate Change," there are many and measurable emotional costs of environmental decline. These include feelings of despair, anxiety, grief, emotional numbness, and "a sense of being overwhelmed or powerless." Ecopsychology posits that our innate affection for nature has been largely lost, or at least impaired, in the unnatural or artificial setting of cities and suburbs, and that this loss engenders feelings of frustration, grief, powerlessness, and the like.

If ecopsychology's program of promoting the mental health of human beings by reconnecting them with nature and natural processes, and the reawakening of a sense of wonder and awe, is new, its message is not. It is at least as old as the Romantic movement of the eighteenth and nineteenth centuries. Before that time, most Westerners viewed wild nature with fear and foreboding. Forests were viewed as dark and threatening, and mountains as obstacles and impediments to human travel. Jean-Jacques Rousseau, the greatest of the Romantic thinkers—and "the first philosopher of the Greens"[39]—challenged that view in a variety of ways. In his widely read novel *Julie, ou La Nouvelle Héloïse*, Rousseau (1712–1778) has its hero Saint-Preux write to Julie:

> I came to the mountains to ponder, but my attention was captured by what was to be seen. At one moment immense rocks hung in ruins above my head. At another, high and rushing waterfalls overcame me with their heavy mist. Then an endless mountain stream opened beside me a ravine too deep for my eyes to penetrate. Now I found myself in the darkness of a somber forest. Then I emerged to find a pretty meadow to delight my eyes... It was at this altitude that I unwound perceptibly in the purity of the air, the true cause of the change of my spirits, the return of that inner peace which I had lost for so long... It seems that in rising above the level where men live, one leaves behind all base earthly feelings, and to the degree that one approaches the ethereal regions of the soul takes in some part of their unchanging purity.[40]

CONCLUSION

We have seen how and for what reasons the Greens criticize many modern mainstream ideologies. We have also noted their reluctance to view their perspective as an ideology. Is their "ethic" an "ideology"? We believe that it is, according to the criteria that we have proposed for identifying and explicating ideologies. First, an ecological ethic fulfills the four functions of an ideology. Second, it proposes and defends a particular view of liberty or freedom. Finally, it advances a particular conception of democracy. Let us briefly consider each of these features in turn.

Ecology as Ideology

An environmental or "green" ideology fulfills the four functions of an ideology, as outlined in Chapter 1. It is, first of all, *explanatory*: it offers an explanation of how the environmental crisis came about. That crisis grew out of the human hubris, or pride, that some Greens call **"anthropocentrism"** and others "humanism." The mistaken belief that human beings are self-sufficient and sovereign masters of nature underlies modern man's rampant and irresponsible disregard for the delicate and interconnected web of life. Second, the emerging green ideology supplies a standard for assessing and *evaluating* actions, practices, and policies. It applauds actions that tend to preserve and protect the natural environment—rain forests, wildlife habitats, wetlands, and other ecosystems—and condemns those that damage and destroy the natural environment. Third, this ideology *orients* its adherents, giving them a sense of identity. Greens think of themselves as members of a species whose health and very existence are deeply dependent upon other species and upon the conditions that nourish and nurture them all. Fourth, their ideology gives Greens a *program* of political and social action. They assume a responsibility for, among other things, promoting practices or policies that protect the natural environment and for educating and enlightening people who are heedless of the health of other species and of the natural environment as a whole. As they see it, only a massive and worldwide change of consciousness can save the planet and its species from heedless human depredation.

Ecology, Freedom, and the Democratic Ideal

As we noted in Chapter 1, every ideology subscribes to its own particular conception of freedom. The "green" or environmental ideology is no exception. Greens believe that human beings and other species can be truly free to flourish and survive only if they overcome, both in theory and in practice, the **arrogance of humanism**—the human-centered outlook that ignores the worth of other species and their environment. The green view of freedom can therefore be encapsulated in our triadic model (see Figure 9.2).

Finally, as we noted in Chapter 1, every modern ideology has its own characteristic interpretation of the democratic ideal. Once again, the Greens are no exception. As we saw earlier, the Greens believe that each of us bears a responsibility for protecting and preserving the environment. This includes not only the natural environment that sustains all creatures but also the social, economic, and political environment in which human beings live and work. People can flourish only within a political system that gives everyone a voice and a vote, thereby maximizing individual participation and personal responsibility. That system, say the Greens, is necessarily democratic. The best kind of democracy, they add, is a decentralized "grassroots" system that encourages and permits the widest possible participation.[41]

But three difficulties with this idealization of local democracy are immediately obvious. The first is that localized or grassroots democracy does not necessarily produce environmentally friendly or "green" outcomes. There is little doubt, for example, that if the decision to drill for oil in the Arctic National Wildlife Refuge were left to Alaskans, a majority would vote to commence drilling in that ecologically pristine region, with little or no regard for environmental protection and the well-being of native wildlife and the ecosystem that sustains it. They are, perhaps understandably, more concerned with jobs and economic "development" in the here-and-now than with environmental preservation for the sake of future generations.

A second difficulty derives from the fact that air and water pollution know no national or local boundaries. Far from staying put, they travel vast distances across oceans and national boundaries. Thus, for example, radioactive waste from

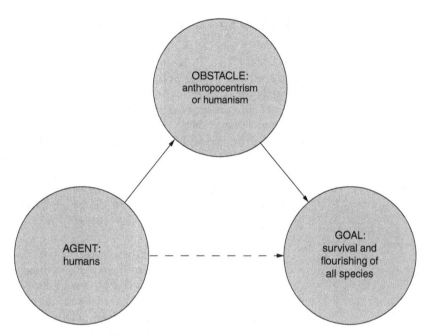

FIGURE 9.2 The "green" view of freedom.

Japan's Fukushima nuclear plant washed ashore on the American and Canadian west coast. And air pollution from China is increasingly appearing in western North America.[42] This suggests that the Green admonition to "Think globally and act locally" must now be amended to emphasize the importance—indeed, indispensability—of acting internationally in concert with other nations.

A third difficulty arises from following out the implications of the ancient adage, "What touches all should be decided by all." That is, everyone should have a say in deliberating about and deciding about matters that affect their interests and well-being. But of course animals—and future generations of human beings—have (or will have) interests but do not and cannot have a voice in present-day democratic discussions, debates, and deliberations. How then can their interests be recognized, respected, and protected in the present for the sake of their future health and well-being? The answer would seem to be some system of representative government which takes into account and protects the interests of non-present people, as well as those of animals and ecosystems. What such a system would look like is the subject of a lively and ongoing debate.[43] Should those now living elect or appoint an ombudsman to look after and represent the inarticulate and as-yet unborn? Or should each of us take responsibility for recognizing and protecting their interests? Perhaps only in such an enlarged democracy—or "biocracy"—can each of us take his or her full, fair, and equal share of responsibility for preserving our planet and all of its species, human and nonhuman, present and future, living and as-yet unborn.

Coda: The End of Environmentalism?

More than two decades ago, critics such as Anna Bramwell predicted "the fading of the Greens" and "the decline of environmental politics in the West."[44] More recently, others, such as Ted Nordhaus and Michael Shellenberger, have predicted not merely the decline but "the death of environmentalism."[45] Critics claimed that the environmental movement either was a passing fad and unable to gain political traction as actual public policy (Bramwell) or was predicated on a false picture of nature as an idyllic and harmonious whole that had been despoiled by heedless human beings. The ensuing predictions of gloom and doom (especially concerning climate change) were more likely to produce pessimism and resignation than to promote environmental activism (Nordhaus and Shellenberger). The former view is more negative and dismissive than the latter, which holds that everyone—even environmentalists—benefits by self-criticism and a rethinking of means if not necessarily of ends.

Environmentalists reply that what both of these viewpoints fail to note is that the environmental movement, far from dying or being already dead, is continuing to evolve and is adapting its ideology to changing conditions and circumstances. Instead of shouting insults from the sidelines they are involved in various political and lobbying organizations and are forging alliances with seemingly unlikely allies. One of these is the alliance between environmentalists and sportsmen—hunters and fishermen in particular, both of whom have a strong and shared interest in preserving wildlife habitat from the predations of developers and others who have scant regard for the well-being of animals and the ecosystems of which they—and we humans—are an integral part. Another is the "black-green" alliance of people of color and (mostly) white environmentalists. The Black Liberation theologian James H. Cone, for one, reminds us that poor African-Americans, Hispanics, and white people (in Appalachia and elsewhere) are much more likely than affluent whites to bear the brunt of environmental degradation. Most toxic waste dumps are located far from homes and businesses owned by affluent Americans and much closer to or even inside neighborhoods occupied by those who are disproportionately poor and people of color. In Appalachia large mining companies strip the tops off of mountains to take the coal, and dump the tops into the streams and valleys, which degrades and destroys the environment in which poor white people live and work. These and other forms of exploitation of the poor are unfair and unjust, and call for remedies that recognize the rights of all God's creatures, whatever their color or creed.[46] Environmentalists have also made common cause with labor unions to promote "fair trade" (instead of unregulated "free trade") in manufactured goods, the end of unfair labor practices in the United States and abroad, and the promotion of sustainable practices in logging, manufacturing, and agriculture. These and other alliances suggest that, far from fading or dying, the environmental movement continues to add a vibrant, vital, and distinctive voice to the oft-times off-key chorus of contemporary politics.

Discussion Questions

1 What are the major differences between "Light" and "Dark" Greens? With whom do you agree more? Why? Be specific.

2 How can Greens claim to be promoting democracy and freedom when they want to limit people's freedom to do as they like, at least with regard to the natural environment?

3 Many Greens see themselves as subscribing to a counter-ideology that tries to correct the mistaken beliefs and assumptions that underlie and inform other ideologies, including liberalism, modern conservatism, socialism, and communism. Are Greens right to trace many modern environmental problems to these ideologies? Why or why not?

4 Some are surprised by the alliance between hunters and fishermen, on the one hand, and environmentalists, on the other—and also between African-Americans and (mostly white) environmentalists. Should they be surprised? Why or why not? What issue(s), if any, makes them real but unlikely allies?

5 What is the new field of ecopsychology and what are its key tenets?

6 What is "creation care," who espouses it, and for what reason(s)?

7 How might "green democracy" differ from democracy as we now know it?

NOTES

1 See, for two very different exemplars, Fritjof Capra and Charlene Spritnak, *Green Politics* (New York: Dutton, 1984), and Robert E. Goodin, *Green Political Theory* (Cambridge: Polity Press, 1992).

2 Gordon K. Durnil, *The Making of a Conservative Environmentalist* (Bloomington: Indiana University Press, 1995); James R. Dunn and John E. Kinney, *Conservative Environmentalism* (Westport, CT: Quorum, 1996); John R. E. Bliese, *The Greening of Conservative America* (Boulder, CO: Westview Press, 2001); John Gray, *Beyond the New Right: Markets, Government, and the Common Environment* (London: Routledge, 1993), Chapter 4; Roger Scruton, "Conservatism," in Andrew Dobson and Robyn Eckersley, eds., *Political Theory and the Ecological Challenge* (Cambridge: Cambridge University Press, 2005); and Scruton, *How to Think Seriously About the Planet: The Case for an Environmental Conservatism* (Oxford and New York: Oxford University Press, 2012). For the original source and inspiration, see Edmund Burke, *Reflections on the Revolution in France*, C. C. O'Brien, ed. (Harmondsworth, U.K.: Penguin, 1969), p. 192.

3 Terry L. Anderson and Donald T. Leal, *Free Market Environmentalism* (Boulder, CO: Westview Press, 1991); William C. Mitchell and Randy T. Simmons, *Beyond Politics* (Boulder, CO: Westview Press, 1994).

4 Max Oelschlaeger, *Caring for Creation: An Ecumenical Approach to the Environmental Crisis* (New Haven, CT: Yale University Press, 1994); Robert Booth Fowler, *The Greening of Protestant Thought* (Chapel Hill: University of North Carolina Press, 1995).

5 Thomas L. Friedman, "The Power of Green," *New York Times Magazine*, April 15, 2007, p. 42.

6 Pope Francis, *Laudato si': On Care for Our Common Home* (The Vatican: Vatican Press, 2015); excerpted in Ball, Dagger, and O'Neill, eds., *Ideals and Ideologies: A Reader*, 10th ed. (New York and London: Routledge, 2016), selection 9.67.

7 Quoted in Neela Banerjee, "Citing Heavenly Injunctions to Fight Warming," *New York Times*, October 15, 2006, p. A19. See also, "'Creation Care' Concerns

Increase Among Evangelicals," *AP Dispatch*, September 8, 2006; and Lani Pearlman, "Evangelicals Embrace 'Creation Care'," *Dallas Morning News*, March 19, 2006.

8 Available at www.npr.org/documents/2006/feb/evangelical/calltoaction.pdf. See, further, Katherine Hayhoe and Andrew Farley, *A Climate for Change: Global Warming Facts for Faith-Based Decisions* (New York: Hachette Book Group, 2011).

9 Laurie Goodstein, "Evangelicals' Focus on Climate Draws Fire of Christian Right," *New York Times*, March 3, 2007, p. A9.

10 Quoted in William Leiss, *The Domination of Nature* (New York: George Braziller, 1972), pp. 58–59.

11 John Locke, *Second Treatise of Government*, para. 42; see excerpt in Terence Ball, Richard Dagger, and Daniel O'Neill, eds., *Ideals and Ideologies: A Reader*, selection 3.12.

12 Karl Marx and Friedrich Engels, *The Manifesto of the Communist Party*, in Lewis S. Feuer, ed., *Marx and Engels: Basic Writings on Politics and Philosophy* (Garden City, NY: Doubleday Anchor, 1959), p. 12; also in Ball, Dagger, and O'Neill, *Ideals and Ideologies*, selection 5.37.

13 Ayn Rand, *The Fountainhead* (New York: Bobbs-Merrill, 1943), p. 10.

14 David Ehrenfeld, *The Arrogance of Humanism* (New York: Oxford University Press, 1978).

15 Aldo Leopold, *A Sand County Almanac* (New York: Oxford University Press, 1968). See, for further discussion of Leopold's "land ethic" and its implications, Leslie Paul Thiele, "Sustainability in the Age of Ecology," in *Ideals and Ideologies*, selection 9.63.

16 See, for example, Christopher Stone, *Earth and Other Ethics* (New York: Harper & Row, 1987).

17 Hans Jonas, *The Imperative of Responsibility* (Chicago: University of Chicago Press, 1984).

18 Wendell Berry, *The Gift of Good Land* (San Francisco: North Point Press, 1981), p. 127.

19 Although this is not the position he takes, this is how Robert Heilbroner poses the challenge facing those who want to curtail present-day consumption. See Heilbroner, "What Has Posterity Ever Done for Me?" *New York Times Magazine*, January 19, 1975.

20 Garrett Hardin, "The Tragedy of the Commons," *Science* 162 (December 13, 1968): 1243–1248.

21 See Andrew Dobson, *Green Political Thought* (London: Unwin Hyman, 2007), pp. 206–213.

22 Arne Naess, "The Shallow and the Deep Long-Range Ecology Movement: A Summary," *Inquiry* 16 (1973): 95–100. See also Naess, *Ecology, Community, and Lifestyle*, trans. and ed. David Rothenberg (Cambridge: Cambridge University Press, 1989).

23 See Roderick Nash, *Wilderness and the American Mind*, 3rd ed. (New Haven, CT: Yale University Press, 1982), pp. 379–388.

24 René Dubos, *The Wooing of Earth* (New York: Scribner, 1980); Wendell Berry, *The Gift of Good Land* (San Francisco: North Point Press, 1981).

25 Wendell Berry, "Getting Along with Nature," in Berry, *Home Economics: Fourteen Essays* (San Francisco: North Point Press, 1987), p. 7; also in Ball, Dagger, and O'Neill, *Ideals and Ideologies*, selection 9.64.

26 Dave Foreman, *Confessions of an Eco-Warrior* (New York: Harmony Books, 1991), p. 92.

27 Dave Foreman and Murray Bookchin, *Defending the Earth: A Dialogue*, ed. Steve Chase (Boston: South End Press, 1991), p. 116.

28 Leopold, *A Sand County Almanac*, p. 240.

29 Ibid., p. 262.

30 George Sessions, ed., *Deep Ecology for the Twenty-First Century* (Boston: Shambhala Publications, 1995).

31 Melissa Lane, *EcoRepublic: What the Ancients Can Teach Us About Ethics, Virtue, and Sustainable Living* (Princeton: Princeton University Press, 2012); John O'Neill,

Ecology, Policy and Politics: Human Well-Being and the Natural World (New York and London: Routledge, 1993).

32 See Peter F. Cannavo and Joseph H. Lane, eds., *Engaging Nature: Environmentalism and the Political Theory Canon* (Cambridge, MA: MIT Press, 2015).

33 See John Seed et al., *Thinking Like a Mountain* (Philadelphia: New Society Publishers, 1988).

34 See Judith Plant, ed., *Healing the Wounds: The Promise of Ecofeminism* (Philadelphia: New Society Publishers, 1989); Val Plumwood, *Feminism and the Mastery of Nature* (London: Routledge, 1993); and Karen J. Warren, ed., *Ecofeminism: Women, Culture, Nature* (Bloomington, IN: Indiana University Press, 1997).

35 See Vandana Shiva, *Staying Alive: Women, Ecology and Development* (London: Zed Books, 1988); Val Plumwood, "Feminism and the Mastery of Nature," in Ball, Dagger, and O'Neill, *Ideals and Ideologies*, selection 9.65.

36 See Murray Bookchin, *The Modern Crisis* (Montreal: Black Rose Books, 1986).

37 For an account of the Sea Shepherd Conservation Society and its founder, Captain Paul Watson, see Raffi Khatchadourian, "Neptune's Navy," *The New Yorker*, November 7, 2007, pp. 56–72. See also Rik Scarce, *Eco-Warriors: Understanding the Radical Environmental Movement* (Chicago: Noble Press, 2006); and Christopher Manes, *Green Rage: Radical Environmentalism and the Unmaking of Civilization* (Boston: Little, Brown, 1990).

38 Edward O. Wilson, *Biophilia* (Cambridge: Harvard Univeristy Press, 1984). See, further, Patricia Hasbach, Peter Kahn, and Jolina Ruckert, eds., *Ecopsychology* (Cambridge: MIT Press, 2011) and a new scholarly journal, *Ecopsychology*. For a useful introduction to and overview of the field, see Daniel B. Smith, "Is There an Ecological Unconscious?" *New York Times Magazine*, January 31, 2010, pp. 36–41.

39 Maurice Cranston, *Jean-Jacques Rousseau* (Chicago: University of Chicago Press, 1991), 3 vols., vol. II, p. ix.

40 Quoted in Cranston, *Jean-Jacques Rousseau*, vol. I, pp. 345–346; we have slightly modified Cranston's translation.

41 See, for example, Rudolph Bahro, *Building the Green Movement*, trans. Mary Tyler (Philadelphia: New Society Publishers, 1986); and Jonathon Porritt, *Seeing Green: The Politics of Ecology Explained* (Oxford: Blackwell, 1984). Some Greens—for example, Dave Foreman—disagree, arguing that local people often wish to "develop" their locale, while outsiders have greater zeal for its preservation. For example, Alaskans are overwhelmingly in favor of oil exploration and drilling in the Arctic National Wildlife Refuge, and most opposition comes from people in the "lower 48" states. See "Alaskans Know Pockets Are Lined with Oil," *New York Times*, March 18, 2001, pp. A1, A14.

42 Edward Wong, "China Is Also an Exporter of Pollution to the Western U.S., Study Finds," *New York Times*, January 21, 2014, p. A6.

43 See Terence Ball, "Democracy," in Andrew Dobson and Robyn Eckersley, eds., *Political Theory and the Ecological Challenge* (Cambridge: Cambridge University Press, 2006), pp. 131–147.

44 Anna Bramwell, *The Fading of the Greens: The Decline of Environmental Politics in the West* (New Haven, CT: Yale University Press, 1994).

45 This self-published essay (2005) by Ted Nordhaus and Michael Shellenberger appears as a chapter of their book, *Break Through: From the Death of Environmentalism to the Politics of Possibility* (New York: Houghton Mifflin Harcourt, 2007).

46 James H. Cone, *Risks of Faith: The Emergence of a Black Theology of Liberation, 1968–1998* (Boston: Beacon Press, 1998); the first chapter of Cone's book—"Whose Earth Is It, Anyway?"—is reprinted in Ball, Dagger, and O'Neill, *Ideals and Ideologies*, selection 9.66.

FOR FURTHER READING

Ball, Terence, "Green Political Theory," in Terence Ball and Richard Bellamy, eds., *The Cambridge History of Twentieth-Century Political Thought*. Cambridge: Cambridge University Press, 2003.

Berry, Wendell. *The Gift of Good Land*. San Francisco: North Point Press, 1981.

Bramwell, Anna. *Ecology in the Twentieth Century: A History*. New Haven, CT: Yale University Press, 1989.

Carson, Rachel. *Silent Spring*. Boston: Houghton Mifflin, 1962.

Catton, William R. *Overshoot: The Ecological Basis of Revolutionary Change*. Urbana: University of Illinois Press, 1980.

Devall, Bill, and George Sessions. *Deep Ecology: Living as if Nature Mattered*. Layton, UT: Gibbs M. Smith, 1985.

Dobson, Andrew, ed. *Fairness and Futurity: Essays on Environmental Sustainability and Social Justice*. New York: Oxford University Press, 1999.

Dryzek, John S. *The Politics of the Earth: Environmental Discourses*. Oxford: Oxford University Press, 1997.

Dryzek, John S., and David Schlosberg, eds. *Debating the Earth: The Environmental Politics Reader*. Oxford: Oxford University Press, 1998.

Ehrenfeld, David. *The Arrogance of Humanism*. New York: Oxford University Press, 1978.

Goodin, Robert E. *Green Political Theory*. Cambridge: Polity Press, 1992.

Hardin, Garrett. *Filters Against Folly*. New York: Viking Penguin, 1985.

Heilbroner, Robert L. *An Inquiry into the Human Prospect*, 3rd ed. New York: Norton, 1991.

Humphrey, Matthew, ed. *Political Theory and the Environment: A Reassessment*. London: Frank Cass, 2001.

Kay, Jane Holz. *Asphalt Nation: How the Automobile Took Over America and How We Can Take It Back*. Berkeley and Los Angeles: University of California Press, 1998.

Kelly, Petra. *Thinking Green! Essays on Environmentalism, Feminism, and Nonviolence*. Berkeley, CA: Parallax Press, 1994.

Leopold, Aldo. *A Sand County Almanac*. New York: Oxford University Press, 1968.

Louv, Richard. *Last Child in the Woods Saving Our Children from Nature-Deficit Disorder*. New York: Workman Publishers, 2005; revised, 2007.

——. *The Nature Principle: Human Restoration and the End of Nature-Deficit Disorder*. New York: Workman Publishers, 2011.

Nash, Roderick Frazier. *The Rights of Nature: A History of Environmental Ethics*. Madison: University of Wisconsin Press, 1989.

Partridge, Ernest, ed. *Responsibilities to Future Generations: Environmental Ethics*. Buffalo, NY: Prometheus Books, 1981.

Porritt, Jonathon. *Seeing Green: The Politics of Ecology Explained*. Oxford: Blackwell, 1984.

Regan, Tom. *All That Dwell Therein*. Berkeley and Los Angeles: University of California Press, 1982.

Regan, Tom, ed. *Earthbound: New Introductory Essays in Environmental Ethics*. New York: Random House, 1984.

Roszak, Theodore. *Person/Planet*. Garden City, NY: Doubleday Anchor, 1978.

Sagoff, Mark. *The Economy of the Earth: Philosophy, Law, and the Environment*. Cambridge: Cambridge University Press, 1988.

Schumacher, E. F. *Small Is Beautiful: Economics As If People Mattered*. Garden City, NY: Doubleday Anchor, 1973.

Seed, John, et al. *Thinking Like a Mountain*. Philadelphia: New Society Publishers, 1988.

Sessions, George, ed. *Deep Ecology for the Twenty-First Century.* Boston: Shambhala Publications, 1995.

Worster, Donald. *Nature's Economy: A History of Ecological Ideas*, 2nd ed. Cambridge: Cambridge University Press, 1994.

From the Ball, Dagger, and O'Neill Reader *Ideals and Ideologies*, Tenth Edition

USEFUL WEBSITES

EarthCare: www.earthcareonline.org
Earth First!: www.earthfirst.org
Earth Liberation Front: http://earth-liberation-front.com
Ecofeminism: http://eve.enviroweb.org
Evangelical Environmental Network: www.creationcare.org
Greenpeace: www.greenpeace.org
The Nature Conservancy: www.nature.org
Sea Shepherd Society: www.seashepherd.org
The Sierra Club: www.sierraclub.org

CHAPTER 10

RADICAL ISLAMISM

The struggle [jihad] between the Believers and their enemies is in essence a struggle of belief

Sayyid Qutb, *Signposts Along the Road*

The twentieth century saw two world wars followed by a Cold War and the fall of the Soviet Union. The advent of the twenty-first century seemed to promise peace of a kind that had not been seen in some long while. But that hope proved illusory. The terrorist attacks of September 11, 2001, in New York and Washington, in Indonesia in 2002, Spain in 2004, England in 2005, Boston in 2013, the bombing of a Russian airliner in 2015, followed weeks later by deadly terrorist attacks in Paris, Mali, and San Bernardino—all these, with the prospect of more to come, have awakened people in the Western world to a new threat to their peace and security. That threat extends to people around the globe, and comes not only from the best-known groups—al-Qaeda (Arabic for "the base") and ISIS (Islamic State of Iraq and Syria)—but from other more obscure organizations as well.

At least some of these terrorist attacks threaten to spark a much larger war. In 2008 suicide bombers (who refer to themselves as "martyrs") from one of these groups, Lashkar-e-Taiba ("Army of the Pure") attacked and occupied several hotels, restaurants, and other establishments in Mumbai (formerly Bombay), India, killing 173 people and wounding more than 300 others. Lashkar-e-Taiba is a radical Islamist organization based in Pakistan and reputed to have the backing of elements in the Pakistani intelligence services. Their aim was apparently to foment further conflict and tension between the governments of India and Pakistan, both of which are democratic nations armed with nuclear weapons. In this exceedingly unstable part of the world, ideologically motivated terrorists are not only able to terrorize civilians but, potentially, to incite nuclear war.[1] And in 2012 radical Islamists affiliated with al-Qaeda attacked the American consulate in Libya, killing the American ambassador and three civilian staff members.

But not all radical Islamists belong to organized groups. As we witnessed in the instance of the bombings at the Boston Marathon, ideologically motivated individuals—so-called "lone wolves" not affiliated with al-Qaeda, ISIS, or any other organization—are quite capable of waging *jihad* and carrying out terrorist attacks. After the April 2013 bombings in Boston, a new word entered the political vocabulary: "self-radicalization." The brothers who made and planted the two bombs apparently had no affiliation, formal or informal, with any Islamist organization. According to the surviving brother, they reportedly radicalized themselves by watching and listening to *jihadist* sermons preached by radical imams on the Internet, from which they also allegedly received bomb-making instructions.

The ideology that inspires and motivates members of ISIS, al-Qaeda, Lashkar-e-Taiba, and other extremist groups—and now self-radicalized individuals as well—is variously called political Islam, radical Islamism, Islamic fundamentalism, or—most controversially and polemically—Islamofascism. Whatever we call it, it is clear that we must understand the main elements of this new ideology if we are to understand the world in which we now live and respond properly to the threat it poses to Muslims and non-Muslims alike. As all of its various names indicate, proponents of this new ideology see themselves as "true" Muslims, and their interpretation of Islam as the only authentic version of it. To understand this ideology, then, we must begin with a brief exploration of the major features of Islam. Before beginning, however, we must emphasize that Islam is a religion, and no more an "ideology," strictly speaking, than Buddhism, Christianity, Hinduism, Judaism, or any other religion. But one minority variant of Islam—Islam*ism*—does qualify as an ideology, for reasons we set out in this chapter. Before we begin, though, we need to be clear about the meaning of the term "Islamism." Islamism comes in several very different varieties. Unfortunately, the most familiar and best-known of these is the radical jihadist Islamism of ISIS (Islamic State), al-Qaeda, and other violent extremist groups. This variant comprises a relatively small and atypical segment within Islamism. Most Islamist parties and movements are nonviolent, working through established institutions to implement Islamist laws and policies—one notable example being the ruling Justice and Development Party in Turkey. Our primary concern in this chapter is to explore the ideas and beliefs—the ideology—of violent jihadist or radical Islamism. But first we need to understand something about the history of the religion from which violent jihadist Islamism is a radical or extremist offshoot.

ISLAM: A SHORT HISTORY

Muslims, as its adherents are called, say that Islam is a religion, but not a religion in the narrower, more restricted sense of the word familiar to people in the modern West. Muslims hold that Islam is a complete way of life, with rules governing everything from manners to morals, marriage, diet, dress, prayer, personal finance, and family life. The religion takes its name from the Arabic word *islam*, which means "submission." It is not submission in general that Islam requires, however, but submission or surrender of the individual's will to Allah, or God. For it is only through submission to God's will that the individual can find peace in this life and paradise in the next.

That is the central belief of Muslims, the people of the Islamic faith. Muslims are people of many different nationalities and inhabit almost every part of the globe, but their numbers are concentrated in North Africa, the Middle- and Near-East, and Indonesia. Islam has dominated most of this territory virtually since the religion began around 620 CE, when the Prophet Mohammed announced in Arabia that he had received a revelation from the Angel Gabriel. The report of this and subsequent revelations make up the *Qur'an* (Koran), the holy book of Islam that Muslims take to be the divine word of Allah, or God. Together with Mohammed's own words and deeds (or *Sunna*), which Muslims are supposed to emulate, the *Qur'an* forms the basis of the Islamic faith—a monotheistic faith, like Judaism and Christianity, that worships one all-knowing, all-powerful, and merciful God.

Within a century of Mohammed's death in 632 CE, Islam had spread from Arabia throughout the Middle East, across North Africa, and through most of Spain. The Muslim rulers of Spain were generally tolerant of other religions, allowing both Christians and Jews to practice their faiths. Spain soon became the chief point of contact between Christian Europe and the Islamic world—a contact that enabled Europeans to enjoy such fruits of Islamic culture as Arabic numerals, which the Arabs themselves had imported from India, algebra, and extraordinary architecture. Islamic universities also preserved many of the works of classical Western philosophy that were lost to Europe for centuries before being rediscovered through contact with Islamic Spain.

Even before Muslims invaded Spain, however, a split had developed within Islam that continues today. This is the split between Sunni and Shi'ite Muslims. The division initially began with a controversy over the question of who was to follow in Mohammed's footsteps as *caliph*, or leader of the Islamic community, but it also raised the further question of what the nature of this leadership should be. Sunnis conceived of the *caliph* or head of the **caliphate** as a kind of elected chief executive, while Shi'ites insisted that the *caliph* is an infallible *imam*, a divinely gifted leader who must be a member of the house of Ali (Mohammed's son-in-law). Today, among Muslims in general, Sunnis are by far the larger of the two groups; but Shi'ites outnumber Sunnis in some countries, such as Iraq and Bahrain, and in Iran they are easily the dominant sect.

For Sunnis and Shi'ites alike, the practice of Islam requires *jihad*, the struggle against evil. Many Muslims, perhaps even most of them, think of *jihad* primarily as the individual's inner struggle to overcome the temptation to be sinful, selfish, and evil. Others, however, take *jihad* to be first and foremost an outward struggle against the enemies of Islam. This latter notion of *jihad* is central, as we shall see, to radical Islamism.

Whether Sunni or Shi'ite, mainstream or radical, most Muslims have believed that religion is not simply a personal matter. Islam is a way of life with profound political and social implications. It draws no hard and fast distinction, as modern Christians and secular Westerners do, between "church" and "state" or religion and politics.[2] The law of the land and the precepts of the faith should be one and the same. Thus the *Shar'ia*—Islamic law derived from the *Qur'an* and the *Sunna*—prohibits usury (lending money at interest), calls for a tax on the wealthy to aid the poor and needy, and prescribes severe punishment for premarital sex and adultery. These and other injunctions are to be enforced by the rulers. Islam calls for a form of rule in which the law of the land is supposed to follow from God's commands. In the case of radical Islamism, the law of the land is *Shar'ia*, narrowly interpreted and strictly enforced by a **theocracy.**

In the twentieth century many predominantly Muslim countries began to separate government and politics from matters of faith, with Turkey probably going the furthest under Mustafa Kemal Ataturk (1881–1938) and his secular successors; this is no longer the case, as the current Turkish regime is rolling back many of Ataturk's reforms. In separating religion from politics or government, Ataturk and his successors followed the example of Western liberals and socialists. In making these liberalizing and modernizing moves, however, Ataturk and other secular-minded reformers provoked a strong reaction by conservative Muslims and, later, radical Islamists, who see **secularism** as a betrayal of their faith.

Muslims in the Middle East and North Africa have long felt themselves and their faith threatened by external enemies. Radical Islamism differs from mainstream Islam largely because the radicals see the threat as greater and the danger more imminent. From the vantage point of many Islamists, these threats have come in four waves. The first wave comprised the Christian Crusades (roughly 1100–1300 CE), or military expeditions to retake the Holy Land for Christendom, to convert or kill "infidels" (that is, non-Christians), and, not least, to gain territory and wealth for Europeans. Untold thousands of Muslim men, women, and children were butchered in the name of Christianity; others were converted to Christianity under threat of death. A second threatening wave came with European imperial expansion into North Africa and the Middle East in the nineteenth and early twentieth centuries. France governed much of North Africa and the Levant, and Britain controlled most of the territory from Egypt through India, including Palestine, Arabia, and Persia (now Iran). The British were also instrumental in paving the way for what many Muslims saw as a third threat: the establishment of the state of Israel in Palestine after World War II. To them, a Jewish state in a predominantly Muslim region was both injury and insult. So too is the stationing of American and other troops in the region since 1990.

More recently, a fourth threatening wave has appeared in the form of influential Western ideas—liberalism, secularism, materialism, religious toleration, and sexual equality among them—that fall under the general heading of "modernity" or "modernism." These ideas are communicated through satellite television, the Internet, home videos, and social media. Reruns of old episodes of *Baywatch*, *Desperate Housewives*, and other (mainly American) programs depict a world in which scantily clad and sexually available women are on socially equal terms with men, and women and men alike live lives in which God and religion play no part whatever. These Western cultural imports are deeply shocking to conservative Muslim sensibilities. Moreover, conservative Muslims fear that such immorality (or amorality) is infectious, with young Muslims being particularly susceptible to the temptations represented by American movies and other cultural media.

Many Muslims also complain that the United States has added military insult to moral injury by using covert operations and military force to topple regimes believed to be unfriendly to American political and business interests. The United States has also supported pro-Western but undemocratic governments headed by hereditary monarchs in Saudi Arabia, Iran, Kuwait, and elsewhere. The monarchs have returned the favor by keeping the oil flowing to the United States and other nations. Following the Gulf War of 1991, moreover, Saudi rulers allowed the United States to station troops inside Saudi Arabia, the home of Mecca and Medina, the most sacred sites in Islam. To many Muslims, including a wealthy Saudi named Osama bin Laden, these military bases were tantamount to an American invasion and occupation of Muslim holy lands and thus a grave threat to Islam itself. Many Muslims have also been alarmed by the United States' strong and long-standing support of Israel, which in their view illegally occupies the land of Palestine and threatens its Arab neighbors.

For these reasons, among others, many Muslims are wary of Western—and particularly American—influence in the Middle East, North Africa, and other parts of the world where Islam is prevalent. What distinguishes moderate or mainstream Muslims from radical Islamists such as bin Laden and the other members of al-Qaeda, or al-Baghdadi of ISIS, or the Taliban of Afghanistan, turns on the question of what is to be done, and how, and by whom. To see how they answer these questions, we must understand the origin and development of radical Islamism.

RADICAL ISLAMISM

Radical or violent jihadist Islamism—which, again, is a small minority within Islamism—is an amalgam of various strands within Islamic thought and culture. Taken together, these strands form an ideology that may be said to represent the Muslim **Counter-Enlightenment**. Just as the European Counter-Enlightenment of the late eighteenth and early nineteenth centuries (discussed in Chapter 7) rejected the scientific and secular ideas of the Enlightenment, so the Muslim Counter-Enlightenment is a reaction against attempts to make Islam and Islamic societies more modern or "enlightened." Like Joseph de Maistre and other leaders of the European Counter-Enlightenment, in other words, radical Islamists adhere to a **reactionary** ideology that aims to restore Islam to its "pure" state, untouched by the secularism and modernism that marks so many of the intellectual, political, and scientific developments of the last several centuries—including those contributed by Muslim scholars and scientists. Thus radical Islamism is directed not only against the West but also against Muslims who subscribe to "Western" ideas and aspirations that would allegedly make Islam into a more open and tolerant religion.

There is no single theorist to whom one can point as the source or fountainhead of radical Islamic thought—certainly not the late Osama bin Laden (1957–2011), who was primarily a practitioner rather than a theorist of radical Islamism. But if there is one especially influential thinker in this movement, it is Sayyid Qutb (1906–1966), the Egyptian author of numerous books, including *Islam and Social Justice* (1949), *The Battle Between Islam and Capitalism* (1950), his multivolume commentary *In the Shade of the Qur'an* (1952–1982), and most notably, *Signposts Along the Road* (1964). Qutb (pronounced "coo-teb") began his career as a novelist, journalist, literary critic, teacher, and high-ranking member of Egypt's Ministry of Education. He was also an outspoken critic of the corruption of the regime of King Faruq, who ruled Egypt from 1936 to 1952. The king sent Qutb into exile in the United States, hoping that exposure to "Western ways" would lead him to cease his criticism. Fluent in Arabic, English, and several other languages, Qutb studied at Colorado State College of Education, earning a master's degree in 1949. Contrary to the king's hopes, however, Qutb's American experience led him in an even more radical direction. Appalled by America's racism and racial segregation, social and economic inequality, sexual promiscuity, alcohol consumption, its secularism and materialism, and its uncritical support of the then-new state of Israel, Qutb reconnected with his early religious upbringing. Upon his return to Egypt in 1951, Qutb joined the anticolonialist Muslim Brotherhood, which had been founded by Hasan al-Banna in 1929 while Egypt was under British imperial domination. Their overriding aim was to oust the British and overthrow the British-backed monarchy as a prelude to establishing a socially and politically conservative Islamist state that would promote non-Western Islamist values. Qutb agreed with al-Banna that Western influence could only be resisted by Muslims who are resolute in their faith and prepared to practice *jihad*. After al-Banna's assassination in 1949, Qutb became the leading thinker of the Muslim Brotherhood's more militant or radical wing.

In 1952 Qutb was fired from the Ministry of Education for his outspoken criticisms of King Faruq's regime. Shortly thereafter Faruq was overthrown by an Egyptian nationalist, Colonel Gamel Abdul Nasser. At first Nasser attempted to curry favor with Qutb and the Muslim Brotherhood, but he rejected Qutb's proposal to turn Egypt into an Islamist state—that is, a state governed in strict accordance with *Shari'a*. Qutb, in turn, was critical of Nasser's program of modernization and reform. In 1954 Qutb was arrested, imprisoned, and tortured. In 1965 he was again arrested and tortured for allegedly plotting the overthrow of Nasser's secular regime. In 1966 he was executed—according to legend he kissed the gallows—and he has ever since been regarded as hero, theorist, and martyr of the radical Islamist cause.

Qutb's massive eight-volume commentary on the *Qur'an*, much of which he wrote while imprisoned in Egypt, is titled *In the Shade of the Qur'an*. The title is intentionally evocative. For desert dwellers in the Middle East and elsewhere, shade is rare, and all the more valued for that. Qutb views the modern world as a spiritual desert—a vast and arid wasteland of secularism, materialism, consumerism, hedonism, egoism, self-centeredness, and selfishness—from which the message of the *Qur'an* comes as a welcome relief. All good Muslims must accordingly flee from this spiritual desert and seek the shade of the *Qur'an*. But of course Qutb and his radical Islamist disciples advocate and adhere to a radical interpretation of the *Qur'an* with which the vast majority of Muslims disagree.

Radical Islamists believe that there is a concerted conspiracy by Christians and Jews to corrupt the morals of Muslims and to destroy Islam itself. More than a decade before the advent of satellite television, and several decades before the Internet and social media, Qutb decried the influence of Western culture on non-Western cultures generally, and on Islamic societies in particular:

> Humanity today is living in a large brothel! One has only to glance at its press, films, fashion shows, beauty contests, ballrooms, wine bars, and broadcasting stations! Or observe its mad lust for naked flesh, provocative pictures, and sick, suggestive statements in literature, the arts, and mass media! And add to this the systems of usury [i.e., lending money at interest] which fuels man's voracity for money and engenders vile methods for its accumulation and investment, in addition to fraud, trickery, and blackmail dressed up in the garb of law.[3]

What Westerners regard as innocent entertainment or information Qutb regarded as part and parcel of a campaign to corrupt young and impressionable Muslims, tempting them to stray from the one true path that is Islam, at least as Qutb and his followers understand and practice it.

In Islam, as we have seen, there are not separate spheres labeled "religion" and "politics" but a single seamless interweaving of all aspects of individual and collective life. Qutb shared this view, and he was highly critical of Muslims who seek to "modernize" and "reform" Muslim societies—and even Islam itself—by introducing Western and secular ideas of religious toleration, individual rights, freedom, sexual equality, and justice.[4] That many Muslims find "reform" attractive only indicates, he thought, the pervasive influence of the West, which is mired in *jahiliyya* ("age of ignorance") and threatens to drag Muslim societies into that darkness. *Jahiliyya* referred originally to the ignorance and spiritual darkness that enveloped the world before the teachings of the *Qur'an* were revealed to the Prophet Mohammed. The "new *jahiliyya*" to which Qutb refers comes from Western ideas and influences. It is a kind of willful and self-imposed darkness, a rejection of divinely revealed truth that is brought about by misplaced pride in the successes of science and technology. This rejection in turn has spawned a mind-set that is a mixture of philosophical skepticism, secularism, and even atheism. People afflicted with this mind-set mistakenly think that human reason can penetrate all mysteries, that they can replace God's will with their own, substitute their judgment for His, with human justice supplanting divine justice. The ideologies of liberalism and communism, in particular, embody this modern Western outlook, which is deeply opposed to the spirit and teachings of Islam. Liberalism emphasizes the sovereignty of the individual, and communism the sovereignty of the proletariat; neither recognizes the true sovereignty of God.

It follows, said Qutb, that "modernizers" and "reformers" in the Middle East are attempting nothing less than the importation of the "new *jahiliyya*" into Muslim societies, thereby subverting and corrupting Islam itself. Qutb's critique of such subversion was not new. What was new was the thoroughness and subtlety of his critique, which in several respects resembles Marx's critique of capitalism and Lenin's vision of a vanguard party. Qutb believed that non-Muslims—and many Muslims—suffer from a kind of **false consciousness** that leads them to see the world and their place in it in an inverted or distorted way. Thus they welcome Western ways and ideas, and call them "progressive." If the Muslim world is to be saved from these so-called "progressives," a small band or **vanguard party** of exceptionally devout Muslims—the *jama'a*—will have to lead the way. That is, they must struggle, or engage in *jihad* against everything that the West stands for—modernity, capitalism, religious toleration, sexual equality, and so on—and be prepared to give their lives in this sacred cause. In short, Muslims must go on the offensive against the "aggressors" who import these ideas into Muslim society. This is the ideological basis of radical Islamism.

Since Qutb's death in 1966, other radical Islamist organizations—including, most notably, al-Qaeda, ISIS, and Boko Haram—have continued to press for a *jihad* against the West and its corrupting ways. How would they conduct this struggle? One way is to attack those Muslims who have supposedly betrayed the faith by adopting secular or Western ideas and institutions. This was their justification, for example, for the assassination of Egyptian President Anwar Sadat in 1981;[5] it also explains their opposition to the "secularist" and "socialist" Saddam Hussein when he ruled Iraq. Another way to wage *jihad* is to launch terrorist attacks directly on Western countries and their troops and civilians. Thus American military barracks in Saudi Arabia have been blown up, the naval ship USS *Cole* was attacked and almost sunk, and U.S. embassies in Kenya and Tanzania were destroyed by suicide bombers, with grave loss of life, mostly African (and many Muslim). Most infamous of all were the terrorist attacks of September 11, 2001, on Washington, D.C., and New York—attacks that killed nearly 3,000 people, most of them Americans— and the subsequent bombings and shootings in France, Mali, Egypt, California, Indonesia, Madrid, London, and elsewhere that have killed thousands of civilians.

The murderers and suicide bombers who are called terrorists in the West are often praised as "martyrs" or "blessed martyrs" in the Middle East, where some regard them as men (and in increasing instances women) who have undertaken the sacred but too often neglected duty of *jihad*.[6] From the perspective of radical Islamism, terrorism is permissible when it promotes the greater good of ridding the Islamic world of Muslim "apostates" and Western "infidels" with their

Osama bin Laden (1957–2011)

pernicious ideas about free speech, sexual equality, and religious toleration. From the perspective of moderate or mainstream Islam, by contrast, suicide and the murder of innocents are strictly forbidden by the *Qur'an* and the *Hadith* (the collected reports of the words and deeds of the Prophet).

A third way in which radical Islamists wage *jihad* is through the education—or, perhaps more precisely, the indoctrination—of young people, and boys in particular. In *madrassas*, or religious schools, in most Middle Eastern countries, students study only one book, the *Qur'an*, which is said to teach everything they need to know. In many of these *madrassas* students are taught a radical interpretation of the *Qur'an*. To take but one example: The *Qur'an* (24:31) states that women (and men) must dress modestly. But what counts as "modest"? Short shorts and bikinis are obviously impermissible, but interpretations differ beyond that point. Moderate or mainstream Muslims are apt to interpret "modest" to mean that women may or may not wear headscarves and expose their faces. By contrast, militant or radical Islamists, such as the Taliban of Afghanistan, insist that "modest" means that women must be completely covered from head to toe; they must wear the *burka*, which conceals even their faces and feet; and any woman who reveals any part of her body in public should be beaten. Here, as elsewhere, a great deal hangs on how the *Qur'an* is interpreted.

THE RISE OF ISIS

The newest organization to promote the radical Islamist cause is ISIS (Islamic State of Iraq and Syria), also known as ISIL (Islamic State of Iraq and the Levant).[7] Its origins are traceable to the American invasion and occupation of Iraq that began in 2003. Although its populace is predominantly Shi'ite, Iraq had long been ruled by Saddam Hussein and the Sunni minority. Saddam's military, which was mostly Sunni, was immediately disbanded and dispersed by the Americans and their allies in the Iraqi Transitional Government. Sunni soldiers and their officers were unemployed. Even before the Shi'ite majority took power in 2006, they and their families were effectively frozen out of the political process. Then the newly elected Shi'ite president, Nouri al-Maliki, and his government made matters even worse. Seeking what they saw as their fair and long-overdue share of political power, Maliki's militias hunted down and murdered peaceful Sunni protesters. Increasingly desperate, impoverished, and powerless, many Sunnis looked to al-Qaeda in Iraq, until 2006 led by Abu Musab al-Zarqawi.

Formerly a hot-headed and violent Jordanian street thug, pimp, and drug dealer, Zarqawi became a devout convert to the extreme jihadist wing of the Salafist sect within Sunni Islam. Although he renounced his previous way of life, he retained one aspect of it—brutal and even spectacular violence directed against anyone who disagreed with him or his religious views. Among these views was the belief that the end of the world was near and that a caliphate or Islamic state would soon appear to wage an apocalyptic war against "crusaders" from the West. For Zarqawi, the American "blessed invasion" and occupation of Iraq was a dream come true and a prayer answered. Prophecy, he thought, was being fulfilled in his own lifetime. Taking advantage of the chaos and civil war in Iraq, he allied himself with al-Qaeda and took charge of its Iraqi operations. Many of Saddam's ousted

Sunni soldiers found employment and the opportunity to wreak revenge on the Shi'ite majority and its increasingly oppressive government.

Too violent and extreme even for al-Qaeda, Zarqawi was disowned, leaving him and his followers free to pursue an even more radical agenda and to wage *jihad*, to conquer and occupy territory and in so doing to bring about the longed-for caliphate. Zarqawi was killed in an American raid in 2006. His place as a charismatic rallying figure for radical Islamists was subsequently taken by Abu Bakr al-Baghdadi, a shadowy figure about whom there remains some disagreement. Introverted and scholarly according to some accounts, or a ruthless Mafioso-like mobster according to others, this cleric proclaimed the caliphate in 2010—with himself as *caliph* or supreme leader[8]—and preached sermons commanding the faithful few to wage all-out war on the unfaithful many, Muslims most especially. ISIS fighters captured the strategically important city of Mosul, in which it found caches of weapons and other resources that made it a military force to be reckoned with. Then came ISIS's biggest break of all—civil war in Syria. For a brief period the Syrian civil war, which came in the wake of the anti-authoritarian "Arab Spring" of 2011, seemed likely to topple the Syrian dictator Bashar Hafez al-Assad. But Assad's brutal repression of rebel forces resulted, not in his downfall, but in utter chaos and a country in ruins. Once again, ISIS saw an opportunity and took it. As a failed state, Syria presented an even more opportune target than neighboring Iraq had, and the two together allowed for an even wider war to be waged to gain territory for the Caliphate and to advance its apocalyptic agenda.

What system of ideas—what ideology—fuels ISIS's agenda? Followers of ISIS believe that no good thing ever comes without sacrifice, without killing and being killed. To die for one's faith is to be a martyr, the highest and holiest title to which mortal humans can aspire. Too many—most—Muslims have strayed from that faith. All Shi'ites and many Sunnis have chosen to adapt to the modern world of secularism, sexual equality, religious toleration, and the rest, instead of turning back the clock and returning to the pure faith of the Prophet himself in the seventh century. Every change since then has been a degeneration and a sacrilege. The greatest threat to "true" Islam—the jihadist Salafist Sunni Islam of ISIS itself—comes from within, from other Muslims who have become apostates, fallen away from the one true faith. Divided within itself, Islam will be unable to resist incursions, invasions, and occupation by the West, which ISIS refers to as "Rome." The day will soon come when the armies of Rome attack the armies of Islam in the final battle which will be a blood bath like no other, with untold millions of deaths—the sacrifice that will usher in the final Caliphate under which the few remaining faithful will live until the world ends. In the meantime, it is ISIS's duty to eliminate "the gray zone"—the zone of compromise and accommodation, of moderation, of peace at almost any price—in which most Muslims now live. By waging an all-out campaign of terror, ISIS will force Muslims to choose sides—there is no middle ground between "true" Islam and "infidelity," between Allah and Satan, good and evil. ISIS's Islamist terror in Europe and elsewhere, its adherents believe, will further marginalize Muslims within their host nations. Already alienated, they will become even more so as politicians and elected officials in France, the United States, and other Western nations condemn and demonize Muslims *en masse*. Then the truly faithful few among them will turn the tables and become terrorists.

ISIS and its agents and allies know that they cannot physically destroy the United States or any other major Western nation; but, they believe, these nations can be led to commit suicide, so to speak, by overreacting to the terrorist threat. This overreaction leads them to roll back constitutional rights and protections, to spend vast sums of money on military and police operations and, in effect, to turn once-democratic nations into police states. And ISIS and its allies can do this cheaply, inasmuch as terrorist attacks are inexpensive—all one needs are a few assault rifles wielded by individuals who are willing and even eager to die—while reactions (or overreactions) are very expensive indeed. The expense is measured not only economically—and those costs are enormous—but psychologically, spiritually, and legally.[9] In all these ways the West will be weakened from within, and the gray zone eliminated. The stage will then be set for the Apocalypse, the penultimate battle between Good and Evil.

This battle will take place in or near Dabiq, a village in northern Syria near the Turkish border. (ISIS calls its glossy monthly magazine, available online and in print, *Dabiq* in anticipation of this coming battle.) At the conclusion of this battle—which the "true" Muslims, with Allah's aid, will win—the Caliphate will go on the offensive, conquer Istanbul in Turkey, and encounter the false prophet Dajjal, who will kill more millions of faithful Muslims, leaving only 5,000 who will be cornered in Jerusalem. At this point, Jesus—a prophet ISIS reveres second only to Muhammad—will return to earth and break the cross to symbolize Christianity's surrender to and merger with Islam as the one true faith. He will then run a spear through the heart of Dajjal, making way for the true Mahdi, or ultimate *caliph*, and bring about Paradise on earth.

HUMAN NATURE AND FREEDOM

As with any ideology, radical Islamism has its own view of human nature and freedom. These are derived not only from its particular way of reading and interpreting the *Qur'an* but also from a particular understanding of the long history of encounters between the Muslim and Christian (or "Western") worlds.

Human Nature. Radical Islamism's view of human nature is rooted in religious belief. Together with the other great monotheistic religions, Judaism and Christianity, whose leading figures they also consider to be prophets, Islam shares the view that there is one God who created the heavens, the earth, and all its creatures, including human beings. Humans are by nature weak and prone to sin. To overcome temptation faithful Muslims must engage in *jihad*, the struggle against evil. As we have noted, this struggle takes place at both an individual and a collective level.

As individuals, Muslims must adhere to a strict regimen that involves praying five times a day, fasting from dawn to dusk during the holy month of Ramadan, practicing zakāt (giving generously to charities to help the poor), making a *hajj* or pilgrimage to the holy shrine at Mecca if possible, and, more generally, living a pious and upright life. Muslims call the struggle to live this way the "greater *jihad*."

Such a life cannot be lived in isolation from others, but only as part of a wider community of believers. If it is to serve its members well, this community must be tightly knit and strict in its enforcement of Islamic law (*Shari'a*). This community engages collectively in *jihad* by helping its members to resist the evil within each individual and the evil without—that is, external enemies who threaten the community by undermining the faith upon which it is based. Muslims often call the struggle against external enemies the "lesser *jihad*." Radical Islamism reverses this order, placing greater emphasis on *jihad* against all enemies of Islam, including (in their view) moderate or reform-minded Muslims as well as "infidels" from the West.

Radical Islamism is anti-liberal in that it is anti-individualist and has no room at all for the liberal-individualist idea of the individual as isolated or distinct from the larger society or community of which he or she is a small and very dependent part. This anti-liberal tendency is especially marked in radical Islamists, who reject "individual rights" or "rights against the larger society" (as in the U.S. Bill of Rights) as perverted ideas utterly foreign or alien to their vision of Islam. To have rights against that which gives you moral guidance and sustenance amounts to having rights against morality, which is absurd.

Once again we must note that Islam is not a unified monolith, no more than Christianity or Judaism is. It is in fact a religion deeply divided within itself—between Sunnis and Shi'ites, liberal modernizers and conservative traditionalists, tolerant moderates and radical extremists. A number of Muslim sects, such as Sufi Islam and the populist Islam practiced in Indonesia and Egypt, favor the toleration of all faiths, a fairly flexible interpretation of the *Qur'an*, and taking full advantage of science and modernity. Other Muslims, such as the Salafis, the Taliban of Afghanistan, and the Wahhabis of Saudi Arabia, reject modernity and seek what they believe to be a return to the pure and authentic Islam preached and practiced in the era of the Prophet Mohammed. The Salafis, for example, hold that the Islam introduced by the Prophet in the seventh century was perfect and needed no further development; hence all later variants of Islam, such as Sufi mysticism, are degenerate, imperfect, and illegitimate. Most radical jihadists follow the Salafist teachings of the fourteenth-century jurist Ibn Tamiyya. They resolutely reject the teachings of Hirith al-Muhaasibi, the founder of Sufism, and Muhammad 'Abduh, who is often considered the most influential Islamist modernist thinker.[10]

Thus, unlike moderate variants of Islam, radical Islamism is, as previously noted, a *reactionary* ideology that seeks to return its adherents—and the wider world—to a culturally and theologically "purer" time. As the Ayatollah Khomeini proclaimed in a sermon shortly before taking power in Iran in 1979:

> Yes, we [radical Islamists] are reactionaries, and you [Western secularists and Muslims who favor "modernizing" Islam] are "enlightened intellectuals." You intellectuals do not want us to go back 1,400 years.[11]

But, Khomeini continued, such a reversal was required if the lessons of the Prophet are to be learned and applied to everyday life. Foremost among these is a repudiation of liberal and Western ideas of "freedom."

Freedom. It might seem that radical Islamism has no conception of, or room for, freedom. Radical Islamism certainly has no room for or sympathy with a *liberal* view of freedom, but that does not mean that it has no view of freedom at all. On the contrary, it has its own distinctive conception of freedom, as Khomeini and Qutb both argued.

Khomeini held that devout Muslims must reject the modern, liberal conception of freedom: "You, who want freedom, freedom for everything, the freedom of [political] parties, you who want all the freedoms, you intellectuals: freedom that will corrupt our youth, freedom that will pave the way for the oppressor, freedom that will drag our nation to the bottom."[12] Muslims must reject this false freedom, Khomeini declared, replacing it with the true freedom that comes only when one surrenders and submits one's will to the supreme will of Allah. This view of freedom-as-submission is a staple feature of Islam generally—again, Islam means "submission"—and of radical Islamism in particular, where it assumes a violent and specifically *political* form. "Islam is not merely 'belief,'" wrote Sayyid Qutb in *Signposts Along the Road*. "Islam is a declaration of the freedom of man from servitude to other men. Thus it strives ... to abolish all those systems and governments which are based on the rule of man over man."[13]

Qutb goes on to argue that to live without Islam is to live as a slave—a slave to sexual desire, to material wants, and to the rule of other human beings—while to live as a faithful Muslim is to be free from these earthly temptations. Only by submitting to the Divine Will of Allah can human beings become truly free.[14] At an individual level, such freedom results from "the greater *jihad*" of internal struggle for spiritual strength and self-control. At a collective level, however, Muslims will become free only if and when they band together in an armed struggle (the "lesser *jihad*") to expel or exterminate "infidels" and "apostates"—Westerners and Muslim moderates and modernizers foremost among them—from predominantly Muslim lands. The radical Islamist conception of freedom thus can be illustrated by way of our triadic model (see Figure 10.1).

These competing conceptions of *jihad* underlie many of the differences between radical and moderate Muslims. Moderate or mainstream Muslims reject radical Islamism, and especially its ready recourse to terrorism, as a perversion of the Prophet's teachings in the *Qur'an* and *Sunna*. These teachings include a prohibition on the killing of innocent noncombatants. How then, moderate Muslims ask, can radical Islamists justify the killing of other Muslims and of innocent civilians? Radical Islamists respond by claiming that their resort to terror and killing is a form of *takfir*—the excommunication of Muslim "apostates" who have fallen away from the one true faith and thus forfeited their status as Muslims and can therefore be justifiably killed. Thus, to cite one of many examples of *takfir*, members of the Muslim Brotherhood declared that Egyptian President Anwar Sadat, a Muslim, deserved to be assassinated because he had negotiated with the Jewish prime minister of Israel. As for the killing of innocent civilians, Osama bin Laden had a ready answer: civilians in Western democracies are not really innocent. In a democracy, he said, the citizens elect leaders and representatives, and the citizens of Western democracies have elected leaders who send soldiers into the Middle East to kill Muslims. "The American people," charged bin Laden, "choose their government by their own free will" and "have the ability and choice to refuse the policies of their government." If they choose a government that pursues anti-Islamic policies in the guise of a "war on terror," they are every bit as responsible as their government and military are, and may therefore be targeted as enemy combatants.[15]

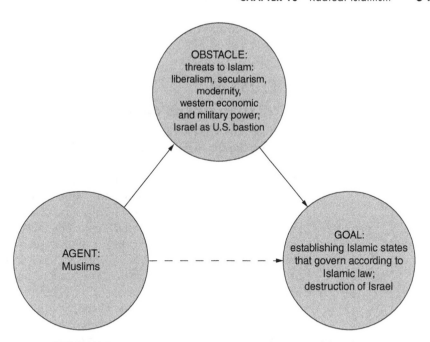

FIGURE 10.1 The radical Islamist conception of freedom.

Another difference between radical Islamists and mainstream Muslims is their way of reading or interpreting the *Qurʾan*. Like Christians and Jews, Muslims are divided over what constitutes the "correct" interpretation of the sacred texts. Other religions have their "fundamentalist" sects—those who believe that their sacred scripture has a definite, unchanging meaning that the faithful can discern by reading it literally rather than figuratively, metaphorically, allegorically, or historically. From the fundamentalists' perspective, those who read scripture in nonliteral ways are apostates or heretics who disavow or deviate from the fundamental truths of the faith.

Sometimes this division appears even within families of the faithful. Hasan al-Banna, the Egyptian founder of the radical Muslim Brotherhood, subscribed to a fundamentalist reading of the *Qurʾan*, according to which *jihad* against "infidels," including many Muslims, is a divine duty. By contrast, his younger brother, Gamal al-Banna (1920–2013), was an eminent Islamic scholar who was highly critical of Islamic fundamentalism. He held that the *Qurʾan* should be interpreted in a more liberal and less literal way than radical Islamists advocate, saying that "man is the aim of religion, and religion is only a means. What is prevalent today [among radical Islamists] is the opposite."[16] Gamal al-Banna was the author or translator of more than 100 books, including *A New Democracy* (1946), in which he criticizes Islamic fundamentalists for looking not at the text of the *Qurʾan* itself but at the earliest interpretations of its meaning, which the fundamentalists then accept as authoritative and eternally valid. His own view was that the *Qurʾan* must be interpreted in light of new knowledge and changing conditions and circumstances. To do otherwise, he contended, is to be hopelessly stuck in the past. Radical

Islamists, by contrast, hope and fight for just such a return to a "purer" past. In that respect radical Islamism is indeed a **reactionary** ideology.

CONCLUSION

Radical Islamism as an Ideology

Like other ideologies, radical Islamism guides and inspires its followers by performing the following four functions in its own distinctive way.

Explanation. Radical Islamism explains the current situation in the parts of the world where Muslims predominate—the Middle and Near East, North Africa, and parts of South and Southeast Asia—in terms of sweeping threats to Islam. The Islamic world and indeed Islam itself are under threat from an enemy that aims to destroy them by all available means: military, economic, intellectual, cultural, and spiritual. The threat of military force, great as it is, pales in comparison to the more insidious ideas with which the West tries to poison the minds of Muslims, especially young Muslims: liberalism, secularism, sexual equality, religious tolerance, materialism, and so forth. There is a concerted, highly organized, global conspiracy to inject these ideas into Islamic culture, with the aim of undermining and ultimately destroying Islam as a religion and way of life.

Evaluation. Radical Islamism supplies its adherents with a view of personal piety, social justice, and communal harmony that provides a perspective from which Western culture can be criticized and its incursions resisted. From this perspective Western ideas—of individualism, liberalism, secularism, sexual equality, material-ism, and so on—are revealed to be transgressive and disrespectful to both body and spirit; they confuse and jumble natural and God-given distinctions between holy and unholy, men and women, rulers and ruled, acceptable and unacceptable behavior. Western liberal individualism dethrones God and attempts to put man or "the individual" in His place as the source of all value—what Immanuel Kant called "the kingdom of ends" and John Stuart Mill the "sovereign self" ("Over himself, over his own body and mind, the individual is sovereign").[17] What in the West is called "religious toleration" really amounts to a pervasive indifference to religion, to God, and to everything that matters most. What is called "sexual equality" represents a confusion or confounding of the God-given sexual and biological differences that leads to an easy familiarity between the sexes, encouraging premarital and extramarital sex (i.e., adultery) and sexual promiscuity. Men and women have deeply different abilities and needs. This means, among other things, that they should be educated separately. Some radical Islamist sects, such as the Taliban and Boko Haram, even say that women should not be educated at all.

Orientation. As a theologically based ideology, radical Islamism supplies its adherents with a sense of individual and collective identity—of who they are and where they belong, who their friends and enemies are, what their purpose in life is. A truly faithful Muslim says, in effect, "I am a Muslim. I belong to and am a small part of a larger community of believers, dependent on that community for my faith, for moral and spiritual guidance. My friends are fellow Muslims who believe and behave as I do. My enemies include any individual, group, or nation that disagrees with or is in any way hostile to the community of which I am a member. My purpose in life is to live an upright life, and my sacred duty is to oppose the enemies of Islam." Radical Islamists differ from moderate or mainstream Muslims whom they identify as "enemies of Islam" and how they propose to deal with them. Radical Islamists believe that only they, and people who agree with them, are truly faithful Muslims. Those who disagree with them—Muslims and non-Muslims alike—are enemies of Islam to be denounced and killed.

Program. The radical Islamist political program is, in a word, *jihad*—a faith-based struggle against the enemies of Islam; that is to say, those who espouse any and all ideas that are inimical to or threaten the ideas and beliefs of Islam: liberalism, secularism, and so on. To protect the Islamic religion and way of life is a sacred duty. To that end radical Islamists believe that any means are permissible—including violence. Terrorism is a weapon of the weak against the strong. To those so-called moderate Muslims who say that the *Qur'an* forbids suicide and the shedding of innocent blood, radical Islamists say that they are following the *Qur'an* in giving like for like: Israelis have shed the blood of innocent Palestinian women and children; the Palestinian "martyrs" are therefore justified in shedding their own and the blood of so-called "innocent" Israeli women and children in whose names and for whose sake the Israeli government has killed or crippled innocent Palestinians. And, as in Israel, so too elsewhere: whoever threatens Muslims and their Islamic faith can—and should—be opposed by any means possible. In a sacred struggle to defend the faith, any means are morally permissible. Moreover, *jihad* is not only to be waged against the West—against the United States and its European and Israeli allies—but also against corrupt and secular governments or regimes in purportedly Muslim countries. This belief supposedly justified the assassination of Egypt's President Sadat. It also explains the hostility of al-Qaeda, ISIS, and other radical Islamists to the royal family of Saudi Arabia, which in their view rules ruthlessly and corruptly, and which for a time even allowed American bases and troops on the sacred soil of Islam. Before Iraq was invaded by the United States and its allies in 2003, moreover, radical Islamists were at odds with Saddam Hussein, who paid only lip service to Islam while ruling a secular state that allowed a measure of religious toleration, sexual equality, the selling of alcohol, and other abominations. More recently, ISIS has emerged as the most militant and violent sect within radical Islamism, targeting non-Sunni Muslims in the Middle East and civilians in France and other Western nations.

In short, radical Islamism lives and flourishes in a world filled with real or imagined threats, of conspiracies and cabals, against Islam and its faithful adherents. It is a response to a real or perceived crisis—the crisis brought about by the clash of West and (Middle) East, of secular modernity and religious tradition. Radical Islamism is at war not only with the West but also with would-be modernizers and reformers within Islam itself.[18] Radical Islamism is thus a *reactionary* ideology, inasmuch as it represents a reaction against the threats posed by the pressures of modernization and secularization.

Radical Islamism and the Democratic Ideal

There is nothing in mainstream Islam that precludes the establishment of democracy, and there are some things that seem to point in the direction of democracy. Islamic teaching suggests, for example, that "consultation" (*shura*) be practiced between rulers and ruled (*Qur'an* 3:159 and 42:38). What form (democratic or otherwise) such consultation might take is not specified, however, which leaves that concept open to radically different interpretations. Radical Islamism tends to be suspicious of if not hostile to democracy, and certainly to *liberal* democracy, in which different factions, parties, and interest groups vie for political power with little apparent concern for some shared or greater good. Liberal democracy, moreover, is avowedly secular inasmuch as it draws a sharp distinction between religion and politics, viewing the former as a purely private or personal matter that has no place in the public or political arena. This is summed up in the phrase "separation of church and state." Liberal democracy, in their view, does not exist for the purpose of making its citizens better or more moral people.[19] Liberal democracy also places a premium on individual rights at the expense of individual and collective duties. Not least, these rights are to be enjoyed by everyone—believers and atheists, women and men, Muslims and Jews and infidels. All this is anathema to radical Islamists.[20]

What then might an Islamic state look like? Would (or could) it be democratic? Views differ, of course. Sayyid Qutb saw democracy as a Western invention to be viewed with suspicion if not outright hostility. After all, democracy rests on the sovereignty of the people and not (necessarily) on the sovereignty of God. Otherwise Qutb had very little to say about democracy or any other form of government.[21] By contrast, Iran's Ayatollah Khomeini (1900?–1989) had quite a lot to say about the structure of an Islamic state, and today we find at least some features of a *radical* Islamic state in the "Islamic Republic" of Iran.[22] Iran has a parliament whose members are elected. But the only candidates eligible to run for public office are those who have been screened and approved by the Council of Guardians consisting of twelve religious elders, or *mullahs*. The *mullahs* also have the power to interpret the Iranian Constitution and to veto any law passed by the parliament. There is virtually no freedom of the press, and journalists and writers who dare to criticize the government are jailed. There is little or no academic freedom, and students and professors who speak their minds are punished harshly. Robbers are routinely punished by having their hands amputated. In some cases a robber's right hand and left foot are amputated, making it impossible for him to walk even with the aid of a cane or crutches, or to be gainfully employed.[23] These and other harsh and oppressive practices are justified on religious grounds. In reality, then, the Republic of Iran is neither a republic nor a democracy but something approaching a theocracy, or what Khomeini called "rule by the clergy" (*velayat-e faqih*).

The supremacy of clerical rule became especially evident in the Iranian presidential election of June 2009 when "Supreme Leader" Ayatollah Ali Khamenei declared the conservative incumbent, Mahmoud Ahmadinejad, the winner a mere two hours after the polls closed and called his victory "divinely ordained." Amid widespread and well-founded allegations of vote rigging, tens of thousands of young supporters of Ahmadinejad's reformist rival, Mir-Hossein Moussavi, took to the streets in peaceful protests. These were met with murderous violence from the religious police and other agents of the state. Untold thousands were beaten, arrested, tortured, and forced to "confess" that their protests were prompted by Western provocateurs. Many others remain in prison and unaccounted for. How many were killed is, as yet, unknown. Supreme Leader Khamenei asserted that the protestors were "acting against God" and got the punishment they deserved. The clergy itself appeared to be divided over the election and the direction in which the country seems to be heading, but the Supreme Leader was then and is now in firm control of the police, the Revolutionary Guards, the *basiji* militias, and the armed forces. Whether or for how long force alone can prevail is an open question. Two of every three Iranians are under thirty years of age. And young Iranians are especially resentful of repression in the name of religion, and many want much greater freedom and an end to theocratic rule.[24] What will happen next is, as always, difficult to predict, but it seems certain that the authority of the *mullahs* and the legitimacy of religious rule were badly tarnished by the 2009 presidential election. And, apparently recognizing this, the *mullahs* allowed the name of a relative moderate, Hassan Rouhani, to appear on the ballot in 2013. Rouhani won in a landslide, and now, as president, appears to be moving Iran in a more moderate and less militant direction. But under the current Iranian constitution his power is limited. Whether, or how long and to what extent, he can prevail against radical Islamists remains to be seen. A crucial test will be the ongoing struggle between moderates and hard-liners over the 2015 treaty banning Iran's development of nuclear weapons.

The Iranian regime is Shi'ite; by contrast, that of the Islamic State (ISIS), as we noted earlier, represents a radical jihadist offshoot of Sunni Islam that seeks a return to the theological purity of the seventh century. And this includes modes or methods of punishment prevalent at that time: crucifixion, beheading, burning alive, and the like. These carefully staged crucifixions, beheadings, and burnings are broadcast worldwide on social media and used as tools to recruit young Muslims from abroad. Alienated, disaffected, and eager to "belong" to a community larger than themselves, these young people are carefully "groomed" by recruiters online. Once recruited, they are told to come to Syria to fight or, failing that, to stay at home and become home-grown terrorists.[25]

The Islamic state envisioned by ISIS is not to be democratic but theocratic. This is not necessarily true of all radical Islamists, some of whom believe, as does the Shi'ite Iranian regime—ISIS's arch-enemy—that a (very) limited form of democracy is legitimate. Whether such a severely circumscribed democracy is really "democracy" is debatable.

For anyone who hopes to establish an Islamic democracy, the status and role of women presents problems. Women in many Islamic countries, such as Jordan, Pakistan, and Egypt, are eligible to vote and hold public office, but in others, including Saudi Arabia, they were not, at least until 2015 when they were partially—and, critics claimed, symbolically—permitted to vote in local elections. Women gained the right to vote in Kuwait in May 2005, despite Islamist opposition, and they did vote in the first free Iraqi election in 2005. If Iraq becomes a conservative Islamic state, however, women there could be forced to revert to "traditional" roles. Traditional views change slowly, if at all, even where radical Islamists have been defeated and discredited, as developments in Afghanistan have shown. When Afghan delegates met to draft a new constitution in late 2003, after the overthrow of the radical Islamist Taliban regime, old misogynist and antifeminist attitudes and beliefs quickly reemerged. Women delegates to the constitutional conference were outnumbered five to one by men, and when the women demanded that at least one of three deputies on the ruling council be a woman, they were outvoted: the new constitution would stipulate that all three deputies would be men. When the women protested, the conference chair—an Islamic scholar reputed to be a moderate—rebuked them. "Don't try to put yourself on a level with men," he said. "Even God has not given you equal rights ... because under His decision two women are counted as equal to one man." (He referred to the passage in the *Qur'an* [2:282], that the testimony of two female witnesses is equivalent to that of one male.) After threatening to walk out and boycott the conference, the women won a victory of sorts: a fourth deputy, who was to be a woman, would be added to the ruling council.[26] And in the wake of the Arab Spring that began in early 2011 and which overthrew repressive regimes in the near and Middle East, once-outlawed radical Islamist parties have secured significant electoral victories.

The fears that followed such victories were especially evident in Egypt, where the former Muslim Brotherhood leader was elected president. Non-traditional Egyptian women had reason to be worried about developments during Morsi's brief time in office, before being overthrown by the Egyptian military. One of these was a statement issued by the Brotherhood in 2013, in response to a proposed United Nations declaration condemning violence against women and advocating equality within marriage. "A woman needs to be confined within a framework that is controlled by the man of the house," said Osama Yehia Abu Salama, a leading Brotherhood member and one of the authors of the statement. A wife who is beaten by her husband typically has only herself to blame. And if the man is mistaken in beating her, she nevertheless "shares 30 [to] 40 percent of the fault." The husband's role is to exercise "guardianship" over his wife, since marriage is not an "equal partnership." A wife needs to ask her husband for permission to— among many other things—travel, use contraceptives, or take a job. "Daughters should not have the same inheritance rights as sons." Claiming the *Qur'an* as its source and authority, the Brotherhood's statement goes on at some length, through a long list of restrictions and prohibitions.[27]

But many women, in Egypt and elsewhere, do not accept this male-dominated or patriarchal way of reading, interpreting, and applying the teachings of the *Qur'an*. Following in the footsteps of prominent Muslim scholars and theologians such as Abu Zayd (1943–), some feminist scholars are challenging interpretations of the *Qur'an* that relegate women to second-class status. Applying critical and historical methods of investigation and interpretation, Amina Wadud, Asma Barlas, Kecia Ali, and others are challenging Islamist readings of the *Qur'an* and the fairly widespread and long-standing male monopoly on interpreting it. They argue that one must separate the patriarchal context in which the *Qur'an* was written (or, as devout Muslims believe, received) and the universalist and egalitarian principles implicit in the text and in the teachings of the Prophet. All human beings are made in Allah's image, and He loves them all equally, men and women alike. Allah commands humans to respect and love each other without regard to race, to differences of wealth, social status, or gender. To discriminate against women, to make them into servants and second-class citizens, is contrary to the spirit and the principles of Islam.[28] Such a feminist rereading of the *Qur'an* has not found favor among traditionalist scholars and has encountered strident resistance and threats of death against women who dare to defy the supposed supremacy of men. To be sure, traditional attitudes about women's proper place in life—attitudes that would keep them out of politics—are not confined to Muslim-majority societies. Those attitudes are especially strong in those societies, however, and they are taken most seriously by radical Islamists. If a society that denies political rights to women can no longer be called a democracy, then radical Islamism cannot be considered a democratic ideology. Indeed, a radical Islamist state would almost certainly deny the vote to women and would probably restrict the political powers and civil rights of men as well. If the examples of Iran and the even more repressive rule of the Taliban in Afghanistan are accurate guides, in sum, it seems safe to say that radical Islamism is, together with fascism, one of those rare ideologies that reject the democratic ideal.

Or so it appeared before the advent of the Arab Spring. Some radical Islamist clerics who had previously contended that democracy and Islam are incompatible subsequently said something quite different. They say that it is not democracy *per se* that is incompatible with Islam but Western-style *liberal* democracy, with its constitutional protections of individual liberty and human rights, sexual equality, and the freedom to worship as one pleases or—even worse—to not worship at all. This has led some observers to speculate that an illiberal Islamist democracy might be as oppressive as any dictatorship. It is, as yet, too early to tell if these fears and forebodings are well-founded. Egypt will almost certainly prove to be an important test case. After the Arab Spring toppled the dictatorial president Hosni Mubarak, even the ultra-conservative Salafi sect—whose leaders had once denounced democracy—organized its own political party and fielded candidates for public office, as did the strict and once-secretive Muslim Brotherhood, whose leading thinker had been Sayyid Qutb.[29] In 2012 Egypt held its first free and fair parliamentary and presidential elections in its 5000-year history. Nearly three-quarters of the parliamentary seats were won by Islamists, and of those half were won by the Islamic Brotherhood's Freedom and Justice Party, and the presidency was won by their candidate, Mohamed Morsi, former leader of the Brotherhood. Shortly thereafter the largely Mubarak-appointed Egyptian judiciary, backed by the military, dissolved the parliament and made the newly elected president a mere figurehead without real power. Morsi attempted to challenge those restrictions, but was subsequently removed from office in a highly controversial military takeover in 2013 that precipitated widespread violence between Islamists and supporters of the military's actions. Both sides claimed to be defending democracy, but the country appeared instead to be careening towards potential civil war. That outcome was prevented as the forces that overthrew the Morsi government consolidated under General Abdel Fattah el-Sisi, who, in a questionable election—he purportedly won 96.9 percent of the vote—became the new president, and a strongman in the mold of Mubarak. In Egypt the once-promising Arab Spring had turned to winter. Morsi and his Muslim Brothers are now in prison, awaiting execution.[30]

Some critics believe that a real or alleged hostility to democracy is not the only feature that radical Islamism and fascism have in common. Former President George

W. Bush and some neoconservatives have even gone so far as to describe radical Islamism as "Islamofascism" or "Islamic fascism."[31] This description, however, has more rhetorical value—"fascism" is, after all, a word with negative connotations—than intellectual merit.[32] Radical Islamism is an ideology rooted in religion, not nationalism or devotion to the state. That is, radical Islamism is a transnational movement that neither recognizes nor respects national boundaries, while fascism is nationalist and state-centered, emphasizing the unity and integrity of the nation-state (as in Italy under Mussolini or Spain under Franco). Radical Islamists look forward to the establishment of a transnational Caliphate or international Muslim community—the *umma*—that encompasses all predominantly Muslim nations in the near and Middle East and in parts of Asia (most notably Indonesia). The fact that Muslims are people of many different nationalities and ethnic groups is of no real concern to them, as it certainly would be to fascists. Moreover, fascism is a form of state-worship that Muslims, both moderate and radical, find idolatrous, abhorrent, and blasphemous. No radical Islamist could agree with Mussolini, for example, when he declared, "for the fascist, everything is in the State, and nothing human or spiritual exists, much less has value, outside the State."[33] Nor can a radical Islamist happily follow the fascist tendency to glorify one supposedly all-wise, all-powerful leader who must be obeyed without doubt or question. On the contrary, Muslims of every stripe believe that no human should command such blind and unquestioning loyalty; only Allah deserves that. For all of these reasons, it is a mistake to brand radical Islamism as a branch from the fascist tree.

Discussion Questions

1   What is the meaning of the Arabic word *jihad*? How do radical Islamists differ from moderate or mainstream Muslims in their interpretations of this word, and what implication does the radical Islamists' interpretation have for their political program?
2   How—i.e., by means of what claims and arguments—do radical Islamists attempt to justify the killings of presumably innocent Israelis and Americans, among many others?
3   What were Sayyid Qutb's main contributions to radical Islamist ideology?
4   The 2013 Boston Marathon terrorist attack brought to the fore the new and heretofore unprecedented phenomenon of "self-radicalization" by and among young Islamists. What does this mean, and how does it come about?
5   What is "the gray zone" and why is ISIS determined to eliminate it?
6   What, according to ISIS, is the significance of a declaration of a Caliphate?

NOTES

1   See Husain Haqqani, "The Ideologies of South Asian Jihadi Groups," *Current Trends in Islamist Ideology*, April 2005, pp. 12–26.
2   As Bernard Lewis and other scholars have observed, the distinction between "church" and "state" is largely a Christian invention, with no clear counterpart in Islam. See Lewis, *What Went Wrong? Western Impact and Middle Eastern Response* (New York: Oxford University Press, 2002), pp. 97–99.

3 Quoted in Daniel Benjamin and Steven Simon, *The Age of Sacred Terror: Radical Islam's War Against America* (New York: Random House, 2003), p. 64.

4 Because most of Qutb's books have not been translated into English, and we do not read Arabic, we have relied on several scholarly sources in developing this account of Qutb's political views, especially the excellent study by Roxanne L. Euben, *Enemy in the Mirror: Islamic Fundamentalism and the Limits of Modern Rationalism* (Princeton, NJ: University Press, 1999). Other helpful sources are: Salwa Ismail, "Islamic Political Thought," in *The Cambridge History of Twentieth-Century Political Thought*, Terence Ball and Richard Bellamy, eds. (Cambridge: Cambridge University Press, 2003); Shahrough Akhavi, "Qutb, Sayyid," *The Oxford Encyclopedia of the Modern Islamic World*, vol. 3 (Oxford: Oxford University Press, 1995), and "The Dialectic in Contemporary Egyptian Social Thought: The Scripturalist and Modernist Discourses of Sayyid Qutb and Hasan Hanafi," *International Journal of Middle East Studies* 29 (1997): 377–401; and William Shepherd, "Islam as a 'System' in the Later Writings of Sayyid Qutb," *Middle Eastern Studies* 25 (1989): 31–50. More recent studies include John Calvert, *Sayyid Qutb and the Origins of Radical Islamism* (Oxford and New York: Oxford University Press, 2013) and James Toth, *Sayyid Qutb: The Life and Legacy of a Radical Islamic Intellectual* (New York and Oxford: Oxford University Press, 2012); both are reviewed by Max Rodenbeck, "The Father of Violent Islamism," *New York Review of Books*, LX: 8 (May 9, 2013), pp. 54–55. For an excerpt from Qutb's *Signposts Along the Road* in English, see Terence Ball, Richard Dagger, and Daniel O'Neill, eds., *Ideals and Ideologies: A Reader*, 10th ed. (London and New York: Routledge, 2016), selection 10.68.

5 As explained in Johannes J. G. Jansen, *The Neglected Duty: The Creed of Sadat's Assassins and the Emergence of Islamic Militance in the Middle East* (New York: Macmillan, 1986).

6 Ibid., pp. 159–234.

7 In this section we have relied on several recent works, including William McCants, *The ISIS Apocalypse: The History, Strategy, and Doomsday Vision of the Islamic State* (New York: St. Martin's Press, 2015); Joby Warrick, *Black Flags: The Rise of ISIS* (New York: Doubleday, 2015); Patrick Cockburn, *The Rise of Islamic State: ISIS and the New Sunni Revolution* (London: Verso, 2015); Michael Weiss and Hassan Hassan, *ISIS: Inside the Army of Terror* (New York: Regan Arts, 2015); Jessica Stern and J. M. Berger, *ISIS: State of Terror* (New York: HarperCollins, 2015); and Graeme Wood, "What ISIS Really Wants," *The Atlantic*, March 2015, pp. 78–94.

8 Abu Bakr al-Baghdadi, "Declaration of a Caliphate," in Ball, Dagger, and O'Neill, eds., *Ideals and Ideologies: A Reader*, selection 10.71.

9 See Andrew Ross Sorkin, "The Hidden Costs of Terror," *New York Times*, November 17, 2015, pp. B1, B4.

10 Lawrence Wright, *The Looming Tower: Al-Qaeda and the Road to 9/11* (New York: Knopf, 2007).

11 Ibid., p. 47.

12 Quoted in ibid., p. 47.

13 Quoted in ibid., p. 108.

14 See Roxanne L. Euben, "Comparative Political Theory: An Islamic Fundamentalist Critique of Rationalism," *Journal of Politics* 59 (February 1997): 28–55.

15 Quoted in Noah Feldman, "Islam, Terror, and the Second Nuclear Age," *New York Times Magazine*, October 29, 2006, pp. 56–57. See also Osama bin Laden and others, "Jihad Against Jews and Crusaders," in Terence Ball, Richard Dagger, and Daniel O'Neill, eds., *Ideals and Ideologies*, selection 10.70; and Peter Bergen, *The Osama bin Laden I Know: An Oral History of Al Qaeda's Leader* (New York: Free Press, 2006).

16 Quoted in Michael Slackman, "A Liberal Brother at Odds with the Muslim Brotherhood," *New York Times*, October 21, 2006, p. A4.

17 Mill, *On Liberty*, in Mill, *Utilitarianism, Liberty, and Representative Government*, A. D. Lindsay, ed. (New York: E. P. Dutton, 1910), p. 96. This passage is included in the

excerpt from *On Liberty* in Ball, Dagger, and O'Neill, *Ideals and Ideologies*, selection 3.18.

18 Michaelle L. Browers and Charles Kurzman, eds., *An Islamic Reformation?* (Lanham, MD: Lexington Books, 2004).

19 Whether this is an accurate characterization of liberal democracy is doubtful, as no less a liberal than John Stuart Mill proclaimed in his *Considerations on Representative Government* that "the most important point of excellence which any form of government can possess is *to promote the virtue and intelligence of the people themselves*" (Mill, *Utilitarianism, Liberty, and Representative Government* [cited earlier, n. 17], p. 259, emphasis added). As we point out in Chapter 3, the question of whether liberal-democratic governments should or should not try to make their citizens better or more virtuous people remains the subject of a vigorous debate among liberal theorists.

20 For a helpful discussion of Islamic liberalism, see Michaelle L. Browers, "Modern Islamic Political Thought," *Handbook of Political Theory*, Gerald Gaus and Chandran Kukathas, eds. (London: SAGE, 2004), esp. pp. 373–377.

21 Roxanne Euben, *Enemy in the Mirror*, pp. 77–78.

22 See *Islam and Revolution: Writings and Declarations of Imam Khomeini*, trans. Hamid Algar (Berkeley, CA: Mizan Press, 1981). Excerpts from this book are included in Ball, Dagger, and O'Neill, *Ideals and Ideologies*, selection 10.69.

23 Nazila Fathi, "Hanging and Amputation Find Favor in Iran Courts," *New York Times*, January 11, 2008, p. A3.

24 Robert F. Worth, "Iranian Protests Turn More Radical—Anger Expands to Include Supreme Leader and Theocratic System," *New York Times*, December 11, 2009, p. A6.

25 Eric Schmitt, "ISIS Followers in U.S. are Diverse and Young," *New York Times*, December 2, 2015, p. A3; Scott Shane, Matt Apuzzo, and Eric Schmitt, "Online Embrace of ISIS, Just a Few Clicks Away," *New York Times*, December 9, 2015, pp. A1, A14.

26 "Meeting on New Constitution, Afghan Women Find Old Attitudes," *New York Times*, December 16, 2003, p. A16.

27 David Kirkpatrick and Mayy El-Sheikh, "Muslim Brotherhood's Statement on Women Stirs Liberal Fears," *New York Times*, March 15, 2013, p. A4.

28 See Anjuman Ali, "Feminists Reread the Qur'an," *The Progressive*, November 2007, pp. 29–31.

29 David D. Kirkpatrick, "Egyptian Campaign Focuses on Islam's Role in Public Life," *New York Times*, May 12, 2012, p. A4.

30 See Thanassis Cambanis, *Once Upon a Revolution: An Egyptian Story* (New York: Simon & Schuster, 2015).

31 See, for example, Norman Podhoretz, *World War IV: The Long Struggle Against Islamofascism* (New York: Vintage Books, 2008).

32 On "fascism" as a "smear" or political swear word, see George Orwell, "Politics and the English Language" in Orwell, *Collected Essays*, eds. Ian Angus and Sonia Orwell, 4 vols. (London: Penguin, 2000), vol. 4.

33 Benito Mussolini, "The Doctrine of Fascism," in Ball, Dagger, and O'Neill, *Ideals and Ideologies*, selection 7.48.

FOR FURTHER READING

Benjamin, Daniel, and Steven Simon. *The Age of Sacred Terror*. New York: Random House, 2002.

Brachman, Jarret M., *Global Jihadism: Theory and Practice*. New York and London: Routledge, 2008.

Browers, Michaelle, *Political Ideology in the Arab World: Accommodation and Transformation*. Cambridge: Cambridge University Press, 2009.

——. "Islamic Political Ideologies," in Michael Freeden, ed., *Oxford Handbook of Political Ideologies*, pp. 627–643. Oxford: Oxford University Press, 2013.

Brown, Nathan J., *When Victory Is Not an Option: Islamist Movements in Arab Politics.* Ithaca, NY: Cornell University Press, 2012.

Cook, David, *Understanding Jihad.* Berkeley and Los Angeles: University of California Press, 2005.

Davidson, Lawrence. *Islamic Fundamentalism.* Westport, CT: Greenwood Press, 1998.

Esposito, John L. *What Everyone Needs to Know About Islam.* Oxford: Oxford University Press, 2002.

——, ed. *Political Islam: Revolution, Radicalism, or Reform?* Boulder, CO: Lynne Rienner, 1997.

Euben, Roxanne L. *Enemy in the Mirror: Islamic Fundamentalism and the Limits of Modern Rationalism.* Princeton, NJ: Princeton University Press, 1999.

Euben, Roxanne L., and Muhammad Qasim Zaman, eds., *Princeton Readings in Islamist Thought.* Princeton, NJ: Princeton University Press, 2009.

Gray, John. *Al Qaeda and What It Means to Be Modern.* London: Faber, 2003.

Ismail, Salwa. "Islamic Political Thought," in Terence Ball and Richard Bellamy, eds., *The Cambridge History of Twentieth-Century Political Thought.* Cambridge: Cambridge University Press, 2003.

——. "Is there an Islamic Conception of Politics?" in Adrian Leftwich, ed., *What Is Politics?* Cambridge: Polity Press, 2004.

——. *Rethinking Islamist Politics: Culture, the State and Islamism,* 2nd ed. London: I. B. Tauris, 2006.

Lewis, Bernard. *What Went Wrong? Western Impact and Middle Eastern Response.* Oxford: Oxford University Press, 2002.

Mawsilili, Ahmad. *Radical Islamic Fundamentalism.* Beirut: American University of Beirut, 1992.

——, ed. *Islamic Fundamentalism: Myths and Realities.* Reading, U.K.: Ithaca Press, 1998.

Sivan, Emmanuel. *Radical Islam: Medieval Theology and Modern Politics,* 2nd ed. New Haven, CT: Yale University Press, 1990.

Wickham, Carrie Rosevsky. *The Muslim Brotherhood: Evolution of an Islamist Movement.* Princeton, NJ: Princeton University Press, 2013.

From the Ball, Dagger, and O'Neill Reader *Ideals and Ideologies*, Tenth Edition

Part X Radical Islamism

USEFUL WEBSITES

Center for Strategic and International Studies: www.csis.org
Federation of American Scientists: www.fas.org
International Crisis Group: www.crisisgroup.org
Middle East Forum: www.meforum.org

CHAPTER 11

POSTSCRIPT: THE FUTURE OF IDEOLOGY

Every boy and every gal
That's born into the world alive
Is either a little Liberal
Or else a little Conservative!

Gilbert and Sullivan, *Iolanthe*

When Gilbert and Sullivan's musical spoof of English politics and society was first performed in 1882, the audience may well have believed that the division between the Liberal and Conservative parties neatly reflected the major ideological divisions of their day. But the range of ideological choices was not so narrow even then. Many socialists were active in North America and Europe—including Karl Marx, who died in England the year following the first performance of *Iolanthe*. Anarchists of different stripes were also active, as were the various nationalists, elitists, and racial theorists who were sowing the seeds of fascism and Nazism. Anyone seeking an alternative to liberalism and conservatism did not have far to look.

Even within the ranks of liberals and conservatives, moreover, there was disharmony and disagreement. This was especially true of the liberals, who were arguing among themselves almost as much as they quarreled with their ideological rivals. Divided into the groups we have called **welfare** and **neoclassical** liberals, they agreed on the value of individual liberty but disagreed strenuously as to whether a strong government was needed to counter the increasing economic and political power of large corporations and to promote liberty—as T. H. Green and the welfare liberals maintained—or, conversely, that the only safe government was a weak government, as Herbert Spencer and the neoclassical liberals insisted.

If ideological conflicts were more complicated in 1882 than Gilbert and Sullivan's spoof suggested, they are even more so today. To the ideological disputes and divisions of the 1800s, the twentieth century added new ones. Beginning with fascism and proceeding through the newly emerging ideologies we discussed in Chapters 8, 9, and 10, the twentieth—and now twenty-first—centuries have been an era of ideological ferment. Newer and older ideologies alike contributed to this

356

ferment as they responded to changing circumstances by shifting their positions, splitting into factions, criticizing and even borrowing from one another—all of which can easily bewilder someone trying to make sense of any one ideology, let alone the wider array of political ideologies in general. Just when one thinks he or she understands what communism is all about, for example, Gorbachev's **glasnost** and the other remarkable changes of the late 1980s in the communist countries come along to upset all expectations. Then in the 1990s communism itself seemed to collapse. As communism all but collapsed, radical Islamism burst onto the political scene. And who knows what history still has in store?

That is why we have taken a historical approach to understanding political ideologies. Political ideologies, as we have emphasized, are dynamic; they do not stand still but change and respond to changing circumstances. Trying to define a particular ideology is thus a little like trying to hit a moving target. But if we look back in history to see how a particular ideology originated, emerged as a political force and how it has responded to changing circumstances and new ideological challenges, we are at least able to use our grasp of what *has happened* to understand what *is happening* now. The past is usually the best guide to the present. It is only in this way, furthermore, that we can hope to understand what is likely to happen in the future of political ideologies—a future that, in one way or another, will play a part not only in our own lives but also in those of our children and grandchildren. With that in mind, our purpose in this final chapter is to take stock of the state of political ideologies today and to try to foresee their future, at least in dim outline.

POLITICAL IDEOLOGIES: CONTINUING FORCES

In Chapter 7 we noted how liberalism and socialism have both followed the lead of the **Enlightenment** philosophers of the eighteenth century in anticipating continuing and ever-accelerating human progress through the exercise of reason. To some extent, of course, their expectations have been met. Whether measured in terms of religious tolerance, freedom of speech, the right to vote and participate in government, or health and life expectancy, the condition of most people in Europe and North America does indeed appear to be better than it was two centuries ago. In other respects, however, it is clear that things have not turned out as the early liberals and socialists expected. In particular, the forces of **nationalism** and religion remain politically powerful.

Liberalism and socialism can both accommodate the kinds of local or parochial sentiments that nationalism embodies, but they do so uncomfortably. In different ways, each represents the universalism of the Enlightenment. Liberals do this by stressing individual liberty—not the liberty of Englishmen or Arabs or Chinese or any other group but of individuals in the abstract. For their part, socialists—or at least democratic socialists—have sought to promote the interests of the working class, but they have tried to do this by overcoming or eliminating class divisions so that every individual may enjoy a free and fulfilling life. In neither case do national loyalties play a part. Yet nationalism has proved to be a persistent and significant factor in modern politics.

Nationalism and Ideology

The nationalist sentiments and ideologies awakened in the nineteenth century grew even more strident and powerful in the twentieth. In the second decade of the twenty-first century, nationalism shows no sign of abating. We saw earlier, in Chapter 7, how nationalism figured in the rise of fascism and Nazism in the last century, but that is only part of the story. Nationalism has also contributed directly to the **anticolonial movements** in Africa, Asia, and Latin America. In the nineteenth century, Latin American colonists joined liberalism to nationalism as they fought to free themselves from Spanish and Portuguese rule. In the twentieth century, Marxist movements often used nationalist appeals, drawing especially on Lenin's theory of imperialism. In the years following World War II, in fact, communist uprisings in the so-called Third World usually took the form of anticolonial "wars of *national* liberation." In Mao Zedong's adaptation of Marx's terms, these were conflicts between "bourgeois" and "proletarian" *nations*.

By the late twentieth century, however, nationalist impulses seemed as likely to frustrate as to further the spread of Marxian socialism. One sign of this trend has been the conflicts between countries that claim to be communist. The long-standing tension between the Soviet Union and the People's Republic of China was one of several examples. China also fought a brief war with its communist neighbor, Vietnam, and Vietnam invaded another neighbor, Cambodia, in order to overthrow its communist Khmer Rouge regime. In all of these cases old antagonisms between different nations proved more powerful than allegiance to a common ideology.

Nationalist antagonisms also provoked dissension *within* the boundaries of communist countries, particularly in the former Soviet Union. About half the population of the Soviet Union was Russian, with the other half consisting of people of various nationalities—Latvian, Ukrainian, Chechen, Armenian, and many others. Many of these people had long resented Russian dominance and sought greater independence for their own national group. (The Ukrainians' "Orange Revolution" provides a particularly vivid example of such nationalist striving, as does the Chechens' even more militant struggle against Russian domination. In 2014 Russia invaded and occupied Crimea, formerly part of Ukraine, and subsequently took over its eastern provinces.) The conflicts and bitterness between these diverse national groups contributed to the breakup of the Soviet Union and the formation in its place of the Commonwealth of Independent States. Nationalist conflicts have appeared in other formerly communist countries as well. They have been especially violent in the former Yugoslavia, where Serbs, Croats, and Bosnian Muslims fought a civil war characterized by **ethnic cleansing**—a euphemism for the systematic expulsion and mass murder of rival nationalities. Even Czechoslovakia split, albeit peacefully, into the Czech Republic and Slovakia. In the late twentieth century, then, nationalism helped to bring down communist regimes and divided neighbors along ethnic lines.

Nor is this a problem only in the communist and formerly communist countries. Nationalism continues to be a powerful force throughout the world, often in the form of **separatist movements.** The Basques in Spain, the Scots in Great Britain, the French-speaking Québécois in Canada—militant members of these and other nationalities occasionally speak up, and in some cases resort to violence, to try to win greater national autonomy or independence for their group. The once-vicious conflict in Northern Ireland is in part a conflict between nationalities. So, too, are many of the disputes in Africa, the Middle East, and Asia, as the civil war between the Hutus and Tutsis that devastated Rwanda in the 1990s and the severe internal conflict in Sri Lanka indicate.

These episodes suggest that nationalism will not simply fade away, no matter how often Marxists say that the workers have no fatherland or liberals describe individuals simply as individuals and not as members of any particular ethnic, racial, or national group. For the foreseeable future, at least, nationalism will doubtless continue to complicate matters. Indeed, there is some reason to believe that nationalistic sentiments may become even more powerful in the twenty-first century. As technological advances in transportation and communication—social media, most especially—make the world a smaller place, with more people crossing more boundaries in search of political refuge or economic opportunity, nationalistic resentments have come to the surface. In Europe, as we noted in Chapter 7, resentment of "guest workers" from other countries, immigrants from former colonies, and the flood of refugees from the civil war in Syria and elsewhere has rekindled fascist sentiments in several countries. Similar concerns about "immigration problems" and the growth of Asian-American and Hispanic populations have led in the United States to the passage of "Official English" laws and restrictions on access to welfare programs, as in California's Proposition 187. More recently, prominent nationalist politicians have advocated mass deportations of millions of undocumented immigrants and the building of a wall along the border to keep them out, the denial of birthright citizenship (in violation of the Fourteenth Amendment), and at least a temporary ban on all Muslim immigration. These concerns have also sparked renewed activity by neo-Nazi and other white-supremacist groups.

For better or worse, then, nationalism promises to be with us for quite some time. The same is true of religion as a political force.

Religion and Ideology

Unlike most conservatives, who have usually regarded religion as an essential part of the social fabric, many liberals and socialists have wanted or expected religion to fade in importance. There have been important exceptions, to be sure, but liberals and socialists have tended to look upon religion in one of two ways. The first is to see it as an obstacle to a full and free life—an outmoded superstition, according to some Enlightenment thinkers, or the **opium of the people** as Marx put it. Once "reason" or "history" or "class struggle" does its work, some say, the obstacle of religion will be removed and left behind. The second way is to declare religion a private matter to be left to the individual's conscience. In this view, religion may be a valuable, even crucial, part of personal life; but church and state must be kept separate to promote tolerance and protect religious freedom.[1]

Yet religion continues to play a major role in political controversies around the world. Far from fading away, as Marx had predicted and Mill had hoped, religion has flourished in most parts of the world. Indeed, many religious people see their religion not as an obstacle but as a pathway to freedom.[2]

Evidence of the continuing strength of religion in politics is abundant. In earlier chapters we discussed the **Religious Right** in American conservatism and liberation theology as it has emerged in Latin America. Further evidence can be found in the Middle East, where the conflict between Israel and the surrounding countries has both religious and nationalistic elements, and in Northern Ireland, where Catholics and Protestants have long been at odds. Finally and most clearly, the political power of religion today is evident in the development of radical Islamism discussed in the previous chapter.

As these and other examples attest, religion is no more likely than nationalism to lose its political appeal. But that is not because religion is a single, united force. To be sure, there is a sense in which fundamentalists within both Christianity and Islam are reacting against the spread of secularism, or "secular humanism." Both groups believe that there is too much attention to human desires and too little to God's commands. This belief has led Islamist radicals to declare a "holy war" on Western "infidels" and Muslim "apostates," while members of the Religious Right have tried to remove books they deem immoral from public libraries and require the teaching of "creation science" or "intelligent design" in public schools.

What they have in common as fundamentalists, however, is more than offset by their differences as Muslims and Christians. As liberation theology demonstrates, furthermore, fundamentalism is not the only active force in religion these days. Liberation theologians and Religious Right fundamentalists share a commitment to Christianity, but their ideas of what it means to be and act as Christians are vastly different. While the Religious Right calls for a strict or literal reading of the Bible and a return to "traditional morality," liberation theology insists that the Bible must be read in the light of the circumstances and knowledge of the day—including knowledge gained from the theories of radicals and atheists such as Karl Marx—and then applied to reshape society in the interests of all, especially the poor. Although many other Christians do not go as far as the liberation theologians, they still see their religion as an inspiration to act in unconventional ways. In the 1980s, for instance, the National Conference of Catholic Bishops of the United States condemned as immoral not only nuclear war but also the use of nuclear weapons even as a deterrent or threat. At about the same time, some American Christians organized the Sanctuary movement, which defied the immigration policies of the United States government by helping refugees from Central America enter and live in the United States. Such sanctuaries continue to prevent the deportation of undocumented immigrants back to their home countries, where their lives may be in danger. In 1991 Pope John Paul II issued an encyclical in which he both welcomed the apparent downfall of communism and warned against "a radical capitalistic ideology" that "blindly entrusts" the solution of "great material and moral poverty" to "the free development of market forces."[3] Pope Francis has been even more outspoken in his critique of capitalism, consumerism, and "the throw-away society."[4]

Religion remains a potent political force, in sum, but it is a force pushing in different directions. We should not expect religion to wither away, as Marx did, but neither should we expect all religious believers to unite in a single political cause.

IDEOLOGY AND PUBLIC POLICY

In Chapter 1 we noted that political ideologies are dynamic—that they change and shift in response to circumstances—and the succeeding chapters have illustrated this point over and over again. Ideologies aim to shape the world, or some significant part of it, but they cannot do this if they fail to respond to changing conditions, including the challenges presented by rival ideologies. One aspect of this dynamism is that ideologies tend to divide into quarreling factions. Within liberalism, as we have seen, there are welfare liberals and neoclassical liberals—and perhaps, nowadays, communitarian liberals, too. Within socialism there are Christian and other non-Marxian socialists, and among the Marxist socialists there are the Marxist-Leninist revolutionaries and the revisionists. And so on for all of the ideologies.

We should be wary, therefore, of the claim that there is a single, unified set of policy positions that all adherents of any ideology accept. We should be skeptical, for example, of anyone who speaks of "*the* conservative position" on abortion, capital punishment, same-sex marriage, or any other issue of law and public policy. Conservatives are more likely to be opposed to abortion and in favor of capital punishment than are liberals, but it would be a mistake to think that all conservatives necessarily hold these views. In the United States, the individualist-conservative group Republicans for Choice holds that a woman's decision to have an abortion is a private matter beyond the legitimate reach of the state—a view strongly opposed by religious-right conservatives. Some self-described "pro-life" conservatives insist that anyone who is truly pro-life must be opposed, as the Roman Catholic Church is, to both abortion and capital punishment. Similarly, some liberals, invoking John Stuart Mill's "harm principle," oppose abortion on the ground that having an abortion is not a self-regarding but an other-regarding act—the "other" in question being the fetus or unborn child—and should therefore be prevented or punished by law. (The Supreme Court decision in the case of *Roe v. Wade* offers a modified version of this view: as the fetus becomes an ever more recognizable human "other," the government's responsibility to protect it/her/him increases.)

On other broadly moral and cultural questions, conservatives and liberals disagree both with each other and among themselves. Therefore one's views about what kinds of laws and public policies should be adopted depend on what *kind* of conservative—or liberal, or socialist, and so on—one is. The study of political ideologies would be simpler if this were not the case, but the dynamic nature of ideologies, compounded by their tendency to develop internal fissures and factions, makes it impossible to reduce any ideology to a single, unified set of policy positions.

IDEOLOGY, THE ENVIRONMENT, AND GLOBALIZATION

Despite their disagreements, liberals and socialists and some conservatives, especially individualist conservatives, have shared a faith in material progress. They have believed, that is, that human life can and will become easier—less subject to starvation, disease, and unremitting labor—through the "mastery of nature." That is why they have usually encouraged industrial and technological development.

In the course of the twentieth century, however, material progress came to be seen as a mixed blessing. Although life is better for many people in many ways, it is now clear that much of this improvement has come at the expense of the natural environment. Nature has not proved so easy to "master" or "harness" as earlier champions of progress had thought. Global warming, the greenhouse effect, acid rain, toxic wastes of various sorts, and the other ecological problems we discussed in Chapter 9 leave no doubt that material progress has produced a host of unanticipated and unhealthy consequences. Life may be better for many people in many ways, but demands on the earth's ecosystems may soon exceed their carrying capacities.

In short, ecological problems have become political problems as well. All ideologies will have to respond to the challenge of these new circumstances in some fashion. One response, as we saw in Chapter 9, is the emergence of a new environmental or "green" ideology. Whether this becomes a major ideology in its own right depends in large part on how the "mainstream" ideologies respond to the ecological crisis. If liberalism, socialism, and/or conservatism address environmental problems in a convincing manner, thereby "stealing the thunder" of the Greens, there will be neither need nor room for a green ideology as such. If none of them does this, however, we should expect green politics to become an increasingly influential presence on the political scene.

Yet another possibility exists. The ecological crisis could conceivably provoke a resurgence of fascism. According to Robert Heilbroner, it may prove impossible to persuade people to make the sacrifices necessary to meet the ecological crisis.[5] Those of us who have grown used to the benefits of material progress—gas-guzzling sport-utility vehicles (SUVs) and air conditioners, for example—will not want to "downsize" or surrender them, and those who do not now enjoy those benefits in India, China, and elsewhere will want them as much as we do. Few people will voluntarily give up what they have; indeed, most people will continue to want more and more. But if these demands continue, the ecological crisis will result in outright ecological disaster. To prevent this from happening, coercion may be necessary. That is, governments may have to force people to lower their expectations and live more modestly. In a democracy, Heilbroner says, this will be all but impossible, for the people are unlikely to elect leaders who promise them hardship. On the contrary, they may turn to leaders who promise to protect them and their economic well-being from foreigners who want what they have. Militant nationalism may thus increase, bringing with it a tendency to silence dissenting opinion, to concentrate power in the hands of a few leaders, and to foster hostile relations among the nation-states of the world—a highly unsettling prospect in the age of nuclear, biological, and chemical weapons.

Heilbroner does not predict that all this will happen, but he does see it as a distinctly possible outcome of the environmental difficulties we now face. Even if there is no broad revival of fascism, moreover, many observers believe that ecological pressures pose a serious challenge to those ideologies that embrace democracy. So too do those pressures that fall under the broad heading of **globalization.**

In the broad sense of the word, "globalization" refers to the cultural and technological changes that seem to draw the peoples of the world more closely together. Advances in transportation and communication, and a corresponding reduction of their costs, have dramatically increased mobility and the opportunity to engage in commercial and social interactions with people in distant places. CNN, the Internet, and social media seem to be everywhere, as do the images of various pop stars and athletes. For better or worse, the distances between peoples seem to be shrinking, as do the differences that have made them distinctive.

"Globalization" also has a narrow or specific sense, however, and in this sense it means the spread of free trade around the world. From the early 1960s to the present, successive American administrations have joined with other countries to lower or eliminate barriers to international trade. Such barriers have included tariffs on imported goods, subsidies to domestic producers, and other measures that aim to protect businesses in one's own country against foreign competition. GATT (the General Agreement on Tariffs and Trade) and, more recently, NAFTA (North American Free Trade Agreement), the TPP (Trans-Pacific Partnership), and other free-trade treaties have committed the United States and other countries to reduce or eliminate all (or almost all) restrictions to the free movement of goods across national boundaries. Countries that do not cooperate may find themselves under pressure from the World Bank and the International Monetary Fund (IMF), two institutions created near the end of World War II to promote a stable, depression-free global economy. Following Adam Smith and the early liberals, advocates of globalization argue that free trade promotes efficiency, rewards producers who manufacture and sell goods at the lowest possible price, and benefits consumers, who can afford to buy more and better goods as competition drives prices down and quality up. Individualist conservatives and neoclassical liberals are thus among the leading proponents of "globalization," which they believe to be the reason for significant gains in health and prosperity in many parts of the world.

Critics—members of labor unions and environmental groups foremost among them—contend that global free trade means that workers in Third World countries, including young children, will be overworked and underpaid, that workers in the United States and other industrial countries will lose jobs as manufacturing moves overseas to take advantage of lower labor costs, and that laws protecting the environment and the safety of workers will be repealed or weakened in the name of higher productivity and reduced costs. Critics call this loss of jobs and lowering of wages and standards a "race to the bottom." These critics complain that the World Trade Organization (WTO), which oversees the international terms of trade, is an unelected and undemocratic body that systematically favors the interests of international corporations to the detriment of workers and the natural environment. According to its critics, the WTO interprets "barriers to trade" to include democratically enacted laws and public policies that promote worker safety and environmental protection. They also complain that free-trade agreements override these same concerns. NAFTA, for example, has touched off a lengthy legal and political battle over trucking safety. According to the agreement, Mexican and American trucks were to be free to travel on the highways of both countries, but the Teamsters Union, the Sierra Club, Public Citizen, and other groups objected that American standards for exhaust emissions and road worthiness were being lowered to accommodate Mexican trucks. After numerous delays, and thirteen years after NAFTA took effect in 1994, the U.S. government won a court case in 2007 that allowed it to proceed with a one-year experiment in which the trucks of pre-inspected Mexican firms would be permitted to operate throughout the United States.[6] If the experiment proved successful—that is, if American roads are as safe as they were before the introduction of Mexican trucks—then the trucking provision of NAFTA was supposed to take effect. This it finally did in 2015. Trucks from Mexico can now cross the border and are held to the same safety and weight requirements as American trucks.

Opposition to NAFTA and other free-trade regimes has produced some ideologically interesting allies who testify to the truth of the old adage, "politics makes for strange bedfellows." In addition to organized labor (including the Teamsters Union and the AFL-CIO) and environmental groups such as the Sierra Club, these allies include anarchists, who have attracted much attention with their attempts, especially in Seattle in 1999, to close down meetings of the WTO and other free-trade organizations. Other allies are Marxists who see globalization as a higher phase of imperialism—and thus of the capitalist exploitation of the working class throughout the world. But there are conservative opponents of globalization, too, such as Pat Buchanan, an American writer and sometime presidential candidate. Buchanan and other traditional conservatives complain that unrestricted free trade reduces or compromises national sovereignty by making national laws subject to international agreements. "Free trade," he charges, "is the serial killer of American manufacturing and the Trojan Horse of world government. It is the primrose path to the loss of economic independence and national sovereignty. Free trade is a bright, shining lie."[7] Some welfare liberals also oppose globalization, largely because of their belief that international free-trade regimes undermine worker safety and democracy. For their part, environmentalists contend that free trade endangers the natural environment by rolling back gains made with the passage and enforcement of the Clean Air and Clean Water Acts, the Endangered Species Act, and other environmental laws in the United States and elsewhere. What is needed, they say, is not merely free trade but "fair trade"—that is, international trade in goods that have been produced by workers who are paid a fair wage, are protected from workplace hazards, and are free to organize themselves into labor unions. Furthermore, such trade must raise rather than lower the standards of environmental protection.

Regarding the sorry state of workplace safety, critics ask us to consider the case of Bangladesh. Approximately 3.5 million Bangladeshis work in that nation's 4500 clothing factories; 80 percent are women. The factories in which they toil to produce inexpensive clothing for Walmart, Gap, and other large American and European retailers are often unclean and sometimes downright dangerous. A particularly egregious example of the hazards faced by workers was the Rana Plaza clothing factory disaster in April 2013. The building was not up to code, and workers had noticed ever more numerous and widening cracks in the walls. When a civil engineer was called in to inspect the building, he strongly recommended its immediate evacuation and closure. The owner refused and the factory remained in operation. When it collapsed 1127 workers died under the debris. Such avoidable accidents are far from rare in Bangladesh and other third-world nations whose workers produce cheap goods for consumption in the developed First World.

No less egregious, critics contend, is the widespread ecological destruction that comes in the wake of drilling for oil. To make its product less expensive, and therefore more attractive on the world market, oil companies cut corners on worker safety and environmental preservation. Pristine forests, rivers, and lakes in Nigeria, Ecuador, and other third-world nations have been polluted with oil and the by-products produced by drilling for it. Native inhabitants' safety, health, and well-being have been harmed, perhaps irreparably, by the extraction and transportation of cheap oil for world markets. This, according to critics, is yet another reason to replace "free trade" with "fair trade."

This controversy over free trade and globalization appears likely to spread and intensify as we move further into the twenty-first century. It promises not only to produce some unusual alliances across ideological divides but also to raise questions about the nature of national sovereignty, democracy, and self-rule.

POLITICAL IDEOLOGIES AND THE DEMOCRATIC IDEAL

And what of the future of democracy? Early in the twenty-first century two things seem clear. The first is that democracy—or at least lip service to the democratic ideal—is more popular than ever. Except for some critics—neo-Nazis, neofascists, and radical Islamists—hardly anyone these days flatly rejects democracy. Indeed, the ideal of democracy is inspiring challenges to established leaders and regimes around the world. Many who helped to dismantle the Marxist-Leninist state in Eastern Europe and the Soviet Union, for instance, acted in the name of democracy, as have those who have rebelled against right-wing dictatorships in Latin America.

The second thing that seems clear about the future of democracy is that it has no place for one of the three versions of the democratic ideal that proved dominant this past century. This version, **people's democracy**, has fallen victim to the general demise of Marxism-Leninism. As we saw in Chapter 2, a people's democracy is supposed to consist of rule by the Communist Party on behalf and in the interests of the people. In this way, the communists argued, the party could both speak for the people and use its powers to defeat their counterrevolutionary enemies. As long as the party itself was a democratic institution, with room for debate and disagreement among the friends of the people, the country would be a people's democracy even though no other party was allowed to compete for power. It became increasingly obvious that the party was *not* a democratic institution, however, but a rigid and hierarchical bureaucratic apparatus in which party members clung to power and privilege, exploiting rather than liberating the people. George Orwell developed this theme in the form of a fable, *Animal Farm*, in 1945. The Yugoslavian Marxist Milovan Djilas also made this argument in the early 1950s in his book, *The New Class*—and was promptly thrown into prison. The student radicals of the 1960s "New Left" in the United States and Europe advanced a similar argument. Indirectly, so too did Alexander Dubček, the communist leader of Czechoslovakia who took steps to loosen the party's control over his country in 1968, only to be removed from office when the Soviet Union sent tanks and troops into Czechoslovakia to put an end to the reforms of the "Prague Spring." The democratically inspired "Arab Spring" of 2011 met with a similar fate, becoming the Arab winter that now exists in Egypt and elsewhere.

The situation in Europe began to change in the 1980s, first with the emergence of the Solidarity trade union in Poland—a noncommunist trade union in a country where the Communist Party controlled all unions. Then came Mikhail Gorbachev and **perestroika** in the Soviet Union itself. Gorbachev's "restructuring" of the Soviet Union amounted to an admission that Marxism-Leninism had failed to achieve its promises economically or politically. Some dissidents inside the party dared to say that the people's democracy was no democracy at all. Once it seemed clear that Gorbachev would not use the military might of the Soviet Union to crush popular uprisings in Eastern Europe, the people's democracies came tumbling down. The so-called domino theory—the idea that if Country A "went communist," neighboring Countries B and C would surely follow—proved to work in reverse. In Eastern Europe the dominoes fell in the other direction, as the people of one country after another toppled their communist regimes in the "Velvet Revolution" of 1989. Most dramatic of all was the literal dismantling of the Berlin Wall, long a symbol of oppressive communist rule. The People's Republic of Hungary dropped "People's" from its name. Hard-line Communist Party leaders in the Soviet Union tried to reverse the direction of change when they attempted to retake power in August 1991, but the popular reaction, led by Boris Yeltsin, defeated their *putsch* and spelled the end of the Soviet Union.

The chief exception to this trend is the People's Republic of China. There, in the country Mao Zedong once called a "people's democratic dictatorship," student protesters who occupied Tiananmen Square in the spring of 1989 called upon Communist Party leaders to relinquish some of their power so that China could become a democracy. What they wanted was not "people's democracy" but something like **liberal democracy**. The party responded by sending troops to suppress the demonstrators. Hundreds, perhaps thousands, died in a single night. Other demonstrators were arrested and imprisoned, and some were even executed. Party leaders have condemned the protestors' plea for democracy as an attempt at "bourgeois liberalization" and have reaffirmed their commitment to people's democracy. To observers throughout the world—and to many of the one billion people of China, one suspects—the events of Tiananmen Square confirmed the view that "people's democracy" is not democracy at all but a front behind which an entrenched elite protects its power and privilege.

The decline of "people's democracy" means that the democratic ideal now survives in two principal forms—**liberal democracy** and **social democracy.** There is some chance that these two forms will converge, because both are committed to freedom of speech, competition for political office, and other civil and political rights. There are also signs that some socialists are adopting some aspects of a capitalist, market-oriented economy. But the differences between them are still quite significant. Those who favor liberal democracy continue to stress the importance of privacy, including private property, so that individuals may be free to choose how to live. The proponents of social democracy, however, continue to emphasize equality as necessary to democracy, claiming that people will not be able to rule themselves unless they have something like an equal voice in the decisions that affect their lives. And the people will not have an equal voice, social democrats say, as long as some have far more wealth and property—and therefore more power—than others. This was the principal theme of Senator Bernie Sanders's campaign for the 2016 Democratic presidential nomination.[8] Senator Sanders's campaign seemed to some to take away the stigma of the "S-word"—

socialism—and to reinsert that once-stigmatized ideology into the American political mainstream.[9]

Even so, in the near future the primary ideological contest will probably continue to pit liberalism and conservatism against each other, and both against socialism, with all proclaiming their devotion to democracy. As more socialists abandon and denounce Marxism-Leninism, it is possible that a realignment may take place along lines that reflect the division of liberalism into its welfare and neoclassical wings. Welfare liberals may come to believe that their views of liberty, equality, and democracy are closer to those of the moderate socialists than to the views of the neoclassical liberals. For their part, neoclassical liberals and conservatives may conclude that they should make common cause against those who favor an active government and a more egalitarian society. The first group would then speak for social democracy, the second for liberal democracy.

But what of the liberation ideologies and the "Greens"? All will almost certainly play a part in the politics of the near future. The main question is whether liberalism or socialism or perhaps conservatism will manage to absorb them, or whether these new ideologies will develop sufficient strength and scope to challenge the older, "mainstream" ideologies. Most liberation ideologies, for instance, share a sense of frustration with liberalism and socialism, but they also owe much of their ideal of liberation to these two ideologies. If either liberalism or socialism can give liberationists—black, women, LGBT, native peoples, or animal—reason to believe that they can make that ideal real, then the liberation ideologies could conceivably merge with one of those ideologies. Otherwise, they will probably continue to follow an independent course as challengers to liberalism, socialism, and, of course, conservatism. But if the aforementioned realignment takes place, it is likely that the liberation ideologies would become part of the social-democratic alliance of welfare liberals and socialists. Conservatives who favor traditional forms of society and individualists who prefer an individualistic, competitive society would then form the opposition, perhaps in the name of liberal democracy. Or perhaps we shall simply see ideologies splinter into many small fragments, with no ideology popular enough to overwhelm the others.

There are, of course, a great many possibilities, and the political world is always capable of surprising us. The opening of the Berlin Wall, the collapse of the Soviet Union, and the demise of apartheid in South Africa are all dramatic examples of events that almost no one had predicted. Political predictions are always precarious. Why, then, have some analysts confidently predicted that ideology itself will soon end?

THE END OF IDEOLOGY?

Amidst all the talk about the end of communism in recent decades, some commentators predicted the end of ideology itself. With the downfall of communism, they declared, not only were the great ideological conflicts of the twentieth century coming to an end, but also all significant ideological conflict was evaporating into a widespread consensus on the desirability of liberal democracy. From this time forward, virtually everyone will agree on the general forms and purposes of political life; the only disagreements will be over how best to achieve the goals—especially the goal of individual liberty, including the liberty to own property—that nearly everyone accepts. Because this change will leave ideology with no useful function to perform, it will simply disappear.

We cannot accept this conclusion. There are, we believe, four reasons why ideologies cannot and will not end. The first is that the "end of ideology" argument has appeared—and failed—before. In the late 1950s and early 1960s, other scholars predicted that a growing consensus on the desirable ends of politics was leading to the end of ideology, at least in the West. As Daniel Bell put it in 1960,

> Few serious minds believe any longer that one can set down "blueprints" and through "social engineering" bring about a new utopia of social harmony. At the same time, the older "counter-beliefs" have lost their intellectual force as well. Few "classic" liberals insist that the State should play no role in the economy, and few serious conservatives, at least in England and on the Continent, believe that the Welfare State is "the road to serfdom." In the Western world, therefore, there is today a rough consensus among intellectuals on political issues: the acceptance of a Welfare State; the desirability of decentralized power; a system of mixed economy and of political pluralism. In that sense, too, the ideological age has ended.[10]

This "consensus," however, was either short-lived or remarkably superficial. The turmoil of the 1960s—and with it the emergence of various liberation movements—suggested that the end of ideology was nowhere in sight. As a prominent philosopher observed, the 1960s marked "the end of the end of ideology."[11] And, far from demonstrating their "acceptance of a Welfare State," conservative governments in the 1980s and 1990s tried to dismantle it. It is possible, of course, that the earlier prediction was premature and that now, the end of ideology has truly come.[12] But the fact that the prediction failed before suggests to us that it is likely to fail again.

A second reason for questioning the prediction is that enough differences remain, even after the demise of Marxism-Leninism, to keep ideological conflict alive for quite some time. Socialism, as we suggested in Chapter 6, could experience a revival of sorts as it sloughs off the soiled mantle of Marxism-Leninism, leaving enough differences between socialists, liberals, and conservatives to fuel many an ideological dispute. In addition to disputes *between* ideologies, there will continue to be differences *within* ideologies. The split between welfare and neoclassical liberals, for one, seems deep enough to prevent the emergence of any widespread consensus on the forms and scope of government activity. Moreover, a great many unresolved issues and tensions continue to press for resolution. What should be the role of religion in public life? Is nationalism something to be encouraged or discouraged? What about the status of those who see themselves as oppressed—black people, gays, women, the poor, indigenous peoples who have been pushed to the margins of society, prevented from acquiring the power they need to liberate themselves and thus to define and celebrate their respective identities? And, as animal rights advocates remind us, what of creatures who cannot speak for themselves? Do they have rights—or at least legitimate interests—that require our recognition and protection? These questions are among many that must be answered before anything like an ideological consensus can be reached. Yet they seem more likely to provoke conflict than agreement.

A third reason to doubt the prediction is that what Bell and others have forecasted is not the *end* of ideology but the *triumph* of one particular ideology—

liberalism. According to Francis Fukuyama, liberalism has now defeated all of its ideological rivals.[13] Some skirmishes remain, but the liberal emphasis on individual liberty, private property, equality of opportunity, and tolerance is rapidly gaining ascendancy throughout the world. This triumph, Fukuyama says, marks "the end of history," in the sense that the major ideological conflicts of the modern world have brought us to a goal or fulfillment. History will continue, of course, in that people will continue to act, argue, quarrel, and reach decisions. Yet nothing fundamental will change or be challenged, because almost everyone will have accepted the basic premises of liberalism. If Fukuyama is right, then we may expect the end of ideological conflict, but not the disappearance of ideology itself.

Fukuyama's claim that we are witnessing the triumph of liberalism over its ideological rivals is not obviously true. To some, the nationalistic and religious conflicts of recent years seem to signal a growing division between two fundamentally different outlooks on life. One outlook stresses religion, with special attention to the contest between people who share a faith and the others, the "infidels" or "unbelievers," who either have a different faith or none at all. The other outlook is more worldly and secular, with its attention devoted to improving life here on earth by using economic competition to bring more and more consumer goods to people around the globe. To those who see the world in fundamentally religious and nationalistic terms, however, this second outlook appears to be converting the whole world into a single, vast, materialistic consumer society. Such a development must be resisted, in their view, for it threatens their religious beliefs and their distinct identities as nations or tribes. Their resistance has led some scholars to observe that the contemporary world is moving toward something quite different from what Fukuyama expects. In place of the "end of history" and the triumph of liberalism, according to one analysis, we are now witnessing a global contest between *jihad* and "McWorld."[14] That is, future conflicts will center on whether (or to what extent) countries and cultures will resist or welcome the forces of globalization. In recent years the rapid rise of radical Islamism strongly suggests that resistance is viewed by some as a real and attractive possibility.

Finally, our fourth reason for believing that ideologies are going to be with us for quite some time is that new challenges and difficulties continue to arise. One great and growing challenge is the environmental crisis, or crises, that we discussed in Chapter 9. Barring some miraculous discoveries—such as a cheap, safe, and nonpolluting source of energy—this crisis will require a political response, and this response will almost certainly take an ideological form. In other words, any adequate response must fulfill the four functions of an ideology. First, people will seek some *explanation* of the nature of the crisis, along with, second, an *evaluation* of the situation they face. Third, they will also need *orientation*—that is, some sense of where they stand with regard to the crisis. Fourth and finally, they will need a *program* for action telling them what they can, and should, do. They will need all of these things to be set out in fairly simple terms. They will need, in short, the guidance of an ideology. If more than one ideology offers this guidance, as seems likely, then ideological conflict will almost certainly persist.[15]

For these reasons, we do not expect to see the end of ideology. Ideologies are too useful, and too important, to wither away. We need ideologies to join thought to action, to provide some vision of human possibilities that will move people to act. As long as we live in a complicated and confusing world, full of challenges and conflicts, we shall need ideologies to (at least allegedly) explain why social conditions are as they are, to evaluate those conditions, to provide a sense of orientation, and to set out a program of action—an attempt to take the world as it is and to remake it as it should be. We shall also need ideologies to give meaning to the democratic ideal and substance to the concept of freedom. With this work still to be done, it is difficult to see how we could do without them. We must conclude, then, that as long as ideologies have these ends to serve, there will be no end of ideology.

Discussion Questions

1   Robert Heilbroner has argued that environmental crises may lead to a revival of fascism. What reasons does he have for saying this? That is, in what ways could environmental problems lead to a crisis of democracy? Do you think that democracies are more or less likely to deal effectively with environmental problems than highly authoritarian or fascist governments?

2   Ball, Dagger, and O'Neill maintain that political ideologies are not about to come to an end. What are the arguments for and against their position? Which point of view do you find more persuasive, and why?

3   What is globalization? Why are some people stridently opposed to it and others more welcoming? Which side do you favor, and why?

4   How is it that some conservatives can support same-sex marriage, even though most conservatives insist that marriage must be between a man and a woman?

5   How is it that some conservatives, such as Pat Buchanan, vigorously oppose NAFTA and other examples of globalization, while other conservatives are very much in favor of such policies?

NOTES

1   This point is as old as John Locke's *Letter Concerning Toleration* (1689), part of which is reprinted in Terence Ball, Richard Dagger, and Daniel O'Neill, eds., *Ideals and Ideologies: A Reader*, 10th ed. (New York and London: Routledge, 2016), selection 3.12.

2   For example, Martin Luther King, Jr., and many others who were active in the civil rights movement in the United States. For an excellent account of the role of religion in the struggle for civil rights, see Taylor Branch, *Parting the Waters: America in the King Years, 1954–1963* (New York: Simon & Schuster, 1988). For a broader account of the role of religious inspiration in political struggles, see Michael Walzer, *Exodus and Revolution* (New York: Basic Books, 1985).

3   Centesimus Annus, in *Origins* 21, no. 1 (May 16, 1991), p. 17.

4   Pope Francis, "Laudato si': On Care for Our Common Home," in Ball, Dagger, and O'Neill, *Ideals and Ideologies*, selection 9.67.

5   Robert Heilbroner, *An Inquiry into the Human Prospect*, 3rd ed. (New York: Norton, 1991). See, further, Luc Ferry, *The New Ecological Order*, trans. Carol Volk (Chicago: University of Chicago Press, 1995).

6   Sean Holstege, "Few Mexican Trucks Poised to Ride into U.S.," *Arizona Republic*, September 3, 2007, p. A1; also Sean Holstege, "Teamsters Continue to Battle Mexican Trucks," *Arizona Republic*, September 3, 2007, p. A2.

7   Patrick Buchanan, *Where the Right Went Wrong: How Neoconservatives Subverted the Reagan Revolution and Hijacked the Bush Presidency* (New York: St. Martin's Press, 2004), p. 171.

8   See Bernie Sanders, "On Democratic Socialism in the United States," in Ball, Dagger, and O'Neill, *Ideals and Ideologies*, selection 6.46.

9   See John Nichols, *The S-Word: A Short History of an American Tradition ... Socialism* (London: Verso, 2011).

10 Daniel Bell, *The End of Ideology: On the Exhaustion of Political Ideas in the Fifties*, rev. ed. (New York: Collier Books, 1961), p. 397.

11 Alasdair MacIntyre, *Against the Self-Images of the Age: Essays on Ideology and Philosophy* (Notre Dame, IN: University of Notre Dame Press, 1978), Chapter 1.

12 Bell defends his end-of-ideology thesis in "The End of Ideology Revisited (Parts I and II)," *Government and Opposition* 23 (Spring and Summer, 1988): 131–150, 321–328, and in the second edition of *The End of Ideology* (Cambridge, MA: Harvard University Press, 2000).

13 Francis Fukuyama, *The End of History and the Last Man* (New York: Free Press, 1992).

14 Benjamin Barber, *Jihad vs. McWorld: Terrorism's Challenge to Democracy* (New York: Times Books, 1995).

15 For an early twenty-first century reassessment of the major ideologies, see Michael Freeden, ed., *Reassessing Political Ideologies* (New York and London: Routledge, 2002).

FOR FURTHER READING

Barber, Benjamin. *Jihad vs. McWorld*. New York: Times Books, 1995.

Cowen, Tyler. *Creative Destruction: How Globalization Is Changing the World's Cultures*. Princeton, NJ: Princeton University Press, 2002.

Fukuyama, Francis. *The End of History and the Last Man*. New York: Free Press, 1992.

Micklethwait, John, and Adrian Wooldridge. *A Future Perfect: The Challenge and Hidden Promise of Globalization*. London: William Heinemann, 2000.

Pfaff, William. *The Wrath of Nations*. New York: Simon & Schuster, 1993.

Steger, Manfred B. *Globalism: Market Ideology Meets Terrorism*, 2nd ed. Lanham, MD: Rowman & Littlefield, 2005.

Stiglitz, Joseph. *Globalization and Its Discontents*. New York: W. W. Norton, 2002.

GLOSSARY

achieved status The condition of earning one's place in society through effort and ability. Contrast with *ascribed status*.

affirmative action The attempt to promote equality of opportunity by providing assistance to members of groups, such as women and racial minorities, that have been the victims of discrimination.

alienation A term Marx adapted from Hegel's philosophy to describe the separation or estrangement of persons or classes of people from their human potential. Under capitalism, Marx claims, the worker's ability to control his or her labor is alienated.

anarchism A term from the Greek *an archos*, meaning "no rule" or "no government." Anarchism aims to abolish the state, replacing political relations with cooperative or voluntary ones.

anarcho-communism The version of anarchism that aspires to a cooperative society in which all property is owned or controlled by the whole community.

anthropocentrism The "human-centered" outlook that Greens say is too selfish and narrow to take into account the well-being of wild creatures and the natural environment. See also *biocentrism* and *ecocentrism*.

anticolonial movements Attempts by people in "Third World" countries to gain their independence from the rule of colonial (usually European) powers.

apartheid The South African policy of "apartness," or separation of the races, with whites holding political power.

aristocratic privilege The policy, based on the belief that one class of people is superior to others, that reserves certain rights and opportunities—such as access to governing power—for the exclusive enjoyment of the nobility.

arrogance of humanism The Green charge that a "humanist" or anthropocentric outlook ignores or devalues the worth of other species of animals and plants and the environment that sustains them.

Aryans Name given to a group of people from whom all Indo-European languages supposedly derive. Nazis believe that this people and their purest descendants are a "master race" whose destiny is to conquer and rule—or exterminate—"inferior" races.

ascribed status A person's being born into a particular social status—such as noble or serf—with little opportunity either to raise or lower his or her social standing. Contrast with *achieved status*.

atomistic conception of society (or **atomism**) The view that society consists of individuals who, like marbles on a tray, are essentially unconnected to or independent of one another. Contrast with the *organic conception of society*.

base (also **material-productive base**) Marx's metaphor for the "social relations" that constitute the "real basis" or foundation of material production. For example, the relationship of landowner to farm-worker is part of the *base* of an agricultural society. See also *superstructure* and *materialist conception of history*.

biocentrism The "life-centered" perspective embraced by Greens because it is broader and more inclusive than the prevailing "anthropocentric" (human-centered) outlook. See also *anthropocentrism* and *ecocentrism*.

bourgeoisie A term that originally referred to those who lived in a market town (*bourg* in French) but later to the middle class—merchants and professional people—in general. In Marx's terms, the bourgeoisie is the ruling class in capitalist society because it owns and controls the *forces* (or *means*) *of production*.

caliphate The idea, according to some (and especially Sunni) interpretations of Islamic teaching, of the

372

leadership of the trans-national Islamic community, or *umma*.

capitalism An economic system in which the major *means of production* are privately owned and operated for the profit of the owners or investors.

center The moderate or "middle of the road" position in political terms, as opposed to the more extreme positions of the *left* and *right*.

centralized control Control of all resources and decisions concerning production and distribution of goods concentrated in the central government.

class A key concept in socialist, and particularly Marxian, analysis, referring to one's socially determined location in the structure of social-economic relations. If you are part owner of the *forces* (or *means*) *of production*, you are a member of the *bourgeoisie* or *capitalist* class; if you are yourself a means of production, then you are a member of the working class, or *proletariat*.

classical or traditional conservatism A belief that the first aim of political action must be to preserve the social fabric by pursuing a cautious policy of piecemeal *reform*. Edmund Burke was a classical conservative.

command economy Favored by the proponents of *centralized control*, the attempt to plan and direct economic production and distribution instead of relying on market forces.

communism A system whereby the major means of production are publicly owned. Originally used to describe any scheme of common or social control of resources, this term is now associated with Marxian socialism. For Marx and the Marxists, the communal ownership and control of the *forces* (or *means*) *of production* represents the fulfillment of human history. The culmination of a long-term revolutionary sequence, a mature communist society subscribes to the principle, "From each according to ability, to each according to need."

communitarian In general terms, anyone who wants to bind people together into a strong, mutually supportive society. In particular, the term is now used to describe those who criticize liberalism for putting too much emphasis on the rights and interests of individuals while ignoring the needs of the community as a whole.

corporativism A policy instituted by Benito Mussolini in Italy in an attempt to bring owners, workers, and government together to promote economic production and social harmony.

Counter-Enlightenment A term referring to a diverse group of thinkers in the early and mid-nineteenth century who rejected all or most of the leading ideas of the *Enlightenment* philosophers.

creation care A phrase used by some evangelical Christians to denote what they believe to be the divine duty to protect the natural environment, which they view as an essential and invaluable part of God's creation.

critical Western Marxism The position taken by a number of twentieth-century scholars, principally European, who accept most of Marx's critique of capitalism as a repressive social and economic system, but who reject Marxism-Leninism and concentrate their efforts on analyzing capitalism as a form of cultural domination that prevents people from being truly free and creative beings.

cultural conservatism Closely connected to *classical conservatism*, a brand of conservatism particularly suspicious of commerce, industry, and "progress," which supposedly threaten our relationship with nature and our respect for cultural traditions.

cunning of reason Hegel's phrase for the process by which intentional actions produce unintended, but nonetheless "rational," consequences that promote the development of "spirit" through history.

decentralized control In contrast to *centralized control*, the dispersion of power by placing control of resources and production in the hands of people at the lowest possible level, such as the town or workplace.

deep ecology A "biocentric" or life-centered philosophical, ethical, and political perspective that places the welfare of human beings on a par with other species and the conditions that nurture and sustain them.

democratic centralism Lenin's attempt to combine democracy with central control of the revolutionary *vanguard party*. The party should encourage debate and discussion within its ranks before decisions are made, Lenin said. Once the leadership reaches a decision, however, debate must stop and all members must follow the party line.

dialectic Generally speaking, the process whereby opposite views or forces come into conflict, which eventually leads to the overcoming or reconciliation of the opposition in a new and presumably higher form. Different versions of this method of reasoning are found in Socrates, Plato, Hegel, and Marx, among others.

dialectical materialism (or sometimes **DiaMat**) The Soviet Marxist-Leninist view that traces all social, economic, and political phenomena to physical matter and its motions. The phrase, never used by Marx, became standard during Stalin's era.

dictatorship of the proletariat (also **revolutionary dictatorship of the proletariat**) The form of government that Marx expected to provide the transition from the revolutionary overthrow of the *bourgeoisie* to the eventual coming of communist society. This interim or transitional state will presumably *wither away*.

ecocentrism An "ecosystem-centered" orientation favored by Greens over and against a human-centered "anthropocentric" outlook. See also *anthropocentrism* and *biocentrism*.

ecofeminism A perspective within Green political thought that combines the principles of feminism with those of environmentalism. Its gender-based approach traces environmental plunder to an "androcentric" (male-centered) view that devalues nature ("Mother Nature") and celebrates its "conquest" by men. Ecofeminists hold that this mind-set—and the actions that follow from it—must be challenged if the earth's ecosystems are to be saved and protected for posterity.

ecology The scientific study of the connections, interdependencies, and energy flows within and between species and ecosystems. In its more recent political sense, however, *ecology* refers to a perspective that values the protection and preservation of the natural environment.

ecotage Short for "ecological sabotage," a form of direct action practiced by Earth First! and other militant environmentalist groups. Such sabotage, or *monkey-wrenching*, ranges from "decommissioning" bulldozers and cutting power lines to "spiking" old-growth trees to save them from loggers.

educative theory of democracy The theory, usually attributed to John Stuart Mill, that citizens' political participation in a democracy is a prime source of civic or political education. By participating with their fellow citizens they learn to take into consideration other interests and different perspectives, thereby broadening their horizons and enabling them to take a broader view of the common or public interest.

elitism A belief that there are a small number of people in any society who either should or necessarily will lead or rule the rest.

empire A political union of several states or peoples governed by a single sovereign power or ruler.

empirical A description or explanation of how things are—for example, "Summers are hotter in Arizona than in Alaska." Usually contrasted with *normative*.

Enlightenment The influential philosophical movement of the eighteenth century, especially in France, that proclaimed the triumph of reason and science over custom and superstition.

essentially contested concept A concept—such as art, religion, or democracy—that generates controversy because it lacks a complete set of clear standards for determining when something falls under the concept. Indeed, this openness or indeterminacy seems to be the nature or essence of these concepts.

ethnic cleansing A euphemism for the systematic murder or removal of members of one nationality or ethnic group by another. Used by militant Serbian nationalists in the early 1990s to justify the expulsion and murder of Bosnian Muslims and members of other ethnic groups supposedly standing in the way of a united Serbian nation-state.

Fabian socialism The British brand of socialism emphasizing the non-revolutionary, peaceful, piecemeal, and gradual transition from a capitalist to a socialist society.

false consciousness A Marxian phrase referring to the false or distorted beliefs of members of the proletariat or working class who fail to understand their real or objective interests. These false beliefs work to the advantage of the ruling class because they prevent the proletariat from seeing the real cause of its oppression.

feudalism Specifically, the social and economic system of medieval Europe that centered on the relationship of the lord, who promised protection and the use of land in exchange for service, and the vassal. More generally, feudalism refers to any similar agricultural society in which a relatively small number of people control the land while most others work it as tenants or serfs. Often associated with *ascribed status*.

forces of production (also **material forces of production, means of production,** or sometimes simply **productive forces**) Marx's phrase for the material means or resources that labor transforms into useful goods or commodities. Examples include trees that are transformed into lumber, ores that are transformed into metal, and the machinery and labor necessary to accomplish the transformation.

gay The orientation of someone who is attracted to or favors exclusive sexual relations with persons of the same sex.

gender A central concept within feminist thought referring to the social construction and meaning of the categories "masculine" and "feminine." That is, what makes something "masculine" or "feminine" is largely determined by social attitudes and beliefs.

glasnost The Russian word for "openness," used by Mikhail Gorbachev in the late 1980s to signal a policy of greater tolerance and freedom in the USSR.

globalization The process of removing restrictions to international trade, resulting eventually in a single global market in which goods move freely across national borders.

government A form of political organization through which people within a defined territory are governed, or govern themselves. Types of government vary enormously, ranging from the highly hierarchical and authoritarian to the extensively egalitarian and participatory.

green politics The use of various strategies to put environmental concerns at or near the top of the political agenda.

greenhouse effect The gradual warming of the earth's atmosphere due to the buildup of carbon dioxide (CO_2) that results from the burning of fossil fuels (oil, gas, coal, and so on) and the destruction of forests.

harm principle The principle, defended by John Stuart Mill and others, that we should be allowed to do whatever we want unless our actions harm or threaten harm to others.

homophobia The fear of homosexuals and/or their real or imagined influence.

ideological superstructure See *superstructure*.

ideologue Someone who is strongly committed to a particular ideology and works to promote its triumph over rival ideologies.

immiseration of the proletariat The Marxian prediction that the working class or proletariat would become progressively worse off under capitalism.

imperialism According to Lenin, the policy whereby capitalist countries conquer, colonize, and exploit third-world countries. It represents, in Lenin's view, the "highest" and last stage of capitalist domination of the world economy. It is also a central concept for Mao Zedong and other Marxist-Leninists.

indigenism The position taken by those who claim to defend and promote the interests of native or indigenous peoples. Those who take this position argue that there is a fundamental unity or common civilization that binds indigenous or native peoples, despite their different languages and cultures. These common elements arise mainly out of native responses to colonialism and domination by Europeans and people of European descent.

individualist conservative Someone who believes that government should promote individual liberty by protecting against foreign threats, but otherwise leave people alone to do as they see fit. Such a view may be closer to *neoclassical liberalism* than to other forms of conservatism.

innovation According to Edmund Burke, a radical change for the sake of change or novelty. The desire to innovate, Burke says, leads people to neglect or reject their time-tested customs. Contrast with *reform*.

intrinsic value The idea that some things—especially the natural environment—have value in and of themselves, quite apart from any instrumental, aesthetic, or economic value they might have for human beings.

invisible hand An image used by Adam Smith to illustrate how markets turn individual vices (e.g., greed) into public benefits: it is as though an "invisible hand" is operating behind the scenes to effect this transformation

Iron Law of Oligarchy A sociological "law" formulated by Robert Michels, according to which no large organization can long remain egalitarian but must sooner or later be ruled by a small elite.

irrationalism The belief, associated with thinkers like Freud and Le Bon, that human beings are moved more by instincts, urges, or subconscious forces than by reason.

jahiliyya An Arabic term referring to the ignorance or spiritual darkness that enveloped the world before the Prophet Mohammed received the revelations that constitute the *Qur'an*. Radical Islamists such as Sayyid Qutb speak of the "new *jahiliyya*" to denote the darkness brought on by modernity, secularism, and science which leads Muslims to stray from the true path of Islam as Qutb and others understand it.

jihad The literal meaning of this Arabic word is "struggle." In Islamic thought, *jihad* refers to an individual's internal struggle to cleanse his or her soul *and* to the collective struggle to wage a "holy war" against Islam's enemies.

land ethic A phrase coined by ecologist Aldo Leopold to refer to an attitude of reverence and respect for the land and the myriad life-forms it sustains.

left (or **left-wing**) In political terms, the belief that a significant, perhaps even radical, change in a new direction will lead to great improvement in social and economic arrangements. In general, socialists are on the left, not the *right* or *center*.

levelling The effort, criticized by many conservatives, to diminish or eliminate the gap between the wealthiest and poorest members of a society. Critics maintain that these efforts promote mediocrity and reduce everyone to the same low level.

liberal democracy In contrast to *people's* and *social democracy*, an emphasis on the importance of individual rights and liberty, including the right to own private property.

libertarianism Generally, the desire to expand the realm of individual liberty. Specifically, "libertarian" is another name for neoclassical liberals, who argue that the only legitimate power of government is to protect the persons and property of its citizens. Some libertarian *anarchists* believe that all governments are illegitimate and immoral.

Malthus's law The assertion that human population tends to grow faster than the resources required to sustain it. Specifically, population grows geometrically and resources grow arithmetically.

market socialism The attempt to combine some features of a competitive market economy with public control of resources. For example, the people who work in a factory may jointly own it, but they must compete for profits with other worker-owned factories.

mass society According to some critics, a dangerously unstable society in which the common people—and the politicians and advertisers who appeal to their tastes—bring everything and everyone down to their own level by abolishing traditional social hierarchies and the secondary associations that Burke called "little platoons."

master-slave dialectic Hegel's account of the confrontation between an all-powerful master and his presumably powerless slave. The conflict between the two reveals that the master is dependent upon his slave; the slave, by winning his struggle for freedom and recognition, liberates both himself and the master. Marx and later "liberation" ideologists also employ this parable of emancipation.

material forces of production (also **forces of production, means of production,** or simply **productive forces**) Marx's phrase for the material means or resources that human labor transforms into useful goods or commodities. Examples include trees that are transformed into lumber, ores into metal, and the labor necessary to accomplish the transformation.

materialism The philosophical doctrine that all reality—social, political, and intellectual—is ultimately reducible to combinations of physical matter. Different versions can be found in Hobbes, in Engels, and in twentieth-century *dialectical materialism*.

materialist conception (or **interpretation**) **of history** The Marxian framework for interpreting or explaining social change. The central idea is that changes in the material-productive *base* bring about changes in the *social relations of production* and the ideological *superstructure*.

mercantilism The economic policy of promoting a country's wealth at the expense of others by establishing *monopolies* and regulating foreign trade to favor domestic industry.

mixed constitution (or **government**) The *republican* policy of combining or balancing rule by one, by the few, and by the many in a single government, with the aim of preventing the concentration of power in any single individual or social group.

monkey-wrenching A form of direct action practiced or advocated by Earth First! and other militant environmentalist groups. Such action ranges from "decommissioning" bulldozers to cutting power lines and "spiking" old-growth trees. See also *ecotage*.

monopoly Exclusive control of a commodity or market by a single firm.

moral hazard The danger that someone who is protected from the consequences of his or her risky behavior may behave recklessly or irresponsibly, leaving others to bear the brunt of his or her bad behavior.

nationalism The belief that people fall into distinct groups, or nations, on the basis of a common heritage or birth. Each nation is then supposed to form the natural basis for a separate political unit, or *nation-state*.

nation-state A political unit that unites the members of a single nation, or people.

natural aristocracy A phrase used by Burke and other thinkers to denote an aristocracy of ability and talent, as distinguished from a purely hereditary aristocracy whose members may or may not be able and talented.

natural right A right that everyone has simply by virtue of being human. Such a right can be neither granted nor taken away by any person or political authority.

negative freedom In contrast to *positive freedom*, negative freedom is the absence of restraint. You are free, in this view, if no one else is preventing you from doing what you want to do.

neoclassical liberalism The belief that government is a necessary evil that should do nothing but protect the persons and property of its citizens. See *libertarianism*.

neoconservatism Beginning among disenchanted *welfare liberals* in the 1960s, a movement advocating less reliance on government, an assertive foreign policy, and an emphasis on the value of work, thrift, family, and self-restraint.

normative A statement or proposition prescribing how things ought to be or judging what is good or bad—for example, "lying is wrong." Usually contrasted with *empirical* and/or descriptive.

opium of the masses (or **people**) Marx's phrase for religion, which he believed dulled the critical capacity of oppressed people by directing their attention and hopes away from this life to an eternal and blissful afterlife.

organic conception of society In contrast to the *atomistic conception*, a view holding that the members of a society are connected and interdependent, like the parts of the body, and that society itself is more than merely the sum of its parts.

original sin The belief in Christian theology that the first sin—Adam's defiance of God in the Garden of Eden—has somehow infected all human beings.

orthopraxis Literally, correct practice or action. Liberation theologians urge the Catholic Church, and Christians in general, to "act correctly" by working for justice for the poor and an end to oppression.

patriarchy (or **patriarchalism**)—or sometimes "sexism" or "male domination"—is the view that men are morally and intellectual superior to women and have a legitimate claim to control their bodies and their lives, supposedly "for their own good." This patronizing attitude toward women is the primary target at which feminist criticism is aimed.

people's democracy Favored by Marxist-Leninists, the view that democracy is government by the Communist Party in the interests of the working class.

perestroika The Russian word for "restructuring," used by Mikhail Gorbachev in the late 1980s to refer in particular to the restructuring of the Soviet Union's economy.

Physiocrats French economic theorists of the eighteenth century who believed that land is the basis of wealth and that unrestricted competition promotes prosperity.

political absolutism Any form of government in which the ruler (or rulers) has nearly complete power, unrestrained by law or other governing bodies.

polity Rule by the many, who are neither wealthy nor poor, in the interests of the whole community. In Aristotle's theory, this is generally the best practically achievable form of government.

positive freedom In contrast to *negative freedom*, the belief that freedom is not simply the absence of restraint but also the power or ability to act and to develop one's capacities.

prejudice In Burke's theory, the "latent wisdom" that societies accumulate through long experience and that usually provides a useful guide to conduct and policy.

proletariat Marx's word for wage-laborers, the industrial working class. The proletariat was originally the lowest class in ancient Rome.

protectionist theory of democracy The theory, espoused by Jeremy Bentham and James Mill, among others, which holds that the point and purpose of democracy is or should be to protect people's interests, and particularly their material or economic interests.

racism The belief that one race (usually one's own) is innately superior to other races or ethnic groups.

reactionary Someone who wants to return to an earlier form of society or government. More generally, a reactionary is an extreme conservative.

reform A gradual and cautious change that corrects or repairs defects in society or government and, according to Edmund Burke, is safer and wiser than *innovation*.

relations of production (or **social relations of production**) Marx's phrase describing the social division of labor—for example, managers, supervisors, laborers—required to transform the *material forces of production* into useful goods.

religious conformity The policy of requiring everyone in a society to follow or acknowledge the same religious beliefs.

religious right The movement of evangelical fundamentalists, such as the Christian Coalition in the United States, who seek to restore "traditional family values."

Renaissance The period of the "rebirth" (re-naissance) of classical learning in fourteenth- and fifteenth-century Europe.

republic A form of government by the people that includes the rule of law, a *mixed constitution*, and the cultivation of an active and public-spirited citizenry.

revisionists The name given to later Marxists who attempted to amend or revise Marxian theory in light of developments after Marx's death.

revolution A sweeping or fundamental transformation of a society. Originally used to describe an attempt to restore or revolve back to a previous condition, the word acquired its present meaning with the French Revolution.

revolutionary dictatorship of the proletariat (also **dictatorship of the proletariat**) The form of government that Marx expected to provide the transition from the revolutionary overthrow of the *bourgeoisie* to the eventual coming of communist society. This interim or transitional state will presumably *wither away*.

right (or **right-wing**) In opposition to the *left* and *center*, the people who occupy the right end of the political spectrum. They often oppose change and prefer an established social order with firmly rooted authority. Both conservatives and reactionaries are usually considered right-wing.

secularism The tendency to turn away from religious considerations and to emphasize the value of earthly life as a good in itself.

separatist movements The attempt by a group of people who see themselves as a distinct nation to break away from another country in order to form their own *nation-state*.

sexism The belief that one sex (almost always the male) is innately superior to the other.

social contract An agreement to form political societies and establish governments, thus creating political authority. How do some people acquire authority over others? Some theorists, such as Thomas Hobbes and John Locke, have answered that individuals in a *state of nature* have in some way entered into a social contract.

Social Darwinists A group of *neoclassical liberals* of the late nineteenth and early twentieth centuries who adapted Darwin's theory of evolution to social and political life, concluding that the struggle for survival between individuals is a natural feature of human life and government should not intervene.

social democracy A view that democracy requires a rough equality of power or influence for every citizen, which may require, in turn, the redistribution of wealth and/or the social control of resources and property. Contrast with *liberal* and *people's democracy*.

social ecology In contrast to *deep ecology*, a view attaching special importance to human life, but also holding that humanity is dependent upon—and responsible for—the environment that sustains it and other species.

social relations of production (or **relations of production**) Marx's phrase describing the social division of labor (for example, managers, supervisors, laborers) required to transform raw materials into useful goods or commodities.

speciesism The belief that the human species is innately superior to other animal species. Speciesists believe that the moral and intellectual superiority of humans over nonhuman animals gives the former the right or liberty to use the latter for food, fur, medical experiments, etc., with little or no regard for their suffering.

state of nature In the theories of Thomas Hobbes, John Locke, and Robert Nozick, among others, the condition in which people live before they create society and government. Everyone is free and equal in this state, and no one has authority over anyone else.

stewardship An orientation emphasizing human beings' responsibility for protecting, preserving, and sustaining the natural and social environment for the sake of future generations.

superstructure (also **ideological superstructure**) Marx's metaphor for the set of beliefs, ideas, and ideals that justifies or legitimizes the social arrangements that constitute the foundation or *base* of society. See also *materialist conception of history*.

takfir An Arabic term referring to the right of faithful Muslims to excommunicate (or, for radical Islamists, kill) Muslims they regard as apostates.

theocracy A form of government in which religious leaders, who see themselves as agents of God (or the gods), try to enforce divine commands by making them the law of the land.

Tory democracy A policy, initiated by the British conservative leader Benjamin Disraeli, supporting voting rights and other benefits for the working class in order to forge an electoral alliance between the upper and the working class against the predominantly middle-class Liberal Party.

totalitarianism The attempt to control every aspect of a country's life—military, press, schools, religion, economy, and so on—by a single, all-powerful party that systematically smothers all opposition.

trade union consciousness A phrase used by Lenin to denote the kind of "false consciousness" that afflicts workers in advanced capitalist countries. They believe—falsely, Lenin asserts—that their interests as a class lies in gaining an ever-larger share of the "superprofits" extracted by the capitalist ruling class by joining trade unions and threatening to strike if their demands are not met. The workers' "real" interest, he says, lies in abolishing capitalism, not profiting from it.

traditional (or classical) conservative Someone, like Edmund Burke, who believes that the first aim of political action must be to preserve the social fabric by pursuing a cautious policy of *reform*.

umma An Arabic term denoting the trans-national community composed of devout Muslims.

Utilitarianism The view that individuals and governments should always act to promote *utility* or, in Jeremy Bentham's phrase, "the greatest happiness of the greatest number."

Utilitarians Those who advocate *Utilitarianism*.

utility Anything that has value, or usefulness, for anyone. As used by Bentham and the *Utilitarians*, utility refers to our tendency to pursue pleasure and avoid pain.

utopia A term coined by Thomas More from Greek words meaning either "good place" (*eu-topos*) or "no place" (*ou-topos*). Utopia now refers to a perfect society from which greed, crime, and other social ills have been banished.

utopian socialism A phrase Marx and Engels used to denote what they saw as the unreasonably idealistic, moralistic, unscientific, and unrealistic schemes of earlier socialists.

vanguard party Lenin's term for the Communist Party, which is to take a tutelary or "leading role" in organizing and educating the proletariat and preparing it to take part in the revolution that will overthrow capitalism and aid the transition to communism.

welfare (or welfare-state) liberalism In contrast to *neoclassical liberalism*, a form of liberalism that regards government as a tool to be used to promote individual freedom, welfare, and equality of opportunity.

withering away of the state Marx's description of the process whereby the interim *dictatorship of the proletariat* loses its reason for being and gradually ceases to exist as a classless communist society comes into being.

NAME INDEX

SUBJECT INDEX

Page numbers in italics refer to figures.